Annabel Ness Evans
Concordia University College of Alberta

Using Basic Statistics in the Behavioral and Social Sciences

Fifth Edition

Los Angeles | London | New Delhi
Singapore | Washington DC

Los Angeles | London | New Delhi
Singapore | Washington DC

FOR INFORMATION:

SAGE Publications, Inc.
2455 Teller Road
Thousand Oaks, California 91320
E-mail: order@sagepub.com

SAGE Publications Ltd.
1 Oliver's Yard
55 City Road
London EC1Y 1SP
United Kingdom

SAGE Publications India Pvt. Ltd.
B 1/I 1 Mohan Cooperative Industrial Area
Mathura Road, New Delhi 110 044
India

SAGE Publications Asia-Pacific Pte. Ltd.
3 Church Street
#10-04 Samsung Hub
Singapore 049483

Acquisitions Editor: Vicki Knight
Associate Editor: Kalie Koscielak
Editorial Assistant: Jessica Young
Production Editor: Eric Garner
Copy Editor: QuADS Prepress
Typesetter: C&M Digitals (P) Ltd.
Proofreader: Stefanie Storholt
Indexer: Jeanne Busemeyer
Cover Designer: Candice Harman
Marketing Manager: Nicole Elliott
Permissions Editor: Karen Ehrmann

Printed in the United States of America

Library of Congress Cataloging-in-Publication Data

Evans, Annabel.
Using basic statistics in the behavioral and social sciences / Annabel Ness Evans, Concordia University College of Alberta. — Fifth edition.

pages cm
Revised edition of the author's Using basic statistics in the social sciences, 4th ed., published in 2008.
Includes bibliographical references and index.

ISBN 978-1-4522-5950-5 (alk. paper)

1. Social sciences—Statistical methods.
2. Psychology—Statistical methods. I. Title.

HA29.E787 2014
300.72′7--dc23   2013009297

This book is printed on acid-free paper.

SUSTAINABLE FORESTRY INITIATIVE
Label applies to the text stock

Certified Sourcing
www.sfiprogram.org
SFI-00341

13 14 15 16 17 10 9 8 7 6 5 4 3 2 1

Using Basic Statistics in the Behavioral and Social Sciences

© 2014

For Marc Daniel and Lucas Garth

Contents

Preface

As a student in psychology, like most, if not all students in the behavioral and social sciences, I had to master courses in statistics designed to separate the "women from the girls." These were courses that I, and my classmates, approached with a certain amount of fear and trepidation. Unlike many students however, I thoroughly enjoyed these courses and felt a great sense of satisfaction when I successfully completed them. One of the things that struck me immediately was that there are right and wrong answers in statistics, a rare state of affairs in the highly theoretical disciplines within the behavioral and social sciences.

I began writing this book because, when it came time for me to teach statistics, I could not find a text that quite suited me. Many were too quantitative and used such complex notation that my students were unable to see through the math to the underlying logic of statistics. Others were what I call "cookbooks" that taught the steps but not the reasons for taking those steps. So I decided to write up my lecture notes and use them as my basic text. Well, as things are wont to do, that initial decision escalated into a major project, and this book is the result.

My writing style is casual. Students are wary of statistics, and I have never understood why authors promote these fears through dry, awkward, and boring prose. I think statistics are fun, and I hope this comes through in my writing. A little humor can do a lot to relax an anxious student.

I do not emphasize mechanical number crunching or rote memorization in my course, and the book reflects this by avoiding unnecessary notation and jargon. I am not particularly interested in ending up with a student who can run a t test or an ANOVA. What I am interested in is ending up with a student who knows which one is appropriate and why. With the technology available today, a trained monkey can push a button to run a particular test of significance, but not even the most sophisticated computer can examine a set of data and decide how best to analyze them in order to answer the questions posed by the researcher.

This book is organized according to the format I use in my course. I begin with descriptive techniques and follow these chapters with several designed to prepare students for inference. Inference is so important to researchers in the behavioral and social sciences that I find it worthwhile to spend a lot of time laying the groundwork before I introduce the topic. The decision to place the chapters on correlation and regression near the end of the text was more or less arbitrary. Some texts introduce these topics early on.

I think one of the key factors that hinders students' success in statistics courses is anxiety. I hope this text will help.

What's New About the Fifth Edition

As always, I considered all the reviewer suggestions when I revised this book. The reviewers of the fourth edition were consistently positive and asked for very few substantive changes. Some things were clarified, some content was added, but very little content was removed. In the fifth edition, I have included more global examples and references than in previous editions.

New Focus on Research Examples: The older Focus on Research sections have been replaced with current research examples and tied more specifically to the chapter concepts.

Inclusion of Excel Output: When appropriate, I have included examples of what the output from Excel looks like for various procedures.

Supplemental Material: There are three supplements, provided free to adopters, that accompany this new edition: the Instructor's Resource Manual With Exercises, the Test Item File, and PowerPoint Slides. All supplements are available online and can be accessed through a password-protected section of www.sagepub.com/evansstats5e. See your local sales representative for details and access.

- *Instructor's Resource Manual With Exercises:* This supplement contains Chapter Outlines and Exercises With Solutions.
- *Test Item File:* This supplement includes an extensive test bank containing Multiple Choice, Short Answer, True-False, and Discussion questions.
- *PowerPoint Slides:* PowerPoint slides outline concepts in each chapter and include a selection of figures and tables from the textbook.

I think that the fifth edition of *Using Basic Statistics in the Behavioral and Social Sciences* is the best one yet, and I hope you will agree. To those of you who have been loyal users of previous editions, thank you so very much for your support over the years.

Annabel Ness Evans
aevans@concordia.ab.ca
Edmonton

Acknowledgments

Thanks, as always, to my colleague, coauthor, and good friend, Dr. Bryan Rooney for his list of errata and thoughts about how to improve this book.

All my colleagues in the Psychology Department at Concordia are truly stellar and have supported me in many ways over the years. They are Dr. Wendy Pullin, Dr. Allison Kulak, Dr. Dorothy Steffler, Dr. Jamie Dyce, and Ms. Lillian Kennedy. Thanks everyone!

I would also like to acknowledge the support given to me by other people at my school. Dr. Gerald Krispin, President of Concordia University College of Alberta, understood that I needed time to meet the expectations of my publisher for two books that were in revision at about the same time, and he graciously gave me that time. Other people who have, over the years, made my life easier and helped me do what I needed to do are Arlene Thompson and Dorota Jakobs. Thank you both so very much.

Sage Publications! What can I say? What a great company and what a great group of people! Thanks to all the fabulous people who worked with me on this edition. I would specially like to mention Vicki Knight, Jessica Young, Kalie Koscielak, Eric Garner, Olivia Weber-Stenis, Candice Harman, and Nicole Elliott.

Each year I challenge my statistics students to find any new errors in the book. Thanks to Jennifer Webber, Gerry Andersen, and Brian Thompson, who found errors in the second edition. Thanks to Steve Wilkinson, Kristy Petersen, and Jess Halyard, who found errors in the third edition. Thanks to Penny Waller, who found errors in the fourth edition.

I would like to thank the following reviewers who helped me decide what needed to be changed, added, and/or deleted:

Michael Latner,
California Polytechnic
State University, SLO

Yating Liang,
Missouri State University

Zandra S. Gratz,
Kean University

Elizabeth Vanner,
Stony Brook University

Mrinal Sinha,
California State University,
Monterey Bay

Tammy Zacchilli,
Saint Leo University

Xin Liang,
University of Akron

Laree J. Schoolmeesters,
Queens University of Charlotte

Christine MacDonald,
Indiana State University

Howard Lune,
Hunter College, CUNY

Margaret A. Herrick,
Kutztown University of
Pennsylvania

Jennifer Marmo,
Arizona State University

Maxwell I. Moholy,
Idaho State University

Dan Ispas,
Illinois State University

Heather T. Mauney,
Florida State University

Amanda O'Dell,
Loyola University Chicago

Arin M. Connell,
Case Western Reserve University

The two psychologists who inspired my love for statistics are Dr. Peggy Runquist and Dr. Stan Rule. Thank you both.

Finally, thanks to all the students who have studied statistics with me for the past 37 years. You continue to inspire me to write a better book and be a better teacher.

ANE
Edmonton

About the Author

 **Annabel N. Evans** received her Ph.D. in cognitive psychology from the University of Alberta in 1979. She is currently Professor and Chair of the Department of Psychology at Concordia University College of Alberta, where she has taught since 1975. She teaches statistics, chairs the department, and directs the undergraduate programs in psychology (3-year B.A. in psychology and 4-year B.A. in psychology with an applied emphasis). She published the first edition of this book in 1984. She has worked with Sage Publications on this, the fifth edition of this book. She published her second book, *Principles of Behavior Analysis*, with Lyle Grant. Her third textbook, *Methods in Psychological Research*, is coauthored by Bryan Rooney and is in its third edition with Sage Publications. She lives in Edmonton, Alberta, with her dogs, Diva and Toasteroven, neither of whom has a clue about statistics.

CHAPTER 1

Introduction to Statistical Concepts

LEARNING OBJECTIVES

After reading this chapter, you should be able to do the following:

1. Explain why we use descriptive, inferential, and correlational/predictive procedures.
2. Define the terms sample and population.
3. Define and provide an example of a constant and a variable.
4. Define and provide an example of an independent, a dependent, a participant, a continuous, and a discrete variable.
5. Define and provide an example of a nominal, ordinal, interval, and ratio variable.
6. Describe three measurement methods used by researchers to collect data.
7. Describe the difference between internal and external validity and list factors that can threaten each type of validity.
8. Describe five research designs typically used by social scientists.
9. State how the following are used in statistics: N, X, X_N, f, Σ.

Have you heard this famous quote, sometimes attributed to Mark Twain but originally written by Disraeli?

There are three kinds of lies: lies, damned lies, and statistics.

I have heard the following comments many times over the years.

Oh, well, it's easy to lie with statistics.

You can prove whatever you want with statistics.

Statistics don't mean anything.

My response is "Not true. Statistics don't lie, you cannot prove whatever you want with statistics, and statistics do mean something." I hope that by the time you have completed your statistics course, you will agree with me.

Researchers have a responsibility to be fair, honest, and objective in all aspects of the research endeavour. And in spite of what you may have read in the more sensational types of media, most researchers take this responsibility to heart.

Statistics as Tools in the Research Process

Statistics are tools for summarizing data, measuring relationships between sets of data, or making inferences about a large set of data by studying a subset drawn from it. In this book, I attempt to show students in various disciplines how to *apply* statistics to problems in their particular area of inquiry. The study of statistics per se is a mathematical discipline, much like geometry or algebra. This text, however, concentrates on how we use these mathematical techniques as tools to help us solve problems, in the same way that we use a pocket calculator or any other mathematical aid.

The Role of Statistics in Research

In a lot of social science research, statistics form the bridge from a question to a conclusion. Researchers begin with a question they wish to answer or a hypothesis they wish to verify. This question or hypothesis is then reworded in terms of data or evidence that might help answer the question or verify the hypothesis. This is where statistics often come into play, helping the researcher simplify or summarize data so that they can more easily be examined. Statistics may be used to evaluate data to determine if they adequately represent what the researcher wants to study.

The final step in research is to interpret the statistical analyses of the data and to make conclusions about the original question asked or hypothesis put forward.

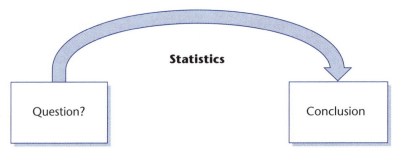

Statistics

Question?   Conclusion

Statistics, then, are tools that the researcher can use to present or interpret information. Researchers use various statistical techniques. We will class these, for the purposes of this text, into three broad categories: (1) *descriptive statistics*, (2) *inferential statistics*, and (3) *correlational and predictive statistics*.

Three Statistical Approaches

Descriptive Statistics

Frequently, researchers need to gather large amounts of data about a variety of events. For example, we may collect outcome measures for various treatment programs designed to help young offenders in Canadian inner cities. Or, perhaps, we interview university students about their views on the relationship between religion and science. When we gather this information, we are soon overwhelmed by numbers. It is very difficult to look at masses of numbers and see any trend or meaning in them. We need to summarize these numbers so that we, and others, can make sense out of them. **Descriptive statistics** serve this purpose. They allow us to describe a mass of numbers in terms of general trends, to tabulate data, and to present data in graphic form.

Using the tools of descriptive statistics, a mass of numbers can be presented in an organized and meaningful way, and data can be simplified so that their general trends can be seen.

Whenever our goal is to *summarize, present,* or *organize* a set of numbers for the purposes of clarification for ourselves, and others, we are using the tools of descriptive statistics.

Inferential Statistics

Suppose that you are a psychologist interested in human memory. You want to know how many numbers people can remember when you read off a list of 20 numbers. One way to answer this question would be to go out and test everyone. You would certainly have your answer, but it would take a lifetime or more for you to test everyone everywhere.

Let's consider a less global question: How sceptical are North American and European consumers about truth in advertising? We could send out a questionnaire to all North American and European consumers and ask them. This might not take a lifetime but it would take a lot more time than most of us would want to spend. A better way to approach this research question would be to ask *some* North American and some European consumers and then *generalize* to all consumers in North America and Europe. This is the inferential approach.

For example, let's consider a water analyst who has come to test your drinking water. She takes a sample from your tap, analyzes that sample, and then gives you her assessment of the water. Although she has not examined all of the water, just a small sample of it, she infers from that sample to all the water. Inferential statistics work like this. We study a subset of items in some detail, the **sample**, and generalize to the complete set of items we are interested in, the

population. In our example, our sample was the water the analyst examined and the population was your water.

Most social science and educational researchers are interested in people, all people. Such research, however, is not conducted on the population at large but rather on some portion of it. Inferential statistics provide tools for generalizing to the population at large by studying only a small sample of it. When used carefully and under appropriate conditions, researchers can use these tools to make *inferences* about populations by examining samples of them.

We use **inferential statistics** whenever we wish to infer things about the population at large, from information taken from a sample of that population.

Descriptive statistics: Procedures used to describe a mass of numbers in terms of general trends, to tabulate data, and to present data in graphic form

Inferential statistics: Procedures used to generalize from a sample to the population from which it was drawn

Population: The entire set of individuals, items, events, or data points of interest

Sample: A subset of a population

CONCEPT REVIEW 1.1

Decide if the examples below use a descriptive or an inferential approach. If you think it is an example of inferential statistics, what is the population?

A. An elementary school teacher keeps careful records about the classroom behavior of his students. At the end-of-the-year school conference, he reports average on-task time, assignments completed, days missed, and tardiness for each student. These data are collected by all the teachers for all the students and are used by the school administrators to evaluate the success of the program.

B. A political scientist is interested in how Californians feel about the recent changes in the health care system put in place by the Obama administration. She mails out a questionnaire to 10 000 randomly chosen people living in California. From their responses, she concludes that Californians are generally in favor of the changes.

Answers on page 27.

Correlational and Predictive Statistics

Every day we notice relationships between things. For example, we all suspect that there is a relationship between poverty and crime and between diet and good health.

Researchers often need to describe these types of relationships. The statistical tools that allow us to measure the strength of various relationships are called correlational statistics. **Correlational statistics** are descriptive when they describe the relationship between two entire sets of observations; they can also be used inferentially to infer, from a sample, the **correlation** in the population.

Universities often use the correlation between high school average and university performance. These two are related in that students with high Grade 12 marks tend to do well in university. This kind of established relationship can be used in predictive statistics. If we know that school grades and university grades are related, then we can look at a student's school grades and *predict* how he or she will do in university. Predictive statistics provide tools for making predictions about an event based on available information. How well or how accurately we can predict depends on how strong the relationship is between the two sets of observations.

When we are describing a relationship between events or when we are predicting from one event to another, we are using correlational and **predictive statistics**, respectively.

Correlational statistics: Describe or infer the relationship between two entire sets of observations

Predictive statistics: Provide tools for making predictions about an event, based on available information

Correlation: Describes a linear relationship between two variables

Preliminary Concepts

Constants Versus Variables

A **constant** is just that—*constant*! A constant is a characteristic of objects, people, or events that *does not vary*. If the temperature of the room in which students wrote their final psychology exam did not vary, it is a constant.

A **variable** is a characteristic of objects, people, or events that can have different **values**. The value can vary in *quantity* (e.g., family income) or in *quality* (e.g., ethnic background). A quantitative (numerical) value is often called a **score**. Variables can be classified in different ways.

Constant: A characteristic of things, people, or events that does not vary

Variable: A characteristic that can have different values

Value: A property of a variable—can be quantitative or qualitative

Score: A quantitative (numerical) value

Classifying Variables

Experimental Classification

Variables are classified according to the function they serve in an experiment. A true experiment requires a true independent variable. A true **independent variable** (**IV**, also called manipulated variable) is one that the researcher directly manipulates or controls. Researchers select the values they wish to study and assign participants to each value or level of the variable.

For example, if I am interested in the effects of practice on problem solving, I might choose to give lots of practice problems to one group and only a few practice problems to a different group of people. After both groups have solved the practice problems, I could measure their performance on a new set of test problems. The IV is *amount of practice*, and I have selected *two values* of that variable to use in my experiment (lots of practice problems and few practice problems).

Perhaps I work in a correctional facility with people who have problems with anger. I might want to evaluate two anger management programs. I could compare the anger management behavior of inmates who received one or the other of the two programs with the behavior of inmates who received neither. The IV would be *type of program*, and I have three values of this variable (the two training programs and the nontrained or control group).

A **dependent variable** (**DV**) depends (we hope) on the levels or values of the IV. The performance of the participants on the test problems is my dependent variable. It is called dependent because we assume their test performance *depends on* the amount of practice they received, the IV. In the second example, the DV would be the measure of anger behavior. We hope that this behavior *depends on* the type or amount of training the inmates received.

In social science and educational research, the DV is often a measure of performance, such as a score on a test, preference measure, rating, or reaction time. DVs could also be physiological measures, such as heart rate, blood pressure, or hormone levels, or psychological measures, such as depression level, mood, or amount of psychopathology. The DV is the response that the researcher measures and expects to be influenced by the IV.

We can think of the relationship between the IV and the DV as *cause and effect*. The DV has this name because its values are expected to *depend on* (or be caused by) the values of the IV. The IV has its name because its values *do not depend* on the values of the DV. Rather, its values are expected to cause changes to the values of the DV (the effect of the manipulation).

There is a special class of variables called **participant variables** that seem like IVs but are not directly manipulated by the experimenter. Instead, the researcher selects groups that already differ with respect to the values or levels of the variable. Participant variables are also called *nonmanipulated* or *comparison* variables.

FYI

Participant variables used to be called subject variables. The American Psychological Association (APA) recommends we use the term *subject* when referring to animals and the term *participant* when referring to humans. I follow that recommendation in this book.

The participant variables age, gender, and ethnicity are often called **organismic variables**. Organismic variables are inherent in the organism. We can study these variables, but we cannot assign participants to different values of these variables. Participants inherently possess a value.

Imagine that I am interested in evaluating different smoking cessation programs. My participants are people who have chosen various programs to help them quit smoking. The type of program the participants enrolled in was their choice, not mine. They selected the program, and I can only compare the outcomes of their selections.

Instead, let's imagine that I selected a group of people and randomly assigned them to different groups. Each group then completed a particular smoking cessation program. Now, we have a true experiment because I selected the levels of the IV (i.e., type of smoking cessation program), and I assigned participants to each level.

Participant variables are not true IVs because, although experimenters can study them, they cannot manipulate them. These variables are traits or characteristics of the participants, and the researcher can only select groups of participants who either possess or have been exposed to different levels or values of these variables. Do not confuse *measurement* of variables with *manipulation* of variables. Imagine that I have measured degree of psychopathology with a personality test. I use the values to create three groups of people who differ in degree (high, moderate, and low pathology). I then gather information about familial histories, socioeconomic status, education, and careers with the goal of finding patterns. Degree of psychopathology is neither an IV nor a DV. Although I measured it to categorize the people, I did not manipulate it.

Researchers who compare groups that differ in levels of participant variables are not conducting true experiments: They are conducting quasi-experiments. Although the statistical analysis of true and quasi-experiments may be the same, the inferences that can be made differ. This is discussed in more detail later in this chapter.

Independent variable: A variable whose values are manipulated by the experimenter and are expected to have an effect on the values of the dependent variable

Dependent variable: A variable whose values are expected to be influenced by values of the independent variable

Participant variable: A variable on which participants differ but which is not manipulated by the experimenter

Organismic variable: Inherent characteristic of the participant that cannot be controlled by the researcher

In an earlier example, I was interested in the effects of amount of practice on problem solving. If I were also interested in whether practice influences younger people more than older people, I might decide to compare younger people who get lots of practice with those who don't and older people who get lots of practice with those who don't. If this were the case, *amount of practice* is still my IV. *Age* would be a new variable in my study, and it would be a *participant variable*, specifically an *organismic variable*, because I don't assign participants to age groups. Age is inherent in the organism. All I can do is select participants of different ages for inclusion in my study. I may find that test performance is influenced not only by amount of practice but also by age. Younger people may benefit more than older people from the opportunity to practice. In this example, a true IV (amount of practice) and a participant variable (age) were combined in one study, a common approach in social science research.

Many researchers study variables that they don't manipulate experimentally. Sociologists are often interested in demographic differences, whereas developmental psychologists may study age differences. Forensic psychologists may study personality trait differences among groups of offenders classified by severity of crime. The study of participant variables is an important part of research in the social sciences.

CONCEPT REVIEW 1.2

In the following examples, determine the IV and the DV, and indicate if any participant variables were involved. Explain why you have categorized a variable as a participant variable.

A. A sports psychologist working with British soccer players has been reading about a new imagery technique in which athletes try to improve their performance by imagining going through the steps to a perfect performance. She decides to do an experiment. She picks, in an arbitrary fashion, 20 of her clients and trains them to use this new technique along with the other strategies she has used in the past. After some time, she compares the performance and attitudes of her 20 "imagery" clients with 20 clients who did not receive the additional imagery instruction. She finds that the imagery-instructed athletes performed better and felt better about their performance than did the athletes who did not receive imagery training. In addition, she noticed that female athletes seemed to benefit even more than men when given imagery training.

B. A sociologist interested in racial profiling interviewed visible minority and White young people in a large Southern U.S. city. She found that Black youth were much more likely to report being stopped and searched by police than young people from other racial backgrounds.

Answers on page 27.

Mathematical Classification

Variables may also be classified in terms of the number of values they may take on in the span between any two points, called an interval. **Continuous variables**, in theory, can take on any value within an infinite series of possible values. Weight, for example, is a continuous variable because there is an infinitely large number of possible values within any weight interval. Similarly, height is a continuous variable. In fact, the values of these continuous variables are limited only by the sensitivity of our scales or rulers, not by the variable itself. My bathroom scale may report my weight to the nearest kilogram but theoretically my weight could be measured to an infinite number of decimals with an infinitely precise scale. Reaction time, blood alcohol level, and temperature are all continuous variables.

Discrete variables can have only a certain defined set of values. Number of children per family is a discrete variable in that certain values are not possible (e.g., 0.5 or 1.5). Gender is also a discrete variable; male and female are the only values possible. Some other examples of discrete variables are socioeconomic status (e.g., upper, middle, lower), psychological diagnosis (e.g., schizophrenia, bipolar disorder, anxiety disorder, depression), and crime type (e.g., homicide, vandalism, major theft, minor theft).

> **Continuous variable:** A variable with, theoretically, an infinite number of values within a given interval
>
> **Discrete variable:** A variable with a finite number of values within a given interval

CONCEPT REVIEW 1.3

Decide if each of the following is an example of a continuous or a discrete variable. Explain your answers.

A. Type of family: two parent, one parent, other

B. Testosterone level of incarcerated men

C. Time-on-task of first graders in Ms. King's class

D. Number of aggressive acts by autistic children in a special needs class

Answers on page XX.

Measurement Classification

Variables can be classified in terms of their scale of measurement. By scale of measurement, I mean degree of *quantification*. Some variables differ only in *quality*; others differ in *quantity*. The degree to which a variable can be quantified defines the kinds of arithmetic, algebraic, and statistical operations that are allowable. The scale of measurement must be known before the appropriate statistical procedure can be determined.

The values of a **nominal variable** differ only in quality. Eye color and gender are nominal variables. For simplicity, we may assign numbers to a nominal variable (e.g., male = 1, female = 2). These numbers, however, provide no quantitative information. The numbers on the sweaters of hockey players are nominal. They are used merely for identification, not to indicate any measure of quantity. We wouldn't claim that a hockey player numbered 99, for example, was 9 times better, bigger, or faster than one numbered 11. Or, would we?

Ethnic background, religious affiliation, and country of origin are also nominal variables.

	Gemstone Type
	Emerald
Nominal	Diamond
	Sapphire

The values of **ordinal variables** differ in quantity. If we ranked 90 students and numbered them from best (1) to worst (90), we would have an ordinal scale. The intervals between the values, however, may not be equal. The second- and third–ranked students are not necessarily the same distance apart as are the first- and second-ranked students. Employment status of workers such as unskilled, skilled, and professional is another example of an ordinal scale. Each value differs in quantity in terms of formal training involved (and probably wages) but the difference between an unskilled worker and a skilled worker in terms of training and wages is probably not the same as the difference between the skilled worker and the professional. Some other ordinal variables are aggressiveness (ranked as highly, moderately, or not aggressive), Piagetian stage of child development (preoperational, concrete operational, formal operational), and outcome prognosis (ranked as excellent, moderate, poor, very poor).

	Gemstone Popularity
	Diamond (most popular)
Ordinal	Emerald (second most popular)
	Sapphire (third most popular)

The intervals between **interval variable** values are equal. The Fahrenheit temperature scale is a good example of an interval variable. The difference between 40 degrees and 50 degrees Fahrenheit is the same as the difference between 60 degrees and 70 degrees; that is, 10 degrees. Interval variables have an *arbitrary* zero point. Zero degree Fahrenheit does not mean zero temperature or the absence of heat; 80 degrees is not twice as hot as 40 degrees. IQ (intelligence quotient) is another interval variable. A person with an IQ of 180 is not twice as smart as someone with an IQ of 90 because a zero IQ outcome on an IQ test does not mean absence of intelligence. But with interval variables, we can say that one observation is larger than another by a certain amount (e.g., 10 degrees or 15 IQ points).

	Gemstone Hardness Rating (1 = softest, 10 = hardest)
	Diamond (10)
Interval	Sapphire (9)
	Emerald (7)

Ratio variables are like interval variables but with a *true* or real zero point. We can say that one observation is not only larger than another by a certain amount (as in interval variables) but also by a certain ratio. For example, length is a ratio variable. One kilometer is half the length of 2 kilometers, and a zero length is a point, not a line. A field goal kicker whose maximum kick is 60 meters can kick *twice as far* (a ratio) as one whose maximum is 30 meters.

Height, weight, and the Kelvin temperature scale are examples of ratio variables (zero degree Kelvin does mean complete absence of heat). Bar pressing rates of rats, time spent in suicidal ideation, and number of suicide attempts are also ratio variables.

	Gemstone Per Carat Value
	Diamond ($3900)
Ratio	Sapphire ($3000)
	Emerald ($900)

Nominal variable: Has values that differ in quality only

Ordinal variable: Has values ordered by quantity

Interval variable: Has values ordered by quantity with equal-sized intervals between each

Ratio variable: Is like an interval variable but with a true zero point

CONCEPT REVIEW 1.4

For each of the following, determine the scale of measurement and explain your answers.

A. Marital status

B. University degree in arts (B.A., M.A., Ph.D.)

C. Level of job satisfaction (very satisfied, moderately satisfied, moderately dissatisfied, very dissatisfied)

D. Number of years of postsecondary education

Answers on page 27.

ALERT

Every year students ask, "How can number of pages in a book be a ratio variable when you can't have a book with zero pages?"

The arbitrary zero point of interval variables does not refer to whether or not such a value can occur; it refers to where we start counting. Think about height of people, a ratio variable. Of course, no one is zero inches tall, but we start measuring height from zero, don't we? We start counting pages from zero also.

The Language of Statistics

Like most science and mathematical disciplines, statistics has its own symbolic language. Different letters are used, sometimes in roman, sometimes in *italics*, sometimes uppercase, sometimes lower. Greek letters are also used, both in upper and lower cases. Symbols often have subscripts. Pay particular attention to the symbols introduced here and throughout the book.

Variables Versus Constants

We use letters at the end of the alphabet such as X, Y, and Z (in *italics*) to refer to variables. Letters at the beginning of the alphabet, such as a, b, and c, are used to refer to constants.

Notation

The use of uppercase letters at the end of the alphabet is reserved for naming collective sets or groups of values. We refer to the X distribution or the Y distribution of numbers, for example. Sometimes, X has a subscript. X_i refers to a particular value in the X distribution; X_1 is the first value in the X distribution; X_7 is the seventh value. Do not use lowercase x when discussing a group of values.

N is the number of values in a distribution. If my psychology class has 42 students enrolled and all wrote the first midterm test, then $N = 42$ for the distribution of scores on that test.

X_N is the last value in a distribution. On the final exam in my psychology class, $X_N = X_{42}$. This refers to the particular score obtained by the last or 42nd student.

f refers to frequency, usually the frequency of a particular value in a distribution. If 13 students got 63% on the final exam in my psychology class, then the f for 63% is 13. Do not use uppercase F when referring to frequency. F has a different meaning entirely.

Σ the Greek uppercase letter sigma is a summation sign. ΣX instructs you to sum or add up all the values in the X distribution.

N: The total number of observations (values) in a population distribution

X_N: The last value in the X distribution

f: The number of times a particular value occurred in a distribution—stands for frequency

Σ: The sign for summation

CONCEPT REVIEW 1.5

Scores on grammar quiz: 10, 9, 9, 8, 7, 7, 5, 5, 4, 3
For the distribution of numbers above:

A. What is the f for the score value of 9?

B. $X_N =$

C. $N =$

D. $\Sigma X =$

Answers on page 28.

Statisticians use one kind of notation when they are referring to a population and a different notation when they are referring to a sample drawn from a population. Descriptive techniques are used to describe entire populations, and so population notation should be used. An *entire* population does not necessarily mean a huge population; it means the population of interest. Inferential techniques are used to make inferences from a sample to a population, and so sample notation should be used. We won't be using sample notation until the chapters on inference, but many textbooks introduce sample notation right away, and some textbooks never make the distinction, using one notation for both descriptive and inferential procedures. My choice is based on my commitment to a conceptual approach in this book. Conceptually, there is a big difference between describing all the members of a population and making inferences about all the members of a population after observing a sample of them.

Table 1.1

Notation for samples versus populations

Measure	Sample	Population
Size	n	N
Mean	$\bar{X}$ or $\bar{Y}$	μ_X or μ_Y
Standard deviation	S or SD	σ
Variance	S^2 or Var	σ^2

Table 1.1 presents some of the standard notation used by statisticians to refer to populations and samples. We will be using these in later chapters.

Conducting Research in the Social Sciences

Some research is conducted in a laboratory setting under highly controlled conditions. Other studies are carried out in the field, a natural setting outside the laboratory. Each technique presents problems to the researcher. Laboratory research, because of its contrived nature, may produce outcomes that would not occur in a more natural setting. People and animals may respond differently in a laboratory than they do in their everyday environment.

Field researchers attempt to study naturally occurring responses in their usual environment. The researcher has much less control over what goes on in a field study than in a laboratory study. Which approach is used depends in part on the research question to be answered. Often, pragmatic needs limit the choices of the researcher.

Regardless of the research setting, research in education and the social sciences is typically concerned with measuring animal or human responses. Some of these responses are overt, such as reaction time, and others more covert, such as brain wave activity. Several methods of measurement are available to the researcher. We will examine three of the more common methods of measurement.

Measurement Methods

Observation

The observation of responses as they occur is one of the primary methods of measurement used by researchers in human and animal behavior. Much of what we know about animal behavior was acquired through observation in the field. Observational methods are used in laboratory settings as well. Watching children engaging in play behavior, perhaps from behind a one-way glass, is an example of observation in the laboratory.

Self-Report

Some things are difficult or impossible to observe directly. People's attitudes about gay marriage, for example, can't really be observed, but we can ask people what their attitudes are. To measure human sexual behavior, Kinsey used the self-report method, whereas Masters and Johnson observed the behavior directly.

Self-report is the method most often chosen by researchers interested in attitudes, beliefs, personality, feelings, and so on. Because participants are reporting on their own inner states, and because it is often difficult to corroborate self-report data, we must be careful when we interpret the results of research using this method of measurement.

Survey researchers gather self-report data with a questionnaire: a standard set of questions given to a large number of people. Opinion poll research is an example of this. The researcher selects a sample of people, measures their opinions on various issues, and generalizes to the population at large. There is always some probability of a sampling error that would bias the outcome, and survey researchers are very aware of the practices to follow to reduce such a possibility.

Some researchers collect self-report data through one-on-one interviews, often with a structured set of questions. The advantage of an interview is that the researcher can vary the questions depending on answers to previous questions. This provides the flexibility that a mail-out questionnaire lacks. Now that most people have access to the Internet, research using this technology is becoming more and more common. Collecting data via the Internet is easy and fast, but there are problems researchers need to be aware of. For example, it is difficult to know who is responding when you use the Internet.

Standardized Tests

There are many psychological, educational, and sociological tests that have been standardized on a large population and can be used to assess an individual against those standards or norms. This method of measurement is typical in educational settings where test performance is used to predict future performance after some sort of educational experience or training. Standardized tests are also commonly used in psychotherapeutic settings to help with diagnosis and treatment of psychological pathology.

It's important to recognize that a single administration of a standardized test to an individual is not normally enough information for accurate prediction or diagnosis. Standardized tests must be corroborated by other measurements.

Interpreting Research Outcomes: Reliability and Validity

However, you have obtained your data, and it is important that your measures be both reliable and valid. A reliable measure is one that is repeatable under similar research conditions; a valid measure is one that measures what it claims to measure. Standardized IQ tests provide quite reliable data. In other words, repeated IQ testing of the same individual tends to produce very similar results. There is some debate, however, about whether or not IQ tests are valid; do they really measure intelligence?

Applying a statistical procedure to a set of numbers is the easy step in the research process. Deciding which procedure is appropriate for the particular data in hand requires expertise in both research design and statistics. But perhaps even more crucial is the interpretation of the statistical outcome, and this issue we will address here. Good researchers are careful to design their studies so that the results can be accurately interpreted. It is necessary to carefully control the research situation so that the results can be attributed to the variables manipulated by the researcher rather than to some other reason. In other words, alternative explanations for the outcome must be ruled out. This is achieved by good research design. If researchers fail to anticipate what the controlling variables are in a study, then their interpretation of which variables are responsible for the outcome may be faulty. The researchers may well believe that the outcome was a result of a particular variable and may be unaware of other variables operating that affected the outcome. When this occurs, we say the study lacks *validity*. Studies can also lack validity when the results do not generalize to other situations or to other participants. A statistically significant outcome from a study does not guarantee that the finding has any importance in the real world.

We say that a research study is valid if (a) the outcome was dependent on the variables specifically studied and (b) the findings generalize to other situations and participants. The former is called **internal validity**, and the latter is called **external validity**.

> **Internal validity:** The extent to which an observed relationship or outcome reflects the manipulations of the research variables
>
> **External validity:** The extent to which research outcomes generalize to other situations and participants

Factors Affecting Internal Validity

An internally valid study is one where the outcomes of importance are a result of the variables manipulated by the researcher. For example, a nursing supervisor who concludes from a study that she conducted that casual clothes, rather than uniforms, worn by her nurses promote a feeling of well-being in her aged patients, must be sure that the change in dress was the responsible variable, rather than something else. Suppose that her nurses were more relaxed in casual clothes than when in uniform and the patients responded favourably. It could be important for the supervisor to realize that the change in attitude on the part of the nursing staff was the critical variable rather than the change in dress. When designing studies, researchers must keep in mind all the factors that can influence the internal validity of their work.

Proactive History

Many researchers compare performance of different groups of participants who have been treated differently in some way. Perhaps one group received a special kind of training and the other group a different type or no training at all. The object is to show that the training was the influencing factor on performance. It is important that the different groups were *initially equivalent* before the training was given. If the groups were different to start with, we should not be surprised to find that the results are different at the end of our study. Proactive history, then, refers to all the differences participants bring with them into the investigation.

Imagine that the Boy Scouts of America organization conducted a study to determine if Scout training influenced social responsibility in young boys. Suppose they found that Scouts were more socially responsible than non-Scout boys. Their conclusion that Scouting experience was responsible for this difference could well be faulty. Boys who join the Scouts may well be different to begin with than boys who do not. If the groups (Scouts and non-Scouts) were indeed initially different, it would be inappropriate to conclude that Scout training had an effect on social responsibility. The fundamental problem with this and all *quasi-experiments* is that there is no assurance of initial equivalence of groups when participant variables are studied. I said earlier that although quasi-experiments are often treated the same as true experiments in terms of the statistical analyses, the inferences that can be made are not the same. In quasi-experimental research, we cannot be sure that the groups were initially equivalent on the outcome variables we measure. Again, if the groups were different to begin with on the variables that we are interested in (in our example, we were interested in social responsibility), then of course they will be different at the end of our study, and Scouting had nothing to do with it.

The most common procedure for controlling the effects of proactive history is random selection of participants and random assignment to groups. Random selection is a method of selecting participants such that all members of the population have an equal probability of being included. Random assignment to groups is done in such a way that participants are independently put into groups.

Retroactive History

Certain events that may influence the participants involved may occur during the time that the research study is conducted. Suppose that a sociologist sends out a questionnaire to compare the attitudes of New Yorkers and Los Angelenos on the issue of capital punishment. Further suppose that during this period of time, a particularly gruesome killing in Los Angeles stimulates a great deal of media attention. The results of the study might show that Los Angelenos have different opinions about capital punishment than do New Yorkers. If the researcher was unaware of the events in Los Angeles, his interpretation of the results might be faulty. Indeed, had he conducted the study at a different time, he might have had quite a different outcome. One of the reasons why many researchers use animals rather than humans is that it is so much easier to control differences in history with animals.

Retroactive history is of particular concern to researchers conducting long-term investigations where the chances of momentous events happening during the course of the study increase.

Maturation

Developmental differences in participants during the course of a research study can affect internal validity. As you might imagine, this is of particular concern in long-term research with children. A finding that children do better at solving math problems after receiving 6 weeks of special training must be carefully evaluated because the maturation of the children may be responsible wholly or in part for the finding rather than the special training itself. The use of an appropriate **control group** is the best way to deal with the influences of maturation.

Control group: The group that is not exposed to the independent variable

Testing

Testing plays an important role in many research studies. A pretest is often used to measure performance level before some special training is given. A posttest follows training to determine if the training had an effect. Sometimes the initial pretest itself can affect performance, and this obscures the role of the training on the posttest scores. For the study to be internally valid, the researcher must find ways to ensure that the training, not the pretest, was responsible for the performance differences following training.

Attrition (Experimental Mortality)

Attrition refers to the differential loss of participants from certain groups in a research study. Participants may be lost for a variety of reasons. If this loss is particularly great for one group, then internal validity may be reduced. A researcher interested in the effects of behavioral intervention with alcoholics might choose to compare two groups—a "problem drinking" group with a "chronic alcoholic" group. Participants are trained in behavioral principles to help them control their drinking over a period of 6 months. Suppose that several members of the "chronic alcoholic" group dropped out of the study for health reasons. This is an example where the internal validity of the study is threatened because we might expect different results had the dropouts been able to continue in the study.

Investigator Bias

Experimenter or investigator bias is an issue of great concern in research today. The expectations of even the most conscientious experimenter may unintentionally influence the results of the study. One way to control for such a bias is through a *double-blind* control procedure, in which neither the individual collecting the data nor the participant participating in the study is aware of the hypotheses or expected outcomes.

Factors Affecting External Validity

An externally valid study is one where the findings can be generalized to participants and situations other than the specific ones studied. Discovering that a third-year anthropology student behaves in a specific way in a highly contrived laboratory context is not all that helpful if this behavior does not occur for most people in most settings. This is where we may ask the question "Is the finding really 'significant' in the real world?" When planning their studies, researchers must consider several factors that can influence external validity.

Sampling Bias

In research, we often study a sample of participants with the objective of generalizing from the sample to the population from which the sample was drawn. Such generalizations have validity only if the sample from which the generalization is made is indeed *representative* of the population being generalized to. One way of increasing the likelihood that the sample is representative of the population is to randomly select the participants to be included in the sample. Unfortunately, much of the time, random selection is not possible. Psychological research, for example, is often conducted on samples of university students. If university students are different in important ways from the general population, then research outcomes from such studies may not have validity in the real world.

The problems that researchers face when designing studies are many. To increase the likelihood of internal validity, one often has to relax concerns about external validity and vice versa. The research design itself provides the best opportunity for increasing validity.

The Hawthorne Effect

Participants who participate in an investigation may behave differently simply because they are singled out for special treatment. The specific treatment may not be responsible for the outcome; rather, the awareness on the part of participants that they are participating in a study may be. This phenomenon is known as the *Hawthorne effect*.

One way to avoid this effect is to use deceptive techniques, so that participants are not aware they are participating. Obviously, this is not always possible or desirable, but researchers do attempt to limit the information available to participants about the nature of the study.

Designing the Study

The choice of a research design is made for a variety of reasons, some of which are pragmatic. Most of us would be delighted if we could always design research where threats to internal and external validity are eliminated. Unfortunately, this is not always possible. Available resources, the nature of the research question, and other variables can limit our choices about design. As long as we are aware of the problems with various designs, we can temper our conclusions about our findings accordingly. A poor design does not necessarily mean poor research. Accurate and fair interpretation of the results is the critical feature of good research.

Experimental Designs

Earlier in this chapter I discussed the experimental classification of variables by the role they play in an experiment. In an experiment, the investigator systematically manipulates an IV(s) and measures some response (the DV) to see if the manipulation of the IV influenced that response. Typically, participants are randomly assigned to an experimental group, which receives one value of the IV, or to a control group, which receives a different value of the IV, often no treatment at all. Assuming that the two groups were initially equivalent, the experimenter can compare their performance. If differences occur, it can be concluded that they were caused by the IV manipulation. This type of research design, called *experimental design*, is the cornerstone of scientific research and is the only design where cause and effect can be claimed with confidence.

Researchers planning to conduct an experiment have many decisions to make. They must decide what IV to investigate and what DV to measure, and they must consider the potential influence of factors other than the IV that might affect the DV. In other words, if variables other than the ones chosen for study, often called *extraneous variables*, influence responding, then the interpretation of the effect of the IV is made much more difficult. Imagine a researcher interested in the effects of alcohol on reaction time in a simulated driving test. She might be wise to consider factors such as previous experience with alcohol and driving competence when she decides how to assign participants to groups. Researchers using people as participants must continually guard against the influence of extraneous variables such as differences in motivation, attention, and ability when they design their experiments. These problems help us understand why some researchers prefer controlled laboratory experiments and animal subjects.

Many research questions, however, do not lend themselves to an experimental design. Medical research, in particular, is often limited by ethical issues that make true experimentation impossible. Suppose that you were interested in the effects of computer radiation on fetal weight gain in pregnant women. It would not be ethical to randomly assign pregnant women to a computer radiation group when you expect this to harm their developing fetuses, would it? This research problem would best be studied with a correlational design.

Correlational Designs

Correlational designs are used to measure the relationship between two or more variables. Participants are not randomly assigned to an IV or control group; rather, they have already been exposed to various levels of some variable. A researcher might study a sample of pregnant women who work on computers for different lengths of time each day as part of their jobs. He wants to determine if there is a relationship between exposure to computer screen radiation and newborn birth weight. Suppose he discovered that the women who spent more time using computers had newborns of lower birth weight than those who spent less time using computers. The researcher might not be able to prove conclusively that the lower birth weights were caused by computer radiation. But if he had carefully controlled other possible variables that might produce the difference, he could suspect that a causal relationship might exist, and he might design further studies to confirm this.

Because correlational designs do not permit strong statements about cause and effect, and because ethical considerations limit the use of the experiment with human participants, many health-related questions are studied with animal populations. Generalizing from animals to humans, however, requires caution.

Case Study Designs

The case study is the design of choice for many who investigate personality and mental illness. Neuropsychology researchers may also use this approach. Freud, a psychoanalyst, used this technique to gather the data he used to develop his theory of personality and psychopathology. You might be interested to know that Freud's theory of personality and personality development was based on case study research of adults in psychotherapy. He rarely studied "normal" adults or children. He based his ideas about childhood development on the recollections of his adult patients!

A case study is an in-depth biography of a specific individual. The researcher uses a variety of methods of measurement, often including observation, self-report, and standardized tests. This design allows for a much more extensive set of data about an individual.

Cross-Cultural Research Designs

Cross-cultural designs are used for research that compares people of different cultures. All of the methods of measurement we have discussed may be used.

Over the past few decades, much has been made of the findings that Blacks tend to score lower on standardized intelligence tests than Caucasians. Less attention has been made to the findings that Asians tend to score higher than Caucasians.

Evaluation Research Designs

Evaluation of educational, therapeutic, and social programs is an important part of the research process. Evaluation research designs are much more prevalent today than in the past. It was not uncommon, a few years ago, for governmental, educational, and other kinds of programs to be introduced with little or no attempt to evaluate the efficacy or cost-effectiveness of the program. For example, some time ago I was employed to evaluate a social services program that had been operating for several years. It was designed to help severely handicapped individuals learn basic skills of daily living. I discovered quite quickly that when the program had initially been designed, there were no provisions made for evaluation. In other words, the program developers failed to build into the program any methods of measuring whether goals were being met or not. No systematic data collection occurred. I was forced to inform the administrators that their program's success or failure in meeting its goals could not be evaluated.

More recently, on the other hand, I was asked to be an evaluation consultant for a program that was not yet developed. This permitted me to be involved in the initial planning of the program, thereby ensuring that appropriate measures were taken to allow for future evaluation of the program's effectiveness. More and more frequently, psychologists, sociologists, and educators are acting as evaluation consultants.

Meta-Analysis

Meta-analysis is more of a strategy than a research design. Researchers combine the data from several studies of a particular topic to better understand the effect of the manipulations. By combining several studies, it is often easier to determine the true effect of the IV on the DV.

Using Computers in Statistics

Computer technology has been a real boon to statisticians. It is a rare researcher who analyzes data by hand these days. Hand-held calculators, PDAs, and even some cell phones are sophisticated enough to do a wide variety of analyses. Many of you probably own calculators, and now is a good time to go back to your instruction booklet and learn how to use the various functions of your calculator. Most medium-priced calculators will sum a list of numbers, sum the squares of those numbers, calculate means and standard deviations, and run a simple t test and correlation test.

For many of you, the first step in using a computer to help with statistical analyses is to learn how to use a spreadsheet. A spreadsheet is an elaborate electronic calculator that can do an enormous number of arithmetical and statistical manipulations almost instantaneously. You enter the data, write formulas to do certain things, and use the built-in functions to do other things. Once a formula is written, the spreadsheet will automatically perform the arithmetic indicated in the formula. Knowing how to use a spreadsheet gives you a lot of flexibility in custom tailoring the analyses you want to do on a set of data.

Many statistical analyses are standard techniques that don't vary from one set of data to another, and there are commercially available programs you can use. The most popular programs include SPSS (Statistical Package for the Social Sciences), SAS (Statistical Analysis System), and MINITAB. Versions of these programs are available for most PCs. As well, numerous smaller statistics programs are available.

Richard Lowry, professor emeritus from Vassar, developed a very useful online statistics program called VassarStats. It will perform most of the statistics described in this book. You can find Dr. Lowry's program at http://vassarstats.net/

It may be well worth your time to learn about the programs available. Which one you choose depends on your needs as well as the type of PC you use. SPSS is considered by most social scientists to be the most comprehensive statistical package. However, Microsoft Excel can perform most of the statistical procedures used in this textbook, and I have included several examples of the output from Excel.

FOCUS ON RESEARCH

Eating disorders such as *anorexia nervosa* have received quite a lot of attention in the media lately. Journalists and magazine writers often speculate about celebrities who they think suffer from these problems. Clinicians typically focus on family problems, body image distortion, and the need for control as factors contributing to eating disorders. One factor that has been neglected is physical activity.

THE RESEARCH PROBLEM

Hechler, Beumont, Marks, and Touyz (2005) were interested in finding out if clinical specialists really understand the link between physical activity and eating disorders.

THE RESEARCH APPROACH

The researchers conducted a *cross-cultural* study. They used a questionnaire to assess the knowledge about eating disorders (ED) of clinicians who were identified as experts in EDs in four country groups: United States/Canada, Europe, Japan/China, and Australia/New Zealand. These experts included psychiatrists, psychologists, physiotherapists, nurses, physicians, and dieticians. The researchers were interested in comparing the responses to the questionnaire of the specialists who had been grouped in categories based on the country of origin. They did not manipulate country of origin, of course, so this is a *quasi-experimental design* with a participant variable as the comparison variable.

THE VARIABLES

The *nonmanipulated variable*: Country of origin is a discrete nominal variable. The *measured variable*: The experts were asked to indicate how important they thought physical activity (PA) was in the development of EDs. They chose from five options. Because the participants chose only one option from a list of five, this is a discrete variable. These options were ordered from *most strongly involved in the development of ED* to *of minor importance*, which is an ordinal variable.

THE RESULTS

Some of the results are presented in Table 1.2.

Table 1.2

Respondents' understanding of the role of physical activity in EDs (%)

Option	United States and Canada	Europe	Japan and China	Australia and New Zealand	Total
PA is fundamental to the development of the ED	0	16.7	0	30.8	15.2
PA and EDs are directly related	40	50	22.2	46.2	39.4
PA and EDs are indirectly related	0	33.3	33.3	23.1	24.0
PA and EDs are variants of each other	60	33.3	22.2	7.7	24.0
PA plays a minor role in EDs	0	16.7	22.2	0	9.1

Note: ED = eating disorder; PA = physical activity. These sample sizes were all very small.

THE CONCLUSIONS

Hechler et al. (2005) concluded that in this small sample, the majority of the experts were aware that PA was an important factor in EDs. The researchers pointed out that there were cultural differences. For example, they noted that the experts from Japan/China thought that PA had a relatively minor role in EDs. The authors suggested that more research should be done in this area.

SUMMARY OF TERMS AND CONCEPTS

Descriptive statistics describe the characteristics of an entire set of data, called a population.

Population is the entire set of individuals, items, events, or data points of interest.

Sample is a subset of individuals, items, events, or data points drawn from the population of interest.

Inferential statistics use sample data to make inferences about populations.

Relationship and predictive statistics describe the relationship between X and Y or predict Y from X.

Variables can take on more than one value but *constants* have only one value.

Independent variables are experimental variables selected and directly altered by the experimenter and expected to affect the values of *dependent variables*.

Continuous variables may have an infinite number of values whereas discrete variables have a finite set of values.

Nominal variables have values that differ in name only, whereas ordinal variables have values that are ordered with respect to quantity.

Interval variables have equal intervals between values and an arbitrary zero point.

Ratio variables are like interval variables with real zero points.

X, Y, Z distribution or X, Y, Z variable refers to a collective set of values. When a subscript accompanies the letter, a specific value is indicated.

N is the total number of values in a distribution of values.

f refers to the frequency with which a value occurred in a distribution of values.

Σ is a summation sign. It is an instruction to sum a set of values as in ΣX.

Research in the behavioral sciences is conducted both in the *field* and in the *laboratory*.

Researchers gather much of their data through *observation*, *self-report*, and *standardized tests*.

Measures must be both *reliable* and *valid* to be useful to researchers. A reliable measure is one that that is repeatable. A valid measure is one that measures what it claims to measure.

A research study is *internally valid* if the outcome was dependent on the specific variables involved in the study. A research study is *externally valid* if the findings generalize to other situations and other participants.

Factors that affect internal validity include *proactive* and *retroactive history, maturation, testing, attrition,* and *investigator bias*. Factors that affect external validity include *sampling bias* and participant awareness (called the *Hawthorne effect*).

Common research designs include *experimental designs, correlational designs, case studies, cross-cultural designs,* and *evaluation research designs*.

CONCEPT REVIEW ANSWERS

1.1. A. Because the school is interested in how *all* its students are doing in the program, this is a descriptive technique. Data are kept on all the students (the population) to describe how they are doing. These data are not used to make generalizations to a larger population.

   B. This is an example of an inferential approach. The political scientist is interested in the attitudes of Californians (all Californians), but she only measures the attitudes of some Californians, the 10 000 in her sample. She examines their opinions about the changes to the health care system and then generalizes to all Californians.

1.2. A. The independent variable is training. The experimental group received additional training in imagery. The other group, the control group, did not. Training is a true independent variable because the sports psychologist controlled it by assigning participants to the levels. Gender is an organismic variable. The sports psychologist could not manipulate gender, but she could look to see if there were differences in attitude and performance (both dependent variables) between men and women.

   B. The researcher grouped young people by their racial background, a participant variable. This is a quasi-experiment with no manipulated IVs.

1.3. Family type and number of aggressive acts are discrete variables. Only certain values exist. Testosterone level and time-on-task are continuous variables. If we had an infinitely precise way to measure testosterone and time, we could measure both to an infinite degree of precision.

1.4. A. Marital status is a nominal variable; the values (married, single, widowed, divorced) differ in quality, not quantity.

B. University degree is best described as ordinal. A Ph.D. is a "higher" degree than an M.A., but the intervals between B.A. and M.A. and M.A. and Ph.D. cannot be considered equal.

C. Level of job satisfaction is best described as an ordinal variable because we cannot assume equal intervals. This type of rating scale is, however, sometimes described as interval.

D. This is a ratio variable because we begin our count of number of years of education from a true zero point (i.e., none).

1.5. A. f of 9 is 2

B. $X_N = 3$

C. $N = 10$

D. $\sum X = 67$

EXERCISES

1. DATA: $X_1, X_2, X_3, \ldots, X_N$
   Describe what you can say about these data if they were measured on a(n)
   a. nominal scale of measurement
   b. ordinal scale (in order from low to high)
   c. interval scale (in order from low to high)
   d. ratio scale (in order from low to high)

2. In a horse race, Two and a Juice came first, Dynamite came second, and Beetlebomb came third.
   a. What scale is involved? Explain your answer.
   b. If we report the time the three horses took to run the race, what kind of scale do we have? Explain your answer.
   c. If we report the gender of the jockeys who rode the horses, what kind of scale do we have? Explain your answer.
   d. If we report the postposition of each horse, what kind of scale do we have? Explain your answer.

3. For each of the following, indicate which category of statistics is most likely involved. Choose from descriptive, inferential, correlational, and predictive. Explain your answers.
   a. A researcher wonders if higher-income Canadians are more likely to be in favor of the free trade agreement with the United States than are lower-income Canadians. In other words, she wonders if income and attitude about free trade are related.
   b. A researcher wonders how New Yorkers feel about the free trade issue. He interviews a selected group of New York residents.

c. A researcher is interested in whether being abused as a child has an effect on whether that person later abuses his own children. He gathers data about the childhood experiences of abusing parents and nonabusing parents.

d. A researcher stationed in a local mall asked every tenth person who passed her whether he or she bought anything that day and from which shop. She wants to compare the popularity of the various shops in the mall.

e. A professor has given the first midterm exam in his first-year anthropology course and wants to present the results to his students.

f. A researcher is hired as a consultant to help with the screening of applicants to police training school. She uses a standard psychological test to determine emotional and psychological health.

4. Label each of the following as a variable or a constant. Why do you think so?

a. The highest temperature of the day in Las Vegas (as measured at the airport) on July 18, 2012

b. The number of children delivered in 2012 at St. Andrews Hospital in London

c. The religious affiliation of students at Boston University

d. Student gender at a preparatory school for boys

e. Species of bird spotted during the Seattle Bird Society's annual Bird Watching Extravaganza

5. For each of the following, decide which is the independent and which is the dependent variable.

a. Reaction time is slower with high blood-alcohol level than with low blood-alcohol level.

b. Policemen trained in conflict mediation are more effective in domestic crisis control.

c. Effective study strategy training improves student grades.

d. Political labels influence how people perceive the motives of the politician.

e. Babies fed on demand gain weight faster than babies fed on a schedule.

f. Aerobic exercise improves physical fitness over no exercise.

6. Label each of the following as discrete or continuous. Explain your answers.

a. academic aptitude
b. number of students in psychology courses
c. reaction time
d. temperature
e. socioeconomic class
f. curriculum subject
g. age
h. gender
i. dress size

7. A researcher wants to study the effects of three different brands of pain reliever on perceived pain relief. He gives one of the three brands to different groups of participants

suffering from chronic headache. He asks all participants to rate the effectiveness of the drug on their headaches. What is the independent variable and what is the dependent variable?

8. Label the following as nominal, ordinal, interval, or ratio.
   a. grading system using A, B, C, F
   b. number correct on a quiz
   c. fur color of dogs
   d. score on an intelligence test
   e. type of housing in an urban center
   f. gender
   g. age
   h. psychopathological diagnosis (e.g., neurotic or psychotic or personality disorder)
   i. the ten healthiest cities in the world, based on weather, pollution, crime rate, and so on.

9. Answer the following questions about the distribution of values below. DATA: 23, 10, 9, 8, 8, 8, 8, 6, 4, 4, 2
   a. $N =$
   b. f for the value $8 =$
   c. $X_8 =$
   d. $X_N =$

10. Label each of the following according to the measurement method used.
    a. A biologist spends her summers on the Montana prairies studying the habits of the ground squirrel.
    b. A sociologist joins a cult to gather information on their practices and rituals without the members being aware of her purpose.
    c. A public health nurse interviews new mothers in their homes to determine the need for more in-hospital education.
    d. A graduate student in education sends a questionnaire to city teachers to determine their satisfaction with their jobs.
    e. A researcher in the department of Native Studies gives a standard IQ test to children on a reserve in the far north.
    f. A speech pathologist sits in on a regular class of special needs children to determine the need for formal speech assessment.

11. List any factors that might threaten the internal validity of the research described below and explain how validity might be threatened. A professor has come to believe that his lectures are boring and need more pizzazz. In particular, he thinks he needs to use more humor in the classroom. He decides to conduct an investigation. In his 8:00 a.m. class he continues with his normal lecturing style. In his 11:00 a.m. class he injects several jokes throughout his lecture. Otherwise he treats the two classes the same way. After a few weeks of this, he has his students assess his lectures with an evaluation form.

12. List any factors that might threaten the internal validity of the research described below and explain how validity might be threatened. An elementary school teacher, having just returned from a seminar in innovative teaching strategies, decides to try out her new skills on her students. She assesses their performance after 2 weeks of innovative instruction.

13. List any factors that might threaten the internal validity of the research described below and explain how validity might be threatened. An elementary school teacher, having just returned from a seminar in innovative teaching strategies, decides to try out her new skills on her students. She assesses their performance both before and after 2 weeks of innovative instruction.

14. List any factors that might threaten the internal validity of the research described below and explain how validity might be threatened.

    A gerontologist investigated a new drug that purports to improve memory performance. He decides to study three different age groups (40–50 yrs, 60–70 yrs, and 80–90 yrs). He randomly selects 50 people in each age group and randomly assigns half of them to an experimental group and the other half to a control group. The experimental participants from each of the three age groups are administered daily doses of the drug for a period of 2 years. The control participants receive a placebo. None of the participants know whether they receive the placebo or the drug. Every 3 months a standard memory test is given to all participants by the gerontologist's assistant, who is unaware of which group the participant is in.

CHAPTER 2

Organizing and Presenting Data

LEARNING OBJECTIVES

After reading this chapter, you should be able to do the following:

1. Describe the difference between simple and grouped frequency distributions and construct either from a given set of data.
2. Define absolute, relative, and cumulative frequency and indicate when each is appropriate.
3. Define mutually exclusive interval, midpoint, and width.
4. Describe how bar graph, histograms, frequency polygons, and ogives are constructed.
5. Obtain exact limits for a given value or interval.
6. Construct a bar graph, histogram, stem-and-leaf diagram, frequency polygon, and an ogive for a given set of data.
7. List examples of and provide sketches of symmetrical and skewed distributions.
8. Describe the difference between a platykurtic and a leptokurtic distribution and provide an example sketch.

A sociologist conducted an Internet survey of 25 heterosexual couples and 25 gay couples. One of the questions he asked was "On a scale from 1 to 9, indicate how satisfied you are, as a couple, with the level of communication in your partnership (1 = *very satisfied* and 9 = *very dissatisfied*)." Here are his data.

7	4	5	6	3
2	9	8	8	2
6	4	7	7	6
9	3	4	3	4
6	9	2	2	9
1	1	6	6	3
4	3	4	3	5
2	8	4	7	4
6	4	8	4	9
4	9	5	6	5

Are the gay couples more satisfied than the heterosexual couples? Can you see any patterns? Neither can I.

In research, we frequently find ourselves with a great many numbers about some event. Only rarely can we simply "scan" these raw data and make any sense out of them. We must organize our numbers into some form that is consistent and understandable not only to us, as data collectors, but also to anyone else who might examine the data that we have collected.

Organizing Raw Data

Options are available to our sociologist for organizing his raw values. He should, of course, organize first by type of couple—gay or heterosexual. Within each category, he can organize by value of the variable. In other words, he can list all the rating values, from highest to lowest. Alternatively, he can organize by participant couple's name or participant couple number, if he has assigned numbers to his couples. As long as his technique is consistent, either method is fine for the initial organization of his data. Table 2.1 shows his satisfaction rating data organized by value; Table 2.2 presents the same data organized by couple number.

Although Table 2.2 has only 50 data points, this initial organization is hard to interpret. We cannot tell at a glance whether gay couples differ from heterosexual couples in their satisfaction with the communication in their partnership. Imagine the chaos if there were hundreds of values. Clearly, we need to have ways to organize data to present our findings.

Presenting Raw Data

Often researchers are called on to report or present their data in journals or at conferences. For uniformity, social scientists follow several conventions, which make it easier for readers of reports and for convention audiences. Raw data are ordered by values of the variable and by group. We do not present data by participant number in most cases.[1] Raw data can be organized and presented in tables or graphs.

---

[1]Data may be presented by participant number when the researcher has used a single-participant design rather than a groups design. This is usually the case in the field of psychology called Experimental Analysis of Behavior.

Table 2.1.

Couple Satisfaction Rating, Organized by Value

Type of Couple	
Gay	Heterosexual
9	9
9	9
8	9
8	9
7	8
7	8
6	7
6	7
6	6
6	6
6	6
5	5
5	5
4	4
4	4
4	4
4	4
4	4
4	3
3	3
2	3
2	3
2	3
2	2
1	1

Table 2.2.

Couple Satisfaction Rating, Organized by Participating Couple Number

Couple Number	Gay	Heterosexual
1	7	8
2	8	9
3	8	9
4	9	9
5	1	9
6	2	8
7	2	7
8	2	7
9	2	6
10	3	6
11	4	4
12	4	4
13	4	4
14	4	4
15	4	5
16	5	5
17	5	6
18	6	4
19	6	1
20	6	3
21	6	3
22	6	3
23	7	2
24	9	3
25	4	3

Presenting Data in a Table: The Frequency Distribution

A frequency distribution is a table indicating the values that a variable can take on and the frequency with which each value occurs. In this chapter, I will discuss *univariate* or one-variable distributions. *Bivariate* frequency distributions are of particular interest in correlational statistics, a topic I will discuss in detail in Chapters 16 and 17. For now, be aware that we have a bivariate distribution if each participant provides one measure on each of two variables. Let's continue with our discussion of univariate distributions where we have one variable, each participant contributing one observation.

Forms of Frequency Distributions

There are several different ways to present data in a frequency distribution. The particular form a researcher selects depends on the type of measurement, the number of values, and the purpose for presenting the data. We will look at two basic forms.

Simple Frequency Distributions

To construct a simple frequency distribution, we list all possible values of the variable in a column and indicate the frequency (*f*) of each value in a second column to the right. All possible values of the variable must be listed, including those that may not have actually occurred. If the variable is nominal, the values may be listed in any order. With ordinal, interval, and ratio data, the values are listed from highest to lowest. All tables should be labelled with a number and a title, and this label is placed above the table. The table title or caption is in italics.

FYI

The *formatting* conventions I use in this book loosely follow the recommendations of the *Publication Manual of the American Psychological Association* (APA). This manual dictates the style and format to be used by researchers submitting papers for publication in psychology journals. If you are a student whose discipline follows the APA style manual, you probably will have noticed that I do not follow *all* of the style recommendations of the APA. Textbook authors have different goals from research paper authors. To demonstrate this difference, all tables and figures in Chapter 2 represent correct APA manuscript style with two exceptions: APA requires double-spacing. We have not done this here for space reasons. We have used color in our tables and figures. APA expects black and white. Please use this chapter as a reference when creating your own APA research manuscripts. The tables and figures in the rest of the text represent how publishers such as Sage translate APA style for print.

There are other style manuals used in other disciplines as you probably have learned already, perhaps to your distress. I sympathize. It would be great if we all followed the same style, but alas, that is not likely to happen any time soon.

Table 2.3 is a simple frequency distribution of the satisfaction ratings given by our gay and heterosexual couples.

As you can see, the rating variable is shown from highest to lowest in the first column, and the groups are separated. Now, we can begin to make some sense out of the data.

The sociologist gathered couple satisfaction ratings from 25 gay and 25 heterosexual couples. What if he had more participants in the heterosexual group

Table 2.3.

Frequency Distribution of Satisfaction
Ratings by Gay and Heterosexual Couples

| Rating | Couple Type | |
	Gay (*f*)	Heterosexual (*f*)
9	2	4
8	2	2
7	2	2
6	5	3
5	2	2
4	6	5
3	1	5
2	4	1
1	1	1
Total	25	25

than the gay group? Suppose that 25 gay couples and 40 heterosexual couples responded to his Internet survey. He would probably want to use all the data and present them in a way that allows him to make meaningful comparisons.

When we want to compare groups of different sizes, **relative frequency** (**rf**) rather than **absolute frequency** (**f**) is preferable. If, for example, I want to compare my class of 100 students with a colleague's class of 350 students, it is difficult to do so using absolute frequency. To say that 3 of my students received A+ compared with 11 students in my colleague's class would not tell us very much because of the huge difference in class size. In such a case, it is much easier to interpret relative or proportionate frequency. If I learn that my colleague assigned a grade of A+ to 0.03 (3%) students, and I see that 0.03 (3%) of my class earned an A+ too, then we have a basis for comparison.

> **Absolute frequency (*f*):** The number of times a value occurs in a distribution
>
> **Relative frequency (*rf*):** The number of times a value occurs in a distribution, divided by the total number of values

Relative frequency is extremely useful when we are comparing groups of different sizes. Relative frequency is also preferable when we are describing the performance of a single group of an unusual size. Reporting that 0.43 of 147 (43%) people think that day care should be heavily subsidized by the government is more meaningful than reporting the absolute frequency of 63. Always keep in mind that the purpose of presenting data is to make it easy for your reader or audience to see the trends in your results. Therefore, you should choose relative frequency or percentage frequency with your audience in mind. Percentage is, of course, just relative frequency multiplied by 100. If you are reporting to a general audience, percentage is a good choice. Both are used in research reports.

Table 2.4 shows how our sociologist might present his data from 25 gay and 40 heterosexual couples on their ratings of satisfaction using relative frequency.

Table 2.4.

Satisfaction Ratings of Communication in Partnership by Gay and Heterosexual Couples (rf)

| | Couple Type | |
Rating	Gay (*rf*)	Heterosexual (*rf*)
9	0.08	0.100
8	0.08	0.050
7	0.08	0.050
6	0.20	0.525
5	0.08	0.050
4	0.24	0.075
3	0.04	0.050
2	0.16	0.050
1	0.04	0.050
Total	1.00	1.000

Now, we can make comparisons between the groups because the measure (*rf*) puts them on an equal footing, so to speak.

ALERT

The sum of the relative frequency must always be 1 within rounding error.

The third way to report frequency, **cumulative frequency (*cf*)**, is used when we are interested in determining relative standing at a glance.

Cumulative frequency distributions add the frequency of each value to the total frequency below. Absolute or relative frequency may be used. Table 2.5 shows the sociologist's data with absolute cumulative frequency.

Table 2.5.

Satisfaction Ratings of Communication in
Partnership by Gay and Heterosexual Couples (cf)

Rating	Couple Type	
	Gay (*cf*)	Heterosexual (*cf*)
9	25	40
8	23	36
7	21	34
6	19	32
5	14	11
4	12	9
3	6	6
2	5	4
1	1	2

Cumulative frequency (*cf*): Summing frequencies from the bottom of a frequency distribution up for each value or interval

ALERT

The top value in the cumulative frequency column must equal the group size because the entire group must have received either the top value or a lower value.

A quick glance at the distribution in Table 2.5 tells us that 21 of the gay couples and 34 of the heterosexual couples rated their satisfaction with the communication in their partnership as a 7 or lower. Although you can probably see that cumulative frequency is useful for determining relative standing, you have no doubt noted that our groups are different sizes. It would be much more meaningful to report the proportion of gay couples who rated communication as 7 or lower. Then, we could compare that proportion with the heterosexual group. What we need is a *cumulative relative frequency (crf)* distribution.

We convert to relative frequency if we are comparing groups of different sizes or if our group size was unusual. Table 2.6 presents the sociologist's data in a form that is easier to understand.

Table 2.6.

Satisfaction Ratings of Communication in Partnership by Gay and Heterosexual Couples (crf)

| Rating | Couple Type | |
	Gay (crf)	Heterosexual (crf)
9	1.00	1.00
8	0.92	0.90
7	0.84	0.85
6	0.76	0.80
5	0.56	0.28
4	0.48	0.23
3	0.24	0.15
2	0.20	0.10
1	0.04	0.05

Now, we can see that 0.84 (84%) of the gay couples and 0.85 (85%) of the heterosexual couples rated their satisfaction level with the communication in their partnership at a 7 or lower. We have an even playing field when we make our comparisons.

ALERT

The top value in any relative cumulative frequency distribution must always be 1 because the entire group must have received either the top value or a lower value.

Grouped Frequency Distributions

Any simple frequency distribution lists all possible values of the variable, even those that did not occur. Often there are too many possible values for a simple frequency distribution to be practical. For example, a typical variable used in schools is percentage. If one student got 0 and another got 100 on a test, a simple frequency distribution of these data would require listing all 101 values in a column. In situations such as these, we often prefer to group data for the sake of clarity. As a rule, whenever we have more than 20 values of the variable or a large number of 0 values in our data, a **grouped frequency distribution** is preferable.

To construct a grouped frequency distribution, the values are grouped into equal-sized intervals, often called **class intervals**. These intervals are then listed from highest to lowest. Intervals must be **mutually exclusive**; each value belongs in one interval only.

When selecting an **interval width**, it is helpful to use an odd-sized one rather than an even-sized one. This makes finding **midpoints**, which we will do shortly, much easier.

Class interval: The span of scores used to group data in a grouped frequency distribution

Mutually exclusive interval: A nonoverlapping interval in a grouped frequency distribution such that each value belongs in one interval only

Interval width: The range of each interval in a grouped frequency distribution

Midpoint: The middle value of an interval in a grouped frequency distribution

Grouped frequency distribution: Table indicating class intervals and their associated frequencies

Imagine that we have recorded the custodial sentencing time (number of days) given to 20 youth under the Young Offenders Act for identical crimes by youth with similar criminal histories. Let's use these data to construct a grouped frequency distribution. We will do this step by step.

DATA: 64, 63, 57, 56, 55, 54, 47, 46, 45, 45, 45, 44, 43, 37, 36, 34, 34, 23, 23, 15

Step 1. Determine how many values are possible (i.e., the range of the variable). The range, or span, of our data is 50 values (i.e., from 15 to 64). There are too many values for a simple frequency distribution to be practical. We would have a column of 50 numbers if we chose to do this.

Step 2. Decide how many intervals to use. It is conventional to use between 10 and 20 intervals. We will use 10.

Step 3. Determine the interval width. The symbol for width is i. We have already decided that we want to have 10 intervals, so we must determine what width will give us 10 intervals. Because we have a range of 50 values, we can see that an interval width of 5 will produce what we want.

Step 4. List the intervals from highest to lowest in a column and the frequencies in a second column.

Table 2.7 presents our data in a grouped frequency distribution using absolute, relative, cumulative, and cumulative relative frequency.

If we look at the cumulative frequency and cumulative relative frequency columns, we can see at a glance that 14 young offenders, or 70%, were sentenced to 49 days or fewer. Cumulative relative frequency, then, is useful when we want to determine relative standing or the location of a particular value in a distribution.

Table 2.7.

Grouped Frequency Distribution of Sentence Length for 20 Young Offenders

Sentence (*Days*)	*f*	*rf*	*cf*	*crf*
60–64	2	0.10	20	1.00
55–59	3	0.15	18	0.90
50–54	1	0.05	15	0.75
45–49	5	0.25	14	0.70
40–44	2	0.10	9	0.45
35–39	2	0.10	7	0.35
30–34	2	0.10	5	0.25
25–29	0	0.00	3	0.15
20–24	2	0.10	3	0.15
15–19	1	0.05	1	0.05

CONCEPT REVIEW 2.1

Decide whether the following data should be presented in a simple or a grouped frequency distribution. Why do you think so? If you decide that a grouped frequency distribution is appropriate, what width would you choose? Would you use absolute or relative frequency?

DATA Sentence length (in days) for minor theft for young offenders with similar histories: 60, 60, 58, 58, 58, 55, 49, 40, 40, 40, 40, 35, 34, 30, 29, 29, 28, 28, 28, 27, 25, 20, 20, 18, 10, 10

Answer on page 61.

Presenting Data in a Graph

Frequency distributions can also be presented in graphic form. Many people find it easier to interpret data presented in a graph rather than in a table.

Graphing Univariate Frequency Distributions

Several conventions in graphing provide consistency in presentation.

1. Graphs are called figures.
2. The figure number and caption are found below the graph, with the word *Figure* and the number in italics followed by the title in roman (i.e., regular type).
3. Frequency is often indicated on the **ordinate** (*y*-axis), and the values of the variable are on the **abscissa** (*x*-axis), but you may reverse this.

4. A ¾ rule is generally used (the ordinate should be ¾ as long as the abscissa).
5. Break axes that do not begin at zero. In other words, if the values of the variable do not start at zero, you should indicate that by marking the axis with a double slash or a zig-zag mark.

There are several ways to graph frequency data. The one you select will depend on your purpose and the type of data you have. Absolute, relative, or cumulative frequency may be used.

Abscissa: The horizontal axis on a graph; x-axis

Ordinate: The vertical axis of a graph; y-axis

Bar Graph

The **bar graph** or bar chart is used to present discrete data. Separate bars represent each value of the variable, and their length or height corresponds to the frequency with which each value occurred. The bars are separated to indicate that the variable is discrete rather than continuous. The discrete values of the variable may be placed on either the abscissa or the ordinate with frequency then plotted on the alternate axis. Which way you choose depends on how you want the graph to look.

Merikangas et al. (2010) collected data on the prevalence of psychological disorders in American youth. They included anxiety, mood, and substance use disorders. Type of disorder is a nominal variable, and we will use a bar graph to display their data (see Figure 2.1).

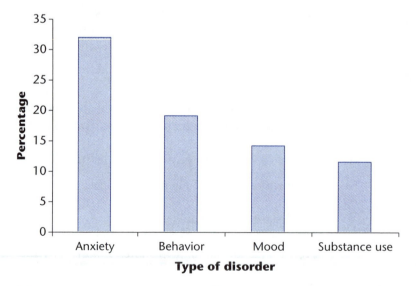

Figure 2.1. Bar graph: prevalence of psychological disorders in American youth

Bar graph: A graph used to depict the frequency distribution of discrete variables

Merikangas, K. R., He, J. P., Burstein, M., Swanson, S. A., Avenevoli, S., Cui, L., . . . Swendsen, J. (2010). Lifetime prevalence of mental disorders in U.S. adolescents: Results from the National Comorbidity Survey Replication—Adolescent Supplement (NCS-A). *Journal of American Academy of Child and Adolescent Psychiatry, 49*(10), 980–989.

As you can see, anxiety disorders were the most common condition (31.9%), followed by behavior disorders (19.1%), mood disorders (14.3%), and substance use disorders (11.4%).

The bar graph can be used to depict discrete ordinal, interval, and ratio data as well. The values of the variable should reflect the natural order. Imagine that we surveyed U.K. citizens to determine their perceptions on the availability of health care services over the past several years. We might present some of the data in a bar graph such as Figure 2.2. As you can see, relative frequency is on the abscissa in this bar graph.

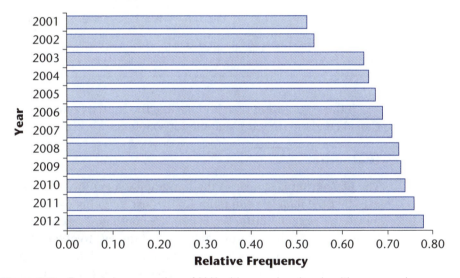

Figure 2.2. Bar graph: proportion of U.K. citizens who view health care service availability as good or excellent over time

If these were real data, the bar graph indicates that things are looking up in terms of health care in Britain.

These simple bar graphs are appropriate when we have only one categorical variable. Often we have more than one variable, in which case we would use a variation of the simple bar graph called a *multiple bar graph.* Suppose we had data on how people living in Canada, the United States, and the United Kingdom view health care service availability over the past 11 years. We might want to present these data in a multiple bar graph so that we could see any changes in opinion over time in all three countries. It might look like Figure 2.3.

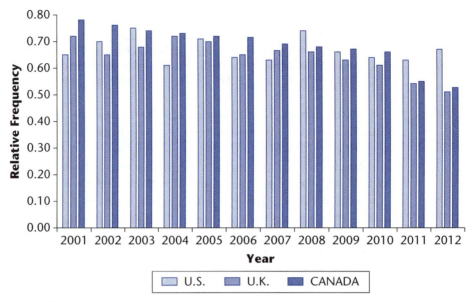

Figure 2.3. Bar graph: proportion of U.S., U.K., and Canadian citizens who view health care service availability as good or excellent over a period of 10 years

If these data were real, it looks like the United States is doing a little better, Canada and the United Kingdom not so much.

Histogram

The **histogram** is similar to the bar graph except the bars are attached to indicate that the data are continuous. To construct a histogram, we need to learn a new term—**exact limits**. When data are continuous, exact limits are the precise beginning and end points of a value or an interval. To obtain the upper exact relative frequency limit, we add half of the smallest unit of measurement to the value or upper limit of the interval. To obtain the lower exact limit, we subtract half of the smallest unit of measurement from the value or lower limit of the interval.

> **Exact limits:** The mathematically precise beginning and end points of a value or interval. Also called real limits.

> **Histogram:** Graph used to depict the frequency distribution of continuous variables

For example, consider a bathroom scale that weighs to the nearest kilogram (kg). The smallest unit of measurement, then, is 1 kg. I weigh 55 kg. The exact limits for my weight are 54.5 kg and 55.5 kg. If this procedure seems obscure, remember that my bathroom scale measures to the nearest kilogram. If, in reality, my weight was 54.62 kg, my scale would report my weight at 55 kg. If I weighed 55.43 kg, my scale would also report me at 55 kg. When my scale says I weigh 55 kg, I may, in reality, weigh anything between 54.5 kg and 55.5 kg.

Here are some other examples.

Variable	Smallest Unit	Amount to + and −	Value or Interval	Exact Limits
Weight (kg)	1	0.50	56	55.5–56.5
Weight (kg)	0.5	0.25	50–53	49.75–53.25
Time (s)	0.1	0.05	15.5	15.45–15.55

FYI

The way a number is written may tell you the precision of measurement. For example, consider the numbers below.

2

2.0

2.00

These three versions of the number 2 indicate three different levels of precision. The first version (2) indicates that we can only measure to the nearest whole number; thus, the exact limits for 2 are 1.5 and 2.5. The second version (2.0) indicates that we can measure to the nearest $\frac{1}{10}$, and so the exact limits are 1.95 and 2.05. The third version (2.00) indicates measurement to the nearest $\frac{1}{100}$, and so the exact limits are 1.995 and 2.005. The smallest unit of measurement, then, may sometimes be determined by examining the way the number is written.

CONCEPT REVIEW 2.2

What are the exact limits for the following?

A. 63 pounds measured to the nearest 1 pound

B. 2.3 inches measured to the nearest $\frac{1}{10}$ inch

C. 75° measured to the nearest 1°

Answers on page 61.

When constructing a histogram, the edges of the bars are at the exact limits, and the middle of the bar is over the middle (midpoint) of the interval. Technically, a histogram should report either the exact limits or the midpoint on the abscissa. I feel, however, that the purpose of the graph and the nature of the audience should be considered. If small violations produce a graph that is more meaningful to the people looking at it, then I think we should go right ahead. We wouldn't want to violate the rules if we were publishing our graph in an academic journal, but if we were producing a report for the general public then I have no problem with making adjustments as long as we don't mislead the reader.

Suppose that we have collected data on how U.S. citizens of different ages perceive the safety of their cities. Imagine that this will be used in a report to be read by average Americans. Relative frequency is not a measure familiar to most people, so we should use percentage, which is a familiar measure. I will use **apparent limits**, rather than exact limits, for the same reason. We first construct a frequency distribution (see Table 2.8).

Apparent limits: The upper and lower scores of a class interval used in the construction of a grouped frequency distribution

Table 2.8.

Americans of Different Ages Who
Perceive Their Cities as Safe or Very Safe

Age (Apparent Class Interval)	Percentage
15–19	80
20–24	81
25–29	65
30–34	76
35–39	72
40–44	64
45–49	58
50–54	54
55–59	62
60–64	60
65–69	55

Now, we can construct a histogram (see Figure 2.4).

Notice that the abscissa does not begin at zero. If it did, the graph would look unattractive. But I have broken the axis to alert the reader to this fact.

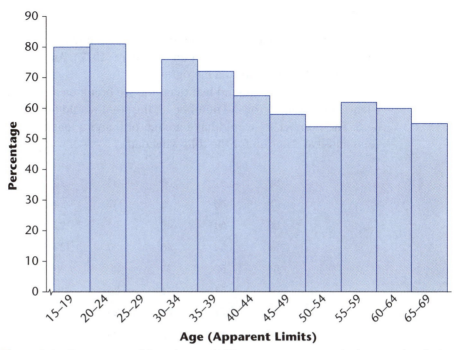

Figure 2.4. Percentage of Americans of different ages surveyed who perceive their cities as safe or very safe

The histogram is a very useful graphing technique for continuous data. Most people have no difficulty interpreting data presented in a histogram.

When constructing a histogram, position each bar over the midpoint to indicate the frequency for that interval. The actual raw values then are not discernible, just the interval within which the values fall.

CONCEPT REVIEW 2.3

For each of the following groups of data, decide what is the appropriate graph.

A. Sociological demographic data such as the socioeconomic status of Floridians versus Californians (i.e., the relative frequency of the population in each status category).

B. Number of babies born in 2013 with the following birth weights to the nearest $\frac{1}{10}$ kilogram: 1.3 to 2.3 kg, 2.4 to 3.4 kg, 3.5 to 4.5 kg, and 4.6 to 5.7 kg.

Answers on page 61.

Stem-and-Leaf Diagrams

A very simple technique for presenting all the data from a distribution is called a stem-and-leaf diagram, developed by Tukey (1977). As you will see, this produces something similar to a histogram.

To construct a stem-and-leaf diagram, we break each value into a stem and a leaf. For example, for the number 18, the stem would be 1, and the leaf would be 8. The number 92 would have a stem of 9 and a leaf of 2. Let's construct a stem-and-leaf diagram for the following data.

80	57	50	38	25
73	55	48	37	24
68	54	46	34	23
66	54	45	30	22
64	52	45	29	20
59	51	41	26	19
58	51	39	25	15
58	50	38	25	15

Because our numbers range from 15 to 80, we will list our stems (the numbers 1 through 8) on the left in a column. The leaves will be placed in ascending order from left to right next to the appropriate stem. For example, the numbers 64, 66, and 68 all have the same stem, so we place the stem (6) on the left and the three leaves (4, 6, and 8) to its immediate right. Here is an example of a stem-and-leaf diagram for our data.

1	5 5 9
2	0 2 3 4 5 5 5 6 9
3	0 4 7 8 8 9
4	1 5 5 6 8
5	0 0 1 1 2 4 4 5 7 8 8 9
6	4 6 8
7	3
8	0

As you read the diagram from left to right starting from the top, you simply append each leaf to the stem on the left to find the values. If we wanted to refine the data, we may prefer to repeat the stems, spreading our diagram out somewhat. We would place leaves from 0 to 4 next to the first stem and the leaves 5 to 9 next to the second identical stem. If we did that, our diagram would look like the following.

1	5	5	9				
2	0	2	3	4			
2	5	5	5	6	9		
3	0	4					
3	7	8	8	9			
4	1						
4	5	5	6	8			
5	0	0	1	1	2	4	4
5	5	7	8	8	9		
6	4						
6	6	8					
7	3						
8	0						

Repeating stems stretches the diagram out. If you bend your head to the right, you will see that a stem-and-leaf diagram looks something like a histogram. It has the advantage that all the data points are readily visible. This technique has a second advantage of being easy for people to understand.

Frequency Polygon

Data presented in a histogram may also be presented in a **frequency polygon**. Points are used instead of bars. When data are grouped, each data point is plotted over the midpoint of the interval; when data are in a simple frequency distribution, each point is plotted over the value. The points are then connected by straight lines. Let's present our perceived city safety data in a frequency polygon. This time we will use relative frequency rather than percentage. First we create a table (see Table 2.9).

Figure 2.5 is the frequency polygon for these data.

It is customary to drop the line to the abscissa at the midpoint of the adjacent interval at both extreme ends. In this way, the polygon is formed. Again, we break the abscissa because it does not start at zero.

Frequency polygon: Graph used to depict the frequency distribution of continuous variables

Table 2.9.

Americans of Different Ages
Who Perceive Their Cities as Safe or Very Safe

Age (Midpoint)	rf
17	0.80
22	0.81
27	0.65
32	0.76
37	0.72
42	0.64
47	0.58
52	0.54
57	0.62
62	0.60
67	0.55

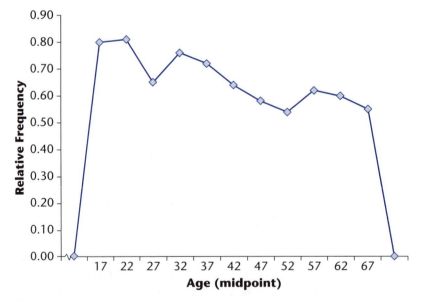

Figure 2.5. Americans of different ages who perceive their cities as safe or very safe

Ogive

I have seen the ogive (pronounced ohgyve with a hard "g") called a cumulative frequency polygon, which I find very strange, because it is not a polygon at all. This graph is constructed from a cumulative frequency distribution. It is appropriate for continuous data and is often used when we wish to locate value position. Questions such as "How have I done compared with the rest of the group?" and "What value would I have needed to be in the top 10% of the group?" can be answered by inspecting the ogive. Cumulative frequencies are plotted as points directly over the upper exact limit of each value or interval, and the points are connected by straight lines. Table 2.10 shows a cumulative frequency distribution of the final grade points of my last statistics class. I have used exact limits and cumulative relative frequency.

Table 2.10.

Cumulative Frequency Distribution of Statistics Grades

Grade (Apparent Value)	Exact Limits	*crf*
4	3.5–4.5	1.00
3	2.5–3.5	0.70
2	1.5–2.5	0.30
1	0.5–1.5	0.05

In the exact limits column, you will see that the bottom left entry is 0.50 and no one got grades at or below that limit. When we plot an ogive, the first point we plot is at the exact lower limit of the distribution. Figure 2.6 shows the ogive.

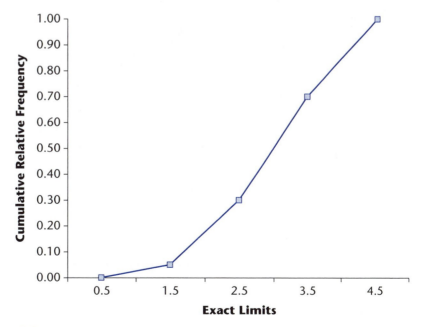

Figure 2.6.   Ogive of statistics grades

The ogive is useful for determining relative standing. A student who earned a grade point of 3 in the course can see, at a glance, that she performed as well as or better than about 0.70 or 70% of the students in the class.

Misleading Graphs

By following the conventions that I have suggested, you should create graphs that are accurate and easily understood. Unfortunately, sometimes graphs are misleading, sometimes deliberately so. Misleading graphs can be caused by incorrect graphing choices or incorrect data choices. For example, a small difference between the values of a variable can be made to look much larger simply by changing the axis.

Look at the two graphs below that show high school dropout rates over the past 5 years.

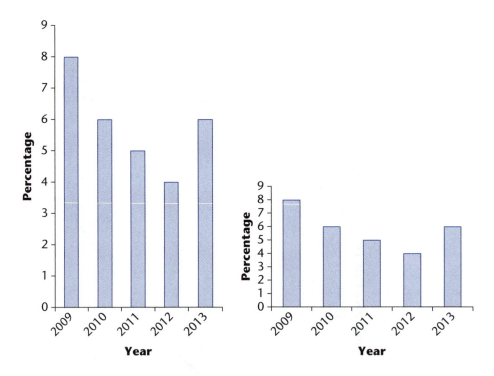

As you can see, changing the length of the axes exaggerates or reduces the apparent differences. Look at what happens when I create two bar graphs of these data and change the starting point of the ordinate without adding a break in the line.

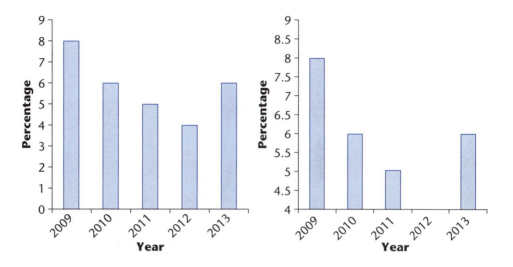

The examples I have shown so far all involve various graphing choices to give different impressions. The *data* you choose to present in a graph can also be misleading. Below are two graphs of exactly the same data, one using absolute frequency and the other using relative frequency. The data are dropout rates in four New England schools for the year 2014 (hypothetical).

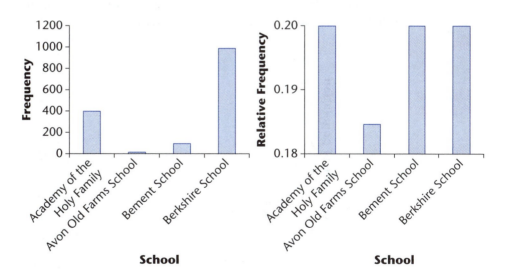

They give quite different impressions, don't they?

Here is another example of problems with both data and graphing choices. This graph shows subscription rates to three newspapers.

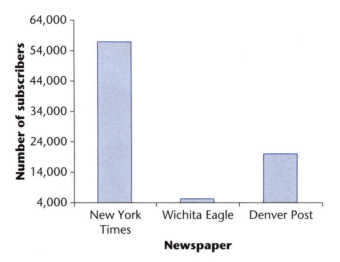

It sure looks as if the *New York Times* is the winner, doesn't it? And perhaps that is the case, but there are problems with the way this graph has been made. Is number of subscribers a fair variable to use to compare the three newspapers? I don't think so. The number of available subscribers in the three cities is very different. A lot more people live in New York City than in Wichita. A fairer measure might be the percentage of the population. Second, the ordinate starts at 4 000, not 0, and there is no break to show that. When the ordinate does not start at zero, smaller differences look larger. Let's see what this graph would look like if we started the ordinate at zero and if we used percentage rather than absolute frequency.

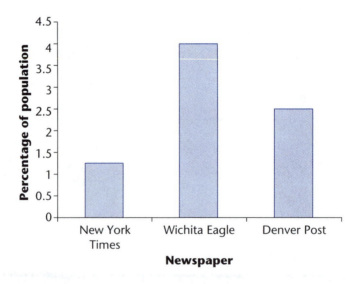

Hmmm, things look rather different now, don't they?
Let's look at another misleading graph.

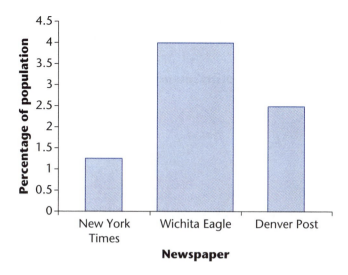

This graph displays bars of different widths, giving the appearance of bigger differences than really exist. The *heights* of the bars indicate the difference in frequency. The *width* should be constant.

I have found each year when I start my statistics class that there are always a few students who are very suspicious. They think that statistics are somehow sneaky and misleading. This is not true. Statistics are always true. It is the user of statistics who might lack integrity. Remember, when you are presenting data, you should strive to present those data honestly and accurately.

And when you read newspapers, magazines, and even scholarly papers, remember to consider the motives, biases, and goals of the publication and writer. A journalist who writes for a newspaper or popular magazine has a least two goals: (1) to impart information and (2) to sell the product. A scholar whose research is supported by a private corporation may also have at least two goals: (1) to contribute to the body of research in the area and (2) to keep her funding. *Consider the source. Be critical consumers of information.*

The Shape of Univariate Frequency Distributions

Univariate frequency distributions have two important shape characteristics: (1) *symmetry* and (2) *kurtosis*.

Symmetry

A **symmetrical distribution** is a mirror image about its center. Some examples of symmetrical distributions used in statistics are the normal distribution and the *t* distribution. Rectangular and U-shaped distributions may also be symmetrical. Figure 2.7 shows what they look like graphically.

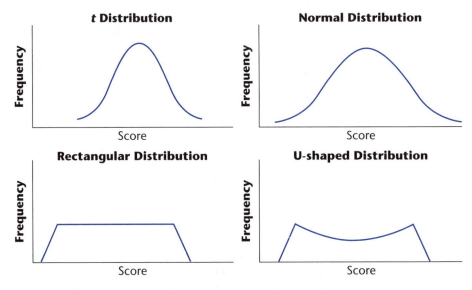

Figure 2.7. Examples of symmetrical distributions

In a skewed distribution, the bulk of the observations (frequency) lies to one side. One side of the distribution is not a mirror image of the other. Skewed distributions are described as having a positive or negative skew. When the extreme end or tail of the distribution points toward the positive side (the right) of the graph, we call this a **positive skew**. When the tail points to the negative, or left, side of the graph, we call this a **negative skew** (see Figure 2.8). Examples used in statistics are the *chi-square* and the *F distribution*, both of which are positively skewed.

Symmetrical distribution: A distribution that is a mirror image about its center

Positively skewed distribution: Graphically presented, a distribution with a tail pointing to the right of the graph

Negatively skewed distribution: Graphically presented, a distribution with a tail pointing to the left of the graph

Kurtosis

Kurtosis is a shape characteristic describing the *spread* or *scatter* of the observations or values. If each value has a similar frequency (i.e., if it occurred the same number of times), the distribution will look flat when it is graphed. Flat

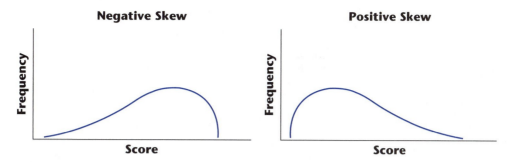

Figure 2.8.   Examples of skewed distributions

distributions are called **platykurtic** (think of the bill of a platypus). Distributions with lots of values bunched in the middle are called **leptokurtic** (see Figure 2.9). In-between distributions are called **mesokurtic**.

> **Kurtosis:** Shape characteristic of a frequency distribution that describes variability or peakedness
>
> **Platykurtic:** Flat compared to the normal distribution
>
> **Leptokurtic:** More peaked with more area in the tails than the normal distribution
>
> **Mesokurtic:** A distribution with moderate peakedness; an example is the normal distribution

Kurtosis is defined in relation to the "normal" distribution, a mesokurtic distribution, which will be discussed later. Basically, a distribution that is flatter or more variable than the normal is platykurtic, and distributions that are less variable, with more area in the tails than the normal, are called leptokurtic (see Figure 2.10).

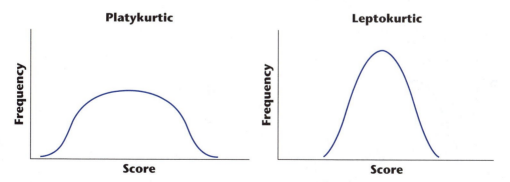

Figure 2.9.   Distributions differing in kurtosis

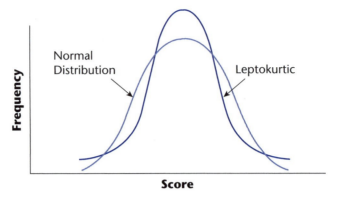

Figure 2.10. The normal distribution versus a leptokurtic distribution

Skewness and kurtosis can be calculated, and both measures may be reported along with other descriptive statistics. The formulas for calculating the skew and kurtosis of a distribution are somewhat complicated and, unless the distribution is very large, may not be useful. Most statistical software packages include both measures in their descriptive statistics. Microsoft Excel, for example, includes these measures when you ask for summary statistics using the data analysis tools. Adventurous students who want to investigate further will find formulas for calculating skewness at http://mathworld.wolfram.com/Skewness.html and formulas for calculating kurtosis at http://mathworld.wolfram.com/Kurtosis.html.

CONCEPT REVIEW 2.4

Describe the shape of each of the following distributions.

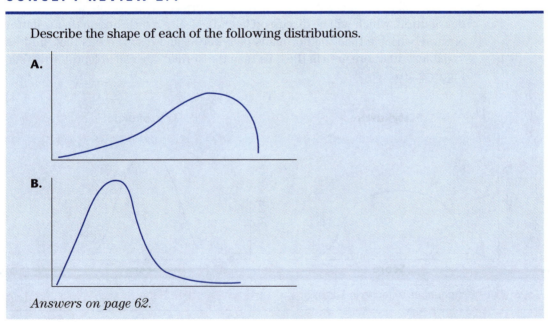

A.

B.

Answers on page 62.

FOCUS ON RESEARCH

Most research institutions and universities have Research Ethics Boards (REB) whose mandate is to ensure that research is ethically sound and that participants, both human and animal, are protected from harm. REBs typically are composed of individuals with expertise in research design.

THE RESEARCH PROBLEM

Thabane, Childs, and Lafontaine (2005) of McMaster University noted that several concerned professionals have suggested that a statistician be included on REBs. Statisticians would be able to advise researchers in areas of research design that could improve the scientific integrity of the work. Statisticians are particularly knowledgeable about sampling techniques, data collection, and statistical analyses. Assessing the ethics of a research project includes assessing its scientific validity. They decided to conduct a national survey of Canadian-based REBs.

THE RESEARCH QUESTIONS

Thabane et al. (2005) were interested in determining the following:

- How many REBs included a statistician.
- For REBs that did not include a statistician, why not, how did the committee deal with statistical issues, and did they think including a statistician would be helpful.

The first question is answered with simple frequency measures. The second question was broken down by the researchers into discrete categories.

THE RESEARCH APPROACH

Thabane et al. (2005) carried out a cross-sectional survey of Canadian-based REBs. From 224 registered REBs in Canada, they randomly selected 140 and sent out a questionnaire, an information form, and a consent form to each contact person.

THE RESULTS

One of the problems with mail-out survey research is low response rate. Thabane et al. (2005) followed up the initial mailing with e-mail and telephone reminders. Seventy-seven REBs responded, giving a final response rate of 55%.

One of the researchers' questions was "How many REBs included a statistician?" Thabane et al. (2005) found that ~78% of the respondents reported that there was no statistician on their REB.

Another question was "For REBs that did not include a statistician, why not?" About 77% of the REBs that did not have a statistician reported that they did not need one. Here are some of the comments by these respondents.

- "We have extensive statistical training."
- "Ethical decisions do not depend on such detailed scrutiny."

Thabane et al. (2005) also wanted to know how REBs without a statistician dealt with statistical issues. They asked respondents to select from a list of options, a discrete variable. Figure 2.11 shows some of the data in a bar graph.

The researchers also asked the REBs if they thought a statistician would be helpful. Some of the comments by the REBs were as follows:

- "Occasionally it would be helpful."
- "We have tried and failed to recruit statisticians."
- "One is preferred but not always available."

THE CONCLUSIONS

Thabane et al. (2005) noted that in general the level of participation by statisticians on Canadian REBs is very low. It appeared that some REBs do not recognize the importance of the involvement of a statistician in these decisions, even though it has been pointed out by several writers. The authors conclude by commenting that they hope this study will highlight the need for statisticians on such boards.

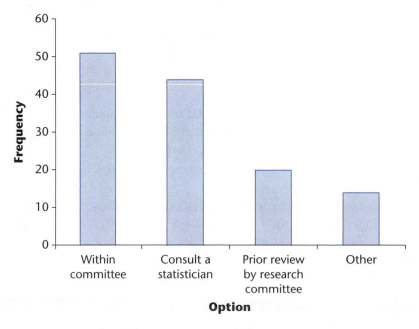

Figure 2.11. How respondents deal with statistical issues

SUMMARY OF TERMS AND CONCEPTS

Raw data are initially organized by *participant number* or from the highest to the lowest value of the variable.

Data are often presented in tables, called *frequency distributions*.

A *simple frequency distribution* lists all possible values of the variable in a column accompanied by the frequencies with which each value occurred. *Absolute, relative,* and *cumulative frequency* may be used.

A *grouped frequency distribution* is used for data that have been grouped into equal-sized intervals. The intervals, which must be *mutually exclusive*, are listed in a column accompanied by the total frequency of values within each.

Discrete variables are presented graphically in a *bar graph*. The separation of the bars indicates the discreteness of the data.

Continuous variables may be presented in a *histogram* or a *frequency polygon*.

A *stem-and-leaf diagram* is easily constructed and similar to a histogram.

The *ogive* is used to present cumulative frequency data and is useful for locating values graphically.

Symmetrical distributions have a left side that is a mirror image of the right.

Positively skewed distributions have the bulk of the frequency on the left side; *negatively skewed distributions* have the bulk of the frequency on the right side.

Distributions that are flatter than the normal distribution are *platykurtic*; distributions that are more peaked, with more area in the tails than the normal, are *leptokurtic*.

CONCEPT REVIEW ANSWERS

2.1. Because these data span 51 values and because several values do not occur at all, a grouped frequency distribution would probably be the best choice. A width of 3 or 5 could be used. With a width of 3, 17 class intervals would be created. With a width of 5, 11 class intervals would be created. The choice would depend on whether the loss of information with the larger width is offset by the economy gained. I would prefer to use relative frequency because the group size, 26, is a bit awkward.

2.2. A. 62.5–63.5

   B. 2.25–2.35

   C. 74.5°–75.5°

2.3. A. The variable "socioeconomic status" is a discrete variable usually including three values (lower, middle, and upper). A bar graph should be used.

B. Weight is a continuous variable, and so a histogram could be used to present these data.

2.4. A. Negative skew and platykurtic

B. Positive skew and leptokurtic

EXERCISES

1. Twenty-five U.S. cities participated in a crime prevention program designed to educate citizens about ways of protecting themselves against theft. The following data are the average number of thefts reported each week before and after the program was completed.

   Before: 66, 57, 56, 48, 48, 48, 42, 41, 41, 40, 39, 35, 34, 33, 32, 31, 31, 30, 30, 29, 26, 24, 24, 21, 20

   After: 50, 46, 41, 40, 40, 40, 39, 39, 33, 31, 30, 29, 28, 26, 25, 25, 24, 24, 23, 22, 22, 20, 19, 18, 17

   a. Construct a grouped frequency distribution for the before and after data. Use a width of 3 and the same intervals for both sets of data.
   b. Plot the grouped data in a frequency polygon.

2. Construct a simple frequency distribution for the following data. Use absolute frequency.

   DATA: 15, 12, 10, 9, 8, 18, 25, 11, 13, 14, 7, 6, 15, 15, 8

3. Construct a simple frequency distribution for the following data. Use relative frequency.

   DATA: 90, 89, 84, 83, 79, 75, 72, 84, 80, 77, 77, 72, 71, 71, 71, 70, 70, 88, 78, 71

4. Construct a simple frequency distribution for the following data. Use cumulative frequency.

   DATA: 10, 10, 10, 11, 13, 13, 16, 17, 17, 16, 18, 19, 19, 21, 20, 15, 15, 15, 14, 14, 14, 16, 16, 13, 13

5. The following data are the proportion of the student body majoring in each of five disciplines. Use the appropriate graph to present the data and explain your choice.

Major	Proportion of Student Body
Psychology	0.36
Sociology	0.32
Biology	0.12
Mathematics	0.12
Anthropology	0.08

6. The following data represent the responses of 100 people asked to indicate their opinion to the following statement on a scale from 1 to 7, where 1 = *strongly agree with the statement* and 7 = *strongly disagree with the statement.*
    "Mandatory AIDS testing should be carried out on all public school teachers."
    Present the data in the appropriate graph and explain your choice.

1	(Strongly agree)	13
2	(Moderately agree)	16
3	(Agree somewhat)	24
4	(Indifferent)	10
5	(Disagree somewhat)	12
6	(Moderately disagree)	5
7	(Strongly disagree)	20

7. A sociologist gathered region-of-birth data on the residents of an inner-city neighborhood in a large Canadian city. Here are her results.

    Construct the appropriate graph to present her data. Explain your choice.

Region of Birth	Percentage of Residents
Canada	48
Europe	22
United States	8
South America	2
Asia	15
Other	5

8. Construct a grouped frequency distribution for the following data in which the interval width (i) is 5 and the upper limits of the intervals are multiples of 5. Use absolute frequency.

    DATA: 50, 44, 36, 12, 23, 14, 8, 10, 5, 45, 36, 9, 9, 9

9. From the grouped frequency distribution in Exercise 8, construct a frequency polygon. Use the midpoints on the abscissa and absolute frequency on the ordinate.

10. From the grouped frequency distribution in Exercise 8, construct a histogram. Use the midpoints and relative frequency.

11. From the grouped frequency distribution in Exercise 8, construct an ogive using the real limits and cumulative frequency.

12. Construct a grouped frequency distribution for the following data. Use an interval width of 7 and relative frequency.

13. Construct a histogram of the data in Exercise 12.

DATA:

90	58	47	28
87	57	47	28
84	56	47	27
78	56	46	27
78	53	46	27
68	53	46	25
67	53	45	25
67	53	45	24
67	52	42	24
65	52	41	21
64	51	39	20
64	51	38	18
61	50	38	14
61	50	37	13
60	50	36	13
60	49	36	8
59	49	36	6
59	49	34	4
59	49	30	3
59	48	29	1

14. State the exact limits for each of the following values or intervals.

a. 2.0 s   c. 2–4 s   e. 24.5–29.5 kg
b. 2.6 s   d. 25–29 kg   f. 24.50–29.50 kg

15. A restaurant owner keeps track of the number of times that each of five dinner entrées is ordered over two 5-day periods, one in midwinter and one in midsummer. A total of 59 customers ordered one of the five dishes during this period in the winter and 47 in the summer. Which type of graph should be used to present these data? Why? What measure of frequency should go on the ordinate? Why?

16. Find the midpoint for the following intervals. Construct a frequency polygon using relative frequency.

X	f
23–25	1
20–22	2
17–19	2
14–16	4
11–13	5
8–10	3
5–7	1
2–4	2

17. A psychiatrist has diagnosed 65 of her patients as suffering from a neurosis, a psychosis, or a personality disorder. She has also classified her patients by gender so that she can see if there is a difference between women and men in terms of the disorders they present. Here are her data.

Disorder	Women (f)	Men (f)
Neurosis	28	17
Psychosis	3	5
Personality disorder	2	10

Construct the appropriate graph to present her data. Explain your choice.

18. Construct a stem-and-leaf diagram for the following data.

DATA:

10	25	37	46	59	66	75	90
10	26	38	48	59	67	77	90
11	27	39	49	59	67	84	93
15	28	39	49	59	68	85	94
16	31	42	50	61	72	85	95
21	32	42	51	64	73	86	96
23	33	43	52	64	73	87	
23	37	46	58	65	74	88	

19. Listed below are the weights of 100 women enrolled in a fitness program.

WEIGHTS:

85	100	105	116	118	128	133	150	154	97
131	119	103	93	108	100	111	130	104	136
122	115	103	90	114	129	96	132	110	116
88	103	108	119	121	131	136	153	157	100
129	117	101	91	106	98	109	128	102	134
86	101	106	117	119	129	134	151	155	98
123	116	104	91	115	130	97	133	111	117
94	109	114	125	127	137	142	159	164	106
136	124	108	98	113	105	116	135	109	141
90	105	110	121	123	133	138	155	159	102

a. Construct a simple frequency distribution of the data.
b. Construct a grouped frequency distribution in which the interval width (i) is 5 and the lower limits of the intervals are multiples of 5.
c. From the grouped frequency distribution, construct a frequency polygon. Use midpoints on the abscissa and absolute frequency on the ordinate. Label both axes and break the abscissa or ordinate if appropriate.
d. From the grouped frequency distribution, construct a histogram. Use midpoints and relative frequency. Label both axes and break them when necessary.

CHAPTER 3

Describing the Central Tendency of Distributions

LEARNING OBJECTIVES

After reading this chapter, you should be able to do the following:

1. Define mode, median, and mean.
2. Describe the assumption that permits calculation of the median by linear interpolation.
3. Determine the mode, median, and mean from a given set of data.
4. Define deviation score, positive deviation, and negative deviation.
5. In terms of the sum of the deviations, describe what is meant by the mean as a balance point in a distribution.
6. Describe the relative position of the mean, median, and mode in a skewed distribution.
7. Describe what is meant by an open-ended distribution.
8. Determine the most appropriate measure of central tendency for a given set of data.

A real estate company reports that the average price of a house in the United States in 2013 was $137 900. But another company reports that the average price of houses in the United States in 2013 was $236 100. Can they both be right? You might be surprised to learn that they can.

Measures of central tendency describe the "average" of a distribution of scores. There are several ways of measuring "average." We will consider the three most commonly used measures: (1) mode, (2) median, and (3) mean.

Three Measures of Central Tendency

Mode

The **mode (*Mo*)** is the most frequently occurring value in a distribution. The mode is the score with a higher frequency than any other score in the distribution. It is the "typical" value in a distribution.

Median

The **median** (*Mdn*) is the point in the distribution at or below which exactly 50% of the scores lie. The median divides the distribution of scores in half.

Mean

The **mean** (μ) is the arithmetic average obtained by summing all the scores and dividing the sum by the total number of scores in the distribution. The mean is the measure most of us think of when we talk about "average." Statisticians use the symbol μ (mu, pronounced "mew") to refer to the population mean.

Note: When means are reported in journal articles, researchers rarely use the symbol; rather, the letter *M* in italics is used to refer to the mean of a distribution of scores.

Mode (*Mo*): The most frequently occurring score in a distribution

Median (*Mdn*): The score at or below which exactly 50% of the scores lie

Mean (μ): The arithmetic average of all the scores

Calculating Measures of Central Tendency

Mode

The mode is easy to determine.

For Ungrouped Data

When data are ungrouped or in a simple frequency distribution, the mode is simply the value with the greatest frequency. A distribution may have more than one mode, and some distributions have no mode; differential frequencies must occur before a mode can be determined. The mode(s) must have a higher frequency than other values. The following examples show numerical and graphic representations of various distributions.

	Data	*Mo*
Unimodal (one mode)	1, 2, 3, 4, 5, 5, 6	5
Bimodal (two modes)	1, 2, 2, 4, 5, 5, 6	2, 5
No mode	1, 2, 3, 4, 5, 6	All scores occur an equal number of times
No mode	3, 3, 4, 4, 5, 5	All scores occur an equal number of times

Unimodal: Term used to describe distributions with one value of highest frequency; graphically having one peak

Bimodal: Describes a distribution with two values of high frequency

Multimodal: A distribution having three or more frequency peaks or points of central tendency

Figure 3.1 shows some examples of smoothed out frequency polygons.

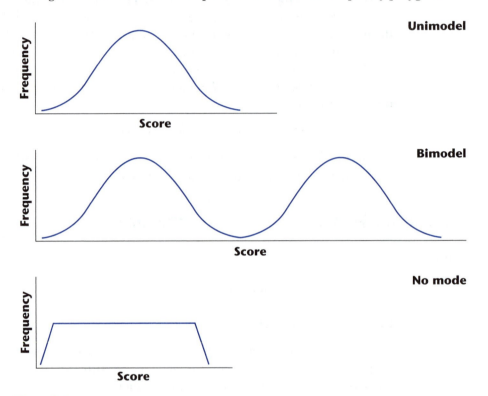

Figure 3.1. Distributions with different modes.

FYI

Some distributions have two (or more) values that occur more frequently than the other values. Consider the following data.

2, 3, 3, 3, 4, 5, 6, 6, 6, 6, 6, 7, 8

If we were to graph these data, we would see two peaks: one at the value of 3, which occurred three times, and another at the value of 6, which occurred five times. Technically, this is a unimodal distribution, and the mode is 6. However, you may see this kind of distribution being called bimodal because that term seems to better describe the shape.

CONCEPT REVIEW 3.1

What is the mode for the following data?

DATA: 3, 4, 5, 6, 7, 7, 7, 9, 12

Answer on page 88.

For Grouped Data

When the data have been placed in a grouped frequency distribution, the mode is the midpoint of the interval containing the highest frequency. The mode of grouped data is often called the "crude" mode, because the midpoint of the interval may or may not be the precise score value with the highest frequency. The midpoint, however, is used to represent the interval. Imagine we have classified 21 attendees at a lecture on investment strategies by age and find the following.

X	f	
50–54	3	
45–49	2	
40–44	7	$Mo = 42$
35–39	4	
30–34	3	
25–29	2	

The interval between 40 and 44 contains the highest frequency, and so the midpoint of that interval (42) is the mode. As with ungrouped data, there must be differential frequency before a mode can be determined. For our example, we would report that the modal age of the attendees at the lecture was 42.

CONCEPT REVIEW 3.2

What is the mode for the following set of data?

X	f
9–11	12
6–8	14
3–5	9
0–2	11

Answer on page 88.

Median

For Ungrouped Data

Median calculation for ungrouped data is a simple matter if there are no repeated values in the middle. If values are repeated, however, certain assumptions must be made.

Data with no repeated middle values. When the score values are arranged from highest to lowest, the median is the middle value (half the score values are above it and half are below it), provided there are no other scores with this value. If there is an even number of scores, the median is the value halfway between the two middle values, providing again that these are not repeated. For example, see the following table:

Data	Mdn
1, 2, 3, 4, 5, 6, 7	4
1, 2, 3, 4, 5, 5, 5	4
1, 2, 3, 4, 5, 6, 7, 8	4.5

Calculation of the median is complicated by certain conditions.

CONCEPT REVIEW 3.3

What is the median for the following data?

DATA: 5, 6, 6, 7, 8, 9, 9, 10

Answer on page 88.

Linear interpolation when middle values are repeated. When repeated middle values occur in a distribution, we must use linear interpolation to determine the median accurately. Linear interpolation assumes that repeated values are *evenly distributed* between the exact or **real limits** of the score. For example, consider a score value of 3 that occurs twice. The exact limits of the score of 3 are 2.5 and 3.5. In other words, a score of 3 could be found anywhere between the precise limits of 2.5 and 3.5. To use linear interpolation in this example, we place the two 3s evenly between these limits. This is the assumption we make when we do this procedure. We divide the interval of one unit (i.e., 2.5 to 3.5) into two halves, and we place one score in each half. We could draw this the following way:

 The *X*s represent the two 3s.

Let's use this method to find the median when we have repeated middle values. Remember, the median is the value at or below which *exactly* half the scores fall.

DATA: 7, 8, 8

Score	Exact Limits
7	6.5–7.5
8	7.5–8.5

Step 1. Draw a line representing the exact limits of the scores.

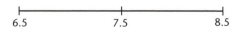

Step 2. Divide each interval into as many equal parts as you have scores.

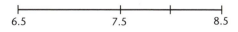

Between 6.5 and 7.5 we have only one score, so we do not divide the interval. Between 7.5 and 8.5 we have two scores, and so we divide the interval into two equal parts and place each score in the middle of each half.

Step 3. Place the scores in the middle of each divided portion.

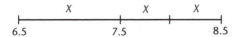

Step 4. Count exactly half the scores and locate the median. One half of 3 is $1\frac{1}{2}$.

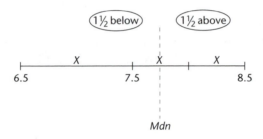

Step 5. Add the lower exact limit of the interval containing the median to the proportion of that interval needed to reach the precise point where the median is located.

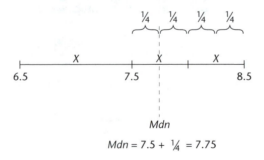

$Mdn = 7.5 + \frac{1}{4} = 7.75$

We need exactly one quarter of the interval to reach the median.
Here are some more examples.

DATA: 1, 2, 2, 2, 3, 4

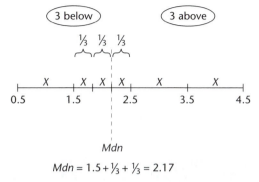

$$Mdn = 1.5 + \frac{1}{3} + \frac{1}{3} = 2.17$$

It is not necessary to draw the line representing all the numbers, but only that portion where the median lies. Consider the following:

DATA: 5, 7, 8, 8, 8, 8, 8

We need ½ of 7 scores above and ½ below the median. This value must lie in the interval from 7.5 to 8.5.

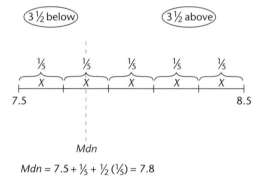

$$Mdn = 7.5 + \frac{1}{5} + \frac{1}{2}\left(\frac{1}{5}\right) = 7.8$$

Two values are below the exact lower limit, 7.5. We need $1\frac{1}{2}$ more to reach the median.

Real limits: Mathematically precise start and end points of numbers or intervals; also called exact limits

For Grouped Data

Linear interpolation is also required to determine the median of grouped data. The procedure is basically the same. We must keep in mind, however, that the interval between the exact limits is no longer one unit long.

ALERT

When data are grouped, the width of the interval is more than one unit. As a result, the proportion of the interval you need is a proportion of its width. For example, if you need one third of the interval to reach the median and the width is 5 units, you need one third of 5.

Here is an example.

Interval	f	cf
60–64	1	28
55–59	0	27
50–54	3	27
45–49	5	24
40–44	3	19
35–39	6	16
30–34	5	10
25–29	1	5
20–24	4	4

We have a total of 28 scores in this grouped frequency distribution. The median is the value at or below which exactly 14 scores fall. It lies somewhere in the interval between 35 and 39. We will draw our line to represent the exact limits of that interval.

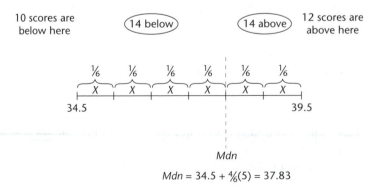

$Mdn = 34.5 + \frac{4}{6}(5) = 37.83$

We need to add $\frac{4}{6}$ of the interval to reach the median. The interval is 5 units long in this case, so we need to add $\frac{4}{6}$ of 5 units to the exact lower limit of the interval.

Linear interpolation is always required when data are grouped or when ungrouped data have repeated values in the middle. Some textbooks do not bother with the details of linear interpolation, because there is a formula that does this for you. I include the details of linear interpolation for the same reason that I have included a lot of other materials in this book. If you understand linear interpolation, you will not be forced to memorize a "meaningless formula" that does magical things that you don't understand. The median is calculated using the following formula:

$$Mdn = L + \frac{\left[N\left(\frac{50}{100}\right) - cf_b\right]i}{f_w}$$

L = lower exact limit of the interval containing the median

cf_b = cumulative frequency below the lower limit of the interval containing the median

f_w = frequency within the interval containing the median. For ungrouped data, this is the number of repeated middle values

i = interval width. For ungrouped data, the width is always 1.

Let's use the formula to verify the previous example.

$$Mdn = L + \frac{\left[N\left(\frac{50}{100}\right) - cf_b\right]i}{f_w}$$

$$= 34.5 + \frac{\left[28\left(\frac{50}{100}\right) - 10\right]5}{6}$$

$$= 34.5 + \left(\frac{4}{6}\right)5 = 37.83$$

To use the formula, you must first find the interval containing the median. The portion of the formula to the right of the plus sign determines the proportion of the interval needed to reach the median. This formula can be used for calculating the median of grouped frequency distributions and distributions that are ungrouped but which have repeated values in the middle.

Let's use our earlier example of ungrouped data to confirm that this is so. Our data were 5, 7, 8, 8, 8, 8, 8, and, using linear interpolation, we found a median of 7.8. When data are ungrouped, $i = 1$.

$$Mdn = L + \frac{\left[N\left(\dfrac{50}{100}\right) - cf_b \right] i}{f_w}$$

$$= 7.5 + \frac{\left[7\left(\dfrac{50}{100}\right) - 2 \right] 1}{5}$$

$$= 7.5 + \left(\frac{3.5 - 2}{5}\right) 1$$

$$= 7.5 + \frac{1.5}{5}$$

$$= 7.5 + 0.3$$

$$= 7.8$$

CONCEPT REVIEW 3.4

What is the median of the following data?

DATA: 4, 5, 6, 6, 6, 6, 7, 7, 7, 7, 8

Answer on page 88.

Mean

For Raw Data

When data are not in a frequency distribution, the mean is calculated by summing all the scores and dividing by the total number of them. The formula for calculating the mean for raw data is

$$\mu = \frac{\sum X}{N}$$

X is a general symbol standing for all the scores in the distribution. The $\sum X$ tells us to sum all the scores in the X distribution. N is the total number of scores. Ready for an example?

Number of tasks Jill completed each day (Max = 5): 5, 4, 3, 4, 3, 0, 2

$\Sigma X = 21$

$N = 7$

$$\mu = \frac{21}{7} = 3$$

I don't think we need to belabor this point, do you?

For Data in a Simple Frequency Distribution

When data are in a frequency distribution, we must multiply each score by its frequency before we sum, then divide by the number of scores. The formula for calculating the mean for data in a frequency distribution is

$$\mu = \frac{\Sigma fX}{N}$$

Here is an example: Seven children in a special needs classroom were asked to rate a classroom experience they had just had from 0 (very boring) to 5 (very interesting).

X	f	fX
5	1	5
4	2	8
3	2	6
2	1	2
1	0	0
0	1	0

$$\Sigma fX = 21$$
$$N = \Sigma f = 7$$
$$\mu = \frac{21}{7} = 3$$

ALERT

Do not sum the X column. This sum has no meaning.

CONCEPT REVIEW 3.5

What is the mean of the X distribution?

X	f
5	2
4	1
3	5
2	2
1	1

Answer on page 88.

For Data in a Grouped Frequency Distribution

When we determined the mode of a grouped frequency distribution, we used the midpoint of the interval with the highest frequency as our mode. Similarly, we use the midpoint of each interval to represent that interval when we determine the mean of a grouped frequency distribution. Here is the number of tokens earned in 1 week by 10 children for appropriate classroom behavior in a class for children diagnosed with behavior disorders.

Interval	Midpoint (X)	f	fX
25–29	27	2	54
20–24	22	2	44
15–19	17	4	68
10–14	12	1	12
5–9	7	0	0
0–4	2	1	2

$$\sum fX = 180$$

$$N = \sum f = 10$$

$$\mu = \frac{180}{10} = 18$$

The mean of a grouped frequency distribution will not exactly equal the mean of the raw data, because midpoints are used to represent the intervals, not the actual scores. The larger the interval width, the greater the degree of error due to grouping.

ALERT

Remember to multiply the midpoint by its frequency before you sum. *Do not* sum the *X* column. *Do* sum the *fX* column.

CONCEPT REVIEW 3.6

Find the mode, median, and mean for the following data.

DATA: 1, 1, 2, 2, 2, 6

Answers on page 88.

Interpreting Measures of Central Tendency

Mode

The mode is interpreted as the "typical" value in a set of scores. If we are interested in the value that occurs more often than any other, then the mode is the only value that is appropriate. A dress manufacturer, for example, who wants to make dresses of only one size would sell the most by using the modal dress size. In this way, he could fit the greatest number of people.

Imagine that we are interested in describing the average American in terms of country of ancestry. We might find that England is the modal country. Neither median nor mean could be used for these data. The mode, a quick way of describing central tendency, is the only measure of central tendency suitable for nominal data. Median or mean hair color makes no sense, but modal hair color does. The mode is also the only sensible measure of average for variables such as socioeconomic status or ethnic background of Americans.

Median

The median is the middle point in a distribution. It divides the number of scores in a distribution exactly in half. If you want to divide a large number of scores into two equal-sized groups, the median is the value to use.

Imagine that we asked residents of Quebec to indicate their opinion of separation from Canada on a scale from 1 to 7, where 1 means "I feel strongly that Quebec should separate" and 7 means "I feel strongly that Quebec should not separate." To indicate the average opinion, we could use the mode, but we could also use the median. We might find that the median rating is 6, with half the respondents indicating that they feel strongly (7) or moderately strongly (6) that Quebec should not be separated from Canada. The median is suitable for ordinal data. It can also be used for interval and ratio data, but the mean, a more sensitive measure of central tendency, is often preferred.

Mean

The mean can be considered the *balance point* of a distribution of scores. The scores below the mean "balance" the scores above the mean. A way to conceptualize the mean is to consider what happens when two children play on a teeter-totter. If one playmate is heavier than the other, she has to sit closer to the middle of the teeter-totter to balance the board. The lighter playmate must sit closer to the end of the board.

The mean acts like the fulcrum of the teeter-totter. The number of times a score occurs represents the weight of the children sitting on the teeter-totter. The distance of the scores above or below the mean represents the distance from the fulcrum that each playmate sits to make the board balance.

The distance between a particular score and the mean of the distribution is its **deviation score**. For example, if a score of 80 comes from a distribution with a mean of 65, then the deviation score value for that raw score is +15. The raw score of 80 is 15 units *above* the mean. A raw score of 60 would have a deviation score value of −5, because 60 is 5 units *below* the mean of 65.

> **Deviation score:** The difference between a score and the mean of its distribution

The formal way of expressing the mean as a balance point is $\Sigma(X - \mu) = 0$. This equation states that if all the scores in a distribution are expressed in terms of deviations from the mean, then the sum of all the deviations is zero. For deviations taken about any mean, the sum of the negative deviations is equal to the sum of the positive deviations.

FYI

Arithmetic and algebraic proofs of $\Sigma(X - \mu) = 0$ appear below.

Arithmetic Proof:

Data: 2, 3, 4, 5, 6

$$\mu = \frac{20}{5} = 4$$

$$\Sigma(X - \mu) = (2 - 4) + (3 - 4) + (4 - 4) + (5 - 4) + (6 - 4)$$
$$= -3 + 3$$
$$= 0$$

Algebraic Proof:

$$\Sigma(X - \mu) = \Sigma X - \Sigma \mu$$
$$= \Sigma X - N\mu^{1}$$
$$= \Sigma X - N(\Sigma X / N)$$
$$= \Sigma X - \Sigma X$$
$$= 0$$

Let's go back to our teeter-totter analogy. The line in Figure 3.2 represents the teeter-totter. The fulcrum is the mean. The raw scores are represented by boxes. The distance of each box from the fulcrum (mean) is the deviation.

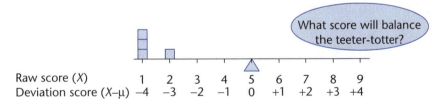

Raw score (X)	1	2	3	4	5	6	7	8	9
Deviation score ($X-\mu$)	−4	−3	−2	−1	0	+1	+2	+3	+4

Figure 3.2. The mean as the balance point in distributions.

In this example, there are three raw scores with a value of 1. Each is 4 points below the mean; the sum of the deviations is 12, 4 for each raw score.

---

[1]The sum of a constant is the constant multiplied by the number of times it appears in the distribution, that is, N. Basic summation rules are presented in Appendix B.

Another raw score is a 2, which is 3 points below the mean; its deviation score value is –3. The sum of the negative deviations is (–12) + (–3) = –15.

To balance, we must have equal "weight" above the mean, so we need a total of +15 deviations. There are several ways this could occur. For example, we could place 15 scores at the value of 6 on our teeter totter. This would produce a total of 15(+1) = +15 deviations, and the board would balance.

Could we balance the board by adding only one more score? Yes; it would have to provide +15 deviations, so it would have to be 15 units above the mean. Because the mean is 5, our single raw score would have to have a value of 20 to balance the distribution.

The sum of the deviations is determined by their size and frequency. A single score far away from the mean may be balanced on the other side by many scores close to the mean.

Shape and Measures of Central Tendency

Symmetrical Distributions

Recall that in a symmetrical distribution, the right half (the side above the mean) is a mirror image of the left half (the side below the mean). For any symmetrical distribution, the mean and median are equal. If the distribution is also unimodal, the mean, median, and mode are equal. Figure 3.3 shows two examples of symmetrical distributions. Notice that the distribution on the right has no mode because each score occurred the same number of times.

Skewed Distributions

Recall that skewed distributions are labelled on the basis of the direction of the tail. When the tail points to the negative or left side of the distribution,

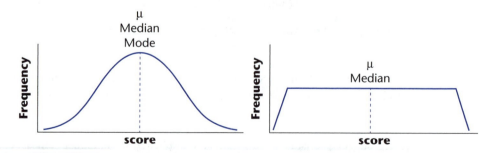

Figure 3.3. The relationship between measures of central tendency in symmetrical distributions.

the distribution is said to have a negative skew. A positively skewed distribution has the tail pointing to the right or positive side. When a distribution is skewed, the mean, mode, and median are not equal. Of the three, the mean always lies closest to the tail. The mode is always at the highest point of the curve, and the median is always between the mean and mode. Here are some examples (see Figure 3.4).

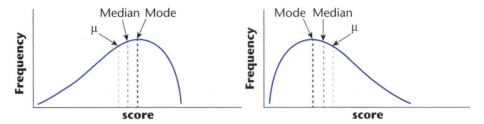

Figure 3.4. The relationship between measures of central tendency in skewed distributions.

Comparing Measures of Central Tendency

Sensitivity to Score Values

The mean is most sensitive to the size and number of score values in a distribution, because all the scores are used to compute the mean. If your objective is to reflect all the scores, then the mean is the most appropriate "average" to use. If, however, you do not want your measure of "average" to be "pushed" toward a few very extreme scores, then the median may be a better choice. The median is not sensitive to the size of each score but only to the number of scores above and below it. It doesn't matter how far above or how far below those scores are. In the example below, the median is the same although the distributions are clearly different.

DISTRIBUTION A: 1, 10, <u>100</u>, 1 000, 10 000

DISTRIBUTION B: 98, 99, <u>100</u>, 101, 102

The median of both distributions is 100, but the mean of Distribution A is 2 222.2, and the mean of Distribution B is 100. The median is not sensitive to the score values, only to their frequencies. The mean, on the other hand, is sensitive to both the size and the number of scores because each score is included in its computation. This requires, of course, that we know the precise value of each score!

Sometimes, we find ourselves in a situation where we do not know the value of each score. In these cases, the median may be the only "average" we can determine. For example, consider an experiment where 100 rats are timed running through a maze. After the experiment is complete, we find that 12 rats got lost in the maze and didn't finish. If we wish to include those rats in our measure of "average running time," we cannot use the mean. We could, however, compute the median. We would count those 12 rats as taking more time than even the slowest rat. This would produce an **open-ended distribution**; there are no values for the extreme end. The median can be calculated for most open-ended distributions because it relies on the number of cases above and below it, not on their distance.

> **Open-ended distribution:** One in which the exact upper or lower limit of the distribution is unknown

The mode is also not sensitive to score values. It is sensitive only to one score, that is, the score with the highest frequency. It is often used as a very quick and somewhat crude measure of central tendency. The mode is the only measure of central tendency appropriate for nominal variables.

Resistance to Sampling Fluctuation

Inferential statistics use samples drawn from a population to make inferences about the properties of that population. We assume that the characteristics of the sample adequately reflect the characteristics of the population from which the sample was drawn. If samples were repeatedly drawn from a population and the three measures of central tendency computed for each sample, the means would be more similar than the medians or modes. The mean fluctuates the least from sample to sample. The greatest variation would occur in the modes. The importance of this will become evident in later chapters.

FYI

THE MEAN OF COMBINED SUBGROUPS

Frequently, it is necessary to find the overall mean of two or more distributions of scores. For example, by the end of the year, my statistics students have written six exams. I always determine the mean on each exam as I record the grades. What if I would like to know the overall mean of the class on the first two exams or on all six? If the same number of students wrote each exam, I would simply compute the mean of the means. Unfortunately, even in my statistics class, some students drop out during the year, and so the number taking each exam often differs. Let's use the data from two exams to illustrate how to compute the **combined mean** of two subgroups.

> **Combined mean (μ_c):** The grand mean of all the scores in all groups when two or more groups are combined

If we have the sum of the raw scores for each exam, we would use the following formula to compute the combined mean (μ_c).

$$\mu_c = \frac{\Sigma X + \Sigma Y}{N_X + N_Y}$$

Mean of combined subgroups when the sums are known

The X distribution will be the scores of the 20 students who wrote the first statistics exam. The Y distribution will be the scores of the 18 who remained to write the second exam.

$$\Sigma X = 1302 \quad \Sigma Y = 1070$$

$$\mu_c = \frac{\Sigma X + \Sigma Y}{N_X + N_Y} = \frac{1302 + 1070}{20 + 18} = 62.42$$

Let's say that we don't happen to have the sums of the raw scores on the exams, but we do have the means for each. The mean for each exam was computed using a different number of students. There were 20 students who wrote the first exam, but only 18 wrote the second. We cannot simply average the two means because they were computed on different group sizes. We must first weight each mean by the number of cases that contributed to its calculation, sum these weighted scores, and then divide by the total number of scores. As you can see, this weighting procedure produces the subgroup sums:

$$\mu = \Sigma X / N$$

and by rearranging things

$$\Sigma X = N\mu$$

(Continued)

(Continued)

To calculate the overall mean, we would use the following formula.

$$\mu_c = \frac{N_X \mu_X + N_Y \mu_Y}{N_X + N_Y}$$

Mean of combined subgroups when the means are known

The mean on the first exam was 65.10, and the mean on the second exam was 59.44.

$$\mu_X = 65.10 \quad \mu_Y = 59.44$$

$$\mu_C = \frac{N_X \mu_X + N_Y \mu_Y}{N_X + N_Y} = \frac{20(65.10) + 18(59.44)}{20 + 18} = 64.42$$

When the subgroups are equal in size, we don't have to weight the means but simply average the means by adding them and dividing by the number of subgroups. If all 20 students had written the second exam and its mean was 59.44, then we could find the combined mean in the following way.

$$\mu_C = \frac{\mu_X + \mu_Y}{2} = \frac{65.10 + 59.44}{2} = 62.27$$

Although this value is close to the value we got when we used the weighted mean formula, it is not exactly the same. The amount of error produced by averaging the means of different-sized groups depends on how different the group sizes are. Larger differences produce larger error.

Measures of central tendency are important techniques for describing the average of distributions. In the next chapter, we will study another important characteristic of distributions: spread or variability.

Misleading With Measures of Average

Students often ask me which measure is the best. As I have said, the mean is typically reported for interval or ratio data, the median for ordinal data, and the mode for nominal data. But always remember that the goal is to describe the central tendency of the distribution honestly and accurately. If a distribution is severely skewed, then the mean, which will fall closest to the extreme end, might not be the best measure of average even if the data are interval or ratio. Perhaps the median might be a more honest measure of average in such a case. What if you have one horrifically extreme score? Again perhaps the mean will not fairly reflect the average. This is not such a concern when you are reporting to sophisticated readers such as readers of scientific literature. But what about newspaper reports, magazine surveys, polls . . .?

I opened this chapter with two measures of average housing prices in the United States and said that they could both be correct. If we looked at a frequency distribution of housing prices, we would find that it is positively skewed. There are some very expensive houses. Consequently, the mean price would be higher than the median or the mode because it is pulled toward those few expensive houses. Think about these things when you read statements about average drug use, average dropout rate, average years of education, and so on.

SUMMARY OF TERMS AND FORMULAS

The *mode (Mo)* is the most frequently occurring value in a distribution.

The *median (Mdn)* is the score value at or below which 50% of the values fall.

The *mean* (μ) is the arithmetic average of all the scores.

Linear interpolation assumes that repeated values are evenly distributed between the exact or real limits of the score.

Deviation score is the difference between a score and the mean of its distribution.

An *open-ended distribution* has no values at the extreme end.

Measure	Formula
Median	$Mdn = L + \dfrac{\left[N\left(\dfrac{50}{100} \right) - cf_b \right] i}{f_w}$
Mean for raw data	$\mu = \dfrac{\sum X}{N}$
Mean for data in a frequency distribution	$\mu = \dfrac{\sum fX}{N}$
Mean for combined subgroups When sums are known	$\mu_C = \dfrac{\sum X + \sum Y}{N_X + N_Y}$
When means are known	$\mu_C = \dfrac{\sum N_X \mu_X + \sum N_Y \mu_Y}{N_X + N_Y}$
When $N_X = N_Y$	$\mu_C = \dfrac{\mu_X + \mu_Y}{2}$

CONCEPT REVIEW ANSWERS

3.1. $Mo = 7$

3.2. $Mo = 7$

3.3. $Mdn = 7.5$

3.4. $Mdn = 5.5 + \dfrac{3.5}{4} = 6.375$

3.5. $\mu = \dfrac{(10 + 4 + 15 + 4 + 1)}{11} = 3.09$

3.6. The mode is 2, the most frequently occurring value. The median is $1.5 + \dfrac{1}{3} = 1.83.$ The mean is $\dfrac{14}{6} = 2.33.$

EXERCISES

1. For each set of raw data, calculate the following.

   a. N
   b. ΣfX
   c. μ
   d. Mo
   e. Mdn
   f. Skew direction

   DATA SET A: 11, 5, 9, 6, 3, 9, 8, 3, 11, 7, 5, 8, 7, 12, 10

   DATA SET B: 4, 3, 7, 2, 1, 0, 2, 0, 1, 2

2. For each set of raw data, calculate a to f:

   a. N
   b. ΣfX
   c. μ
   d. Mo
   e. Mdn
   f. Skew direction

DATA SET A

X	f
10	1
9	3
8	4
7	6
6	3
5	2

DATA SET B

Midpoints	f
52	2
47	5
42	2
37	3
32	6
27	3
22	12
17	15
12	11
7	4
2	2

3. Construct a frequency polygon for Data Set B in Exercise 2.

4. Calculate the mean, mode, and median for the following set of raw data. What direction is the skew?

    DATA: 10, 5, 8, 7, 3, 5, 9, 8, 3, 8, 11

5. Calculate the mean, mode, and median for the following set of raw data. What direction is the skew?

    DATA: 5, 3, 8, 2, 1, 0, 2

6. Calculate the combined mean of the distributions in Exercise 1.

7. Calculate the mean, mode, and median for the following set of raw data. What direction is the skew?

    DATA: 35, 32, 32, 31, 28, 27, 27, 26, 26, 24, 23, 23, 22, 20, 19, 18, 18, 17, 15, 15, 14, 14, 13, 12, 12, 12, 11, 11, 8, 7

8. Calculate the mean, mode, and median for the following set of data. What direction is the skew?

X	f
10	3
9	1
8	2
7	2
6	5
5	6

9. Calculate the mean, mode, and median for the following set of data. What direction is the skew?

Interval	f
150–154	2
145–149	1
140–144	2
135–139	5
130–134	7
125–129	9
120–124	8
115–119	13
110–114	11
105–109	14
100–104	12
95–99	4
90–94	5
85–89	5
80–84	2

10. For the following data, calculate the mean, mode, and median. ($N = 30$)
    What direction is the skew?

X	rf
16–18	0.2
13–15	0.1
10–12	0.2
7–9	0.3
4–6	0.1
1–3	0.1

11. Income is a positively skewed distribution.
    a. Why do you think this is so?
    b. If the United States wants to impress the world with its standard of living, which measure of central tendency should it use to report average income of U.S. citizens? Why?

12. Sixty gerbils were timed as they ran through a complicated maze, at the end of which was a reward of gerbil treats. The data are presented below. Compute the mean, median, and mode. What direction is the skew?

Interval	f
15.0–15.2	3
14.7–14.9	2
14.4–14.6	1
14.1–14.3	0
13.8–14.0	0
13.5–13.7	4
13.2–13.4	8
12.9–13.1	8
12.6–12.8	7
12.3–12.5	7
12.0–12.2	5
11.7–11.9	10
11.4–11.6	0
11.1–11.3	2
10.8–11.0	2
10.5–10.7	1

13. Which measure of central tendency should be reported for each of the following examples? Explain your answers.

   a. A dress manufacturer wants to know the average dress size of women.
   b. A researcher wants to separate people on the basis of a personality test into two groups of equal sizes: a high-anxiety group and a low-anxiety group.
   c. Students rated a professor as an effective instructor, using a scale of 1 to 5, with 1 meaning strongly agree and 5 meaning strongly disagree.
   d. In a timed problem-solving experiment, some of the participants failed to solve the problem within a reasonable period of time. The experimenter would like to include these participants in his measure of average time to solve the problem.

CHAPTER 4

Describing the Variability of Distributions

LEARNING OBJECTIVES

After reading this chapter, you should be able to do the following:

1. Describe what is meant by the term variability.
2. Define range and semi-interquartile range.
3. Determine the range and semi-interquartile range of a given set of data.
4. Define variance.
5. Compute the variance of a given set of data.
6. Define standard deviation.
7. Compute the standard deviation of a given set of data.
8. Compare distributions with different variances.

You just received your midterm exam score in your criminology class. You got 78%, and the class average was only 65%. Your friend Charlie, who got 78% on his last exam in statistics, tells you that the class average on his exam was the same as your class average, but he says that, relatively speaking, he did a lot better than you! He could be right. After reading this chapter, you will understand why.

Chapter 3 dealt with measures of central tendency—methods for indicating the "average" of a distribution. Measures of variability are methods for describing the variation in scores, the amount of scatter around the center of a distribution. These measures indicate whether scores are clustered closely around the middle of the distribution or whether they are scattered far from the middle. To adequately describe a distribution of scores, we require a measure of variability as well as a measure of central tendency. There are several ways of measuring variations in scores. We will consider four of these: (1) range, (2) semi-interquartile range, (3) variance, and (4) standard deviation.

Measures of Variability

Range

The **range** of a distribution is the number of values over which the distribution spans. The range gives us a quick measure of variability.

Semi-Interquartile Range

The **semi-interquartile range** provides a kind of an average of the span of a distribution. It is more sensitive than the range.

Variance and Standard Deviation

Variance is the *average of the squared deviations of scores from the mean* of the distribution. The symbol for the variance is σ^2, "sigma squared." Standard deviation is the *average deviation of scores from the mean*. It is the square root of the variance, and its symbol is σ, "sigma." You may be wondering why we have these two measures when one is the square of the other. Well, **standard deviation** is typically used descriptively, and variance is used inferentially, as you will see later on.

> **Range:** The span of a distribution
>
> **Semi-interquartile range:** Half the span of the middle 50% of the distribution
>
> **Variance (σ^2):** The average squared deviation of scores from the mean
>
> **Standard deviation (σ):** The average deviation of scores from the mean

Calculating Measures of Variability

Range

Range is by far the easiest measure to determine. It is the difference between the highest and lowest score, plus one unit. In a distribution of test scores, if someone got 1% and someone else got 100%, then the range would be $(100 - 1) + 1 = 100$. In other words, the scores would range over a total of 100 possible values. We determined the range of an interval, which we called the width, in Chapter 2, when we constructed a grouped frequency distribution. The range, as a measure of variability, can be thought of as the width of the entire distribution.

CONCEPT REVIEW 4.1

What is the range for the data below?

8, 12, 24, 6, 11, 3, 7, 25, 4, 6, 6, 10

Answer on page 113.

ALERT

Statistical software programs do not report range this way. Rather, most programs simply report the range as the difference between the highest and lowest score.

Semi-Interquartile Range

Calculating the semi-interquartile range requires determining two percentiles, the 75th percentile (also called the third quartile or Q_3) and the 25th percentile (also called the first quartile or Q_1). Percentiles and percentile ranks are discussed in depth in Chapter 5. For now, think about a distribution sectioned into fourths, or quartiles. Q_1 is the score value at or below which 25% of the cases fall. Q_2 is the score value at or below which 50% of the cases fall (you will recall that this is the median). Q_3 is the score value at or below which 75% of the cases fall, and Q_4 is the highest score value. One-hundred percent of the cases fall at or below Q_4.

The distance between the third and first quartiles (i.e., $Q_3 - Q_1$) is called the **interquartile range**. This measure excludes the lower and higher 25% of the distribution. To calculate the semi-interquartile range, we determine the interquartile range and divide by 2. The semi-interquartile range is $(Q_3 - Q_1)/2$.

For example, if 75% of the scores in a distribution fall at or below a value of 84 and 25% of the scores fall at or below 30, then the semi-interquartile range would be $(84 - 30)/2 = 27$.

Here is an example.

DATA: 2 2 3 3 3 **4**   **5** 5 5 5 5 5   5 5 5 5 5 **5**   **6** 6 7 8 8 8
$\qquad\qquad\quad Q_1 = 4.5$ $\qquad\qquad\qquad\qquad\qquad\qquad Q_3 = 5.5.$

There are 24 scores in this distribution. Dividing the distribution into quartiles leaves six scores in each quartile. Q_1 lies midway between the 6th and 7th score (i.e., 4.5), and Q_3 lies midway between the 18th and 19th score (i.e., 5.5). The interquartile range is $5.5 - 4.5 = 1$, and the semi-interquartile range = 0.5.

With most data, it is rarely this simple to determine the semi-interquartile range. Formulas for computing Q_1 and Q_3 are provided in Chapter 5 when percentiles and percentile ranks are discussed in detail.

The semi-interquartile range as a measure of variability is limited but may properly accompany the median when the distribution is extremely skewed. It is often used when the researcher is working with ordinal data. In such cases, the range itself may be of little value in describing spread.

> **Interquartile range:** The distance between the 75th and 25th percentiles; a measure of variability

Variance and Standard Deviation

In the previous chapter, I described the mean as the balance point of any distribution because the sum of the negative deviations equals the sum of the positive deviations. We will need the concept of the deviation score again, this time to calculate variance and standard deviation.

Defining Formulas

The deviation of a score from its mean is determined by subtracting the mean from the score. This operation can be expressed as $X - \mu$.

Variance is the average of the squared deviations of the scores from the mean of the distribution. The defining formula for the variance of the population is

$$\sigma^2 = \frac{\Sigma (X - \mu)^2}{N}$$

To use the variance formula, follow these steps:

Step 1. Subtract the mean from each raw score.

Step 2. Square each difference.

Step 3. Sum all the squared differences.

Step 4. Divide this sum by N (the total number of cases).

The result of Step 3 gives us the sum of squared deviations of scores from the mean. This is called, for short, the **sum of squares**, a term frequently used in statistics. Soon we will use **SS** to refer to the sum of squares. It will make life much easier. Recall in Chapter 3 that one way to define the mean is as the value about which the sum of the deviations is equal to zero. Another way to define the mean is as *the value about which the sum of squares is a minimum*. This means that the sum of squared deviations from the mean will be less than the sum of squared deviations taken around any other value. This *least squares* concept will turn up again in Chapter 17.

> **Sum of squares (*SS*):** The sum of the squared deviations of scores from the mean

Standard deviation is simply the square root of the variance, so to determine it, we add the following step:

Step 5. Take the square root of the number obtained in Step 4.

The defining formula for the standard deviation of the population is

$$\sigma = \sqrt{\frac{\sum(X - \mu)^2}{N}}$$

Let's use an example to show the steps for calculating variance and standard deviation of a distribution of scores. Before I do, let me remind you again that a population is the entire set of individuals, items, events, or data points of interest to the researcher. Although we think of a population as being very large, this is not necessary from a statistical point of view. It is not its size that makes a population a population or a sample a sample. Of course, in reality, populations are usually much larger than the examples I give in this book. It's important to recognize, however, that describing large populations is no different than describing little populations. Let's compute the variance and standard deviation for the little population below. Let's also use the much simpler notation, *SS*, to stand for $\sum(X - \mu)^2$.

X	X − μ	(X − μ)²
1	−9	81
4	−6	36
7	−3	9
13	+3	9
16	+6	36
19	+9	81
μ = 10	$SS = \sum(X - \mu)^2 = 252$	

$$\sigma^2 = \frac{SS}{N} = \frac{\sum(X - \mu)^2}{N} = \frac{252}{6} = 42$$

$$\sigma = \sqrt{\sigma^2} = \sqrt{42} = 6.48$$

The middle column of numbers contains the deviation scores for each raw score. These deviations are then squared in the right-hand column. The sum of the squared deviations is divided by N for the variance. The standard deviation is the square root of the variance.

CONCEPT REVIEW 4.2

Compute the variance, standard deviation, range, and semi-interquartile range for the following data:

$$SS = \sum(X - \mu)^2 = 81$$
$$N = 99$$

Highest score = 87

Lowest score = 23

$$Q_3 = 80$$
$$Q_1 = 25$$

Answer on page 113.

Computational Formulas: Raw Data

The defining formulas for these two measures of variability are helpful because they show us exactly what we are doing when we compute a variance or standard deviation. By examining the defining formulas we can see that both measures tell us how far the scores vary around the mean, the variance in squared units, and the standard deviation in the same units as the raw scores. These formulas, however, are not often used in calculation. The computational formulas for variance and standard deviation have been derived from the defining ones and are easier to use.

When data have not been organized into a frequency distribution but appear as single raw scores, the computational formulas for calculating the population variance and population standard deviation for the raw data are as follows:

$$\sigma^2 = \frac{SS}{N} = \frac{\sum X^2 - (\sum X)^2 / N}{N}$$

$$\sigma = \sqrt{\frac{SS}{N}} = \sqrt{\frac{\sum X^2 - (\sum X)^2 / N}{N}}$$

ΣX^2 is the sum of the squared raw scores. To calculate ΣX^2, follow these steps:

Step 1. Square all the scores.

Step 2. Sum the squared scores.

The computational formulas for variance and standard deviation are, of course, equivalent to the defining formulas. Using either one will produce the same value. I like to use the defining formulas in teaching because they show my students exactly what is being computed, whereas the computational formulas often don't seem so clear. You will notice that the only difference between the defining and the computational formula for variance and standard deviation is in the numerator of the ratio, the sum of squares.

FYI

To prove the equivalence of the defining and computational formulas requires that we show that the numerators are algebraically equivalent. The proof for the equivalence of the defining and computational formulas for the sum of squares is as follows:

Algebraic Rules:

$$(X - Y)^2 = X^2 - 2XY + Y^2$$
$$\Sigma(X - Y) = \Sigma X - \Sigma Y$$
$$\Sigma c = Nc \qquad \text{where } c \text{ is a constant.}$$

Algebraic Proof:

$$SS = \Sigma(X - \mu)^2 = \Sigma\left(X^2 - 2X\mu + \mu^2\right)$$
$$= \Sigma X^2 - \Sigma 2X\mu + \Sigma \mu^2$$
$$= \Sigma X^2 - 2\Sigma X \frac{(\Sigma X)}{N} + N\mu^2$$
$$= \Sigma X^2 - 2\frac{(\Sigma X)^2}{N} + N\frac{(\Sigma X)^2}{N^2}$$
$$= \Sigma X^2 - 2\frac{(\Sigma X)^2}{N} + \frac{(\Sigma X)^2}{N^2}$$
$$= \Sigma X^2 - \frac{(\Sigma X)^2}{N}$$

Using the computational formulas, let's compute the variance and standard deviation for a distribution of scores. We will use the data we used earlier when we computed variance and standard deviation with the defining formulas.

Step 1. Square all the scores.

Step 2. Sum the squared scores.

X	X^2
1	1
4	16
7	49
13	169
16	256
19	361
$\Sigma X = 60$	$\Sigma X^2 = 852$

Now we have what we need to compute the variance and standard deviation.

$$\sigma^2 = \frac{SS}{N} = \frac{\Sigma X^2 - (\Sigma X)^2 / N}{N}$$

$$= \frac{852 - 60^2 / 6}{6}$$

$$= 42$$

$$\sigma = \sqrt{42}$$

$$= 6.48$$

For this distribution then, the scores vary on average 6.48 points from 10 (i.e., 60/6), the mean of the distribution.

CONCEPT REVIEW 4.3

Compute the variance for the following.

$\Sigma X = 50$

$\Sigma X^2 = 300$

$N = 10$

Answer on page 113.

ALERT

Occasionally, students come to me with a problem in their calculation of the variance. Typically, they have computed a negative variance. Now, of course, we know you cannot have negative variability.
If all the scores are the same, then you will have zero variability but
you can't have less than zero, can you? So how does this happen?
Almost always the student has put the wrong sum in the wrong
place. The first term in the numerator of the computational formula
for the variance tells you to square the scores first, and then sum
the squares. The second term tells you to sum the scores and then
square the sum. If you reverse these two sums, then you will get a
negative number.

Computational Formulas: Data in a Frequency Distribution

When data have been organized into a frequency distribution, the computational
formulas for variance and standard deviation are as follows:

$$\sigma^2 = \frac{SS}{N} = \frac{\sum X^2 - \left(\sum X\right)^2 / N}{N}$$

$$\sigma = \sqrt{\frac{SS}{N}} = \sqrt{\frac{\sum X^2 - \left(\sum X\right)^2 / N}{N}}$$

When we calculated the mean for data in a frequency distribution, we multiplied each score by its frequency. We must do the same here.

To calculate $\sum fX^2$, follow these steps:

Step 1. Square each X value.

Step 2. Multiply each square by its frequency.

Step 3. Sum these products.

ALERT

Remember to square the X values first and then multiply each
value by its frequency before summing.

To calculate $\left(\sum fX\right)^2$, follow these steps:

Step 1. Multiply each X value by its frequency.

Step 2. Sum these products.

Step 3. Square the sum.

Let's follow these steps to calculate the variance and standard deviation for the frequency distribution (Table 4.1) of marital satisfaction scores for 60 couples in first marriages and 60 couples in second marriages (higher scores reflect higher satisfaction).

Table 4.1

Marital satisfaction scores for first and second marriages

Marital Satisfaction Score	First Marriage (*f*)	Second Marriage (*f*)
25	2	8
24	1	6
23	2	4
22	4	2
21	3	5
20	4	7
19	6	5
18	1	4
17	0	4
16	8	2
15	6	0
14	5	2
13	2	1
12	0	3
11	3	3
10	4	0
9	5	0
8	1	1
7	0	1
6	1	0
5	1	1
4	1	1

To calculate ΣfX^2, follow these steps:

Step 1. Square each X value (see Table 4.2, columns 1 and 2).

Step 2. Multiply each square by its frequency (Table 4.2, columns 4 and 6).

Step 3. Sum these products (last row in Table 4.2).

Table 4.2

Calculating ΣfX^2 for data in Table 4.1

		First Marriage		Second Marriage	
X	**X²**	**f**	**fX²**	**f**	**fX²**
25	625	2	1 250	8	5 000
24	576	1	576	6	3 456
23	529	2	1 058	4	2 116
22	484	4	1 936	2	968
21	441	3	1 323	5	2 205
20	400	4	1 600	7	2 800
19	361	6	2 166	5	1 805
18	324	1	324	4	1 296
17	289	0	0	4	1 156
16	256	8	2 048	2	512
15	225	6	1 350	0	0
14	196	5	980	2	392
13	169	2	338	1	169
12	144	0	0	3	432
11	121	3	363	3	363
10	100	4	400	0	0
9	81	5	405	0	0
8	64	1	64	1	64
7	49	0	0	1	49
6	36	1	36	0	0
5	25	1	25	1	25
4	16	1	16	1	16
Sum		60	16 258	60	22 824

To calculate $(\sum fX)^2$, follow these steps:

Step 1. Multiply each X value by its frequency (Table 4.3, columns 3 and 5).

Step 2. Sum these products (last row in Table 4.3).

Table 4.3

Calculating $(\sum fX)^2$ for the data in Table 4.1

	First Marriage		Second Marriage	
X	f	fX	f	fX
25	2	50	8	200
24	1	24	6	144
23	2	46	4	92
22	4	88	2	44
21	3	63	5	105
20	4	80	7	140
19	6	114	5	95
18	1	18	4	72
17	0	0	4	68
16	8	128	2	32
15	6	90	0	0
14	5	70	2	28
13	2	26	1	13
12	0	0	3	36
11	3	33	3	33
10	4	40	0	0
9	5	45	0	0
8	1	8	1	8
7	0	0	1	7
6	1	6	0	0
5	1	5	1	5
4	1	4	1	4
		0		
Sum	60	938	60	1 126

Step 3. Square the sum of the *fX* columns.

First marriage: $\left(\sum fX\right)^2 = 938^2 = 879\ 844$

Second marriage: $\left(\sum fX\right)^2 = 1126^2 = 1\ 267\ 876$

Now we have everything we need to compute the variance and standard deviation for each group. First marriage group:

$$\mu = \sum fX\ /\ N = 938\ /\ 60 = 15.63.$$

$$\sigma^2 = \frac{\sum fX^2 - \left(\sum fX\right)^2 /\ N}{N}$$

$$= \frac{16258 - 938^2\ /\ 60}{60}$$

$$= 26.56$$

$$\sigma = \sqrt{26.56}$$

$$= 5.15$$

Second marriage group:

$$\mu = 1126\ /\ 60 = 18.77.$$

$$\sigma^2 = \frac{22824 - 1126^2\ /\ 60}{60},$$

$$= 28.21.$$

$$\sigma = \sqrt{28.21} = 5.31.$$

If we were reporting our findings in a formal paper, we would write something like the following, using the notation for means and standard deviation preferred by the APA (American Psychological Association). "Couples in second marriages reported higher levels of marital satisfaction ($M = 18.77$, $SD = 5.31$) than couples in first marriages ($M = 15.63$, $SD = 5.15$)."

Standard deviation, rather than the variance, is reported descriptively because it is on the same scale as the raw score units and is therefore easier to understand. Generally when we report means, we also report standard deviations when we are describing our data.

We will find later that in inference, the variance rather than standard deviation is typically used.

CONCEPT REVIEW 4.4

Compute the variance for the data in the frequency distribution given below:

X	f
5	1
4	2
3	5
2	2

Answer on page 113.

FYI

When calculating variance and standard deviation of data in a grouped frequency distribution, we represent each interval by its midpoint just as we did earlier when computing the mean. I include the following example to illustrate this concept because there may be occasions when you do not have access to the original data.

Interval	Midpoint	f	fX	X^2	fX^2
155–159	157	1	157	24 649	24 649
150–154	152	2	304	23 104	46 208
145–149	147	1	147	21 609	21 609
140–144	142	7	994	20 164	141 148
135–139	137	4	548	18 769	75 076
130–134	132	5	660	17 424	87 120
125–129	127	3	381	16 129	48 387
120–124	122	2	244	14 884	29 768
115–119	117	1	117	13 689	13 689
Sums		26	3552		487 654

$$\sigma^2 = \frac{SS}{N} = \frac{\sum fX^2 - \left(\sum fX\right)^2 / N}{N}$$

$$= \frac{487654 - 3552^2 / 26}{26}$$

$$\sigma = \sqrt{92.16}$$

$$= 9.60$$

Interpreting Measures of Variability

Range

Range indicates the total number of possible values over which the raw scores span. Because the range uses only the highest and lowest scores in its calculation, it is a relatively crude measure of variability. When the median has been used as the measure of central tendency of a distribution, the range may be an appropriate measure of variability unless the distribution is very skewed. If we were reporting median house price or median income, we would want to include range as well.

Semi-Interquartile Range

Semi-interquartile range may be a more useful measure of variability when the median is used as a measure of average and the distribution is extremely skewed. The median plus and minus the semi-interquartile range approximates the values that include 50% of the cases in the distribution. In other words, if a distribution had a median of 35 and a semi-interquartile range of 5, then about 50% of the cases would lie between the values of 30 and 40. But, like the range, the semi-interquartile range is not sensitive to precise score position.

Variance and Standard Deviation

Variance is a number reflecting the "average squared" distance or deviation of scores from the mean of the distribution. Because the deviations are squared, variance can be hard to interpret because it is not in the same arithmetic units as the raw scores.

Standard deviation indicates the "average" distance or deviation of the scores from the mean. Because standard deviation is the square root of the variance, it is in the same units as the raw scores and is easier to interpret. A standard deviation of 6, for example, means that, on average, the scores vary 6 points from the mean. Because of this, when we are describing the variability of a distribution, we report standard deviation rather than variance.

Standard deviation is a quick way of locating the bulk of the scores in a distribution. In any distribution, regardless of the shape, at least 75% of the scores are within two standard deviations of the mean and at least 89% are within three standard deviations of the mean. Thus, a distribution with a standard deviation of 6 has at least 75% of its scores between 12 points below and 12 points above the mean and 89% between 18 points below and above the mean.

For a fairly symmetrical distribution, more than 90% of the observations fall within two standard deviations of the mean, and almost all the observations are within three standard deviations of the mean.

For a normal distribution, which we will study further in later chapters, the following is true:

$$\mu \pm 3\sigma = 99.74\%$$
$$\mu \pm 2\sigma = 95.44\%$$
$$\mu \pm 1\sigma = 68.26\%$$

This means that in a normal distribution, 99.74% of the scores fall between three standard deviations above and below the mean; 95.44% of the scores are within two standard deviations; 68.26% of the scores are within one standard deviation of the mean. These facts will provide a basis for several statistical techniques that we will study in the chapters on inference.

Whenever we describe a distribution of raw scores, we should include a measure of variability along with a measure of central tendency. It is not sufficient to state the "average" only. For example, two distributions may have the same "average" but may be very different in terms of spread. I opened this chapter with a claim by Charlie that despite equal test scores and class averages, one score was better than the other.

Look at Figure 4.1. The scores on the sociology exam were more spread out than the scores on the statistics test. In the statistics class, people tended to be closer to the class average and so Charlie's score of 78% is really very good. Charlie was right. His score of 78% is better than yours because fewer people outperformed him in the statistics test than outperformed you on the sociology test. We need to know both average and variability to understand how well we have done compared with everyone else.

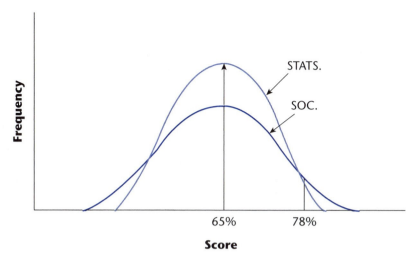

Figure 4.1.   Charlie's score in statistics versus his score in sociology.

FYI

THE VARIANCE AND STANDARD DEVIATION OF COMBINED SUBGROUPS

When we studied central tendency, we discovered that finding the combined mean of two or more groups is often not as simple as taking the average of the means of each group. Finding the overall variance and standard deviation of several subgroups is similar. We cannot just average the measures.

Variance and standard deviation are measures of spread around the mean of a distribution of scores. To find the variance or standard deviation of combined subgroups, we must determine the average spread of *all the scores around the combined mean*. We cannot simply average the subgroups' variances or standard deviations because each refers to the spread of group scores around the mean of that group. Rather, we must determine the spread of *all* the scores from *all* the subgroups to find the pooled variance or pooled standard deviation. The formula for determining the pooled variance of three groups is presented below. This formula may be modified for any number of subgroups. The square root of the pooled variance gives the pooled standard deviation.

(Continued)

(Continued)

$$\sigma_C^2 = \frac{N_W \sigma_W^2 + N_X \sigma_X^2 + N_Y \sigma_Y^2 + N_W (\mu_W - \mu_C)^2 + N_X (\mu_X - \mu_C)^2 + N_Y (\mu_Y - \mu_C)^2}{N_W + N_X + N_Y}.$$

Combined or pooled variance

Each subgroup variance must be weighted by the number of scores in the group, and the squared deviation of each subgroup mean from the combined mean must also be weighted by the group size. To illustrate this, let us determine the pooled variance for the following data:

$$\mu_W = 8, \sigma_W^2 = 2, N_W = 10$$

$$\mu_X = 6, \sigma_X^2 = 1, N_X = 12$$

$$\mu_Y = 10, \sigma_Y^2 = 3, N_Y = 15$$

The first step is to determine the combined mean discussed in Chapter 3. With three groups, the formula for the combined mean is as follows:

$$\sigma_C = \frac{N_W \mu_W + N_X \mu_X + N_Y \mu_Y}{N_W + N_X + N_Y}$$

$$= \frac{10(8) + 12(6) + 15(10)}{10 + 12 + 15}$$

$$= \frac{302}{37}$$

$$= 8.16$$

Now we can go ahead and compute the combined variance.

$$\sigma_C^2 = \frac{N_W \sigma_W^2 + N_X \sigma_X^2 + N_Y \sigma_Y^2 + N_W (\mu_W - \mu_C)^2 + N_X (\mu_X - \mu_C)^2 + N_Y (\mu_Y - \mu_C)^2}{N_W + N_X + N_Y}$$

$$= \frac{10(2) + 12(1) + 15(3) + 10(8 - 8.16)^2 + 12(6 - 8.16)^2 + 15(10 - 8.16)^2}{10 + 12 + 15}$$

$$= \frac{(77 + 107.03)}{37}$$

$$= 4.97$$

Notice that the combined variance is *not an average* of the subgroup variances. Rather, it is a measure of the spread of *all* the subgroup scores around the combined mean.

FOCUS ON RESEARCH

THE RESEARCH PROBLEM

Ambrose, Fey, and Eisenberg (2012) were interested in speech and language development in young children with cochlear implants. More specifically, they wanted to compare phonological awareness and print knowledge of preschool children with cochlear implants to children with normal hearing.

THE PARTICIPANTS, DESIGN, AND VARIABLES

Forty-seven children between 3 and 5 years of age participated in the study. Twenty-four of these children who had severe hearing loss and had cochlear implants for a minimum of 18 months constituted the cochlear implant group (CI).

The normal hearing (NH) group included 23 children with no hearing difficulties.

This study was a quasi-experiment because the comparison variable (CI vs. NH) was a participant variable, not a true independent variable.

The Test of Preschool Early Literacy (TOPEL; Lonigan, Wagner, Torgesen, & Rashotte, 2007) as cited in Ambrose et al. (2012) was used to assess phonological awareness and print knowledge.

Phonological awareness was tested by asking the children to identify words with missing letters (e.g., find the word kitty without the Y), blend two words into one (e.g., ice-cream), and to identify the word that certain sounds make (e.g., kit-ee).

To test print knowledge, the researchers asked the children to name letters (e.g., Which one is A?) and to provide the sound that letters make (e.g., What does B sound like?).

THE RESULTS

I will present some of the results here. Means and standard deviations were computed for each group on each of the two language variables (phonological awareness and print knowledge). These data are in Table 4.4.

As you can see, the mean print knowledge scores were very similar but the phonological awareness mean was lower for the CI group. The variability in the scores for both groups was quite similar.

THE CONCLUSIONS

The researchers concluded that intervention programs be used to help children with cochlear implants improve their phonological awareness.

Ambrose, S. E., Fey, M. E., & Eisenberg, L. S. (2012). Phonological awareness and print knowledge of preschool children with cochlear implants. *Journal of Speech, Language, and Hearing Research, 55*(3), 811–823.

Table 4.4

Language comparisons (means, standard deviations) for the Cochlear Implant and Normal Hearing Groups

Group	Mean	Standard Deviation
Phonological awareness		
CI	87.33	10.53
NH	102.96	13.97
Print knowledge		
CI	99.25	16.90
NH	101.09	16.09

SUMMARY OF TERMS AND FORMULAS

Measures of *variability* describe the spread or scatter of the scores in a distribution.

The *range* measures the span of the distribution.

The *semi-interquartile range* provides an estimate of the range of half the scores from the median.

The *variance* and *standard deviation* measure how far, on the average, the scores are from the mean of the distribution.

The sum of squared deviations of scores from the mean is often called the *sum of squares (SS)*.

When the *mean* is used as the measure of central tendency, the *standard deviation* usually accompanies it as the measure of variability. When the *median* is used, it is usually accompanied by the *range* or the *semi-interquartile range*.

Pooled variance and *pooled standard deviation* are measures of spread around the combined mean of all scores from two or more groups.

Measure	Computational Formula	Defining Formula
Range	$H - L + 1$	
Semi-interquartile range	$\dfrac{(Q_3 - Q_1)}{2}$	
Variance for raw data	$\dfrac{\sum X^2 - (\sum X)^2 / N}{N}$	$\dfrac{\sum (X - \mu)^2}{N}$

Measure	Computational Formula	Defining Formula
Variance for data in a frequency distribution	$\dfrac{\sum fX^2 - (\sum fX)^2 / N}{N}$	
Standard deviation for raw data	$\dfrac{\sum X^2 - (\sum X)^2 / N}{N}$	$\sqrt{\dfrac{\sum (X - \mu)^2}{N}}$
Standard deviation for data in a frequency distribution	$\sqrt{\dfrac{\sum fX^2 - (\sum fX)^2 / N}{N}}$	
Pooled variance for three combined subgroups	$\sigma_C^2 = \dfrac{N_W \sigma_W^2 + N_X \sigma_X^2 + N_Y \sigma_Y^2 + N_W (\mu_W - \mu_C)^2 + N_X (\mu_X - \mu_C)^2 + N_Y (\mu_Y - \mu_C)^2}{N_W + N_X + N_Y}$	

CONCEPT REVIEW ANSWERS

4.1.   The highest score is 25, and the lowest is 3. The range is $H - L + 1 = 25 - 3 + 1 = 23$.

4.2. $\sigma^2 = \dfrac{81}{9} = 9 \quad \sigma = \sqrt{9} = 3$

Range $= (87 - 23 + 1) = 65$

Semi-interquartile range $= \dfrac{(80 - 25)}{2} = 27.5$

4.3. $\sigma^2 = \dfrac{\left(300 - 50^2 / 10\right)}{10} = 5$

4.4. $\sum fX = 5 + 8 + 15 + 4 = 32$

$\sum fX^2 = 25(1) + 16(2) + 9(5) + 4(2) = 110$

$\sigma^2 = \dfrac{\left(110 - 32^2 / 10\right)}{10} = 0.76$

EXERCISES

1. For each set of raw data, calculate a. to g.

DATA SET A: 13, 15, 21, 12, 45, 30, 10, 19, 28, 7
DATA SET B: 12, 12, 8, 7, 6, 3, 1

    a. ΣX

    b. N

    c. μ

    d. $\Sigma(X - \mu)$

    e. SS

    f. σ^2

    g. σ

2. For each set of data, calculate a. to f.

   DATA SET A: 10, 9, 7, 7, 5, 3, 1
   DATA SET B:

X	f
10	3
9	1
8	2
7	2
6	5
5	6
4	4
3	2
2	0
1	1

    a. ΣX

    b. ΣX^2

    c. $(\Sigma X)^2$

    d. $(\Sigma X)^2 / N$

    e. σ^2

    f. σ

3. For the following distributions, determine the deviation scores for each raw score.

   X: 2, 4, 6, 7, 4, 3, 2
   Y: 12, 23, 50, 35, 20

4. Use the defining formulas to calculate variance and standard deviation of the following data. What is the range?

   DATA: 10, 8, 4, 4, 8, 5, 2

5. Use the defining formulas to calculate variance and standard deviation of the following data. What is the range?

   DATA: 6, 4, 8, 2, 1, 0, 0, 3

6. Use the computational formulas to calculate the variance and standard deviation for the following data.

   DATA: 6, 4, 8, 2, 1, 0, 0, 3

7. Use the computational formulas to calculate variance and standard deviation for the following data. What is the range?

X	f
10	3
9	1
8	2
7	2
6	5
5	6

8. Calculate variance and standard deviation for the following grouped frequency distribution.

X	f
23–25	1
20–22	2
17–19	2
14–16	4
11–13	5
8–10	3
5–7	1
2–4	2

9. Compute the pooled variance for the data in Exercises 4 and 5.

10. You received a test score of 112. In which of the following distributions of test scores would you prefer to be? Explain your answer.

   DISTRIBUTION A: Mean = 98   Standard Deviation = 4

   DISTRIBUTION B: Mean = 98   Standard Deviation = 16

11. The following data are the test results for two different groups of students. Compute the mean and standard deviation for each group. Provide a rough sketch of the two distributions to show how they differ.

   GROUP 1:

   25, 25, 25, 25, 25, 25, 25, 25, 25, 25, 25, 25, 25, 25, 24, 24, 24, 24, 24, 24, 24, 24, 24, 24, 24, 24, 24, 23, 23, 23, 23, 23, 23, 22, 22, 22, 22, 22, 22, 21, 21, 17, 16

   GROUP 2:

   25, 25, 25, 25, 24, 24, 24, 24, 24, 24, 24, 24, 24, 23, 23, 23, 23, 23, 22, 22, 22, 22, 22, 22, 21, 21, 21, 21, 21, 21, 21, 21, 21, 21, 20, 20, 20, 19, 18, 15, 12, 8

12. Compute the mean and standard deviation for the following data. Plot the data in a histogram. What is the skew direction?

   DATA: 9, 9, 9, 9, 8, 8, 8, 8, 8, 8, 7, 7, 7, 7, 7, 7, 7, 7, 7, 6, 6, 6, 6, 6, 6, 6, 6, 6, 6, 6, 6, 5, 5, 5, 5, 5, 5, 5, 4, 4, 4, 4

13. Determine the semi-interquartile range for each of the following sets of data.

   a. DATA: 25, 24, 23, 22, 20, 12, 10, 8
   b. DATA: 25, 24, 23, 22, 22, 20, 19, 18, 10, 10, 9, 8

Describing the Position of Scores in Distributions

LEARNING OBJECTIVES

After reading this chapter, you should be able to do the following:

1. Define the term derived score.
2. Define percentile and percentile rank, and provide an example for each.
3. Compute percentiles from a given set of data.
4. Compute percentile ranks from a given set of data.
5. Define the term *z* score.
6. Calculate *z* scores for a given set of data.
7. List the properties of a *z* distribution.
8. Use *z* to locate the position of scores in a distribution.

When my friend Millie took her infant son Jake for his 6-week checkup, she learned that his body size was at the 50th percentile but his head circumference was at the 99th percentile!

It has been estimated that home-schooled students, on average, score at the 80th percentile in reading, at the 76th percentile in language, and at the 79th percentile in mathematics.

What exactly does this mean? Well, in Jake's case, it means that half the babies were the same size or smaller than Jake at 6 weeks in body size, but 99% of babies had the same or smaller heads than Jake.

Home-schooled children seem to perform as well as or better in reading, language, and mathematics than more than three quarters of the population of kids.

Percentiles and **percentile ranks** use percentage to describe score position. After taking a test, you may wish to know how well you did compared with the rest of the class. You might find, for example, that your performance on a test was as good as or better than 80% of the class. Your test score would have a percentile rank of 80.

Alternatively, you might ask, "What score did I need to be in the top 10% of the class?" You might find that to be in the top 10%, you would have had to score 78 points on the test. The score of 78, then, would be the 90th percentile.

These techniques rely on how many cases are above and below certain points in the distribution of scores. Recall that the median also does this by indicating the point at or below which half the cases fall; the median is the 50th percentile (P_{50}). In Chapter 4, we learned about the semi-interquartile range, a measure of variability that relies on two percentiles, P_{25}, also called Q_1 (the first quartile) and P_{75}, also called Q_3 (the third quartile).

Another way of locating the position of a score is to compare that score with the mean of the distribution. **z scores** do this by indicating how far above or below the mean a particular raw score value lies. z scores rely on distance from the mean; percentiles and percentile ranks rely on number of cases.

Percentile ranks and z scores are **derived scores** because they are derived from the raw scores in the distribution. They help us determine the relative standing of a particular score in a distribution of scores.

Derived scores: Scores obtained by transforming raw scores

Percentile or **percentile point (P):** Score point at or below which a particular percentage of cases fall

Percentile rank (PR): The percentage of cases falling at or below a particular score

Percentiles and Percentile Ranks

Percentiles

A percentile is a *score point* at or below which a particular percentage of cases fall. P_{PR} is the abbreviation for percentile. The subscript indicates the percentage of cases falling at or below a particular score. A percentile can range over the possible values in the distribution. For example, P_{75} is the score value in a distribution at or below which 75% of the cases fall, also called Q_3. P_{50} is the score value at or below which 50% of the cases fall, also called Q_2. P_{50} or Q_2 is also the median of a distribution.

Percentile Ranks

The percentile rank (PR_X) of a score is a number indicating the percentage of cases falling at or below a particular score value. It is a *percentage value* and can only range from 0 to 100. The subscript is the score value, and PR indicates what percentage of the distribution is at or below that score value. For example, if the percentile rank of a score of 115 is 65 ($PR_{115} = 65$), then we know that 65% of the cases lie at or below the score of 115. Alternatively, we could say that 115 is the 65th percentile ($P_{65} = 115$).

Earlier, we found that we could divide a distribution exactly in half using the median or the 50th percentile. Similarly, we could divide a distribution into quarters using the 25th, 50th, 75th, and 100th percentiles, producing four equal-sized groups. As we saw in Chapter 4, these are called **quartiles**.

Quartile: The 25th, 50th, 75th, and 100th percentile of a distribution

CONCEPT REVIEW 5.1

Emily scored a 586 on her police procedures exam. Only 15% of those taking the exam did better than Emily. What is Emily's percentile rank? For this particular test, what is the 85th percentile point?

Answer on page 129.

Calculating Percentiles and Percentile Ranks

Percentiles

The general formula for computing percentiles from a grouped frequency distribution is

$$P_{PR} = L + \frac{\left[N\left(\dfrac{PR}{100}\right) - cf_b\right]i}{f_W}$$

L = lower exact limit of the score or interval containing the percentage of cases of interest

N = total number of cases in the distribution

cf_b = cumulative frequency below the score or interval containing the percentile

f_w = number of cases within the interval containing the percentile

i = interval width

This formula is almost the same as the one we used for calculating the median which makes sense because the median is the 50th percentile. The procedure we will follow is the same as we used when computing the median. Ready for an example? Below is a grouped frequency distribution.

Interval	f	cf	
155–159	1	25	
150–154	0	24	
145–149	2	24	P_{90}
140–144	2	22	
135–139	3	20	
130–134	4	17	
125–129	6	13	
120–124	4	7	
115–119	2	3	
110–114	1	1	

Let's determine P_{90}. When we were finding medians, the first step was to determine where half the cases fell. To determine P_{90}, we must find where 90% of the cases fall.

Step 1. Determine what 90% of the total is. 90% of 25 is 22.5.

Step 2. Find the interval containing the 22.5th score. Looking at the cumulative frequency column, we see that this score is in the interval 145–149.

Step 3. Determine the lower limit of this interval and substitute into the formula.

$$P_{PR} = L + \frac{\left[N\left(\dfrac{PR}{100}\right) - cf_b \right] i}{f_W}$$

$$P_{90} = 144.5 + \frac{\left[25\left(\dfrac{90}{100}\right) - 22 \right] 5}{2}$$

$$= 144.5 + \frac{(22.5 - 22)5}{2}$$

$$= 145.75$$

Therefore, 145.75 is the point in the distribution at or below which 90% of the scores fall.

Earlier we calculated the median by formula and by linear interpolation. We can use linear interpolation to find any other percentile. Using the above example, let's verify that the 90th percentile is 145.75.

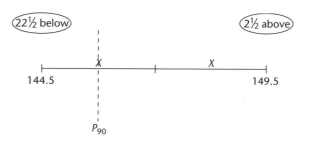

$$P_{90} = 144.5 + \frac{1}{4}(5) = 144.5 + 1.25 = 145.75$$

We can see that there are two scores within the interval containing the 90th percentile. We need exactly one half of one of these scores so that they are 22.5 below and 2.5 above. We need, then, one quarter of the entire interval, which is 5 units long. This method can be used to determine any percentile for a grouped frequency distribution. Recall in Chapter 4, the discussion of the semi-interquartile range. Q_1 and Q_3 were needed to compute this measure of variability. Q_1 is the 25th percentile and Q_3 is the 75th percentile. We can easily tailor our general percentile formula for these two quartiles.

$$Q_1 = L + \frac{\left[N\left(\dfrac{25}{100}\right) - cf_b \right] i}{f_w}$$

$$Q_3 = L + \frac{\left[N\left(\dfrac{75}{100}\right) - cf_b \right] i}{f_w}$$

Once these are determined, the semi-interquartile range is easy to determine:

$$\frac{Q_3 - Q_1}{2}$$

Percentile Ranks

The formula for determining the percentile rank of any score is

$$PR_X = \frac{\left[f_w \dfrac{(X-L)}{i} + cf_b \right] 100}{N}$$

X = score value whose rank you wish to determine

L = lower exact limit of the interval in which the score falls

f_w = number of scores in that interval

cf_b = cumulative frequency below that interval

i = interval width

N = total number of scores in the distribution

To illustrate this, let's use the same example we used earlier. Recall that the 90th percentile was 145.75. This means that the percentile rank of 145.75 must be 90. Let's use our percentile rank formula to prove that this is true.

$$PR_X = \frac{\left[f_w \dfrac{(X-L)}{i} + cf_b \right] 100}{N}$$

$$PR_{145.75} = \frac{\left[\dfrac{2(145.75-144.5)}{5} + 22 \right] 100}{25}$$

$$= \frac{\left[\dfrac{2.50}{5} + 22 \right] 100}{25}$$

$$= 22.5(4)$$

$$= 90$$

Percentile ranks are derived scores that provide information about relative standing. They indicate the percentage of cases that are found at or below a particular score value. They do not, however, indicate the *distance* of the scores from the score in question. For example, a score with a percentile rank of 80 indicates that 80% of the cases were at or below that score but not how far below those cases were. A derived score that does indicate the actual distance a raw score is from the mean is the *z score.*

CONCEPT REVIEW 5.2

For the data below what is PR_5? What is P_{70}?

Interval	f
10–12	9
7–9	16
4–6	6
1–3	4

Answer on page 129.

The *z* Score

The *z* score is a derived score that indicates how many standard deviations a raw score is from the mean and in what direction. This derived score is often more meaningful than the percentile rank of a score because it tells us how far above or below the mean the score value is. A raw score value above the mean has a positive *z* score. A raw score below the mean has a negative *z* score. A *z* score of –1, for example, tells us that the raw score equivalent is exactly one standard deviation *below* the mean of the distribution.

> ***z* score:** A derived score that indicates how many standard deviations a raw score is from the mean and in what direction

Calculating *z* Scores

The general formula for determining the *z*-score equivalent of any raw score is

$$z = \frac{X - \mu}{\sigma}$$

This formula simply divides the deviation score by the standard deviation of the distribution. In this way, the *z* value tells us whether the raw score was above or below the mean and exactly how far in standard deviation units.

Consider the distribution below. Its mean is 50, and its standard deviation is 7. Each raw score has been translated into its *z*-score equivalent, using our formula.

Raw Scores	$X - \mu$	z
68	18	2.57
54	4	0.57
51	1	0.14
50	0	0.00
50	0	0.00
48	-2	-0.29
48	-2	-0.29
46	-4	-0.57
45	-5	-0.71
40	-10	-1.43

$$\Sigma_z = 0$$

$$\mu = 50$$

$$\sigma = 7$$

Notice that a raw score of 40 is nearly $1\frac{1}{2}$ standard deviation units below the mean. A score of 54 is more than $\frac{1}{2}$ a standard deviation above the mean. Because z indicates distance from the mean, a score that is equal to the mean (in this case 50) will always have a z score of zero, regardless of the standard deviation.

Notice also that the sum of the z scores is zero. This is true of any distribution of z scores. You will recall that the sum of the deviations about any mean is zero. Thus, because z scores are deviation scores divided by the standard deviation (a constant), their sum must also be zero.

Properties of a *z* Distribution

A z distribution is a distribution where all raw scores have been converted to their z-score equivalents. All z distributions have certain unchanging properties.

The Mean

The mean of any z distribution is zero. This makes sense because the mean of the distribution does not deviate from itself.

$$\mu_z = 0$$

The Variance and Standard Deviation

The variance and standard deviation of any z distribution are always equal to 1.

$$\sigma_z^2 = \sigma_z = 1$$

The Shape

When a distribution of raw scores is converted to z scores, its shape does not change. After all, we are simply subtracting a constant (the mean) from the raw score and then dividing that difference by another constant (the standard deviation).

This is not true of all derived scores. The "dreaded" stanine system, used in many colleges and universities, changes the shape of the raw score distribution to a bell-shaped curve. The grading scheme used at my college changes the shape of the raw score distribution to a negatively skewed curve. Converting a raw score distribution to z scores, however, has no effect on its shape.

Using z to Locate Scores in a Distribution

The z score is extremely useful for indicating the location or the relative standing of a score in a distribution of scores. Let's consider an example.

Elmer obtained 80% in his psychology midterm exam. He was quite pleased with this grade. He was not so pleased, however, when he received 40% in his anthropology midterm. Although, at first glance, it is tempting to believe that 80% is the better grade, we are statistically sophisticated enough now not to jump to conclusions. First, we must ask a couple of questions. We need to know the mean and standard deviation of each exam. Consider the following data:

Psychology Midterm	Anthropology Midterm
$\mu = 70\%$	$\mu = 35\%$
$\sigma = 20$	$\sigma = 2$
Elmer's score = 80%	Elmer's score = 40%

In the anthropology test, most of the students were clustered around the mean, and few got high marks. In the psychology test, the students' scores were much more variable. Several students got high marks. It is difficult to evaluate Elmer's grades by glancing at the data. Certainly, he was above the mean in both cases, but how far? This question can be answered by converting his raw scores to z scores.

$$z \text{ in anthropology} = \frac{X - \mu}{\sigma} = \frac{40 - 35}{2} = +2.5$$

$$z \text{ in psychology} = \frac{80 - 70}{20} = +0.5$$

In the anthropology test, Elmer's mark was $2\frac{1}{2}$ standard deviations above the class mean. In his psychology test, his mark was only $\frac{1}{2}$ a standard deviation above the mean. Clearly, Elmer's performance, compared with his classmates, was far superior in the anthropology test.

Consider another example. Elmer got 80% in a math test and 80% in a chemistry test. The class average was 60% on both tests. It would be tempting to conclude that Elmer performed equally well on both tests, but we know better. Remember Charlie in Chapter 4? The data we need are as follows:

Math Test	Chemistry Test
$\mu = 60\%$	$\mu = 60\%$
$\sigma = 15$	$\sigma = 5$
Elmer's score = 80%	Elmer's score = 80%

These two distributions might look like the following:

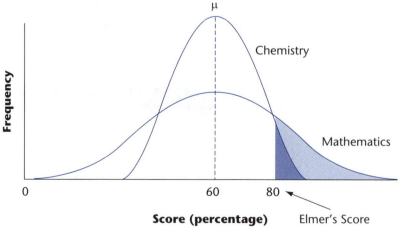

Figure 5.1. Position of a score in two distributions with equal means but different variability.

As you can see, the standard deviations differ considerably. In the math exam, several students got 80% and higher but in the chemistry test, very few students did as well as Elmer. Converting Elmer's grades to z scores we find

$$z \text{ (in math)} = \frac{80 - 60}{15} = +1.33$$

$$z \text{ (in chemistry)} = \frac{80 - 60}{5} = +4.00$$

Elmer's score of 80% on the chemistry test was 4 standard deviations above the mean; his score on the math test was $1\frac{1}{3}$ units above the mean. It is necessary to know both the central tendency and the amount of spread in a distribution to determine relative standing.

CONCEPT REVIEW 5.3

Zack obtained a score of 60 on a test of verbal fluency. He obtained a 540 on a test of mathematical aptitude. Given the data below, is language or math Zack's strength?

| Verbal fluency test | $\mu = 70$ | $\sigma = 10$ |
| Mathematical aptitude test | $\mu = 500$ | $\sigma = 35$ |

Answer on page 129.

In Chapters 1 to 5, I have shown you the typical statistics that researchers use when they are describing a population of scores. And I have shown you how those statistics are computed so that you have a good understanding of what they really mean. You may never compute any of these by hand again. Rather you will use a statistical package to do the work. The most useful package is the Statistical Package for the Social Sciences (SPSS). Unless you are taking a statistics course, you probably will not have access to SPSS but most students have access to Excel, a component of Microsoft Office. Let's see what Excel would produce if you ask for descriptive statistics for the following data.

DATA: 9, 5, 8, 8, 7, 5, 4, 6, 9, 5, 8, 4, 8, 7, 6, 6,

Score		
9	**Score**	
5		
8	Mean	6.5625
8	Standard error	0.41801864
7	Median	6.5
5	Mode	8
4	Standard deviation	1.67207456
6	Sample variance	2.795833333
9	Kurtosis	1.259322632
5	Skewness	0.075250828
8	Range	5
4	Minimum	4
8	Maximum	9
7	Sum	105
6	Count	16
6		

As you can see, Excel provides a number of statistics with the click of your mouse. Note the measures of skewness and kurtosis. In Excel, the normal curve would have a skewness of 0 and a kurtosis of 0. Positive skewness indicates the tail of the distribution lies to the right; a negative measure indicates the tail lies to the left. Positive kurtosis means the distribution is more peaked than the normal curve; negative kurtosis means it is flatter.

Measures of skewness and kurtosis may have limited meaning unless the distribution is very large. This is one of the reasons I do not show you how these are typically measured. Also note that Excel gives a range of 5. As I mentioned in Chapter 4, the range is actually $H - L + 1 = 6$ but like some other packages Excel uses $H - L$ for the range.

In the next three chapters, we will be doing foundational work to get ready to tackle inferential statistics.

SUMMARY OF TERMS AND FORMULAS

The measures discussed in this chapter are useful for determining the location of a score in a distribution.

The *percentile* is a score value at or below which a certain percentage of the scores fall. The *percentile rank* is a value indicating the percentage of scores at or below a particular score value.

Because the 25th, 50th, and 100th percentiles divide a distribution into four equal-sized groups, they are known as *quartiles.*

The *z score* indicates the distance, above or below the mean of a distribution, that a particular score falls in units of standard deviation. A *z distribution* is a distribution where all raw scores have been converted to *z* scores.

Percentile ranks and *z* scores are examples of *derived scores.*

Measure	Formula
Percentile	$P_{PR} = L + \dfrac{\left[N\left(\dfrac{PR}{100} \right) - cf_b \right] i}{f_w}$
Percentile rank	$PR_X = \dfrac{\left[f_w \left(\dfrac{X - L}{i} \right) + cf_b \right] 100}{N}$
z score	$z = \dfrac{X - \mu}{\sigma}$

CONCEPT REVIEW ANSWERS

5.1. Eighty-five percent of the group writing the test did as well as or more poorly than Emily, and 15% did better. Therefore, $PR_{586} = 85$ and $P_{85} = 586$.

5.2. $PR_5 = 20$ $P_{70} = 9.22$

5.3. z for verbal fluency test $= \dfrac{60 - 70}{10} = -1$

z for math $= \dfrac{540 - 500}{35} = 1.14$

Zack appears to be more mathematically inclined than verbally fluent.

EXERCISES

1. Determine the 50th, 75th, and 90th percentiles for the following frequency distribution. What is the percentile rank of 117?

Interval	f
135–139	3
130–134	12
125–129	9
120–124	10
115–119	15
110–114	7
105–109	2
100–104	2

2. John got 45 on his spelling test. If the class mean was 57 and the standard deviation was 6, what was John's z score?

3. For the following data, determine the z scores for each raw score.

    Data: 4, 6, 8, 9, 11, 3

4. Maria got 87% in her grammar test and 76% in her math test. Using the following data, determine if she did better in her grammar test than in her math test.

    Grammar test mean = 85   standard deviation = 2
    Math test mean = 70   standard deviation = 4

5. It is possible for a score to have a percentile rank of 65 and a negative z score. What kind of distribution must this score come from?

6. The percentile rank of a score of 89% is 62. Describe this in words.

7. Dan got 80% in an English test for which the mean was 70. He got 70% in a French test for which the mean was 80. The standard deviation for both tests was 10, and the median for both was 65. Which of the following is undeniably true?

    a. The English test was easier.
    b. The two distributions differ in skew direction so we can't make comparisons.

c. Dan's absolute z score for each test is 1.00. Therefore, his relative position in the two classes is the same.

d. None of the above.

8. A criminology midterm exam has a mean of 54 and a standard deviation of 3. What raw score would you need to be three standard deviations above the mean?

9. A student received a z score of 1.30 in her education foundations exam. If the class mean was 64% and the variance was 9, what was her raw score in the test?

10. For the data below:

a. Compute P_{30}, P_{45}, and P_{85}.
b. Determine the percentile rank of 83, 54, and 78.
c. Compute the mean and standard deviation.
d. Convert the midpoints to z scores.

Interval	f	cf
96–100	1	40
91–95	3	39
86–90	1	36
81–85	5	35
76–80	7	30
71–75	7	23
66–70	1	16
61–65	2	15
56–60	4	13
51–55	5	9
46–50	4	4

11. Below is the grouped frequency distribution for Chapter 2, Exercise 19 (b). Calculate the following:

a. P_{30}
b. P_{95}
c. PR_{127}
d. PR_{139}

Apparent Limits	Exact Limits	Midpoints	f	rf	cf	crf
160–164	159.5–164.5	162	1	0.01	100	1.00
155–159	154.5–159.5	157	5	0.05	99	0.99
150–154	149.5–154.5	152	4	0.04	94	0.94
145–149	144.5–149.5	147	0	0.00	90	0.90
140–144	139.5–144.5	142	2	0.02	90	0.90
135–139	134.5–139.5	137	6	0.06	88	0.88
130–134	129.5–134.5	132	10	0.10	82	0.82
125–129	124.5–129.5	127	7	0.07	72	0.72
120–124	119.5–124.5	122	6	0.06	65	0.65
115–119	114.5–119.5	117	13	0.13	59	0.59
110–114	109.5–114.5	112	7	0.07	46	0.46
105–109	104.5–109.5	107	12	0.12	39	0.39
100–104	99.5–104.5	102	12	0.12	27	0.27
95–99	94.5–99.5	97	6	0.06	15	0.15
90–94	89.5–94.5	92	6	0.06	9	0.09
85–89	84.5–89.5	87	3	0.03	3	0.03

12. Construct an ogive for the following data using cumulative relative frequency on the ordinate. Determine the percentile rank of a raw score of 130 using dotted lines from the score up to the curve and across to the ordinate value. Confirm your result with the formula. Using solid lines, indicate the value of the median. Confirm this with the formula.

Interval	f
145–149	2
140–144	4
135–139	6
130–134	13
125–129	16
120–124	7
115–119	2

13. For the data below, calculate the following:

    Data: 28, 35, 28, 38, 40, 40, 39, 27, 40, 37, 40, 38, 39, 38, 21

    a. ΣX
    b. ΣX^2
    c. N
    d. $(\Sigma X)^2$
    e. μ
    f. $(\Sigma X)^2/N$
    g. σ^2
    h. σ
    i. List the z scores
    j. $\Sigma(z \text{ scores})$

14. a. Spencer got 60 in his first statistics test and 74 in his second. The mean and standard deviation for the first test were 56 and 12, respectively. The mean and standard deviation for the second test were 68 and 15, respectively. In which test did Spencer do better? Why do you think so?

    b. Ben of Baltimore makes $45 000 a year. Tom of Toronto makes $42 500. If the mean income in the United States is $28 000 with a standard deviation of $6 000 and the mean income in Canada is $30 000 with a standard deviation of $4 000, who is richer? Why?

CHAPTER 6

Introduction to Inference: The Normal Curve

LEARNING OBJECTIVES

After reading this chapter, you should be able to do the following:

1. Describe the difference between empirical and theoretical distributions.
2. List the properties of the normal curve.
3. Find areas under the normal curve, given z scores.
4. Find z scores, given areas under the normal curve.
5. Find areas, given z scores with normal distributions.
6. Find z scores, given areas with normal distributions.

It seems that life goes by, resembling somewhat of a bell curve of what is considered successful.

At age 4, success is: not peeing in your pants.

At age 10, success is: making your own meals.

At age 12, success is: having friends.

At age 16, success is: having a driver's license.

At age 20, success is: having sex.

At age 35, success is: having money.

At age 50, success is: having money.

At age 60, success is: having sex.

At age 70, success is: having a driver's license.

At age 75, success is: having friends.

At age 80, success is: making your own meals.

At age 85, success is: not peeing in your pants.

The Psi Café: *www.psy.pdx.edu/PsiCafe*

The normal curve is a bell-shaped, theoretical, relative-frequency distribution. A normally distributed variable has few observations at either extreme end; the bulk of the observations lie in the middle.

Many variables of interest to social scientists distribute themselves according to this bell-shaped curve. Height and weight of people, along with their IQs, for example, are variables that take a bell shape. For these variables, most of the scores cluster around the middle or the mean of the distribution, and only a few scores lie at the extreme ends.

Empirical and Theoretical Frequency Distributions

Empirical means data based. An empirical frequency distribution is a distribution constructed from real data. Therefore, it has a finite number of values along the abscissa. **Theoretical** means based on theory or hypothetical observations. Theoretical frequency distributions are composed of theoretical observations and may have an infinite number of values on the abscissa. The normal curve is a theoretical distribution.

> **Empirical:** Based on real observations
>
> **Theoretical:** Based on theoretical or hypothetical observations

The Normal Curve

The normal curve is not a single distribution, but rather a family of curves. Just as the mathematical function of a circle describes a family of circles, the mathematical function of the normal curve describes a family of curves.

Because many statistical procedures rely on the normal curve, the curve has been standardized and should, more properly, be called the **standard normal curve**. The standard normal curve has z scores along the abscissa and relative frequency along the ordinate. In this form, all normal curves are identical. Figure 6.1 illustrates the standard normal curve.

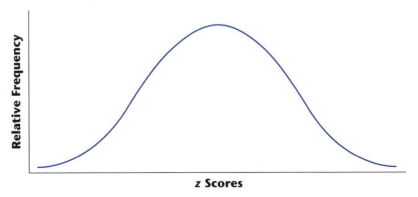

Figure 6.1. The standard normal curve.

FYI

The normal curve is defined by a mathematical function. It is included here for your interest.

$$Y = \frac{1}{\sqrt{2\pi\sigma^2}} e^{-(X-\mu)^2/2\sigma^2}$$

Equation for the normal curve

Y = height of curve at point X
X = any point on abscissa
μ = the mean
σ^2 = the variance
π = a constant (pi) = 3.14159
e = the base of Napierian logarithms = 2.71828

Standard normal curve: Theoretical bell-shaped distribution, often simply called the normal curve

Properties of the Standard Normal Curve

The standard normal curve has certain unchanging properties, as follows:

1. It is symmetrical.
2. It is unimodal; the mean, median, and mode are equal.
3. The values along the abscissa are continuous.
4. The curve is asymptotic to the abscissa: Because there are an infinite number of values in the distribution, the curve never touches the abscissa.
5. The mean is zero.
6. The variance and standard deviation equal 1.
7. The area under the curve is 1.

If the ordinate used percentage, then all of the cases (i.e., 100%) must be contained under the curve. Because the ordinate uses relative frequency or proportion, the entire area under the curve equals 1, the sum of the relative frequency of the entire range of z scores. Because the curve is symmetrical, .50 of the area is on each side of the mean.

Using the Normal Curve to Solve Problems

Because these properties don't change, we can solve problems by using the standard normal curve. Examine the normal curve in Figure 6.2.

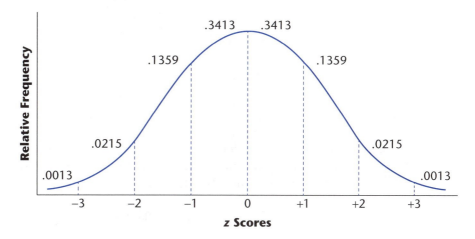

Figure 6.2. Areas under the normal curve.

You can see that .3413 of the total area lies between a z score of +1 and the mean of the curve. Because the curve is symmetrical, the same proportion of the area, that is, .3413, lies between a z score of −1 and the mean.

Table B.1 in Appendix B presents the exact areas under the standard normal curve for z scores from 0 to 4.00. The first column provides areas between the mean of the curve (i.e., 0) and any particular z score. The second column provides areas beyond a particular z score. Only positive z scores are given because the curve is symmetrical. The area beyond (i.e., to the right of) a z score of +1.00, for example, is the same as the area beyond (i.e., to the left of) a z score of −1.00.

Finding Areas Under the Curve

If we are given a particular z score, we can use Table B.1 in Appendix B to find out how much of the area lies between it and the mean, and how much of the total area lies beyond that score. When solving problems with the normal curve, you need to first draw a rough picture. This will help you see exactly what you are doing. Ready for some examples?

Example A: How much of the total area under the curve lies between the mean and a z score of 1.05? We will solve these problems in steps.

Step 1. Draw a curve and shade in the area of concern.

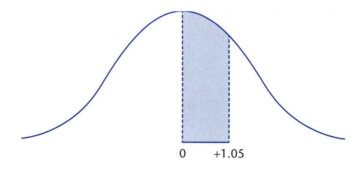

Step 2. Go to Table B.1 to look up the area between the mean and a z score of 1.05. In the z column find 1.05. Read the area in the first normal curve–area column (Column 2) of the table.

Area = .3531

Approximately 35% of the total area is found between a z score of 0 (the mean) and a z score of 1.05.

Example B: How much of the total area under the curve is found between the mean and a z score of –1.74?

Step 1. Draw a curve and shade in the area of concern.

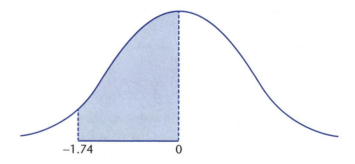

Step 2. Look up the area in Table B.1. Because the curve is symmetrical, we can ignore the minus sign.

Area = .4591

Approximately 46% of the total area is found between a *z* score of –1.74 and the mean of the distribution.

Example C: How much of the area is found beyond (i.e., to the right of) a *z* score of 3.24?

Step 1. Draw a curve and shade in the area of concern.

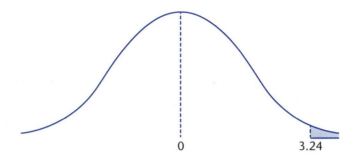

Step 2. Now we need to use the second curve-area column (Column 3) of Table B.1. Under the *z* column, find 3.24 and look for the area.

Area = .0006

As you can see, very little of the area is found beyond a *z* score of 3.24.

Example D: How much of the area is found between the *z* scores of 1.74 and 3.24? This problem illustrates the importance of drawing a curve first.

Step 1. Draw a curve and shade in the area of concern.

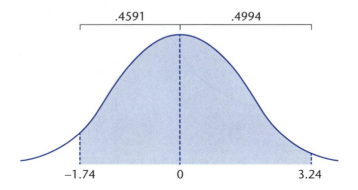

Step 2. We have already determined that .4591 of the area lies between a z score of 1.74 and the mean. Look up the area between the mean and a z score of 3.24. There is .4994 of the area between these points. We add these two areas together to solve our problem.

$$Area = .9585$$

There is .9585 or about 96% of the total area between these two scores.

As long as you have specific z scores, you can always determine the exact proportions of the total area under the curve.

CONCEPT REVIEW 6.1

How much of the area lies between a z score of 1.4 and 1.8 under the normal curve?

Answer on page 147.

Finding z Scores With the Curve

We can also solve problems when the value of z, not the area, is the unknown.

Example E: What z score has .1915 of the total area between it and the mean? Our step-by-step procedure is as follows:

Step 1. Draw a curve and shade in the area of concern.

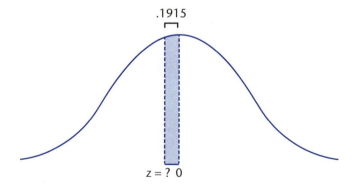

I have shaded an area below the mean. This is arbitrary. There are, of course, two z scores, one positive and one negative, that will solve our problem.

Step 2. Look in the first curve-area column (Column 2) of Table B.1 for the area of .1915. Look across to the left (Column 1) for the z value. Either the positive or the negative value is appropriate, because both solve the problem.

$$z = +0.50 \text{ or } -0.50$$

There is .1915 of the total area between either z score and the mean.

Example F: Let's find the two z scores that separate the middle 95% of the area from the extreme 5%. We will have 2.5% or .025 of the area in each tail.

Step 1. Draw a curve and shade in the area of concern.

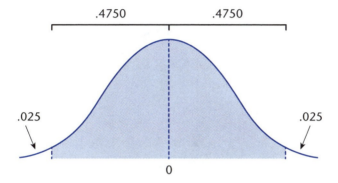

Step 2. Using the second curve-area column, find .025 and read the z in the z column.

$$z = 1.96$$

Because the curve is symmetrical, we know that 95% of the total area is between the z's of +1.96 and −1.96.

Because the standard normal curve has unchanging properties, we can always determine exact areas when we have z scores, and we can find z scores when we have exact areas. Whenever we have a real distribution that is normal in shape, we can use these procedures.

CONCEPT REVIEW 6.2

Find the two z scores that separate the middle 60% of the area from the extreme 40% of the normal curve.

Answer on page XX.

Working With Empirical Data That Are Normally Distributed

If we know that a particular distribution of scores is normal in shape, we can use the normal curve table to learn about our distribution. We simply translate our data into z-score form and then use the normal curve table to solve problems about our specific distribution.

As you know, the distribution of IQ scores is normal in shape with a mean of 100 and a standard deviation of 15.

Example G: Let's find the proportion of scores (or area) below an IQ of 95.

Step 1. Draw a curve and shade in the area of concern.

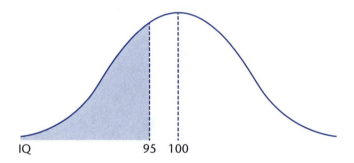

Step 2. Find the z score. We must transform our raw score into a z score so that we can use Table B.1. Recall that the formula for converting a raw score to a z score is

$$z = \frac{X - \mu}{\sigma}$$

Our z score is

$$z = \frac{95 - 100}{15} = -0.33$$

Step 3. Look up the area beyond (to the left of) a z of –0.33.

Area = .3707

Approximately 37% of the distribution of IQ scores is below an IQ of 95.

Example H: What proportion of the IQ scores lies between 95 and 115?

Step 1. Draw a curve and shade in the area of concern.

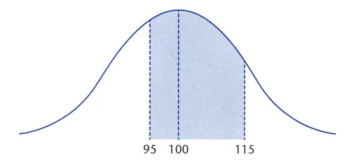

95 100   115

Step 2. We already know that .3707 of the area lies below 95, so we can just subtract this from .50 to find the area between 95 and the mean of 100. This
is .1293. Next, we need to translate the score of 115 into a *z* score.

$$z \text{ of } 115 = \frac{X - \mu}{\sigma} = \frac{115 - 100}{15} = 1$$

Step 3. We look up the area between the mean and a *z* of 1.00 and find it is .3413.

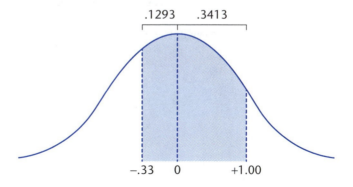

.1293   .3413

−.33   0   +1.00

We add these two areas together and find that .4706 of the area is found
between the scores of 95 and 115.

Example I: Now, let's find the proportion of IQ scores between 115 and 130.

Step 1. Draw a curve and shade in the area of concern.

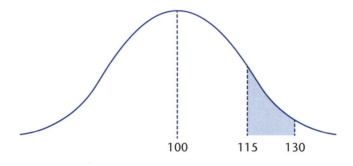

Step 2. Translate the scores into z scores.

$$z \text{ of } 115 \text{ is } + 1.00$$

$$z \text{ of } 130 = \frac{X - \mu}{\sigma} = \frac{130 - 100}{15} = +2.00$$

Step 3. There are several ways to solve this problem. Let's look up the area between the mean and a z of + 2.00. Then, we'll subtract the area between the mean and a z of +1.00 from that value.

Area between mean and z of 2.00 is .4772

Area between mean and z of 1.00 is .3413

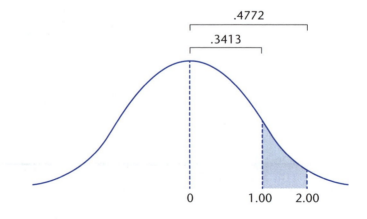

By subtraction, we find that .1359 (i.e., .4772 − .3413) of the area lies between the z's of 1.00 and 2.00. Approximately 14% of the scores lie between IQs of 115 and 130.

Example J: To continue, let's find the two IQ scores that separate the middle 90% of the distribution from the extreme 10%. We have the area and must find the scores.

Step 1. Draw a curve and shade in the area of concern.

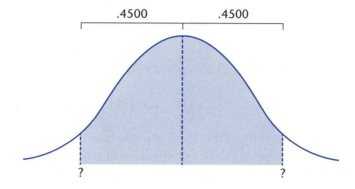

Step 2. Look up the tabled value that has .4500 of the area between it and the mean.

$$z = \pm 1.645$$

Step 3. We have the two z values and we now convert them to the raw scores. Rearrange the z formula so that X is the unknown.

$$X = \mu \pm z\sigma$$
$$= 100 \pm 1.645(15)$$
$$= 124.675 \text{ and } 75.325$$

We find that 90% of the scores lie between the values of 124.675 and 75.325 and 10% lie outside these two values.

Example K: What two IQ scores cut off the middle 95% from the extreme 5%?

Step 1. Draw a curve and shade in the area of concern.

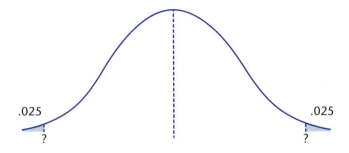

Step 2. Look up the appropriate z scores.

$$z = \pm 1.96$$

Step 3. Convert the z's to raw scores.

$$z = 100 \pm 1.96(15) = 129.40 \text{ and } 70.60$$

We find 95% of the distribution between IQs of 129.40 and 70.60.

Whenever we have a distribution of scores that we know is normally distributed, we can use the standard normal curve as a model to solve problems about our distribution. We only need the mean and standard deviation of our distribution to use the normal curve table. Many "real" distributions are similar in shape to the normal curve, and so the normal curve table is a very useful device for solving a variety of problems.

CONCEPT REVIEW 6.3

Using the IQ data of above, determine the percentage of the population with scores of 130 or greater.

Answer on page 147.

SUMMARY OF TERMS AND FORMULAS

The *normal curve* is an extremely useful tool for many statistical procedures because it has certain unchanging properties.

Empirical frequency distributions consist of actual observations and the distribution has a fixed size. In contrast, *theoretical frequency distributions* consist of theoretical observations and may have an infinite number of values.

The *standard normal curve* is a *symmetrical distribution* with a mean, median, and mode of zero. The observations along the abscissa of the curve are *infinite* and *continuous* and consist of z scores.

Because the area under the normal curve represents *relative frequency* and is equal to 1, the curve can be used as a model for solving a variety of problems about normally distributed variables.

CONCEPT REVIEW ANSWERS

6.1. Area $.4641 - .4192 = .0449$

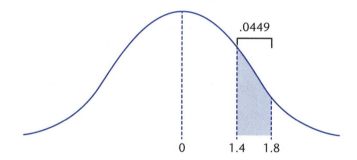

6.2. z's are ± 0.84

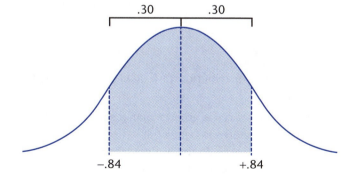

6.3. $z_{130} = \dfrac{130 - 100}{15} = +2$

Area beyond a z of $+2 = .0228$

About 2% of the population has IQ scores of 130 or greater.

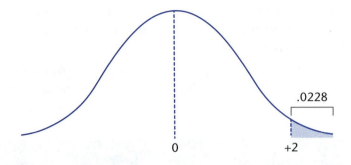

.0228

0   +2

EXERCISES

1. Determine the area under the normal curve between $z = \pm 2.50$.

2. Determine the area under the normal curve between $z = \pm 1.87$.

3. Determine the area under the normal curve beyond (to the right of) $z = 1.96$.

4. Find the two z scores that separate the middle .90 of the area from the extreme .10.

5. Find the z score below which (to the left of) .90 of the area lies.

6. Determine the percentile rank of each of the following z scores. (*Hint*: area under the curve can be converted to percentage.)
   a. −2.58
   b. −1.96
   c. 0
   d. 1.64
   e. 2.33

7. Assume you have a normal distribution of 5 000 test scores with a mean of 72 and a standard deviation of 12.
   a. What percentage of the scores is greater than a score of 80?
   b. What percentage of the scores is below 66?
   c. Between what two test scores do the middle 60% of the scores lie?
   d. The lower 5% of the scores falls below what score?
   e. How many scores lie below the score in part (d) above?
   f. What score is exceeded by only four students (round to the nearest whole number)?
   g. What test score is at the 25th percentile? (*Hint*: What exactly is a percentile; what does it tell you?)

8. In a normal distribution with a mean of 50 and standard deviation of 10, find PR_{63}.

9. Find the score at the 20th percentile for the distribution in Exercise 8.

10. In a normal distribution with a mean of 112 and a variance of 144, what proportion of the area lies between the scores 70 and 150?

11. A distribution of 10 000 test scores is normally distributed with a mean of 550 and a standard deviation of 60. Determine the two z scores that separate the middle 9 000 scores from the extreme 1 000 scores.

12. For the distribution described in Exercise 11, determine the two raw scores that separate the middle 90% from the extreme 10% of the distribution.

13. For the distribution described in Exercise 11, find the raw score below which only 50 scores fall.

14. For the distribution described in Exercise 11, determine how many raw scores fall between scores of 500 and 600.

CHAPTER 7

Introduction to Inference: Probability

LEARNING OBJECTIVES

After reading this chapter, you should be able to do the following:

1. Define the term simple probability, and determine simple probability for a given example.
2. Describe conditional probability, and determine conditional probability for a given example.
3. Define and categorize events as dependent and independent.
4. Determine the probability of *A* and *B* and *A* or *B* for a given example.
5. Define and categorize events as mutually exclusive or not mutually exclusive.
6. Determine the number of permutations and the number of combinations for a given example.
7. Describe and provide an example of a dichotomous variable.
8. Use the formula to determine probability with a binomial distribution.
9. Describe how a frequency distribution can be viewed as a distribution of probabilities.

Location: Roulette table in Las Vegas.

Marjorie to Leonard: "Why are you betting so much on red?"

Leonard to Marjorie: "It was black the last five rounds. It's bound to be red this time!"

Leonard's logic demonstrates what is called the Gambler's Fallacy, the belief that independent events are dependent. In roulette, each trial is independent. Where the ball fell on previous trials has no effect on the probability of where it will fall next.

You will soon learn that statistical inference is all about probabilities. To really understand inference, we first need to understand basic probability.

Simple Probability

The probability of a particular event or outcome occurring is the number of ways that the event can occur, divided by the total number of possible outcomes that could occur in a situation where all outcomes are equally likely.

$$p(A) = \frac{\text{number of ways } A \text{ can occur (\#}A)}{\text{total number of outcomes (\#}O)}$$

In a single toss of a coin, the probability of getting a head is the number of ways a head can occur (1) over the total number of outcomes possible (2).

$$p(H) = \frac{1}{2}$$

In the roll of a die (one of a pair of dice), the probability of rolling a four is the number of ways a four can occur (1) over the total number of possible outcomes (6).

$$p(4) = \frac{1}{6}$$

Both of these examples have outcomes that are equally likely. In a single toss of a fair coin, a head is as likely to occur as a tail. With a fair die, the likelihood of rolling a four is the same as for a 1, 2, 3, 5, or 6.

What would be the probability of obtaining an even number on a single roll of a fair die? Using the same approach, we would determine the number of ways that an even number could occur over the total number of outcomes. There are three ways an even number could show up (i.e., 2, 4, 6), and the total number of outcomes remains the same (six).

$$p(\text{even number}) = \frac{3}{6} = \frac{1}{2}$$

If we rolled a die many times then, we would expect to get an even number half the time *on the average*, because the probability on a single roll is one half.

CONCEPT REVIEW 7.1

In a single roll of a die, what is the probability of getting an odd number?

Answer on page 168.

Conditional Probability

When the probability of a given event is *dependent on* or *influenced by* the occurrence or nonoccurrence of a previous event, it is called conditional probability. In other words, the likelihood of a given event occurring is conditional on what went on before.

Let's determine the probability of drawing a jack from a well-shuffled deck of playing cards. Because all cards are equally likely to be drawn, we can determine the probability of drawing a jack by using our simple probability formula.

$$p(J) = \frac{\text{number of ways a jack can be drawn}}{\text{total number of outcomes or cards}}$$

There are four jacks in a deck of 52 cards, and so

$$p(J) = \frac{4}{52}$$

Now let's draw a second card from our deck without putting the first one back. What is the probability of drawing another jack if the first card drawn was a jack? Because there are only three jacks left, the number of ways we can draw a second jack is three, and the total number of cards is only 51.

$$p(\text{jack given the first card was a jack}) = p(J\,/\,J) = \frac{3}{51}$$

This is an example of conditional probability, because the outcome (jack on second draw) is conditional on or dependent on what happened in the first draw. The general formula for this kind of conditional probability is

$$p(B\,/\,A) = \frac{\text{number of ways } B \text{ can occur given } A \text{ has occurred}}{\text{total number of outcomes given } A \text{ has occurred}}$$

In our example,

$$p(J\,/\,J) = \frac{3}{51}$$

What if a jack was not drawn the first time? The probability of getting a jack on the second draw, given a jack was not drawn on the first draw, would be the number of ways to draw a jack (four, because all four are still in the deck) over the total number of outcomes (51, because one card was already drawn and not replaced).

$$p(\text{jack/non-jack}) = \frac{4}{51}$$

Dependent events are events in which the occurrence of one alters the probability of occurrence of the other. Conditional probability involves dependent events. In contrast, independent events are those where the occurrence of one does not affect the probability of occurrence of the other. In our example, had we returned the first card drawn to the deck, the probability of drawing a jack on the second draw would have been unaffected by the outcome of the first draw. In this case, the probability of drawing a second jack would be a matter of simple probability—the number of ways of drawing a jack (four) over the total number of outcomes (52).

$$p\left(\text{jack on second draw given the first drawn jack was replaced}\right) = \frac{4}{52}$$

These two events are independent, because the outcome of the second draw is not influenced by what happened on the previous draw. Conditional probability refers only to dependent events. By replacing our first drawn card, we have made the second draw independent of the first and, therefore, not a conditional event. We could describe this situation of independent events by using our formula. When events are independent, then the probability of event B occurring, given A has already occurred, is the same as the probability of B.

If $p(B/A) = p(B)$, then the events are **independent.**

This underlies the "gambler's fallacy" that this chapter opened with. Many gambling games (e.g., roulette) involve independent events. The fact that the ball has just stopped on the 34 has absolutely no effect on its next stopping place. I am, of course, assuming a fair roulette wheel, which may be naive! Unfortunately, many gamblers think that these events are dependent, and they have a multitude of schemes for trying to determine probabilities. It's really very simple. If a roulette wheel has 36 numbers, the probability of the ball stopping on the number 34 is $\frac{1}{36}$ (i.e., the number of ways a 34 can occur, 1, over the number of possible outcomes, 36), no matter what numbers have previously occurred. I should mention that this knowledge has never stopped me from betting on my favourite number—7!

Dependent events: Two events are dependent when the occurrence of one affects the probability of occurrence of the other.

Independent events: Two events are independent when the occurrence of one has no effect on the probability of occurrence of the other.

CONCEPT REVIEW 7.2

You hold the A, K, Q, and J of hearts in your hand. One more card is dealt to you from the remaining 48 cards in the deck, which has been shuffled. What is the probability that you will get a royal straight flush (i.e., you are dealt the 10 of hearts)? What is the probability that you will make your straight (i.e., you are dealt any 10)?

Answer on page 168.

Probability of Compound Events

Probability of *A* and *B*

Many situations involve questions about the probability of two or more specified events occurring rather than just a single event. This is called the probability of *A* and *B*. We may wonder what the probability might be of obtaining a jack on the first draw and another jack on the second draw from our deck of 52 cards. The general formula for the probability of two specified events occurring is

$$p(A \text{ and } B) = p(A) \bullet p(B/A)$$

The probability of both *A* and *B* occurring is the product of the probability of *A* and the probability of *B*, given *A* has occurred. We use a dot to indicate multiplication, because large brackets are somewhat messy looking. We can now determine the probability of drawing two jacks in a row without replacing the first one from a deck of 52 cards:

$$p(J \text{ and } J) = p(J) \bullet p(J/J)$$

$$p(J \text{ and } J) = \frac{4}{52} \bullet \frac{3}{51} = 0.0045$$

On the first draw, the probability of a jack is simply the number of ways a jack can occur (4) over the total number of outcomes (52). On the second draw, there are only three ways to get a second jack out of a total of 51 cards, because the first jack was not replaced.

If we had replaced the first jack, making the two events independent, then the probability of the second jack would not be affected by the first draw, and the probability of getting two jacks in a row would be

$$p(J \text{ and } J) = p(J) \bullet p(J)$$

$$p(J \text{ and } J) = \frac{4}{52} \bullet \frac{4}{52} = 0.0059$$

The general formula for the probability of two independent events occurring is

$$p(A \text{ and } B) = p(A) \bullet p(B)$$

This procedure can be used for more than two events as well. If all events are independent, then the probability of all of them occurring is the product of their individual probabilities. If I tossed a coin, for example, and it turned up heads 10 times in a row, would you wonder about what kind of coin I had? I would. Let's determine what the probability is of obtaining 10 heads in a row with 10 tosses of a fair coin. This is just the probability of getting a head *and* a head *and* a head, and so on.

$$p(10 \text{ heads in a row}) = p(H) \bullet p(H) \bullet p(H) \bullet p(H) \bullet p(H) \bullet p(H) \bullet$$
$$p(H) \bullet p(H) \bullet p(H) \bullet p(H)$$

$$= \frac{1}{2} \bullet \frac{1}{2} \bullet \frac{1}{2} \bullet \frac{1}{2} \bullet \frac{1}{2} \bullet \frac{1}{2} \bullet \frac{1}{2} \bullet \frac{1}{2} \bullet \frac{1}{2} \bullet \frac{1}{2}$$

$$= \frac{1}{1024} = 0.00098$$

As you can see, this is a mighty unlikely series of events!

CONCEPT REVIEW 7.3

A. In two draws from a 52-card deck, what is the probability of drawing the ace of hearts and then a seven without replacing the first card?

B. The probability that a young offender's father is an alcoholic is 0.20. The probability that a young offender's mother is an alcoholic is 0.05. If these two events are independent, what is the probability that a young offender's parents are both alcoholics?

Answer on page 168.

Probability of *A* or *B*

We have seen how to determine the probability of two (or more) events occurring together. We can also ask questions about the probability of *either* of two events occurring. This is called the probability of *A* or *B*, and the general formula is

$$p(A \text{ or } B) = p(A) + p(B) - p(A \text{ and } B)$$

Let's go back to our deck of playing cards. What would be the probability of drawing a jack or a red card in a single draw from our deck of 52? Half of the deck (26) is red, and two of the cards are black jacks, so the number of ways to get a jack *or* a red card must be 28 out of the total number of outcomes (52). Let us use our general formula to verify this.

$$p(J \text{ or } R) = p(J) + p(R) - p(R \text{ and } J)$$

$$= \frac{4}{52} + \frac{26}{52} - \frac{2}{52} = \frac{28}{52} = 0.54$$

This formula is always used when two events can occur together. We needed to subtract the $p(R \text{ and } J)$, so that we didn't count the red jacks twice. A red card can also be a jack, so these events can occur together. When two events cannot occur at the same time, they are said to be **mutually exclusive**. Drawing a jack or a queen, for example, would be mutually exclusive events, because you cannot draw a jack and a queen in one draw. If one event has occurred, the other cannot have occurred.

Mutually exclusive events: Events that cannot occur together

In the case of mutually exclusive events, the last term in the above formula is zero, because *A* and *B* cannot occur at the same time. The probability of drawing a jack or a queen in a single draw is simply the sum of their individual probabilities.

$$p(J \text{ or } Q) = p(J) + p(Q)$$

$$= \frac{4}{52} + \frac{4}{52} = 0.1538$$

The general formula, then, for determining the probability of one event or the other event occurring (probability of A or B) when events are mutually exclusive is

$$p(A \text{ or } B) = p(A) + p(B)$$

CONCEPT REVIEW 7.4

What is the probability of drawing the three of clubs or the six of diamonds in a single draw from a deck of 52 cards?

Answer on page 169.

The examples we have looked at have been quite simple. We began by learning that the probability of occurrence of a given event A is found by dividing the number of ways A can occur by the total number of outcomes possible. The total number of outcomes and the number of ways A can occur are easy to determine when you are dealing with dice, coins, or a couple of draws from a deck of playing cards. What if I ask you to determine the probability of being dealt a royal straight flush (i.e., A, K, Q, J, and 10 all in the same suit) from a deck of 52 cards? Could you do it?

It's not too tricky to figure out how many ways you could get a royal straight flush. There are four suits, so there are only four ways—one for each suit. However, determining the total number of five-card hands possible would daunt most of us! Luckily, we have methods for doing just this sort of thing without the necessity of enumerating every possibility. Our royal flush problem is a combinations problem. We will now examine permutations and combinations: methods for counting things.

Methods of Counting

Permutations

A **permutation** is an *ordered sequence* of things, objects, or events. A different order of the same objects is a different permutation of those objects. Consider a relay swim team whose members are Hewey, Dewey, and Susan. There are several ways we could arrange our three swimmers in terms of position. Let's diagram the different teams we could have (see Figure 7.1).

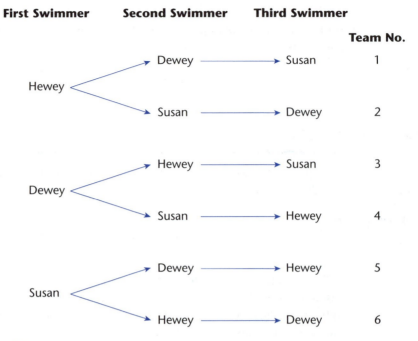

Figure 7.1. Number of swim teams with three swimmers.

There are six different arrangements that could be made with our three swimmers. We are simply arranging our three objects (swimmers) into different orders or permutations.

What would happen if we added one more swimmer (Lewey)? We would end up with a lot more possibilities, 24 in total. As you can imagine, it would get quite tedious to delineate all the possible arrangements. Fortunately, we have a formula to do this work for us. The formula for calculating permutations is

$$_nP_r = \frac{n!}{(n-r)!}$$

n = the total number of objects we have to work with

r = the number of objects we need in a single arrangement

The number of ordered sequences of r objects that can be selected from a total of n objects is symbolized by $_nP_r$. The symbol $_nP_r$ can be read as the number of permutations of n objects taken r at a time.

The exclamation mark means *factorial*, which I have always thought was a somewhat mysterious operation. Here is how it is done.

$$n! = n(n-1)(n-2)(n-3)\ldots 1$$

For example, $6! = 6(5)(4)(3)(2)(1) = 720$

At this point, it is important to mention that 0 factorial (0!) *is always* 1. Just accept this on faith.

To illustrate this, let's use our four swimmers, Hewey, Dewey, Lewey, and Susan. We can determine how many different teams of two swimmers can be selected from our total of four when order makes a difference in the following way (see Figure 7.2):

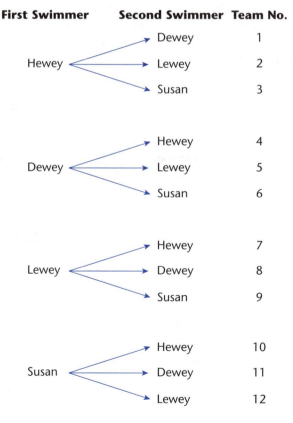

First Swimmer	**Second Swimmer**	**Team No.**
	Dewey	1
Hewey	Lewey	2
	Susan	3
	Hewey	4
Dewey	Lewey	5
	Susan	6
	Hewey	7
Lewey	Dewey	8
	Susan	9
	Hewey	10
Susan	Dewey	11
	Lewey	12

Figure 7.2.   The number of permutations of two objects from a total of four.

Note that each two swimmers produce two permutations. The different order makes them *different permutations*.

By counting up our teams, we can see that there are 12 permutations when four objects are taken two at a time. We can use our formula to verify this.

$$_4P_2 = \frac{n!}{(n-r)!} = \frac{4!}{(4-2)!} = \frac{4 \bullet 3 \bullet 2 \bullet 1}{2 \bullet 1} = 12$$

Let us look at a more useful example. Those of you interested in horse racing may find this profitable. What is the probability of selecting the first, second, and third in a race with a field of 10 horses? In horse-racing terminology, this is called picking the win, place, and show horse. Our general approach tells us that we must divide the number of ways we could pick first, second, and third by the total number of outcomes in such a race. Clearly, there is only one way of selecting the first three horses in the correct position. However, the total number of possible sequences of 3 horses from a field of 10 is not so obvious. It is a very large number, so large that diagramming the sequences as we have done before would be an onerous task, indeed. Luckily, we can use our formula to solve this problem.

Total number of outcomes $\quad p(\text{exactly } 2H \text{ in 10 tosses}) = 45 \bullet \dfrac{1}{1024} = 0.0439$

There are 720 ordered sequences of 10 horses selected in threes. We can now determine the probability of picking the winning three horses in the correct order.

$$p\left(\text{picking win, place, and show}\right) = \frac{\text{number of ways to pick 1st, 2nd, and 3rd}}{\text{total number of outcomes}}$$

$$= \frac{1}{720} = 0.00139$$

You might want to consider this the next time you gamble on a Trifecta! Of course, it is important to point out that the above example assumes we are randomly choosing the three horses from the field. Most of us, I am sure, never behave so frivolously when it comes to betting on horses. We use important information such as the attractiveness of the horses' names and their color to determine our choices!

Permutation: In probability, an ordered sequence of events

CONCEPT REVIEW 7.5

How many different ways can we arrange seven books on a bookshelf?

Answer on page 169.

Combinations

A **combination** is a set of things, objects, or events. Order is not important. *AB* and *BA is the same combination.* The formula to determine the number of combinations of n objects taken r at a time is

$$_nC_r = \frac{n!}{(n-r)!\,r!}$$

Back to our tireless swimmers. Let's determine the number of teams of two swimmers we can combine from our total of four. Remember that order is not important.

Swimmers	Teams
Hewey and Dewey	1
Hewey and Lewey	2
Hewey and Susan	3
Dewey and Lewey	4
Susan and Dewey	5
Susan and Lewey	6

There are only *6 combinations*, but there were *12 permutations*. For every 1 combination, then, there were 2 permutations. *In any situation, there will be r! permutations for every one combination.* This is why you find $r!$ in the denominator of the combinations formula.

We can verify our example by using the combination formula for four objects selected two at a time.

$$_4C_2 = \frac{4!}{(4-2)!\,2!} = \frac{4 \bullet 3 \bullet 2 \bullet 1}{2 \bullet 1 \bullet 2 \bullet 1} = 6$$

Using four objects, let us determine the number of combinations and permutations of three objects that can be selected. Let's forgo our swimmers this time.

Objects	Combinations of Three	Permutations of Three
A, B, C, D	ABC, ABD, ACD, BCD	ABC, ABD, ACD, BCD,
		ACB, ADB, ADC, BDC,
		BAC, BAD, CAD, CBD,
		BCA, BDA, CDA, CDB,
		CBA, DBA, DCA, DBC,
		CAB, DAB, DAC, DCB

We have 24 permutations but only 4 combinations. There are 6 permutations for every 1 combination. Note that $r!$ is 6, so there are $r!$ permutations for every combination.

Using the formulas to verify the example above, we have

$$_4C_3 = \frac{n!}{(n-r)!r!} = \frac{4!}{1!3!} = \frac{4 \bullet 3 \bullet 2 \bullet 1}{1 \bullet 3 \bullet 2 \bullet 1} = 4$$

$$_4P_3 = \frac{n!}{(n-r)!} = \frac{4!}{1!} = \frac{4 \bullet 3 \bullet 2 \bullet 1}{1} = 24$$

Combination (C): In probability, a set of events where order or sequence is irrelevant

CONCEPT REVIEW 7.6

A student has 16 different university subjects to choose 5 from. How many combinations of 5 are there?

Answer on page 169.

Binomial Probability

When I was an undergraduate student taking statistics, the topic of binomial probability almost defeated me. I could not understand why it was important.

It is important, however, because many things in this world have only two outcomes, for example, on/off, yes/no, or pregnant/not pregnant. It's really not very complicated at all.

Binomial probability is a special case in probability in which we are determining the number of combinations when two outcomes of interest exist for each of several trials. A variable having only two outcomes of interest is also called a *dichotomous variable*. Consider coin tossing again. You may be wondering if all statisticians spend a lot of time tossing pennies. Well, some do and some don't.

Coin-tossing experiments have only two outcomes of interest, heads and tails. If I were to toss a coin 10 times in a row, what would be the probability of obtaining only two heads? This is a case of binomial probability. We are talking about combinations, not permutations, because the question does not specify the order in which the events must occur. We are specifying that only 2 of the 10 tosses must be heads. To determine the probability of such an event, we must first determine the probability of any one arrangement of 2 heads and 8 tails, and then determine how many such arrangements or sequences are possible.

One sequence that fits our requirements could be the following:

$$H, H, T, T, T, T, T, T, T, T$$

What is the probability of tossing this sequence of 10 coins? We learned earlier that the probability of several specified events occurring is the product of their individual probabilities when the events are independent. The events in the above example are definitely independent: Earlier events do not alter the probability of later events occurring. The probability of getting a head in a single toss of a coin is ½, and the probability of tossing a tail is also ½, so the probability of the above sequence of heads and tails is

$$p(H, H, T, T, T, T, T, T, T, T) = \frac{1}{2} \bullet \frac{1}{2} \bullet \frac{1}{2} \bullet \frac{1}{2} \bullet \frac{1}{2} \bullet \frac{1}{2} \bullet \frac{1}{2} \bullet \frac{1}{2} \bullet \frac{1}{2} \bullet \frac{1}{2}$$

$$= \frac{1}{2^{10}} = \frac{1}{1024}$$

Another sequence of events that would satisfy our requirement of exactly two heads in 10 tosses is

$$H, T, H, T, T, T, T, T, T, T$$

The probability of this sequence occurring is also $\frac{1}{1024}$. In fact, the probability of *any* particular sequence of two heads and eight tails is $\frac{1}{1024}$.

Now that we know the probability of any one sequence occurring, we need to figure out how many sequences fit our requirement of two heads and eight tails.

The number of sequences of two heads in 10 tosses of a coin is simply the number of combinations of 10 things taken two at a time. Using our combinations formula:

$$_{10}C_2 = \frac{n!}{(n-r)!r!} = \frac{10!}{(10-2)!2!} = 45$$

There are 45 different ways that we can get exactly two heads in 10 tosses of a coin. Each way has a probability of occurring of $\frac{1}{1024}$. The probability, then, of getting two heads in 10 tosses of a coin is

$$p(\text{exactly } 2H \text{ in 10 tosses}) = 45 \bullet \frac{1}{1024} = 0.0439$$

This may seem like a rather long and drawn out way to solve a seemingly simple problem. It is! Fortunately, we have a formula for determining binomial probabilities.

In a sequence of **n** independent trials with only two outcomes of interest (we call them "success" and "failure") or binomial probability, the probability of exactly r successes is

$$_{n}C_r p^r q^{n-r} = \frac{n!}{(n-r)!r!} p^r q^{n-r}$$

Success and failure are mutually exclusive events. p is the probability of success, and q is the probability of failure. q *always equals* $1-p$.

The terms *success* and *failure* are really quite arbitrary. In general, success is the event in which you are interested. In our example above, a success is getting a head. Therefore, p is the probability of getting a head in one trial (i.e., $\frac{1}{2}$), and q is the probability of not getting a head (i.e., a failure). In our case, that probability is also $\frac{1}{2}$. The probability of a success does not have to equal the probability of a failure; however, their individual probabilities must add up to 1 (i.e., they must be mutually exclusive events).

Back to our coin-tossing experiment. We have already determined the probability of getting exactly two heads in 10 tosses of a coin. Now, let's verify this with our formula.

$$p(2H \text{ in 10 tosses}) = {}_{10}C_2\, p^r q^{n-r}$$

$$= \frac{n!}{(n-r)!r!}p^r q^{n-r}$$

$$= \frac{10!}{(10-2)!2!}\left(\frac{1}{2}\right)^2\left(\frac{1}{2}\right)^8$$

$$= 45\left(\frac{1}{2}\right)^{10} = \frac{45}{1024} = 0.0439$$

As you can see, we ended up with the same number. So, now, you can go ahead and determine the probability of getting exactly 13 heads with 54 tosses of a fair coin, or 43 heads with 100 tosses of a fair coin, or . . .

n: The total number of observations in a sample

Binomial variable: A variable having only two outcomes of interest (also called dichotomous)

Frequency Distributions as Probability Distributions

Any frequency distribution can be viewed as a distribution of probabilities. Below are the final grades for one of my statistics classes. The grades range from A+ through F.

Grade	f	rf
A+	2	0.06
A	6	0.19
A–	5	0.16
B+	6	0.19
B	3	0.09
C+	3	0.09
C	5	0.16
D	2	0.06
F	0	0.00
	N = 32	

Viewing this distribution as a probability distribution, we can see that the probability of a *randomly selected* student receiving a grade of A– is .16. Furthermore, the probability of a student receiving a grade of B+ or better would be $p(B+) + p(A–) + p(A) + p(A+) = .60$.

Let's examine another frequency distribution. Imagine that a sociology researcher has classified 100 young offenders by type of crime, gender, and level of education attained. Table 7.1 presents the data.

Table 7.1

Young offenders classified by education, crime, and gender

Type of Crime	Gender	Elementary School Incomplete	High School Incomplete	High School Graduate	Row Sum
Simple theft	Male	.22	.09	.01	0.32
	Female	.04	.03	0	0.07
Break and enter	Male	.16	.08	.03	0.27
	Female	0	.01	0	0.01
Assault	Male	.18	.06	.02	0.26
	Female	.04	.02	.01	0.07
Column sum		.64	.29	.07	1.00
					$N = 100$

This is a relative frequency distribution, and we can view it as a probability distribution. For example, the probability is .36 (.29, .07) that a randomly selected young offender has at least some high school education. This is so because 36% or 0.36 of the entire group have some high school education. Likewise, the probability that a randomly selected young offender would be a woman who committed assault is .07, because only 7% of the young offenders were women who had committed assault—4%, 2%, and 1% in each category of education level.

CONCEPT REVIEW 7.7

Given the data in Table 7.1, determine the probability that a randomly selected young offender is a

A. male high school graduate

B. female thief

C. male *or* a thief

Answer on page 169.

The Normal Curve as a Probability Distribution

The normal curve is a relative-frequency distribution and as such is a probability distribution. With continuous variables such as z scores, the probability of an event A is found by

$$p(A) = \frac{\text{area under the curve associated with } A}{\text{total area under the curve}}$$

Suppose we have a normal distribution of scores with a mean of 100 and a standard deviation of 10. Let's determine the probability of randomly selecting a score of 112 or higher. We have already learned how to solve problems like this in Chapter 6. The only difference here is the terminology. In Chapter 6, we would have phrased the question as, "What proportion of the area lies beyond a score of 112?" Using the same procedure, we first convert the raw score to a z score and then look up the proportion of the total area beyond that z score.

$$z = \frac{112 - 100}{10} = +1.2$$

$$\text{Area} = .1151$$

The probability, then, of randomly selecting a single score of 112 or greater is .1151.

If we were to randomly select a single score from this distribution, what is the probability that it would be between 90 and 110? We could write this problem in the following way:

$$p(90 \leq X \leq 110) = ?$$

Using our usual procedure,

$$z = \pm 1$$

$$\text{Area} = .6826$$

$$p(90 \leq X \leq 110) = .6826$$

The probability, then, of randomly selecting one score between 90 and 110 is .6826. About two thirds of the time, if we were to repeatedly draw a single score, replacing the score each time before the next draw, we would expect it to fall between these two values.

Any frequency distribution can be viewed as a probability distribution. This underlies some important procedures that we will study later.

SUMMARY OF FORMULAS

Simple probability	$p(A) = \dfrac{\#A}{\#O}$
Conditional probability	$p(B/A) = \dfrac{\#B/A \text{ has occured}}{\#O/A \text{ has occured}}$
Compound probability	
Dependent events	$p(A \text{ and } B) = p(A) \bullet p(B/A)$
Independent events	$p(A \text{ and } B) = p(A) \bullet p(B)$
Not mutually exclusive	$p(A \text{ or } B) = p(A) + p(B) - p(A \text{ and } B)$
Mutually exclusive	$p(A \text{ or } B) = p(A) + p(B)$
Permutations	$_nP_r = \dfrac{n!}{(n-r)!}$
Combinations	$_nC_r = \dfrac{n!}{(n-r)!r!}$
Binomial probability	$_nC_r p^r q^{n-r} = \dfrac{n!}{(n-r)!r!} p^r q^{n-r}$

CONCEPT REVIEW ANSWERS

7.1. $p(\text{odd number}) = p(1 \text{ or } 3 \text{ or } 5) = 3/6$

7.2. $p(\text{you are dealt the 10 of hearts/the A, K, Q, J of hearts have been dealt to you already}) = 1/48$

$p(\text{any } 10/A, K, Q, J) = 4/48$

7.3. A. $p(AH \text{ and } 7) = p(AH) \bullet p(7/AH) = 1/52 \bullet 4/51 = .001508$

B. $p(A \text{ and } B) = p(A) \bullet p(B) = 0.20 \bullet 0.05 = .01$

7.4. Because these two events are mutually exclusive, the probability is easy to determine:

$$p(3C \text{ or } 6D) = p(3C) + p(6D) = \frac{1}{52} + \frac{1}{52} = .0385$$

7.5. $_7P_7 = 7!/0! = 7 \bullet 6 \bullet 5 \bullet 4 \bullet 3 \bullet 2 = 5\,040$

7.6. $_{26}C_5 = \dfrac{16!}{(11!)5!} = 4368$

7.7. A. $p = 0.01 + 0.03 + 0.02 = .06$

To answer this question, we need to add the relative frequencies for each of the three types of crime committed by male high school graduates.

B. $p = .04 + .03 + 0 = .07$

To answer this question, we need to add the relative frequencies of the three levels of education of the thieving women.

C. Using our formula for $p(A \text{ or } B)$, we find that $p = p(\text{male}) + p(\text{thief}) - p(\text{male and thief}) = .85 + .39 - .32 = .92$. This probability includes all the men in the group (85%) plus the female thieves (7%).

EXERCISES

1. Which of the following pairs of events are mutually exclusive?
   a. Rolling a six: Rolling an odd number in one roll of a die
   b. Drawing an ace: Drawing a red card in one draw from a deck
   c. Flipping a head: Flipping a tail in one flip of a coin
   d. Being pregnant: Not being pregnant

2. Which of the following pairs of events are independent?
   a. Flipping a head on the first flip: flipping a head on the second flip of a coin
   b. Drawing an ace first: Drawing a red card second in two draws from a deck without replacement
   c. Drawing an ace first: Drawing a red card second in two draws from a deck with replacement
   d. Being accepted by Harvard University: Being accepted by Yale University

3. Imagine that the probability of your getting married in the next 5 years is .80, and the probability that you will be a parent within the next 5 years is .70.
   a. What is the probability that you will be both married and a parent?
   b. What are your chances of being either married or a parent?

4. A certain (unenlightened) company wants to hire a chief executive. The probability that they will hire a woman is .15. The probability that they will hire an unmarried person is .25. What is the probability that this company will hire

   a. a single woman?
   b. a single man?
   c. either a woman or a married person? (Are these events mutually exclusive?)
   d. a married woman?

5. Sheila wants to move to another city. If Sheila's chance of getting a job in New York is .10 and her chance of getting one in Seattle is .25, what is the probability that Sheila will be offered both jobs? What is the probability that Sheila will get either the New York position or the Seattle position?

6. My glove compartment contains three red fuses, four green fuses, and six blue fuses.

   a. I need a green fuse. What is the probability that I will grab a green one if I don't look?
   b. If I grab three fuses without looking, what is the probability that they are all red?
   c. What is the probability that I will grab a green one if I have already grabbed a blue one and not replaced it?
   d. What is the probability that in three grabs I will draw one red, one blue, and one green fuse in that order?

7. My glove compartment contains three red fuses and five green fuses. If I take six fuses with replacement, what is the probability of getting exactly two red and four green fuses?

8. In a horse race with six horses and six post positions, how many different orders of horses can we have?

9. How many different teams of five volleyball players could be made from eight players?

10. In "Over-the-Line" baseball, there is a pitcher, batter, left fielder, and right fielder. If we have 10 players, how many different teams could we have if putting the same players in different positions makes a different team?

11. From a standard deck of shuffled playing cards, you have been dealt the seven, eight, nine, and ten of hearts, which you are holding. If you are dealt one more card, what is the probability that it will be

    a. the six of hearts?
    b. the jack of hearts?
    c. either the six or the jack of hearts?
    d. neither the six nor the jack of hearts?
    e. any six?

12. From a standard deck of shuffled playing cards, you have been dealt the seven, eight, nine, and ten of hearts, which you are holding. If you are dealt two more cards, what is the probability that you will get

    a. the six of hearts followed by the jack of hearts?
    b. the six of hearts and the jack of hearts?
    c. two sixes?

13. Determine the number of possible outcomes if (a) a pair of dice is rolled and (b) two coins are tossed.

14. If a pair of dice is rolled, what is the probability of rolling a one and a five?

15. If two coins are tossed, what is the probability that they will both be heads? What is the probability that one is a head and the other is a tail?

16. A six-shooter has been loaded randomly with two bullets. You are going to squeeze the trigger twice.

    a. Determine the total number of possible outcomes (B = bullet, E = empty).
    b. What is the probability of firing both bullets if the cylinder is spun after the first shot is made?

17. The following table shows a breakdown of a statistics class in terms of grade received and major.

Grade	Psychology	Premed	Business
9	3	1	0
8	6	4	3
7	15	10	8
6	9	6	10
5	22	12	11
4	2	3	1
3	0	0	0
2	0	1	1
1	1	0	0

    a. If a student is selected at random from the class, what is the probability that he or she is a psychology major?
    b. If a student is selected at random from the class, what is the probability that he or she is a business student with a grade of 7 or better?

    c. If 3, 2, and 1 are failing grades, what is the probability of randomly selecting a premed student who failed the course?

    d. Ignoring major, what is the probability that a randomly selected student passed the course?

18. You are dealt five cards from a well-shuffled deck of playing cards. What is the probability of getting

    a. a flush (five cards all in the same suit)?

    b. the ace of spades as your first card?

    c. the ace of clubs as your second card, given you got the ace of spades as your first card?

CHAPTER 8

Introduction to Inference: The Random Sampling Distribution

LEARNING OBJECTIVES

After reading this chapter, you should be able to do the following:

1. Describe the difference between a parameter and a statistic.
2. Describe how a random sample is selected.
3. List the steps required to construct a random sampling distribution.
4. State the central limit theorem.
5. Define the mean and standard error of the sampling distribution of the mean, and state how they are related to the mean and standard deviation of the population.
6. Define the mean and standard error of the random sampling distribution of the difference, and state how they are related to the mean and standard deviation of the populations.
7. Define the mean and standard error of the random sampling distribution of the proportion, and state how they are related to the mean and standard deviation of the population.
8. Use the z formulas for the sample mean, the difference between means, and the proportion to solve a given problem.

Assume that I am going to toss a coin and bet with you about the outcome. If I bet on heads, how many heads in a row would I have to toss before you started getting suspicious? Let's say I toss the coin three times, and all three times it comes up heads. Would you accuse me of trickery? How about five heads in a row? Now would you start to doubt my honesty? What if I tossed the coin 10 times, and it came up heads each time? What would you have to say about that, given the probability we calculated in Chapter 7 for this very event?

Probably, most people would doubt that a fair coin would turn up heads 10 times in a row. Most people would think that this is too much for coincidence. What they are really deciding is that it is highly *improbable* that a fair coin would turn up heads as many as 10 times in a row *by chance alone*. A betting person would probably conclude that the coin was not fair at all! Now, it is possible that a fair coin could behave this way, but if I had money on it, I think I would be better off rejecting such a hypothesis. It seems much more reasonable to conclude that something fishy is going on.

This simple example demonstrates the underlying logic of all statistical inference. Statistical inference involves determining the probability that a particular outcome (e.g., 10 heads in a row) occurred by chance alone, given a specific hypothesis about the nature of things (e.g., a fair coin was used). We can easily determine probabilities for coin tossing. These probabilities then tell us how a fair coin should behave. A distribution of probabilities for a coin toss is a **random sampling distribution**. We cannot judge the fairness of any given coin unless we know how fair coins behave.

Random sampling distributions have a central role in inferential statistics. Although it may seem that we have spent a lot of time introducing statistical inference, it is important to have a thorough understanding of the basic concepts before we start doing inference.

> **Random sampling distribution:** A theoretical relative frequency distribution of the values of some statistic computed for all possible samples of some fixed size(s) drawn with replacement from a population; important in statistical inference

Statistical Inference

As you know, we use descriptive procedures when we can collect all the observations in the population that we are interested in. It is not always practical, and often not even possible, to collect all the observations in an entire population of observations. In such cases, we will use inferential rather than descriptive procedures. Statistical inference allows us to draw conclusions about values of population **parameters** by calculating the values of **statistics** from samples drawn from the population.

> **Parameter:** A summary value (e.g., mean, variance, standard deviation, etc.) of a population of observations
>
> **Statistic:** A summary value of a sample

Descriptive Versus Inferential Statistics

Descriptive statistics require

1. Specifying the population of interest
2. Collecting all observations from the population

3. Computing summary values (parameters), such as the mean and standard deviation
4. Using these summary values to describe the properties of the population

Technically, because descriptive statistics examine the entire population, we should not use the word "statistics." Rather, we should talk about "descriptive parameters." However, it has become common to use the term *statistics* even when describing entire populations.

Inferential statistics require

1. Obtaining one or more samples from the population(s) of interest
2. Computing estimates of parameters from the sample data
3. Making inferences about the corresponding population parameters from which the sample was drawn

Descriptive statistics: Procedures for summarizing the characteristics of populations

Random Sampling

A **random sample** is a sample that is drawn in such a way that all observations in the population have an equal likelihood of being included in the sample. The term *random sample* does not define what the sample is like. Rather, it describes *how* the members of the sample were selected.

Random sampling is a procedure for collecting observations from a population. It is a common technique in inferential statistics. There are many other ways of selecting observations to be included in a sample. I focus on random sampling in this book because many statistical procedures assume that observations were randomly selected.

Note: In reality, researchers rarely, if ever, use a true random sampling procedure. There has been a certain amount of debate about this for a long time. I could write a book (well may be a chapter or two) about this controversy. It is complicated, but I am reasonably comfortable in saying that when we are testing hypotheses (which is what we do most of the time as researchers in psychology), where we are comparing groups under different **treatment** conditions, random assignment of participants to groups is usually more important than random selection of participants. If you want to make your statistics professor crazy, initiate a discussion of this in class!

Random sample: A sample collected such that all members of the population are equally likely to be included

Treatment: Refers to some manipulation by the researcher; an independent variable

Two samples randomly drawn from the same population are rarely identical. It is a fundamental fact that samples vary. This is called **sampling fluctuation** or sampling error. Consider the population of IQ scores of Americans. It has been determined that the mean of the population is 100 and the standard deviation is 15. Let's put all these IQ scores in a hat, shake them up, and select 10 scores. We compute the mean of our sample to be 95. If we used this value as our inference about the population mean, we would be wrong. Let's randomly sample another 10 observations. This time we might compute a mean of 102. If we used this value to infer the population mean, we'd be wrong again. Whenever we make a statistical inference, *we may be wrong!*

The key is to discover what values of a statistic would occur, and with what frequency, when sampling repeatedly from the same population. If we know what outcomes are likely to occur, then we can make conclusions about the particular outcome we have found. In this chapter, we treat random sampling distributions theoretically. In later chapters, we will discuss how to use sampling distributions.

> **Sampling fluctuation:** Refers to the fact that samples drawn from the same population will yield summary measures that vary; variability of these measures depends on sample size

The Random Sampling Distribution

The random sampling distribution is critical in inferential statistics. It is a *relative frequency distribution* of the values of some statistic, calculated for *all possible samples of a fixed size* drawn at random and with replacement from a given population. With replacement means that each observation selected from the population is returned to the population before the next observation is selected.

Let's return, for a moment, to our bogus coin. How many heads in a row could I toss before you became suspicious about the fairness of my coin? Perhaps you would start feeling doubtful after the sixth head in a row. Let's analyze this situation as a statistician might.

We obtain a coin that we know is fair, toss it six times, and record how many heads occur. If we repeat this experiment enough times, we will get six heads in a row, even though our coin is fair. However, this outcome will be quite rare. If we could determine how often six heads occur when we toss a fair coin, we would know the *probability* of such an outcome in a single experiment of six tosses. If we computed the frequency of all possible outcomes of six coin tosses, we would have a frequency distribution. We could convert this to a relative frequency distribution, giving us a random sampling distribution for six tosses of a fair coin, repeated many times.

Let's say that the relative frequency of six heads in a row when the experiment is repeated an infinite number of times is $\left(\dfrac{1}{2}\right)^6 = .016$. This probability is very low. If we were betting on the fairness of a coin that came up heads six times in a row, we should put our money on the bogus side, not on the fair side. It is extremely unlikely that a fair coin would produce such an outcome.

Random sampling distributions describe the probabilities of outcomes in specified situations. When we know what is likely to occur in a given situation, we are able to make informed decisions about a particular outcome that has occurred.

A random sampling distribution can be constructed for any statistic. The general procedure for constructing a random sampling distribution is the following:

Step 1. Randomly select (with replacement) one (or more) sample(s) of observations of some fixed size from a given population.

Step 2. Calculate some statistic for that sample.

Step 3. Repeat Steps 1 and 2 until all possible different samples have been drawn.

Step 4. Place all statistics in a relative frequency distribution.

A random sampling distribution is named after the statistic of interest. For example, if the statistic calculated on the samples was the median, we would call the relative frequency distribution "the random sampling distribution of the median." If the mode was calculated, it would be the "random sampling distribution of the mode."

In our studies, we will learn about many random sampling distributions. One very useful sampling distribution in inferential statistics is the *random sampling distribution of the mean*.

The Random Sampling Distribution of the Mean

To construct the random sampling distribution of the mean, follow these steps:

Step 1. Randomly select with replacement a sample of some fixed size from the population of interest.

Step 2. Calculate the sample mean.

Step 3. Repeat Steps 1 and 2 until all possible different samples have been drawn.

Step 4. Place the sample means in a relative frequency distribution.

Let's follow these steps to create a random sampling of the mean for the tiny population below.

Population of scores: 1, 2, 3.

Step 1. Let's fix our sample size at two. We will put our three numbers in a hat and draw out two numbers replacing the first number after it is drawn. Let's imagine our first sample is 1, 1.

Step 2. Our sample mean is 1, $\frac{1+1}{2}$.

Step 3. Repeat until all possible different samples have been drawn.

Here are all the possible different samples that could be drawn from our population:

1,1	2,1	3,1
1,2	2,2	3,2
1,3	2,3	3,3

And here are all the sample means:

1	1.5	2
1.5	2	2.5
2	2.5	3

Step 4. Here is our random sampling distribution. We list each sample mean and its relative frequency.

Mean	f	rf
1	1	0.11
1.5	2	0.22
2	3	0.33
2.5	2	0.22
3	1	0.11

We now have a distribution of sample means. This random sampling distribution of the mean has certain invariable characteristics.

The Mean

Recall that the symbol μ stands for the mean of a population of observations. To refer to the mean of a sample drawn from a population, we use $\bar{X}$. The random sampling distribution of the mean is the relative frequency distribution of the means calculated for all possible samples drawn with replacement from a population. This distribution of sample means also has a mean. The symbol for the mean of the random sampling distribution of the mean is $\mu_{\bar{X}}$.

The mean of the random sampling distribution of the mean $\left(\mu_{\bar{X}}\right)$ equals the mean of the raw score population (μ). To summarize,

μ = mean of the population

$\bar{X}$ = mean of the sample

$\mu_{\bar{X}}$ = mean of the random sampling distribution of the mean

$\mu_{\bar{X}} = \mu$

The Variance

The symbol for the variance of a population of raw scores is σ^2. The variance of the random sampling distribution of the mean is the variability of the sample means around the mean of the distribution. The symbol for the variance of a random sampling distribution of the mean is $\sigma_{\bar{X}}^2$. The variance of the random sampling distribution of the mean is *not* equal to the variance of the population. The variability of the means around $\mu_{\bar{X}}$ is less than the variability of the raw scores around μ. In fact, the variance of the sampling distribution $\sigma_{\bar{X}}^2$ will be less than that of the population by a factor of 1 over the size of the sample. We will use lowercase n to refer to sample size. The variance of the sampling distribution is related to the variance of the population in the following way:

$$\sigma_{\bar{X}}^2 = \frac{\sigma^2}{n}$$

The variance of the sampling distribution is 1 nth of the variance of the population of raw scores. Note that the variance of the sampling distribution is less for a distribution constructed from large samples than for a distribution constructed from small samples. As sample size increases, the variance of the random sampling distribution of the mean decreases. To summarize,

σ^2 = variance of the population

$\sigma_{\bar{X}}^2$ = variance of the random sampling distribution of the mean

$\sigma_{\bar{X}}^2 = \dfrac{\sigma^2}{n}$ where n is the sample size

The Standard Deviation

The symbol for the standard deviation of a population is "σ." The symbol for the standard deviation of the random sampling distribution of the mean is $\sigma_{\bar{X}}$. This measure is used so frequently that it has a special name—the *standard error of the mean*. It is easier to say "standard error of the mean" than "standard deviation of the random sampling distribution of the mean." The term **standard error** (*SE*) is used to refer to the standard deviation of any random sampling distribution.

Standard error: Standard deviation of a random sampling distribution

Recall that the variance of the sampling distribution is related to the variance of the population by $\sigma_{\bar{X}}^2 = \dfrac{\sigma^2}{n}$. You can see, then, that the standard error is related to the standard deviation of the population in the following way:

$$\sigma_{\bar{X}} = \frac{\sigma}{\sqrt{n}}$$

The standard error is smaller than the standard deviation of the population by a factor of $1 / \sqrt{n}$.

To summarize,

σ = standard deviation of a population

$\sigma_{\bar{X}}$ = standard deviation of the sampling distribution of the mean (called the standard error of the mean)

$\sigma_{\bar{X}} = \dfrac{\sigma}{\sqrt{n}}$ where n is the sample size

Note: As I have mentioned before, APA expects researchers to report statistics such as sample means and either standard deviations or standard errors. The notation we are using here is not typically used in such reports. Rather, *M*, *SD*, and *SE* are used to report means, standard deviations, and standard errors, respectively.

The Shape: The Central Limit Theorem

The **central limit theorem** is critically important to inferential statistics. At this point in our studies, the central limit theorem tells us the following:

1. The random sampling distribution of the mean tends toward a normal distribution, irrespective of the shape of the original raw score population.
2. This tendency increases as sample size increases.

In other words, no matter what the shape of the original population of raw scores, the relative frequency distribution of means, computed for all possible samples drawn with replacement from that population, will approach the normal distribution. Furthermore, the shape will be closer to normal for larger sample sizes.

In Chapter 6, we studied the characteristics of the standard normal distribution. Those same characteristics hold for the random sampling distribution of the mean when the sample size is large enough. The normal curve may be used as a model, then, for any sampling distribution of means when

1. the original population is normal or close to normal in shape, or
2. the original population is not normal, but the sample size is large.

The central limit theorem is important because it allows us to use the theoretical normal curve as our model to solve problems about real or empirical distributions.

Central limit theorem: Defines the relationship between various random sampling distributions and the normal distribution

CONCEPT REVIEW 8.1

Here is a tiny population of scores: 2, 4, 6. Construct the random sampling distribution of the mean with $n = 2$.

Answer on page 199.

Solving Problems With the Random Sampling Distribution of the Mean

In Chapter 6, we learned how to convert a raw score into a z score to solve problems using the normal curve table. Recall that the formula to convert a raw score to its corresponding z is

$$z = \frac{X - \mu}{\sigma}$$

We were able to find the proportion of the total area under the curve between two z scores and to find z scores when we knew the area. We learned to use Table B.1 in Appendix B to solve problems with any raw score distribution that was normal in shape.

We know that the random sampling distribution of means is normal in shape under certain conditions; therefore, we can use the same procedure and table to solve problems about means of samples that we used to solve problems about raw scores. We need only to convert the sample mean to its corresponding z score, so that we can use the normal curve table.

We convert a sample mean to a z score in a similar manner to converting a raw score to a z score. The mean of the distribution is subtracted from the corresponding sample statistic, and this difference is divided by the standard deviation of the distribution of the statistic. In the case of a sample mean, our formula for calculating the z score is

$$z = \frac{\overline{X} - \mu_{\overline{X}}}{\sigma_{\overline{X}}}$$

We need to know the value of the population mean (μ) and the value of the population standard deviation (σ). We know the mean of the sampling distribution $\left(\mu_{\overline{X}}\right)$ is equal to the population mean (μ). We can find the standard error $\left(\sigma_{\overline{X}}\right)$ by dividing σ by the square root of n.

Ready for an example?

Example A: Consider a normal population of scores whose mean is 130 and whose standard deviation is 10. Let's randomly select several samples of 25 observations from this population and compute the mean for each. How often would we expect to get sample means between 128 and 132? We will solve this problem with the same strategy that we used in Chapter 6. Remember the following sequence of steps.

$$\text{DATA: } \mu = 130$$
$$\sigma = 10$$
$$n = 25$$

Step 1. Draw a curve and shade in the area of concern.

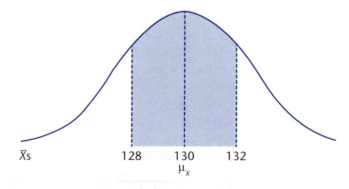

We know that the mean of the sampling distribution is 130, because it is equal to the mean of the population.

Step 2. Convert the sample means to z scores.

$$z = \frac{\bar{X} - \mu_{\bar{X}}}{\sigma_{\bar{X}}}$$

$$z_{128} = \frac{128 - 130}{10/\sqrt{25}} = -1$$

$$z_{132} = \frac{132 - 130}{2} = +1$$

Step 3. Look up the area between the two z values in the normal curve table.

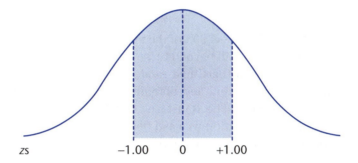

Area between the mean and a z of +1.00 is .3413
Area between the mean and a z of −1.00 is .3413
Area between the two z values is .6826

Therefore, when we draw many samples from this population, we would expect to get means between 128 and 132 about 68% of the time.

If I told you that I had randomly selected one sample of 25 observations from this population and calculated the sample mean of 131, would you be surprised? Not particularly, I don't imagine.

Example B: Let's try another example. Between what two values would we expect 99% of the means of samples from our population to fall?

Step 1. Draw a curve and shade in the area of concern.

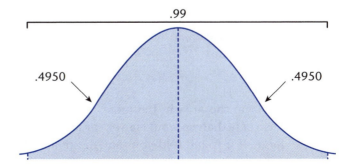

Step 2. Look up the two z values between which .99 of the total area lies (i.e., .4950 on each side of the mean).

$$z = \pm 2.58.$$

Step 3. Rearrange the formula so that $\bar{X}$ is the unknown.

$$\bar{X} = \mu_{\bar{X}} \pm z\sigma_{\bar{X}}$$
$$= 130 \pm 2.58\left(10 / \sqrt{25}\right)$$
$$= 130 \pm 5.16$$
$$= 124.84 \text{ and } 135.16$$

We would expect 99% of the means to fall between 124.84 and 135.16 and the remaining 1% to fall beyond these two points.

If I told you that I had randomly selected one sample of 25 observations from this population and obtained a sample mean of 137, would you be surprised? You should be. It just isn't very likely that I would get a sample mean that high if the population was as I described it. In fact, I would get a sample mean that high less than 1% of the time.

Example C: How often would we expect to draw sample means as large or larger than 145 from our population?

Step 1. Draw a curve and shade in the area of concern.

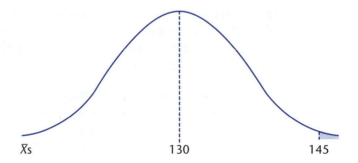

Step 2. Convert the sample mean to a z score.

$$z_{145} = \frac{\left(145 - 130\right)}{2} = 7.5.$$

Step 3. Look up the area in the table. The tables don't go this far. Our best answer is that we would never (or hardly ever) expect to get means this large. If a friend told you that she randomly selected 25 observations from a normal population whose mean is 130 and whose standard deviation is 10, and computed a sample mean of 145, your skepticism would be understandable. The probability of such an outcome, given that the information about the population is true, is incredibly low.

However, what if your friend could prove that her calculation of the mean was correct and that she did, in fact, randomly select 25 observations with a sample mean of 145? What can you conclude? Two possibilities come to mind. Either she obtained an amazingly rare outcome or the information about the population from which she drew her sample is wrong.

Remember the coin-toss experiment where six heads occurred in a row? Two explanations again come to mind. Either an extremely rare outcome occurred with a fair coin or the coin was bogus. In the latter explanation, expectations about how the coin should behave were wrong. This describes the logic of many inferential techniques. Inferences are based on the probability of a particular sample outcome occurring when certain hypotheses are made about the population from which the sample was selected.

In the next chapter, we are going to learn about hypothesis testing, an important inferential technique used by researchers in the social sciences and other disciplines. Researchers often have hypotheses, or educated guesses, about many things. These hypotheses come from existing research, theory, and sometimes common sense. To test whether or not a hypothesis about a population is likely to be correct, we need to know what is likely and what is not likely when we draw samples from populations similar to the one we are hypothesizing about. The random sampling distribution of the mean tells us how means calculated for samples drawn from populations with assumed (hypothesized) characteristics should behave. Once we know how they should behave, we can assess a particular sample outcome as "behaving in the expected manner or not."

The random sampling distribution of the mean is very important in statistical inference. Knowing its properties allows us to make decisions about outcomes of experiments.

CONCEPT REVIEW 8.2

Test scores for a standardized aptitude test are normally distributed with a mean of 85 and a standard deviation of 7. A random sample of 49 elementary students takes the test. Their mean is 88. What is the likelihood of getting this particular mean or a higher one if these students are a random sample from the given population?

Answer on page 200.

The Random Sampling Distribution of the Difference Between Means

Another important random sampling distribution involves the differences between means drawn from two populations with equal means, the random sampling distribution of the difference between means. If we draw samples from populations of raw scores having equal means, we would not expect the sample means to be identical. Remember sampling fluctuation? The question we must ask is "How different would we expect sample means to be, when the samples are drawn from populations with equal means?" To answer this question, we need to determine the kinds of differences that would occur. We must construct a random sampling distribution of differences between pairs of means drawn from two populations with equal means. This distribution is constructed in the following manner:

Step 1. Randomly draw one sample with replacement, of a fixed size, from each of two populations with equal means. (The two samples don't have to be of equal size.)

Step 2. Calculate the mean of each sample and record the difference.

Step 3. Repeat Steps 1 and 2 until all possible pairs of samples have been drawn.

Step 4. Place the mean differences in a relative frequency distribution.

The result is a random sampling distribution of the difference between means. This distribution of differences has several unvarying properties related to the original populations.

The Mean

When we compute the mean of all the differences we collected, we find it is zero. This makes sense because we drew our samples from two populations with the same mean.

Staying with our usual notation,

$\bar{X}_1 - \bar{X}_2$ is the difference between the means of a pair of samples

$\mu_1 - \mu_2$ is the mean of the population of differences

$\mu_{\bar{X}_1-\bar{X}_2}$ is the mean of the sampling distribution of differences

The means of the raw score populations are equal, so the mean of the distribution of differences is zero.

$$\mu_1 - \mu_2 = 0$$
$$\mu_{\bar{X}_1-\bar{X}_2} = 0$$

ALERT

Let's talk subscripts.

We will be dealing with lots of subscripts from now on. Do not treat these as arithmetic operations. The subscript for the mean of the sampling distribution of the difference (i.e., $\mu_{\bar{X}_1 - \bar{X}_2}$) must not be interpreted as a difference.

That is, we do not subtract sample means. This is just a way of designating that this particular mean is the mean of the sampling distribution of differences. It acts as an identifier, not as a mathematical instruction.

The Variance

Because we have a frequency distribution of values (i.e., differences), we can calculate the variance of that distribution. How much do the differences vary around the mean difference of zero? The variance of the sampling distribution of the difference between means is related to the variances of the populations. It is smaller than in the original populations because we are dealing with sample means, not raw scores. As we saw with the sampling distribution of the mean, when the samples become larger, the variance of the sampling distribution of the difference becomes smaller. The variance of the sampling distribution of the difference between means is related to the population variances in the following manner:

$$\sigma^2_{\bar{X}_1 - \bar{X}_2} = \sigma^2_{\bar{X}_1} + \sigma^2_{\bar{X}_2} = \frac{\sigma^2_1}{n_1} + \frac{\sigma^2_2}{n_2}$$

When we compute the variance of the sampling distribution of the difference from the sums of squares of the groups, our computational formula is as follows:

$$\sigma^2_{\bar{X}_1 - \bar{X}_2} = \left\{ \frac{\left[\sum X_1^2 - \frac{\left(\sum X_1 \right)^2}{n_1} \right] + \left[\sum X_2^2 - \frac{\left(\sum X_2 \right)^2}{n_2} \right]}{n_1 + n_2} \right\} \left\{ \frac{1}{n_1} + \frac{1}{n_2} \right\}$$

$$\text{or} = \frac{\left[\sum X_1^2 - \frac{\left(\sum X_1 \right)^2}{n} \right] + \left[\sum X_2^2 - \frac{\left(\sum X_2 \right)^2}{n} \right]}{n(n)} \quad \text{if } n_1 = n_2$$

Recall that in Chapter 4, I started to use SS to refer to $\sum X^2 - \dfrac{(\sum X)^2}{n}$, the sum of squares. Now you will appreciate why. Our formulas for the variance of the sampling distribution of the difference are simplified by the use of SS. They are as follows:

$$\sigma^2_{\bar{X}_1 - \bar{X}_2} = \frac{SS_1 + SS_2}{n_1 + n_2}\left(\frac{1}{n_1} + \frac{1}{n_2}\right)$$

$$\text{or } = \frac{SS_1 + SS_2}{n(n)} \quad \text{if } n_1 = n_2$$

$$\text{where } SS = \sum X^2 - \frac{(\sum X)^2}{n}$$

If the populations from which the samples were drawn have equal variances as well as equal means, and if the samples were of equal sizes, then the relationship between the population variance and the variance of the sampling distribution is

$$\sigma^2_{\bar{X}_1 - \bar{X}_2} = \frac{2\sigma^2}{n}$$

To summarize

σ^2_1 = variance of the first population

σ^2_2 = variance of the second population

$\sigma^2_{\bar{X}_1 - \bar{X}_2}$ = variance of the sampling distribution of differences between means. The relationship between them is

$$\sigma^2_{\bar{X}_1 - \bar{X}_2} = \frac{\sigma^2_1}{n_1} + \frac{\sigma^2_2}{n_2}$$

The Standard Deviation

You will recall that the standard deviation of a random sampling distribution is called a standard error. The standard deviation of the sampling distribution of the difference is called the standard error of the difference between means, but I often just call it the **standard error of the difference**. The standard error is simply the square root of the variance. To summarize,

σ_1 = standard deviation of the first population

σ_2 = standard deviation of the second population

$\sigma^2_{\bar{X}_1-\bar{X}_2}$ = standard deviation of the sampling distribution of differences between means

The standard error of the random sampling distribution of the difference is related to the populations in the following way:

$$\sigma_{\bar{X}_1-\bar{X}_2} = \sqrt{\sigma^2_{\bar{X}_1} + \sigma^2_{\bar{X}_2}}$$

$$= \sqrt{\frac{\sigma_1^2}{n_1} + \frac{\sigma_2^2}{n_2}}$$

$$\text{or} = \sqrt{\frac{2\sigma^2}{n}} \quad \text{if } \sigma_1 = \sigma_2 \text{ and } n_1 = n_2$$

The computational formulas for the standard error of the difference are as follows:

$$\sigma_{\bar{X}_1-\bar{X}_2} = \sqrt{\frac{SS_1 + SS_2}{n_1 + n_2}\left(\frac{1}{n_1} + \frac{1}{n_2}\right)}$$

$$\text{or} = \sqrt{\frac{SS_1 + SS_2}{n(n)}} \quad \text{if } n_1 = n_2$$

$$\text{where } SS = \Sigma X^2 - \frac{(\Sigma X)^2}{n}$$

The Shape

Remember the central limit theorem? It governs the shape of the random sampling distribution of the difference between means in the same way it does with the sampling distribution of the mean. This distribution is normal if the populations are normal or if the samples are reasonably large. We can use the normal curve to solve problems about the sampling distribution of the difference as we did with the sampling distribution of the mean.

Solving Problems With the Random Sampling Distribution of the Difference

Once again, to use the normal curve table (Table B.1 in Appendix B), we need to convert our statistic to its z-score equivalent. The mean of the sampling distribution is subtracted from its corresponding sample statistic, and this difference is divided by the standard deviation of the sampling distribution of the statistic. Because our statistic is the mean difference, the z-score formula for the difference between means is

$$z = \frac{\left(\bar{X}_1 - \bar{X}_2\right) - \mu_{\bar{X}_1 - \bar{X}_2}}{\sigma_{\bar{X}_1 - \bar{X}_2}}$$

In practice, we will omit the right part of the numerator because the mean of the sampling distribution of the difference is equal to the mean difference in the population: zero.

When the shape of the distribution of mean differences is normal, we can solve problems about mean differences in the same way we solved problems with single means as the examples that follow indicate.

Example D: Consider two normally distributed raw score populations with means of 100 and standard deviations of 10. Let us randomly select a sample of 25 observations from each population and compute the difference between the sample means. How often would we expect to get mean differences between 5 and –5? Using the same procedure we applied earlier, we take these steps:

Step 1. Draw the curve and shade in the area of concern.

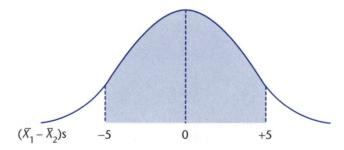

$(\bar{X}_1 - \bar{X}_2)$s   –5   0   +5

Step 2. Compute the z scores.

Because we have drawn equal-sized samples from populations with equal variances, our formula is

$$z \text{ of } \pm 5 = \frac{\pm 5}{\sqrt{\dfrac{2(10)^2}{25}}} = \frac{\pm 5}{2.83} = \pm 1.77$$

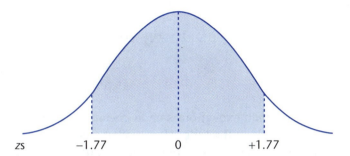

zs   −1.77   0   +1.77

These two z scores correspond to mean differences of 5 points or less between the two samples in either direction.

Step 3. Look up the area in the normal curve table (Table B.1 in Appendix B).

Area between the mean of 0 and a z of ± 1.77 is $2(.4616) = .9232$

About 92% of the time, we would expect to get samples whose means differ by 5 points or less either way, when drawing from such populations. This much sampling fluctuation, then, is quite likely.

If I told you that I had drawn two samples of 25 observations from these populations and calculated one mean to be 101 and the other to be 104, would you be surprised? You wouldn't, would you? A difference of three points is not at all unusual.

Example E: Now let's try another question. Beyond what two values would we expect only the extreme 5% of the mean differences to fall, 2.5% on either side?

Step 1. Draw the curve and shade in the area of concern.

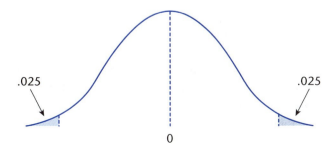

.025   .025

0

Step 2. Look up the z values that separate the middle 95% from the extreme 5% of the area.

$$z = \pm 1.96$$

Step3. Convert the z scores to mean differences by rearranging the formula:

$$\bar{X}_1 - \bar{X}_2 = \left(\mu_{\bar{X}_1 - \bar{X}_2}\right) \pm z \left(\sigma_{\bar{X}_1 - \bar{X}_2}\right)$$
$$= 0 \pm 1.96(2.83)$$
$$= \pm 5.55$$

We would expect our sample means to differ 5.55 points or more in either direction, 5% of the time. Thus, you should be surprised if I told you that I had drawn two samples and found a mean difference of 6 points. This would not be likely if I had randomly drawn the observations and if the assumptions about the populations were true.

Solving problems about mean differences follows the same logic as solving problems about single means. The central limit theorem assures us that the shape of the sampling distribution of the difference is normal if the populations are normal or close to normal, or when the samples are reasonably large.

CONCEPT REVIEW 8.3

What is the probability that two samples, randomly drawn from a normal population, would have means that differ by five points or more if the standard error of the difference is 10?

Answer on page 200.

The Random Sampling Distribution of a Proportion

Recall our coin toss experiment. In one toss of a coin, only two outcomes are possible. You will recall from Chapter 7 that this is called a dichotomous variable. Dichotomous variables are ones where only two mutually exclusive outcomes are of interest. Up to now, we have been discussing random sampling distributions where means of samples have been computed. Dichotomous variables can be placed in a random sampling distribution as well. We'll call this the *random sampling distribution of a proportion*. Any dichotomous variable can be thought of in terms of proportions.

We construct the random sampling distribution of a proportion in the following manner:

Step 1. Randomly select, with replacement, a sample of some fixed size from the population of a dichotomous variable.

Step 2. Determine the proportion of times the value of interest occurs.

Step 3. Repeat Steps 1 and 2 until all possible samples have been drawn.

Step 4. Place these sample proportions in a relative frequency distribution.

If we were interested in setting up the random sampling distribution of our simple but illustrative experiment of 6 tosses of a coin, we would:

Step 1. Toss the coin 6 times. (Our sample size is 6.)

Step 2. Count the number of times a head occurs and record this as a proportion (e.g., .5 or $\frac{3}{6}$).

Step 3. Repeat Steps 1 and 2 an infinite number of times.

Step 4. Place our proportions in a relative frequency distribution.

If you suspect that this distribution has certain unvarying properties, you are quite correct.

The Mean

In our coin toss experiment, the outcome that will occur most frequently is three heads in six tosses. With a fair coin, we would expect to get half heads and half tails more often than any other outcome. Occasionally, we will get an unlikely outcome, such as six heads in a row, but not often. The mean of the random sampling distribution of a proportion (P_p) is equal to the proportion of times the outcome of interest is expected to occur in the population (P). In the case of a coin, we would expect to get heads 50% or 0.50 of the time. This is also the probability of a head; proportions can be thought of as probabilities. (You may recall our discussion of a relative frequency distribution as a probability distribution.) We will use lowercase "p" to refer to the proportion of times the outcome of interest occurred in the sample. The mean of all the sample proportions determined from all possible samples is equal to the expected value of the outcome of interest in the population (P). To summarize,

P = proportion for the outcome of interest in the population or the probability of the outcome of interest

p = proportion of times the outcome of interest occurred in the sample

P_P = mean of the random sampling distribution of the proportion

$P_P = P$

FYI

In this discussion of the sampling distribution of a proportion, I have not italicized all the "p"s and "P"s. This is to distinguish these from the *P* we use to stand for percentile and the *p* we use to stand for probability.

The Variance

All the sample proportions vary around the mean of the distribution. The variance of sampling distribution of a proportion is

$$\sigma_p^2 = PQ / n$$

If we think of P as the probability of the outcome of interest, then Q is the probability of the other outcome. Q is always equal to $1 - P$.

The Standard Deviation

As you might expect, the standard deviation of the random sampling distribution of a proportion is called the *standard error of the proportion*. It is the square root of the variance.

$$\sigma_p = \sqrt{PQ / n}$$

The Shape

Once again the central limit theorem governs the shape of the sampling distribution of a proportion. When the sample size is large, the distribution is normal in shape. Let's repeatedly toss our coin 6 times in a row. Now, let's repeatedly toss the coin 50 times in a row. The relative frequency distribution constructed in the second experiment would be closer to the normal distribution than the one constructed in the first experiment. Samples must be about 30 or larger for the sampling distribution to be normal enough to use the normal curve as a model.

Solving Problems With the Random Sampling Distribution of a Proportion

Let's toss our coin 50 times and record the number of heads we get. If we did this over and over again, how often would we expect to get 40 or more heads in 50 tosses? We can solve this problem using the same procedure we used earlier. To use the normal curve table to find areas, we must have a z score. Because the general formula for z is to subtract the mean of the sampling distribution from the sample statistic and divide this difference by the standard error, our z formula is

$$z = \frac{p - P}{\sigma_p}$$

Now, let's apply the procedure.

Example F: How often should we expect to get 40 or more heads in 50 tosses of a coin?

Step 1. Draw a curve and shade in the area of concern.

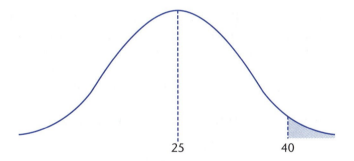

Because we are tossing our coin 50 times, 50 is our sample size. The mean of the sampling distribution of the proportion (P_p) equals the expected proportion in the population. If the coin is fair, we would expect to get heads on half of the tosses, or 25 times in 50 tosses, on the average.

Step 2. Compute the z score. Our sample proportion is $40/50$ or .80. The mean of the sampling distribution is $25/50$ or .50.

$$z = \frac{p - P_p}{\sigma_p} = \frac{.80 - .50}{\sqrt{\dfrac{(.50)(.50)}{50}}} = \frac{.30}{.07} = 4.29$$

Step 3. Look up the z value. Once again our z value is too large for the table. It is extremely unlikely to get 40 heads in 50 tosses of a fair coin. This outcome would occur so rarely that our best bet is that the coin is not fair.

Let's reword this using the terms of hypothesis testing. We begin by hypothesizing that a coin is fair. Once we make this assumption, we know how the coin should behave when it is tossed 50 times, over and over again. We know this because we know that the probability of a head on any one toss is 0.50, and so we expect to get heads about half the time. We have tossed this particular coin 50 times (our sample) and we counted 40 heads (our sample outcome). Because we know how the coin should behave (our sampling distribution), we can evaluate how the coin did behave. It behaved very oddly, indeed. It did not behave like a fair coin should. As hypothesis testers, we *could* conclude that this was a fluke and that our hypothesis that the coin was fair is correct. But I think, as I imagine you do, that we would be wiser to conclude that our hypothesis that the coin was fair is not correct. We would be wise to reject that hypothesis and accept another—the coin is not fair.

Example G: Let's look at a different kind of problem. Remember Mendel's laws of genetics? Consider a variety of garden pea for which Mendel's laws state that 25% of the peas are yellow in color and the rest are green. If we were to randomly select many samples of 400 peas each, how often would we expect to get 79 or fewer yellow peas in the 400 we picked?

Step 1. Draw a curve and shade in the area of concern.

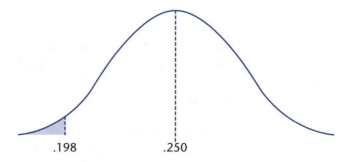

The mean of the sampling distribution is .25, because Mendel's laws state that 25% or 100 of the 400 peas should be yellow. We are interested in the area under the curve for proportions of 79 / 400 , or .198, or less.

Step 2. Compute the z score.

$$z = \frac{\text{p} - \text{P}_\text{p}}{\sigma_\text{p}} = \frac{.198 - .25}{\sqrt{\dfrac{(.25)(.75)}{400}}} = \frac{-.052}{.022} = -2.36$$

Step 3. Look up the area in Table B.1.

$$\text{Area} = .0091$$

We would expect to get 79 or fewer yellow peas out of 400 less than 1% of the time.

What would you conclude about Mendel's laws if we had found fewer than 79 yellow peas out of 400? Our sample did not behave the way it should have if Mendel (our hypothesis) was correct. We could conclude that we had an unlikely outcome and that Mendel was correct. We could, but we might be wiser to conclude that in this case Mendel's laws were not correct.

CONCEPT REVIEW 8.4

Claire Voyant claims that she has ESP (extrasensory perception). We shuffle a deck of 30 index cards. Of the 30 cards, 10 cards have stars on them, 10 have circles, and 10 have squares. Claire, who is blindfolded, guesses what is on each card presented one at a time. What is the probability that Claire will guess 20 or more cards correctly?

Answer on pages 200–201.

Knowing the shape of the random sampling distribution of a statistic allows us to determine the likelihood of different kinds of sample outcomes. Here, we have looked at the normal distribution. Later, we will discuss sampling distributions of statistics that are not normally shaped. The logic of the procedure, however, will not change. When we know the frequency of the expected outcomes, we can make informed decisions about particular outcomes.

The normal curve is a very useful tool in inferential statistics. It can be used to approximate several different random sampling distributions. It is a model of what will happen when we randomly sample from populations with certain characteristics. So, if we have reason to believe that a population has certain characteristics, we can sample from that population and use that sample information to decide if our belief (hypothesis) about the population is reasonable or not.

SUMMARY OF TERMS AND FORMULAS

A summary value of a population is called a *parameter*. A summary value of a sample is called a *statistic*.

A *random sample* is a sample collected such that each member of the population has an equal likelihood of being included.

Standard error is the standard deviation of a random sampling distribution.

According to the *central limit theorem*, the random sampling distributions of means, mean differences, and proportions tend toward a normal distribution, regardless of the shape of the original raw score population. This tendency increases as sample size increases.

Random Sampling Distribution of:	Mean	Variance	Standard Deviation	z formula
The mean	$\mu_{\bar{X}_1}$	$\sigma^2_{\bar{X}_1}$	$\sigma_{\bar{X}}$	$\dfrac{\bar{X} - \mu_{\bar{X}}}{\sigma_{\bar{X}}}$
The difference	$\mu_{\bar{X}_1 - \bar{X}_2}$	$\sigma^2_{\bar{X}_1 - \bar{X}_2}$	$\sigma_{\bar{X}_1 - \bar{X}_2}$	$\dfrac{\bar{X}_1 - \bar{X}_2}{\sigma_{\bar{X}_1 - \bar{X}_2}}$
The proportion	P_p	σ^2_p	σ_p	$\dfrac{p - P_p}{\sigma_p}$

Computation formulas for the standard error of the difference

$$\sigma_{\bar{X}_1 - \bar{X}_2} = \sqrt{\frac{SS_1 + SS_2}{n_1 + n_2}\left(\frac{1}{n_1} + \frac{1}{n_2}\right)}$$

$$= \sqrt{\frac{SS_1 + SS_2}{n(n)}} \quad \text{if} \quad n_1 = n_2$$

$$\text{where } SS = \sum X^2 - \left(\sum X\right)^2 / n$$

Relationship between properties of the random sampling distribution (RSD) and properties of the population

RSD of the mean	$\mu_{\bar{X}} = \mu$
	$\sigma_{\bar{X}} = \sigma / \sqrt{n}$
RSD of the difference	$\mu_{\bar{X}_1 - \bar{X}_2} = \mu_1 - \mu_2 = 0$
	$\sigma_{\bar{X}_1 - \bar{X}_2} = \sqrt{\dfrac{\sigma_1^2}{n_1} + \dfrac{\sigma_2^2}{n_2}}$
RSD of the proportion	$P_p = P$
	$\sigma_p = \sqrt{\dfrac{PQ}{n}}$

CONCEPT REVIEW ANSWERS

8.1.

Samples	Sample Means
2, 2	2
2, 4	3
2, 6	4
4, 2	3
4, 4	4
4, 6	5
6, 2	4
6, 4	5
6, 6	6

Means	*rf*
6	0.11
5	0.22
4	0.33
3	0.22
2	0.11

8.2. $z = \dfrac{88-85}{7/\sqrt{49}} = 3/1 = 3$

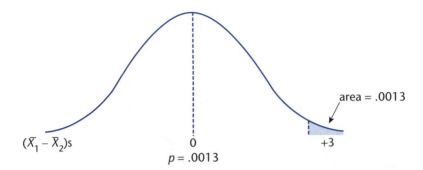

$(\bar{X}_1 - \bar{X}_2)s$ 0   +3

area = .0013

$p = .0013$

It's not very likely that these students are a random sample from the given population.

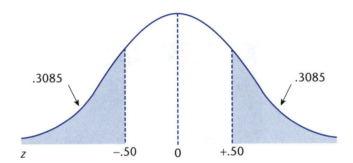

.3085   .3085

z −.50   0   +.50

$$z = \pm 5/10 = \pm 0.50.$$

$$p = .3085(2)$$

8.3. We would expect to get mean differences of 5 points or more about 61% of the time.

8.4. Because one third of the cards display each of the three symbols, we would expect that by sheer chance alone, Claire would guess about 10 cards correctly. So our P = 1/3. If Claire guessed 20 cards correctly, p = 20/30 or 2/3. Using our z formula we find

$$z = \frac{2/3 - 1/3}{\sqrt{\dfrac{(1/3)(2/3)}{30}}} = \frac{0.33}{0.086} = 3.837$$

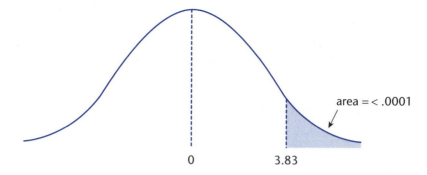

area = < .0001

0   3.83

We would expect someone who is not clairvoyant to guess 20 or more cards correctly less than .01% of the time.

EXERCISES

1. Given the following population of scores, calculate a to f.

   DATA: 10, 13, 15, 17, 20, 25, 30

   a. ΣX
   b. $\left(\Sigma X\right)^2/N$
   C. N
   d. ΣX^2
   e. μ
   f. σ

2. The following data are a population of raw scores. Compute the mean and standard deviation of this population.

   DATA: 1, 2, 4, 7, 11

3. Using the population of scores in Exercise 2, list the 25 possible samples of size two that can be drawn from this population with replacement. Find the mean of each sample.

4. Place the sample means from Exercise 3 into an absolute frequency distribution. Find the mean of the distribution and the standard deviation of the distribution using the following formulas: (*Hint:* $N = 25$)

$$\mu_{\overline{X}} = \frac{\Sigma f\overline{X}}{N}$$

$$\sigma_{\overline{X}} = \sqrt{\frac{SS}{N}} = \sqrt{\frac{\Sigma f\overline{X}^2 - \left(\Sigma f\overline{X}\right)^2 / N}{N}}$$

You will find that the mean of the sample means ($\mu_{\bar{X}}$) is equal to the mean of the original population that you computed in Exercise 2 (namely, μ). Check to make sure that the standard deviation or standard error you computed on your distribution of sample means is equal to $\sigma/\sqrt{n}$, where n is the sample size of two.

5. Using the distribution of sample means from Exercise 4, determine the probability of drawing at random a single sample of two scores whose mean is

   a. equal to 5
   b. >5
   c. >4 and<6

6. A distribution of scores has a mean of 75 and a standard deviation of 15. If all possible samples were drawn with replacement from this population, calculate the mean and standard deviation of the sampling distribution if

   a. $n = 225$
   b. $n = 100$
   c. $n = 25$

7. What is the probability of drawing a single sample of 25 scores whose mean is between 70 and 80 from the population in Exercise 6?

8. A normal population has a mean of 100 and a standard deviation of 16. What is the probability of randomly selecting 25 observations from this population and computing a mean

   a. equal to or larger than 112?
   b. between 95 and 105?
   c. equal to or less than 90?

9. Using the distribution described in Exercise 8, determine

   a. between what two means, 95% of the means will lie.
   b. between what two means, 99% of the means will lie.

10. Using the data below, solve the following problems. Assume the populations are normally distributed with equal means. What is the probability of randomly selecting a sample from each population and getting a mean difference as far as or farther above zero than indicated in each of the following?

    $SS_1 = 57600 \; SS_2 = 45400 \; n_1 = n_2 = 20$

    a. $\bar{X}_1 = 59$ $\bar{X}_2 = 37$
    b. $\bar{X}_1 = 65$ $\bar{X}_2 = 35$
    c. $\bar{X}_1 = 73.9$ $\bar{X}_2 = 26.7$

11. Using the data below, solve the following problems. Assume the populations are normally distributed with equal means.

$$\sigma_1^2 = 16 \quad n_1 = 36$$
$$\sigma_2^2 = 25 \quad n_2 = 50$$

a. $\bar{X}_1 = 123.72$ $\bar{X}_2 = 124.01$

b. $\bar{X}_1 = 124$ $\bar{X}_2 = 126$

c. $\bar{X}_1 = 122.5$ $\bar{X}_2 = 123.0$

12. An investigator decides to test a die for fairness. She rolls the die 40 times and counts the number of times a four turns up. If the die is fair, what is the probability that she will count

a. ten or more fours?

b. six or fewer fours?

c. two or fewer fours?

13. A sociologist randomly selects 500 New England families and categorizes each according to its socioeconomic status (SES). According to U.S. census data, 75% of the population are from middle-to-upper SES and the rest are from lower SES. If New Englanders are similar to the rest of the population, what is the probability that the sociologist would find 339 or fewer middle-to-upper SES families in his sample?

CHAPTER 9

Inference With the Normal Curve

LEARNING OBJECTIVES

After reading this chapter, you should be able to do the following:

1. Define the following terms: a priori, post hoc, critical value, Type I error, Type II error, and power.
2. List the critical values for one-tailed and two-tailed tests at the .05 and the .01 levels of significance.
3. Set up the 95% and 99% confidence intervals for a population mean, the difference between means, and the population proportion for a given set of data.
4. Define and provide examples of conceptual, research, and statistical hypotheses.
5. Describe the difference between an experimental and a correlational research hypothesis.
6. Define and provide examples of null and directional and nondirectional alternative hypotheses.
7. List the steps for testing the null hypothesis.
8. Indicate on a diagram the region of rejection and the region of acceptance for one-tailed and two-tailed tests of significance.
9. Run a z test for a single mean, the difference between means, and the proportion for a given set of data.
10. Determine the appropriate test of significance for a given research problem.

How satisfied is the American public with Barack Obama's presidency?

Are North American airports more secure than European airports?

Does banning cell phone use by drivers reduce traffic accidents?

In Chapters 6, 7, and 8, I discussed topics that are basic to inferential statistics. You now know the properties of the normal curve and several other random sampling distributions. You understand probability and how it applies to frequency distributions. It's now time to apply this knowledge to address questions such as those above. It is time to put our knowledge about inference to work.

Hypothesis Testing and Interval Estimation

Hypothesis testing and **interval estimation** are two inferential techniques that are based on the concept of random sampling distributions. They both use sample statistics to make inferences about population parameters.

In hypothesis testing, we have an **a priori** (before the fact) hypothesis about the value of some parameter or the relationship between parameters. Sample data are used to determine whether or not this hypothesis is reasonable—in other words, to "test our guess."

With interval estimation, we do not have any a priori hypotheses about the value of the parameter(s). We use the sample data to infer what the value of the parameter might be. Interval estimation, then, is a **post hoc** (after the fact) technique. Because interval estimation is a simpler technique, I will discuss it first.

When we use interval estimation with the normal curve, we are asking, "What is the value of this population parameter?" or "What is the relationship between parameters?" Interval estimation provides us with a method to set up a *range of values* within which the parameter will likely fall. Although the size of the range of values is arbitrary, most researchers in the social sciences use two ranges, the 95% and the 99% **confidence intervals**.

> **Interval estimation** Inferential procedure that estimates the probable location of population parameters or relationships between parameters from sample data
>
> **a priori:** Before the fact
>
> **post hoc:** After the fact
>
> **Confidence interval:** A range of values computed from sample data within which a parameter of interest has a known probability of falling

Setting Up Confidence Intervals Using the Normal Distribution

Setting Up the Confidence Interval for a Population Mean

In Chapter 8, we saw that means, calculated from random samples drawn from a population, distribute themselves normally within the limits of the central limit theorem. A single sample mean, if selected randomly, may be viewed as a *single random case* drawn from the distribution of all sample means. Recall that in the random sampling distribution of the mean, 95% of the sample means fall within ± 1.96 standard deviations of the mean of the sampling distribution, and 99% of the means fall within ± 2.58 standard deviations of the mean of this distribution. These two values, ± 1.96 and ± 2.58, are called **critical values** in inferential statistics.

When we know the population standard deviation and the mean of a single random sample, we can estimate where the population mean (μ) is likely to fall. All we do is rearrange our z formula such that the mean of the sampling distribution (which equals μ) is the unknown. The formulas for setting up the 99% and the 95% confidence intervals (CI) for the mean are as follows:

$$95\% \text{ CI:} \quad \bar{X} \pm 1.96\sigma_{\bar{X}}$$

$$99\% \text{ CI:} \quad \bar{X} \pm 2.58\sigma_{\bar{X}}$$

Let's examine a specific example. Suppose we have drawn a random sample from a population whose standard deviation is 15. We find that the mean of our 25 observations is 100. We now wish to determine a range of values within which we are reasonably sure that the population mean will fall. Likely the population mean will not equal 100, because we know that sample means vary somewhat from the population mean. If we claimed that $\mu = 100$, the chances are we would be wrong. To make a better guess, use the two formulas above to provide the 95% and 99% CI's.

$$\text{DATA: } \sigma = 15$$
$$n = 25$$
$$\bar{X} = 100$$

Before we use the formulas, we need to find the standard deviation of the sampling distribution (the standard error).

$$\sigma_{\bar{X}} = \sigma / \sqrt{n}$$
$$= 15 / \sqrt{25}$$
$$= 3$$

$$95\% \text{ CI:} \bar{X} \pm 1.96\sigma_{\bar{X}}$$
$$= 100 \pm 1.96(3) = 100 \pm 5.88 = 94.12 \text{ and } 105.88$$

We are 95% confident that the population mean lies between 94.12 and 105.88. In other words, our confidence is .95 that the population mean is greater than or equal to 94.12 and less than or equal to 105.88. This can be expressed in notation as follows:

$$C(94.12 \leq \mu \leq 105.88) = .95$$

If we wanted to be more confident, we could set up a 99% confidence interval by

$$99\%CI : \bar{X} \pm 2.58\sigma_{\bar{X}} = 100 \pm 2.58(3) = 100 \pm 7.74 = 92.26 \text{ and } 107.74$$

and express this in notation as

$$C(92.26 \leq \mu \leq 107.74) = .99$$

As you can see, the 99% CI sets a wider range of values within which the population mean is likely to fall.

Critical value: The value of a statistic corresponding to a given significance level determined by its sampling distribution

FYI

Why do we use the term *confidence* instead of *probability*? This is a good question. When we set up the 95% CI, for example, we know that 95% of the sample means will lie within ±1.96 standard error units from the mean of the sampling distribution. Therefore, 5% of the sample means will be further away from $\mu_{\bar{X}}$ than $\pm 1.96\sigma_{\bar{X}}$. For these few sample means, the limits set up by our procedure will *not* encompass μ. (Remember that $\mu_{\bar{X}} = \mu$.) In other words, 5% of the time we will obtain a sample mean that lies so far from the mean of the sampling distribution that our confidence interval will not include μ. *Before* we draw our sample to set up the 95% CI, we can say that the *probability* that our interval will contain μ is .95. However, once the data have been collected and we have set our limits, a given interval *either does or does not* contain μ.

Probability is a term that we use to express the likelihood of future outcomes. Once the event has taken place, we cannot use the term *probability*. A good analogy is one toss of a fair coin. While the coin is still up in the air, we can say that the *probability* of getting a head is $^1/_2$. Once the coin has landed, however, either a head or a tail has occurred. The event has taken place, and we can no longer use the term *probability*. When setting up limits for μ, then, we use the term *confidence* rather than probability.

With any inferential technique, there is some probability of error. When we set up confidence intervals, there is always a possibility that our limits will not encompass the parameter of interest.

Consider a population of raw scores with a mean of 100 and a standard deviation of 20. If we randomly draw all possible samples of 100 observations from this population, and place the sample means in a relative frequency distribution, we will have the random sampling distribution of the mean for a sample size of 100. Suppose we draw a single sample of 100 observations from the population and compute a sample mean of 103. Let's go ahead and set up the 95% CI for this sample mean.

$$95\% \; CI : 103 \pm 1.96 \left(20 / \sqrt{100} \right) = 103 \pm 3.92 = 99.08 \text{ and } 106.92$$

We would claim that we are 95% confident that the population mean lies between these two values, and, of course, our claim would be true.

Now, let's draw another sample from the population and compute the mean of the sample. We find it is 95. Now, we set up the 95% CI for this sample mean.

$$95\% \; CI: 95 \pm 1.96(2) = 91.08 \text{ and } 98.92$$

We would claim that μ lies between these two values. Are we correct? Not this time. The limits do not include μ. Figure 9.1 illustrates what happened.

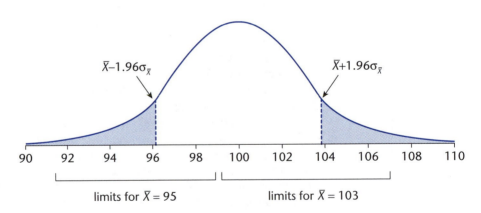

Figure 9.1. Confidence intervals for two sample means.

Look at the range of values we set up for the two sample means. You can see that for the mean of 103, our limits included μ, but for the mean of 95, they did not. Whenever a sample mean is further away from the mean of the sampling distribution than $\pm 1.96 \sigma_{\bar{X}}$, the limits set up by the 95% CI will not contain the population mean. If, on the other hand, the sample mean is within $\pm 1.96 \sigma_{\bar{X}}$ of

μ, the population mean will be included in our interval. We know that 5% of the time a single sample mean will be further away than $\pm 1.96\sigma_{\bar{X}}$ of μ, and so 5% of the time we make an incorrect inference about the location of the population mean. Obviously, if we want to be very careful about error, we would use a stricter criterion. The 99% CI is more conservative, and we will be in error only 1% of the time.

CONCEPT REVIEW 9.1

Set up the 95% CI for the following:

Sample mean is 85

Standard error is 5

Answer on page 234.

Setting Up the Confidence Interval for the Difference Between Population Means

Similarly, confidence intervals can be determined for the difference between population means. The random sampling distribution of the difference tells us what kinds of differences we can expect between sample means when they come from populations with equal means. If we draw two random samples and compute the mean difference, we can set up a range of values between which we are reasonably confident the mean difference in the population lies. Again, we simply rearrange our z formula to solve the mean difference of the sampling distribution. The formulas for 95% and 99% confidence intervals for the difference between means are as follows:

$$95\% \text{ CI}: \left(\bar{X}_1 - \bar{X}_2\right) \pm 1.96\left(\sigma_{\bar{X}_1 - \bar{X}_2}\right)$$

$$99\% \text{ CI}: \left(\bar{X}_1 - \bar{X}_2\right) \pm 2.58\left(\sigma_{\bar{X}_1 - \bar{X}_2}\right)$$

Again, we are simply using the sample statistic—the mean difference—to set up a range of values within which we think the population parameter $(\mu_1 - \mu_2)$ lies. Ready for an example?

In a sixth-grade special needs class, 16 students are randomly selected and randomly assigned to two experimental conditions. Both groups of 8 students each are given the same normally distributed, 25-item multiple-choice test.

Group 1 is given hints on taking multiple-choice tests; Group 2 is not. We want to set up the 99% CI for the difference. Here are the data.

$$\text{DATA}: \bar{X}_1 = 13.25 \qquad \bar{X}_2 = 14.75$$
$$SS_1 = 43.5 \qquad SS_2 = 75.5$$
$$n_1 = n_2 = 8$$

$$99\% \text{ CI} : \left(\bar{X}_1 - \bar{X}_2\right) \pm 2.58\left(\sigma_{\bar{X}_1 - \bar{X}_2}\right)$$

We first need to compute the standard error of the difference. Because the samples are of the same size, we can use the following equation:

$$\sigma_{\bar{X}_1 - \bar{X}_2} = \sqrt{\frac{SS_1 + SS_2}{n(n)}}$$
$$= \sqrt{\frac{43.5 + 75.5}{8(8)}}$$
$$= 1.36$$

Now, we can go ahead and set up the confidence interval.

$$99\% \text{ CI} : \left(13.25 - 14.75\right) \pm 2.58(1.36) = -1.50 \pm 3.51 = 2.01 \text{ and } -5.01$$

We are 99% confident that the true mean difference in the population lies somewhere between −5.01 and 2.01 or, expressed in notation:

$$C(-5.01 \le (\mu_1 - \mu_2) \le 2.01) = 0.99$$

CONCEPT REVIEW 9.2

Set up the 99% CI for the following:

Mean difference = 6

Standard error of the difference = 2

Answer on page 234.

Setting Up the Confidence Interval for a Population Proportion

We can set up confidence intervals for the proportion using the same logic and procedure. The formulas are as follows:

$$95\% \text{ CI:} \qquad p \pm 1.96\sigma_p$$

$$99\% \text{ CI:} \qquad p \pm 2.58\sigma_p$$

In this case, we are setting up a range of values within which we are reasonably sure that the population proportion lies. Let's do an example.

You randomly select 52 friends and ask each to guess the color (red or black) of the playing card you are holding behind your back. Thirty-eight people guess correctly. You are interested in knowing the proportion of people in the population who would guess correctly. You decide to set up the 95% CI. For each participant, we assume that the probability of guessing correctly is $\frac{1}{2}$.

$$\text{DATA: } p = 38/52 = 0.73$$

$$\sigma_p = \sqrt{PQ/n} = \sqrt{\frac{(0.5)(0.5)}{52}} = 0.07$$

$$95\% \text{ CI: } 0.73 \pm 1.96(0.07) = 0.59 \text{ and } 0.87$$

You are 95% confident that the true percentage of correct guesses in the population is between 59% and 87%, at least under the conditions of your experiment. We might wonder about how you conducted this study, however!

CONCEPT REVIEW 9.3

Set up the 95% CI for the following:

$p = 0.6$

$\sigma_p = 0.03$

Answer on page 234.

Confidence intervals can be set up for many population parameters. All we need is the sample statistic, the standard deviation of the sampling distribution of that statistic, and knowledge of the shape of that sampling distribution. The general formula for any confidence interval is

$$\text{CI for parameter} = \text{statistic} \pm \text{critical value (standard error)}$$

We use confidence intervals when we have no a priori hypothesis about the value of the population parameter. However, when we have a hypothesis about some parameter and we wish to test its validity, we use a different inferential technique.

Hypothesis Testing With the Normal Curve

In research, we often have hypotheses about events or phenomena. These "educated guesses" may come from theories, previous research, or good old common sense. So let's see how we proceed to test our guess.

Types of Hypotheses

Three levels of hypotheses can be distinguished in terms of the degree of quantification involved.

Conceptual Hypotheses

A **conceptual hypothesis** is a statement about the relationship between theoretical concepts. Hypotheses such as "Punishment facilitates learning" or "Criminality is related to poverty" are examples of conceptual hypotheses. Punishment, learning, criminality, and poverty are theoretical concepts. They can never be directly tested because they are not measurable as defined. Conceptual hypotheses must be **operationalized** or made measurable before we can test them.

> **Conceptual hypothesis:** States relationship between theoretical concepts
>
> **Operationalize:** To make observable or measurable

Research Hypotheses

A **research hypothesis** is a statement about the expected relationship between *observable* or *measurable* events. An **experimental research hypothesis** states expected relationships between independent and dependent variables. For example, "Shock, following errors, will decrease the number of errors made," is an experimental research hypothesis.

A **correlational research hypothesis** states the expected relationship between two or more variables. "The lower the income, the higher the number of convictions" is an example of a correlational research hypothesis. A research hypothesis restates the conceptual hypotheses in observable or measurable terms.

Research hypothesis: States expected relationship between measurable variables

Experimental hypothesis: States expected relationship between an independent variable and a dependent variable

Correlational hypothesis: States expected relationship between two or more variables

Statistical Hypotheses

A **statistical hypothesis** states an expected relationship between numbers that represent statistical properties of data (e.g., mean, variance, correlation). This type of hypothesis is always a guess about the value of a population parameter or about the relationship between values of two or more parameters, at least in parametric hypothesis testing. Nonparametric hypothesis testing is quite different as you will see in later chapters.

Examples of statistical hypotheses include "The mean number of errors is the same under shock and no-shock conditions" and "The correlation between number of convictions and income is zero."

Researchers usually begin with a conceptual hypothesis derived from some theory or published work. They then determine the best way to collect observations or measurements appropriate to their conceptual hypothesis. Data collection follows; then, statistical procedures commence.

Statistical hypothesis: States expected relationship between statistical properties of data

CONCEPT REVIEW 9.4

Categorize each of the following as a research, conceptual, or statistical hypothesis.

A. Violence on television increases aggressiveness in children.

B. Mean verbal fluency scores are higher for girls than for boys.

C. Teenage boys have longer jail sentences than teenage girls for similar crimes.

Answer on page 234.

The Logic and Procedure for Testing a Hypothesis

The steps for testing hypotheses are as follows:

Step 1. If you have a conceptual hypothesis, restate it as a research hypothesis. (Operationalize the concepts.)

Step 2. Make a statement about expected values of parameters of interest. (State the statistical hypothesis.)

Step 3. Collect and summarize the data.

Step 4. Test the statistical hypothesis.

Step 5. Draw conclusions about the conceptual hypothesis.

We will start at Step 2. A statistical hypothesis includes the hypothesis that you wish to disprove (the **null hypothesis**) and the hypothesis that you wish to confirm (the **alternative hypothesis**).

Null and Alternative Hypotheses

The null hypothesis (H_0) is the one you test and hope to prove wrong, reject, or nullify. If the null is rejected, the alternative hypothesis (H_1) is accepted. The aim of hypothesis testing is to show that the null is false, and, therefore, you accept an alternative hypothesis.

Null hypothesis (H_0): States expected value of a parameter or expected relationship between parameters

Alternative hypothesis (H_1): States a value or relationship different from the null

ALERT

The alternative hypothesis corresponds to the research hypothesis. Confirmation of the research hypothesis lies in *rejecting the null*. We cannot confirm the null, but we can confirm the alternative. For example, we cannot "prove" that a coin is fair, but we can "prove" that it is *not fair*. This may seem to be a pretty strange way of doing things, but it will become clearer to you, I hope!

The null hypothesis specifies the expected value of a single population parameter or the expected relationship between two or more parameters. Some examples of null hypotheses are as follows:

$$H_0: \mu = 100$$
$$P = 1/2$$
$$\sigma_1^2 / \sigma_2^2 = 1$$
$$\mu_1 = \mu_2$$

The alternative hypothesis asserts that the value of relationship specified by the null is not true. You test the null hypothesis, and if it is rejected, you accept an alternative hypothesis. An alternative hypothesis that simply negates the null is called a **nondirectional alternative**. If it specifies the direction of the difference, it is called a **directional alternative**. Some examples are as follows:

H_0	Nondirectional H_1	Directional H_1
$\mu = 100$	$\mu \neq 100$	$\mu < 100$ or $\mu > 100$
$\mu_1 = \mu_2$	$\mu_1 \neq \mu_2$	$\mu_1 < \mu_2$ or $\mu_1 > \mu_2$

Nondirectional alternative: Hypothesis that negates the null

Directional alternative: Hypothesis that specifies the direction of the difference from the null

ALERT

The type of alternative hypothesis used depends on the research hypothesis. If the researcher's interest is in finding a difference only in a particular direction, then a directional alternative is appropriate. Otherwise, a nondirectional alternative hypothesis is used.

CONCEPT REVIEW 9.5

For each of the following, determine the type of statistical hypothesis to which the statement best corresponds.

A. Violent criminals have higher testosterone levels than nonviolent criminals.

B. Boys and girls differ in spatial ability.

C. Children who view violent television programs are not different in aggression from children who view nonviolent programs.

Answer on page 234.

Testing the Null

The null hypothesis is tested in a clearly defined series of steps:

Step 1. Define the H_0 and the H_1.

Step 2. Select one or more random samples from the population(s) of interest and calculate the value of the statistic that corresponds to the parameter specified in the null.

Step 3. Determine the probability of getting a sample outcome, by chance alone, that is as far or further from the value hypothesized by the null as the one you obtained. This is done in reference to the sampling distribution of the statistic specified by the conditions of the null hypothesis.

Step 4. If the probability is low, reject the null and accept the alternative. If the probability is high, do not reject the null.

Let's try to analyze this procedure conceptually. The null hypothesis is the one we want to prove wrong. Suppose we believe that women are more intelligent than men! The null hypothesis might state that women are equal in intelligence to men, and the alternative might state that they are more intelligent. (Remember that the alternative corresponds to the researcher's hypothesis.) Let's assume, for the moment, that men and women are equal in intelligence. If this is true, then two random samples, one of men and one of women, should have similar mean intelligence scores. Of course, we wouldn't expect the sample means to be exactly the same because samples do vary. The question is "How much greater does the mean of the sample of women have to be to conclude that women are more intelligent than men?" To answer this question, we need to find out what kinds of mean differences are likely to occur when we draw two samples from populations with equal means. Then, if our difference is much larger than what we would expect by chance alone, we may feel free to conclude that, in fact, the populations do not have equal means.

The null hypothesis, then, provides us with a sampling distribution that *we know a lot about*. We know what kinds of sample outcomes are likely to occur under the conditions assumed by the null. If our sample outcome is very different from what we would expect, we say that the null hypothesis is probably wrong and an alternative hypothesis is true.

Step 4 says that we reject the null if the probability of getting a sample outcome as deviant as the one we got is very low. How do we decide if the probability is low enough?

Decision Criteria

The tradition in the social sciences has been to use two probability values when testing hypotheses. These levels, symbolized by α (alpha) are called **significance levels**. The 1% level of significance (α = .01) allows us to reject the null hypothesis if our sample outcome was likely to have occurred 1% or less of the time if the null were true. The 5% level of significance allows us to reject the null if the probability of our outcome occurring is equal to or less than .05.

FYI

Most introductory statistics texts take the position that the significance level is set a priori—that is, before the outcomes are known. I also take this position in this book because I think it is preferable for teaching purposes. The reality is that researchers report the significance level post hoc. In other words, the specific probability is usually reported for outcomes most of us would think of as "rare." Outcomes that would be expected to occur more than 10% of the time are sometimes reported as nonsignificant (*ns*), but sometimes the actual level is given (e.g., *p* = .09). The reader is then given the information to judge for him or herself the meaning of the finding. I tend to prefer this practice; but, as usual, there are pros and cons. On the one hand, the reader is given the opportunity to judge for herself. On the other, if the reader is not statistically "savvy," he may be confused.

Significance level: The level of probability at which we will reject the null hypothesis

When we test hypotheses with the normal curve as our sampling distribution, we do not need to determine the exact probability of our sample outcome. We know that the z scores of ±1.96 separate the middle 95% of the distribution from the extreme 5%. In other words, z values lying in the tails beyond ±1.96 will occur less than 5% of the time. Once we have calculated our z value, we only need to compare it with ±1.96. If our z value is larger (ignoring the sign) than these critical z values, then we know that the probability of occurrence of our outcome is low—less than .05—and we can reject the null hypothesis.

The same is true for a significance level of .01. The critical values for $\alpha = .01$ are ±2.58 because these two values separate the middle 99% from the extreme 1% of the distribution. In summary,

$$\text{critical } z \text{ values: } \alpha = .05 \qquad z_{crit} = \pm 1.96$$
$$\alpha = .01 \qquad z_{crit} = \pm 2.58$$

Critical values, then, cut off the appropriate areas in the tails of the distribution corresponding to the level of significance selected by the researcher. Any obtained z value that falls beyond these critical values is said to lie in the **region of rejection** or the **critical region**. z values falling between the critical values are said to lie in the **region of acceptance**. This is illustrated in Figure 9.2.

Critical region or region of rejection

Region of acceptance or non-rejection

Critical region or region of rejection

Figure 9.2. Hypothesis testing with the normal curve: Regions of rejection and acceptance.

We reject the null when the obtained z value lies in the critical region because the probability of getting an outcome that far from the expected outcome specified in the null, by chance alone, is low—that is, less than alpha. Otherwise, we *fail to reject the null hypothesis*. We never say that we accept the null; rather we always state that we have failed to prove it wrong. The term *region of acceptance* implies that we do accept the null. I think it is more appropriate, if a bit awkward, to call this area the *region of nonrejection*.

Region of rejection or critical region: Area beyond the critical value(s). Outcomes lying in this area lead to rejection of a null.

Region of nonrejection or region of acceptance: Outcomes in this area lead to nonrejection of the null.

One-Tailed and Two-Tailed Tests

Recall that the alternative hypothesis may be either a nondirectional alternative and, therefore, negate the null or it may be a directional alternative and specify the direction of the difference.

The critical region of a nondirectional alternative lies in both tails, and the test of the null is a **two-tailed test** of significance. The critical region of a directional alternative is on one side only, and we run a **one-tailed test** of significance. We are interested in one side of the distribution only, because we have specified this in the alternative hypothesis. We may reject the null only if our outcome is in the critical region of that tail.

The critical values given earlier were for a two-tailed test with a nondirectional alternative hypothesis. Recall that ±1.96 separates the middle 95% of the distribution from the extreme 5% with 2.5% in each tail. These are the critical values for a two-tailed test at $\alpha = .05$. However, if the alternative hypothesis is directional, these critical values won't work.

The significance level of .05 for a one-tailed test requires that the extreme 5% lies in *one tail only*, whichever tail is specified in the alternative. When $\alpha = .01$, we need one z value, which cuts off 99% from the extreme 1% in one tail only. These critical values must be smaller than the corresponding ones for a two-tailed test because all the area is in one tail. Looking in Table B.1 in Appendix B, we find that the z values are + 1.64 or − 1.64 ($\alpha = .05$), and +2.33 or −2.33 ($\alpha = .01$).

Figures 9.3 and 9.4 illustrate the critical region for a one-tailed test with alpha levels of .05 and .01, respectively.

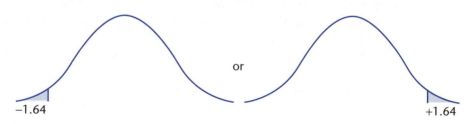

−1.64   or   +1.64

Figure 9.3. Critical values for a one-tailed test at $\alpha = .05$.

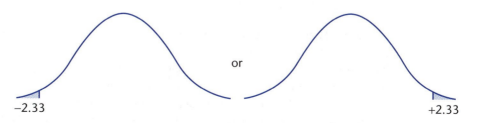

−2.33   or   +2.33

Figure 9.4. Critical values for a one-tailed test at $\alpha = .01$.

In summary,

critical z values	$\alpha = .05$	$\alpha = .01$
Two-tailed test	± 1.96	± 2.58
One-tailed test	$+$ or -1.64	$+$ or -2.33

Note that the critical values are smaller for a one-tailed test of significance. This means that a smaller z value is required to reject the null hypothesis. So why don't researchers always do one-tailed tests if it's easier to reject the null?

Part of the answer to this question is that *if our outcome was extremely deviant, but in the wrong direction, we might not reject the null hypothesis!* For example, had we hypothesized that women are smarter than men, and had we found that our female sample mean of IQ scores was very much lower than the mean for the male sample, we would not be able to say that "women are less smart than men." Our outcome was not in the region of rejection specified by the alternative hypothesis. So, although we suspect something is happening here, we may not make the obvious inference, which may be a good thing anyway!

Generally, in research, we use nondirectional alternatives unless we have absolutely no interest in finding a difference in the other direction, or unless finding a difference in the opposite direction to that specified by the alternative *has no real meaning.* For example, if we were interested in testing Claire Voyant's claim that she has ESP (extrasensory perception), we may run a one-tailed test because a finding that Claire performed significantly *lower* than chance level has no meaning. All we could say was that Claire was a pretty poor guesser—poorer than chance level.

Now that we have covered some of the basics, let's put these skills to work.

One-tailed test: A statistical test where the region of rejection lies in one tail only; the outcome is expected to be in a specific direction

Two-tailed test: A statistical test where the region of rejection lies in both tails

Testing a Hypothesis About a Population Mean

M. Pierre Theroux wants to compare elementary students in Paris with those in the rest of the country on a test of mathematical achievement. Specifically, he wonders if his special new math program has had an effect on the students' mathematical skills. The national norms for a normally distributed standardized math test are $\mu = 85$ and $\sigma = 20$. One hundred randomly selected students attending school in Paris are tested, and the mean of the sample is 89. Let's use our steps to help Pierre answer his question. We will test the null at $\alpha = .05$.

Step 1. State the null and the alternative. Remember that the null must state that the students are *not* different from the national norm. The alternative states that they are different. The mean of the population on the math test is 85, and so

$$H_0: \mu = 85$$
$$H_1: \mu \neq 85$$

Step 2. Draw a random sample from the population and calculate the statistic corresponding to the null hypothesis. We have done this, and the sample statistic is

$$\bar{X} = 89$$

Step 3. Determine the probability of getting an outcome as far, or farther, from the hypothesized value as the one obtained: in this example, a mean math score of 89 or higher. We don't actually have to do this; rather, we simply compare our value with the critical value. To do this, we need to convert our sample mean to a z score so we can compare it with the critical z value. Recall the z formula for a sample mean:

$$z = \frac{\bar{X} - \mu_{\bar{X}}}{\sigma_{\bar{X}}}$$

Step 4. If the probability is low enough, reject the null hypothesis. This is the decision step. We can see that our obtained z value (z_{obt}) is larger numerically than the critical value (z_{crit}) of ±1.96, and we will reject the null hypothesis at $\alpha = .05$. Our sample outcome is **statistically significant**. If we were reporting this in a paper to be published, we might say that the Parisian students ($M = 89$, $SE = 2$) are *significantly different* from the national norm on the test of mathematical achievement, $z = 2$, $p < .05$.

Statistically significant outcome: An outcome leading to rejection of the null hypothesis

What we have really found out is that the students in the Paris sample would not have produced a mean so deviant from the national mean if they were the same as the students in the rest of the country. We conclude that they are not the same. To prove that a sample is from a different population, we must prove that it does not behave in the way a sample from the hypothesized population would, and so it is unlikely to be from the hypothesized population. In this example, we had one sample, and we made an inference about the mean of the population from which the sample was drawn. Often in research, we have two samples, and our interest is in the difference between the means of their respective populations.

SUMMARY OF z TEST FOR A SINGLE MEAN

Hypotheses

H_0: μ = specified value
H_1: $\mu \neq$, $\mu <$, or $\mu >$ specified value

Assumptions

Participants are randomly selected.
Population distribution is normal.
Population standard deviation is known.

Decision Rules

If $z_{obt} \geq z_{crit}$ reject the H_0
If $z_{obt} < z_{crit}$ do not reject H_0

Formula

$$z = \frac{\overline{X} - \mu_{\overline{X}}}{\sigma_{\overline{X}}}$$

CONCEPT REVIEW 9.6

A special education teacher gives her students a normally distributed, standardized achievement test and does a *z* **test** to determine their standing with respect to the national norms. Her obtained *z* value is –1.98. What can she conclude?

z **test:** Parametric test of significance of means, mean differences, or proportions

Answer on page 234.

Testing a Hypothesis
About the Difference Between Population Means

To test whether two samples come from populations with different means, we assume the null hypothesis that the samples come from populations with equal means. Even if we drew two random samples from the same population, we would not expect to get identical sample means because samples vary. The question is "How different would we expect sample means to be when they are drawn from populations with equal means?" Once we know what kinds of mean differences to expect under these conditions, we can compare a specific obtained difference with the expected difference. If our sample means differ more than chance alone would predict, we may conclude that our samples come from populations with unequal means. We would reject the null hypothesis and claim a significant difference between the population means from which our samples were drawn.

To find out what kinds of sample mean differences would occur with repeated sampling from populations with equal means, we need the random sampling distribution of the difference between means so that we can compare our obtained difference with that distribution. Recall that this distribution is normal within the limits of the central limit theorem, so the normal curve is an appropriate model for this test.

If the null hypothesis is true and the population means don't differ, we would expect the mean difference of our two samples to be close to zero. If it is far from zero, we would claim the null is false and accept the alternative hypothesis. Hypothesis testing for the difference follows the same general procedure that we have been using. We must compute a z score for the difference and compare it with the critical values. The critical values for the test for the difference are the same as those we used for the test for a single mean.

Recall the z formula for the difference between means:

$$z = \frac{\left(\bar{X}_1 - \bar{X}_2 \right) - \left(\mu_{\bar{X}_1 - \bar{X}_2} \right)}{\sigma_{\bar{X}_1 - \bar{X}_2}}$$

You may recall from Chapter 8 that the mean of the sampling distribution of the difference is equal to the difference between population means (i.e., zero), so we can leave off the right-hand portion of the numerator in our z formula, and our formula simplifies to

$$z = \frac{\bar{X}_1 - \bar{X}_2}{\sigma_{\bar{X}_1 - \bar{X}_2}}$$

and the formulas for the standard error of the difference are

$$\sigma_{\bar{X}_1 - \bar{X}_2} = \sqrt{\sigma_{\bar{X}_1}^2 + \sigma_{\bar{X}_2}^2}$$

$$\text{or} = \sqrt{\frac{\sigma_1^2}{n_1} + \frac{\sigma_2^2}{n_2}}$$

$$\text{or} = \sqrt{\frac{2\sigma^2}{n}} \quad \text{if } \sigma_1^2 = \sigma_2^2 \text{ and } n_1 = n_2$$

Ready for an example? A school board member is interested in the outbreak of "free" high schools where students are given a much more flexible curriculum and allowed to study independently. She decides to select a random sample of 25 students from a "free" school and another sample of 25 students from a traditional high school. All students are given a standardized achievement test, which is normally distributed and has a standard deviation of 15. The mean score of the "free" school students on this test is 145, and the mean score for the traditional high school students is 148. Let's test the hypothesis that "free" school and traditional school students don't differ in achievement. We will use $\alpha = .01$.

Step 1. State the null and the alternative.

$$H_0: \mu_1 = \mu_2$$

This is always the null for a test of the difference.

$$H_1: \mu_1 \neq \mu_2$$

We will use a nondirectional alternative.

Step 2. Draw two random samples from the populations and calculate the statistic corresponding to the null hypothesis. We have done this, and the sample statistic is

$$\overline{X}_1 - \overline{X}_2 = 145 - 148 = -3$$

Step 3. Convert the sample statistic to a z score and compare it with the critical values. The critical values for a two-tailed test at $\alpha = .01$ are ± 2.58. We first find the standard error of the difference and then compute the z ratio.

$$\sigma_{\overline{X}_1 - \overline{X}_2} = \sqrt{\frac{2\sigma^2}{n}} = \sqrt{\frac{2(15)^2}{25}} = 4.24$$

$$z = \frac{\overline{X}_1 - \overline{X}_2}{\sigma_{\overline{X}_1 - \overline{X}_2}} = \frac{145 - 148}{4.24} = -0.71$$

Step 4. Make a decision. Our obtained z value is not larger numerically than the critical value. Because it does not fall in the critical region, we do not reject the null hypothesis. The probability of getting a sample outcome as far as or farther from the hypothesized population difference than the one we got is greater than .01. We have no statistical evidence that our samples come from populations with different means. Thus, there is no significant difference between "free" school students and students from traditional schools. If we were reporting this in a paper, we might say that the performance of "Free School" students ($M = 145$) did not differ from that of the "Traditional School" students ($M = 146$), $z = -0.71$, *ns*.

SUMMARY OF z TEST FOR INDEPENDENT MEANS

Hypotheses

H_0: $\mu_1 = \mu_2$
H_1: $\mu_1 \neq \mu_2$, $\mu_1 < \mu_2$, or $\mu_1 > \mu_2$

Assumptions

1. Participants are randomly selected and independently assigned to groups.

2. Population distributions are normal.

3. Population standard deviations are known.

Decision Rules

If $z_{obt} \geq z_{crit}$ reject the H_0
If $z_{obt} < z_{crit}$ do not reject H_0

Formula

$$z = \frac{\bar{X}_1 - \bar{X}_2}{\sigma_{\bar{X}_1 - \bar{X}_2}}$$

CONCEPT REVIEW 9.7

A researcher measures the testosterone levels of a sample of men convicted of violent crimes and a sample of men convicted of nonviolent crimes. She uses the z test for the difference because she has normative data regarding testosterone levels in the population. Her obtained z is 0.84. What can she conclude?

Answer on page 234.

Testing a Hypothesis About a Population Proportion

To test a hypothesis about a population proportion, we assume, in the null hypothesis, that the population proportion has some specified value. Thus, we use the same general approach as we used earlier. Let's use our steps to test a hypothesis based on Mendel's Laws (remember Mendel's peas?). Three hundred garden peas were randomly selected. According to Mendel's Laws, 15% of the stock the peas were taken from should exhibit the recessive characteristic of sterility. Of the 300 peas selected, 65 were found to be sterile. Let's test the hypothesis that the peas came from a new hybrid stock. We will use $\alpha = .05$.

Step 1.

$$H_0: P = 0.15$$
$$H_1: P \neq 0.15$$

Step 2. $\quad$ p = 65/300 = 0.22

Step 3.

$$z = \frac{p - P}{\sqrt{PQ/n}} = \frac{0.22 - 0.15}{\sqrt{\dfrac{(0.15)(0.85)}{300}}}$$

$$= \frac{0.07}{0.02} = 3.5$$

Step 4. Our obtained z value falls in the critical region, and we will reject the null hypothesis. We have evidence that the stock from which our sample was selected is significantly different from the stock hypothesized in the null.

Testing the null hypothesis involves determining the probability of a particular sample statistic occurring with respect to the sampling distribution of that statistic. The general approach is to calculate the z value corresponding to the statistic and compare it with the critical values. The general z formula we use is

$$z = \frac{\text{statistic} - \text{hypothesized parameter value}}{\text{standard error}}$$

In summary,

If $z_{obt} \geq z_{crit}$ then $p \leq \alpha$, and we reject the null.

If $z_{obt} < z_{crit}$ then $p > \alpha$, and we fail to reject the null.

SUMMARY OF z TEST FOR A PROPORTION

Hypotheses

H_0: P = specified value
H_1: P $\neq$, <, or > specified value

Assumptions

1. Participants are randomly selected.

2. Sampling distribution of the statistic is normal.

3. Observations are dichotomous.

Decision Rules

If $z_{obt} \geq z_{crit}$ reject the H_0
If $z_{obt} < z_{crit}$ do not reject H_0

Formula

$$z = \frac{p - P}{\sigma_p}$$

CONCEPT REVIEW 9.8

A researcher in women's issues wonders about hiring equity in corporate America. He finds after surveying many U.S. corporations that more men than women are in executive positions. In fact, he finds that 84% of the CEOs in his sample are men. How might he test this for statistical significance?

Answer on page 235.

Consequences of Statistical Decisions

Whenever we make an inference, there is some probability that we will be wrong! A careful researcher is well aware of the consequences of statistical decisions.

Statistical Significance

The null hypothesis states that a given parameter has some value. When the null is rejected, we claim that the parameter is unlikely to have that value. In other words, there is a *difference between the true population value and the hypothesized population value.*

In practice, any sample outcome that occurs by chance alone 5% of the time (in the case of $\alpha = .05$), or 1% of the time (in the case of $\alpha = .01$) when the null is true, will lead us to conclude incorrectly that the null is false!

Type I and Type II Errors

A decision as to whether the null is true or false is never made with certainty. A **Type I error** occurs when the null hypothesis is true but our sample outcome leads us to reject it. In other words, we obtain a rare sample outcome that leads us to make an error. Romeo made a Type I error when he wrongly rejected his hypothesis "Juliet is alive." His error was tragic. The probability of making a Type I error (i.e., the Type I error rate) is set by alpha. For example, if the null is true and our alpha level is .05, we will make a Type I error 5% of the time. If alpha is .01, we will make a Type I error only 1% of the time. Obviously, to reduce the probability of a Type I error, we need to lower the value of alpha (e.g., from .05 to .01).

Unfortunately, it doesn't stop here! A **Type II error** is made when the null is false but we fail to reject it. In other words, a difference between the true parameter value and the hypothesized value exists, but our test did not discover this. Julius Caesar made a Type II error when he wrongly failed to reject the null hypothesis "Brutus is my buddy." Hence, his response, "Et tu, Brute?" His error, too, was tragic. The probability of a Type II error (i.e., the Type II error rate) is related to alpha and is called beta (β). The exact relationship between α and β is not determined empirically, because the nature of the alternative or true "state of affairs" is unknown, but generally the lower the level of β, the higher the level of α. To reduce the probability of making a Type II error, we need to increase the alpha level (e.g., from .01 to .05).

> **Type I error:** Rejecting a null hypothesis that is true
>
> **Type II error:** Failing to reject a null hypothesis that is false

CONCEPT REVIEW 9.9

A researcher has decided to use an alpha level of .25. What seems to be this researcher's priority?

Answer on page 235.

The problem is one of balance. By lowering α, we increase β. In preliminary or pilot research, the general rule is to use a higher level of significance such as $\alpha = .05$. In a well-developed field, with lots of experimental control, we tend to use stricter, lower significance levels such as $\alpha = .01$.

In summary,

As α decreases, p(Type I) decreases and p(Type II) increases.

As α increases, p(Type I) increases and p(Type II) decreases.

A Type II error is made when the null is false but we do not reject it. This is not a desirable state of affairs because the whole reason for testing hypotheses is to reject the null when it is false. Fortunately, there is another way to reduce the probability of making a Type II error.

Increasing the number of observations in the sample(s) reduces β. With larger samples, the standard error (the denominator of the z formula) tends to be reduced. This is because there is less variability in larger samples. When the denominator is smaller, the z value will be larger, and so it is more likely that the obtained z value will be larger than the critical z value. In other words, by increasing sample size, we increase the probability of rejecting a false null, which is what we are trying to do. When a test of significance has a high probability of rejecting false null hypotheses, it is said to be a *powerful test*.

Power

If β is the probability of *not rejecting a false null*, then, clearly, the probability of *rejecting a false null* must be $1 - \beta$. The probability of rejecting a false null hypothesis is called **power**. Power, then, is the capability of our test to reject the null when it should be rejected. Increasing the alpha level (e.g., from .01 to .05) and the sample size(s) increases power.

Figure 9.5 illustrates what can happen when we test hypotheses about population parameters.

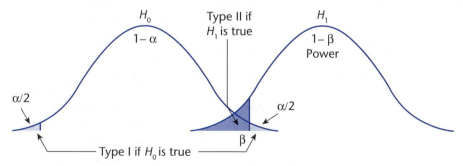

Figure 9.5.   Examples of decision outcomes in hypothesis testing.

The curve on the left represents the random sampling distribution when the null hypothesis is true. The curve on the right represents one of many possible alternative hypotheses. You can see that if the null is true, occasionally we will obtain an outcome in the region of rejection, which will lead us to reject the null and make a Type I error. This will occur α of the time. Most of the time $(1 - \alpha)$, however, we will not reject a true null and will make a correct decision. Look at the curve on the right. Here, we see what could happen if the null is false and the alternative is true. If our sample outcome lies in the "region of nonrejection," we will not reject the null even though it is false. This will occur β of the time, and we will make a Type II error. However, $1 - \beta$ of the time, when the alternative is true, we will get a sample outcome in the critical region, reject the null, and make a correct decision. This is power.

We can summarize this as follows:

	True State of Affairs	
Decision	H_0 **is true**	H_0 **is false**
Reject H_0	Type I error $p = \alpha$	Correct decision $p = 1 - \beta$ (Power)
Do not reject H_0	Correct decision $p = 1 - \alpha$	Type II error $p = \beta$

The concept of power is an important one in hypothesis testing. All researchers want to maximize power when they test hypotheses. We have seen that power is affected by the significance level chosen and by the sample size. Let's look more closely at the relationship between sample size and power. In effect, increasing the number of participants in the sample serves to decrease the size of the denominator of the z ratio. When the denominator of the z ratio decreases, the z value must increase. It is more likely, then, that the obtained z value will be larger than the critical value, resulting in rejection of the null.

The denominator of the z ratio, the standard error, is a measure of the variability of the random sampling distribution. Recall that the random sampling distribution of the mean, for example, is a distribution of sample means drawn from a population. Sample means vary even when the samples are drawn from a single population. This variation, which I have called sampling fluctuation, is sometimes called **error variance**. In much social science research, the main source of error variance is individual differences between people. People differ in ability, motivation, attention, and so on. The more the individuals vary, the more the sample means will vary. Anything that the researcher can do to reduce individual variability will serve to increase the power of his or her statistical procedure. Good research technique is the critical factor here. Many researchers prefer laboratory experiments to field experiments because they allow more control over extraneous variables that might increase variability between the participants. Testing people in a laboratory where distractions can be minimized, for example, will help reduce variability.

We have learned that significance level, sample size, and individual differences all affect the power of the test. The most important factor to consider when we talk about power, however, is the effect of the independent variable, the experimental treatment. Clearly, an independent variable that has a small effect on the dependent variable will be harder to detect than an independent variable that has a large effect. Researchers, of course, hope that the independent variable they have chosen to study will have a large effect on the dependent variable, but they certainly don't know in advance if this is so. If they did, they wouldn't be doing the research to begin with! We will look at this dilemma again as we learn more about tests of significance. For now, just remember that the significance level chosen, the size of the sample, the inherent differences among participants, and the effect of the independent variable all influence the power of any statistical test of significance.

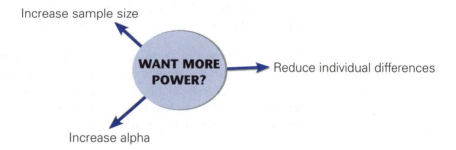

Power (1 − β): The probability that a significance test will lead to rejection of a false null hypothesis

Error variance: Variability between participants that is free of treatment effects

Assumptions Underlying Inference With the Normal Curve

The inferential statistical procedures using the normal curve as a model that I have discussed here assume certain conditions.

1. The sampling distribution of the statistic is normally distributed.

2. The sample observations have been randomly selected.

3. With two samples, observations have been independently assigned.

We know from the central limit theorem that the sampling distribution will be normally distributed if the population is normal or if the sample(s) is large enough.

The assumptions of random sampling and independent assignment are important ones. In research, we are careful not to violate these assumptions. Random sampling and independent assignment of participants to groups allow us to use very powerful statistical techniques. When these assumptions have been badly violated, other procedures are available, but these may not be as powerful as the techniques we have been studying.

Choosing the Appropriate Test of Significance

Knowing which test to use for a given research problem is the special skill of statisticians. In this chapter, we discussed three z tests. Deciding which is appropriate is a matter of determining what kind of data are involved and how many groups participated in the experiment. If the data are proportion, frequency, or percentage data, the z test for a proportion is called for. If the data are measures for which we will compute means, then we choose the z test for a single mean for an experiment with one group of participants and the z test for two independent means for an experiment with two groups of participants. Let's try a few examples.

Example A: Suppose the Board of Education has decided to compare students in two different schools using a standardized test of writing competence for which normative statistics are available. A sample is randomly selected from each school, and the mean test results are compared. Let's go through the steps involved in choosing the appropriate test of significance.

Step 1. Determine the kind of data collected in the experiment.

In this example, the scores of all the students were collected, and the means were computed for each group.

Step 2. Determine the number of groups in the experiment.

There were two samples taken, one from each school, and so the Board should run a z test for two independent means.

Example B: The School of Political Science at Texas State University is concerned that its students are not performing at the same level as the rest of the student body. A random sample of the grade point averages of 200 political science students is collected. A comparison is made between the average performance of this group and the performance of the student body at large. Statistics are available for the entire student population.

Step 1. Determine the kind of data collected in the experiment.

The mean grade point average of the political science students is to be compared with the average of the entire student body.

Step 2. Determine the number of groups in the experiment.

Although, at first glance, you might think there are two groups in this study, there is only one randomly selected group. The entire student body of Texas State is the population, and the 200 political science students comprise the sample. A z test for a single mean should be used to determine whether the political science students differ from the norm (i.e., the whole university).

Example C: A hospital administrator is concerned about the increased length of hospital stays for women who have cesarean sections versus vaginal deliveries. Eighty percent of the women who deliver vaginally stay in hospital 2 days or less. He selects a random sample of 80 women who had cesareans and makes a note of the number of women who stayed 2 days or less. How would he test his hypothesis that cesarean section increases hospital stay?

Step 1. Determine the kind of data collected in the experiment.

The hospital administrator has simply counted the number of women staying 2 days or less. He has frequency data that he will use in a z test for a proportion.

Developing skills in making decisions about the appropriate test of significance to use for a given research problem is an important part of learning statistics. With only three tests to choose from, it is not very difficult to decide which one to use. As you learn about other tests of significance, however, you will find it becomes an increasingly more complicated process.

SUMMARY OF FORMULAS

	Hypothesis Testing	Interval Estimation
The mean	$z = \dfrac{\bar{X} - \mu_{\bar{X}}}{\sigma_{\bar{X}}}$	$\mu = \bar{X} \pm z\sigma_{\bar{X}}$
The difference	$z = \dfrac{\bar{X}_1 - \bar{X}_2}{\sigma_{\bar{X}_1 - \bar{X}_2}}$	$\mu_1 - \mu_2 = \left(\bar{X}_1 - \bar{X}_2\right) \pm z\sigma_{\bar{X}_1 - \bar{X}_2}$
The proportion	$z = \dfrac{p - P}{\sigma_p}$	$P = p \pm z\sigma_p$

(Continued)

(Continued)

	Hypothesis Testing	Interval Estimation
Formulas for the standard error		
The mean	$\sigma_{\bar{X}} = \dfrac{\sigma}{\sqrt{n}}$	
The difference	$\sigma_{\bar{X}_1 - \bar{X}_2} = \sqrt{\dfrac{\sigma_1^2}{n_1} + \dfrac{\sigma_2^2}{n_2}}$	
The proportion	$\sigma_p = \sqrt{\dfrac{PQ}{n}}$	

CONCEPT REVIEW ANSWERS

9.1. $85 \pm 1.96(5) = 85 \pm 9.8 = 94.8$ and 75.2

$C(75.2 \leq \mu \leq 94.8) = 0.95$

9.2. $6 \pm 2.58(2) = 6 \pm 5.16 = 0.84$ and 11.16

$C(0.84 \leq (\mu_1 - \mu_2) \leq 11.16) = 0.99$

9.3. $0.6 \pm 1.96(0.03) = 0.6 \pm 0.06 = 0.54$ and 0.66

$C(0.54 \leq P \leq 0.66) = 0.95$

9.4. A. This is a conceptual hypothesis because neither term is measurable as stated.

B. This is a statistical hypothesis stating a relationship between means.

C. This is a research hypothesis because the terms are measurable.

9.5. A. This statement corresponds to a directional alternative hypothesis.

B. This statement corresponds to a nondirectional alternative.

C. This is most likely a null hypothesis.

9.6. The probability that her class would perform so poorly by chance alone is less than 5%. She has evidence that her students' achievement is below the norm.

9.7. She has no evidence that violent criminals have different testosterone levels than nonviolent criminals.

9.8. Because percentage is easily converted to proportion, he could run a z test for a proportion. His null might be that the proportion of men in executive positions is 0.5. His alternative might be that the proportion is greater than 0.5.

9.9. This researcher is more worried about "false acceptance" than false rejection. He is probably exploring new terrain—so to speak, looking for potential areas for further research. Once his research program is well established, and he has better control over variables, he will use a more stringent alpha level.

EXERCISES

1. The graduating averages of high school students in Boston are normally distributed with a mean of 79 and a standard deviation of 14. A random sample of 25 students from one of the schools has a mean of 85. Use a two-tailed test at $\alpha = .01$ to test the hypothesis that students from this school are at par with the city average.

2. Using the data from Exercise 1, set up the 95% and 99% confidence intervals for the sample of 25 students.

3. Claire Voyant claims to have ESP. An investigator tests her with a deck of 52 cards—half red and half black. Claire guesses whether successive cards, turned over out of her sight, are red or black. On 52 independent trials, she guesses correctly 29 times. Use a one-tailed test at $\alpha = .05$ to find out if Claire is doing significantly better than chance.

4. A seat belt manufacturer, who provides seat belts for Volkswagen cars, claims that his product has a mean breaking strength of 250 kg with a standard deviation of 3.5 kg. You select a random sample of 49 of his seat belts and compute the mean breaking strength of your sample to be 245 kg. Test the manufacturer's claim at $\alpha = .05$.

5. A realtor in Florida claims that more than 75% of retired couples prefer apartment living to single-unit housing. A random sample of 100 couples shows that 81 prefer apartment living. Test the claim of the realtor at the 5% level of significance. (*Hint:* The realtor's claim, that more than 75% prefer apartment living, corresponds to the alternative hypothesis. The null will state that 75% prefer apartment living.)

6. A normal population has a standard deviation of 20. A researcher collects a random sample of 100 scores and computes a mean of 48. Between what two values can the researcher be 99% confident that the population mean lies?

7. A toothpaste company claims that 70% of European dentists use its toothpaste. Of 50 randomly selected dentists across Europe, 30 reported that they use this brand of toothpaste. Test the null hypothesis that the true proportion is 70% at $\alpha = .01$.

8. A total of 173 students attending Kansas State University were polled for an upcoming election and asked to state their preference for one of two candidates. Candidate A received 98 votes and B got 75. Test at $\alpha = .05$ whether Candidate A is ahead of Candidate B. (*Hint:* If A is not ahead of B, then what proportion of the total votes would we expect A to get?).

9. The Friendly Fitness Club recorded the weights of its members before they began their fitness program. They discovered that the weights were normally distributed with a mean of 85 kg and a standard deviation of 9.5. After the fitness program was finished, the director of the club randomly selected 49 participants and recorded their weights. She found that the mean weight for this group was 82 kg. Use a one-tailed test at $\alpha = .05$ to determine if the program was effective in reducing weight. Put your statistical decision in words.

   a. H_0:
      H_1:
   b. Critical z value
   c. Obtained z value
   d. Decision

10. Brad was unprepared for his first exam in forensic psychology. He decided to guess on the multiple-choice exam. Each of the 25 questions had four alternatives, and Brad got 16 correct. Use a one-tailed test at $\alpha = .01$ to see if Brad was a better-than-chance guesser. Provide the following:

    a. H_0:
       H_1:
    b. Critical z value
    c. Obtained z value
    d. Decision
    e. Put your statistical decision in words.

11. A cereal company advertises that "there is a cup of raisins in each box of Raisin Surprise." You decide to investigate. After contacting the cereal company, you find that they claim that the mean is 1.1 cups of raisins with a standard deviation of 0.79. You randomly select 100 boxes of Raisin Surprise and measure the raisin content. You find your sample to have a mean of 0.90 cups of raisins. At $\alpha = .01$, use a two-tailed test to test the claim of the company. Give H_0, H_1, critical z value, obtained z value, and decision, and put your statistical decision in words.

12. Set up the 99% confidence interval for the difference with the following data. Data are as follows:

$$\bar{X}_1 = 115$$
$$\bar{X}_2 = 118$$
$$\sigma_{\bar{X}_1 - \bar{X}_2} = 2$$

CHAPTER 10

Inference With the *t* Distribution

LEARNING OBJECTIVES

After reading this chapter, you should be able to do the following:

1. Define the terms unbiased estimate of a parameter and degrees of freedom.
2. Describe the difference between the *t* distribution and the normal distribution.
3. Set up the 95% and 99% confidence intervals for a population mean and the difference between population means for a given set of data.
4. Run a *t* test for a single mean, the difference between independent means, and the difference between dependent means for a given set of data.
5. Describe the difference between an independent-groups design and a dependent-groups design.
6. Describe the difference between a matched-groups design and a within-participants design.
7. Describe how effect size, sample size, and power are related.
8. Calculate Cohen's *d* for estimating effect size.
9. Determine the appropriate test of significance for a given research problem.

Internet marketers of acai berry weight loss pills and colon cleansers will pay $1.5 million to settle charges of deceptive advertising and unfair billing, the Federal Trade Commission announced today.

The Phoenix-based Central Coast Nutraceuticals marketed acai berry supplements, colon cleansers, and other products using allegedly fraudulent free trial offers and phony endorsements from Oprah Winfrey and Rachael Ray. The company will pay $1.5 million as part of a settlement with the Federal Trade Commission, and the money will be made available for consumer refunds.

Kyle Hill, *Science-Based Life*, January 2012

We all see claims for weight loss, antiaging, antismoking, and dozens of other products. How many of these products have actually been scientifically tested? Probably not many. In this chapter, we will study procedures that could be used to determine if acai berries have any effect on weight loss.

To use the normal curve for estimating the value of population parameters and testing hypotheses about population parameters, a standard score called a **z score** must be determined. To test hypotheses about the value of μ, for example, we used the following to determine z:

$$z = \frac{\bar{X} - \mu_{\bar{X}}}{\sigma_{\bar{X}}}$$

This formula follows the general format for testing the null hypothesis:

$$\text{Standard score} = \frac{\text{value of statistic} - \text{hypothesized value of the parameter}}{\text{standard deviation of the distribution of the statistic}}$$

To estimate the value of μ from sample data, we used the following formula:

$$\mu = \bar{X} \pm z\sigma_{\bar{X}}$$

The general formula, then, for estimating the location of parameter values from samples is as follows:

$$\text{Estimate of parameter} = \text{statistic} \pm (\text{standard score}) \times$$
$$(\text{standard deviation of the distribution of the statistic})$$

z score: The deviation of a particular value from the mean of its distribution expressed in relationship to the standard deviation of that distribution

Let's look more closely at the two formulas. $\bar{X}$, the sample mean, is determined from the data that we collect. μ is the hypothesized value of the population mean or, in the case of confidence interval estimation, it is unknown. $\sigma_{\bar{X}}$ is the standard deviation of the sampling distribution of means calculated for all possible samples drawn at random with replacement from the population of raw scores. We called this the *standard error*. The standard error for any given example is calculated by dividing σ, the standard deviation of the raw score population by the square root of the sample size, n.

Here is the problem. *Because we don't know enough about the original population to know its mean, how likely are we to know its standard deviation?* Practically speaking, if we don't know μ, we probably don't know σ either!

To determine σ, we would have to look at all the raw scores in the population. If we could, we would also know the mean of that population and wouldn't need to make inferences about what it might be. Instead, we would use descriptive techniques, not inferential techniques.

When we do not know the value of σ, we cannot calculate the standard error or use z to estimate where μ may lie or to test hypotheses about the value of μ.

In most research, we do not know the value of σ, and the normal curve *cannot* be used as our model of expected outcomes for making inferences about population parameters. And, as you have probably figured out already, we use a different curve or distribution as our model of expected outcomes when we do not know the value of σ.

The *t* Distribution and Unbiased Estimates

You will recall that the normal curve is the sampling distribution of the *z* statistic. Similarly, the *t* distribution is the sampling distribution of the *t* statistic. We use the *t* distribution as a model when we do not know the value of the population standard deviation and must estimate its value from our sample data. We use lowercase *s* to indicate that we are estimating the value of the population standard deviation.

> ***t* score:** The deviation of a particular value from the mean of its distribution expressed in relationship to an unbiased estimate of the standard deviation of that distribution

The estimate of the population standard deviation used in the *t* ratio is the square root of the **unbiased estimate** of the population variance. An unbiased estimate of a parameter is one that, *on average*, will equal exactly the parameter being estimated. To determine whether an estimate is unbiased, we follow these steps:

Step 1. Draw all possible samples of some fixed size, with replacement, from the population.

Step 2. Calculate a statistic for each sample.

Step 3. Compute the mean of the statistics.

If this mean has the same value as the parameter to which it corresponds, then the estimate is unbiased. Otherwise, it is a biased estimate.

Earlier, we saw that the mean of the sampling distribution of means ($\mu_{\bar{X}}$) is exactly equal to the mean of the population from which the samples were drawn (μ). In other words, the mean of all the sample means ($\bar{X}$s) exactly equals the population mean. $\overline{X}$, then, is an *unbiased estimate* of μ because, on average, it exactly equals the parameter it is estimating, that is, μ.

For a moment, let's talk about the variance of a sample. You will remember, I hope, that the formula for calculating the variance of a population is

$$\sigma^2 = \frac{SS}{N} = \frac{\Sigma(X - \mu)^2}{N}$$

Using our sample notation, we can adjust this formula to compute the variance of a sample. We'll call this S^2.

$$S^2 = \frac{SS}{n} = \frac{\Sigma(X - \overline{X})^2}{n}$$

Unbiased estimate: An estimate of a parameter that, on average, exactly equals the value of the parameter

Sample Variance

Now, if we used this s^2 formula to calculate the variance for all possible samples drawn with replacement from some population, and computed the mean of all these sample variances, we would find that this mean value is consistently *smaller* than σ^2. Although the mean of all the sample means *will exactly equal* the population mean, the mean of all the sample variances *will not equal* the population variance. For this reason, we say that sample variance is a *biased estimate* of σ^2. It is biased because it always underestimates σ^2. Because t requires an unbiased estimate in its calculation, we cannot use the sample variance as that estimate.

Fortunately, we have an arithmetic adjustment to correct this problem. Rather than calculating sample variance by the formula above, we calculate s^2, the unbiased estimate of σ^2.

$$s^2 = \frac{SS}{n-1} = \frac{\Sigma(X - \overline{X})^2}{n-1}$$

Unbiased Estimate of Population Variance

As you can see, the denominator of the s^2 formula is $n-1$ instead of n. Because we are dividing the same numerator we used in the S^2 formula by a slightly smaller denominator, we end up with a slightly larger value.

Now, if we randomly select all possible samples from a population, calculate s^2 for each sample, and compute the mean of all the s^2s, we would have a value that *exactly* equals σ^2. This s^2 formula, then, produces an unbiased estimate of σ^2 because, on average, it exactly equals σ^2. If this strikes you as a bit mysterious, it is indeed. This is one of a few magical things in statistics that I will ask you to accept on faith☺

Recall that the *t* ratio is the deviation of a value from the mean of its distribution, expressed in relationship to an estimate of the standard deviation of that distribution. This estimate is always based on the unbiased estimate of the population variance. Some unbiased estimates used in inference with the *t* distribution are as follows:

Unbiased Estimate of Parameter	Parameter Being Estimated
$\overline{X}$	μ
s	σ
s^2	σ^2
$s_{\overline{X}}$	$\sigma_{\overline{X}}$
$s_{\overline{X}_1 - \overline{X}_2}$	$\sigma_{\overline{X}_1 - \overline{X}_2}$

Relationship Between the Normal and the *t* Distribution

Both the normal and the *t* distribution have the following characteristics:

1. They are symmetrical.
2. They are unimodal.
3. They have means of zero.

Recall that the *z* formula for a sample mean is

$$z = \frac{\overline{X} - \mu_{\overline{X}}}{\sigma_{\overline{X}}}$$

Substituting in our unbiased estimate of the standard error in the denominator, you can see that the *t* formula for a sample mean must be

$$t = \frac{\overline{X} - \mu_{\overline{X}}}{s_{\overline{X}}}$$

t Ratio for a Sample Mean

If you drew all possible samples of some fixed size from a population, calculated z scores and t scores for each sample mean, and placed the z scores and t scores in separate frequency distributions, the zs would follow a normal distribution and the ts would follow a t distribution.

The difference between the normal and the t distribution is mainly in the tails. The t distribution is leptokurtic (i.e., more peaked) and tends to have more area in the tails than does the normal distribution.

Are you wondering why the two distributions are different? Well, let's think about how these two distributions are formed.

The z distribution is normal in shape because μ and σ are fixed (and therefore don't affect the shape) and the sample means are normally distributed or close to it (remember the central limit theorem). Because μ and σ do not change, the distribution of z values follows the shape of the distribution of the sample means: They are the only values that vary. We know that the distribution of sample means is close to normal, regardless of the shape of the original population, when sample size is reasonably large.

The t distribution, on the other hand, departs from normality in a regular fashion even though the sample means are normally distributed. μ is still fixed, but the value of the standard error used in the denominator of the t ratio is determined from the sample data and differs from sample to sample. It is not fixed but is a variable. The variability of the *standard error* is directly affected by sample size—smaller samples produce greater variability.

So the z distribution is normal in shape because the means are normally distributed, within the limits of the central limit theorem, and μ and σ are fixed. Because σ is fixed, the standard error is also fixed. With the t distribution, however, the standard error (actually, the unbiased estimate of it) is not fixed but varies, and so the distribution is not normal in shape.

The exact shape of the t distribution depends on **degrees of freedom (*df*)**. Recall that the normal curve is a family of curves that has been standardized to the standard normal curve with z scores on the abscissa and relative frequency on the ordinate.

The t distribution is also a family of curves, the shape of each depending on degrees of freedom. Unless the number of degrees of freedom is infinitely large, the shape of the t distribution is *not* normal. Now, with lots and lots of degrees of freedom, the t distribution does look close to normal, but with very few degrees of freedom, the t distribution is leptokurtic with respect to the normal curve. You can see from the examples in Figure 10.1 that the t distribution has more area in the tails than the normal distribution has.

Degrees of freedom are related, but not identical, to sample size. When degrees of freedom are infinitely large, the shape of the t distribution is normal and the value of the t ratio equals exactly the value of the z ratio. In

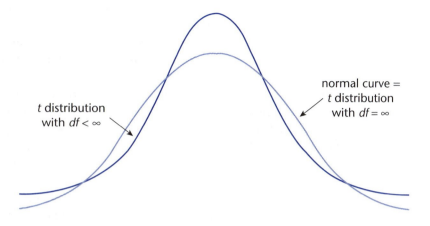

Figure 10.1.   Comparing the normal and a *t* distribution.

such cases, there is no *mathematical* distinction between calculating *z* and calculating *t*.

When degrees of freedom are less than infinity, the *t* distribution has more area in the tails than does the normal distribution, and the value of the *t* ratio will not equal the value of the *z* ratio. When testing the null hypothesis, somewhat larger *t* values are required to reject the null hypothesis whenever degrees of freedom are less than infinity. The critical values of *t* are larger than the critical values of *z* and depend on degrees of freedom. You are probably wondering what the heck are degrees of freedom? Well, read on.

> **Degrees of freedom (*df*):** The number of values free to vary once certain constraints have been placed on data; important in several statistical procedures

Degrees of Freedom When Estimating Parameters

Suppose your statistics instructor commented on your performance on a test. The feedback included the following information:

1. You scored 150 points on your statistics exam.
2. You missed 50 points.
3. A perfect score on the test was 200.

You now have three pieces of information:

1. Your score
2. The number of points you missed
3. The total number of points possible

Actually, you could have determined the third piece of information from the first two. Knowing that you scored 150 and missed 50 points is all you need to know to figure out that the total number of points on the test was 200. In fact, knowing any two of the three values allows you to determine the remaining one. For example, if you heard that you lost 50 points on the test and there were 200 points available, you could easily determine that you got 150 points.

For this example, statisticians would say that two pieces of information fixed the third. They also say that two of the values are independent and one is dependent. Statisticians tend to state the same thing in as many ways as possible; many statisticians will also say that in our example, two values are free to vary and one is fixed.

Degrees of freedom, then, in any particular situation, are determined by the number of values free to vary. This concept is important when we estimate parameter values from sample data. When we estimate σ with our s formula, which we must do to determine the t ratio for a single mean, we use the sample mean ($\bar{X}$) as an estimate of μ, and by doing so, we *use up* one degree of freedom. In other words, calculating $\bar{X}$ and using it in our computation of s fixes one value in that it is no longer free to vary.

FYI

This above point is clear if we consider the following distribution of scores. The first column provides the original raw scores, and the second column shows the deviation of each score from the mean of the distribution.

X	$(X - \bar{X})$
15	2
14	1
13	0
12	−1
11	−2
$\bar{X} = 13$	$\Sigma (X - \bar{X}) = 0$

I hope you remember that the sum of the positive deviations must exactly equal the sum of the negative deviations for deviations taken around the mean of any distribution. The mean of this X distribution is 13, and the sum of the negative deviations equals the sum of the positive deviations around 13. How many score values could we change without changing the value of the mean?

Let's change the first value from 15 to 20, the second from 14 to 17, the third from 13 to 10, and the fourth from 12 to 8. Before we go further, let's determine the deviation scores. Remember, we cannot change the value of the mean.

X	(X – X̄)
20	7
17	4
10	–3
8	–5
?	?
X̄ = 13	Σ (X – X̄) = 0

Keeping the mean at 13, then, we have a total of 11 positive deviations [i.e., (20 – 13) + (17 – 13) = 11] and so far 8 negative deviations [i.e., (10 – 13) + (8 – 13) = –8]. Because the sum of the negative deviations must equal the sum of the positive deviations around any mean, our fifth score value must be 3 deviations below the mean. Our fifth value, then, can only be a 10. No other value will do! We have only four degrees of freedom. Once four values are changed, the fifth value is fixed.

When we estimate the population standard deviation using the sample mean, we constrain the data and use up a degree of freedom. Degrees of freedom (*df*) are determined by the number of constraints placed on our data by our calculations. When computing a *t* for the mean of a single sample, we estimate the population standard deviation from our sample data; in doing so, we use up one degree of freedom. Degrees of freedom in this case are equal to $n - 1$, the number of values free to vary.

When computing a *t* score for the difference between means, we estimate population standard deviation using the means of both samples; in doing so, we use up a degree of freedom for each mean used. Degrees of freedom in this case are equal to $(n_1 - 1) + (n_2 - 1)$.

Note: Degrees of freedom is a topic that most students find quite confusing and mysterious. I have tried to give you a basic idea of what this is all about, but do not worry if you are still a bit mystified. A good friend who has a Ph.D. in educational psychology, with several courses in statistics under her belt, told me that the first inkling she had about what degrees of freedom really means was when she edited the first edition of this textbook. Teaching you the meaning of this concept in any more detail is not suitable or even possible in this book. Interested students should consult a high-level statistics textbook for more information about degrees of freedom when estimating parameters.

CONCEPT REVIEW 10.1

How many degrees of freedom are associated with the following?

A. $n = 46$

B. $n_1 = 22$ $n_2 = 30$

Answer on page 276.

When to Use the *t* Distribution

Just as the normal curve may be used as a model of expected outcomes when making inferences or testing hypotheses about the value of population parameters under certain conditions, so can the *t* distribution be used as a model for such procedures. The choice depends on whether or not the population standard deviation is known. If it is, the normal curve may be the appropriate model. If the population standard deviation must be estimated, then *t* may be the appropriate distribution. See Figure 10.2.

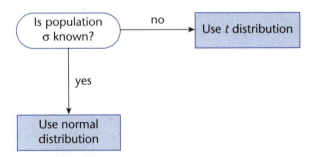

Figure 10.2. Deciding between the normal and the *t* distribution.

Setting Up Confidence Intervals Using the *t* Distribution

The *t* distribution is the sampling distribution of the *t* statistic. Like *z*, *t* is calculated for all possible samples of some fixed size drawn from a population. Setting up confidence intervals with the *t* distribution is essentially the same as it was using the normal curve and *z*.

Setting Up the Confidence Interval for a Population Mean

You will recall that the normal curve formula for setting up a confidence interval to locate the population mean is

$$\mu = \bar{X} \pm z_{crit}\sigma_{\bar{X}}$$

The formula for setting up a confidence interval to locate the population mean using the *t* distribution is

$$\mu = \bar{X} \pm t_{crit}s_{\bar{X}}$$

Rather than using the standard error, we must use an estimate of the standard error. The critical value of *t* changes with the significance level chosen (as does the critical value of *z*) and with the degrees of freedom (unlike with *z*). So, unless you are going to use the same sample size whenever you do research, you will need to look up the critical value of *t* for each confidence interval you set up. Table B.2 in Appendix B lists critical values of *t* depending on degrees of freedom and alpha level.

Ready for an example? The chairperson of the Ski Jump Preparation Committee is in the process of making decisions about the facilities for the next Olympics. She is not sure how long the landing platform should be. She decides to set up a 95% confidence interval for the mean length required for landing by world-class ski jumpers. (Don't ask me why she didn't confer with the chairperson of the previous Ski Jump Preparation Committee!) She selects a random sample of 25 world-class ski jumpers and measures the distance required by each for landing. Then, she calculates the mean and the estimate of the population standard deviation using her sample data. Here are her calculations:

$$\text{Mean distance: } \bar{X} = 125 \quad n = 25 \qquad df = n - 1 = 24$$
$$s = 15 \quad t_{.05} = \pm 2.064$$

The appropriate formula to use is

$$\mu = \bar{X} \pm t_{crit}s_{\bar{X}}$$

Notice that she has calculated the estimate of the population *standard deviation* (i.e., *s*). But our formula requires that we use the estimate of the *standard error* ($s_{\bar{X}}$). You may recall that in Chapter 9, the standard error was computed by dividing the population standard deviation by the square root of the sample size. We do the same here to obtain the estimate of the standard error. We compute $s_{\bar{X}}$ by dividing s by the square root of n.

$$s_{\bar{X}} = \frac{s}{\sqrt{n}}$$

$$= \frac{15}{\sqrt{25}}$$

$$= 3$$

Now, we can proceed to set up the 95% CI for μ:

$$\mu = 125 \pm (2.064)\ (3)$$

Limits are 118.81 and 131.19

Using the "official" format we present the confidence interval limits as follows:

$$C(118.81 \leq \mu \leq 131.19) = .95$$

The Chairperson of the Ski Jump Preparation Committee can claim, in the next meeting, that her confidence that the average world-class ski jumper clears distances of 118.81 to 131.19 meters is 95%.

Now, in the example above, it was simple to compute the estimate of the population standard error because we were given the estimate of the population standard deviation and we just divided it by the square root of n. Here are some other formulas we may need.

$$s_{\bar{X}} = \sqrt{\frac{s^2}{n}} \quad \text{where } s^2 = \frac{SS}{n-1}$$

or

$$s_{\bar{X}} = \sqrt{\frac{SS}{n(n-1)}}$$

CONCEPT REVIEW 10.2

Set up the 99% CI for the following:

$\bar{X} = 100$

$n = 41$

$s_{\bar{X}} = 1.2$

Answer on page 276.

Setting Up the Confidence Interval for the Difference Between Independent Population Means

Setting up a confidence interval for the difference between population means follows the same general pattern. The appropriate formula is

$$\mu_1 - \mu_2 = \left(\bar{X}_1 - \bar{X}_2\right) \pm t_{crit}\left(s_{\bar{X}_1 - \bar{X}_2}\right)$$

The trickiest part of this procedure is determining the estimate of the standard error of the difference. Here are some formulas you will need.

$$s_{\bar{X}_1 - \bar{X}_2} = \sqrt{s_{\bar{X}_1}^2 + s_{\bar{X}_2}^2} = \sqrt{\frac{s_1^2}{n_1} + \frac{s_2^2}{n_2}}$$

This is all very well if we have already calculated the unbiased estimates of the variance for each sample. If we have not, however, the following computational formula is appropriate to estimate of the standard error of the difference when $n_1 \neq n_2$:

$$s_{\bar{X}_1 - \bar{X}_2} = \sqrt{\frac{SS_1 + SS_2}{n_1 + n_2 - 2}\left(\frac{1}{n_1} + \frac{1}{n_2}\right)} \quad \text{where } SS = \sum X^2 - \frac{\left(\sum X\right)^2}{n}$$

This formula is appropriate when the two samples are not the same size. The formula to estimate the standard error of the difference when $n_1 = n_2$ simplifies somewhat to

$$s_{\bar{X}_1 - \bar{X}_2} = \sqrt{\frac{SS_1 + SS_2}{n(n-1)}}$$

A researcher wonders what the difference might be between artists and mathematicians on a test of creativity. He randomly selected a sample of 18 artists and 20 mathematicians from a list of professors working at a large university. After everyone had completed the creativity test, the researcher organized the scores and computed the SS for each group. Here are those data.

X_1 (Artists)	X_1^2	X_2 (Mathematicians)	X_2^2
16	256	15	225
13	169	15	225
14	196	14	196
12	144	14	196
18	324	15	225
10	100	16	256
18	324	16	256
18	324	17	289
15	225	13	169
16	256	12	144
14	196	14	196
13	169	15	225
17	289	13	169
17	289	13	169
15	225	15	225
15	225	17	289
18	324	12	144
17	289	12	144
		13	169
		14	196
Sum 276	4324	285	4107

$$SS_1 = \sum X_1^2 - \frac{\left(\sum X_1\right)^2}{n_1}$$

$$= 4324 - \frac{(276)^2}{18}$$

$$= 4324 - 4232 = 92$$

$$SS_2 = \sum X_2^2 - \frac{\left(\sum X_2\right)^2}{n_2}$$

$$= 4107 - \frac{285^2}{20}$$

$$= 4107 - 4061.25$$

$$= 45.75$$

To compute the estimate of the standard error of the difference, he used the following formula because the sample sizes were not the same.

$$s_{\bar{X}_1 - \bar{X}_2} = \sqrt{\frac{SS_1 + SS_2}{n_1 + n_2 - 2}\left(\frac{1}{n_1} + \frac{1}{n_2}\right)}$$

$$= \sqrt{\frac{92 + 45.75}{36}\left(\frac{1}{18} + \frac{1}{20}\right)}$$

$$= 0.635$$

Now the 99% CI can be determined.

$$\bar{X}_1 = 15.33$$

$$\bar{X}_2 = 14.25$$

$$t_{.01} = \pm 2.72$$

$$\mu_1 - \mu_2 = \left(\bar{X}_1 - \bar{X}_2\right) \pm 2.72(0.635)$$

$$= 1.08 \pm 1.73 = 2.81 \text{ and } -0.645$$

The researcher may say, with 99% CI, that the mean difference between artists and mathematicians on his test of creativity is somewhere within those limits. To present these data formally,

$$C(-0.645 \leq (\mu_1 - \mu_2) \leq 2.81) = .99$$

Hypothesis Testing With the *t* Distribution

Testing hypotheses about the value of a population parameter(s) with the *t* distribution follows the same logic and procedure as it does with the normal curve. The general form of the *t* ratio is similar to the general form of the *z* ratio.

$$t = \frac{\text{value of statistic} - \text{hypothesized value of parameter}}{\text{estimate of standard deviation of distribution of the statistic}}$$

If $\bar{X}$ is the statistic in question, then the t ratio for a single mean is

$$t = \frac{\bar{X} - \mu_{\bar{X}}}{s_{\bar{X}}}$$

If $\bar{X}_1 - \bar{X}_2$ is the statistic in question, then

$$t = \frac{\left(\bar{X}_1 - \bar{X}_2\right) - \left(\mu_{\bar{X}_1 - \bar{X}_2}\right)}{s_{\bar{X}_1 - \bar{X}_2}}$$

but as in the z ratio for the difference, the hypothesized mean of the sampling distribution of the difference is zero, and so we drop the right side of the equation and the t ratio for the difference between means is

$$t = \frac{\bar{X}_1 - \bar{X}_2}{s_{\bar{X}_1 - \bar{X}_2}}$$

Let's go ahead and test some hypotheses using the t distribution.

Testing Hypotheses About Population Means

A nationwide survey conducted in the 1960s reported that young people listened to rock music an average of 2 hours per day. Let's hypothesize that the youth of today rock longer than the youth of yesterday. We will randomly select a sample of twenty-five 16-year-olds and record the numbers of hours per day each spends listening to rock music over a period of 6 months. Let's use a one-tailed test to test our hypothesis at $\alpha = .01$.

$$H_0: \mu = 2$$

$$H_1: \mu > 2$$

$$df = 25 - 1 = 24$$

$$t_{.01} = +2.492$$

Here are our data.

Number of Hours (*X*)	*X²*
4.5	20.25
3.8	14.44
0.9	0.81
3.5	12.25
4.2	17.64
3.8	14.44
4.2	17.64
3.0	9
3.0	9
4.0	16
3.5	12.25
3.9	15.21
2.6	6.76
3.8	14.44
3.5	12.25
3.4	11.56
3.2	10.24
2.9	8.41
3.0	9
3.0	9
4.0	16
2.5	6.25
3.8	14.44
2.8	7.84
4.6	21.16
$\Sigma X = 85.4$	$\Sigma X^2 = 306.3$

We will need to compute the sample mean and the sum of squares. Then, we compute the standard error and finally our *t* statistic.

To compute the standard error of the mean, we use the computational formula given below.

$$s_{\bar{X}} = \sqrt{\frac{SS}{n(n-1)}} = \sqrt{\frac{\sum X^2 - (\sum X)^2 / n}{n(n-1)}}$$

Let's finish our calculations.

$$\Sigma X = 85.4$$

$$(\Sigma X)^2 = 7293.16$$

$$SS = \Sigma X^2 - \frac{(\Sigma X)^2}{n}$$
$$= \frac{306.3 - 7293.16}{25} = 14.55$$

$$s_{\bar{X}} = \sqrt{\frac{SS}{n(n-1)}} = \sqrt{\frac{14.55}{25(24)}} = 0.156$$

$$\bar{X} = \frac{\Sigma X}{n} = \frac{85.4}{25} = 3.42$$

And now, we can calculate our t statistic.

$$t = \frac{\bar{X} - \mu}{s_{\bar{X}}} = \frac{3.42 - 2.0}{0.156} = 9.09$$

Because our obtained t value of 9.09 is larger than the critical value for a one-tailed test with 24 df, we reject the null hypothesis. The probability is low (<.01) that, by chance alone, our sample mean of 3.2 hours is that much larger than the hypothesized mean of 2. Because the probability that we would get this outcome by chance alone is low, we reject the null and conclude that the youth today "rock longer than the youth of yesterday." Well, being professionals of course, we would say that youth today spend significantly more time listening to music than the youth of the 1960s.

The APA (American Psychological Association) has specified how we should report statistics in research papers submitted for publication in journals. For example, sample means are notated by the letter M in italics. Standard deviations are notated by SD and standard errors by SE. The rules are very specific, and you should consult the APA publication manual for details.

If we were reporting our teen rocker data in a research paper that we hoped to publish, we might report our result in the following way:

Teens today spend significantly more hours per day ($M = 3.42$, $SE = 0.156$) listening to music than they used to, $t(24) = 9.09$, $p < .01$.

You can see that this method of reporting is very efficient. In one sentence, we have provided the mean and standard error for our sample and reported that we found a significant difference between our hypothesized mean of 2 and our sample outcome, including df, t value, and probability level.

SUMMARY OF *t* TEST FOR A SINGLE MEAN

Hypotheses

H_0: μ = specified value
H_1: $\mu \neq, <,$ or $>$ specified value

Assumptions

1. Participants are randomly selected.
2. Population distribution is normal.

Decision Rules

$df = n - 1$

If $t_{obt} \geq t_{crit}$ reject the H_0

If $t_{obt} < t_{crit}$ do not reject H_0

Formula

$$t = \frac{\overline{X} - \mu}{s_{\overline{X}}}$$

CONCEPT REVIEW 10.3

A family therapist believes that families who come for therapy have poorer communication skills than other families. He has read in a reputable journal about a test of communication skills that has been standardized on a large number of families. The mean on this test is available to the therapist. What statistical procedure might he use?

Answer on page 276.

Testing a Hypothesis
About the Difference Between Independent Population Means

A *t* **test** for the difference between two independent means follows the same general logic and procedure as the normal curve test. Let's consider the following example.

An education professor is interested in knowing whether there is a difference in final exam performance between students who take their introductory education psychology course under a personalized system of instruction (PSI) and those who study under the more conventional, lecture-discussion format (L). He randomly selects a sample of 30 students and randomly assigns 15 of them to each of two groups. One group studies under PSI conditions and the other under L conditions. Unfortunately, two of the PSI students dropped out of school before they wrote the final exam. Nevertheless, he goes ahead and tests his hypothesis.

$$H_0: \mu_1 - \mu_2 = 0$$

$$H_1: \mu_1 - \mu_2 \neq 0$$

Here are the final exam scores in percentage and the values needed to calculate the t ratio. The professor needs both means and the standard error of the difference.

t **test:** Parametric test of significance of means or mean differences

	$X_1(PSI)$	X_1^2	$X_2(L)$	X_2^2
	78	6 084	64	4 096
	75	5 625	69	4 761
	72	5 184	68	4 624
	79	6 241	62	3 844
	82	6 724	75	5 625
	65	4 225	68	4 624
	76	5 776	60	3 600
	69	4 761	60	3 600
	72	5 184	63	3 969
	75	5 625	66	4 356
	79	6 241	70	4 900
	86	7 396	65	4 225
	65	4 225	64	4 096
	59	3 481		
	75	5 625		
Sum	1107	82 397	854	56 320
Mean	73.8		65.69	

To compute the standard error of the difference, he first finds the *SS* for each group.

$$SS_1 = \sum X_1^2 - \frac{\left(\sum X_1\right)^2}{n_1}$$

$$= 82397 - \frac{1107^2}{15}$$

$$= 700.4$$

$$SS_2 = 56320 - \frac{854^2}{13}$$

$$= 218.77$$

$$s_{\bar{X}_1 - \bar{X}_2} = \sqrt{\frac{SS_1 + SS_2}{n_1 + n_2 - 2}\left(\frac{1}{n_1} + \frac{1}{n_2}\right)}$$

$$= \sqrt{\frac{700.4 + 218.77}{26}\left(\frac{1}{15} + \frac{1}{13}\right)}$$

$$= 2.25$$

$$t = \frac{\bar{X}_1 - \bar{X}_2}{s_{\bar{X}_1 - \bar{X}_2}} = \frac{73.8 - 65.69}{2.25} = 3.60$$

$$df = n_1 + n_2 - 2 = 26$$

$$t_{.05} = \pm 2.056$$

Because the obtained value of *t* is numerically larger than the critical value, he may reject the null hypothesis. If he were reporting this in a research paper, he would write something like the following. There was a significant difference in performance under PSI ($M = 73.8$, $SD = 6.83$) versus L conditions ($M = 65.69$, $SD = 4.10$), $t(26) = 3.60$, $p < .05$.

If we input these data to Excel and ask for a *t* test, we get the following output:

t Test: Two-Sample Assuming Equal Variances		
	PSI	**L**
Mean	73.8	65.69230769
Variance	50.02857143	18.23076923
Observations	15	13
Pooled variance	35.35266272	

(Continued)

(Continued)

	PSI	L
Hypothesized mean difference	0	
df	26	
t stat	3.598524664	
P(T ≤ t) one-tail	0.000659764	
t critical one-tail	1.705617901	
P(T ≤ t) two-tail	0.001319528	
t critical two-tail	2.055529418	

In Excel, the obtained value of t is called t stat.

SUMMARY OF t TEST FOR INDEPENDENT MEANS

Hypotheses

H_0: $\mu_1 = \mu_2$
H_1: $\mu_1 \neq \mu_2$, $\mu_1 < \mu_2$, or $\mu_1 > \mu_2$

Assumptions

1. Participants are randomly selected and independently assigned to groups.
2. Population variances are equal.
3. Population distributions are normal.

Decision Rules

$df = n_1 + n_2 - 2$
If $t_{obt} \geq t_{crit}$ reject H_0
If $t_{obt} > t_{crit}$ do not reject H_0

Formula

$$t = \frac{\overline{X}_1 - \overline{X}_2}{s_{\overline{X}_1} - s_{\overline{X}_2}}$$

CONCEPT REVIEW 10.4

The mean yearly income for a random sample of 50 families living on the East Coast is $26 000. A random sample of 60 families living in the Midwest yields a mean income of $28 000. From the sample data, the estimate of the standard error of the difference is determined to be 1245.

Is there a difference in annual income between East Coasters and Midwesterners? Use the .05 level of significance.

Answer on page 276.

Assumptions Underlying Inference With the *t* Distribution

The use of the *t* distribution in making inferences about population parameters assumes certain conditions:

1. The observations were randomly selected from the population(s) of interest.
2. The estimate of the standard error is based on an unbiased estimate of the population variance.
3. The sampling distribution of the statistic (i.e., the sample mean or difference between means) must be normally distributed. This is true (according to the central limit theorem) as long as either the population is normal or the sample size(s) is large enough.

A further assumption with *t* tests for the difference between means is that the populations from which the two samples were collected have equal variability. This is called the assumption of **homogeneity of variance**. We want to know if we are sampling from distributions with different means, not different variances. It will probably occur to you that, in real-life research, it is unlikely that we will know whether the populations are equally variable or not. Not to worry! The *t* test is quite robust, and so violations of this assumption are not a problem as long as our sample size(s) is large enough and in the case of a test for the difference between means, *approximately equal*.

Homogeneity of variance: Equal variances in populations

FYI

The *t* test I discuss in this chapter (Student's *t* test) uses a pooled variance estimate in the denominator of the *t* ratio. This test has an assumption of equal variances in the populations from which the samples were selected. If that assumption has not been met, then another test (Welch's *t*) may be more appropriate. Students should consult an higher-level statistics text for more information on this approach.

For the *t* test for the difference between two independent means, we have another very important assumption. It is assumed that the observations have not only been randomly selected but that they have been *assigned randomly* to the two samples. In other words, the samples are independently formed. The observations in the first sample must not be correlated or dependent on observations in the second sample.

Sometimes we don't have independent samples. Perhaps we have used the same participants in both our groups or we may have used matched participants. For these situations, we have another procedure for making inferences with the *t* distribution. When two samples are dependent or correlated, we use the *t* test for dependent samples.

Dependent or Correlated Samples

Probably the major grievance of researchers in the social sciences is the extreme variability of the data. People, for example, do not behave like molecules. Chemists are fortunate: When they repeat experiments, they get identical results every time. Research in the social sciences is much less precise.

All statistical inference is really asking the same question. Is our obtained outcome likely to be due to chance? When we obtain a sample outcome that seems highly unlikely to have occurred if the assumptions of the null are true, we say we have a *significant* result. It seems more reasonable to conclude that the null is not true than to conclude that we got such an unlikely result by chance alone. In other words, the participants in our experiment did not respond the way we would expect them to if the assumptions of the null were correct. Let's look more closely at the response of a participant. Whether we are dealing with an animal, an insect, or a person, the response of any single participant in a research study reflects at least three factors:

1. Random error
2. The effects of the experimental variable
3. Individual differences among participants

Random error is one of the factors that make some social science research so imprecise (I call this the slop factor). We do our best to control this factor by using good experimental techniques.

The effect of the experimental variable on our participants' responses is the factor of interest in any experiment. We would like our experimental variable to have a big effect on responses.

The third factor, individual differences, is often the largest factor contributing to the scores and their variability in research in the social sciences. People, for example, differ psychologically, physiologically, and behaviorally in many ways. Many researchers try to reduce the effects of this factor by using participants who do not differ very much. Animals raised for research purposes, for example, have similar histories and are generally not as complex as people. Those of us doing research with people, however, must deal with this factor all the time.

In a great deal of research in the social sciences, individual differences in *ability* on the task are the largest source of variability in scores. Finding ways to control for these differences is important if we hope to assess the effects of an experimental variable. One way is *random assignment of participants to groups*. Random assignment allows us to assume *initial* "between-group" equality. In other words, if we have randomly assigned participants to each group in our experiment, we may assume that the groups, on average, do not differ much in ability on whatever our task is or in any other ways for that matter. If randomly assigned, why would one group of people be more motivated, physically fitter, or smarter than another? So, by randomly assigning participants to groups, we can assume the groups are initially equivalent on whatever our response measure is going to be. If we find that our groups differ after we introduce our experimental variable, then we may conclude that this difference was caused by the variable we introduced. Random assignment of participants to groups is not the only way to control for between-group individual differences. The use of *correlated or dependent samples* is another way of controlling for individual differences.

Note: As mentioned elsewhere in this book, the APA prefers that the term *participants*, rather than *subjects*, be used to refer to human participants in research. The term *subjects* is preferred for animals. I have followed this recommendation.

Within-Participants Designs

Many studies of the effects of an experimental variable use the same participants in both the **treatment** (experimental) **group** and in the **control group**. Measuring performance of participants before and after they receive some instructional training is an example of a **within-participants design**. Rather than measuring performance between two groups, of which one receives the training and the other does not (a **between-participants design**), we measure performance of the same participants under no-training conditions and again under training conditions. This reduces the between-participants variability because a participant will respond more like himself or herself than anyone else. The effect is that the two groups do not differ initially on whatever variable we are measuring.

> **Treatment group:** The group in an experiment that is exposed to one level of the independent variable
>
> **Control group:** The group that is exposed to a different level of the independent variable (often a no-treatment group)
>
> **Within-participants design:** The same participants serve in both the control group and the treatment group
>
> **Between-participants design:** Different participants are randomly assigned to the control and treatment group

Matched-Groups Designs

Another way of reducing between-participant variability is to *match* participants on some variable known to be related to the response measure (usually the dependent variable). Giving participants a practice task similar to what they will be doing in the experiment, for example, allows us to match participants on initial ability on the task and to assign one participant to our control group and another of equal ability to our experimental group. In this way, we end up with groups that are initially equal on our response measure. A family therapist who wants to evaluate the effectiveness of different kinds of therapy on marital discord (the response measure) might first match her couples on degree of marital discord before beginning therapy. In this way, she ensures that the groups are similar to begin with so she can compare the groups after therapy to see if they are now different.

> **Matched-groups design:** Participants are matched on some variable related to the response measure

When to Use Dependent-Groups Designs

Both the within-participant and the matched-groups techniques control for initial individual differences between groups, and, therefore, let us better estimate the effects of the experimental variable on our response measure. Arithmetically speaking, these procedures reduce the size of the denominator (**error term**) in the *t* test. The standard error will be smaller because there is less variability between participants. With a smaller denominator, the *t* ratio tends to be larger. The dependent samples approach, therefore, may be a more *powerful* test of significance of an experimental variable. You will recall that *power* is the term we use to describe the ability of the test to reject a false null. I'm sure you are saying to yourself, "Why don't we always do dependent sample research?" Clearly, if the *t* ratio tends to be larger with a dependent sample approach, then we are more likely to reject the null, right? Well, not necessarily!

Error term: The denominator of the significance test ratio

It is true that the *t* ratio for dependent samples tends to be larger than for independent samples. However, you will recall that the critical value of *t*, to which we compare our obtained value, depends on degrees of freedom. As degrees of freedom get larger our critical value gets smaller. Remember that for a *t* test for two independent samples, the degrees of freedom are $n_1 + n_2 - 2$. With dependent samples, degrees of freedom are $n_p - 1$ (number of *pairs* of scores − 1).

For example, if we did a study with two groups, 20 participants in each group, we would have 38 *df* for an independent *t* test but *only* 19 *df* for a dependent *t* test. Why this is so will become clear to you shortly. Although using a dependent sample approach may increase the value of the obtained *t* score, *the critical value of t needed for rejection of the null is also increased.* On the one hand, we increase the power of our test by reducing the error term. But, on the other hand, we decrease power by losing degrees of freedom. This is one of the reasons why we do not always use a dependent-samples approach.

Dependent-groups designs are very useful in social science research. In most cases, between-participant variability is the largest source of error, and the dependent-groups approach is, overall, a more sensitive test of the null in spite of the loss of degrees of freedom. The reduction of the error term (the denominator of the ratio) usually has a greater impact on the outcome of the statistical procedure than does the loss of degrees of freedom.

There are situations, however, where within-participants designs should not be used. Sometimes the performance of the control task *carries over* to the experimental task. Measuring performance on a problem-solving task before and after instruction on some problem-solving strategy would be an example of such a case. The practice effects of working on the problems first under control conditions may carry over to the experimental condition and thus mask the effects of the independent variable (i.e., the training).

Matched-groups designs avoid the problem of carry-over effects because they use different participants in each group, matched on some initial measure.

ALERT

It is critical, with a matched-groups design, that the matching variable be an important contributing factor to response variability. If it is not, then the dependent t test will be less powerful than an independent t test because of the loss of degrees of freedom.

Generally speaking, a matched-groups design will be more powerful than an independent-groups design when the variable used to equate participants is strongly related to the response measure. If we match participants on some variable unrelated to whatever we are measuring, then we will have a less powerful test of the null hypothesis. For example, say we are interested in the effects of reward on the arithmetic performance of children. We decide to use two groups of children and have them do a whole series of arithmetic problems. One group receives a treat for each correct answer; the other group receives nothing. We count the number of problems solved by each child at the end of the session. Suppose that, for some obscure reason, we believe height may be an important contributing factor to task performance. So we measure the heights of a group of children and find 20 pairs of children of the same height. We assign one child of each matched pair to the control (no reward) condition and the other child of the same height to the experimental condition (reward).

This somewhat silly example illustrates a *weak* test of the null hypothesis. Our matching variable is probably unrelated to task performance, so we have not reduced the size of the error term in the t ratio. Our obtained t value, then, will be smaller, and we have many fewer degrees of freedom ($df = 19$) than if we had not matched participants ($df = 38$). Matched-groups designs can be powerful, but we must be careful in selecting our matching variable.

If we have matched participants or used the same participants under both control and experimental conditions, we run a dependent or correlated t test on our data.

t Test for the Difference Between Two Dependent Samples

One of the formulas you were given for the standard error used in the denominator of the t ratio for the difference between means was

$$s_{\bar{X}_1 - \bar{X}_2} = \sqrt{s^2_{\bar{X}_1} + s^2_{\bar{X}_2}}$$

Actually, this formula is not accurate!

The real formula for any *t* test of the difference, whether it be a dependent-groups or an independent-groups test, is

$$s_{\bar{X}_1 - \bar{X}_2} = \sqrt{s_{\bar{X}_1}^2 + s_{\bar{X}_2}^2 - 2\rho s_{\bar{X}_1} s_{\bar{X}_2}}$$

You will appreciate why I didn't show you this earlier! Consider an independent *t* test for the difference. This test requires that participants be independently assigned to groups. If this is done, we would not expect the responses of the two groups to be correlated in any way. A measure of correlation, which I discuss in Chapter 16, is symbolized by ρ (Greek letter "rho"). With independent samples, we expect no correlation between the populations from which the groups were selected ($\rho = 0$). For this reason, we do not include the third term under the square root sign because it is assumed to be zero when samples are independent.

When samples are dependent, however, the correlation will *not* be zero, and the full form of the standard error formula must be used. This formula requires that we determine (actually we estimate) the correlation before we can calculate the standard error. If you do not have a computer handy that can do this for you, there is a convenient technique for computing the *t* ratio for dependent samples. This technique is called the *direct difference method*. The *t* ratio for dependent means using the direct difference method follows the same general format we have been using:

$$t = \frac{\bar{D} - \mu_{\bar{D}}}{s_{\bar{D}}}$$

The data are the differences (*D*) between the pair of measures for each participant. We take the mean difference between our two groups (i.e., $\bar{D}$) and subtract from that the hypothesized mean difference (i.e., $\mu_{\bar{D}}$). Then, we divide this by the standard error of the difference (i.e., $s_{\bar{D}}$). As with any two-sample *t* test, the hypothesized difference stated by the null is zero, and so we often leave out the last term ($\mu_{\bar{D}}$), and our *t* ratio becomes

$$t = \frac{\bar{D}}{s_{\bar{D}}}$$

Ready for an example? A consulting psychologist has been hired by an inner-city school principal to assess the effects of an educational video on students' views about bullying in schools. He hopes that the video will help students better understand how serious bullying can be. He decides to measure the attitudes of a random sample of students before and after they view the video. Because the same participants are tested before and after, he will analyze his data with a dependent t test. Higher scores indicate that bullying is perceived as more serious. His data are shown below and in Table 10.1.

$$H_0: \mu_1 = \mu_2$$

$$H_1: \mu_1 < \mu_2$$

$$\alpha = .01$$

$$t_{.01} = -2.82$$

$$df = 9$$

Table 10.1

Perceived Seriousness of Bullying

	Before	After	D	D²
	25	28	-3	9
	23	19	4	16
	30	34	-4	16
	7	10	-3	9
	3	6	-3	9
	22	26	-4	16
	12	13	-1	1
	30	47	-17	289
	5	16	-11	121
	14	9	5	25
Sum			-37	511
Mean	17.11	20.8		
SD	10.20	12.92		

The standard error of the difference is

$$s_{\bar{D}} = \frac{\sqrt{\sum D^2 - \left(\sum D\right)^2 / n}}{n(n-1)}$$

$$= \sqrt{\frac{511 - \left(-37\right)^2 / 10}{10(9)}}$$

$$= 2.04$$

Now, he computes mean difference and the *t* ratio.

$$\bar{D} = \frac{\Sigma D}{n}$$

$$= \frac{-37}{10} = -3.7$$

$$t = \frac{\bar{D}}{s_{\bar{D}}} = \frac{-3.7}{2.04} = -1.81$$

The obtained *t* value is not in the critical region; the null is not rejected. The principal must conclude that he has no evidence that the students perceived bullying to be more serious after viewing the video ($M = 20.8$, $SD = 12.92$) than they did before ($M = 17.1$, $SD = 10.20$), $t(9) = -1.81$, *ns*.

If we input our data to Excel and ask for a paired samples test, the output would look like this:

t Test: Paired Two Sample for Means		
	Before	**After**
Mean	17.1	20.8
Variance	104.1	166.8444444
Observations	10	10
Pearson correlation	0.870242132	
Hypothesized mean difference	0	
Df	9	
t stat	−1.81480148	
$P(T \leq t)$ one-tail	0.051474218	
t critical one-tail	2.82143792	
$P(T \leq t)$ two-tail	0.102948435	
t critical two-tail	3.24983554	

The direct difference method uses difference scores to compute the standard error (denominator) and the mean difference between the groups to compute the numerator of the *t* ratio. This technique takes into account the expected correlation.

Now, you probably understand why degrees of freedom for a dependent *t* test are "number of pairs of scores minus one." We used the 10 differences as our data for calculating the *t* ratio. The standard error for the **dependent samples *t* test** uses the *mean difference* in the computation of the sum of squares. In our example, we had 10 differences, and we used the mean difference in calculating the sum of squares. Only 9 of these differences are free to vary because the mean difference is fixed. Statistically, we are operating as if we had only one group of scores, that is, the difference scores. Therefore, the degrees of freedom are equal to the number of difference scores minus one.

SUMMARY OF t TEST FOR DEPENDENT MEANS

Hypotheses

H_0: $\mu_1 = \mu_2$
H_1: $\mu_1 \neq \mu_2$, $\mu_1 < \mu_2$, or $\mu_1 > \mu_2$

Assumptions

1. Participants are randomly selected.
2. Population distributions are normal.
3. Population variances are homogeneous.
4. Repeated measures or matched participants are used.

Decision Rules

$df = n_{pairs} - 1$

If $t_{obt} \geq t_{crit}$ reject H_0

If $t_{obt} < t_{crit}$ do not reject H_0

Formula

$$t = \frac{\bar{D}}{s_{\bar{D}}}$$

CONCEPT REVIEW 10.5

A sociologist has collected socioeconomic status (SES) data on a large number of families living in a community on the West Coast. He is interested in how people's perceptions about issues can be influenced by the way questions are framed by an interviewer. He intends to interview family members to determine their views on the availability and quality of health services in their community. For half the families, his interview questions will be framed in a positive manner, and for the other half, the questions will be framed in a negative manner. He believes that SES might be a factor. For example, he thinks that lower-SES people might feel more negatively about health services in general. What should he do?

Answer on page 277.

Power Revisited

Recall the discussion of power concerning hypothesis testing with the normal curve. We learned that the power of a test is affected by the alpha level, the independent variable or treatment, the sample size, and the error variance (the variability between participants due to inherent individual differences). We learned that we can increase power by using research techniques that reduce error variance. In this chapter, we have seen that a dependent-groups design serves to increase power by reducing error variance, either by using the same participants in both the experimental and the control group or by matching participants on a variable known to contribute to error variance. The significance level can be selected by the experimenter to increase the power of a test, and sample size can be increased as well.

So to produce a powerful test, we can select the appropriate alpha level, increase sample size, and use a dependent-groups design. All these choices will increase the probability that we will reject a false null. But what about the effect of the independent variable? This is the critical factor in any experiment. We want to know if the independent variable has a significant effect on the dependent measure. Statistical significance and "real-world" significance are not the same. If we can use these techniques to increase power to the point where the effect of the independent variable becomes trivial, then we might wonder about the "real-world" significance of our research. For example, it's possible to increase our sample size (and, therefore, power) to such an extent that even tiny differences between population means will be detected in our test of significance. Sometimes a "significant" effect is not all that significant!

The term *statistical significance* should never be confused with the everyday use of the term *significance*, which means important. A statistically significant finding may not be very important in the real-world scheme of things! So the question must be, how big must an effect be to be important?

Effect Size

Imagine that we have calculated our statistic and concluded that there is a significant difference between groups. But how large is that difference? How large a difference should we expect? Is the difference important? Remember, a statistically significant difference is not necessarily an important difference. An important difference should be a large difference. In other words, the manipulation of the independent variable in an experiment should have a large effect on the dependent variable to be considered important. A tiny difference between the null and the alternative that reaches statistical significance may or may not be important.

Imagine that we have determined that drinking a cup of coffee before writing a final exam in statistics significantly improved students' performance compared with a control group of students who drank a decaffeinated beverage. The mean for the coffee group was 78.6%, and the mean for the control group was 77.5 %. This difference could reach significance if the sample sizes were very large and there wasn't a lot of variability in the scores. But is this significant difference important enough that we should provide coffee to all students writing final exams? Probably not.

Now, there may be times when small differences are important, but at the very least, we should think about the minimum effect size that is worth our effort as we design our study and choose our statistical procedures.

Effect size: An estimate of the strength of the treatment or relationship

So how would we determine our desired effect size? There are several ways. If you check the APA manual, you will find about 13 different effect size estimates used by psychology researchers. I will discuss two here.

Remember that a significant effect is not necessarily a large effect. The difference between group means is important, but the variability of the scores is also important. If there is hardly any variability, then tiny differences between the means may reach statistical significance.

One common measure of effect size is Cohen's d, which compares the difference between the means of two groups and takes into account the sample variability. The formula is as follows:

$$\text{Cohen's } d = \frac{M_1 - M_2}{SD}$$

Cohen suggested that either sample standard deviation can be used (assuming homogeneity of variance), but some researchers suggest that an average of the two sample standard deviations should be used.

This formula can be used to calculate effect size when you have conducted a t test. Cohen (1992) suggests that a d of about .20 is a small effect. A medium effect would be a d of .50, and a large effect would be a d of .80.

Let's use our PSI versus L example earlier in this chapter to calculate Cohen's effect size estimate. We will use the average standard deviation of the groups.

$$\begin{aligned}
\text{Cohen's } d &= \frac{M_1 - M_2}{SD} \\
&= \frac{73.8 - 65.69}{5.74} \\
&= 1.41
\end{aligned}$$

As you can see, the effect is large.

Another measure of effect size, used in correlational research, is the *coefficient of determination* (ρ^2). When we have calculated a correlation coefficient, we can square it, and this coefficient tells us how much of the variance in one variable is explained by its correlation with another variable. I will discuss this in more detail in Chapter 16.

FYI

The APA recommends that researchers provide effect size estimates along with the other statistics in research papers submitted for publication. You will find a very handy effect size calculator at this website.

http://web.uccs.edu/lbecker/Psy590/escalc3.htm

Effect Size and Sample Size

Students often ask me if a significant finding might have been *more significant* if the samples had been larger. Well, not necessarily. We need to consider the size of the effect. If the relationship between the independent and dependent variable was strong and experimental control was tight, then a significant result might be found with quite small samples. This would mean that the effect size was large. On the other hand, if your independent variable has a small effect on the dependent variable, then you'll need larger samples to reach statistical significance.

The weaker the treatment and the weaker the experimental control, the larger the samples must be to get significance. Of course, we don't know in advance whether we have a large or a small effect. Yes, it is a bit of a conundrum.

There is some controversy in psychology these days about our reliance on tests of significance. Because an effect does not reach statistical significance does not necessarily mean that the effect is not important. If you think I sound like I am arguing against what I just said, you are quite right. Both arguments are valid. Some significant findings are simply not "significant," and some non-significant findings probably are! Recently, researchers have begun to conduct what are called meta-analyses on previously published findings. A meta-analysis examines the findings of many studies of the same phenomenon. Such analyses then involve much larger samples. Some interesting conclusions have been made as a result of meta-analyses. Marginally significant or nonsignificant effects are found to be significant in some meta-analyses.

Choosing the Appropriate Test of Significance

You now have learned about six different tests of significance: three z tests (the z test for a single mean, for the difference between two independent means, and for a proportion) and three t tests (t test for a single mean, for the difference between independent means, and for the difference between dependent means). Let's examine the steps we need to go through to make decisions about the appropriate test of significance. Then, we will consider some examples.

Step 1. Determine the kind of data collected in the experiment.

If the data are proportions, frequencies, or percentages, we use the z test for a proportion. If the data are measures that are used to compute means and if there is only one group in the experiment, we go to Step 2. If there are two groups, we go to Step 4.

Step 2. Determine whether repeated measures have been taken.

If there is only one group of participants, then you must determine whether each participant provided one observation or two observations. In other words, you have to determine if repeated measures were taken. If each participant contributed two data points, you run a t test for dependent samples. If you have determined that each participant in the group provided only one data point or observation, go to Step 3.

Step 3. Determine if the population standard deviation is known.

Run a z test for a single mean if the population standard deviation is known and a t test for a single mean if it must be estimated.

Step 4. Determine whether participants have been matched.

With two groups of participants, you need to determine whether participants were matched (a matched-groups design). If they have, you run a t test for dependent means. If participants have not been matched but, rather, have been independently assigned to the two groups, you have one more question to answer.

Step 5. Determine if the population standard deviations are known.

If you know the population standard deviations, you run a z test for independent means. If you do not know the population standard deviations, you run a t test for independent means.

Example A: You are comparing the average performance of two randomly selected groups of nurses, one group of RNs (registered nurses) and the other of BS nurses, on a new test of general nursing practice. Let's go through the steps to determine the appropriate test of significance for this research problem.

Step 1. Determine the kind of data collected in the experiment.

The data are measures from each nurse, which will be used to compute the mean performance of each group. Because the data are measures and not frequencies, a *z* test for the proportion will not be appropriate. There are two groups, RNs and BSs, so we skip Steps 2 and 3 and go to Step 4.

Step 4. Determine whether participants have been matched.

The two groups of nurses were randomly selected. A matched-groups design was not used.

Step 5. Determine if the population standard deviations are known.

There was no information in the problem suggesting that the test was standardized with available norms, so we assume the population standard deviations are not known, and we run a *t* test for independent means.

Example B: The Stanford-Binet IQ (intelligence quotient) test has a mean of 100 and a standard deviation of 15. A randomly selected group of teenagers from a juvenile offenders program are compared with the norm.

Step 1. Determine the kind of data collected in the experiment.

We can assume that the teenagers provided IQ data and the average IQ of the group was computed. There is one group, so we go to Step 2.

Step 2. Determine whether repeated measures have been taken.

Repeated measures have not been taken. Each teenager provided one data point.

Step 3. Determine if the population standard deviation is known.

Because the Stanford-Binet is a standardized IQ test, the mean and standard deviation are both available. A *z* test for a single mean should be used to compare the juvenile offender group with the general population.

Example C: A sociologist has randomly selected a large group of people and collected information regarding SES, annual income, and years of education for each individual. She randomly assigns participants in pairs to an experimental or a control group, such that each pair is equal in terms of SES, income level, and years of education. The experimental participants receive special training in logical problem solving. She is interested in the effects of the training on average problem-solving performance.

Step 1. Determine the kind of data collected in the experiment.

The data are mean performance on the problem-solving tasks. There are two groups, so we go to Step 4.

Step 4. Determine whether participants have been matched.

The participants have been matched on three variables: (1) SES, (2) income, and (3) education. The experimenter will run a *t* test for dependent groups.

Example D: A medical researcher is testing an experimental drug that purports to improve muscle development. She injects half of the dogs in the left leg and half of the dogs in the right leg. This procedure continues for 6 weeks. Muscle mass is measured for both legs of all dogs to see if the drug increased the average amount of muscle tissue.

Step 1. Determine the kind of data collected in the experiment.

Average amount of muscle tissue is measured. There is only one group in the experiment, and so we go to Step 2.

Step 2. Determine whether repeated measures have been taken.

The researcher is comparing left-leg versus right-leg muscle mass in each of her dogs. This is a repeated measures design because each participant is contributing two data points. She will run a *t* test for dependent samples.

FOCUS ON RESEARCH

THE RESEARCH PROBLEM

When separating or divorcing, parents are in conflict over the custody of their children, the courts will often require that a psychologist assess each parent for suitability for custody. Likewise, the courts may mandate assessments of parents whose children may have been removed from their homes for reasons of neglect and abuse. The Minnesota Multiphasic Personality Inventory–2 (MMPI-2) is a common tool used in these assessments. Resendes and Lecci (2012) wondered if these two groups of parents might differ in important ways on some of the subscales of the MMPI-2.

THE DESIGN AND VARIABLES

A sample of parents who were assessed for competency was compared with a sample of parents who were litigating for custody of their children. The MMPI-2 was used as the assessment instrument, and **independent samples *t* tests** were used to compare the groups.

> **Dependent samples *t* test:** Parametric test for the significance of the difference between means of samples of same or matched participants

> **Independent samples *t* test:** Test for the significance of the difference between means of samples of independent (uncorrelated) participants

THE RESULTS

Resendes and Lecci (2012) found several differences between the groups. I will report some of those findings here.

The Parental Competency group ($M = 62.4$, $SD = 14.1$) scored significantly higher on the L scale than the Parental Custody group ($M = 56.01$, $SD = 10.56$), $t = 6.0$, $p < .003$, $d = .53$. (*df*s were not reported.) The Parental Competency group ($M = 58.9$, $SD = 16.01$) also scored significantly higher on the *F* scale than the Custody group ($M = 44.67$, $SD = 6.82$), $t = 15.38$, $p < .003$, $d = 1.15$.

Both of these scales assess "honesty." The *L* scale is referred to as the lie scale, and the *F* scale is referred to as the faking good = faking bad scale. You are aware I am sure from your studies in psychology about the notion of social desirability. People often try to appear "better" than they are. These scales are measures of aspects of that tendency. It seems that the parents who were being assessed by the courts for their competence as parents "tried harder" to appear to be good people than the parents who were involved in custody litigation with each other.

THE CONCLUSIONS

Resendes and Lecci suggest that psychologists and courts should be aware that parents involved in custody conflict may be quite different from those involved in competency matters.

Resendes, J., & Lecci, L. (2012). Comparing the MMPI-2 scale scores of parents involved in parental competency and child custody assessments. *Psychological Assessment.* Advance online publication. doi:10.1037/a0028585

SUMMARY OF FORMULAS FOR THE ESTIMATES OF:

Population standard deviation

$$s = \sqrt{\frac{SS}{(n-1)}} = \sqrt{\frac{\sum X^2 - (\sum X)^2/n}{n-1}}$$

Standard error of the mean

$$s_{\bar{X}} = \sqrt{\frac{SS}{n(n-1)}} = \sqrt{\frac{\sum X^2 - (\sum X)^2/n}{n(n-1)}}$$

Standard error of the difference

$$s_{\bar{X}_1 - \bar{X}_2} = \sqrt{s_{\bar{X}_1}^2 + s_{\bar{X}_2}^2}$$

Independent samples

$$s_{\bar{X}_1 - \bar{X}_2} = \sqrt{\frac{SS_1 + SS_2}{n_1 + n_2 - 2}\left(\frac{1}{n_1} + \frac{1}{n_2}\right)} \quad n_1 \neq n_2$$

$$s_{\bar{X}_1 - \bar{X}_2} = \sqrt{\frac{SS_1 + SS_2}{n(n-1)}} \quad n_1 = n_2$$

where $SS = \sum X^2 - \frac{(\sum X)^2}{n}$

Dependent samples

$$s_{\bar{D}} = \sqrt{\frac{\sum D^2 - (\sum D)^2/n}{n(n-1)}}$$

Estimate of treatment effect

Cohen's $d = \frac{M_1 - M_2}{SD}$ with t test

ρ^2 with correlation test

CONCEPT REVIEW ANSWERS

10.1. A. 45

B. $21 + 29 = 50$

$t_{.01} = \pm 2.704$

10.2. $100 \pm 2.704(1.2) = 100 \pm 3.24 = 103.24$ and 96.76

$C(96.76 \leq \mu \leq 103.24) = .99$

10.3. He would probably want to run a t test for a single sample using the population mean provided with the test. If the standard deviation were also available, he would use a z test.

$df = 50 + 60 - 2 = 108$

10.4. $t = \frac{(26000 - 28000)}{1245} = -1.61$

The *t* table doesn't give a critical *t* for 108 *df*, but we can see that with 120 *df* we would need a *t* value beyond −1.98. Because our *t* value is not large enough, we can't reject it. We cannot say that the East Coasters and people in the Midwest have different yearly incomes.

10.5. He should match his families on SES so that his two groups are equivalent in terms of SES at the outset. In this way, he can better evaluate the effects of his independent variable, the way in which he has framed his questions.

EXERCISES

Note: Some of the exercises have smaller samples than advisable in real research.

1. A group of 23 participants was given a list of 30 one-word anagrams to solve. Half the solution words were emotionally neutral in meaning and half were unpleasant. Which *t* test should you run to determine if the affective or emotional meaning of the solution words has any effect on the time taken to solve the anagrams?

2. A psychologist wanted to find out whether the development of the ability to formulate abstract concepts could be hastened by special training. She selected 10 sets of 5-year-old identical twins to be her participants. The 20 children were given 25 conceptual problems to solve, and it was found that none of them could offer any correct solutions. Following this initial test, one twin in each set was given a 30-minute training session every day for 3 weeks. Six months after the training was complete, all 20 children were given a new set of 25 conceptual problems. The measure was the number of correct solutions on this second test. Assume that all participants improved on the second testing. Which *t* test should you use to determine if the special training had any additional effect?

3. A school counselor is interested in the effects of two teaching methods in a learning task. She believes, however, that intelligence and gender may be involved. She randomly selects 20 boys, all with IQs more than 120. She randomly assigns them into two groups, one of which is taught with one method and the other with the second method. She measures the amount of time to learn required by each child. Which *t* test should be used to determine if teaching method makes a difference in performance?

4. Indicate the degrees of freedom and the critical value of *t* at $\alpha = .05$ for the following:

   a. two-tailed *t* test for independent means; $n_1 = 18$, $n_2 = 12$
   b. two-tailed *t* test for dependent means; $n_1 = 16$, $n_2 = 16$

5. Sixteen inmates incarcerated for violent crimes are assigned randomly to two conflict resolution treatment programs, one of which is expected to be more effective. Following the treatment program, the participants complete a questionnaire that measures how well the respondents deal with conflict. At $\alpha = .01$, run a *t* test on the data below. Indicate your null and alternative hypothesis and the critical *t* value. What will be your statistical decision?

   Program A: 12, 17, 15, 13, 11, 10, 16, 12

   Program B: 16, 14, 18, 19, 17, 13, 11, 10

6. Fifteen randomly selected students from a political science class at the University of Toronto are given two forms of an attitude questionnaire, one before and the other after listening to a speaker discuss the separation of Quebec from the rest of Canada. Run a t test on the data below to determine if the speaker had an influence on student attitude regarding separation (higher numbers indicate more accepting attitudes). Indicate your null and alternative hypothesis and the critical value of t at $\alpha = .01$. What is your statistical decision?

   Attitude Score Before Speaker: 13, 17, 14, 17, 23, 20, 13, 25, 24, 18, 17, 15, 21, 19, 28

   Attitude Score After Speaker: 22, 14, 23, 21, 20, 26, 14, 27, 20, 21, 15, 29, 30, 22, 28

7. Women being treated for depression were recruited to participate in a study. Twenty were randomly selected from a list of survivors of acquaintance rape, and 20 were randomly selected from a list of women who had not been assaulted. Self-esteem was measured. Conduct the appropriate statistical analysis to test the hypothesis that depressed women who have suffered acquaintance rape have lower self esteem (lower scores) than depressed women who were not assaulted. Use $\alpha = .01$. Indicate your null, alternative, and critical value of t. What is your statistical decision? What is your conclusion?

   Date Rape: 4, 4, 5, 5, 4, 4, 6, 5, 5, 5, 5, 4, 4, 3, 3, 2, 4, 4, 5, 5

   No Assault: 6, 5, 5, 5, 7, 7, 7, 8, 6, 6, 4, 6, 5, 5, 6, 7, 4, 5, 5, 5

8. Set up the 95% CI for the difference between means for the following data:

   $$\bar{X}_1 = 25 \qquad\qquad \bar{X}_2 = 20$$
   $$n_1 = 15 \qquad\qquad n_2 = 10$$
   $$SS_1 = 225 \qquad\qquad SS_2 = 200$$

9. Define and give the probability for each of the following:
   a. Type I error
   b. Type II error
   c. Power

10. List three things we can do to increase the power of the t test.

11. A sociologist uses a standardized test of assertiveness to assess 16 randomly selected students from a class who had completed an assertiveness-training seminar. The normative mean for the test is 28. The sociologist wants to know if the seminar had an effect on the assertiveness of the graduates. Use the data below to answer his question. What is your conclusion?

$$\bar{X} = 25.75$$
$$\sum X^2 = 11290$$
$$\sum X = 412$$
$$\alpha = .05$$

a. H_0:
    H_1:
b. *df*
c. Critical *t* value
d. *s*
e. Obtained *t* value
f. Decision

12. Sixteen students are randomly selected from a class in the philosophy of ethics and are assigned randomly to two experimental conditions. Both groups are given the same aptitude test designed to measure logical decision making. Prior to this test, one group attends a hands-on workshop in logical decision making and the other group attends a lecture covering the same content. Determine if the practical experience of the workshop affected test performance at $\alpha = .01$. Higher scores are better. State your conclusion.

    Workshop: 13, 11, 15, 10, 12, 15, 12, 10

    Lecture: 18, 14, 10, 11, 17, 17, 19, 16

    a. H_0:
        H_1:
    b. *df*
    c. $t_{.01}$
    d. t_{obt}
    e. $p <$ or $> \alpha$?
    f. Decision

13. Ten randomly selected rats are run through a maze before and after being injected with DNA from proven "fast runners." Test the hypothesis that the DNA from the "fast rats" improved running speed. Use $\alpha = .05$. Put your decision in words.

Rat	Before	After
1	24	22
2	21	23
3	24	21
4	28	26
5	22	22
6	29	28
7	26	21
8	22	23
9	27	23
10	28	24

a. H_0:
    H_1:
b. *df*

c. $t_{.05}$
d. t_{obt}
e. $p <$ or $> \alpha$?
f. Decision

14. A neuropsychologist compares cognitive test performance of two groups of adults who have been diagnosed with schizophrenia. She is interested in the effects of the level of sensory stimulation on their performance. She collected data in the form of the number of problems solved by each group. She randomly assigned 10 participants to each of two conditions. All the participants wore headphones. One group heard silence (Low Stim) and the other heard white noise (High Stim). Unfortunately, her research assistant lost some of the data. Run a t test on the remaining data to see if the amount of sensory simulation affected performance. Use $\alpha = .05$. What is your statistical decision? Did the white noise make a difference? Put your decision in words.

High Stim: 12, 14, 16, 13, 10, 17, 18, 15, 15, 13

Low Stim: 10, 8, 18, 12, 10, 16, 14, 17

a. H_0:
   H_1:
b. df
c. $t_{.05}$
d. t_{obt}
e. $p <$ or $> \alpha$?
f. Decision

15. Set up the 95% and 99% CIs for the difference between means for the following data.

$\bar{X}_1 = 21.78$ $\bar{X}_2 = 19.45$
$n_1 = 18$ $n_2 = 11$
$SS_1 = 221.70$ $SS_2 = 197.30$

a. df
b. $t_{.05}$
   $t_{.01}$
c. $s_{\bar{X}_1 - \bar{X}_2}$
d. 95% CI
e. 99% CI

CHAPTER 11

Inference With the *F* Distribution

After reading this chapter, you should be able to do the following:

1. List the steps to construct the *F* distribution.
2. Describe the shape of the *F* distribution.
3. Describe how the variance and degrees of freedom are partitioned in a one-way analysis of variance (ANOVA).
4. Run a one-way ANOVA for a given set of data.
5. Describe the difference between main effects and interaction effects.
6. Describe how the variance and degrees of freedom are partitioned in a two-way ANOVA.
7. Run a two-way ANOVA for a given set of data.
8. Complete an ANOVA summary table for a given analysis.
9. Determine the appropriate test of significance for a given research problem.

Are there differences in time-on-task behavior for kids diagnosed with behavior disorders who have received drug therapy, counselling, or mindfulness-based cognitive behavioral therapy?

Does the number of bystanders witnessing a crime affect their willingness to testify in court (e.g., one other, two others, or five others present)?

Are there differences in time spent one-on-one with patients among nurses, orderlies, volunteers, and physicians?

These examples deal with comparisons among more than two groups of participants. A statistical approach that can help us answer these kinds of questions is called analysis of variance (ANOVA). **ANOVA** is a family of statistical techniques specifically designed for assessing mean differences among several groups of participants.

ANOVA: A significance test for the difference between means of two or more groups

ANOVA is the appropriate technique for evaluating the differences between the means of two or more populations. ANOVA may be used for interval or ratio data. You may wonder why we don't simply compare pairs of samples with several t tests. This is a good question.

Consider an experiment in which we gave different doses of an experimental drug to five groups of cancer patients and evaluated the effects on tumor growth. We could measure the effect of each dose level by comparing every pair of means using a separate t test. Remember the formula for the number of combinations of five things taken two at a time?

$$_5C_2 = \frac{5!}{3!2!} = 10$$

We would need 10 t tests. There are several problems with this approach. It would be a lot of work, but there is a statistical problem with it, which is more critical. Running multiple t tests in a single experiment is inappropriate, because the probability of an inferential error is high. I will discuss this in more detail later on.

Recall that inference with the normal curve involved computing z scores. Inference with the t distribution required the computation of t scores. ANOVA is an inferential technique that uses the F distribution and requires the computation of F scores.

The *F* Distribution

Just as the normal distribution is the random sampling distribution of the z statistic, and the t distribution is the random sampling distribution of the t statistic, the **F distribution** is the random sampling distribution of the F statistic.

In Chapter 10, we saw that when we collect all possible samples from a population, calculate z and t for each sample mean, and place the z values and the t values in separate relative frequency distributions, the z values follow a normal curve, and the t values follow the t distribution. The F distribution, like the normal and t distribution, is a theoretical distribution that is mathematically derived. But if we wanted to construct an empirical random sampling distribution of the F statistic, we would use a procedure much as we did to construct empirical z and t distributions.

F distribution: In ANOVA, the relative frequency distribution of the F statistic

Constructing an Empirical *F* Distribution

The *F* distribution is a little different from what you are used to, and as you learn more about ANOVA, the reasons for this will become clearer. An empirical sampling distribution of the *F* statistic is constructed in the following way:

Step 1. Randomly select, with replacement, two samples of fixed sizes from a population.

Step 2. Calculate an *unbiased estimate of the variance* (s^2) for each sample.

Step 3. Divide the first variance estimate (s_1^2) by the second variance estimate (s_2^2). *This is the F statistic or* **F ratio**.

Step 4. Repeat Steps 1 to 3 until all possible pairs of samples have been drawn.

Step 5. Place the *F* ratios in a relative frequency distribution.

The random sampling distribution of the *F* statistic has certain important properties that allow us to make inferences about population means.

F ratio: In ANOVA, the ratio of two unbiased variance estimates

Characteristics of the *F* Distribution

The *F* distribution is the relative frequency distribution of the *F* statistic. The *F* statistic is a ratio between two variance estimates. Because an estimate of the variance cannot be negative (zero variability is as low as it goes), the frequency distribution is limited at zero. The other end of the distribution, however, is not limited, and so the distribution is positively skewed.

Notice that the variance estimates are calculated for samples drawn from a single population. On average, then, we would expect the two estimates to be equal. The expected value of *F* is 1 because we are computing a ratio between two variance estimates, each of which estimates the same population variance. In summary,

The *F* ratio $= \dfrac{s_1^2}{s_2^2}$.

The *F* distribution is positively skewed with a limit at zero.

The expected value of *F* is 1.

The *F* distribution, like the *t* distribution, is a family of curves whose shape depends on degrees of freedom. Figure 11.1 presents an example of an *F* distribution.

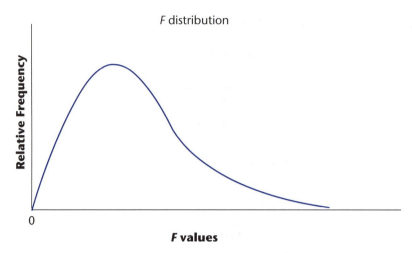

Figure 11.1. An example of an *F* distribution.

CONCEPT REVIEW 11.1

Why can't we obtain negative *F* values? What does it mean to say that the expected value of *F* is 1?

Answer on page 324.

Using the *F* Distribution

Recall that ANOVA is used to make inferences about the means of the populations from which samples have been drawn. Often, these samples have been treated differently by the researcher who wishes to know if the treatment or independent variable (IV) had an effect on the dependent variable (DV). If the IV didn't work, we would expect the samples and their means to be similar, differing from each other only by chance. In other words, if the IV has no effect, the samples are simply different samples drawn from the same population, and their means will differ due to sampling fluctuation only.

If, however, the treatment has an effect, the samples then come from populations with different means, and we would expect the sample means to be quite different.

Are you beginning to see why this analysis is called "Analysis of Variance?" ANOVA examines how much sample means vary from each other compared with what would be expected by chance sampling fluctuation.

Null and Alternative Hypotheses

When we made inferences about means with the normal or the t distribution, the null hypothesis stated that all the means were equal. The same is true when we make inferences about means using the F distribution. The null hypothesis is

$$H_0 : \; \mu_1 = \mu_2 = \mu_3 = \cdots = \mu_k$$

where k is the number of samples in the experiment.

When an analysis compares only two means, we distinguish between directional and nondirectional alternative hypotheses. In ANOVA, however, the null hypothesis may be false because two means are different, although all the rest are equal, or three means may be different and all the rest the same, for example. ANOVA does not tell us where the difference(s) lies; it just tells us that there is a difference between at least two of the means. Therefore, the alternative hypothesis for ANOVA is always

$$H_1: H_0 \text{ is false}$$

We do not distinguish between directional and nondirectional alternative hypotheses in ANOVA. Once ANOVA has determined that a significant difference exists, we must do further analyses to find out which means are responsible for the outcome of ANOVA. In Chapter 13, I will discuss some of the statistical techniques commonly used after ANOVA.

ANOVA is a family of techniques. We will study two of these in this chapter: One-way ANOVA for one independent variable and a two-way ANOVA for two independent variables.

CONCEPT REVIEW 11.2

What does it mean to reject the null in ANOVA?

Answer on page 324.

One-Way Analysis of Variance

One-way ANOVA is a statistical procedure that tests for differences between two or more means.

With only two samples, it is appropriate to compute either t or F. Comparing two means with a t test is a special case of one-way ANOVA. In fact, the outcome (not the actual value) of an ANOVA done on two samples is identical to the outcome of a t test done on those two samples.

Let's examine the logic of one-way ANOVA. Consider three groups of 10 participants each. All the participants were randomly selected from a population and independently assigned to groups. Each group was treated differently. Now imagine, for the moment, that the treatment (IV) *had no effect* on the DV. We might find the following kinds of results:

```
GROUP 1    X  XX  XXXXX  X    X
                   X̄₁
GROUP 2    XXXX XX    X   XX
                 X̄₂
GROUP 3    X   X XXXXX  X  XX
                   X̄₃
```

Each X represents the score for a single participant, and the placement of the mean indicates its value relative to the individual scores. As you can see, within each group, the individual scores vary around that group mean. The means of the three groups are similar but not identical.

Now, let's consider what kind of data we might have if the treatment *did have an effect* on the groups. We might see something like this:

```
GROUP 1              X  XX  XX    XXXXX
                          X̄₁
GROUP 2    X XXX XXX X X X
                X̄₂
GROUP 3                        XXX  XXXX  X   XX
                                       X̄₃
```

Within each group, the scores vary around the group mean. But the group means are not as similar as when the treatment had no effect. However, we would not expect the means to be identical even if the treatment had no effect. They would vary somewhat because of sampling fluctuation. The question is "How different must the group means be before we can conclude that the differences are probably not due to sampling variation alone?" In other words, "How much variation is expected when the groups come from populations with equal means?"

If there is no treatment effect, the populations from which the groups were drawn would have identical means, and thus, we may treat the samples as if they come from the same population. Any variation in the sample means would be considered chance variation. If, however, the treatment did have an effect, then the samples come from populations with different means, and we would expect the variation between the sample means to be quite large.

Partitioning the Variance

Looking at the examples given in the previous section, we can identify three kinds of variation.

1. The individual scores *vary around their subgroup means*. The participants within each group are different, and so their scores are different. This is variation inherent in the participants themselves. *Inherent variation* or **error variance** is free of the effects of the treatment. It is the variation we see because of individual differences among our participants.

Error variance: Variability among participants that is free of treatment effects

2. The subgroup means are not the same. *The subgroup* means *vary around the combined mean*, the overall mean of the experiment. These group means are different for two reasons: (1) inherent variation of the participants and (2) the effect of the treatment, if indeed it had an effect. The variation between subgroup means is due to *inherent variation plus variation due to treatment.*
3. Finally, the individual scores *vary around the combined mean* of the entire distribution. Each score varies from the overall mean. This is the *total variation in the experiment.*

We have three kinds of variations:

1. Variation of the scores within each group from their own group mean
2. Variation of the group means from the combined mean
3. Total variation as reflected in the difference between the scores and the combined mean

The first kind of variation is due to inherent variability only. The second kind of variation is due to inherent variation and the effect of the treatment. If the treatment had no effect, we would expect the first and second kinds of variation to be equal. In other words, if the treatment had no effect, then these two measures should be more or less the same, given some amount of sampling fluctuation. This is the logic of ANOVA.

The **total variability** in an experiment may be partitioned into:

1. Variability of participants within groups
2. Variability between groups

Any individual score in any group can vary from the combined mean of all the groups ($X - \bar{X}_C$). Any score can vary from the mean of its own group ($X - \bar{X}$). Each group mean can vary from the combined mean ($\bar{X} - \bar{X}_C$). If we squared each of these differences and summed the squares, we would have three measures of variability in "sum of squares" form. ANOVA involves computing various sums of squares and comparing them. We will continue to use **SS** to stand for **sum of squares** in ANOVA.

> **Total variability:** Variability of all the scores from the combined mean
>
> **Within-group variability:** Variability of scores within groups from the group mean
>
> **Between-group variability:** Variability of group means from the combined mean

Calculating the Sums of Squares

Because we have three measures of variability, we compute three separate sums of squares. The measure of total variability (called SS_{TOT}) is composed of two parts:

1. Variability within groups (called SS_{WG})
2. Variability between groups (called SS_{BG})

The defining formula that partitions the total variability in an experiment into its two component parts is

$$SS_{TOT} = SS_{BG} + SS_{WG}$$

$$\sum^{k}\sum^{n}\left(X_i - \bar{X}_c\right)^2 = \sum_{n}^{k}\left(\bar{X}_k - \bar{X}_c\right)^2 + \sum^{k}\sum^{n}\left(X_i - \bar{X}_k\right)^2$$

where $\bar{X}_c$ is the combined mean

$\bar{X}_k$ is the group mean

X_i is the raw score

Now, don't let this throw you! I include it because I believe it is the best way to understand what ANOVA is really doing. As with other techniques, the computational formulas do not help us understand the logic.

Examine the expression to the left of the equals sign. This tells us to subtract the combined mean from each score in the entire experiment, square these differences, and sum them. This is the total variability in the experiment. The first expression to the right of the equals sign tells us to subtract the combined mean from each group mean, square each difference, multiple each difference by n, and sum these. The defining formula for the between-group sum of squares is

$$SS_{BG} = n_1 \left(\bar{X}_1 - \bar{X}_c \right)^2 + n_2 \left(\bar{X}_2 - \bar{X}_c \right)^2 + \cdots + n_k \left(\bar{X}_k - \bar{X}_c \right)^2$$

The last expression tells us to subtract the group mean from each score in the group, square these differences, sum them, and to do this for all the groups. In other words, compute the sum of squares within each group. The defining formula for the within-group sum of squares is

$$SS_{WG} = SS_1 + SS_2 + \cdots + SS_K$$

In the past, we have found that the defining formulas are not usually used computationally. This is also true here. Simplified formulas are used in the actual computation of the sums of squares. The computational formula for the total sum of squares is

$$SS_{TOT} = \Sigma X_{tot}^2 - \frac{\left(\Sigma X_{tot} \right)^2}{n_{tot}}$$

X_{tot} = all the raw scores in the experiment

n_{tot} = the total number of observations in the experiment

To use this formula, follow these steps:

Step 1. Square all the raw scores in the experiment.

Step 2. Sum the squared raw scores.

Step 3. Sum the raw scores, square the sum, and divide by the total number of observations in the experiment.

Step 4. Subtract the result of Step 3 from that of Step 2.

The computational formula for the between-group sum of squares is

$$SS_{BG} = \frac{\left(\Sigma X_1 \right)^2}{n_1} + \frac{\left(\Sigma X_2 \right)^2}{n_2} + \cdots + \frac{\left(\Sigma X_K \right)^2}{n_k} - \frac{\left(\Sigma X_{tot} \right)^2}{n_{tot}}$$

To use this formula, follow these steps:

Step 1. Sum the raw scores in each group.

Step 2. Square each group sum and divide each by its group size.

Step 3. Sum the values obtained in Step 2.

Step 4. Sum the scores in the entire experiment, square this sum, and divide by the total number of observations.

Step 5. Subtract the result of Step 4 from that of Step 3.

Because the total sum of squares is composed of the between-group sum of squares plus the within-group sum of squares, we can obtain the sum of squares within groups by subtraction ($SS_{TOT} - SS_{BG}$).

FYI

If we wished to calculate the within-group sum of squares directly, we would determine the sum of squares within each of our groups using our usual formula for any sum of squares:

$$SS = \sum X^2 - \frac{(\sum X)^2}{n}$$

We would compute this value for each group and then sum the resulting values. The computational formula for within-group sum of squares would look like this:

$$SS_{WG} = \left[\sum X_1^2 - \frac{(\sum X_1)^2}{n_1} + \sum X_2^2 - \frac{(\sum X_2)^2}{n_2} \right] + \cdots + \left[\sum X_K^2 - \frac{(\sum X_K)^2}{n_K} \right]$$

Calculating the Mean Squares

In the past, we have divided sums of squares by degrees of freedom to obtain unbiased estimates of the population variance (s^2). We will do the same here. Dividing each sum of squares by its associated degrees of freedom produces unbiased estimates of the population variance called **mean squares** in ANOVA.

Mean square: Estimate of the population variance found by dividing sum of squares by df

When we compute the total sum of squares, we effectively ignore the groups and treat all the scores as one large group. We subtract each raw score from the overall or combined mean, square each difference, and sum the squared differences. Because we use the combined mean in our calculation, it is fixed, and we use up one degree of freedom. Therefore, $(n_{tot} - 1)$ scores are left free to vary. When computing the degrees of freedom for total sum of squares,

$$df_{tot} = n_{tot} - 1$$

Computing the sum of squares between groups requires that we subtract the combined mean from each subgroup mean, square each difference, and sum the squared differences. Because we use the combined mean in our computations, it is fixed. We have as many difference values as we have groups (k), but we have used up one degree of freedom. When computing the degrees of freedom for between-group sum of squares,

$$df_{bg} = k - 1$$

The sum of squares within groups is found by measuring the amount of variability of the group scores around their own means. We subtract the subgroup mean from all the scores in its group, square the differences, and sum them. We do this for each group in our experiment. Because we use the subgroup means in our calculation, each is fixed, and we use up one degree of freedom for each group mean used. When computing the degrees of freedom for within-group sum of squares,

$$df_{wg} = n_1 - 1 + n_2 - 1 + \cdots + n_k - 1 = n_{tot} - k$$

In an experiment, the total sum of squares can be partitioned into the sum of squares between groups plus the sum of squares within groups. The total number of degrees of freedom in the experiment can be partitioned into two parts as well: degrees of freedom between groups plus degrees of freedom within groups. Therefore,

$$df_{tot} = df_{bg} + df_{wg}$$
$$n_{tot} - 1 = k - 1 + n_{tot} - k$$

The partitioning of the variability and degrees of freedom in a one-way ANOVA is illustrated in Figure 11.2.

Dividing each sum of squares by its associated degrees of freedom produces unbiased estimates of the population variance: mean squares (MS). If the treatment in our experiment had no effect on the DV, we would expect the estimate of the variance between groups (MS_{BG}) to be similar to the estimate of the variance within groups (MS_{WG}). This is because the variance estimate between

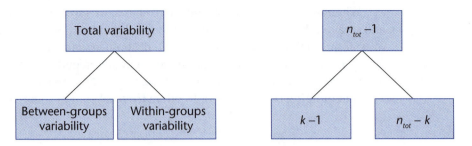

Figure 11.2. Partitioning the variability and degrees of freedom for a one-way ANOVA.

groups reflects inherent variation plus treatment, while the variance estimate within groups reflects inherent variation only. If the treatment has no effect, these two measures are estimating the same thing: *inherent variation.* We are interested, then, in these two unbiased estimates: (1) the mean square between groups and (2) the mean square within groups. Each is found by dividing the sum of squares by degrees of freedom.

In summary, the mean squares for a one-way ANOVA are computed as follows:

$$MS_{BG} = \frac{SS_{BG}}{df} = \frac{SS_{BG}}{k-1}$$

$$MS_{WG} = \frac{SS_{WG}}{df} = \frac{SS_{WG}}{n_{tot} - k}$$

Now, we can compare these two variance estimates to determine the effect of the treatment. If the treatment didn't work, each estimates the same population variance. If the treatment did work, then the between-group mean square would be larger than the within-group mean square because it reflects not only inherent variation but also treatment effects.

CONCEPT REVIEW 11.3

$SS_{BG} = 44$

$SS_{WG} = 60$

$k = 5$

$n_{tot} = 25$

What are the mean squares for the above?

Answer on page 325.

Calculating and Interpreting the *F* Ratio

The *F* ratio is the ratio between the between-groups variance estimate and the within-groups variance estimate:

$$F = \frac{MS_{BG}}{MS_{WG}}$$

Clearly, if the treatment had no effect, we would expect this ratio to be 1 on average. If the treatment did have an effect, we would expect this value to be greater than 1. Table B.3 in Appendix B provides the critical values of *F* for the 5% and 1% level of significance. This table is read by locating the degrees of freedom associated with the numerator (between-group mean square) along the top and locating the degrees of freedom associated with the denominator (within-group mean square) along the side. As usual, to reject the null hypothesis, the obtained *F* value must be equal to, or larger than, the critical value. If the null is rejected, we conclude that the treatment had a significant effect on the DV. In other words, the between-group mean square is so much greater than the within-group mean square that we claim that this is not due to chance but is caused by the treatment variable.

CONCEPT REVIEW 11.4

What is the critical *F* value at $\alpha = .01$ when the *df* for the between-group sum of squares are 8 and the *df* for the within-group sum of squares are 65?

Answer on page 325.

Let's work our way through an example in detail to see how ANOVA is done.

Running a One-Way Analysis of Variance

As a psychology instructor, I am always looking for ways to help students improve their study skills and test performance. Let's assume that I have randomly selected three groups of 15 students each and have given special training to two of the groups. In one group, I have concentrated their training on test-taking skills (Group T). Another group has been trained in study skills (Group S). The third group, the control group (Group C), received no special training. The trained groups have been instructed to use their new skills when studying and taking weekly tests for a period of 1 month. At the end of this time, all the students take a common test to measure their knowledge about the preceding month's work. Here are the data:

	Group T	Group S	Group C	X_1^2	X_2^2	X_3^2
	64	56	45	4 096	3 136	2 025
	78	76	60	6 084	5 776	3 600
	68	55	65	4 624	3 025	4 225
	57	53	67	3 249	2 809	4 489
	76	76	54	5 776	5 776	2 916
	75	75	53	5 625	5 625	2 809
	73	51	58	5 329	2 601	3 364
	66	62	59	4 356	3 844	3 481
	87	69	49	7 569	4 761	2 401
	89	63	72	7 921	3 969	5 184
	68	52	63	4 624	2 704	3 969
	59	53	69	3 481	2 809	4 761
	72	81	61	5 184	6 561	3 721
	83	90	53	6 889	8 100	2 809
	61	84	58	3 721	7 056	3 364
Sum	1076	996	886	78 528	68 552	53 118
Mean	71.73	66.40	59.07			

We have all the raw scores and their squares. Now let's run a one-way ANOVA on these data.

Step 1. Compute the sums of squares.

$$SS_{TOT} = \sum X_{tot}^2 - \frac{\left(\sum X_{tot}\right)^2}{n_{tot}}$$

$$\sum X_{tot}^2 = 78528 + 68552 + 53118 = 200198$$
$$\sum X_{tot} = 1076 + 996 + 886 = 2958$$
$$n_{tot} = 45$$

$$SS_{TOT} = 200198 - \frac{(2958)^2}{45}$$

$$= 200198 - 194439.20 = 5758.80$$

$$SS_{BG} = \frac{(\sum X_1)^2}{n_1} + \frac{(\sum X_2)^2}{n_2} + \cdots + \frac{(\sum X_k)^2}{n_k} - \frac{(\sum X_{tot})^2}{n_{tot}}$$

$$= \frac{1076^2}{15} + \frac{996^2}{15} + \frac{886^2}{15} - 194439.20$$

$$= 195652.53 - 194439.20 = 1213.33$$

$$SS_{WG} = SS_{TOT} - SS_{BG}$$

$$= 5758.80 - 1213.33 = 4545.47$$

We can verify the within-group sum of squares by computing it directly.

$$SS \text{ within Group T} = \sum X_T^2 - \frac{(\sum X_T)^2}{n_T} = 78528 - \frac{1076^2}{15} = 1342.93$$

$$SS \text{ within Group S} = \sum X_S^2 - \frac{(\sum X_S)^2}{n_S} = 2417.60$$

$$SS \text{ within Group C} = \sum X_C^2 - \frac{(\sum X_C)^2}{n_C} = 784.93$$

$$SS_{WG} = 1342.93 + 2417.60 + 784.93 = 4545.47$$

Step 2. Compute the mean squares.

To calculate the *F* ratio, we use the within-group mean square and the between-group mean square. We have a total of $(n_{tot} - 1)$ *df* $(45 - 1 = 44)$. Because we have three groups, the between-group mean square has 2 *df*. The within-groups mean square has 42 *df* (i.e., $n_{tot} - k$).

$$MS_{BG} = \frac{SS_{BG}}{df_{bg}} = \frac{1213.33}{2} = 606.67$$

$$MS_{WG} = \frac{SS_{WG}}{df_{wg}} = \frac{4545.47}{42} = 108.23$$

Step 3. Compute the F ratio.

$$F = \frac{MS_{BG}}{MS_{WG}} = \frac{606.67}{108.23} = 5.61$$

Step 4. Compare the obtained F value with the critical value and make a decision.

$$F_{crit} = F(2,42) = 5.15 \text{ at } \alpha = .01$$

Because our obtained value is larger than the critical value, we reject the null hypothesis. We have evidence that there is a significant difference between the means of the populations from which our samples were drawn. We can say that training makes a difference in test performance. The next step would be to find out exactly where that difference lies. This requires that we follow our ANOVA with another statistical technique designed to compare individual means. The more common comparison procedures are discussed in Chapter 13.

The outcome of any ANOVA can be summarized in a table called an ANOVA summary table. The summary table for the analysis we just did would look like this:

Source of Variance	Sum of Squares	df	Mean Squares	F	p
Between groups	1 213.33	2	606.67	5.61	<.01
Within groups	4 545.47	42	108.23		
Total	5 758.80	44			

We can see at a glance that the F value was significant, because the p column information tells us that the probability of getting a value that is large or larger if the null were true is very low, in fact less than 1%. So we reject the null. If we were reporting our ANOVA finding in a research paper, we would write something like this:

There was a significant effect of training on performance, $F(2, 42) = 5.61, p < .01$.

Let's enter our data into Excel and ask for a one-way ANOVA (called Single Factor in Excel). Here is what Excel provides:

ANOVA: Single factor

Summary

Groups	Count	Sum	Average	Variance
Group T	15	1076	71.73	95.92
Group S	15	996	66.4	172.69
Group C	15	886	59.07	56.07

ANOVA

Source of Variation	Sum of Squares	*df*	Mean Squares	*F*	*p* value	*F* crit
Between groups	1213.33	2	606.67	5.6	0.007	5.61
Within groups	4545.47	42	108.22			
Total	5758.8	44				

SUMMARY OF ONE-WAY ANOVA

Hypotheses

H_0: $\mu_1 = \mu_2 = \ldots = \mu_k$
H_1: H_0 is false.

Assumptions

1. Participants are randomly selected and independently assigned to groups.
2. Population distributions are normal.
3. Population variances are homogeneous.

Decision Rules

$df_{bg} = k - 1$

$df_{wg} = n_{tot} - k$

If $F_{obt} \geq F_{crit}$ reject the H_0

If $F_{obt} < F_{crit}$ do not reject H_0

Formula

$$F = \frac{MS_{BG}}{MS_{WG}}$$

CONCEPT REVIEW 11.5

Fill in the missing numbers in the ANOVA summary table.

Source of Variance	Sum of Squares	df	Mean Squares	F	p
Between groups	96	4	—	—	—
Within groups	450	45	—		

How many treatment groups are there in this analysis?

Answer on page 325.

Two-Way Analysis of Variance

One-way ANOVA is a method for comparing groups receiving different treatments or different levels of *one* IV. Another ANOVA technique, called the two-way ANOVA, allows us to simultaneously study the effects of *two* IVs.

Suppose we have been hired by a large corporation to determine if the readability of four fonts typically used in its published documents differs under fluorescent versus incandescent light. We could do two experiments: one to study the readability of the four fonts under fluorescent light and a second to study readability under incandescent light. This approach is not very efficient, however. Two-way ANOVA allows us to investigate the two IVs (light and font) at the same time in a single experiment. This design is particularly important because it provides an analysis of the interaction between the two variables.

The Logic of Two-Way Analysis of Variance

A two-way ANOVA provides three different *F* tests to answer three different questions about the effects of the treatments. Using the previous example, let's consider the questions we can ask. First, Are some fonts easier to read than others, overall? Second, Regardless of font, is it easier to read text under incandescent versus fluorescent light? Third, Whatever the difference in readability of the four fonts, is this difference the same under both light conditions? The first two questions are asking about **main effects**. The third question asks whether or not there is an **interaction effect** between font and lighting conditions.

Main effect: In ANOVA, the effect of an independent variable on the dependent variable

Interaction effect: In ANOVA, the effect of the combination of levels of the independent variables on the dependent variable

Main Effects

Main effect refers to the effect of each IV. If font made a difference in readability, we would say there is a *main effect of font*. If light conditions also made a difference, we would say there is a *main effect of lighting*. The readability scores from our experiment are as follows:

Light	Chicago	Geneva	Monaco	Princeton	Sum	Mean
Fluorescent	35	22	20	31	108	27
Incandescent	28	23	8	29	88	22
Sum	63	45	28	60		
Mean	31.5	22.5	14.0	30.0		

Let's consider the main effect of font: Does font make a difference overall? To determine this, we examine the sums (or means) for each font, ignoring light conditions for the moment. We can see that the readability score is highest for Chicago and lowest for Monaco. Let's graph the main effect of font (see Figure 11.3).

Note: In Chapter 2, we learned that discrete data should be graphed in a bar graph. I am violating that rule here for a good reason. I find main effects and interactions are easier to understand with the graphs I have used in the next sections.

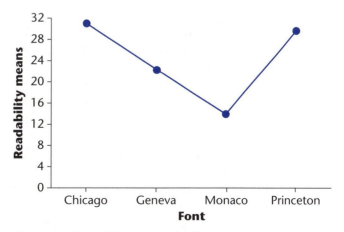

Figure 11.3.   The main effect of font on readability.

Figure 11.3 indicates that readability is poorest for Monaco, best for Chicago and Princeton, and intermediate for Geneva. If the line were flat, there would be no main effect due to font.

The second IV was light condition. If we graphed the data on readability under the two kinds of lighting, we could examine the main effect of lighting. Figure 11.4 indicates that readability was better under fluorescent lighting conditions.

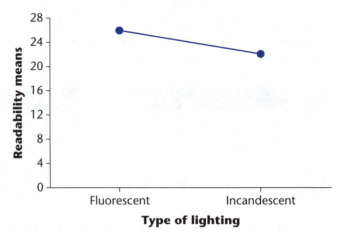

Figure 11.4. The main effect of lighting on readability.

The third question we asked was "Whatever the effect of one of the IVs, is it the same under the levels of the other IV?" In other words, "Is there an interaction between the two IVs?"

The Interaction

Main effects must be interpreted in light of any interaction effect. An interaction, in our example, means that the effect of font on readability is different under fluorescent and incandescent lighting. To graph the interaction, we separate the scores under the two lighting conditions (see Figure 11.5).

Figure 11.5 indicates that the Monaco font was particularly hard to read under incandescent light. It appears to be the font most affected by the change in lighting conditions. If the effect of lighting was the same for all fonts, the two lines of our graph would be more or less parallel. As you can see if we just looked at the main effects, we would not properly interpret our findings.

The *F* test for the interaction measures the degree to which the lines are parallel. If it is significant, we conclude that the lack of parallelism is not due to chance alone. Of course, we would not expect the lines to be exactly parallel; we would expect some deviation. If the deviation is very large, however, we have a significant interaction.

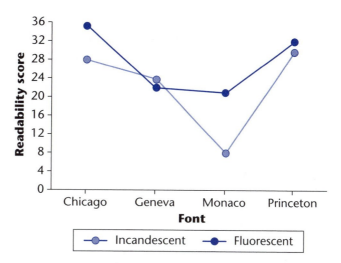

Figure 11.5. The interaction between lighting and font.

Finding a significant interaction affects how we interpret our data. Consider an example where two teachers are interested in the effectiveness of two instructional methods on student performance. Professor A is very effective when she uses a small-group discussion approach. When she uses a straight lecture approach, however, her students do not do very well. Professor B, on the other hand, is a very effective lecturer, and students do much better when he lectures than when he uses a small-group approach. If we obtained overall performance scores from the students under each teaching method, we might find the situation shown in Figure 11.6.

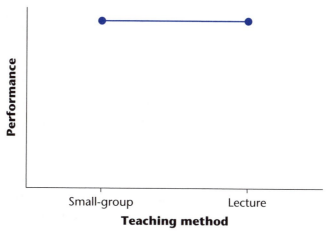

Figure 11.6. The main effect of teaching method on performance.

This graph indicates that there is no difference in overall performance under the two teaching methods—that is, there is *no main effect of teaching method*. When we look at the two professors, ignoring method, the data might look like Figure 11.7.

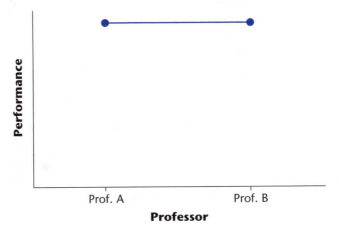

Figure 11.7. The main effect of professor on performance.

This graph indicates that there is no difference in performance between Professor A's students and Professor B's students—that is, there is *no main effect of teacher*. If our interpretation of the data stopped here, it would be misleading. The lack of main effects does not necessarily mean that there are no differences. We must also examine the interaction between teacher and the method. The graph of the interaction would look like Figure 11.8.

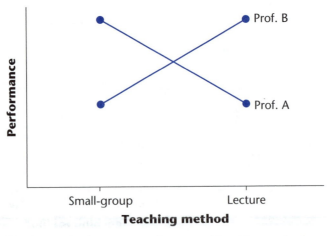

Figure 11.8. The interaction between professor and teaching method.

Now, we can see what really happened. Professor A was very effective with the small-group approach, and Professor B was very effective with the lecture approach. The teaching method *interacted* with the teacher using it. If we had looked only at the main effects we would have concluded, incorrectly, that neither teacher nor the method made a difference in student performance. Two-way ANOVA allows us to examine the interaction between the two IVs. It provides us with important information that we do not have with a one-way ANOVA.

CONCEPT REVIEW 11.6

Examine the following illustration of the results of a study of the effects of anonymity and group size on helping behavior. The people in the anonymous groups were dressed in hooded jackets so that their faces were obscured. Large groups were composed of 10 people; small groups had only 3 people. Don't worry about the details of how the measures were taken. Can you describe what seems to have gone on in this study?

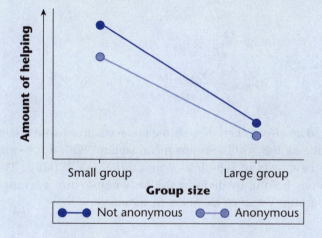

The effects of anonymity and group size on helping behavior.

Answer on page 325.

Partitioning the Variance

Let's consider an experiment with two IVs (*A* and *B*), each having two levels (1 and 2). This design is called *a* 2 × 2 *complete factorial*. We have two variables or factors, each of which has two levels. In total, we have four groups of participants. As with a one-way ANOVA, we can partition the total variance in the experiment into its component parts. The total sum of squares can be divided into the sum of squares between groups (often called the treatment sum of squares) and the sum of squares within groups.

What is new with a two-way ANOVA is that the *sum of squares between groups can be partitioned into three sums of squares* ($SS_{BG} = SS_A + SS_B + SS_{A \times B}$):

1. The sum of squares associated with the first IV (SS_A)
2. The sum of squares associated with the second IV (SS_B)
3. The sum of squares associated with the interaction ($SS_{A \times B}$)

Each sum of squares, when divided by its associated degrees of freedom, gives us an unbiased estimate of the population variance. These variance estimates are called mean squares as before. The mean squares for a two-way ANOVA are

$$MS_A = \frac{SS_A}{df_a}$$

$$MS_B = \frac{SS_B}{df_b}$$

$$MS_{A \times B} = \frac{SS_{A \times B}}{df_{a \times b}}$$

If neither A nor B had an effect, then these three mean squares estimate the same population variance as the within-groups mean square. With a two-way ANOVA, we have three new tests of significance and three new F ratios. The F ratios are determined, as before, by dividing the **between-group variance** estimates by the within-groups variance estimate. In summary,

$$F \text{ for the } A \text{ main effect} = \frac{MS_A}{MS_{WG}}$$

$$F \text{ for the } B \text{ main effect} = \frac{MS_B}{MS_{WG}}$$

$$F \text{ for the interaction} = \frac{MS_{A \times B}}{MS_{WG}}$$

Each F ratio is compared with the critical value in Table B.3 to determine its significance.

Let's look at an example to see how we would calculate the sums of squares for our three tests of significance.

Calculating the Sums of Squares

Below is an example of a 2×2 factorial design layout. Thirty-two participants are randomly selected and independently assigned to four groups, with eight participants in each.

> **Completely randomized factorial design:** In ANOVA, a fully crossed experimental design in which different participants serve in each treatment combination

Participant	Groups			
	A_1		A_2	
	B_1	B_2	B_1	B_2
1	X			
2				
3				
4				
5				
6				
7				
8				
Sum	A_1B_1	A_1B_2	A_2B_1	A_2B_2

The X would be the score of the first participant in the A_1B_1 group.

Step 1. Calculate the total sum of squares.

This is done in the same way as before. Recall the formula for the total sum of squares.

$$SS_{TOT} = \sum X_{tot}^2 - \frac{\left(\sum X_{tot} \right)^2}{n_{tot}}$$

Once again, we square all the raw scores, add them up, and subtract from this value the square of the sum divided by the total number of scores in the experiment.

Step 2. Calculate the between-groups and within-groups sums of squares.

We use the same procedure as we did with a one-way ANOVA. We'll modify our earlier formula for the between-groups sum of squares to fit our needs. The between-groups sum of squares formula for a general two-way ANOVA is

$$SS_{BG} = \frac{\left(\sum X_{A_1B_1}\right)^2 + \left(\sum X_{A_1B_2}\right)^2 + \cdots + \left(\sum X_{A_aB_b}^2\right)}{n} - \frac{\left(\sum X_{tot}\right)^2}{n_{tot}}$$

n = number of participants in each group

a = number of levels of the A IV

b = number of levels of the B IV

The within-group sum of squares is easily found by subtraction.

$$SS_{WG} = SS_{TOT} - SS_{BG}$$

Step 3. Calculate the sums of squares for the main effects and the interaction.

Recall that we have three between-groups tests of significance because we partitioned the between-group sum of squares into three parts: the two main effects and the interaction. We must determine the sum of squares for the A main effect, for the B main effect, and for the $A \times B$ interaction. The general formula for computing the sum of squares for the A main effect is

$$SS_A = \frac{\left(\sum X_{A_1}\right)^2 + \left(\sum X_{A_2}\right)^2 + \cdots + \left(\sum X_{A_a}\right)^2}{bn} - \frac{\left(\sum X_{tot}\right)^2}{n_{tot}}$$

where bn is the total number of participants in each level of the A IV.

For the A main effect in our 2×2 design, we must sum over the two levels of B for A_1 and over the two levels of B for A_2, square each sum, and divide by the number of participants contributing to that sum, that is, bn. We ignore the B IV and look only at the difference between the levels of A. We then subtract the same term: the square of the sum of all the scores in the experiment divided by the total number of scores. Our formula for our 2×2 design is

$$SS_A = \frac{\left(\sum X_{A_1}\right)^2 + \left(\sum X_{A_2}\right)^2}{bn} - \frac{\left(\sum X_{tot}\right)^2}{n_{tot}}$$

To calculate the B main effect sum of squares, the general formula is

$$SS_B = \frac{\left(\sum X_{B_1}\right)^2 + \left(\sum X_{B_2}\right)^2 + \cdots + \left(\sum X_{B_b}\right)^2}{an} - \frac{\left(\sum X_{tot}\right)^2}{n_{tot}}$$

where an is the total number of participants in each level of B. For our 2×2 design, this formula is simplified to

$$SS_B = \frac{\left(\sum X_{B_1}\right)^2 + \left(\sum X_{B_2}\right)^2}{an} - \frac{\left(\sum X_{tot}\right)^2}{n_{tot}}$$

Here, we ignore the A IV and look only at the difference between the two levels of B.

Remember that the between-group sum of squares is composed of the sum of squares for A, the sum of squares for B, and the sum of squares for the $A \times B$ interaction. The interaction sum of squares, then, can be found by subtraction. The formula is

$$SS_{A \times B} = SS_{BG} - SS_A - SS_B$$

Calculating the Mean Squares

Each sum of squares is divided by its degrees of freedom to provide mean squares. Recall that the total degrees of freedom in the experiment is $n_{tot} - 1$. The within-group sum of squares has $(n_{tot} - k)$ df, and the between-group sum of squares has $(k - 1)$ df. Recall that k for a two-way ANOVA is the product of a and b (i.e., the number of levels of A times the number of levels of B).

Because the between-group sum of squares is partitioned into three sums of squares, we might expect the degrees of freedom between groups to be partitioned as well; and this is so. The degrees of freedom for the A main effect are found by subtracting 1 from the number of levels of A. If there are two levels of A, we have 1 df for the A main effect. The same is true for the main effect of B. The degrees of freedom are the number of levels of B minus 1. The remaining degrees of freedom between groups are taken by the interaction. The interaction, then, has $k - 1 - df_a - df_b$. The degrees of freedom for the interaction can also be obtained by $(df_a)(df_b)$. A 2×2 experiment with four groups would have a 3 df between groups: 1 df for the A main effect, 1 df for the B main effect, and 1 df for the interaction. In summary,

$$df_{bg} = df_a + df_b + df_{a \times b}$$

The mean squares are now easy to obtain.

$$MS_A = \frac{SS_A}{df_a}$$

$df = (a-1)$ where a is the number of levels of A

$$MS_B = \frac{SS_B}{df_b}$$

$df = (b-1)$ where b is the number of levels of B

$$MS_{A\times B} = \frac{SS_{A\times B}}{df_{a\times b}}$$

$$df_{a\times b} = (df_{bg} - df_a - df_b) \text{ or } (df_a)(df_b)$$

Partitioning of the variability and degrees of freedom for a two-way ANOVA is illustrated in Figure 11.9.

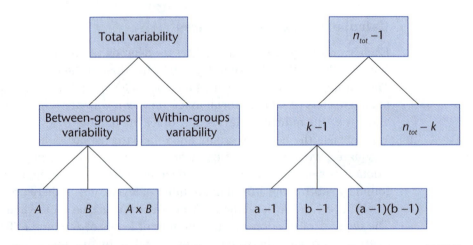

Figure 11.9. Partitioning the variability and degrees of freedom for a two-way ANOVA.

Calculating and Interpreting the *F* Ratios

Now, we can test the three mean squares for significance. The *F* ratios for a two-way ANOVA are:

$$F_A = \frac{MS_A}{MS_{WG}}$$

$$F_B = \frac{MS_B}{MS_{WG}}$$

$$F_{A \times B} = \frac{MS_{A \times B}}{MS_{WG}}$$

All three F ratios use the mean square within groups in the denominator. Each is tested for significance by locating the appropriate critical value in Table B.3. The between-groups, or treatment mean square itself, may be tested for significance with the within-groups mean square in the denominator. Lack of significance of the between-groups mean square does not preclude a significant result in the other tests, however. Often, we don't test the between-groups mean square in a two-way ANOVA, because our interest is in the main effects and the interaction rather than in the overall treatment mean square.

As in one-way ANOVA, we would expect the F ratios to be 1, on average, if the IVs had no effect on performance. With a two-way ANOVA, however, we have three questions to ask.

1. Did our first IV have an overall effect?
2. Did our second IV have an overall effect?
3. Was the effect of the first IV the same under each level of the second IV?

If the F ratio for the A main effect was significant, then we know that A made a difference in performance. If the B main effect was also significant, we know that B affected performance. If the interaction is significant, we know that the A IV affected performance differently under the different levels of the B IV.

Running a Two-Way Analysis of Variance

Let's do a two-way ANOVA. Once again, we'll use a 2×2 factorial design. A researcher decides to investigate the effect of ethnic background and gender of victim on attribution of responsibility. She randomly selects 32 young adults and randomly assigns them to two groups of 16 each. All the youth read scenarios describing a situation in which a young person has been attacked by two teenagers. For one group, the victim of the attack is a First Nations American. For the other group, no mention is made of the victim's ethnic background. In addition, for half of each group, the victim is identified as female and for the other half as male, making four groups of eight. The participants are asked to rate how responsible they think the victim is for the attack. Here are her data. Higher scores indicate that the victim is more responsible.

Ethnicity of Victim	Ethnicity Unspecified (A_1)		First Nations (A_2)	
Gender of Victim	Male	Female	Male	Female
	B_1	B_2	B_1	B_2
	6	6	12	9
	9	5	9	8
	6	7	9	8
	9	4	8	9
	8	6	7	7
	6	2	9	9
	8	4	8	5
	4	7	6	6
Sum	56	41	68	61
Mean	7.00	5.13	8.50	7.63

Step 1. Compute the total sum of squares.

$$\sum X_{tot} = 56 + 41 + 68 + 61 = 226$$

$$SS_{TOT} = \sum X_{tot}^2 - \frac{\left(\sum X_{tot}\right)^2}{n_{tot}}$$

$$= 6^2 + 9^2 + 6^2 + \cdots + 6^2 - \frac{226^2}{32}$$

$$= 1726 - 1596.125 = 129.88$$

Step 2. Compute the between-group sum of squares.

$$SS_{BG} = \frac{\left(\sum X_{A_1B_1}\right)^2 + \left(\sum X_{A_1B_2}\right)^2 + \left(\sum X_{A_2B_1}\right)^2 + \left(\sum X_{A_2B_2}\right)^2}{n} - \frac{\left(\sum X_{tot}\right)^2}{n_{tot}}$$

$$= \frac{56^2 + 41^2 + 68^2 + 61^2}{8} - \frac{226^2}{32}$$

$$= 1645.25 - 1596.125 = 49.13$$

Step 3. Compute the within-group sum of squares.

$$SS_{WG} = SS_{TOT} - SS_{BG}$$

$$= 129.88 - 49.13 = 80.75$$

Step 4. Compute the A, B, and $A \times B$ sums of squares.

$$SS_A = \frac{\left(\sum X_{A_1}\right)^2 + \left(\sum X_{A_2}\right)^2}{bn} - \frac{\left(\sum X_{tot}\right)^2}{n_{tot}}$$

$$= \frac{97^2 + 129^2}{16} - \frac{226^2}{32} = 32$$

$$SS_B = \frac{\left(\sum X_{B_1}\right)^2 + \left(\sum X_{B_2}\right)^2}{an} - \frac{\left(\sum X_{tot}\right)^2}{n_{tot}}$$

$$= \frac{124^2 + 102^2}{16} - \frac{226^2}{32} = 15.13$$

$$SS_{A \times B} = SS_{BG} - SS_A - SS_B = 49.13 - 32 - 15.13 = 2$$

Step 5. Compute the mean squares.

$$MS_A = SS_A / df$$
$$= 32 / 1 = 32$$
$$MS_B = SS_B / df$$
$$= 15.13 / 1 = 15.13$$
$$MS_{A \times B} = SS_{A \times B} / df$$
$$= 2 / 1 = 2$$
$$MS_{WG} = SS_{WG} / df$$
$$= 80.75 / 28 = 2.88$$

Step 6. Compute the *F* ratios.

$$F_A = MS_A / MS_{WG}$$
$$= 32 / 2.88 = 11.10$$
$$F_B = MS_B / MS_{WG}$$
$$= 15.13 / 2.88 = 5.25$$
$$F_{A \times B} = MS_{A \times B} / MS_{WG}$$
$$= 2 / 2.88 = 0.69$$

Step 7. Complete the ANOVA summary table given below.

Source of Variance	Sum of Squares	df	Mean Squares	F	p
Between					
A	32.00	1	32.00	11.10	<.01
B	15.13	1	15.13	5.25	<.05
A × B	2.00	1	2.00	0.69	ns
Within	80.75	28	2.88		
Total	129.88	31			

What does all this mean? Our researcher has two significant main effects, one at $\alpha = .05$ and one at $\alpha = .01$, and no significant interaction. The A main effect tells her that ethnic background of the victim affected the ratings of responsibility for the attack. Because there were only two levels of this variable, we know that the raters attributed more responsibility to victims who were identified as First Nations, $F(1, 28) = 11.10$, $p < .01$. The probability that this was a chance outcome is less than 1%. The B main effect tells her that gender of the victim also made a difference. Female victims were perceived as less responsible for their fate than male victims were, $F(1, 28) = 5.25$, $p < .05$. The probability that this was a chance outcome is less than 5%. The lack of significance of the interaction means that the two variables, ethnicity and gender of victim, did not interact. The ratings of responsibility between the First Nations and no-background groups were similar whether the victim was identified as male or female, $F(1, 28) = 0.69$, ns. Let's graph both main effects and the interaction.

When we graph a main effect, we collapse across the subgroups of the other variables. In our example, we determine the mean of the two First Nations groups, the mean of the two no-background groups, and plot those two points to examine the main effect of ethnic background. Next, we determine the mean of the two female victim groups and the mean of the two male victim groups, and plot these two points to examine the main effect of victim gender. We might create a table like the one below for victim ethnicity and gender.

	Victim Ethnicity		
Victim Gender	None Specified	First Nations	Mean
Male	7	8.5	7.75
Female	5.13	7.63	6.38
Mean	6.06	8.06	

Let's examine the ethnicity main effect by plotting the means of the two groups (Figure 11.10).

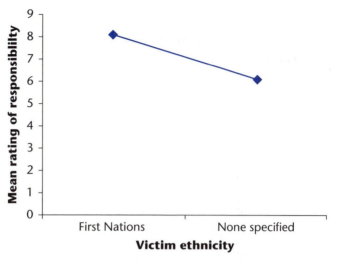

Figure 11.10.   The main effect of victim ethnic background on responsibility ratings.

We can easily see from Figure 11.10 that the ratings of responsibility were higher when the victim was identified as First Nations. Let's look at the main effect of gender (Figure 11.11).

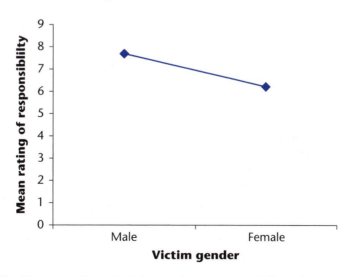

Figure 11.11.   The main effect of victim gender on responsibility ratings.

As you can see, more responsibility was assigned to male victims.

Recall that the test of significance of the interaction involves testing whether the two lines depart significantly from parallelism. The interaction between victim ethnicity and gender was not significant. As you can see in Figure 11.12, the two lines do not depart from parallel more than expected by chance. They don't look exactly parallel, but, nevertheless, they are not divergent enough for statistical significance.

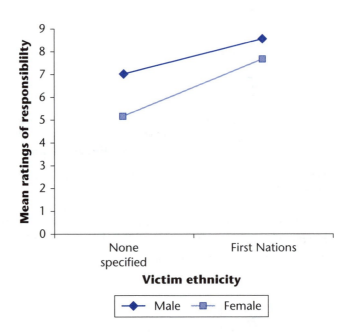

Figure 11.12. The interaction between victim ethnic background and gender.

Let's look at another example. Suppose I am interested in dog training. I may wonder if some breeds are easier to train than others. I also may wonder if type of training makes a difference and, more specifically, if some breeds of dogs respond differently to different training methods. Let's imagine I have selected four breeds of dogs and two training methods. I assign six dogs (in real research, I would use larger samples) of each breed to each training method. I train the dogs assigned to Method 1, using positive reinforcement only. The dogs in Method 2 are trained with a more punitive approach where I also use reprimands. I train all the dogs for the same length of time, and then, I test them for obedience. I do this by saying "sit/stay" and counting the number of seconds that the dog stays in the sitting position. The data below are the number of seconds each dog stayed, so higher numbers mean a more obedient dog.

	B_1	B_2	B_3	B_4	Sum	A Sum
A_1	1	7	6	9	23	
Positive reinforcement	4	10	9	7	30	
	3	10	7	10	30	
	1	9	8	10	28	
	2	6	5	8	21	
	2	8	10	9	29	
Sum	13	50	45	53	161	161
A_2	5	9	1	2	17	
Reprimands	1	9	0	6	16	
	4	8	3	3	18	
	1	10	1	4	16	
	2	5	2	5	14	
	3	8	4	3	18	
Sum	16	49	11	23	99	99
B sum	29	99	56	76	260	260

We first compute the total sum of squares.

$$SS_{TOT} = \sum X^2_{tot} - \frac{\left(\sum X_{tot}\right)^2}{n_{tot}}$$

$$= 1^2 + 4^2 + 3^2 + \cdots + 3^2 - \frac{260^2}{48}$$

$$= 1896 - 1408.33 = 487.67$$

Now, we compute the between- and within-group sums of squares.

$$SS_{BG} = \frac{(\Sigma X_{A_1B_1})^2 + \cdots + (\Sigma X_{A_2B_4})^2}{n} - \frac{(\Sigma X_{tot})^2}{n_{tot}} = \frac{13^2 + 16^2 + \cdots + 23^2}{6} - \frac{260^2}{48}$$

$$= 1801.67 - 1408.33 = 393.34$$

$$SS_{WG} = 487.67 - 393.34 = 94.33$$

Finally, we partition the between-group sum of squares into A (type of training), B (breed of dog), and $A \times B$ (interaction).

$$S_A = \frac{(\Sigma X_{A_1})^2 + (\Sigma X_{A_2})^2}{bn} - \frac{(\Sigma X_{tot})^2}{n_{tot}}$$

$$= \frac{161^2 + 99^2}{24} - \frac{260^2}{48} = 80.08$$

$$SS_B = \frac{(\Sigma X_{B_1})^2 + (\Sigma X_{B_2})^2 + (\Sigma X_{B_3})^2 + (\Sigma X_{B4})^2}{an} - \frac{(\Sigma X_{tot})^2}{n_{tot}}$$

$$= \frac{29^2 + 99^2 + 56^2 + 76^2}{12} - \frac{260^2}{48} = 221.17$$

$$SS_{A \times B} = SS_{BG} - SS_A - SS_B = 92.08$$

We compute the mean squares and the F values and summarize our analysis in the ANOVA summary table given below.

Source	Sum of Squares	df	Mean Squares	F	p
A	80.08	1	80.08	33.96	<.01
B	221.17	3	73.72	31.26	<.01
A × B	92.08	3	30.69	13.02	<.01
WG	94.33	40	2.36		
TOT	487.67	47			

As you can see, both main effects and the interaction were significant. I find the best way to interpret these kinds of findings is to graph the interaction.

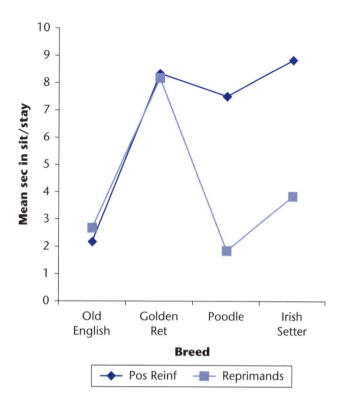

So, what does this mean. Well, the main effect of type of training was significant. Because we have only two types of training, we know that positive reinforcement produced better obedience, overall, than reprimands, $F(1, 40) = 33.96$, $p < .01$. Type of breed was also significant, $F(3, 40) = 31.26$, $p < .01$, as was the interaction of breed with type of training, $F(3, 40) = 13.02$, $p < .01$. If we were reporting these results in a journal article, we would have to follow our ANOVA with other analyses to know which specific means differ, but let's just look at the graph. It seems that Old English Sheepdogs don't learn much regardless of type of training used. They leave the sit position in a matter of seconds. It seems that Golden Retrievers obey well regardless of training. The source of the interaction lies with the Poodles and the Irish Setters. Both of these breeds do well with positive reinforcement but fall apart when they are reprimanded. So as you can see, main effects must be understood in terms of any significant interaction effects.

I would have shown you the output from Excel for a two-way ANOVA, but Excel does not appear to provide this analysis.

You may have noticed that all my examples of two-way ANOVA have had groups of equal sizes. This is not necessary; however, the calculations for a design with unequal group sizes are beyond the scope of this book.

SUMMARY OF TWO-WAY ANOVA

Hypotheses

H_0: No main effects and no interaction.
H_1: H_0 is false.

Assumptions

1. Participants are randomly selected and independently assigned to groups.
2. Population distributions are normal.
3. Population variances are homogeneous.

Decision Rules

$df_a = a - 1$
$df_b = b - 1$
$df_{a\times b} = (a-1)(b-1)$
If $F_{obt} \geq F_{crit}$ reject the H_0
If $F_{obt} < F_{crit}$ do not reject H_0

Formulas

$$F_A = \frac{MS_A}{MS_{WG}}$$

$$F_B = \frac{MS_B}{MS_{WG}}$$

$$F_{A\times B} = \frac{MS_{A\times B}}{MS_{WG}}$$

CONCEPT REVIEW 11.7

Fill in the missing blanks for the ANOVA summary table below.

Source of Variance	Sum of Squares	df	Mean Squares	F	p
Between					
A	36	1			
B	14	2			
A × B	2	2			
Within	648	54			

How many treatment groups were there in this experiment?

Answer on page 325.

Assumptions Underlying Inference With the *F* Distribution

The ANOVA techniques that we have studied assume that the populations from which the samples were drawn are normally distributed. The central limit theorem assures us that the assumption of normality won't be seriously violated as long as our samples are reasonably large and the same size.

ANOVA also assumes that the populations from which the samples are drawn have equal variances. The *F* test is quite robust, however, in that it is relatively insensitive to heterogeneity of variances as long as participants have been randomly selected and independently assigned to groups.

FYI

There are ways to determine if we have violated the assumption of homogeneity of variance. But generally, these kinds of violations tend to make our significance test less powerful. So if we have a significant outcome, we need not worry too much about whether or not we have violated this assumption.

Inferential Error

One of the important concerns in research is that of inferential error. You may recall the discussion, in Chapter 9, of Type I and Type II errors in statistical inference. A Type I error occurs when a true null hypothesis is rejected. The Type I error rate is set by alpha. Earlier in this chapter, I mentioned that one of the problems with using multiple *t* tests was the increased probability of making an error. When many *t* tests are run within a single experiment, the probability of rejecting at least one true null hypothesis is greater than alpha. The advantage of ANOVA is that the probability of a Type I error is maintained at alpha over the entire experiment. This is often referred to as the **experiment-wise error rate** (i.e., the probability of making at least one Type I error). In ANOVA, the experiment-wise error rate is alpha or less.

Experiment-wise error rate: Probability of a Type I error overall in an experiment

Calculating Effect Size

In Chapter 10, I discussed the importance of effect size estimates and mentioned that the *APA* expects researchers to provide these in their papers. An estimate of effect size often used with ANOVA designs is eta squared. This measures the proportion of the total variability in the DV that is accounted for by the manipulation of the IV. The formula for eta squared is as follows:

$$\eta^2 = \frac{SS_{TREATMENT}}{SS_{TOTAL}}$$

We would use this formula to calculate the effect size for each main effect and the interaction. A small effect would be $\eta^2 = .01$, a moderate effect is $\eta^2 = .06$, and a large effect would be $\eta^2 = .14$.

Let's calculate the main effect sizes for our ratings of responsibility example: victim ethnicity and gender. We use the sums of squares from our ANOVA summary table.

Effect size estimate for the victim ethnicity variable is

$$\eta^2 = \frac{SS_A}{SS_{TOT}} = \frac{32}{129.88} = 0.246$$

Effect size estimate for the victim gender variable is

$$\eta^2 = \frac{15.13}{129.88} = 0.116$$

Ethnicity had a large effect on ratings of responsibility, and gender had a moderate effect.

Choosing the Appropriate Test of Significance

In this chapter, we learned about two new tests of significance, one-way ANOVA and two-way ANOVA. Deciding which of these two analyses is appropriate for a given research study is a matter of determining how many IVs are operating. We will assume that the experiment has more than two groups of participants.

If you have a situation with two or more groups in the study, you must determine how many IVs are involved. Do you have several groups of participants under different levels of one IV, or do you have groups being treated with more than one IV?

With more than two groups of participants and each group under a different level of a single IV, choose a one-way ANOVA. If you determine that the experimental design involves two IVs, where participants have been randomly and independently assigned to all levels of both IV's, choose a two-way ANOVA.

Example A: A biology student has three groups of randomly selected, corpulent rats. This is a strain of rats that become obese quite naturally and are affectionately called "fat rats" by many researchers. The student is interested in the effects of a new drug on controlling weight gain. He uses three dosages of the drug, one dose level for each group. The rats are weighed before and after the period of drug administration. He will compare the average weight gain of the groups.

This study has one IV and one dosage level, and a one-way ANOVA is the appropriate analysis.

Example B: Another biology student has three groups of "fat rats" and three groups of normal (thin) rats. He is interested in the differential effects of the new drug on controlling weight gain. He wonders if the drug may have different effects on the corpulent groups than on the thin groups. He uses three dosage levels—high, medium, and low—on the fat rat groups and the same three levels on the thin rat groups. He compares weight gain after the drug administration period is over.

In this study, there are two IVs. The student is interested in the effects of the three levels of drug dose (first IV) and the type of rat being tested (second IV). He will use a two-way ANOVA, allowing him to examine the overall effect of dosage, the overall effect of rat type, and the interaction between the two. For example, he might find that the high-dosage level has a greater effect on the fat rats than on the thin rats, and that the low- and medium-dosage levels have similar effects on fat and thin rats.

This chapter has dealt with statistical techniques for research involving more than two groups of different participants. The next chapter describes the use of ANOVA in research where participants serve in more than one group. These are called dependent groups designs or repeated measures designs.

FOCUS ON RESEARCH

THE RESEARCH PROBLEM

Eyewitnesses to crimes often have very different recollections about what the perpetrator(s) looked like, and they may even disagree about what happened. Eyewitness error in identification of perpetrators in lineups is a problem for law enforcement. Suggestions that have been made to reduce these kinds of errors include

telling the eyewitness that the perpetrator may or may not be in the lineup,

using fillers who match the eyewitness description of the perpetrator,

recording the confidence of the eyewitness immediately after identification, and

using a double blind procedure where the people administering the lineup do not know the identity of the suspected perpetrator

Dysart, Lawson, and Rainey (2012) were particularly interested in the influence of postidentification feedback (i.e., confirmation given to the witness that he or she selected the bad guy) on witness confidence in their judgments. I will discuss part of their study here.

Mock witnesses watched a staged video of a theft in a research lab. They then were shown a lineup of potential thieves and asked to identify the thief who they had seen in the video. After their identification, they either were given feedback about their identification or not and were asked to make judgments about their confidence in their identification.

THE DESIGN AND VARIABLES

Introductory psychology students were the "eye witnesses." The design was a 2 (presumed blind/nonblind) × 2 (feedback/no-feedback) design. Participants in the presumed blind groups selected a video from a stack of unmarked videos and watched the "theft" alone. Participants in the presumed nonblind groups were given a video by the experimenter who remained in the room when they watched it. Participants were asked to identify the thief who they had seen commit the crime from a lineup of six. Participants in the feedback groups were told after the identification that they were "great witnesses," and participants in the no-feedback groups received no information.

Participant confidence and other kinds of judgments were then assessed.

THE ANALYSIS AND RESULTS

The data analyses were complicated and extensive, and only some of the results are reported here. Dysart et al. (2012) used ANOVA and reported a significant interaction between the blind condition and feedback, $F(6, 218) = 2.22$, $p = .04$, but no main effects of blind condition or feedback condition. Feedback increased the witnesses' confidence in their identifications and other judgments in the nonblind condition but had no effect on these judgments in the blind conditions. Let's look at the confidence in identification data graphically.

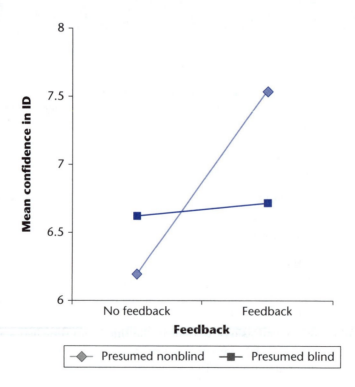

As you can see, postidentification feedback had little influence on the participants' confidence in their identification of the thief in the presumed blind condition. In the presumed nonblind condition, however, the eyewitnesses were more confident in their identification of the thief when they had been given positive feedback about their judgment.

THE CONCLUSIONS

The researchers note that their results show that witnesses who think the administrator does not know the identity of the suspect are not influenced by feedback from such administrators. However, when the eyewitnesses have reason to think that the administrator knows who the suspect is, then feedback increases their confidence that they identified the bad guy. Dysart et al. (2012) suggest that double blind procedures be used in lineup identifications.

Dysart, J. E., Lawson, V. Z., & Rainey, A. (2012). Blind lineup administration as a prophylactic against the postidentification feedback effect. *Law and Human Behavior*, *36*(4), 312–319. doi:10.1037/h0093921

SUMMARY OF FORMULAS

One-way ANOVA: Computational formulas
Sums of squares
Total $$SS_{TOT} = \sum X_{tot}^2 - \frac{\left(\sum X_{tot}\right)^2}{n_{tot}}$$
Between groups $$SS_{BG} = \frac{\left(\sum X_1\right)^2}{n_1} + \frac{\left(\sum X_2\right)^2}{n_2} + \cdots + \frac{\left(\sum X_k\right)^2}{n_k} - \frac{\left(\sum X_{tot}\right)^2}{n_{tot}}$$
Within groups $$SS_{WG} = SS_{TOT} - SS_{BG}$$
Mean squares
Between groups $$MS_{BG} = \frac{SS_{BG}}{k-1}$$
Within groups $$MS_{WG} = \frac{SS_{WG}}{n_{tot} - k}$$
F ratio $$F = \frac{MS_{BG}}{MS_{WG}}$$
Two-way ANOVA: Computational formulas
Sums of squares
Total $$SS_{TOT} = \sum X_{tot}^2 - \frac{\left(\sum X_{tot}\right)^2}{n_{tot}}$$

Between groups	$$SS_{BG} = \frac{\left(\sum X_{A_1B_1}\right)^2 + \left(\sum X_{A_2B_2}\right)^2 + \cdots + \left(\sum X_{A_aB_b}\right)^2}{n} - \frac{\left(\sum X_{tot}\right)^2}{n_{tot}}$$
A	$$SS_A = \frac{\left(\sum X_{A_1}\right)^2 + \left(\sum X_{A_2}\right)^2 + \cdots + \left(\sum X_{A_a}\right)^2}{bn} - \frac{\left(\sum X_{tot}\right)^2}{n_{tot}}$$
B	$$SS_B = \frac{\left(\sum X_{B_1}\right)^2 + \left(\sum X_{B_2}\right)^2 + \cdots + \left(\sum X_{B_b}\right)^2}{an} - \frac{\left(\sum X_{tot}\right)^2}{n_{tot}}$$
A × B	$$SS_{A\times B} = SS_{BG} - SS_A - SS_B$$
Within groups	$$SS_{WG} = SS_{TOT} - SS_{BG}$$
Mean squares	
A	$$MS_A = \frac{SS_A}{a-1}$$
B	$$MS_B = \frac{SS_B}{b-1}$$
A × B	$$MS_{A\times B} = \frac{SS_{A\times B}}{(a-1)(b-1)}$$
Within groups	$$MS_{WG} = \frac{SS_{WG}}{n_{tot} - k}$$
F ratios	$$F_A = \frac{MS_A}{MS_{WG}}$$ $$F_B = \frac{MS_B}{MS_{WG}}$$ $$F_{A\times B} = \frac{MS_{A\times B}}{MS_{WG}}$$

CONCEPT REVIEW ANSWERS

11.1. The F statistic is a ratio between two variance estimates. Variance cannot be negative, so neither can the F statistic. If the treatment has no effect on the scores, then the variance calculated within groups and the variance calculated between groups are estimating the same thing, inherent variability. Therefore, we would expect the F value to be 1 on average.

11.2. When the null is rejected in ANOVA, we know that at least one mean is significantly different from at least one other.

11.3.
$$MS_{BG} = \frac{SS_{BG}}{k-1} = \frac{44}{4} = 11$$

$$MS_{WG} = \frac{SS_{WG}}{n_{tot} - k} = \frac{60}{20} = 3$$

11.4. $F_{crit} = 2.79$

11.5.

Source of Variance	Sum of Squares	df	Mean Squares	F	p
Between groups	96	4	24	2.4	ns
Within groups	450	45	10		

Because *df* for the between-groups variance is 4 (i.e., $k - 1$), we know that there were five groups in this study.

11.6. We cannot say much for sure without doing the appropriate statistical analysis. But we can describe the apparent trends. First, it seems that when there aren't a lot of other people around, we tend to give help. Anonymity seems to make a small difference; when we feel anonymous, we tend to give less help. There seems to be an interaction. It seems that when we are in a small group and we feel anonymous, we give less help, but when we are in a large group, anonymity doesn't seem to matter much. Perhaps, the largeness of the group already makes us feel anonymous. This last statement is highly speculative.

11.7.

Source of Variance	Sum of Squares	df	Mean Squares	F	p
Between					
A	36	1	36	3.00	ns
B	14	2	7	0.58	ns
A × B	2	2	1	0.08	ns
Within	648	54	12		

The degrees of freedom column tells us that there were two levels of *A* and three levels of *B*. There were six treatment groups in this experiment.

EXERCISES

1. The data below reflect the outcome of a one-way ANOVA.

$$SS_{BG} = 141.3$$
$$k \quad = 4$$
$$SS_{WG} = 1278$$
$$n_1 = n_2 = n_3 = n_4 = 25$$

   a. Determine the MS_{BG}.
   b. Determine the MS_{WG}.
   c. Determine F.
   d. What is the critical F value at $\alpha = .05$?
   e. What is your decision?

2. Complete the ANOVA summary table.

$$SS_{TOT} = 540.30 \quad \alpha = .01$$
$$SS_{BG} \quad = 433.20 \quad n_1 = 5, n_2 = 6, n_3 = 4$$

3. An investigator measures the running speed through a maze of two groups of cockroaches. One group had been pretrained in the maze, and the other group was a control group. Run a one-way ANOVA at $\alpha = .05$ on the data (speeds in seconds). (*Note:* With two groups a t test or an ANOVA may be run).

   Pretrained roach: 7, 9, 12, 10, 10, 9, 8, 8, 8, 4

   Control roach: 9, 11, 10, 10, 13, 14, 12, 12, 13, 14

4. Sketch a rough graph for each of the following outcomes of a two-way ANOVA:
   a. One main effect and no interaction
   b. Two main effects and no interaction
   c. One main effect and an interaction
   d. Two main effects and an interaction

5. The following data were obtained from a two-way ANOVA. Sketch each main effect and the interaction.

	Mean Score	
	B_1	B_2
A_1	22	3
A_2	14	8

6. A social psychologist was interested in the effects of (a) televised violence on the aggressive behavior of children and (b) the presence of an authority figure on their behavior. She decided to investigate the two variables simultaneously. She randomly selected four groups of eight children each. Two of the groups were exposed to a violent cartoon show (V groups), and the other two groups were shown a neutral cartoon show (N groups). All the children were then allowed to play in a common area. Their behavior was monitored by a "blind" judge who counted the number of aggressive acts performed by each child. For one V group and one N group, an adult authority figure was present during the play period. For the other two groups, no authority figure was present. Run a two-way ANOVA on the data at $\alpha = .05$.

Violent Groups		Neutral Groups	
Authority	**No Authority**	**Authority**	**No Authority**
2	6	0	0
1	3	1	2
3	7	2	3
2	5	0	1
3	4	1	1
1	6	2	3
2	4	1	1
1	5	7	4

7. Run an ANOVA on the following data with $\alpha = .05$.

Group A: 7, 3, 1, 4, 4, 8, 2

Group B: 1, 3, 6, 8, 5, 5, 5

Group C: 7, 9, 10, 8, 7, 5, 9

a. SS_{TOT}
b. SS_{BG}
c. SS_{WG} SS_{WG} $(to\ check) = SS_{TOT} - SS_{BG}$
d. H_0:
   H_1:
e. $F_{.05}$
f. Complete the ANOVA summary table.
g. Put your decision in words.

8. Complete the ANOVA for the following data.

Group	1	2	3	4
ΣX	45	38	32	32
ΣX^2	310	217	185	210
n	7	7	7	7

a. SS_{TOT}
b. SS_{BG}
c. SS_{WG}
d. H_0:
   H_1:
e. $F_{.05}$
f. Complete the ANOVA summary table.
g. Put your decision in words.

9. Run a two-way ANOVA on the following data.

	A_1		A_2	
B_1	B_2	B_1	B_2
49	61	71	80
64	72	72	47
77	83	69	67
52	77	75	56
73	82	78	89
70	65	58	43

a. SS_{TOT}
b. SS_{BG}
c. SS_{WG}
d. SS_A
e. SS_B
f. $SS_{A \times B}$
g. Complete the ANOVA summary table.
h. Plot the interaction using the group means.

10. The Canadian military hired a consultant to conduct research on obedience to authority. The consultant was asked to determine the effects of perceived arbitrariness of a command and the effects of the authority figure on obedience to the command. Eighty randomly selected members of the armed forces were independently assigned to groups, such that there were 20 participants in each of four groups. All participants

read a story describing a situation where military personnel issued a command to other military personnel. For two of the four groups (*A*), the story described commands that were arbitrarily based. In other words, no apparent rationale for the commanded behavior was provided. For the other two groups (*R*), the story included a rationale for the commanded behavior. In addition, for one *A* group and one *R* group, the command was issued to a subordinate by a superior-ranking officer (*S*). For the remaining groups, the command was issued by an equal-ranked person (*E*). After the story was read, participants were required to predict whether or not the individual being commanded would obey the command, using a rating scale, where 1 = *definitely would obey* and 7 = *definitely would not obey*. The mean ratings of each group are provided below. Run a two-way ANOVA to determine if authority figure and arbitrariness had an effect on the participants' predictions. Graph the interaction.

Arbitrary			Rationale	
S	*E*		*S*	*E*
6	4		7	6
6	3		6	6
6	4		6	5
5	1		5	5
5	3		6	7
7	2		7	3
1	2		2	7
7	4		6	6
6	3		5	5
2	4		5	4
5	3		3	7
5	2		3	1
5	2		6	5
5	1		5	7
6	3		5	5
1	4		2	6
6	2		5	6
6	3		1	2
7	4		6	5
5	2		6	6

Means		
	S	*E*
A	5.10	2.80
R	4.85	5.20

CHAPTER 12

Analysis of Variance With Repeated Measures

LEARNING OBJECTIVES

After reading this chapter, you should be able to do the following:

1. Describe the partitioning of the variance for a one-way analysis of variance (ANOVA) with repeated measures and indicate the associated degrees of freedom.
2. Provide the *F* ratio tested in a one-way ANOVA with repeated measures.
3. Run a one-way ANOVA with repeated measures.
4. Describe the partitioning of the variance for a two-way ANOVA with repeated measures and indicate the associated degrees of freedom.
5. Provide the *F* ratio tested in a two-way ANOVA with repeated measures.
6. Run a two-way ANOVA with repeated measures.
7. Complete an ANOVA summary table for a given analysis.
8. Determine the appropriate test of significance for a given research problem.

Does our frontal-lobe brain activity differ when we are reading comics, editorials, or featured articles in a newspaper?

How happy is each member of cohabiting couples during the 1st year, the 3rd year, the 5th year, and the 10th year of the relationship?

Does our body image improve as we view more and more realistic images in popular media?

These kinds of research questions might be best assessed by measuring responses from participants who serve under all the different conditions (or levels of the independent variable [IV]) in the study. When we measure responses from the same participants in all conditions of a study, we have a **repeated measures design**.

Researchers in education and the social sciences tend to study organisms whose responses are quite variable even under identical experimental conditions. As you know, people are generally more variable than rats, pigeons, or chemical compounds. People bring their different backgrounds and experiences into the experimental situation. In Chapter 10, we discussed the use of dependent-groups designs to reduce the effects of individual differences as a source of variability.

Recall that ANOVA is a family of analyses, some of which are appropriate when the same participants serve under more than one condition. In this chapter, we will look at two repeated-measures ANOVA designs.

> **Repeated measures design:** An experimental design where participants serve in more than one treatment group

One-Way ANOVA With Repeated Measures

In a one-way ANOVA with repeated measures, all participants serve under two or more levels (called treatments) of one independent variable. The order of treatment may not be the same for all participants, but instead, it may be counterbalanced or randomized in some way. Because each participant is tested under all treatment levels, differences in performance *between* the participants should reflect treatment differences, not individual differences. Any repeated-measures design allows us to remove the variability due to individual differences from the estimate of experimental error. Thus, it is a more powerful test of the treatment effect. We assume that the error variance based on repeated measures of the same participant, when the effects of the treatment are removed, will be less than the error variance based on different participants under the same treatment.

Null and Alternative Hypotheses

The null and alternative hypotheses are the same as those for any one-way ANOVA. The null assumes no difference between population means, and the alternative specifies that the null is false. As with other ANOVAs, specific differences between treatment means must be determined by a multiple comparison procedure.

Partitioning the Variance

The total variability in a one-way ANOVA repeated-measures experiment is partitioned into two parts. The variability between participants reflects individual differences. The variability within participants reflects variation due to differences in treatments and to uncontrolled variation when the same participant is tested repeatedly.

The second component, variability within participants, can be partitioned into (1) variability between treatments and (2) error variability (called "participant by treatment" or $P \times T$).

As you might expect, degrees of freedom can be partitioned similarly. Figure 12.1 illustrates the partitioning of variability and degrees of freedom for a one-way ANOVA with repeated measures, where k is the number of treatment groups and n is the number of participants in the experiment.

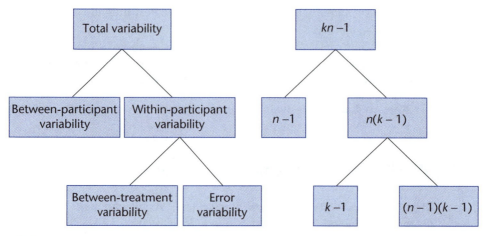

Figure 12.1. Partitioning the variability and degrees of freedom for a one-way ANOVA with repeated measures.

CONCEPT REVIEW 12.1

Twenty participants are tested on five different occasions. What are the degrees of freedom for the total sum of squares?

Answer on page 361.

Calculating the Sums of Squares

Below is an example of a one-way ANOVA repeated-measures design with three levels of independent variable and five participants tested under each level.

Participants	Independent Variables			Sums
	1	**2**	**3**	
1				ΣX_{P_1}
2				ΣX_{P_2}
3				ΣX_{P_3}
4				ΣX_{P_4}
5				ΣX_{P_5}
Sum	ΣX_{T_1}	ΣX_{T_2}	ΣX_{T_3}	

We begin our analysis by following these steps:

Step 1. Calculate the total sum of squares.

This is done in the usual way. We square all the scores, sum them, and subtract from this value the square of the sum of all the scores divided by the total number of scores (kn) in the experiment.

$$SS_{TOT} = \sum X_{tot}^2 - \frac{\left(\sum X_{tot}\right)^2}{kn}$$

Step 2. Calculate the between-participants sum of squares.

For simplicity, we'll call this the participant sum of squares. The general formula for calculating the participant sum of squares is

$$SS_p = \frac{\left(\sum X_{P_1}\right)^2 + \left(\sum X_{P_2}\right)^2 + \cdots + \left(\sum X_{P_n}\right)^2}{k} - \frac{\left(\sum X_{tot}\right)^2}{kn}$$

This formula tells us to

1. square each participant's sum,
2. sum the squares,
3. divide this sum by the number of treatments (k), and
4. subtract from the obtained value the square of the sum of all the scores divided by the total number of scores.

Step 3. Calculate the within-participants sum of squares.

This can be done using the following formula:

$$SS_{WP} = \frac{\sum X_{tot}^2}{kn} - \frac{\left(\sum X_{P_1}\right)^2 + \left(\sum X_{P_2}\right)^2 + \cdots + \left(\sum X_{P_n}\right)^2}{k}$$

You can see that both parts of this formula have been calculated previously in determining the total and the participant sum of squares. Because the total sum of squares is composed of the within-participants and the participant sum of squares, the within-participants sum of squares can be easily obtained by subtraction. The formula for calculating the within-participants sum of squares is

$$SS_{WP} = SS_{TOT} - SS_P$$

Step 4. Partition the within-participants sum of squares into the between-treatment (or simply, treatment) sum of squares and the error (or $P \times T$) sum of squares.

The formula for the treatment sum of squares is

$$SS_T = \frac{\left(\sum X_{T_1}\right)^2 + \left(\sum X_{T_2}\right)^2 + \cdots + \left(\sum X_{T_k}\right)^2}{n} - \frac{\left(\sum X_{tot}\right)^2}{kn}$$

This formula tells us to

1. square each treatment sum and sum the squares,
2. divide the value computed in Step 1 by the number of participants (n), and
3. subtract from this sum the square of the sum of all the scores divided by the total number of scores.

This is the source of variability we are interested in, because it reflects the effect of the experimental treatment.

The error or $P \times T$ sum of squares is easily found by subtracting the treatment sum of squares from the within-participants sum of squares.

$$SS_{P \times T} = SS_{WP} - SS_T$$

This source of variability will be used in the denominator of the F ratio to test for the significance of the treatment effect.

Calculating the Mean Squares

The two mean squares used in the F ratio are obtained as always by dividing the sum of squares by the appropriate degrees of freedom.

The between-treatment mean square is

$$MS_T = \frac{SS_T}{k-1}$$

The $P \times T$ or error mean square is

$$MS_{P \times T} = \frac{SS_{P \times T}}{(n-1)(k-1)}$$

ALERT

Note that the degrees of freedom for the $P \times T$ sum of squares are the product of the degrees of freedom for the participant sum of squares (i.e., $n - 1$) and the treatment sum of squares (i.e., $k - 1$).

Calculating the F Ratio

The F ratio to test the significance of the experimental treatment is found in the usual way.

$$F = \frac{MS_T}{MS_{P \times T}}$$

The obtained F value is evaluated for significance against the critical value of F from Table B.3 in Appendix B, with $(k - 1)$ df in the numerator and $(n - 1)$ $(k - 1)$ df in the denominator.

CONCEPT REVIEW 5.2

The mean square treatment is 12, and the mean square participant by treatment $(P \times T)$ is 4. What is the treatment F value?

Answer on page 361.

Running a One-Way ANOVA With Repeated Measures

The following data are the scores obtained by 10 participants under each of three treatment conditions. Participants were tested for problem-solving performance: alone, with 1 other person present, or with 10 other people present. The researcher was interested in the effect of the presence of others (i.e., the treatment) on performance. The order of the three treatments was randomly determined for each participant.

	Treatment			
Participant	**Alone**	**1 Other Present**	**10 Others Present**	**Sum**
1	90	90	70	250
2	95	85	85	265
3	95	70	65	230
4	85	90	65	240
5	95	75	30	200
6	85	85	60	230
7	85	70	75	230
8	80	80	70	230
9	85	80	80	245
10	95	90	75	260
Sum	890	815	675	2 380

Step 1. Compute the total sum of squares.

$$SS_{TOT} = \sum X_{tot}^2 - \frac{\left(\sum X_{tot}\right)^2}{kn}$$

$$= 90^2 + 95^2 + \cdots + 75^2 - \frac{2380^2}{30}$$

$$= 194100 - 188813.33$$

$$= 5286.67$$

Step 2. Compute the participant sum of squares.

$$SS_P = \frac{\left(\sum X_{P_1}\right)^2 + \left(\sum X_{P_2}\right)^2 + \cdots + \left(\sum X_{P_{10}}\right)^2}{k} - \frac{\left(\sum X_{tot}\right)^2}{kn}$$

$$= \frac{250^2 + 265^2 + \cdots + 260^2}{3} - \frac{2380^2}{30}$$

$$= 189850 - 188813.33$$

$$= 1036.67$$

Step 3. Compute the within-participants sum of squares.

$$SS_{WP} = SS_{TOT} - SS_P$$

$$= 5286.67 - 1036.67 = 4250$$

Step 4. Compute the treatment and participant by treatment sum of squares.

$$SS_T = \frac{\left(\sum X_{T_1}\right)^2 + \left(\sum X_{T_2}\right)^2 + \left(\sum X_{T_3}\right)^2}{n} - \frac{\left(\sum X_{tot}\right)^2}{kn}$$

$$= \frac{890^2 + 815^2 + 675^2}{10} - \frac{(2380)^2}{30}$$

$$= 191195 - 188813.33 = 2381.67$$

$$SS_{P \times T} = SS_{WP} - SS_T$$

$$= 4250 - 2381.67 = 1868.33$$

Step 5. Compute the mean squares and F ratio.

$$MS_T = \frac{SS_T}{k-1}$$

$$= 2381.67 / 2 = 1190.83$$

$$MS_{P \times T} = \frac{SS_{P \times T}}{(n-1)(k-1)}$$

$$= 1868.33 / 18 = 103.80$$

$$F = \frac{MS_T}{MS_{P \times T}}$$

$$= 11.47$$

With 2 and 18 df, the obtained F value is larger than the critical value at the .01 level of significance, and so we reject the null hypothesis. We have statistical evidence that the presence of others affects problem-solving performance. We could report our analysis in an ANOVA summary table.

ANOVA Summary Table					
Source of Variance	Sum of Squares	df	Mean Squares	F	p
P	1 036.67	9			
WP	4 250.00	20			
T	2 381.67	2	1 190.83	11.47	<.01
P × T	1 868.33	18	103.80		
Total	5 286.67	29			

If we were reporting the ANOVA results in a formal paper, we might say something like this:

People performed significantly differently under the three conditions, $F(2, 18) = 11.47, p < .01$.

Following the ANOVA, we would use one of the tests discussed in Chapter 13 to compare specific pairs of means.

CONCEPT REVIEW 12.3

Twenty people participated in a driving simulation study under four different levels of difficulty. Difficulty was determined by speed limit, road hazards, number of other vehicles on the road, and so on. What are the degrees of freedom for the following:

A. Participant sum of squares

B. Within-participants sum of squares

C. Treatment sum of squares

D. $P \times T$ sum of squares

Answer on page 361.

SUMMARY OF ONE-WAY ANOVA WITH REPEATED MEASURES

Hypotheses

H_0: $\mu_1 = \mu_2 = \ldots = \mu_k$
H_1: H_0 is false.

Assumptions

1. Participants are randomly selected.
2. Population distributions are normal.
3. Population variances are homogeneous.
4. Population covariances are equal.

Decision Rules

$df_t = k - 1$
$df_{p \times t} = (n - 1)(k - 1)$
If $F_{obt} > F_{crit}$ reject the H_0
If $F_{obt} < F_{crit}$ do not reject H_0

Formula

$$F = \frac{MS_T}{MS_{P \times T}}$$

FYI

In general, a repeated-measures one-way ANOVA is a more powerful design than its between-participants counterpart (i.e., a simple one-way ANOVA). This is because the error term, the denominator of the F ratio, tends to be smaller because same participants are less variable than different participants. A repeated-measures design is also more economical because it requires fewer participants. Many research questions are suitable for a repeated-measures approach, but some are not. When the randomizing or counterbalancing of order-of-treatment conditions cannot be done or will not remove order effects, a repeated-measures design is not appropriate.

Two-Way ANOVA With Repeated Measures on One Factor

In Chapter 11, I discussed two-way ANOVA as a useful design for simultaneously analyzing the effects of two experimental variables with three tests of significance: two tests for the main effect of each variable and one test for the interaction between the variables.

Two-way ANOVA can also be used to analyze experiments where repeated measures are taken on one or both experimental variables. We will concern ourselves with the case where one variable or factor has repeated measures and the other does not, a mixed design. Why am I switching terms from variable to factor? Well, only because the term **factor** is the more common usage these days.

We may be interested in the effect of training on the performance of groups of participants who differ with respect to job experience. Suppose that we are investigating the effects of four drug dosages on visual acuity performance of three groups of participants, each group having received different instructions about the task. If we randomly assigned participants to instruction groups and tested each under all four dosage levels, we would have a 4×3 mixed design with repeated measures on Factor B (drug dosage).

A 2×3 experiment with repeated measures on Factor B may be represented as

	P	B_1	B_2	B_3
A_1	1	X_{111}	X_{112}	X_{113}
	2	X_{211}	X_{212}	X_{213}
	3			
	.			
	.			
	.			
	n			X_{n13}
A_2	1	X_{121}	X_{122}	X_{123}
	2	X_{221}	X_{222}	X_{223}
	3			
	.			
	.			
	.			
	n			X_{n23}

The first subscript refers to the participant number, the second to the A condition, and the third to the B condition. This illustration indicates that there were n participants in A_1, all of whom participated under each level of B, and there were n different participants in A_2, all of whom participated under each level of B. Therefore, A is a between-participants factor, and B is a within-participants factor. Note that the score X_{111} represents the score that the first participant in A_1 received in the B_1 treatment condition. X_{112} is her score in the B_2 condition, and X_{113} is her score in the B_3 condition. The score symbolized by X_{121} is the score that the first participant in the A_2 condition received in the B_1 treatment condition. If you feel confused, please read on.

Let's take the design above and relate it to something we can all understand. Imagine that we have 40 children diagnosed as learning disabled. Half of these kids have been randomly assigned to a highly structured instructional program (Formal); the rest are in a less structured program (Informal). We want to know if the program structure makes a difference in academic achievement. We decide to target three curriculum areas: (1) language, (2) math, and (3) science. We obtain three achievement scores for each child. Let's use the illustration that confused us earlier to sort out what is happening.

Factor: In ANOVA, an independent variable

Program	Language (B_1)	Math (B_2)	Science (B_3)
Formal (A_1)			
Christiaan	X_{111}	X_{112}	X_{113}
Marc Dan	X_{211}	X_{212}	X_{213}
Lucas			
.			
.			
$n = 20$			X_{2013}
Informal (A_2)			
Matthew	X_{121}	X_{122}	X_{123}
Ben	X_{221}	X_{222}	X_{223}
Nick			
.			
.			
$n = 20$			X_{2023}

ALERT

This repeated-measures design reduces error variance for tests of the within-participants factors. Differences in performance found between the different levels of Factor B under each level of A, for example, cannot be due to differences between participants, because the same participants serve under all levels of *B*. In other words, variability due to individual differences is removed from the analysis of the main effect of Factor *B*. This is also true of the interaction effect. Statisticians say that the *B* treatment effect and the *A* × *B* interaction are *unconfounded* by between-participants differences. For this reason, the test of significance for Factor *B* and the *A* × *B* interaction is more sensitive than the test of significance for the *A* main effect. This design is particularly suitable for researchers who are more interested in the *B* factor than the *A* factor.

Null and Alternative Hypotheses

The null and alternative hypotheses are the same as those for any two-way ANOVA. The null assumes no main effects and no interaction.

Partitioning the Variance

The total variability can be partitioned in a manner similar to that used for the one-way design. Figure 12.2 illustrates the partitioning of the variability for a two-way ANOVA with repeated measures on Factor *B*.

The total degrees of freedom can be partitioned as shown in Figure 12.3, where *a* is the number of levels of Factor *A*, *b* is the number of levels of Factor *B*, and *n* is the number of participants in each group.

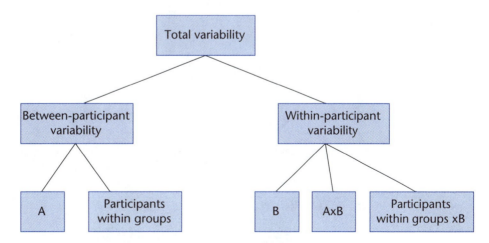

Figure 12.2. Partitioning the variability for a two-way ANOVA with repeated measures on Factor B.

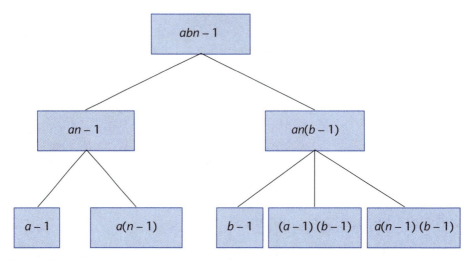

Figure 12.3. Partitioning the degrees of freedom for a two-way ANOVA with repeated measures on Factor B.

Calculating the Sums of Squares

Below is an example of a 2×3 mixed design, with two levels of the between-participant factor (A), three levels of the within-participants factor (B), and a total of 10 participants in the experiment.

Participant	B_1	B_2	B_3	Sum
A_1				
1				P_1
2				P_2
3				P_3
4				P_4
5				P_5
Sum	A_1B_1	A_1B_2	A_1B_3	A_1
A_2				
6				P_6
7				P_7
8				P_8
9				P_9
10				P_{10}
Sum	A_2B_1	A_2B_2	A_2B_3	A_2
Sum	B_1	B_2	B_3	

Step 1. Calculate the total sum of squares.

$$SS_{TOT} = \sum X_{tot}^2 - \frac{\left(\sum X_{tot}\right)^2}{abn}$$

We square all the raw scores, sum them, and subtract from this value the square of the sum of all the scores divided by the total number of scores in the experiment. For a two-way mixed design, there is a total of abn scores in the experiment.

Step 2. Calculate the participant sum of squares (SS_P) and its component parts, the sum of squares for A (SS_A), and the sum of squares for participants within groups ($SS_{P(gps)}$).

$$SS_P = \frac{\left(\sum X_{P_1}\right)^2 + \left(\sum X_{P_2}\right)^2 + \cdots + \left(\sum X_{p_{an}}\right)^2}{b} - \frac{\left(\sum X_{tot}\right)^2}{abn}$$

The participant sum of squares is found by

1. summing across all levels of B for each participant in the experiment,
2. squaring each sum,
3. adding all these squared sums,
4. dividing the value in Step 3 by the number of levels of B, and
5. subtracting from the value in Step 4 the same value we used to obtain the total sum of squares in Step 1 (i.e., the squared sum of all the scores in the experiment divided by the total number).

This participant sum of squares can now be partitioned into its component parts. We first find the sum of squares for Factor A.

$$SS_A = \frac{\left(\sum X_{a_1}\right)^2 + \left(\sum X_{a_2}\right)^2 + \cdots + \left(\sum X_{a_a}\right)^2}{bn} - \frac{\left(\sum X_{tot}\right)^2}{abn}$$

This sum of squares is found by

1. summing across all participants and levels of Factor B for each level of Factor A,
2. squaring each of these sums,
3. summing the squares,
4. dividing this value by the number of scores contributing to the sum (i.e., bn), and
5. subtracting the same value as we used before.

The participants within-groups sum of squares can now be found by subtraction.

$$SS_{P(gps)} = SS_P - SS_A$$

Step 3. Calculate the within-participant sum of squares and its component parts, the B, $A \times B$, and participants within-groups $\times B$ sums of squares.

The within-participant sum of squares is easily obtained by subtracting the participant sum of squares from the total sum of squares.

$$SS_{WP} = SS_{TOT} - SS_P$$

Now, we compute the sum of squares for Factor B.

$$SS_B = \frac{\left(\sum X_{b_1}\right)^2 + \left(\sum X_{b_2}\right)^2 + \cdots + \left(\sum X_{b_b}\right)^2}{an} - \frac{\left(\sum X_{tot}\right)^2}{abn}$$

You can see that the procedure for calculating the sum of squares for Factor B is much the same as that for Factor A. We sum across all participants and levels of A for each level of B, square each sum, add the squares, and divide by the total number of participants in each level of B (i.e., an).

Next, we compute the sum of squares for the $A \times B$ interaction.

$$SS_{A \times B} = \frac{\left(\sum X_{a_1b_1}\right)^2 + \left(\sum X_{a_1b_2}\right)^2 + \cdots + \left(\sum X_{a_ab_b}\right)^2}{n} - \frac{\left(\sum X_{tot}\right)^2}{abn} - SS_A - SS_B$$

The interaction sum of squares is found first by computing the sum for each combination of A and B. For a 3×2 design, we would have six sums. Then, we add up the squares of all the sums, divide by the number of participants in each group (i.e., n), and subtract from this value the same value we have used before. Then, we subtract the SS_A and the SS_B.

Finally, we find the third component of the within-participant sum of squares, the participants within-groups $\times B$ sum of squares ($SS_{P(gps) \times B}$), by subtraction.

$$SS_{P(gps) \times B} = SS_{WP} - SS_B - SS_{A \times B}$$

Now, we have all the components we need to calculate the mean squares that we will use in our significance tests.

Calculating the Mean Squares

As with any two-way ANOVA, we have three tests of significance, one for each main effect and one for the interaction.

The between-participants main effect of interest is the A main effect. The mean square for A is tested for significance with the mean square for participants within groups (i.e., the error mean square for between-participant comparisons).

The within-participants tests are for the main effect of B and for the interaction of A and B. Both mean squares are compared with the mean square for participants within groups $\times B$ (i.e., the error mean square for the within-participants comparisons).

All mean squares are found by dividing the sums of squares by the appropriate degrees of freedom.

$$MS_A = \frac{SS_A}{a-1}$$

where a is the number of levels of Factor A

$$MS_{P(gps)} = \frac{SS_{P(gps)}}{a(n-1)}$$

where n is the number of participants in each group

$$MS_B = \frac{SS_B}{b-1}$$

where b is the number of levels of Factor B

$$MS_{A \times B} = \frac{SS_{A \times B}}{(a-1)(b-1)}$$

$$MS_{P(gps) \times B} = \frac{SS_{P(gps) \times B}}{a(n-1)(b-1)}$$

Calculating and Interpreting the F Ratios

Now, the three mean squares can be tested for significance.

$$F_A = \frac{MS_A}{MS_{P(gps)}}$$

$$F_B = \frac{MS_B}{MS_{P(gps) \times B}}$$

$$F_{A \times B} = \frac{MS_{A \times B}}{MS_{P(gps) \times B}}$$

Each F ratio is compared with the critical value from Table B.3 in Appendix B by entering the appropriate degrees of freedom. Interpretation of the outcome of a two-way ANOVA is discussed in Chapter 11. A repeated-measures design is interpreted in much the same way. Recall, however, that because participants serve under all levels of B, tests of the within-participants treatment effects will be more sensitive than tests of the between-participants effects.

Running a Two-Way ANOVA With Repeated Measures on One Factor

Carla has been hired by the police department to assess the performance of its officers in several areas related to their jobs. The department is primarily interested in three areas of competence: (1) general knowledge of police procedure, (2) general knowledge about the law and justice system in the state, and (3) decision-making ability in "real-life" situations. The department has a secondary interest in whether "time on the force" is an important factor.

Carla decides to use standardized tests available from the police department. All the multiple-choice tests are scored out of a maximum of 40 points. She randomly selects 10 officers from each of four categories of "time on the job": (1) 1 year, (2) 2 to 4 years, (3) 5 to 10 years, and (4) >10 years on the police force.

All officers are tested in each of the three areas of competence. Carla, being a well-trained researcher, is concerned about the effects of previous testing on later test performance, so she randomizes the order of the three tests in such a way that an equal number of officers within each group receive each order. In this way, she feels confident that the effects of repeated testing will be balanced among her groups. Carla's design is a 3×4 mixed design with repeated measures on a Factor B type of test. Table 12.1 shows her design and data.

Table 12.1

Carla's 3 × 4 mixed design

A (Time on Force)	P	B (Type of Test) B₁	B₂	B₃	Sum	A (Time on Force)	P	B (Type of Test) B₁	B₂	B₃	Sum
	1	37	15	12	64		21	30	39	23	92
	2	28	20	11	59		22	22	33	27	82
	3	30	24	13	67		23	13	31	26	70
	4	22	25	12	59		24	15	25	15	55
$A_{1\ (1\ yr)}$	5	33	21	14	68	$A_{3\ (5-10\ yrs)}$	25	17	30	18	65

A (Time on Force)	P	B₁	B₂	B₃	Sum	A (Time on Force)	P	B₁	B₂	B₃	Sum
	6	29	30	12	71		26	35	28	19	82
	7	27	35	13	75		27	33	22	18	73
	8	31	21	11	63		28	10	27	20	57
	9	36	22	11	69		29	18	32	24	74
	10	33	25	11	69		30	26	24	20	70
	11	25	28	13	66		31	26	22	23	71
	12	28	21	14	63		32	22	36	25	83
	13	30	30	17	77		33	21	33	28	82
	14	19	31	16	66		34	30	32	23	85
	15	22	36	13	71		35	15	27	27	69
A_2 (2–4 yrs)	16	29	22	13	64	A_4 (>10 yrs)	36	18	25	27	70
	17	31	15	26	72		37	21	37	29	87
	18	13	20	13	46		38	27	20	26	73
	19	15	18	14	47		39	22	21	29	72
	20	20	30	15	65		40	16	17	27	60

Let's sum the scores for the participants within each combination of A and B.

	B₁	B₂	B₃	Sum
A_1	306	238	120	664
A_2	232	251	154	637
A_3	219	291	210	720
A_4	218	270	264	752
Sum	975	1050	748	2773

Step 1. Calculate the total sum of squares.

$$SS_{TOT} = \sum X_{tot}^2 - \frac{\left(\sum X_{tot}\right)^2}{abn}$$

$$= 37^2 + 28^2 + \cdots + 27^2 - \left(\frac{2773^2}{120}\right)$$

$$= 70349 - 64079.41$$

$$= 6269.59$$

Step 2. Calculate the SS_P and its component parts, SS_A and $SS_{P(gps)}$.

$$SS_P = \frac{\left(\sum X_{P_1}\right)^2 + \left(\sum X_{P_2}\right)^2 + \cdots + \left(\sum X_{P_{an}}\right)^2}{n} - \frac{\left(\sum X_{tot}\right)^2}{abn}$$

$$= 64^2 + 59^2 + \cdots + 60^2 - 64079.41$$

$$= 65349.00 - 64079.41 = 1269.59$$

$$SS_A = \frac{\left(\sum X_{a_1}\right)^2 + \left(\sum X_{a_2}\right)^2 + \cdots + \left(\sum X_{a_a}\right)^2}{bn} - \frac{\left(\sum X_{tot}\right)^2}{abn}$$

$$= \frac{664^2 + 637^2 + 720^2 + 752^2}{30} - 64079.41$$

$$= 64352.30 - 64079.41 = 272.89$$

$$SS_{P(gps)} = SS_P - SS_A = 996.70$$

Step 3. Calculate SS_{WP} and its component parts, the B, $A \times B$, and participants within-groups ×B sums of squares.

$$SS_{WP} = SS_{TOT} - SS_P = 5000.00$$

$$SS_B = \frac{\left(\sum X_{b_1}\right)^2 + \left(\sum X_{b_2}\right)^2 + \cdots + \left(\sum X_{b_b}\right)^2}{an} - \frac{\left(\sum X_{tot}\right)^2}{abn}$$

$$= \frac{975^2 + 1050^2 + 748^2}{40} - 64079.41$$

$$= 65315.73 - 64079.41 = 1236.32$$

$$SS_{A \times B} = \frac{\left(\sum X_{a_1 b_1}\right)^2 + \left(\sum X_{a_1 b_2}\right)^2 + \cdots + \left(\sum X_{a_a b_b}\right)^2}{n} - \frac{\left(\sum X_{tot}\right)^2}{abn} - SS_A - SS_B$$

$$= \frac{306^2 + 238^2 + \cdots + 264^2}{10} - 64079.41 - 272.89 - 1236.32$$

$$= 67208.30 - 64079.41 - 272.89 - 1236.32 = 1619.68$$

$$SS_{P(gps) \times B} = SS_{WP} - SS_B - SS_{A \times B} = 2144.00$$

Step 4. Calculate the mean squares.

$$MS_A = \frac{SS_A}{a - 1}$$

$$= 272.89 / 3 = 90.96$$

$$MS_{P(gps)} = \frac{SS_{P(gps)}}{a(n-1)}$$
$$= 996.70 / 36 = 27.69$$

$$MS_B = \frac{SS_B}{b-1}$$
$$= 1236.32 / 2 = 618.16$$

$$MS_{A \times B} = \frac{SS_{A \times B}}{(a-1)(b-1)}$$
$$= 1619.68 / 6 = 269.95$$

$$MS_{P(gps) \times B} = \frac{SS_{P(gps) \times B}}{a(n-1)(b-1)}$$
$$= 2144.00 / 72 = 29.78$$

Step 5. Calculate the F ratios.

$$F_A = MS_A / MS_{P(gps)} \quad = 90.96 / 27.69 \quad = 3.29$$
$$F_B = MS_B / MS_{P(gps) \times B} \quad = 618.16 / 29.78 = 20.76$$
$$F_{A \times B} = MS_{A \times B} / MS_{P(gps) \times B} = 269.95 / 29.78 = 9.07$$

Step 6. Enter the results in an ANOVA summary table.

ANOVA Summary Table					
Source of Variance	**Sum of Squares**	**df**	**Mean Squares**	**F**	**p**
Between participants	1269.59	39			
A	272.89	3	90.96	3.29	<.05
$P(gps)$	996.70	36	27.69		
Within participants	5000.00	80			
B	1236.32	2	618.16	20.76	<.01
$A \times B$	1619.68	6	269.95	9.07	<.01
$P(gps) \times B$	2144.00	72	29.78		
Total	6269.59	119			

Now, of course, we need to interpret these results. Because both main effects are significant, we know that the type of test, $F(3, 36) = 3.29$, $p < .05$, and the length of time on the force, $F(3, 72) = 20.76$, $p < .01$, both made a difference in performance. However, the presence of a significant interaction, $F(6,72) = 9.07$, $p < .01$, tells us that the test difference pattern is not identical for the four groups. The best way I know of determining what went on in a design as complicated as this one is to present the data graphically.

Interpreting a Two-Way ANOVA With Repeated Measures

First we will look at the main effect of time on force, illustrated in Figure 12.4.

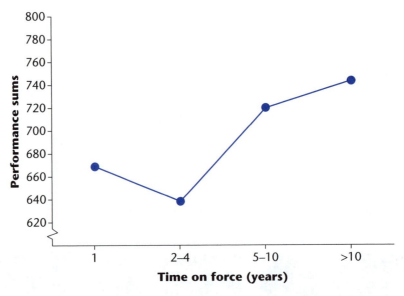

Figure 12.4. The main effect of time on force.

We can see that, overall, the more senior officers tended to do better; however, the 1st-year group did better than the 2- to 4-year group. To determine which groups are significantly different, this analysis would be followed by a multiple comparison technique as discussed in Chapter 13.

Let's look at the main effect of type of test, shown in Figure 12.5.

Overall, we see that the officers performed best on the law test and worst on the decision-making test.

Both these main effects must be interpreted somewhat cautiously because of the existence of a significant interaction between the variables. Let's look at the interaction.

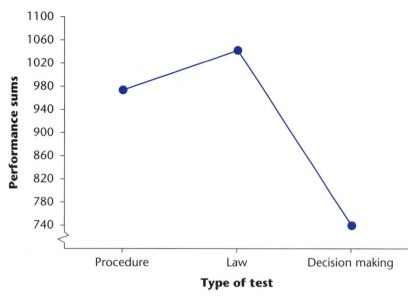

Figure 12.5. The main effect of type of test.

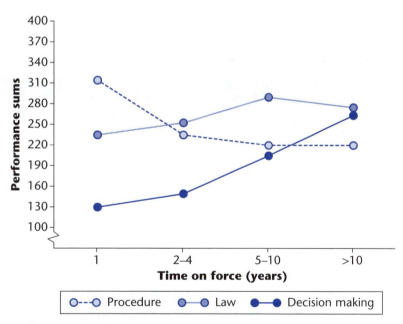

Figure 12.6. The interaction between time on force and type of test.

Examination of Figure 12.6 indicates that as experience (i.e., years on the force) increases, performance on the decision-making test also increases.

The new officers did particularly well on the procedure test. We might speculate that the years of experience in the field improved the scores of the senior officers in "real-life" decision-making tests but that they tended to be a little complacent about matters involving procedure and law. We might also speculate that the new officers, on the other hand, lack real-life experience but are keener about "book learning."

ALERT

We should comment on specific trends only if we have supporting statistical results from a multiple comparison analysis. The statistical results do not provide us with any help in terms of interpretation. That is the researcher's domain. The usefulness of the interpretation of the outcome of a statistical analysis depends entirely on the expertise of the researcher. Different researchers may interpret the same results quite differently. That is the nature of scientific inquiry.

CONCEPT REVIEW 12.4

Complete the ANOVA summary table below.

Source of Variance	Sum of Squares	df	Mean Squares	F
A	18	2		
$P_{(gps)}$	64	16		
B	4	2		
$A \times B$	80	4		
$P_{(gps)} \times B$	96	32		

Answer on page 361.

SUMMARY OF A TWO-WAY ANOVA MIXED DESIGN

Hypotheses

H_0: No main effects and no interaction.
H_1: H_0 is false.

Assumptions

1. Participants are randomly selected with repeated measures on Factor B.
2. Population distributions are normal.
3. Population variances are homogeneous.
4. Population covariances are equal.

Decision Rules

$df_a = a - 1$

$df_b = b - 1$

$df_{a \times b} = (a - 1)(b - 1)$

$df_{P(gps)} = a(n - 1)$

$df_{P(gps) \times b} = a(n - 1)(b - 1)$

If $F_{obt} \geq F_{crit}$ reject the H_0

If $F_{obt} < F_{crit}$ do not reject H_0

Formulas

$$F_A = \frac{MS_A}{MS_{P(gps)}}$$

$$F_B = \frac{MS_B}{MS_{P(gps) \times B}}$$

$$F_{A \times B} = \frac{MS_{A \times B}}{MS_{P(gps) \times B}}$$

Assumptions Underlying ANOVA With Repeated Measures

One of the assumptions of ANOVA is that the populations from which the samples are drawn are normally distributed with equal variances. We discussed this assumption of homogeneity of variance in Chapter 11, where we learned that the F test is quite robust (i.e., insensitive to violations of this assumption) when the participants have been randomly selected and independently assigned to groups, and when samples are about the same size.

With repeated-measures designs, participants are not independently assigned to groups, so the assumption of homogeneity of variance takes on added importance. Another assumption of ANOVA is that the population correlations (often called covariances) are constant. If participants are independently assigned to groups, it is reasonable to assume that the population correlations are constant. When the same participants take part in all treatment levels, however, this is unlikely to be true. When there is reason to believe that both assumptions (homogeneity of variances and covariances) have been violated, a more conservative test is recommended (e.g., Geisser & Greenhouse, 1958).[1] Discussions of the problems of homogeneity of variances and covariances can be found in most higher-level statistics textbooks.

Choosing the Appropriate Test of Significance

You have now learned about four F tests of significance: One- and two-way ANOVA with repeated measures in this chapter, and one- and two-way ANOVA without repeated measures in Chapter 11. Let's go through the steps we need to decide which of these four analyses is appropriate. We will not include two-group studies in the present discussion.

Step 1. Determine the number of groups in the experiment.

If there is only one group of participants and each participant contributes several observations, then repeated measures have been taken, and you will choose a one-way ANOVA with repeated measures. If there are more than two groups, we go to Step 2.

Step 2. Determine the number of independent variables.

If you have more than two groups in the study, you must determine how many independent variables are involved. Do you have several groups of participants under different levels of one independent variable, or do you have groups being treated with more than one independent variable? With more than two groups of participants, where each group is under a different level of a single independent variable, you choose a one-way ANOVA. If the experiment has two independent variables, we must go to Step 3.

Step 3. Determine whether repeated measures have been taken on one of the two independent variables.

If participants have been randomly and independently assigned to all levels of both IVs, you choose a two-way ANOVA. If one of the independent variables involves measures on the same participants—that is, a repeated-measures design—then you will run a two-way ANOVA with repeated measures.

Let's go through the steps to decide which analysis to use in the following examples.

---

[1]Geisser, S., & Greenhouse, S. W. (1958). An extension of Box's results on the use of the F distribution in multivariate analysis. *Annals of Mathematical Statistics, 29,* 885–891.

Example A: A researcher has randomly selected 40 participants for a learning experiment. All participants are required to learn three different lists of words. The lists differ in terms of the relationship between the items. For example, in List S, the items are semantically similar—that is, they have similar meanings. In List R, the words rhyme. The last list (C) is a control condition in which the words are not related to each other in any way. The number of trials it takes for the participants to learn each list is the dependent variable.

Step 1. Determine the number of groups in the experiment.

There is only one group of participants in this experiment, and each participant contributes three observations (the number of trials needed to learn each of the three lists). Repeated measures have been taken, and the researcher will use a one-way ANOVA with repeated measures.

Example B: A provincial board of health has decided to investigate three treatment programs for treating alcohol abuse. Three groups of abusers of alcohol are randomly selected: one group of heavy abusers, a second of moderate abusers, and a third of light abusers. Each group participates in a 6-month treatment program. For the first 2 months, the participants receive training in behavioral observation and in the monitoring of their drinking behavior. For the next 2 months, the participants receive group therapy. For the final 2 months, participants receive individual therapy. Measures of drinking behavior and attitude are taken after each treatment period.

Step 1. Determine the number of groups in the experiment.

There are three groups of participants in this study: (1) a heavy abusing group, (2) a moderate abusing group, and (3) a light abusing group. We go to Step 2.

Step 2. Determine the number of independent variables.

This experiment has two independent variables: (1) level of abuse and (2) treatment program, and so we must go to Step 3. Actually, level of abuse is a participant variable, not a true IV, but the analysis is the same.

Step 3. Determine whether repeated measures have been taken on one of the two independent variables.

The three levels of abuse groups were randomly selected, and all participants went through the three phases of the treatment program. Repeated measures, therefore, were taken from all participants after each treatment period.

The appropriate analysis is a two-way ANOVA with repeated measures on type of treatment. The researcher will discover whether level of abuse overall makes a difference, whether treatment program overall makes a difference, and whether the two variables interact in some way. For example, perhaps the heavy abusers benefit more from one-on-one individual therapy than do the other groups.

Example C: A provincial board of health has decided to investigate two treatment programs for treating alcohol abuse. Six groups of abusers are randomly selected: two groups of heavy abusers, two groups of moderate abusers, and two groups of light abusers of alcohol. Each group participates in a 2-month treatment program. One group of each pair is randomly assigned to one of two treatment programs: (1) behavioral treatment or (2) group therapy. In other words, one group of heavy abusers, one group of moderate abusers, and one group of light abusers receive behavioral treatment for 2 months. A second set of abusers (i.e. heavy, moderate, and light) receive group therapy for 2 months. Following the therapy period, measures of drinking behavior and attitude are taken.

Step 1. Determine the number of groups in the experiment.

There are six groups of participants in this study: two heavy abusing groups, two moderate, and two light abusing groups.

Step 2. Determine the number of independent variables.

This experiment has two independent variables, level of abuse and treatment program, and so we must go to Step 3. Like the example above, level of abuse is not a true IV but the analysis is the same.

Step 3. Determine whether repeated measures have been taken on one of the two independent variables.

Repeated measures have not been taken. Groups were randomly assigned to treatment condition. A two-way ANOVA is the appropriate analysis for this study.

CONCEPT REVIEW 12.5

A researcher measures the anxiety level of 15 soccer players in each of three divisions (*A*, *B*, and *C*) before a practice game, before a preseason game, and before a tournament game. What type of ANOVA should she use?

Answer on page 361.

FOCUS ON RESEARCH

"It's a boy! Rob and Kris are thrilled to announce the safe arrival of Jack Morgan Tinker. Proud grandparents are Hollis and Marilyn Clifton of Ottawa and Larry and Rosemary Tinker of Montreal. Welcome little one!"

"It's a girl! Barbara Lofton and Scott Hasler are delighted to announce the birth of their lovely daughter, Madison Evelyn Hasler. Grandparents are both joyful and overwhelmed" (Gonzalez & Koestner, 2005, p. 407).[2]

THE RESEARCH PROBLEM

Reading birth announcements like these led Gonzalez and Koestner (2005) of the University of Montreal to wonder if baby gender and parents' positive affect are related. Specifically, they wanted to determine if type of affect (happiness vs. pride) that parents seem to display in their birth announcements was linked to the gender of their new baby.

THE VARIABLES AND DESIGN

Birth announcements for 194 girls and 192 boys were selected from a Calgary and a Montreal newspaper. Gender information was deleted, and the announcements were assessed by two independent raters for happiness and pride. Their scores were very similar (high interrater reliability). The researchers wanted to compare the ratings, treated as an interval variable, for boys versus girls and Calgary versus Montreal, both *nominal participant* variables.

The design was a $2 \times 2 \times 2$ repeated-measures ANOVA with baby gender (boy vs. girl) and city (Calgary vs. Montreal) as *between-participants* variables and type of affect (happiness vs. pride) as a *within-participants* variable.

THE RESULTS

Some of the results are as follows. The researchers reported a significant main effect for type of affect, $F(1, 382) = 115.90$, $p < .0001$. Overall, the birth announcements were rated higher for happiness ($M = 1.30$) than pride ($M = 0.70$).

There was no main effect for baby gender, $F(1, 382) = 0.016$, *ns*. The birth announcements for boys ($M = 0.99$) reflected about the same amount of affect as those for girls ($M = 1.01$).

There was a significant interaction between city and type of affect, $F(1, 382) = 16.64$, $p < .0001$. As you can see in Figure 12.7, Montreal announcements were rated as happier ($M = 1.44$) and less proud ($M = 0.61$) than Calgary announcements (happiness $M = 1.16$; pride $M = 0.79$).

Baby gender and type of affect also interacted, $F(1, 382) = 5.85$, $p < .05$. As Figure 12.8 indicates, parents of boys expressed more pride ($M = 0.76$) than parents of girls ($M = 0.64$), and parents of girls expressed more happiness ($M = 1.38$) than parents of boys ($M = 1.23$).

---

[2]Gonzalez, A. Q., & Koestner, R. (2005). Parental preference for sex of newborn as reflected in positive affect in birth announcements. *Sex Roles, 52*(5/6), 407–411.

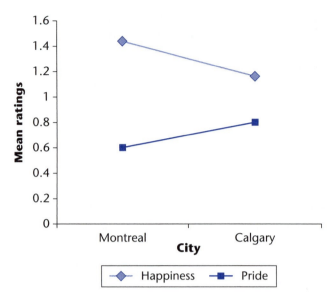

Figure 12.7. Interaction of city and type of effect.

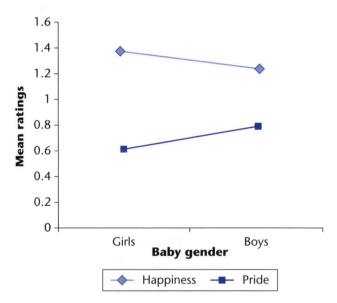

Figure 12.8. Interaction of baby gender and type of affect.

CONCLUSIONS

The researchers concluded that, as they expected, parents in Canada express more pride at the birth of boys than girls and more happiness at the birth of girls than boys.

They speculated that parental pride at the birth of boys might be related to social standing and that parental happiness at the birth of girls might be related to attachment; perhaps, girls are perceived as more expressive and warmer than boys.

SUMMARY OF FORMULAS

One-way ANOVA with repeated measures—Computational formulas

Sums of squares	
Total	$SS_{TOT} = X_{tot}^2 - \dfrac{(\sum X_{tot})^2}{Kn}$
Between participants	$SS_P = \dfrac{(\sum X_{P_1})^2 + (\sum X_{P_2})^2 + \cdots + (\sum X_{P_n})^2}{k} - \dfrac{(\sum X_{tot})^2}{kn}$
Within participants	$SS_{WP} = SS_{TOT} - SS_P$
Treatment	$SS_T = \dfrac{(\sum X_{T_1})^2 + (\sum X_{T_2})^2 + \cdots + (\sum X_{T_k})^2}{n} - \dfrac{(\sum X_{tot})^2}{kn}$
Participant by treatment	$SS_{P \times T} = SS_{WP} - SS_T$
Mean squares	
Treatment	$MS_T = \dfrac{SS_T}{k-1}$
Participant by treatment	$MS_{P \times T} = \dfrac{SS_{P \times T}}{(n-1)(k-1)}$
F ratio	$F = \dfrac{MS_T}{MS_{P \times T}}$

Two-way ANOVA with repeated measures—Computational formulas

Sums of squares	
Total	$SS_{TOT} = \sum X_{tot}^2 - \dfrac{(\sum X_{tot})^2}{abn}$
Between participants	$SS_P = \dfrac{(\sum X_{P_1})^2 + (\sum X_{P_2})^2 + \cdots + (\sum X_{P_{an}})^2}{b} - \dfrac{(\sum X_{tot})^2}{abn}$

(Continued)

(Continued)

A	$$SS_A = \frac{\left(\sum X_{a_1}\right)^2 + \left(\sum X_{a_2}\right)^2 + \cdots + \left(\sum X_{a_a}\right)^2}{bn} - \frac{\left(\sum X_{tot}\right)^2}{abn}$$
Participants within groups	$$SS_{P(gps)} = SS_P - SS_A$$
Within participants	$$SS_{WP} = SS_{TOT} - SS_P$$
B	$$SS_B = \frac{\left(\sum X_{b_1}\right)^2 + \left(\sum X_{b_2}\right)^2 + \cdots + \left(\sum X_{b_b}\right)^2}{an} - \frac{\left(\sum X_{tot}\right)^2}{abn}$$
A × B	$$SS_{A \times B} = \frac{\left(\sum X_{a_1 b_1}\right)^2 + \left(\sum X_{a_1 b_2}\right)^2 + \cdots + \left(\sum X_{a_a b_b}\right)^2}{n} - \frac{\left(\sum X_{tot}\right)^2}{abn} - SS_A - SS_B$$
Participants within groups × B	$$SS_{P(gps) \times B} = SS_{WP} - SS_B - SS_{A \times B}$$
Mean squares	
A	$$MS_A = \frac{SS_A}{a-1}$$
Participants within groups	$$MS_{P(gps)} = \frac{SS_{P(gps)}}{a(n-1)}$$
B	$$MS_B = \frac{SS_B}{b-1}$$
A × B	$$MS_{A \times B} = \frac{SS_{A \times B}}{(a-1)(b-1)}$$
Participants within groups × B	$$MS_{P(gps) \times B} = \frac{SS_{P(gps) \times B}}{a(n-1)(b-1)}$$
F ratios	
A	$$F_A = \frac{MS_A}{MS_{P(gps)}}$$
B	$$F_B = \frac{MS_B}{MS_{P(gps) \times B}}$$
A × B	$$F_{A \times B} = \frac{MS_{A \times B}}{MS_{P(gps) \times B}}$$

CONCEPT REVIEW ANSWERS

12.1. $df_{tot} = kn - 1 = 99$

12.2. $F = \dfrac{12}{4} = 3$

12.3. A. Between participants $df = 19$
       B. Within-participants $df = 60$
       C. Treatment $df = 3$
       D. $P \times T\ df = 57$

12.4.

Source of Variance	Sum of Squares	df	Mean Squares	F
A	18	2	9	2.25
P(gps)	64	16	4	
B	4	2	2	0.67
A × B	80	4	20	6.67
P(gps) × B	96	32	3	

12.5. There are three groups, one group of players in each of three divisions. Each player's anxiety level is measured on three different occasions. She should use a two-way ANOVA with repeated measures.

EXERCISES

1. Below is a layout for a one-way ANOVA with repeated measures.

	Treatment				
Participants	1	2	3	4	5
1					
.					
.					
.					
20					

Give the number of degrees of freedom for the following:

a. Total SS
b. Between-participants SS

    c. Within-participants SS

    d. Between-treatment SS

    e. Participant by treatment SS

2. Run a one-way ANOVA at $\alpha = .05$ on the following data. All participants served under each treatment condition.

Participant	Treatment 1	Treatment 2	Treatment 3
1	22	34	21
2	35	36	20
3	31	40	17
4	17	41	23
5	22	33	27
6	20	36	29
7	35	28	31
8	21	29	22
9	33	34	15
10	10	30	28

3. Complete the ANOVA summary table for the following. There were four levels of A and three levels of B with nine participants under each level of A. Use $\alpha = .05$.

Sum of Squares	
Total	3500
Participants	250
A	50
$P_{(gps)}$	200
WP	3250
B	700
$A \times B$	550
$P_{(gps)} \times B$	2000

4. A sociology professor was interested in the effects of socioeconomic status on three different areas of marital satisfaction. She randomly selected eight couples from each of two SES groups: upper/middle and lower SES. She wanted to compare their perception as a couple on three areas of marital relationships: (1) communication (C), (2) domestic chore equity (DE), and (3) personal self-esteem (SE). She used a questionnaire that yielded the following scores out of 100. Run a two-way ANOVA with repeated measures on the marital satisfaction category at $\alpha = .01$.

SES	Marital Area		
Upper/Middle	C	DE	SE
1	88	87	90
2	76	75	80
3	65	70	75
4	40	68	65
5	76	75	70
6	78	84	80
7	40	56	60
8	80	83	79
Lower			
1	75	75	80
2	72	78	80
3	56	63	70
4	69	74	70
5	63	76	75
6	71	70	72
7	73	69	69
8	64	69	78

5. Graph the two main effects and the interaction from Exercise 4. Use group means on your graphs.

6. Run a two-way ANOVA on the following data where repeated measures are taken on Factor B. Calculate a to f and answer g and h.

	Participant	B_1	B_2	B_3	B_4		Participant	B_1	B_2	B_3	B_4
A_1	1	2	4	5	7	A_2	9	8	2	6	6
	2	4	5	5	8		10	4	3	5	5
	3	7	6	2	6		11	6	6	3	7
	4	6	4	3	5		12	5	7	6	4
	5	5	3	4	4		13	7	6	7	6
	6	2	7	3	7		14	3	8	9	7
	7	9	8	2	9		15	9	9	5	3
	8	7	9	1	9		16	10	10	4	8

a. SS_{TOT}

b. SS_P

    c. SS_A

    d. $SS_{P(gps)}$

    e. SS_{WP}

    f. SS_B

    g. $SS_{A \times B}$

    h. $SS_{P(gps) \times B}$

    i. Complete the ANOVA summary table.

    j. Using the group sums, graph the interaction.

7. A clinical psychologist was interested in the influence of psychotherapeutic labels on people's judgments of mental health. She randomly assigned 10 participants to each of three groups. All the participants read short stories about people with various psychological problems. After each story was read, participants were required to rate the mental health of the person described in the story, where low ratings = *poor mental health* and high ratings = *good mental health*. A third of the stories described people with anxiety disorders (*AD*), a third described people with personality disorders (*PD*), and a third described people with depressive disorders (*DD*). For one of the three groups, each story ended with a behavioral label diagnosing the disorder (*BL*). In another group, a psychiatric label from the *Diagnostic and Statistical Manual of Mental Disorders* (*DSM*) was used. In the last group, no label was given. Run the appropriate ANOVA on the mean rating data from this study.

	No Label			DSM			BL		
Diagnosis	**AD**	**PD**	**DD**	**AD**	**PD**	**DD**	**AD**	**PD**	**DD**
	5.6	5.8	4.7	5.6	3.5	5.0	5.9	6.3	5.3
	4.3	6.1	4.3	5.1	3.7	3.0	4.8	5.7	5.4
	3.8	6.7	4.7	4.6	2.8	3.0	4.5	6.0	4.8
	5.9	6.1	2.7	5.8	1.6	6.0	6.0	5.6	6.1
	5.0	5.4	5.2	5.0	3.9	5.0	5.6	5.9	6.2
	5.1	5.8	6.0	6.1	4.0	5.0	6.7	6.2	5.7
	4.1	6.8	4.8	5.7	5.3	4.2	4.8	4.6	5.0
	3.7	1.8	2.5	4.9	4.6	3.6	6.2	6.3	6.1
	6.2	6.4	5.1	4.7	3.4	4.5	5.9	5.2	5.2
	4.8	5.3	5.3	4.0	4.2	5.1	1.7	5.2	5.0

8. The academic dean of a large university decided to do some research to see whether there was a difference in student performance in three different classes of a senior seminar in organic chemistry. He selected three senior classes, each taught by a different professor. All three professors used the same term exams. The dean collected the term exam

scores of the students in each of the three classes. His primary interest was whether the professor had an influence on the scores. He expected that performance would improve over the term. Run the appropriate ANOVA on the data he collected.

	Student	Exam 1	Exam 2	Exam 3
Professor A	1	87	74	35
	2	77	58	45
	3	45	50	55
	4	68	50	67
	5	90	63	70
	6	86	76	45
	7	86	80	55
	8	80	78	65
	9	63	77	69
	10	59	68	62
Professor B	1	85	65	50
	2	75	55	65
	3	65	48	45
	4	58	69	50
	5	50	45	60
	6	60	55	40
	7	60	58	55
	8	59	65	45
	9	68	45	60
	10	60	50	52
Professor C	1	60	63	53
	2	67	57	50
	3	64	60	48
	4	70	56	55
	5	60	55	47
	6	63	65	69
	7	58	60	55
	8	63	55	43
	9	63	51	49
	10	54	49	50

Multiple Comparison Procedures

After reading this chapter, you should be able to do the following:

1. Describe experiment-wise error rate.
2. Describe the difference between a priori and post hoc comparisons.
3. Use the planned comparison approach to test for differences between means.
4. Use the Scheffé method to test for differences between means.
5. Use the Tukey method to test for differences between means.
6. Describe the hypotheses, assumptions, and decision rules for each multiple comparison technique.
7. Describe the appropriate conditions in which to use each multiple comparison technique.

We have analyzed our data with an ANOVA, and we find that there is a significant main effect of mood state (very positive, positive, neutral, negative, and very negative) on assignment of blame. But which means are significantly different? ANOVA doesn't answer that question. We need to do more statistical analyses.

In Chapters 11 and 12, we learned that the outcome of ANOVA tells us whether or not a significant difference exists. It does not tell us where that difference lies.

Controlling the Error Rate

One of the important concerns in doing inferential statistics is the possibility of making an error. A Type I error, you will recall, is made when we reject a null hypothesis that should not have been rejected. ANOVA keeps the Type I error rate at alpha over the entire experiment. If, on the other hand, we do multiple t tests, rather than ANOVA, the Type I error rate is higher than alpha. Although the probability of a Type I error for each individual t test is alpha, the probability of making at least one Type I error with many t tests within one experiment is higher than alpha. The **experiment-wise error rate** is higher than the error rate for each t test comparison. The experiment-wise error rate depends on the number of t test comparisons that are made within a single experiment. Because researchers must control the overall experiment-wise error rate, procedures other than the t test are recommended for comparing group means following ANOVA. Some common multiple comparison procedures are discussed in the following sections.

> **Experiment-wise error rate:** Overall probability in an experiment that the null will be rejected in error (Type I error)

A Priori (Planned) Comparisons

A priori, as you know, means before the fact, and so **a priori** (planned) comparisons are those planned in advance of the experiment, usually on the basis of some theory or previous research. It is not required that the ANOVA yield a significant result for **planned comparisons** to be made.

> **Planned comparisons:** Statistical comparisons among means planned in advance of data collection; a multiple comparison procedure

FYI

As is often the case in statistics, there is some disagreement about the specifics of a planned comparison analysis. Interested students should consult a higher-level statistics text for clarification. In this chapter, I have assumed that comparisons need not be orthogonal.

Each planned comparison is evaluated for significance with a t ratio. For our purposes we will assume that the means to be compared are based on equal sample sizes. In this case, the numerator of the t ratio is simply the difference between the pair of means of interest, and the denominator uses the error mean square from the ANOVA to compute the standard error of the comparison. The t ratio for a planned comparison is

$$t = \frac{\bar{X}_1 - \bar{X}_2}{\sqrt{2MS_{error}/n}}$$

We have used ANOVA to see if type of training in critical thinking (Authentic vs. Fictional examples) made a difference in participants' ability to critically evaluate research methods and outcomes. A control group received no special training. There were 15 students in each group. The relevant data are presented below (higher scores are better).

ANOVA Summary Table					
Source of Variance	**Sum of Squares**	**df**	**Mean Squares**	**F**	**p**
Between groups	1213.33	2	606.60	5.61	<.01
Within groups	4545.47	42	108.23		
Total	5758.80	44			

$$\bar{X}_1 \text{ (Control)} = 59.07$$

$$\bar{X}_2 \text{ (Fictional)} = 66.40$$

$$\bar{X}_3 \text{ (Authentic)} = 71.73$$

Let's use a planned comparison technique to compare the control group with each of the trained groups. We first compute the standard error for the t ratio. It will be the same for both comparisons.

$$\text{Standard error} = \sqrt{2MS_{error} / n}$$
$$= \sqrt{2(108.23) / 15}$$
$$= \sqrt{14.43} = 3.80$$

The t ratio for the planned comparison of the control group with the Fictional group is

$$t = \frac{\bar{X}_2 - \bar{X}_1}{\text{standard error}}$$
$$= \frac{66.40 - 59.07}{3.80}$$
$$= 1.93$$

The t ratio for the planned comparison of the control group with the Authentic group is

$$t = \frac{\bar{X}_3 - \bar{X}_1}{\text{standard error}}$$
$$= \frac{71.73 - 59.07}{3.80}$$
$$= 3.33$$

To evaluate the comparisons for significance, let's use the .05 level of significance. We enter the degrees of freedom associated with the error mean square (i.e., 42) into Table B.2 of Appendix B, and we find that the critical value of t for a two-tailed test is approximately $\pm\ 2.02$.

We conclude that although critical thinking training with fictional examples ($M = 66.40$) did not improve performance over no-training ($M = 59.07$), $t(42) = 1.93$, ns, critical thinking training with authentic examples ($M = 71.73$) did, $t(42) = 3.33$, $p < .05$.

SUMMARY OF PLANNED COMPARISONS

Hypotheses

H_0: No difference between population means.
H_1: H_0 is false.

Assumptions

The outcome of the ANOVA need not be significant.

Decision Rules

If $t_{obt} \geq t_{crit}$ reject H_0
If $t_{obt} < t_{crit}$ do not reject H_0

Formula

$$t = \frac{\bar{X}_1 - \bar{X}_2}{\sqrt{2MS_{error} / n}}$$

CONCEPT REVIEW 13.1

The error mean square from a one-way ANOVA was 125. There were 10 participants in each group (two types of treatment for impulse control problems and a nontreated control group). The means for the three groups in the experiment are as follows:

Control group	Treatment 1	Treatment 2
65	75	85

Use planned comparisons to determine if the control group differed from each treatment group. Use a two-tailed test at the .05 level of significance.

Answer on page 378.

A Posteriori or Post Hoc Comparisons

A posteriori (or post hoc) means after the fact, so post hoc comparisons are usually not planned until after the researcher has examined the data and noted trends. Post hoc comparisons require the *F* ratio from the ANOVA to be significant.

The Scheffé Method

The Scheffé method is appropriate for making *any* or *all* comparisons on a set of means. This method is considered superior to some of the other techniques when complex comparisons are of interest and/or when sample sizes are not equal. When samples are of the same size and when simple comparisons are of interest, the Scheffé method is more conservative (less powerful) than some of the other techniques.

Constructing the Comparison

The Scheffé method allows comparisons between any and all means. In any comparison, two quantities are contrasted. These quantities may both be sample means or averages of means. For example, a researcher who used a control group and two experimental groups may wish to compare the control group mean with the average of the experimental group means. This could be expressed as

$$\overline{X}_c \text{ compared with } \frac{\overline{X}_1 + \overline{X}_2}{2}$$

Or she may wish to compare the two experimental group means with each other:

$$\overline{X}_1 \text{ compared with } \overline{X}_2$$

To construct a comparison, each quantity is multiplied by a coefficient. In the first example, the researcher wants to compare the control group with the average of the two experimental groups, so +1 is the coefficient for the control mean and $-\frac{1}{2}$ is the coefficient for each experimental group mean. Because the null hypothesis is at the population level, for this example it is

$$H_0 : 1\mu_c - \frac{1}{2}\mu_1 - \frac{1}{2}\mu_2 = 0$$

For the second example, the researcher wants to compare the two experimental groups, and so the coefficients are +1 and –1, and the null hypothesis is

$$H_0: 1\mu_1 - 1\mu_2 = 0$$

Alternative hypotheses are always nondirectional.

In general, any comparison (C) may be expressed by the following, where c is the coefficient for each mean and k is the number of groups.

$$C = c_1\overline{X}_1 + c_2\overline{X}_2 + \cdots + c_k\overline{X}_k$$

Note that the sum of the coefficients must be zero, that is ($c_1 + c_2 + \ldots + c_k = 0$). Group means not included in the comparison are assigned coefficients of zero.

CONCEPT REVIEW 13.2

Construct the planned comparison between a control group mean ($\overline{X}_c$) and the average of four treatment group means (i.e., $C = ?$).

Answer on page 379.

The Standard Error of the Comparison

To test the significance of a comparison, we need to determine the standard error (s_c). The general formula to calculate the standard error for a Scheffé test is as follows:

$$s_c = \sqrt{MS_{error}\left(\frac{c_1^2}{n_1} + \frac{c_2^2}{n_2} + \cdots + \frac{c_k^2}{n_k}\right)}$$

MS_{error} is the appropriate error variance estimate from the ANOVA

c is the coefficient for the group mean

n is the sample size

Evaluating the Comparison for Significance

To evaluate a comparison for significance, we first must calculate F_s, the critical value of F used for a Scheffé comparison.

$$F_s = \sqrt{(k-1)F_{crit}}$$

In this equation, k is the number of groups, and F_{crit} is the tabled value of F from Table B.3 in Appendix B, with $(k-1)$ df in the numerator and the degrees of freedom associated with the MS_{error} from the analysis of variance in the denominator.

Now we can go ahead and test our comparison for significance. The formula for calculating the F statistic for a Scheffé test is

$$F' = C / s_c$$

As usual, if the obtained F value for any comparison (i.e., F') is equal to or larger than the critical value (i.e., F_s), we reject the null hypothesis.

Running a Scheffé Test

Let's use the same example we analyzed with a planned comparison approach in the preceding section to see how the Scheffé method differs. The data were as follows:

ANOVA Summary Table					
Source of Variance	Sum of Squares	df	Mean Squares	F	p
Between groups	1213.33	2	606.60	5.61	<.01
Within groups	4545.47	42	108.23		
Total	5758.80	44			

$$\bar{X}_1 \ (\text{Control}) = 59.07$$

$$\bar{X}_2 \ (\text{Fictional}) = 66.40$$

$$\bar{X}_3 \ (\text{Authentic}) = 71.73$$

The ANOVA told us that there was a significant difference between the three groups: (1) those trained in critical thinking with fictional examples (F), (2) those trained with authentic examples (A), and (3) those receiving no training (C). Six comparisons can be examined:

F versus A	F versus C	A versus C
FA versus C	FC versus A	AC versus F

Let's run a Scheffé test to determine whether the training made a difference. In other words, we will compare the control group with the two trained groups. The null hypothesis will be H_0: $\frac{1}{2}\mu_2 + \frac{1}{2}\mu_3 - 1\mu_1 = 0$.

Step 1. Construct the comparison for FA versus C.

$$C = c_1\bar{X}_1 + c_2\bar{X}_2 + c_3\bar{X}_3$$

$$= \left(\frac{1}{2}\right)(66.40) + \left(\frac{1}{2}\right)(71.73) + (-1)(59.07)$$

$$= 69.07 - 59.07$$

$$= 10$$

Step 2. Determine the standard error.

$$s_c = \sqrt{MS_{WG}\left(\frac{c_1^2}{n_1} + \frac{c_2^2}{n_2} + \frac{c_3^2}{n_3}\right)}$$

$$= \sqrt{108.23\left(\frac{\left(\frac{1}{2}\right)^2}{15} + \frac{\left(\frac{1}{2}\right)^2}{15} + \frac{(-1)^2}{15}\right)}$$

$$= 3.29$$

Step 3. Determine Scheffé's critical F.

$$F_s = \sqrt{(k-1)F_{crit}}$$

F_{crit} can be found in Table B.3 in Appendix B, with $(k-1)$ df in the numerator and the df associated with the MS_{WG} (i.e., the error mean square from ANOVA) in the denominator.

$$F(2,42) \text{ at } \alpha = .05 \text{ is } 3.22$$
$$F_s = \sqrt{2(3.22)} = 2.54$$

Step 4. Test the comparison for significance.

$$F' = C / s_c$$
$$= 10 / 3.29$$
$$= 3.04$$

Step 5. Make a decision.

Because the obtained F' is larger than the critical value, we reject the null; we have statistical evidence that the training improved performance.

The Scheffé method is particularly appropriate when complex combinations of sample means are being compared.

CONCEPT REVIEW 13.3

If $C = 8$ and $s_c = 4$, what is the value of F'?

Answer on page 379.

SUMMARY OF THE SCHEFFÉ TEST

Hypotheses

H_0: No difference between population means.
H_1: H_0 is false.

Assumptions

The outcome of the ANOVA was significant.

Decision Rules

If $F' \geq F_s$ reject the H_0

If $F' < F_s$ do not reject H_0

Formulas

$F' = C / s_c$

$F_s = \sqrt{(k-1) F_{crit}}$

The Tukey Method

The Tukey method is more powerful than Scheffé's for comparing pairs of means. However, it is less powerful for comparing combinations of means. The Tukey method compares the difference between each pair of means with a value called the **honestly significant difference (HSD)**. The value of HSD is found by

$$\text{HSD} = q\left(\alpha, df_{error}, k\right) \sqrt{MS_{error} / n}$$

q = value from Table B.5 in Appendix B

df_{error} = degrees of freedom associated with the MS_{error} from ANOVA

k = number of groups

n = number of participants within a group

The value of q is found by entering the α level, the df associated with the MS_{error} from the ANOVA, and the number of groups involved in the analysis into Table B.5 Appendix B. The differences between pairs of means can then be compared with the value of HSD. If any difference is greater than or equal to the value of HSD, the two means are significantly different or "honestly significantly different."

As with the Scheffé test, the null hypotheses specify no difference between the population means, and the alternative hypotheses are nondirectional.

Honestly significant difference (HSD): Value used in the Tukey test to assess the significance of mean differences

Running a Tukey Test

Let's use the same example we used earlier to run a Tukey test at $\alpha = .05$ on each pair of means. The three samples had 15 observations each, and the outcome of the ANOVA was as follows:

ANOVA Summary Table					
Source of Variance	**Sum of Squares**	**df**	**Mean Squares**	**F**	**p**
Between groups	1213.33	2	606.60	5.61	<.01
Within groups	4545.47	42	108.23		
Total	5758.80	44			

$\overline{X}_1$ (Control) = 59.07

$\overline{X}_2$ (Fictional) = 66.40

$\overline{X}_3$ (Authentic) = 71.73

Step 1. Determine the difference between each pair of group means.

$$F - C = 66.40 - 59.07 = 7.33$$
$$A - C = 71.73 - 59.07 = 12.66$$
$$A - F = 71.73 - 66.40 = 5.33$$

Step 2. Compute the value of HSD.

$$\text{HSD} = q\left(\alpha, df_{wg}, k\right)\sqrt{MS_{WG} / n}$$
$$= q(.05, 42, 3)\sqrt{108.23 / 15}$$
$$= 3.44(2.69)$$
$$= 9.25$$

Step 3. Compare differences with the value of HSD, and make a decision.

Because the only mean difference larger than HSD is that between the Authentic group and the Control group, we conclude that training in critical thinking with authentic examples ($M = 71.73$) had a significant effect on performance compared with no training ($M = 59.07$) (HSD $= 9.25$, $p < .05$).

CONCEPT REVIEW 13.4

ANOVA error mean square $= 180$ $k = 3$

$df_{error} = 60$, $\alpha = .05$

What is the value of q? If $n = 20$, what is the value of HSD?

Answer on page 379.

Several other techniques for post hoc multiple comparisons have been developed, but the Scheffé and Tukey methods are probably the most commonly used because of their generality and utility.

SUMMARY OF THE TUKEY TEST

Hypotheses

H_0: No difference between population means.
H_1: H_0 is false.

Assumptions

The outcome of the ANOVA was significant.

Decision Rules

Any mean difference $\geq$ HSD reject the H_0

Formula

$$\text{HSD} = q\left(\alpha, df_{error}, k\right)\sqrt{MS_{error} / n}$$

SUMMARY OF TERMS AND FORMULAS

Planned comparisons are made *a priori* and do not require a significant outcome from the ANOVA. Common post hoc comparisons include the *Scheffé* and *Tukey* tests, which do require a significant outcome from the ANOVA.

The *Scheffé method* is suitable for comparing any or all pairs of means as well as complex combinations of means. Samples need not be the same size. The Scheffé test requires computation of the *F statistic* for each comparison of interest. Each *F* statistic is then compared with *Scheffé's critical F value* for significance.

The *Tukey method* is used for comparing pairs of means; it requires samples to be of the same size. For simple comparisons, the Tukey method is considered to be more powerful than the Scheffé method. The Tukey test compares the difference between each pair of sample means with the value of the *honestly significant difference (HSD)*. Any mean differences equal to or larger than the HSD are considered to be significant.

Test Formulas	
Planned comparisons	$t = \dfrac{\bar{X}_1 - \bar{X}_2}{\sqrt{2MS_{error}/n}}$
Scheffé F'	$F' = C/s_c$
Critical F	$F_s = \sqrt{(k-1)F_{crit}}$
Comparison	$C = c_1\bar{X}_1 + c_2\bar{X}_2 + \cdots + c_k\bar{X}_k$
Standard error	$s_c = \sqrt{MS_{error}\left(\dfrac{c_1^2}{n_1} + \dfrac{c_2^2}{n_2} + \cdots + \dfrac{c_k^2}{n_k}\right)}$
Tukey	
Honestly significant difference	$HSD = q(\alpha, df_{error}, k)\sqrt{MS_{error}/n}$

CONCEPT REVIEW ANSWERS

13.1.

Comparison	Mean Difference	t Ratio
$C - T_1$	−10	−2
$C - T_2$	−20	−4

$$\text{denominator} = \sqrt{2(125/10)} = \sqrt{25} = 5$$

$$t_{.05} = \pm 2.052 \text{ two-tailed test}$$

The Control Group differed significantly from Treatment Group 2 but was not significantly different from Treatment Group 1.

13.2. $C = \frac{1}{4}\bar{X}_1 + \frac{1}{4}\bar{X}_2 + \frac{1}{4}\bar{X}_3 + \frac{1}{4}\bar{X}_4 - \bar{X}_c$

13.3. $F' = C / s_c = 8 / 4 = 2$

13.4. $q = 3.40$

$$\text{HSD} = 3.40\sqrt{180 / 20} = 3.40\sqrt{9} = 3.40(3) = 10.20$$

EXERCISES

1. Below is the outcome of a two-way ANOVA. Use a planned comparisons approach to test the six possible comparisons for significance at the .05 level. There were six participants in each group.

Source of Variance	Sum of Squares	df	Mean Squares	F	p
A	16.67	1	16.67	0.11	ns
B	8.17	1	8.17	0.05	ns
A × B	383.99	1	383.99	2.58	ns
WG	2 981.00	20	149.05		
Total	3 389.83	23			

$\bar{X}_{A_1 B_1} = 64.17$ $\bar{X}_{A_1 B_2} = 73.33$

$\bar{X}_{A_2 B_1} = 70.50$ $\bar{X}_{A_2 B_2} = 63.67$

2. Below is the outcome of an ANOVA. Use the planned comparisons approach to see if Group 2 is significantly different from each of the other groups at the .01 level of significance. There were 20 participants in each group.

Source of Variance	Sum of Squares	df	Mean Squares	F	p
A	23.11	1	23.11	9.41	<.01
B	19.01	1	19.01	7.74	<.01
A × B	35.11	1	35.11	14.29	<.01
WG	186.75	76	2.46		

$$\bar{X}_1 = 5.10 \qquad \bar{X}_3 = 4.85$$
$$\bar{X}_2 = 2.80 \qquad \bar{X}_4 = 5.20$$

3. The outcome of a one-way ANOVA is provided below. Run a Scheffé test at $\alpha = .05$ for the following null hypotheses.

   a. $1\mu_1 - 1\mu_2 = 0$
   b. $1\mu_3 - 1/2\mu_1 - 1/2\mu_2 = 0$
   c. $1\mu_2 - 1\mu_3 = 0$

Source of Variance	df	Mean Squares	F	p
Between groups	2	32.6	7.36	<.05
Within groups	12	4.43		

$$\bar{X}_1 = 4.60 \qquad \bar{X}_3 = 8.00$$
$$\bar{X}_2 = 3.00 \qquad n_1 = n_2 = n_3 = 5$$

4. Run a Tukey test on the following data for all possible comparisons at $\alpha = .05$.

Participant	Control	Group A	Group B
1	6	1	4
2	4	3	4
3	9	3	5
4	10	2	6

5. For the following data, complete the ANOVA summary table and run Scheffé's test for all possible comparisons ($\alpha = .05$).

Source of Variance	SS	df	MS	F	p
Between	28.40	2			
Within	9.20	6			

$$\bar{X}_1 = 6.30 \qquad \bar{X}_3 = 2.40$$
$$\bar{X}_2 = 1.70 \qquad n_1 = n_2 = n_3 = 3$$

6. A kayak manufacturer measured the time taken by professional racers in four different types of kayak to complete six trials of a race course. Here are the data.

Eclipse	Mirage	Dancer	Mark IV
1.4	1.7	2.0	3.0
1.2	1.8	2.1	3.1
1.0	1.9	2.0	2.9
1.6	2.2	2.4	2.8
1.8	2.4	2.6	3.4
1.0	2.7	2.8	3.5

a. Run a one-way ANOVA on the data above at $\alpha = .05$.
b. Compare the Eclipse with the Mirage using Scheffé's test ($\alpha = .05$). Do they differ?
c. Compare the Eclipse with the average of the other three boats. Use Scheffé's test ($\alpha = .05$). What is your conclusion?
d. Compare all possible means with Tukey's test ($\alpha = .05$). What are your conclusions?

7. The following data are from a two-way ANOVA. Compare the means with a Tukey test at $\alpha = .05$. Compute a and b.

No Feedback		Corrective Feedback	
High Practice	**Low Practice**	**High Practice**	**Low Practice**
7.00	5.13	8.50	7.63

MS error $= 2.88$ with 28 *df n* $= 8$ for each group

a. HSD
b. NH − NL; CH − NH; CL − NH; CH − NL; CL − NL; CH − CL
c. Which means are significantly different?

8. Using the data below and the Scheffé test at $\alpha = .05$, compare the average of means 1 and 2 with the average of means 3 and 4. Compute a to d.

$$\bar{X}_1 = 6.43 \ \bar{X}_2 = 5.43 \ \bar{X}_3 = 4.57 \ \bar{X}_4 = 4.57 \ MS_{error} = 5.58$$

a. C
b. s_c
c. F_s
d. F'
e. What is your decision?

CHAPTER 14

Inference With the Chi-Square Distribution

LEARNING OBJECTIVES

After reading this chapter, you should be able to do the following:

1. Describe the difference between a parametric technique and a nonparametric technique.
2. List the steps for constructing the chi-square distribution.
3. Describe the shape of the chi-square distribution.
4. Determine degrees of freedom for a chi-square test for goodness of fit and a chi-square test for independence.
5. Run a chi-square test for goodness of fit and a chi-square test for independence for a given set of data.
6. Provide the formula for determining expected values for a chi-square test for independence.
7. Determine the appropriate test of significance for a given research problem.

In the previous chapters on inference, we have learned about several parametric techniques for comparing means. But often researchers are not interested in comparing means. Sometimes they want to compare frequencies or percentages. Which political candidate is the most popular? Are people in favor of private health care? How prevalent is depression in winter than in summer? Consider the report below.

Medical Brain Drain Puts Southern Africa in a Quandary: The Figures Tell It All

In South Africa, 37 percent of the country's doctors and seven percent of its nurses have migrated to Australia, Canada, Finland, France, Germany, Portugal, Britain and the United States.

In Zimbabwe, 11 percent of doctors and 34 percent of nurses have left in search of greener pastures.

Moyiga Nduru, Inter Press Service (Johannesburg), April 2006

But do the figures tell it all? Is there really a medical brain drain in South Africa? Are these percentages higher than usual? The techniques we will study in this chapter could help answer this question.

When we make inferences about the mean of a population or the difference between means of two or more populations, we are using parametric techniques. We are inferring the values of population parameters. Some research questions do not involve specific parameters of a distribution, but rather the entire frequency distribution. For example, an automobile dealer might be interested in the relative popularity of six of her car models. If her data showed that one model was more popular with her customers than the others, she might use this information when ordering new cars from the manufacturer. In this example, the data that interest the dealer are not mean scores; rather, they are the number of cars sold of each type.

If we are interested in the nature of the entire population, we may find a **nonparametric technique** to be appropriate. The **chi-square** (χ^2) **test** is a nonparametric test that allows us to make inferences about population frequencies from sample frequencies. Nonparametric tests are useful for analyzing data measured on nominal and ordinal scales because they do not make as many assumptions as parametric tests.

Chi-square tests compare obtained sample frequencies with those expected according to the null hypothesis. Chi-square can be used with frequency data or with proportion data, because proportions can always be converted into frequencies. Chi-square tests can be used for discrete variables or for continuous variables that have been categorized into discrete intervals.

The chi-square test compares the frequencies obtained in a sample with those expected if the null hypothesis were true. The null hypothesis states the expected frequencies of sample data based on certain assumptions about the population from which the sample was drawn. Of course, we would not expect sample frequencies to be *exactly* equal to expected frequencies, even if the null were true. Sample frequencies will vary somewhat from their hypothesized values. The question is "How much variation between obtained sample frequencies and their expected values would likely occur if the null were true?" To answer this question, we need a sampling distribution.

Nonparametric techniques: Used to make inferences about populations rather than population parameters

Chi-square test: A nonparametric analysis used to test hypotheses about frequencies of categorical or discrete variables

The Chi-Square Distribution

Like the t and F distributions, the chi-square distribution is a family of distributions; the shape of each is determined by degrees of freedom. The chi-square distribution is a relative frequency distribution based on discrepancies between obtained frequencies and their expected values. The value of chi-square will be smaller when the obtained and expected frequencies are similar, and the value will be larger when they are not. If the hypothesized frequencies are not true population frequencies, the discrepancies between obtained and expected values will be large and so will the value of chi-square. We need to discover what values of chi-square would occur with random sampling when the null is true. We can then compare our obtained chi-square value with this distribution of values and determine whether our outcome is a likely one or not according to the null hypothesis.

Constructing the Sampling Distribution of Chi-Square

The random sampling distribution of chi-square is constructed in the following manner:

Step 1. Randomly select a sample, with replacement, from a population of a discrete variable whose expected frequencies are known. Record the frequency for each category.

Step 2. Subtract the expected frequency (E) for each category from the observed frequency (O). Square each difference and divide it by the associated expected frequency (i.e., $[O - E]^2/E$). Sum these values for all categories of the variable. This is the chi-square statistic.

Step 3. Repeat Steps 1 and 2 until all possible samples have been drawn from the population.

Step 4. Place the chi-square values in a relative frequency distribution. This relative frequency distribution is the random sampling distribution of the chi-square statistic.

Characteristics of the Chi-Square Distribution

Because the chi-square value is computed by squaring the differences between the observed and expected values, it can never be negative.

The null hypothesis states that the category frequencies in the population equal a set of values. A sample selected from that population should reflect that set of values.

ALERT

When the obtained frequencies are either larger or smaller than those expected, the value of chi-square increases. For this reason, the region of rejection always appears in the upper tail of the distribution, as illustrated in Figure 14.1. Although the critical region lies in one tail, the chi-square test is nondirectional. A very low chi-square value simply means that the obtained frequencies are closer to the expected values than chance would predict.

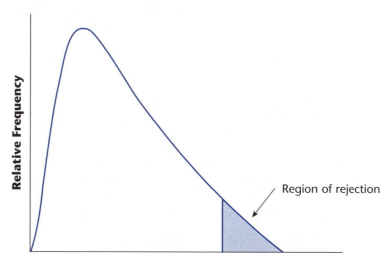

Figure 14.1. An example of a chi-square distribution.

The chi-square distribution changes shape depending on degrees of freedom. In the other distributions that we have looked at, degrees of freedom have been determined in relation to sample size. Degrees of freedom for the chi-square test are not related to sample size but rather are related to the number of discrepancies, $(O - E)$s, that are independent and free to vary. In a chi-square test, we assume that the total number of observations or total frequency is fixed and determine how many discrepancies are free to vary.

Using the Chi-Square Distribution

We will discuss two chi-square tests: (1) the chi-square test for goodness of fit and (2) the chi-square test for independence. The first is used when we have one variable. The second test is used when we wish to discover whether two variables are related.

The Chi-Square Test for Goodness of Fit

This test is used when we have two or more categories or levels but only one variable. We are interested in knowing whether the frequencies we obtain for each category in our sample match the expected frequencies specified by the null hypothesis.

Null and Alternative Hypotheses

The null and alternative hypotheses for a chi-square test of goodness of fit are determined before data collection—that is, a priori. How the null and alternative are stated depends on the research question. For example, a tavern owner may be interested in customer preference for four types of beer. He may decide to have 100 customers taste each beer and indicate their preference. If the population from which his customers came had no preference for any of the four types, he would expect 25 people to choose each one. These would be the expected frequencies. The null hypothesis would specify "no difference in preference," and the expected value for each brand would be 25. The alternative hypothesis would state that "preference differs" and that the true frequencies in the population were different from those hypothesized in the null.

H_0: No difference in preference for types of beer.

H_1: Preference for types of beer differs.

Calculating Chi-Square

Let's run a chi-square test for goodness of fit to answer the tavern owner's question. Suppose he finds, after 100 customers choose which of the four types of beer they prefer, the following frequencies.

Frequencies	Ale	Beer	Lager	Porter	Row Sum
Observed	10	20	55	15	100
Expected	25	25	25	25	100

We find the value of chi-square as follows:

$$\chi^2 = \Sigma \frac{(O-E)^2}{E}$$

$$\chi^2 = \frac{(10-25)^2 + (20-25)^2 + (55-25)^2 + (15-25)^2}{25} = 50$$

Now he needs to compare the obtained χ^2 value with the critical value. The critical values for chi-square are found in Table B.4 in Appendix B for various degrees of freedom. As usual, if the obtained value is equal to or larger than the critical value, the null hypothesis is rejected.

Recall that degrees of freedom for chi-square are determined by the number of comparisons between observed and expected frequencies that are free to vary. The total frequency is fixed. Looking at our example, we can see that three frequencies can vary, but the fourth must be fixed to keep the sum at 100. Three discrepancies can vary, but the fourth cannot. One degree of freedom is used so that the total can stay at 100. This problem, then, has 3 *df*.

The critical value of chi-square ($\chi^2_{.01}$) for 3 *df* is 11.34 at $\alpha = .01$. Because the obtained value of 50 is greater than the critical value, the null is rejected. The tavern owner has statistical evidence of a significant difference in population preference for his four types of beer.

In this example, the expected frequencies for each category were equal. This is not always the case. Remember Mendel? Imagine a botanist has determined that seedlings should show four particular characteristics in the ratio of 4:3:2:1. The first characteristic should appear in $\frac{4}{10}$ of the seedlings, the second in $\frac{3}{10}$, and so on. If the botanist collected a random sample of 200 seedlings, the expected frequencies for each characteristic would be 80, 60, 40, and 20. The obtained (*O*) values could then be compared with these expected (*E*) values.

CONCEPT REVIEW 14.1

Conduct a chi-square test for the seedling data given below.

Frequencies		Characteristic			
	1	2	3	4	5
O	90	30	50	30	200
E	80	60	40	20	200

Answer on page 401.

Both of these examples have four categories and 3 df. A special situation exists when there are two categories and 1 df. With only two categories of frequencies, either a chi-square test for goodness of fit or a z test for a proportion may be used, as long as the assumptions of z have been met. The outcome will be the same. For example, suppose a social worker counts the number of her clients who prefer in-home visits and the number who prefer office visits. Of her 50 clients, 33 prefer in-home visits and 17 prefer meeting at her office. She wants to know if there is a significant difference in client preference for the two meeting places. If there is no difference in preference, we would expect equal numbers of clients choosing each place to meet. This experiment has one variable (meeting place), two categories of that variable (home, office), and 1 df; we may run a chi-square test or a z test for a proportion because our frequencies can be easily converted to proportion. Let's do both at $\alpha = .01$. The null and alternative hypotheses for a chi-square test are as follows:

H_0: Equal preference for in-home and office meetings

H_1: Preference differs

$$\chi^2 = \frac{(33-25)^2 + (17-25)^2}{25} = 5.12$$

With 1 df, the critical value of $\chi^2_{.01}$ is 6.64; we would not reject the null hypothesis. Her clients, evidently, have no preference for the place where they meet with her, $\chi^2(1) = 5.12$, ns.

With a z test for a proportion, we hypothesize that the proportion of clients in the population who prefer in-home meetings is 0.50. In our sample, the proportion of clients who preferred in-home meetings was $\frac{33}{50} = .66$. Our hypotheses are as follows:

H_0: $P = .50$

H_1: $P \neq .50$

Then, we conduct a z test for a proportion.

$$z = \frac{p - P_p}{\sqrt{PQ/n}} = \frac{.66 - .50}{\sqrt{(.5)(.5)/50}} = \frac{.16}{.07} = 2.29$$

The critical value of z is ± 2.58 at $\alpha = .01$, so we cannot reject the null. There is no evidence that the proportion of clients preferring in-home meetings is different from 0.50, $z = 2.29$, ns.

Interpreting Chi-Square

The tavern owner interested in customer preference chose to test 4 types of beer. What if he had decided to test 10 types? The degrees of freedom would be 9, not 3. The computed chi-square value would be larger because there were six more discrepancies in its calculation.

We found in the t and F distribution that as degrees of freedom increase, the critical value decreases. Perhaps you are wondering why we don't just add more categories, increasing the value of our obtained chi-square and making it easier to reject the null. A good point! If you examine the chi-square table, you will notice that as degrees of freedom increase, the critical value of chi-square *gets larger, not smaller.* Adding more categories does not make it easier to reject the null. The table takes the number of degrees of freedom into account when it determines the critical value. With more degrees of freedom in your experiment, you must obtain a larger chi-square value to reject the null.

The chi-square test for goodness of fit compares obtained frequencies with a priori expected values stated by the null hypothesis. As we will see in the next section, the chi-square test for independence makes a different comparison.

SUMMARY OF THE CHI-SQUARE TEST FOR GOODNESS OF FIT

Hypotheses

H_0: Os = Es
H_1: Os ≠ Es

Assumptions

1. Participants are randomly selected.
2. Categories are mutually exclusive.

Decision Rules

df = number of categories − 1

If $\chi^2_{obt} \geq \chi^2_{crit}$ reject H_0

If $\chi^2_{obt} < \chi^2_{crit}$ do not reject H_0

Formula

$$\chi^2 = \Sigma \frac{(O-E)^2}{E}$$

The Chi-Square Test for Independence

The chi-square test for independence is used to measure the association between two variables. This is often called the "two-variable case." The question asked is "Are the two variables independent?" Suppose the tavern owner discussed earlier wished to know if preference for his four types of beer depended on whether the customer was female or male. His research question in this case would be "Are gender and beer preference independent?" Similarly, the social worker may wonder if preference for meeting place depends on the distance between the clients' homes and her office. Her research question in this case would be "Does preference for meeting place depend on travel distance?"

Null and Alternative Hypotheses

In the chi-square test for independence, the null hypothesis always states that the two variables are independent, and the alternative hypothesis states that they are dependent.

In the one-variable case (goodness of fit), expected frequencies were determined a priori by some theoretical assumption. In the two-variable case, the expected values are determined after data collection, or post hoc, from the values of the obtained or observed frequencies.

Determining Expected Frequencies

Let's call on our tavern owner again to illustrate how expected frequencies are determined in a chi-square test for independence. Suppose he randomly selected 150 men and 100 women and asked each to declare his or her preference for the four types of beer. Here are his data for observed frequencies.

	Ale	Beer	Lager	Porter	Row Sum
Women	35	25	15	25	100
Men	20	30	70	30	150
Column sum	55	55	85	55	250

To find the expected frequencies for this problem, we must determine the frequencies we would expect in each category if gender made no difference to preference. If we examine the column totals, we see that lager is the "preferred type" over all, and the other three are ranked equally. If gender and preference are independent, then that pattern of results would be expected for both genders. In other words, if gender didn't matter, how many women and how many men would prefer each type, considering the size of our two samples? The formula for determining these expected values for chi-square test for independence is

$$E = \frac{(\text{row sum})(\text{column sum})}{\text{total}}$$

Using this formula, our expected frequencies for each group would be

	Ale	Beer	Lager	Porter	Row Sum
Women	22	22	34	22	100
Men	33	33	51	33	150
Column sum	55	55	85	55	250

Note that the row and column totals are the same as those of the observed frequencies. This is always true. Now we are ready to compute our chi-square.

Calculating Chi-Square

$$\chi^2 = \Sigma \frac{(O-E)^2}{E}$$
$$= \frac{(35-22)^2}{22} + \frac{(25-22)^2}{22} + \frac{(15-34)^2}{34} + \frac{(25-22)^2}{22}$$
$$+ \frac{(20-33)^2}{33} + \frac{(30-33)^2}{33} + \frac{(70-51)^2}{51} + \frac{(30-33)^2}{33}$$
$$= 31.86$$

Now, we need to look up the critical value of chi-square and compare it with our obtained value. However, we need to know the degrees of freedom. Degrees of freedom are determined by the number of $O - E$ differences that are free to vary. In a chi-square test for independence, we assume that the row and column sums are fixed. Degrees of freedom are equal to the number of cells in the table of expected values that are independent and, therefore, free to vary. One way to determine degrees of freedom is to ask how many expected values must be calculated before we can obtain the rest by subtraction. Let's look at our table of expected values, for a moment.

	Ale	Beer	Lager	Porter	Row Sum
Women	*				100
Men					150
Column sum	55	55	85	55	250

Let's calculate the expected frequency for the box marked with an asterisk.

$$E = \frac{(\text{row sum})(\text{column sum})}{\text{total}}$$
$$= \frac{(100)(55)}{250} = 22$$

We can find the expected value for men choosing ale by subtraction. It must be $55 - 22 = 33$. This value, then, is not free to vary. How many more values must we compute before we can obtain the rest by subtraction? Clearly, we need to calculate only two more values. Three expected values, altogether, must be calculated before the rest are fixed. Our problem, then, has 3 *df*.

For any chi-square test of independence, degrees of freedom are calculated by

$$df = (\text{number of rows} - 1)(\text{number of columns} - 1)$$

Returning to our problem,

$$df = (2 - 1)\ (4 - 1) = 3$$

The critical value of χ^2 is 7.82 at $\alpha = .05$. Our obtained value is larger than the critical value, and so, we reject the null hypothesis. We have evidence that gender and preference for four types of beer are dependent. In other words, women and men do not prefer the same types of beer, $\chi^2(3) = 31.75, p < .05$.

CONCEPT REVIEW 14.2

Determine the expected frequencies for the following.

	Column 1	Column 2	Column 3	Column 4	Row Sum
Row 1					30
Row 2					20
Row 3					20
Column sum	10	20	10	30	70

Answer on page 402.

Let's do another example.

Imagine that we have surveyed men and women to determine their perceptions about the causes of marital discord. Our survey specifies several reasons why marriages fail, and we ask our respondents to select the one that they believe is at the root of most marital problems. Here are the data for the observed frequencies.

	Men	Women	Row Sum
Financial problems	40	10	50
Sexual problems	40	15	55
Poor communication	5	50	55
Differences in basic values	5	30	35
Boredom	10	10	20
Column sum	100	115	215

To determine the expected frequencies, we multiple the row sum by the column sum and divide by the total. The expected frequencies are as follows:

	Men	Women	Row Sum
Financial problems	23.26	26.74	50
Sexual problems	25.58	29.42	55
Poor communication	25.58	29.42	55
Differences in basic values	16.28	18.72	35
Boredom	9.30	10.70	20
Column sum	100	115	215

Here are the squared differences divided by the expected frequencies, that is $\dfrac{(O-E)^2}{E}$:

	Men	Women
Financial problems	12.05	10.48
Sexual problems	8.13	7.07
Poor communication	16.56	14.40
Differences in basic values	7.81	6.79
Boredom	0.05	0.045

Now, we sum these to obtain our chi-square statistic:

$$\chi^2 = \Sigma \frac{(O-E)^2}{E} = 83.4$$

Our chi-square value of 83.4 is significant at the .01 level. In a research report, we might say that the perceptions about why marriages fail depends on gender, $\chi^2(4) = 83.4$, $p < .01$.

Interpreting Chi-Square

Like the goodness-of-fit test, as categories are added to one or both variables, the χ^2 value will increase. The table takes this into account; the critical values increase with larger degrees of freedom.

FYI

A significant value of χ^2 means that the two variables are related in some systematic way. When two variables are related, we often say they are *correlated*. Correlation, as a statistical technique, is discussed in detail in Chapter 16. A significant value of chi-square, then, tells us that the variables depend on each other or are correlated. But how dependent or correlated are they? A statistic that has been developed to measure the strength of this relationship is called *Cramer's measure of association* (φ). This statistic is appropriate for computing the strength of the relationship when the chi-square test for independence produces a significant result. This statistic ranges from 0 (when the two variables are not related) to 1 (when the variables are perfectly related). Students should consult an upper-level statistics text for detailed information on this measure.

SUMMARY OF THE CHI-SQUARE TEST FOR INDEPENDENCE

Hypotheses

H_0: The population variables are independent.
H_1: The population variables are dependent.

Assumptions

1. Participants are randomly selected.
2. Observations have been classified simultaneously on two independent categories.

Decision Rules

$df = (\text{number of rows} - 1)\ (\text{number of columns} - 1)$

If $\chi^2_{obt} \geq \chi^2_{crit}$ reject H_0

If $\chi^2_{obt} < \chi^2_{crit}$ do not reject H_0

Formula

$$\chi^2 = \Sigma \frac{(O - E)^2}{E}$$

Assumptions Underlying Inference With the Chi-Square Distribution

Chi-square assumes that the sample was randomly selected from the population, the observations are independent, and the variable is discrete. Each particular observation can only be recorded in one cell. In other words, the categories are *mutually exclusive*.

In repeated experiments, chi-square requires that observed frequencies be normally distributed around their expected frequencies. This makes sense, because if we have an expected frequency of 15, occasionally we would observe a much higher or lower frequency, but most of the time we would see frequencies close to the expected value, given the null is true.

ALERT

This assumption may cause problems when expected frequencies are very small. With an expected frequency of 3, for example, the observed frequencies would be positively skewed around 3 because the distribution is limited at 0. Some statisticians recommend that all expected frequencies should be 5 or greater.

FYI

A special correction has been developed for the chi-square test for independence when we have 1 *df*. This correction, called *Yates Correction for Discontinuity*, may be appropriate when sample sizes are small. The effect of **Yates correction** is to prevent the overestimation of statistical significance when frequency counts are low. There is some debate that Yates correction may be too conservative even when counts are low. The correction consists of subtracting 0.5 from the absolute difference between each observed and expected value before squaring. Rather than summing

$$\frac{(O-E)^2}{E}$$

we sum

$$\frac{(|O-E|-0.5)^2}{E}$$

This method provides a more appropriate test of the null hypothesis for these special cases. Using Yates correction, the chi-square value is found by

$$\Sigma \frac{(|O-E|-0.5)^2}{E}$$

Yates correction: An adjustment used in special cases of chi-square tests when expected frequencies are small

Choosing the Appropriate Test of Significance

This chapter has dealt with two nonparametric tests of significance: (1) chi-square test for goodness of fit and (2) chi-square test for independence. Deciding which of these two tests should be used is not difficult for most students. What many students have trouble with is deciding whether the data in a particular research study lend themselves to a parametric or a nonparametric approach. This decision is made by examining the kinds of data collected in the study.

In this section, we will go through the steps involved in deciding whether ANOVA or chi-square is the appropriate analysis. I did not include ANOVA designs where repeated measures have been taken.

Step 1. Determine the kind of data collected in the experiment.

The first step in deciding between chi-square and ANOVA is to examine the dependent variable data to see if measures of performance or categories of frequencies have been collected. If *participants* provided measures that will be used to compute means, then ANOVA is the likely analysis. On the other hand, if *participants* have been categorized into frequency groups, then chi-square is the likely approach.

Step 2. Determine the number of independent variables.

If you have two or more groups in the study, you must determine how many independent variables are involved. With two or more groups or categories of *participants*, with each group under a different level of a single independent variable, you will choose one-way ANOVA if the data are measures, and you will choose chi-square test for goodness of fit if the data are frequency counts.

If you determine that the experimental design involves two independent variables, then you will run a two-way ANOVA if the data are measures, and you will run a chi-square test for independence if the data are frequency counts.

Let's use the steps to decide which analysis is appropriate for the following research studies.

Example A: An investigator has classified 400 randomly selected business executives, according to their profiles from a standardized personality test, into high-anxious, medium-anxious, and low-anxious. He wonders if the proportions of each type are similar.

Step 1. Determine the kind of data collected in the experiment.

This is an easy one. The term *classified* and the term *proportions* are clues that these data are frequency counts. Although measures have been taken, they have not been used directly in any computation of average; they have been used to categorize the *participants*.

Step 2. Determine the number of independent variables.

There is only one variable in this example: level of anxiety. A chi-square test for goodness of fit will be used to determine if there is a difference in proportion among the three levels.

Example B: The music department at a large college classifies a randomly selected group of music students into expert, intermediate, and novice pianists. Half of the students in each group are given intensive piano training using an innovative approach to teaching. The other half are given standard training for the same length of time. Following the training period, all students are required to give a piano recital, and the number of errors made by each student is recorded. The average number of errors made by each group is compared.

Step 1. Determine the kind of data collected in the experiment.

Although the use of the term *classifies* might have led you to think the data are frequency data, you can see that this is not the case. "Number of errors made" was the measure, and averages for each group were computed.

Step 2. Determine the number of independent variables.

There are two variables in this study: (1) level of expertise and (2) type of training. The investigator will run a two-way ANOVA to see if expertise overall made a difference in performance, if training overall made a difference, and if the two variables interact. For example, perhaps the innovative training was particularly helpful to the novice students.

Example C: The music department at a large college is hosting a recital by its piano students. Each performance at the recital is categorized, by an impartial member of the department, as excellent, fair, or poor. Some of the students had received intensive piano training using an innovative teaching approach for several weeks before the recital. Others had been given standard training for the same length of time. A researcher tallies the students in terms of what kind of training they had received—innovative or standard—and what rating they were given for their recital—excellent, fair, or poor.

Step 1. Determine the kind of data collected in the experiment.

In this version, the data are clearly frequency counts. The researcher has counted the number of students in each category.

Step 2. Determine the number of independent variables.

Two variables are involved: (1) training type and (2) performance category. Students have been simultaneously categorized by type of training and recital rating. A chi-square test for independence will tell the music department whether recital performance and type of training are independent or dependent. If type of training wasn't important, we'd expect the same number of excellent, fair, and poor performances from each group.

Example D: The Dolphin Show manager at Ocean Realm has become concerned about the influence of the trainer on the dolphins' performance. He has noticed that some of the dolphins seem to perform differently with different trainers.

He randomly assigned 20 dolphins to each of three trainers. Their trainers signal the dolphins, one at a time, to perform a high leap out of the water. Impartial judges are on hand to determine if each jump was successful (reached a certain height) or not.

The number of dolphins succeeding and the number failing are counted for each of the three trainers.

Step 1. Determine the kind of data collected in the experiment.

These data are frequency data. The manager is interested in how many dolphins perform successfully with each trainer.

Step 2. Determine the number of independent variables.

There are two independent variables. The dolphins have been categorized into two groups based on whether they succeeded or not in their jumps and simultaneously on a second variable—which trainer was present. A chi-square test for independence will help the manager determine if success or failure depends on the trainer involved.

Example E: The Dolphin Show manager at Ocean Realm has become concerned about the influence of the trainer on the dolphins' performance. He has noticed that some of the dolphins seem to perform differently with different trainers. He randomly assigned 20 dolphins to each of three trainers. Their trainers signal the dolphins, one at a time, to perform a high leap out of the water. Impartial judges are on hand to measure the height of the jump against a backdrop ruler. The average jump height of the dolphins assigned to each trainer is compared.

Step 1. Determine the kind of data collected in the experiment.

In this example, a measure for each subject is collected (i.e., height of jump), and a mean will be computed for each group (i.e., mean height under each trainer).

Step 2. Determine the number of independent variables.

There is only one independent variable in this study, the trainer. The analysis will compare the mean performance of the animals under three different trainers. A one-way ANOVA is the appropriate test of significance. The dolphins were randomly assigned to a trainer, and so if Trainer 1's dolphins jumped significantly higher than the rest, the manager might have reason to believe that Trainer 1 is a more effective trainer than the others.

FOCUS ON RESEARCH

THE RESEARCH PROBLEM

The notion that men and women differ in IQ (intelligence quotient) has been around for a long time. In general, it seems that there really is no gender difference in IQ, although there may be some specific components of intelligence that differ between men and women.

Szymanowicz and Furnham (2011) of University College in the United Kingdom were interested in cultural stereotypes about the intelligence of men versus women. More specifically, they wanted to know if men and women perceive a target person differently, depending on the gender of the target.

THE DESIGN AND VARIABLES

I will describe part of the study here.

Participants (57 women and 64 men) were given the following information about the target person who was identified as either John or Jane.

Jane (John) Evans, aged 32, had recently taken an intelligence test. She (he) has just received her (his) results and found out that she (he) scored high enough to become a member of MENSA—an international organisation associating highly intelligent people whose IQ is in the top 2% of the population.

Participants were then asked to respond "Yes" or "No" to questions, including the following, and to elaborate their answers.

Should Jane (John) tell her (his) friends about her IQ?

Jane (John) is planning to place an advertise(ment) on a dating website—should she (he) include the information about being a member of MENSA?

THE ANALYSIS AND RESULTS

Data included frequency counts for various parts of the answers that the participants gave, and so chi-square tests for goodness of fit were used to assess differences.

The researchers found several significant differences between the responses of the men and the women. Overall, more women than men thought that the target should tell friends about IQ, $\chi^2(1) = 7.31$, $p < .01$, and more women than men thought friends would react positively to the information about IQ, $\chi^2(1) = 5.88$, $p < .01$. Interestingly, women called disclosing the IQ score as something to be proud of—significantly more often—when they were talking about Jane than when they were talking about John, $\chi^2(1) = 6.31$, $p < .01$.

Significantly, more men than woman had doubts about the importance of IQ testing, $\chi^2(1) = 6.14$, $p < .01$, and they thought that Jane would suffer more negative consequences from men on the dating website by disclosing her IQ than John would, $\chi^2(1) = 10.24$, $p < .001$.

CONCLUSIONS

Szymanowicz and Furnham conclude that gender stereotypes related to intelligence exist and that more research should be conducted to determine how those stereotypes affect behavior in Western and other cultures.

Szymanowicz, A., & Furnham, A. (2011). Do intelligent women stay single? Cultural stereotypes concerning the intellectual abilities of men and women. *Journal of Gender Studies*, *20*(1), 43–54.

SUMMARY OF TERMS AND FORMULAS

The *chi-square tests* are *nonparametric* analyses used to test hypotheses about frequencies of categorical or discrete variables.

The *test for goodness of fit* is used to evaluate the discrepancy between observed and expected frequencies for categories of a single variable.

The *test for independence* evaluates the relationship between two variables, with a null hypothesis that the variables are unrelated.

Degrees of freedom for chi-square tests are determined by the number of discrepancies used in the computation, which are independent and free to vary.

$$\text{Chi-square formula} \qquad \chi^2 = \Sigma \frac{(O-E)^2}{E}$$

Degrees of freedom	
Test for goodness of fit	number of categories − 1
Test for independence	(number of rows − 1)(number of columns − 1)
Expected values	$E = \dfrac{\text{row sum} - \text{column sum}}{\text{total}}$
Yates correction for discontinuity when $df = 1$	$\Sigma \dfrac{(|O-E|-0.5)^2}{E}$

CONCEPT REVIEW ANSWERS

14.1.

$(O-E)$	10	230	10	10
$(O-E)^2$	100	900	100	100
$\dfrac{(O-E)^2}{E}$	1.25	15	2.5	5

$$\chi^2 = 23.75$$

The critical value of chi-square at $\alpha = .01$ is 11.34. Evidently the seedlings do not follow the values expected by the botanist.

14.2.

	Column 1	Column 2	Column 3	Column 4	Row Sum
Row 1	4.29	8.57	4.29	12.86	30
Row 2	2.86	5.71	2.86	8.57	20
Row 3	2.86	5.71	2.86	8.57	20
Column sum	10	20	10	30	70

EXERCISES

1. For each of the following, determine the degrees of freedom and the critical value of chi-square.
    a. Test for goodness of fit, 6 categories, $\alpha = .05$
    b. Test for goodness of fit, 2 categories, $\alpha = .01$
    c. Test for independence, 4 categories for one variable and 5 categories for the second variable, $\alpha = .05$
    d. Test for independence, 2 categories for each variable, $\alpha = .01$

2. A local brewer observes that in a random sample of 100 women, 35 prefer light ale, 20 prefer pilsner, and 45 prefer a heavier malt brew. Test the hypothesis that women's preference is equal for the three types of beer. Compute a to d, and put your decision in words.
    a. H_0:
       H_1:
    b. df
    c. $\chi^2_{.05}$
    d. χ^2
    e. Decision

3. A biologist wants to determine if a rare strain of rat will perform better on a problem-solving task than the more common strain. The results showed that 24 of the 30 rare rats succeeded in solving the problems, and the remaining 6 failed. Twelve of the common strain solved the problem, and the remaining 15 failed. With $\alpha = .05$, run a test for independence. Compute a to d, and put your decision in words.

	Observed Frequencies	
	Success	**Failure**
Rare	24	6
Common	12	15

a. H_0:
   H_1:
b. df
c. $\chi^2_{.05}$
d. χ^2
e. Decision

4. A psychologist administers a test assessing strength of religious values to 120 randomly selected churchgoers. He then administers a second questionnaire assessing their attitude toward censorship of rock videos. Use a χ^2 test to see if "piety" and attitude toward censorship are related at $\alpha = .01$. Compute a to d, and put your decision in words.

	Observed Frequencies of Piety		
Censorship Attitude	**High**	**Medium**	**Low**
Pro	23	7	5
Neutral	20	20	20
Anti	8	22	25

a. H_0:
   H_1:
b. df
c. $\chi^2_{.01}$
d. χ^2
e. Decision

5. A breakfast cereal manufacturer observed that in a random sample of 60 children, 27 preferred a cornflake product, 19 preferred a shredded wheat product, and 14 preferred a high-fiber product. Use chi-square to test the hypothesis that there is no difference in children's preference for the three cereals. Use $\alpha = .05$.

6. A census determined that 60% of Americans vote regularly in state elections, 30% vote occasionally, and 10% never vote. A survey of an American college of political science determined that of the 500 students enrolled, 300 vote regularly in state elections, 190

vote occasionally, and 10 never vote. Test the hypothesis at $\alpha = .05$ that the students are a random sample of the American population.

7. When offered a choice between Popsicles and ice cream, 35 children chose Popsicles and 15 chose ice cream. At $\alpha = .01$, test the hypothesis that children's preference does not differ for the two treats.

8. A sporting goods manufacturer wants to determine if there is a relationship between gender and the riskiness of the sport each engages in. Over a 6-month period, he records whether the equipment purchased is for a high-risk sport (kaya-king, downhill skiing, skydiving) or a low-risk sport (cross-country skiing, skating, windsurfing), and whether the purchaser was male or female. He records his data in the following table. Test at $\alpha = .05$ to know whether riskiness and gender are independent.

	High Risk	Low Risk
Men	22	37
Women	18	28

9. A psychologist administers a test to 120 randomly selected churchgoers to assess the strength of their religious values. A second test is then administered to the same group to assess attitude toward legalization of marijuana. Use a chi-square test to see if the two variables are related at $\alpha = .01$. The data are as follows:

Marijuana Attitude	Piety			Row Sum
	High	Medium	Low	
In favor	5	10	20	35
Neutral	15	20	10	45
Against	20	10	10	40
Column sum	40	40	40	120

10. A sociologist wonders if "blondes have more fun." She selects a random sample of 50 blondes, 40 brunettes, and 35 redheads. She records the number of dates each girl has over a 6-month period and classifies them into three categories. Test the hypothesis that hair color and "popularity" are independent, at $\alpha = .05$. The data are as follows:

Number of Dates	Blondes	Brunettes	Redheads	Row Sum
50	39	15	13	67
25–50	8	20	10	38
<25	3	5	12	20
Column sum	50	40	35	

11. A scientist has been experimenting with black gerbils. He claims that as a result of certain injections, when two black gerbils are mated, the offspring will be black, white, and grey in the proportion 5:4:3. Many gerbils were mated after being injected with the chemical. Of 170 newborn gerbils, 61 were black, 69 were white, and 40 were grey. Test the scientist's claim at $\alpha = .01$.

12. Two kayaking buddies, Dan and Peter, enjoy racing each other down river. Over several years, they have been very evenly matched. Each has won about half the races. Last season, Peter read a book called *How to Win in Kayak Racing*. Since then, Peter has lost 18 out of 20 races against Dan. Use chi-square, at $\alpha = .05$, to test the hypothesis that the book had no effect on Peter's performance.

13. A faculty member and his wife are getting ready to attend a garden party given by his university. He wants to dress casually, but his wife thinks he should wear a suit. He explains to her that although most of the administrative staff attending the party will be in suits, most of the faculty will not. He lost the argument, but when they arrived at the party, he made a careful tally of who (administrators vs. faculty) were wearing what (suit or no suit). At $\alpha = .01$, test the hypothesis that position and style of dress are independent. The data are as follows:

	Position at University		
	Administrator	Faculty	Row Sum
Suit	45	8	53
No suit	10	32	42
Column sum	55	40	95

14. A criminologist categorizes 315 randomly selected inmates, incarcerated in prisons across the United States, by type of offence and family structure of parental home. Are the variables independent? Use $\alpha = .05$.

Family Structure	Crimes of		
	Violence	Theft	Drug Trafficking
Two-parent	2	87	60
Single parent	4	93	40
Other	8	12	9

15. A political scientist randomly selects 200 people from each of three occupational categories and determines their political affiliation. Are the variables independent? Use $\alpha = .01$.

Occupational Categories	Political Affiliation			
	Conservative	Liberal	NDP	Row Sum
Professional	30	85	85	200
Skilled	80	80	40	200
Unskilled	72	85	43	200
Column sum	182	250	168	600

CHAPTER 15

Additional Nonparametric Techniques

LEARNING OBJECTIVES

After reading this chapter, you should be able to do the following:

1. Describe the relationship between the Mann-Whitney U test and the t test for independent groups.
2. Run the Mann-Whitney U test for a given set of data and provide the z ratio for the U statistic.
3. Describe the relationship between the Wilcoxon test and the t test for dependent groups.
4. Run the Wilcoxon test for a given set of data and provide the z ratio for the T statistic.
5. Describe the relationship between the one-way ANOVA and the Kruskal-Wallis test.
6. Run the Kruskal-Wallis test for a given set of data.
7. Describe the relationship between the one-way repeated measures ANOVA and the Friedman test.
8. Run the Friedman test for a given set of data.
9. Determine the appropriate test of significance for a given research problem.

Top Six Healthiest Cities in the United States: Minneapolis; Washington, DC; Boston; Portland; Denver; and San Francisco

www.travelchannel.com/interests/wellness-and-renewal/photos/americas-top-20-healthiest-cities

Top Six Sexiest Women in the World: Tulisa Contostavios, Cheryl Cole, Rihanna, Rosy Jones, Georgia Salpa, and Katy Perry

www.fhm.com/girls/news/2012s-fhm-100-sexiest-01—tulisa-83165#pagetitle

I have no idea how the lists above were actually created, but they are presented as rank-order data (i.e., first to sixth). Rank-order data are considered to be ordinal, and inferences about means, for example, are inappropriate because the underlying assumptions of parametric analyses cannot be met. When we have ordinal measures, we must use procedures specifically developed for them. Chapter 14 presented the chi-square test, a nonparametric technique appropriate for frequency data. This chapter presents some additional nonparametric analyses.

The Mann-Whitney *U* Test

The **Mann-Whitney *U* test** is used to make inferences about the difference between two populations. The test is sensitive to the entire distributions from which the samples were drawn as well as their central tendencies.

This test, used for ordinal data, is the nonparametric alternative to the *t* test for the difference between independent groups.

> **Mann-Whitney *U* test:** Nonparametric alternative to the *t* test for independent groups, used for rank-order data

Null and Alternative Hypotheses

The null hypothesis states that the populations from which the samples were drawn are identical. The alternative hypothesis states they are different.

H_0: The populations are identical.

H_1: The populations are not identical.

If the population distributions are similar in shape, the test compares their central tendencies. If the central tendencies are similar, the test compares the entire distributions. As you can see, these hypotheses are slightly different from those used in inference with the *t* distribution.

The Mann-Whitney *U* test requires that participants be randomly selected and independently assigned to groups and that the scores be ranked in order.

The *U* Statistic

The Mann-Whitney test computes the *U* statistic, which follows the *U* distribution. The obtained *U* value is evaluated in terms of the sampling distribution of the *U* statistic. The Mann-Whitney *U* statistic that is tested for significance is the smaller of the following two values:

$$U_1 = n_1 + n_2 + \frac{n_1(n_1+1)}{2} - \Sigma R_1$$

$$U_2 = n_1 + n_2 + \frac{n_2(n_2+1)}{2} - \Sigma R_2$$

n_1 = sample size of Group 1

n_2 = sample size of Group 2

ΣR_1 = sum of the ranks for Group 1

ΣR_2 = sum of the ranks for Group 2

The critical values of U are found in Table B.6 in Appendix B for one- and two-tailed tests of significance. Enter the sample size for the first group along the top of the table and the sample size of the second group along the side of the table. Unlike our previous tests, the obtained U value must be smaller than the critical value to be significant.

Running the Mann-Whitney *U* Test

Step 1. Assign ranks to the scores in the groups.

This is done by combining and arranging the scores from both groups in order from the smallest to the largest and assigning a rank where 1 is the smallest score. For example, if a participant in Group 1 had the smallest score, then that participant's rank would be 1. If the next smallest score was obtained by a participant in Group 2, then that participant would be assigned a rank of 2.

Step 2. Calculate the U statistic.

Step 3. Compare the obtained value with the critical value.

The obtained value (U_{obt}) is the smaller of U_1 and U_2. If the obtained U value is smaller than the critical value, reject the null hypothesis; otherwise, do not reject the null hypothesis.

Ready for an example? Ten psychology professors and 10 biology professors were given a questionnaire designed to measure their attitudes toward various controversial issues about the influence of heredity and environment on human behavior. Here are the data arranged in order for each group.

Scores on the questionnaire:

BIOLOGY PROFESSORS: 2, 3, 11, 13, 15, 25, 27, 33, 39, 45

PSYCHOLOGY PROFESSORS: 6, 8, 16, 17, 23, 24, 26, 37, 38, 49

Let's follow our step-by-step procedure.

Step 1. Assign ranks to the scores in the groups.

The smallest score, 2, appears in the biology professors' group, and that score is assigned a rank of 1. Here are the rank-order data.
Ranks:

BIOLOGY PROFESSORS: 1, 2, 5, 6, 7, 12, 14, 15, 18, 19; Total = 99

PSYCHOLOGY PROFESSORS: 3, 4, 8, 9, 10, 11, 13, 16, 17, 20; Total = 111

Step 2. Calculate the U statistic.

Now, we can use the formulas to compute each U value.

$$U_1 = n_1 n_2 + \frac{n_1 (n_1 + 1)}{2} - \sum R_1$$
$$= 10(10) + \frac{10(11)}{2} - 99$$
$$= 100 + 55 - 99 = 56$$
$$U_2 = n_1 n_2 + \frac{n_2 (n_2 + 1)}{2} - \sum R_2$$
$$= 10(10) + \frac{10(11)}{2} - 111$$
$$= 100 + 55 - 111 = 44$$

Step 3. Compare the obtained value with the critical value.

The second U value is smaller, so we compare it with the critical value. At $\alpha = .05$, the critical value is 23 for a two-tailed test (as listed in Table B.6 in Appendix B). Because the smaller obtained U value is larger than the critical value, the null hypothesis is not rejected. We have no evidence that biology and psychology professors differ in terms of their attitudes toward the effect of heredity and environment on behavior ($U = 44$, ns).

ALERT

Remember that for this test, the obtained U must be smaller than the critical value before we can reject the null.

Running the Mann-Whitney *U* Test for Large Sample Sizes

The sampling distribution of the U statistic approaches the normal distribution when both samples have 20 or more observations. In such cases, we can compute a z value and use the normal curve tables in our test of significance.

After ranks have been assigned to the scores, we can run the Mann-Whitney U statistic in the following way:

Step 1. Determine the mean and standard deviation of the U statistic.

The sampling distribution of the U statistic has a mean of

$$\mu_U = \frac{n_1 n_2}{2}$$

and a standard deviation of

$$\sigma_U = \sqrt{\frac{n_1 n_2 (n_1 + n_2 + 1)}{12}}$$

Step 2. Compute the z statistic.

Subtract the mean of the sampling distribution of our statistic (μ_U) from the obtained sample outcome (U) and divide by the standard error of the sampling distribution (σ_U). In notation, the z formula for the U statistic is

$$z = \frac{U - \mu_U}{\sigma_U}$$

Step 3. Compare the obtained z value with the critical value.

If the obtained value is equal to or larger than the critical value, reject the null hypothesis; otherwise, do not reject the null hypothesis.

Ready for an example? Twenty randomly selected women and 20 randomly selected men are given a questionnaire designed to assess their feelings about the status of women in the workplace. The data are considered ordinal. Arranged from lowest to highest (where higher scores indicate higher status), here are the scores and ranks.

Scores		Ranks	
Women	Men	Women	Men
3	5	1	3.5
4	7	2	6
5	9	3.5	8.5
6	10	5	10
8	11	7	11
9	18	8.5	17
12	19	12	18
14	20	13.5	19.5
14	21	13.5	21
16	23	15	23
17	24	16	24
20	29	19.5	27
22	31	22	28
27	34	25	30
28	37	26	33
32	39	29	35
35	41	31	36
36	46	32	38
38	48	34	39
43	52	37	40
		$\Sigma = 352.5$	$\Sigma = 467.5$

ALERT

You will notice that some of the scores are equal. For example, two scores of 5 occurred, one in the women's group, the other in the men's. A common way to deal with tied scores is to assign the average of the ranks whose positions they take. Look at the two 5s that occurred. If these two scores were different, they would take positions 3 and 4. Because they are the same, they are assigned the average of those two rank positions—that is, 3.5. If three 5s had occurred, each would be given the rank of 4, the average of positions 3, 4, and 5.

We can now go ahead and run our test. We first need to compute U_1 and U_2.

$$U_1 = n_1 + n_2 + \frac{n_1(n_1+1)}{2} - \Sigma R_1$$

$$= 20(20) + \frac{20(21)}{2} - 352.5$$

$$= 257.5$$

$$U_2 = n_1 + n_2 + \frac{n_2(n_2+1)}{2} - \Sigma R_2$$

$$= 20(20) + \frac{20(21)}{2} - 467.5$$

$$= 142.5$$

Because U_2 is the smaller value, we use 142.5 as the U value in our z test.

$$z = \frac{U - \mu_U}{\sigma_U}$$

$$= \frac{U - n_1 n_2 / 2}{\sqrt{\dfrac{n_1 n_2 (n_1 + n_2 + 1)}{12}}}$$

$$= \frac{142.5 - (20)(20)/2}{\sqrt{(20)(20)(41)/12}}$$

$$= \frac{-57.5}{36.97}$$

$$= -1.56$$

The critical value for a z test is ± 1.96 for a two-tailed test at the .05 level of significance (as we discussed in Chapter 9). Because our obtained z value was numerically less (smaller when you ignore the sign) than the critical value, we do not reject the null hypothesis. In other words, we have no evidence that men and women feel differently about the status of women in the workplace, $z = -1.56$, *ns*.

The Mann-Whitney test is the nonparametric alternative to the t test for independent groups. It requires that the two samples be independent. If the two groups are dependent (for instance, the participants are matched on certain characteristics or repeated measures have been taken), then a different nonparametric test is required.

SUMMARY OF THE MANN-WHITNEY U TEST

Hypotheses

H_0: Populations are identical.
H_1: Populations are not identical.

Assumptions

1. Participants are randomly selected and independently assigned to groups.
2. Measurement scale is ordinal.

Decision Rules

If $U_{obt} < U_{crit}$ reject the H_0
If $U_{obt} \geq U_{crit}$ do not reject the H_0

Formulas

$$U_1 = n_1 n_2 + \frac{n_1(n_1+1)}{2} - \sum R_1$$

$$U_2 = n_1 n_2 + \frac{n_2(n_2+1)}{2} - \sum R_2$$

U_{obt} is the smaller of U_1 and U_2.

The Wilcoxon Signed-Ranks Test

The Wilcoxon signed-ranks test is used for ordinal data obtained on the same or matched participants. It is the nonparametric alternative to the t test for dependent means.

Null and Alternative Hypotheses

The null and alternative hypotheses for the Wilcoxon test are identical to those in the Mann-Whitney test.

H_0: The populations are identical.

H_1: The populations are not identical.

The *T* Statistic

The Wilcoxon test computes the *T* statistic.

ALERT

The Wilcoxon *T* is not the same as the *t* statistic. The *T* statistic follows the sampling distribution of *T*, not *t*.

The following procedure is used to conduct the Wilcoxon test.

Step 1. Calculate the difference between the two scores for each participant.

Step 2. Rank the absolute values (i.e., ignore the + or – sign of each value) of the difference scores from lowest to highest. Assign a sign to the ranking by referring to the differences and placing the corresponding sign (+ or –) next to each rank.

Step 3. Sum the ranks with the less frequent sign. In other words, if there are fewer positive ranks than negative ranks, sum the values of the positive ranks. This is the *T* statistic.

Step 4. Compare the obtained value with the critical value.

Table B.7 in Appendix B provides the critical values of *T* for one- and two-tailed tests at various levels of significance. As with the Mann-Whitney test, the obtained *T* value must be *less* than the critical value for rejection of the null hypothesis.

Running the Wilcoxon Signed-Ranks Test

Let's work through an example. A French professor rated the pronunciation accuracy of 10 randomly selected students based on a pretest. Scores could range from 0 to 15, with 15 representing excellent pronunciation. The students were then trained in correct French pronunciation with audio correction technology and re-rated their accuracy on a posttest. Let's run a two-tailed test at $\alpha = .05$.

Step 1. Calculate the difference between the two scores for each participant.

Student	Pretest	Posttest	Difference	Rank
1	10	10	0	dropped
2	4	7	−3	−3.5
3	11	8	3	3.5
4	9	10	−1	−1
5	2	6	−4	−5
6	6	1	5	6
7	8	2	6	7
8	12	5	7	8
9	3	12	−9	−9
10	4	2	2	2

Step 2. Rank the absolute values (i.e., ignore the + or − sign of each value) of the difference scores from lowest to highest.

Like the Mann-Whitney test, tied difference scores are assigned shared ranks. Note that when the two scores are equal and the difference is 0, the pair of scores is dropped from the analysis and n, the number of paired scores, is reduced accordingly.

Step 3. Sum the ranks with the less frequent sign.

There are fewer negatives than positives, so we sum all the ranks with negative signs. Our T value is 18.5.

Step 4. Compare the obtained value with the critical value.

To determine the critical value, we enter Table B.7 in Appendix B with the number of pairs of scores used in the final analysis. In our example, we dropped one pair of scores, and so $n = 9$. We find that the critical value of T for a two-tailed test at $\alpha = .05$ is 5. Because our obtained T value is greater than the critical value, we do not reject the null. Remember that, for this test, the obtained value must be smaller than the critical value to reject the null. There is no evidence that the professor's instruction affects students' pronunciation accuracy, $T = 18.5$, ns.

Running the Wilcoxon Signed-Ranks Test for Large Sample Sizes

Like the Mann-Whitney test, when the samples are reasonably large (>20), the sampling distribution of T approaches the normal distribution, and the z statistic is used in the test for significance.

Step 1. Determine the mean and standard deviation of the T statistic.

The mean of the sampling distribution of T is

$$\mu_T = \frac{n(n+1)}{4}$$

and, the standard deviation is

$$\sigma_T = \sqrt{\frac{n(n+1)(2n+1)}{24}}$$

Step 2. Compute the z statistic.

The formula for converting the T statistic to z is the following:

$$z = \frac{T - \mu_T}{\sigma_T}$$

Step 3. Compare the obtained z value with the critical value.

If the obtained z value is equal to or larger than the critical value, reject the null hypothesis; otherwise, do not reject the null.

Inmate	Rating Before	Rating After	Difference	Rank
1	34	40	−6	−9.5
2	23	30	−7	−12
3	56	55	1	1.5
4	46	50	−4	−4.5
5	33	40	−7	−12
6	38	39	−1	−1.5
7	25	25	−12	−16
8	26	30	−4	−4.5
9	22	25	−3	−3

(Continued)

(Continued)

Inmate	Rating Before	Rating After	Difference	Rank
10	37	43	−6	−9.5
11	19	36	−17	−20
12	27	34	−7	−12
13	45	50	−5	−7
14	33	47	−14	−18
15	29	38	−9	−15
16	30	25	5	7
17	20	15	5	7
18	25	38	−13	−17
19	15	31	−16	−19
20	50	42	8	14

Let's look at an example. Twenty inmates in a minimum-security facility who had anger management problems were enrolled in a conflict resolution program. Prior to beginning the program, they were assessed, by impartial judges, on their conflict resolution skills in a variety of simulated conflict situations. After completing the program, each inmate was again assessed in a series of similar conflict situations. Higher scores reflect better conflict resolution skills. Let's test the null hypothesis that the program had no effect on the conflict resolution skills. The scores received by each inmate appear on page 417.

In this example, there are fewer positively signed ranks than negative ranks, so we sum the positive ranks. Our obtained T value is 29.5, the sum of the four positive ranks.

To compute the z value,

$$z = \frac{T - \mu_T}{\sigma_T}$$

$$= \frac{T - (n)(n+1)/4}{\sqrt{\dfrac{n(n+1)(2n+1)}{24}}}$$

$$= \frac{29.5 - 20(21)/4}{\sqrt{20(21)(41)/24}}$$

$$= \frac{-75.5}{26.79}$$

$$= -2.82$$

The critical z at $\alpha = .01$ is -2.33 for a one-tailed test. Our obtained z value is larger numerically than the critical value so we reject the null hypothesis and accept the alternative. Conflict resolution skills were statistically significantly better after training, $z = -2.82$, $p < .01$.

The Mann-Whitney and Wilcoxon tests are alternative analyses to t tests. When the assumptions underlying inference with the t distribution have not been met (e.g., the data are ordinal in scale), then these tests are appropriate for testing hypotheses about the difference between two population distributions.

SUMMARY OF THE WILCOXON SIGNED-RANKS TEST

Hypotheses

H_0: Populations are identical.
H_1: Populations are not identical.

Assumptions

1. Participants are randomly selected.
2. Same or matched participants.
3. Measurement scale is ordinal.

Decision Rules

If $T_{obt} \leq T_{crit}$ reject the H_0
If $T_{obt} > T_{crit}$ do not reject the H_0

Formula

n is the number of pairs with nonzero differences.
T is the sum of the absolute ranks with the less frequently appearing sign.

The Kruskal-Wallis Test

In Chapter 11, you learned how to use the F distribution to test hypotheses about several population means. When the assumptions underlying ANOVA have not been met, an alternative analysis is appropriate. The nonparametric analog to the one-way ANOVA is the **Kruskal-Wallis test**.

The Kruskal-Wallis test is used for ordinal data when participants have been randomly selected and independently assigned to groups. The calculations for this test are similar to those used in the Mann-Whitney test.

Kruskal-Wallis test: Nonparametric alternative to the one-way ANOVA, used for rank-order data

Null and Alternative Hypotheses

The null hypothesis of the Kruskal-Wallis test states that all populations have identical distributions. The alternative is that the populations are not identical.

H_0: Populations are identical.

H_1: Populations are not identical.

The *H* Statistic

The statistic computed in the Kruskal-Wallis test is the H statistic. The sampling distribution of the H statistic follows the chi-square distribution with $(k-1)$ degrees of freedom, where k is the number of samples or groups in the experiment.

The computational formula for the Kruskal-Wallis H statistic is as follows:

$$H = \frac{12}{n_{tot}(n_{tot}+1)}\left[\frac{(\Sigma R_1)^2}{n_1} + \frac{(\Sigma R_2)^2}{n_2} + \cdots + \frac{(\Sigma R_k)^2}{n_k}\right] - 3(n_{tot}+1)$$

n_{tot} = total number of observations

ΣR = sum of the ranks of the scores in the group

k = number of groups

Running the Kruskal-Wallis Test

The following lists the steps for running the Kruskal-Wallis test.

Step 1. Assign ranks to the scores in the groups.

All the scores are rank-ordered from the smallest to the largest, regardless of group membership. Ties are treated in the usual way.

Step 2. Calculate the H statistic.

Step 3. Compare the obtained H value with the critical value of χ^2.

If the obtained value is equal to or larger than the critical value, reject the null hypothesis; otherwise, do not reject the null.

Let's look at an example. The president of a small junior college has obtained teaching evaluation ratings of eight professors in each of three faculties: (1) arts, (2) science, and (3) education. Let's compute the Kruskal-Wallis H to test the hypothesis that the ratings for these professors don't differ. Here are the data.

ARTS PROFESSORS: 13, 12, 16, 27, 19, 18, 15, 31

SCIENCE PROFESSORS: 23, 30, 29, 14, 11, 9, 24, 32

EDUCATION PROFESSORS: 17, 10, 28, 20, 22, 21, 8, 26

Step 1. Assign ranks to the scores in the groups.

These evaluation scores must be combined and then ranked from smallest to largest. The smallest score was obtained by the seventh education professor, so this score is assigned the rank of 1. Here are the rank data.

ARTS PROFESSORS: 6, 5, 9, 19, 12, 11, 8, 23; Total 93

SCIENCE PROFESSORS: 16, 22, 21, 7, 4, 2, 17, 24; Total 113

EDUCATION PROFESSORS: 10, 3, 20, 13, 15, 14, 1, 18; Total 94

Step 2. Calculate the H statistic.

Using our formula for the H statistic,

$$H = \frac{12}{n_{tot}\left(n_{tot}+1\right)}\left[\frac{\left(\sum R_1\right)^2}{n_1}+\frac{\left(\sum R_2\right)^2}{n_2}+\frac{\left(\sum R_3\right)^2}{n_3}\right]-3\left(n_{tot}+1\right)$$

$$= \frac{12}{24\left(24+1\right)}\left(\frac{93^2}{8}+\frac{113^2}{8}+\frac{94^2}{8}\right)-3\left(24+1\right)$$

$$= 0.02\left(3781.75\right)-75 = 0.63$$

Now, we can complete our analysis.

Step 3. Compare the obtained H value with the critical value of χ^2.

The obtained H value is compared with the critical value of χ^2 with $(k - 1)$ degrees of freedom. In our example, $k = 3$, and the critical value of χ^2 for 2 degrees of freedom at $\alpha = .05$, is 5.99 (as listed in Table B.4 in Appendix B). The obtained value is smaller than the critical value, so we do not reject the null hypothesis. We have no evidence that student evaluations of professors in arts, science, and education are different, $H = 0.63$, *ns*.

SUMMARY OF THE KRUSKAL-WALLIS TEST

Hypotheses

H_0: Populations are identical.
H_1: Populations are not identical.

Assumptions

1. Participants are randomly selected and independently assigned to groups.
2. Measurement scale is ordinal.

Decision Rules

$df = k - 1$

If $H_{obt} \geq \chi^2_{crit}$ reject the H_0

If $H_{obt} > \chi^2_{crit}$ do not reject the H_0

Formula

$$H = \frac{12}{n_{tot}\left(n_{tot} + 1\right)} \left[\frac{\left(\sum R_1\right)^2}{n_1} + \frac{\left(\sum R_2\right)^2}{n_2} + \cdots + \frac{\left(\sum R_k\right)^2}{n_k} \right] - 3\left(n_{tot} + 1\right),$$

where k is the number of columns of ranked scores,
n is the number of rows—that is, the number of participants or matched participants
$\sum R$ is the sum of the ranks in a column.

The Friedman Test

In Chapter 12, you learned how to use the F distribution when repeated measures have been taken. When the assumptions underlying ANOVA have not been met, an alternative analysis is appropriate. The nonparametric analog to the one-way repeated measures ANOVA is the Friedman test for three or more ordinal distributions from the same or matched participants. Like the Kruskal-Wallis test, the scores are converted to ranks. The scores are ranked within each row—that is, by participant rather than across groups. Tied scores are treated in the usual way.

Null and Alternative Hypotheses

H_0: Populations are identical.

H_1: Populations are not identical.

The Chi-Square Statistic

To calculate the Friedman χ_r^2, we follow these steps.

Step 1. Rank-order the scores for each participant or matched set. In other words, rank-order within each row.

Step 2. Sum the ranks for each column.

Step 3. Compute the χ_r^2 statistic.

$$\chi_r^2 = \frac{12}{nk(k+1)}\left[\left(\sum R_1\right)^2 + \left(\sum R_2\right)^2 + \left(\sum R_3\right)^2 + \cdots + \left(\sum R_k\right)^2\right] - 3n(k+1)$$

Step 4. Compare the obtained value with the critical value of chi-square with $k - 1$ *df*.

Step 5. If the obtained value is equal to or larger than the critical value, reject the null.

ALERT

The Friedman χ_r^2 follows the chi-square distribution when we have at least 10 scores in each of three columns or at least 5 scores in each of four columns. Critical values can thus be found in Table B.4 in Appendix B. For smaller sample sizes, you must consult Table B.10 in Appendix B for the critical value.

Running the Friedman Test

A political scientist is interested in education and political party affiliation. She suspects that better-educated citizens might be more liberal than citizens with less education. Because people with more education tend to be older than those with less education, she decides to match her participants on age. She randomly selects members of the New Democratic Party, Liberal, and Conservative parties in Canada and notes the age of each. She then creates 10 triads of one New Democratic Party member, one Liberal, and one Conservative who are roughly the same age. She then notes the number of years of education for each individual. Here are her data.

	Number of Years of Education		
Triad Matched on Age	**New Democratic Party**	**Liberal**	**Conservative**
1	16	14	12
2	15	12	14
3	16	14	12
4	16	15	14
5	18	16	17
6	20	16	14
7	15	14	16
8	16	14	12
9	14	12	11
10	16	12	10

Step 1. Rank-order the scores for each participant or matched set.

In our case, we will rank-order the scores from 1 to 3 within each triad.

Step 2. Sum the ranks for each column.

	New Democratic Party	**Liberal**	**Conservative**
	R_1	R_2	R_3
	1	2	3
	1	3	2
	1	2	3
	1	2	3
	1	3	2
	1	2	3
	2	3	1
	1	2	3
	1	2	3
	1	2	3
Sum	11	23	26

Step 3. Compute the χ_r^2 statistic.

$$\chi_r^2 = \frac{12}{nk(k+1)}\left[(\Sigma R_1)^2 + (\Sigma R_2)^2 + (\Sigma R_3)^2\right] - 3n(k+1)$$

$$\chi_r^2 = \frac{12}{10(3)(4)}\left[11^2 + 23^2 + 26^2\right] - 3(10)(4)$$

$$= 0.1(1326) - 120 = 132.6 - 120 = 12.6$$

Step 4. Compare the obtained value with the critical value of chi-square with $k - 1$ *df*.

The critical value of chi-square with 2 degrees of freedom at the .01 level of significance is 9.21.

Step 5. If the obtained value is equal to or larger than the critical value, reject the null.

We can reject the null and conclude that the amount of education is significantly different for members of the three political parties, $\chi_r^2(2) = 12.6$, $p < .01$.

SUMMARY OF THE FRIEDMAN TEST

H_0: Populations are identical.
H_1: Populations are not identical.

Assumptions

1. Participants are randomly selected.
2. Same or matched participants.
3. Measurement scale is ordinal.

Decision Rules

If $\chi_r^2 \geq \chi_{crit}^2$ reject the H_0

If $\chi_r^2 < \chi_{crit}^2$ do not reject the H_0

Formula

$$\chi_r^2 = \frac{12}{nk(k+1)}\left[(\Sigma R_1)^2 + (\Sigma R_2)^2 + (\Sigma R_3)^2 + \cdots + (\Sigma R_k)^2\right] - 3n(k+1)$$

Choosing the Appropriate Test of Significance

In this chapter, you learned about four tests of significance that are the non-parametric equivalents to parametric tests. The Mann-Whitney U test is the nonparametric alternative to the t test for independent means. The Wilcoxon Signed-Ranks test is the alternative to the t test for dependent means. The Kruskal-Wallis test is the nonparametric alternative to the one-way ANOVA, and the Friedman test is the nonparametric alternative to the one-way repeated measures ANOVA. The more difficult aspects of making decisions between parametric and nonparametric approaches will be addressed elsewhere in this book; however, serious students should consult upper-level textbooks for clarification on issues concerning violation of parametric assumptions.

Let's go through the steps required to decide if an analysis should be a parametric or a nonparametric approach.

Step 1. Determine the number of groups in the experiment.

If more than two groups are involved in the experiment, determine whether the data are measures from participants in all groups or are ranks of participants in all groups.

Step 2. Determine if repeated measures have been taken or if participants have been matched in some way.

If different participants have been ranked, the appropriate analysis is the Kruskal-Wallis procedure. If measures have been taken from different participants and means will be computed, the appropriate analysis is the one-way ANOVA. If repeated measures have been taken and those measures are ranks, the Friedman test is used. If repeated measures have been taken and means will be computed, a one-way repeated measures ANOVA should be used.

If there are only two groups or fewer in the study, we go to Step 3.

Step 3. Determine if repeated measures have been taken or if participants have been matched in some way.

If participants have contributed more than one observation, or if participants have been matched on some variable, determine whether the data are measures from participants in all groups or if the data are ranks of participants in all groups. For data that are measures from participants that will be used to compute means, a t test for dependent means should be used. If the data are ranks, then the Wilcoxon test is appropriate. If there are two independent groups, we go to Step 4.

Step 4. Determine the kind of data involved.

If repeated measures have not been taken and groups have not been matched, you have an independent groups design. With rank data you will run a Mann-Whitney U test, and with measurement data you will run a t test for independent groups.

Example A: Six groups of randomly assigned laboratory rats have received different reinforcement experiences for running a maze. The amount of reinforcement varied from one pellet (Group 1) to six pellets (Group 6) of rat treats for each trial. After 2 weeks of experience, all the rats were placed in a maze that they had not experienced previously. Each rat was given 30 trials in the new maze, and the number of trials in which the rat completed the maze within a given period of time was recorded. After all the rats had been tested, they were rank-ordered according to the number of trials where completion occurred so that a rat that completed all 30 trials under the time limit was ranked number 1 and so on.

Step 1. Determine the number of groups in the experiment.

There are six groups in this experiment, each group receiving different amounts of reinforcement. Because the investigator rank-ordered the animals, he will use the Kruskal-Wallis test to analyze the difference among the six groups.

Example B: Six groups of randomly assigned laboratory rats have received different reinforcement experiences for running a maze. The amount of reinforcement varied from one pellet (Group 1) to six pellets (Group 6) of rat treats for each trial. After 2 weeks of experience, all the rats were placed in a maze that they had not experienced previously. Each rat was given 30 trials in the new maze, and the time to complete the maze was recorded. After all the rats had been tested, the average time to complete the maze was computed for each group.

Step 1. Determine the number of groups in the experiment.

There are six groups of animals in this experiment. The data consisted of the mean time to complete the maze. The group performance will be compared using a one-way ANOVA.

Example C: An industrial psychologist was hired by a large company to investigate employee morale. The company was interested in whether morale would improve if its employees could share in the profits of the company. The psychologist measured the morale of 20 company employees with a rating scale. Six months after a profit-sharing scheme was introduced, morale was measured again.

Step 1. Determine the number of groups in the experiment.

With only one group in this experiment, the 20 employees, we go to Step 2.

Step 2. Determine if repeated measures have been taken or if participants have been matched in some way.

The 20 employees provided two observations: morale rating before and after the introduction of the profit-sharing program. Rating scale data are usually considered ordinal, and the preferable analysis for this study is likely a Wilcoxon test.

Example D: A sociologist measured the psychosocial well-being of 30 randomly selected single mothers and 30 randomly selected married mothers using an ordinal scale with several subscales. She wanted to compare the two groups.

Step 1. Determine the number of groups in the experiment.

There are two groups in the study, so we go to Step 2.

Step 2. Determine if repeated measures have been taken or if participants have been matched in some way.

There are two independent groups, so we go to Step 3.

Step 3. Determine the kind of data involved.

The ordinal scale data involved in this study would most likely be analyzed using a Mann-Whitney U test.

Example E: A criminologist compared the number of crimes committed per year in 10 western cities with crimes in 10 eastern cities. All cities had approximately the same population. He was interested in determining whether the average yearly crime rate differed between the east and the west.

Step 1. Determine the number of groups in the experiment.

There are two groups, so we go to Step 2.

Step 2. Determine if repeated measures have been taken or if participants have been matched in some way.

The participants are cities, the groups are independent, so we go to Step 3.

Step 3. Determine the kind of data involved.

The data are mean crime rates, and the appropriate analysis is a t test for independent groups.

Example F: Thirty children attending a day care program were given a token for each sharing behavior seen by the day care staff. They could trade in the tokens for various treats. At the end of each week for a 6-week period, the total number of tokens earned by each child was counted. The children were then rank-ordered according to the number of tokens earned each week.

Step 1. Determine the number of groups in the experiment.

There is one group of children.

Step 2. Determine if repeated measures have been taken or if participants have been matched in some way.

Each child has contributed six measures, one per week.

Step 3. Determine the kind of data involved.

The children have been rank-ordered, and the Friedman test is appropriate.

FOCUS ON RESEARCH

Teaching is a tough job. Teacher "burnout" is a serious problem. This is the topic that interested Austin, Shah, and Muncer (2005).[1]

THE RESEARCH PROBLEM

One of the objectives of Austin et al. (2005) was to identify the strongest sources of stress for teachers.

THE VARIABLES

Teachers completed a questionnaire designed to measure stress in four areas (e.g., work related, time management, discipline, and motivation). Because the researchers' measures were *ordinal*, they chose various nonparametric procedures to test their hypotheses.

THE RESULTS

Using the **Friedman test**, Austin et al. (2005) reported a statistically significant difference in the amount of stress associated with the five areas, $\chi_r^2(4) = 61.95, p < .001$. The **Wilcoxon**

---

[1]Austin, V., Shah, S., & Muncer, S. (2005). Teacher stress and coping strategies used to reduce stress. *Occupational Therapy International, 12*(2), 63–80.

test was used for various comparisons. For example, work-related stress was significantly greater than time management stress, $z = 3.96$, $p < .001$.

THE CONCLUSIONS

The researchers concluded that the main stressor for teachers was work related from heavy caseloads, administrative duties, class preparation, and parents. They suggested that teachers need to be aware of these sources of stress and be taught effective coping strategies for dealing with them.

> **Friedman test:** Nonparametric alternative to one-way repeated measures ANOVA

> **Wilcoxon test:** A nonparametric equivalent to the t test for independent samples

SUMMARY OF TERMS AND FORMULAS

When the underlying assumptions of parametric analyses have not been met, a *nonparametric approach* may be appropriate.

The *Mann-Whitney U test* is analogous to the t test for the difference between independent means.

For two samples that are correlated or dependent, the *Wilcoxon signed-ranks test* is appropriate and is the nonparametric equivalent to the t test for dependent means.

When the assumptions of ANOVA have not been met, the *Kruskal-Wallis test* may be used for independent groups and the *Friedman test* may be used if repeated measures have been taken.

Test	Computational Formula
Mann-Whitney	$U_1 = n_1 n_2 + \dfrac{n_1(n_1+1)}{2} - \Sigma R_1$ $U_2 = n_1 n_2 + \dfrac{n_2(n_2+1)}{2} - \Sigma R$ $z = \dfrac{U - \mu_U}{\sigma_U}$ z formula for the U statistic
Wilcoxon z formula	$z = \dfrac{T - \mu_T}{\sigma_T}$ z formula for the T statistic

Test	Computational Formula
Kruskal-Wallis	$H = \dfrac{12}{n_{tot}(n_{tot}+1)} \left[\dfrac{(\sum R_1)^2}{n_1} + \dfrac{(\sum R_2)^2}{n_2} + \cdots + \dfrac{(\sum R_k)^2}{n_k} \right] - 3(n_{tot}+1)$
Friedman	$\chi_r^2 = \dfrac{12}{nk(k+1)} \left[(\sum R_1)^2 + (\sum R_2)^2 + (\sum R_3)^2 + \cdots + (\sum R_k)^2 \right] - 3n(k+1)$

EXERCISES

1. A random sample of students from a liberal arts college and another random sample from a church-work training college are given a questionnaire designed to measure their attitude toward capital punishment. The scores are given below. A high score reflects pro-capital punishment. Run a Mann-Whitney U test on these data with $\alpha = .01$. What are your conclusions?

   LIBERAL ARTS STUDENTS 10, 11, 12, 14, 18, 8, 9, 7

   CHURCH-WORK STUDENTS: 6, 5, 3, 7, 6, 2, 4, 10

2. A social psychologist used an aggression scale to rate the aggressiveness of children before and after they viewed a violent cartoon show. Run a Wilcoxon test on the data below at $\alpha = .05$. What are your conclusions?

Aggressiveness Rating	
Before	After
2.0	2.5
3.5	2.5
1.5	2.0
2.5	2.5
3.0	1.5
4.0	4.5
1.0	2.5
3.0	2.5
1.5	3.0

3. Kayakers have been asked to rate the quality of three different boats. Run a Kruskal-Wallis test to see if the ratings differ ($\alpha = .05$).

   RATINGS

   ECLIPSE: 6.0, 6.5, 5.2, 4.8, 6.1

MIRAGE: 5.3, 5.4, 4.7, 3.1, 3.9

DANCER: 3.5, 3.3, 3.6, 2.9, 4.0

4. Run a Mann-Whitney U test on the following data. Because there are more than 20 observations in each group, you will run the test for large sample sizes.

GROUP 1: 64, 78, 68, 57, 76, 75, 73, 66, 87, 89, 68, 59, 72, 83, 61, 56, 76, 55, 53, 76, 75, 51

GROUP 2: 62, 69, 63, 52, 53, 81, 90, 84, 45, 60, 65, 67, 54, 53, 58, 59, 49, 72, 63, 69, 61, 53

a. $\sum R_1 \sum R_2$
b. $U_1 \quad U_2$
c. z_{obt}
d. Decision

5. Run a Kruskal-Wallis test on the data given below.

GROUP 1: 45, 49, 51, 52, 53, 53, 53, 53, 54, 55, 56, 57, 58, 58, 59

GROUP 2: 59, 60, 61, 61, 62, 63, 63, 64, 65, 66, 67, 68, 68, 69, 69

GROUP 3: 72, 72, 73, 75, 75, 76, 76, 76, 78, 81, 83, 84, 87, 89, 90

a. $\sum R_1 \sum R_2 \sum R_3$
b. H

c. $\chi^2_{.05}$

d. Decision

6. In a longitudinal study of quality of life, ordinal data were collected from eight individuals at four times over a period of 20 years. Run a Friedman test to determine if quality of life changes as people age. Use an alpha level of .05. What is your conclusion? Notice the tied scores in Row 2.

Time 1	Time 2	Time 3	Time 4
43	46	47	50
40	42	40	45
39	40	42	43
44	39	45	40
36	40	35	41
42	43	45	46
39	42	40	38
37	40	35	41

Correlational Techniques

LEARNING OBJECTIVES

After reading this chapter, you should be able to do the following:

1. Describe the difference between a positive and a negative correlation.
2. Compute Pearson's coefficient using the raw-score, the deviation-score, and the z-score formulas.
3. Define linearity of regression, homoscedasticity, and discontinuity, and describe how these factors affect the correlation.
4. Define and provide a formula for the coefficient of determination.
5. Provide the t ratio for the Pearson correlation coefficient.
6. Run the Pearson correlation test of significance for a given set of data.
7. Describe the kind of research problem suitable for the Spearman rank-order correlation test.
8. Run the rank-order correlation test for a given set of data.
9. Construct a bivariate frequency distribution and scattergram for a given set of data.

Colorado Police Link Rise in Violence to Music

After a spate of shootings, and with a rising murder rate, the police [in Colorado] are saying gangsta rap is contributing to the violence, luring gang members and criminal activity to nightclubs.

New York Times, September 3, 2007

Eat your broccoli . . . ; and ward off cancer

Leslie Beck

Special to *The Globe and Mail*, April 05, 2011

What do you think of these news excerpts? Does rap change the way young people act? Are violent youth drawn to rap music? Or is another factor at work? Does eating broccoli reduce cancer incidence? These are the kinds of questions that we must address when we have correlations.

Did you know that there is a correlation between years of education and hair loss in men? Yes, indeed! Do you think going to school makes men's hair fall out? Of course not! This example demonstrates the adage that all social science students hear at some point in their academic career: *Correlation does not imply causation.* The fact that two variables are correlated does not tell us the cause of that relationship. We cannot infer that the first variable (education) causes changes in the second (hair loss). We also cannot infer that the second causes changes in the first. In fact, we cannot infer cause at all. In the example above, it seems reasonable to suspect that a third variable (age) is the causal variable. A correlation, no matter how strong, does not tell us anything about cause. A strong correlation only tells us that two variables tend to vary together. Why they do is a question that only a well-controlled *experiment* can answer.

Check your newspaper and magazine articles, and you will no doubt find many cases where it seems likely that cause has been assumed for correlational relationships.

Correlational techniques are used to determine if two variables are related. Correlation is a valuable statistical technique used in a great deal of research, particularly in medical research. For example, the general health of pregnant women is correlated with the birth weight of their babies. Stress is correlated with heart problems in men. Education is correlated with income. When we say that two variables are *positively correlated*, we mean that the values of these variables tend to increase and decrease together. For example, studying is positively correlated with grades. In other words, increasing study time tends to be associated with increasing grades.

When two variables are *negatively correlated*, the values of the first variable tend to increase as the values of the second variable decrease. Age and visual acuity are negatively correlated. As people get older, their vision tends to get poorer.

CONCEPT REVIEW 16.1

There is a negative correlation between using crack cocaine during pregnancy and neonatal health. Pregnant women who are heavy crack users tend to have babies with more health problems. Can you think of any variables other than crack use that might affect the health of the newborns of crack users (compared with those of non–crack users)?

Answer on page 457.

The correlation between high school grades and postsecondary performance may be of interest to you. After many years of collecting data, most colleges and universities have found that their students with higher high school grades tend to do better than those with poorer grades. In other words, there is a **positive correlation** between high school grades and college grades. Colleges and universities use this correlation for screening applicants to their programs. We will look at how correlational information is used to predict future events from current events in the next chapter.

Correlational techniques can be used not only to describe the relationship between two variables but also to make inferences about the correlation between two variables in a population from a sample drawn from that population. We will start by discussing correlation as a descriptive technique. We will then discuss correlation as an inferential technique.

Positive correlation: Describes two variables that increase and decrease together in a linear fashion

Correlation as a Descriptive Technique

When two variables are correlated, the values of the first variable tend to increase or decrease in a regular fashion with the values of the second variable. When high values of one variable are associated with high values of another, and low values of the first are associated with low values of the second, the two variables are *positively* correlated. On the other hand, when high values of one variable are associated with low values of another, the two variables are *negatively* correlated.

Constructing Bivariate Frequency Distributions

In Chapter 2, we constructed a univariate frequency distribution of English proficiency scores of students taking ESL (English as a Second Language). What if we collected data on our ESL students regarding the length of time each student had been living in the United States? We might want to construct a distribution that shows both proficiency score and time residing in the United States (see Table 16.1). Because we have two variables, we would construct a bivariate frequency distribution.

Note that the students who had only been in the United States for 6 months or less tended to score lower on the proficiency test. For example, no one who had lived in the United States for less than 14 months got the top score of 70. Students who had been here for longer tended to do better.

Table 16.1

Bivariate frequency distribution of proficiency scores and duration of residence in the United States

English Proficiency Score	Number of Months of Residence in the United States			
	0–6	7–13	14–20	21–27
70	0	0	1	8
69	0	0	1	26
68	1	0	25	30
67	0	3	18	19
66	0	2	34	12
65	2	0	12	10
64	1	0	9	18
63	0	19	5	5
62	3	26	6	8
61	9	35	0	2
60	8	20	0	3
59	15	14	2	1
58	16	9	0	0
57	13	5	1	0
56	25	6	1	1
55	30	2	1	0
54	45	3	1	0

Graphing Bivariate Frequency Distributions: The Scattergram

The graph used for bivariate frequency distributions is called a **scattergram** or scatterplot. Recall that a bivariate frequency distribution reports frequencies for two variables. Graphing bivariate data in a scattergram can show us, at a glance, whether or not the variables seem to be related or correlated.

The values of the first variable are located on the abscissa and the values of the second on the ordinate. The points are not connected.

As an example, imagine that I have asked 10 married couples to rate their marriage in terms of how well they communicate and how satisfied they are in the marriage. Let's use a scale from 1 to 10, where 1 = *very poor communication* and 10 = *excellent communication*. We'll use a similar scale for their ratings of marital satisfaction. I could then plot the data in a scattergram to see if there might be a relationship. For example, perhaps, couples who communicate well with each other are also very satisfied with their marriages (see Figure 16.1). The data might look something like this:

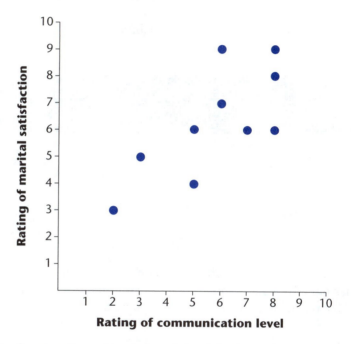

Figure 16.1. Couple ratings of level of marital satisfaction and communication.

Each point represents the rating each couple selected on the two scales. It looks as though there might be some relationship. Couples who rate their communication level as poor also tend to be dissatisfied with the marriage. Those who think they communicate well seem to be quite satisfied with their marriages.

A quick inspection of a scattergram will give some indication of the degree of relationship between variables. Now let's learn how to quantify that relationship.

Scattergram: A graphic representation of a bivariate frequency distribution; sometimes called scatterplot or scattergraph

CONCEPT REVIEW 16.2

Tim, a student of mine, conducted a study to determine if men and women differ in their liking for various sports. He was particularly interested in whether the violence of the sport made a difference. He asked women and men to rate various sports on (a) how violent they perceived the sport to be and (b) how much they liked watching the sport being played. He hypothesized that men preferred sports that they perceived as being violent, whereas women liked sports that they perceived as being less violent. Specifically, he expected a positive correlation between rated violence and preference for men and a negative correlation between rated violence and preference for women. Here are his data:

Sport	Men		Women	
	Violence Rating	Preference Rating	Violence Rating	Preference Rating
Football	4.20	4.20	4.33	2.47
Hockey	4.07	4.40	4.27	3.33
Soccer	2.00	2.47	2.53	2.73
Basketball	1.93	2.67	2.00	2.93
Baseball	1.60	2.60	1.93	3.20

Plot Tim's data in two scattergrams, one for the men and another for the women. Tim has only five data points for each scattergram, so we really can't conclude too much, but do you think he might be onto something?

Answer on page 457.

Quantifying the Bivariate Relationship

A coefficient of correlation is a statistic that tells us how strongly two variables are related and in what fashion. All correlation coefficients range from +1 to −1. A correlation coefficient of +1 or −1 is a perfect correlation and means that values of one variable are exactly related to values of another variable. A correlation coefficient of zero indicates that the values of the first variable are unrelated to the values of the second variable.

Several ways of computing correlation coefficients have been developed. The choice of one over another depends on the variables of interest. When both variables are continuous, Pearson's product-moment coefficient of correlation is used.

Pearson's Product-Moment Coefficient of Correlation

Pearson's product-moment correlation coefficient is used to determine the extent of relationship between two variables. Pearson developed this coefficient by fitting a straight line to a bivariate frequency distribution. The line is called the *straight line of best fit*. The next chapter describes how Pearson fitted this line to the data.

Basically, the coefficient of correlation (ρ, pronounced "rho") is a number describing how closely the points in a bivariate frequency distribution fit the straight line of best fit. If all the points fall on the line, the correlation is +1 or −1: a perfect correlation. If all the points do not fall on the line, the correlation coefficient will approach zero.

Calculating the Pearson Coefficient of Correlation

The formula for calculating Pearson's coefficient of correlation varies depending on the data. We will look at versions of the formula for three types of data: (1) raw scores, (2) deviation scores, and (3) z scores.

Data in Raw-Score Form

For raw data, the formula for Pearson's ρ is

$$\rho = \frac{\sum XY - (\sum X)(\sum Y)/N}{\sqrt{(SS_X)(SS_Y)}}$$

$\sum XY$ = sum of the *cross products* of the values for each variable

$(\sum X)(\sum Y)$ = product of the sum of X and the sum of Y

N = number of pairs of scores.

$$SS_X = \sum X^2 - (\sum X)^2 / N_X$$
$$SS_Y = \sum Y^2 - (\sum Y)^2 / N_Y$$

Ready for an example? Suppose I gathered data about the television habits of 10 children in a kindergarten class. I asked the teachers to rate the aggressiveness of each child, on a scale from 1 to 10, during each recess period for 1 month. Variable X is the mean rating per week for each child. I also asked the parents of these children to determine the amount of violent television programs their children watch each week. The mean number of hours watched by each child per week is my Y variable. I am interested in determining whether those children who are rated as most aggressive are also the children who watch a lot of violent television programs. Let's determine whether these two variables, aggressiveness (X) and TV-viewing habits (Y), are related.

Child	X	Y	X²	Y²	XY
Ben	8.5	5.8	72.3	33.6	49.30
Christiaan	4.3	3.6	18.5	13.0	15.48
Linda	5.6	4.0	31.4	16.0	22.40
Luke	2.2	1.5	4.8	2.3	3.30
Hiro	6.5	6.3	42.3	39.7	40.95
Matthew	8.2	7.5	67.2	56.3	61.50
Mia	9.7	8.0	94.1	64.0	77.60
Ashley	1.0	2.2	1.0	4.8	2.20
Daniel	3.5	3.1	12.3	9.6	10.85
Padraic	5.0	3.0	25.0	9.0	15.00
Totals	54.5	45.0	368.8	248.2	298.58

$$\rho = \frac{\sum XY - (\sum X)(\sum Y)/N}{\sqrt{[\sum X^2 - (\sum X)^2 / N][\sum Y^2 - (\sum Y)^2 / N]}}$$

$$= \frac{298.58 - (54.5)(45)/10}{[368.8 - (54.5)^2 / 10][248.2 - (45)^2 / 10]}$$

$$= \frac{53.33}{(8.47)(6.76)} = .93$$

The correlation between teachers' ratings of the children's aggressiveness and the number of hours watching violent television programs, recorded by the parents, is .93. This suggests that the children who are rated most aggressive watch a lot of violent television programs, according to their parents. The scattergram of these data is shown in Figure 16.2.

As you can see, as TV viewing increases, so do aggressiveness ratings.

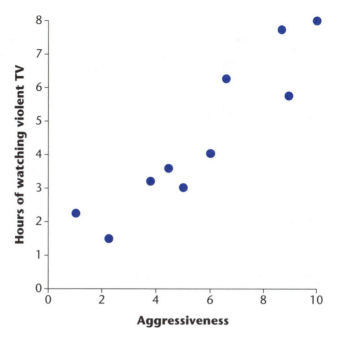

Figure 16.2. Scattergram of the relationship between aggressiveness and television habits.

Data in Deviation-Score Form

When the data are in deviation-score form, the formula for Pearson's coefficient is

$$\rho = \frac{\sum[(X - \mu_X)(Y - \mu_Y)]}{\sqrt{(SS_X)(SS_Y)}}$$

Here, the numerator is the sum of the cross products of the deviation scores for each variable: SS_X is the sum of the squared deviations in X, and SS_Y is the sum of the squared deviations in Y.

Let's use the previous example to verify our formula. Here are the data in deviation score form.

Child	$(X - \mu_X)$	$(Y - \mu_Y)$	$(X - \mu_X)^2$	$(Y - \mu_Y)^2$	$(X - \mu_X)(Y - \mu_Y)$
Ben	3.0	1.3	9.0	1.7	3.9
Christiaan	−1.2	−0.9	1.4	0.8	1.1

(Continued)

(Continued)

Child	$(X - \mu_X)$	$(Y - \mu_Y)$	$(X - \mu_X)^2$	$(Y - \mu_Y)^2$	$(X - \mu_X)(Y - \mu_Y)$
Linda	0.1	−0.5	0.0	0.3	−0.1
Luke	−3.3	−3.0	10.9	9.0	9.9
Hiro	1.0	1.8	1.0	3.2	1.8
Matthew	2.7	3.0	7.3	9.0	8.1
Mia	4.2	3.5	17.6	12.3	14.7
Ashley	−4.5	−2.3	20.3	5.3	10.3
Daniel	−2.0	−1.4	4.0	2.0	2.8
Padraic	−0.5	−1.5	0.3	2.3	0.8
Totals			71.8	45.9	53.3

Using the deviation score formula,

$$\rho = \frac{\Sigma[(X - \mu_X)(Y - \mu_Y)]}{\sqrt{(SS_X)(SS_Y)}}$$

$$= \frac{53.3}{\sqrt{(71.8)(45.9)}} = \frac{53.3}{57.4} = .93$$

As you can see, the result is the same as that for the raw score data.

Data in z-Score Form

When the data are in z-score form, the formula for Pearson's correlation is

$$\rho = \frac{\Sigma(z_X z_Y)}{N}$$

The cross products of the z scores are summed and divided by the number of scores.

To show how this formula works, we will use the same data. Now, the scores have been converted to z scores.

Child	z_X	z_Y	$z_X z_Y$
Ben	1.12	0.61	0.68
Christiaan	−0.45	−0.42	0.19
Linda	0.04	−0.23	−0.01
Luke	−1.23	−1.40	1.73
Hiro	0.37	0.84	0.31
Matthew	1.01	1.40	1.41
Mia	1.57	−1.64	2.56
Ashley	−1.68	−1.07	1.80
Daniel	−0.75	−0.65	0.49
Padraic	−0.19	−0.70	0.13
Total			9.30

$$\rho = \frac{\Sigma(z_X z_Y)}{N}$$

$$= \frac{9.30}{10} = .93$$

Once again, the result is the same because this formula is algebraically equivalent to the others.

Factors Influencing the Correlation Coefficient

I am sure every statistics student and most introductory psychology students have been told over and over that *correlation does not imply causation*. You know that the coefficient of correlation measures the degree to which two variables are related. It does not tell you anything about the reason for the relationship. If variable A is correlated with variable B, then we know that values of A tend to be associated with values of B. We do not know if A causes B, if B causes A, or if some other variable is responsible for the relationship. Earlier, the correlation between hair loss and educational level of men was mentioned. It appears that as men become more educated, they tend to lose more hair. Now, if we were naive, we might think that education *causes* hair loss; perhaps studying causes stress, which causes hair loss. Or perhaps hair loss *causes* men to seek more education; bald men do not date much, so they have more time, so they take more courses. Clearly, this is ridiculous. What we are actually seeing is a relationship between two variables, hair loss and education, which is no doubt caused by a third variable, age. Older men tend to have more years of education. Similarly, because they are older, they have less hair!

CONCEPT REVIEW 16.3

Consider the following statements:

A. "People who brush with 'Brand X' toothpaste have fewer cavities."

   This statement implies that the use of a product will cause certain wonderful things to happen. What is your assessment of the meaning of this statement?

B. I found this in a local newspaper some years ago: "Women! Don't study engineering. Research has shown that female engineers are less likely to marry than women in other disciplines."

   This statement implies that somehow studying engineering will reduce the likelihood that women will marry. What is your assessment of the meaning of this statement?

Answer on page 458.

Linearity of Regression

Linearity of regression means that the best way to describe the relationship between two variables is a straight line. In a particular set of data, however, a straight line may or may not describe the relationship between the variables. A straight line is appropriate for variables that are linearly related. But what if X and Y are not linearly related?

Figure 16.3 presents scattergrams of two bivariate frequency distributions.

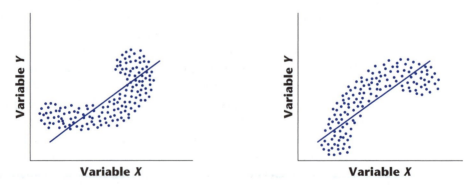

Figure 16.3. Examples of curvilinear relationships.

If we calculated the correlation coefficient, ρ, for either of these distributions, it would be quite low; the points do not fit a straight line very well. In both cases, a curvilinear function best describes the relationship between the variables. Whenever the relationship between two variables is not linear, ρ will *underestimate* the strength of the relationship.

Let's look at a scattergram of a relationship often seen in social science research, the relationship between physiological arousal and performance on cognitive tasks. Imagine that we have ratio measures of arousal and performance for 31 college students taking a final exam in their criminology course (see Figure 16.4).

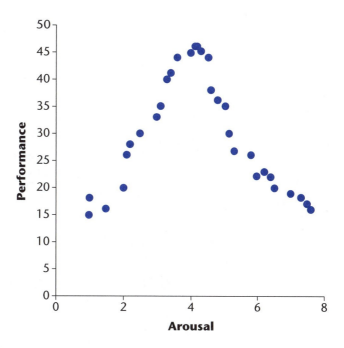

Figure 16.4. Cognitive performance and arousal.

If you are almost asleep, you won't do well on your final exam, will you? Likewise, if you are frantic with anxiety, you also won't do very well. For most cognitive tasks, a moderate level of arousal is associated with optimal performance.

Now, let's see what happens when we calculate Pearson's coefficient.

Arousal	Performance	X^2	Y^2	XY
1.0	15	1.0	225	15.0
1.5	16	2.3	256	24.0
1.0	18	1.0	324	18.0
2.0	20	4.0	400	40.0
2.1	26	4.4	676	54.6
2.2	28	4.8	784	61.6
2.5	30	6.3	900	75.0
3.0	33	9.0	1 089	99.0
3.1	35	9.6	1 225	108.5
3.3	40	10.9	1 600	132.0
3.4	41	11.6	1 681	139.4
3.6	44	13.0	1 936	158.4
4.0	45	16.0	2 025	180.0
4.1	46	16.8	2 116	188.6
4.2	46	17.6	2 116	193.2
4.3	45	18.5	2 025	193.2
4.5	44	20.3	1 936	198.0
4.6	38	21.2	1 444	174.8
4.8	36	23.0	1 296	172.8
5.0	35	25.0	1 225	175.0
5.1	30	26.0	900	153.0
5.3	27	28.1	729	143.1
5.8	26	33.6	676	150.8
6.0	22	36.0	484	132.0
6.2	23	38.4	529	142.6
6.4	22	41.0	484	140.8
6.5	20	42.3	400	130.0
7.0	19	49.0	361	133.0
7.3	18	53.3	324	131.4
7.5	17	56.3	289	127.5
7.6	16	57.8	256	121.6
Sum 134.9	921	697.9	30 711	3907.2

$$\rho = \frac{\sum XY - (\sum X)(\sum Y)/N}{\sqrt{[\sum X^2 - (\sum X)^2/N]}\sqrt{[\sum Y^2 - (\sum Y)^2/N]}}$$

$$= \frac{3907.2 - (134.90)(921)/31}{\sqrt{697.6 - 134.9^2/31}\sqrt{30711 - 921^2/31}}$$

$$= \frac{-100.63}{609.15} = -0.16$$

Pearson's coefficient is quite low, indicating that there isn't much of a relationship. This is not true of course. The problem is that this is the wrong way to measure this curvilinear relationship.

This upside-down, U-shaped relationship is clearly not linear, and Pearson's ρ is not the appropriate way to measure its strength. There are other techniques for measuring curvilinear relationships, which you will find discussed in upper-level statistics books.

> **Linearity of regression:** In regression, refers to a relationship between two variables that is best described by a straight line

Homoscedasticity

When the amount of scatter is the same throughout a bivariate distribution, it is said to have the property of homoscedasticity or equal variability.

Examine the two scattergrams in Figure 16.5. The distribution illustrated in the scattergram on the left is homoscedastic. No matter which value of X is chosen, the corresponding Y values are equally scattered around the straight line of best fit. In the scattergram on the right, however, this is not the case. If X is low, Y does not vary much around the line; for higher values of X, the corresponding Y values vary a great deal.

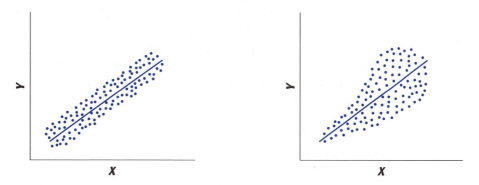

Figure 16.5. Bivariate distributions differing in homoscedasticity.

Pearson's ρ reflects the "average" degree to which the scores hug the line of best fit. For the scattergram on the right, ρ will underestimate the strength of the relationship for low values of X and overestimate it for high values of X. In other words, for low X values, Pearson's ρ will indicate that the relationship between X and Y is weaker than it is, and for high values of X, Pearson's ρ will indicate that the relationship is stronger than it is.

> **Homoscedasticity:** In regression, equal variability of Y values around the regression line throughout the bivariate distribution

Discontinuous Distributions

Whenever the range of one or both variables is restricted in some way, ρ will be affected. For example, if the middle of a distribution is excluded, the ρ will be higher than if the middle had been included. This might occur if we were to correlate the high and low scores without including the middle scores. Suppose the dean of arts wished to know if the grade point average of his first year arts students correlated with their high school grades. He has data for students who failed and for those who received honors in their first year, but has no data for the middle students. If he calculates Pearson's ρ for this *discontinuous* distribution, it will be somewhat higher than if he had all the data available. Similarly, if the extreme scores are omitted from the calculation, ρ tends to be lower. The full range of both variables should be included when calculating correlation coefficients.

Interpreting the Coefficient of Correlation

Unless ρ is 1, the coefficient of correlation does not directly indicate the association between Y and X. For example, a ρ value of .50 does not mean that there is a 50% association between the two variables. However, the square of ρ does indicate the degree of the association.

The **coefficient of determination**, ρ^2, reflects the degree of association between Y and X. For a correlation coefficient of .50, the coefficient of determination (ρ^2) is .25. This indicates the strength of the association. Specifically, .25 or ¼ of the total Y variance is explained by the correlation of Y with X. The coefficient of determination will be discussed in detail in the next chapter. For now, remember that ρ^2 reflects the amount of association between the two variables.

> **Coefficient of determination:** Indicates the strength of relationship between two variables

Correlation as an Inferential Technique

When we draw samples from a population, determine the correlation between two variables, and make inferences about the value of the correlation in the population, we are using correlation as an inferential technique. Like any inferential technique, we do this when we can't obtain all the observations in a population.

We will examine one test involving correlation—testing the hypothesis that the population correlation is zero. As you will see, the formulas and notations change when we use correlation in inference.

Null and Alternative Hypotheses

The null hypothesis states that, in the bivariate population from which the sample was selected, the correlation is zero.

H_0: $\rho = 0$.

The alternative hypothesis may be directional or nondirectional.

H_1: $\rho \neq 0$, < 0, or > 0.

You will recall that whenever we sample from a population, the sample statistics vary from sample to sample. This is called sampling fluctuation. Even if the correlation in a population was truly zero, we would not expect a sample correlation of exactly zero. We would expect some variability. Our question here, as with any inferential technique, is "How far from zero would our sample correlation be expected to vary if the true population correlation is indeed zero?"

To answer this question, we need a distribution of correlations based on samples drawn from a population with a correlation of zero, the *random sampling distribution of the correlation coefficient*. The mean of this sampling distribution will be zero. We use the letter "r" to designate the coefficient of correlation computed on a sample. The estimate of the standard deviation or standard error of this sampling distribution is denoted as s_r. When the null hypothesis is true, the sampling distribution of the correlation coefficient is close to the normal distribution for reasonably large samples.

Testing the Significance of the Correlation

To test the significance of a correlation, we need to compute r from the sample data. The formula to calculate the coefficient of correlation for a sample is

$$r = \frac{\sum XY - (\sum X)(\sum Y)/n}{\sqrt{(SS_X)(SS_Y)}}$$

The obtained r value may be compared with the critical value of r by entering the degrees of freedom into Table B.9 of Appendix B. The degrees of freedom for testing the correlation are the number of pairs minus two ($n_p - 2$).

The significance of the correlation can also be determined with a t test when n is large and r is small. However, if n is small and r is reasonably large, it is easier and probably more accurate to use Table B.9 in Appendix B.

Nonlinearity: In regression, a relationship between two variables that is best described as a curve rather than a straight line

To use a t test to determine the significance of a correlation, we must convert our sample statistic, r, to a standard score. As you recall, this is done by subtracting the hypothesized parameter from the sample statistic and dividing the difference by the standard error of the sampling distribution of the statistic.

$$t = \frac{r - \rho}{s_r}$$

The estimate of the standard deviation, the standard error, is found by the following formula:

$$s_r = \sqrt{\frac{1 - r^2}{n - 2}}$$

When we do this for r, we obtain standard scores that follow the t distribution with ($n_p - 2$) degrees of freedom, where n_p refers to the number of pairs of scores.

After computing the t value, we test our coefficient for significance by looking up the critical value of t for ($n_p - 2$) degrees of freedom.

Let's do an example. A social worker randomly selects 10 homeless people from inner-city shelters in Houston, Texas. He uses a standardized assessment test to measure each person's level of overall health (a continuous measure), and he determines how long each person has been on the streets. He discovers that the correlation between the two variables is 0.80. He wants to test whether the general health of homeless people is negatively correlated with the length of time that they have been homeless: the longer they have been homeless, the worse their health.

$$H_0: \rho = 0$$
$$H_1: \rho < 0$$

$$s_r = \sqrt{\frac{1 - r^2}{n - 2}} = \sqrt{\frac{1 - (-.8)^2}{8}} = -0.21$$

$$t = \frac{r - \rho}{s_r} = \frac{-.8 - 0}{0.21} = -3.81$$

The critical value of t is -2.896 with 8 df at $\alpha = .01$ (as listed in Table B.2). Because the obtained t falls in the region of rejection, the null hypothesis is rejected. The social worker concludes that the general health of the homeless is significantly correlated with the length of time that they have been homeless, $t(8) = -3.81$, $p < .01$.

Assumptions Underlying Inference About Correlations

The assumptions underlying tests of significance of correlation coefficients are similar to those of several parametric analyses we have discussed previously. First, the participants are assumed to be randomly selected from the population. Second, normal population distributions of both X and Y are assumed. When the sample is reasonably large (30 or more), this assumption will not be badly violated, because the sampling distribution of r tends to be normal, regardless of population shape.

SUMMARY OF THE PEARSON CORRELATION TEST

Hypotheses

H_0: $\rho = 0$
H_1: $\rho \neq 0$, $\rho < 0$, or $\rho > 0$

Assumptions

1. Participants are randomly selected.
2. Both populations are normally distributed.

Decision Rules

If $t_{obt} \geq t_{crit}$ reject H_0
If $t_{obt} < t_{crit}$ do not reject H_0

Formula

$$t = \frac{r - \rho}{s_r}, \text{ where } s_r = \sqrt{\frac{1 - r^2}{n - 2}}$$

The Spearman Rank-Order Correlation Test

Pearson's correlation test is a procedure for determining the strength of association between two continuous variables. An adaptation of this test, the

Spearman rank-order correlation test, is used when values of an ordinal variable have been rank-ordered. The rank-order test is a very useful test for many research situations.

When ordinal variables have been ranked and you wish to determine the relationship between the ranks, the Spearman rank-order correlation test, often called *Spearman's Rho,* is appropriate.

Null and Alternative Hypotheses

The null hypothesizes no correlation between the ranks. The alternative hypothesis may be nondirectional (i.e., the correlation is not zero) or directional (i.e., the correlation is greater or less than zero).

H_0: *Rho* = 0

H_1: *Rho* ≠ 0, < 0, or > 0

The *Rho* Statistic

To be consistent, we will differentiate between the correlation in the population (*Rho*) and the correlation in the sample (*rho*).

The *rho* statistic is calculated on rank data with the following formula:

$$rho = 1 - \frac{6\sum d^2}{n\left(n^2 - 1\right)}$$

n = number of paired ranks

d = difference between the paired ranks

Running the Spearman Rank-Order Correlation Test

The following describes the steps for running the rank-order correlation test:

Step 1. Determine the difference between the ranks for each participant.

Step 2. Square each difference and sum them.

Step 3. Calculate the *rho* statistic.

Step 4. Compare the obtained *rho* value with the critical value.

If the obtained value is equal to or larger than the critical value, reject the null hypothesis; otherwise, do not reject the null. Table B.8 in Appendix B provides the critical values of *rho* for various sample sizes and levels of significance.

ALERT

Remember that the sample size is the number *of pairs* of ranks.

Ready for an example? A sociologist has conducted a survey of how people perceive the prestige of different occupations. She wonders if people perceive high-income occupations as more prestigious. Her survey data have provided rank-orders of prestige, and she has rank-ordered each occupation according to mean income. The data are given below.

She follows these steps.

Step 1. Determine the difference between the ranks for each participant.

Step 2. Square each difference and sum them.

Occupation	Prestige	Income	d	d^2
Physician	1	1	0	0
Lawyer	2	2	0	0
Banker	3	3	0	0
Professor	4	4	0	0
Teacher	5	7	−2	4
Nurse	6	6	0	0
Accountant	7	5	2	4
Secretary	8	9	−1	1
Postal worker	9	8	1	1
Day care worker	10	10	0	0
				$\sum d^2 = 10$

Step 3. Calculate the *rho* statistic.

Using our formula,

$$rho = 1 - \frac{6\sum d^2}{n\left(n^2 - 1\right)} = 1 - \frac{6(10)}{10(100 - 1)}$$

$$= 1 - \frac{60}{990} = .94$$

Step 4. Compare the obtained *rho* value with the critical value.

The critical value of *rho* is .65, at a = .05 for a two-tailed test, when there are 10 participants (see Table B.8 in Appendix B). The obtained value is larger than the critical value, and the null hypothesis is rejected. There is a significant correlation between perceived prestige and income of these 10 occupations, *rho* = .94, *p* < .05.

The rank-order correlation test is very useful for ranked data. If the original data are not in rank-order form, they must be converted to use the *rho* formula.

SUMMARY OF THE SPEARMAN RANK-ORDER CORRELATION TEST

Hypotheses

H_0: *Rho* = 0
H_1: *Rho* ≠ 0, <, or >0.

Assumptions

1. Participants are randomly selected.

2. Observations are rank-ordered.

Decision Rules

n = number of pairs of ranks

If $rho_{obt} \geq rho_{crit}$ reject H_0

If $rho_{obt} < rho_{crit}$ do not reject H_0

Formula

$$rho = 1 - \frac{6\sum d^2}{n(n^2 - 1)}$$

FYI

Several other correlation coefficients have been developed that are suitable for a variety of types of variables. In Chapter 14, we referred to a correlation coefficient used to determine the strength of the relationship between variables following a chi-square test for independence. Although it is beyond the scope of this book to discuss additional coefficients in detail, mention of some of the available techniques might be in order. The

Pearson coefficient, you will recall, measures the degree to which the points in a scattergram hug the line of best fit. The line of best fit is a straight line. In other words, Pearson's coefficient appropriately measures only linear relationships. We have seen that when the relationship between two variables is nonlinear, Pearson's coefficient is inappropriate. For curvilinear relationships, a *polynomial regression equation* must be used, but this topic is beyond our scope.

Other coefficients that have been developed include *Kendall's tau* (τ) for monotonically related ranks; the *point biserial* (r_{pb}) for quantitative versus dichotomous variables; the *biserial* (r_b) for quantitative variables, where one has been made dichotomous; the *tetrachoric* (r_t), where quantitative variables have both been dichotomized; and the *phi* (φ) coefficient, where both variables are dichotomous. Interested students are encouraged to consult upper-level statistic texts for information on these correlation coefficients.

FOCUS ON RESEARCH

THE RESEARCH PROBLEM

What does the average Swiss Joe and Jill know about nutrition and health? And does this knowledge affect what he or she chooses to eat? This is the topic that interested Swiss researchers Dickson-Spillman and Siegrist (2011).

THE VARIABLES

The researchers surveyed 1 043 Swiss consumers to find out what they knew about healthy eating and what kinds of foods they consumed. They wanted to know if knowledge about food nutritional value was related to diet and other variables.

THE ANALYSIS AND RESULTS

They used correlational analyses to examine several variables. Some of their results are as follows: Consumers with more knowledge about nutrition ate more vegetables than consumers with less knowledge, $r = .029$, $p < .001$; younger consumers knew more about nutrition than older consumers, $r = .34$, $p < .001$; and better-educated consumers knew more about nutrition than less well-educated consumers, $r = .28$, $p < .001$. They also found out that consumers who were following physician-prescribed diets knew significantly less about nutrition ($M = 32.3$, $SD = 5.1$) than those who were not ($M = 34.2$, $SD = 4.3$), $t(1008) = 4.4$, $p < .001$.[1]

---

1. What do you think about this finding, given the degrees of freedom?

THE CONCLUSION

Spillmann and Siegrist (2011) concluded that knowledge about nutritional value is related to diet, age, and education and that consumers need to be better informed about these relationships.

Dickson-Spillmann, M., & Siegrist, M. (2011). Consumers' knowledge of healthy diets and its correlation with dietary behaviour. *Journal of Human Nutrition and Dietetics, 24*, 54–60. doi:10.1111/j.1365-277X.2010.01124.x

SUMMARY OF TERMS AND FORMULAS

Pearson's product-moment correlation coefficient (ρ) is used to determine the extent of the relationship between two variables. The numerical size of the coefficient indicates the strength, and the sign indicates the direction of the relationship. The square of the coefficient, the *coefficient of determination* (ρ^2), indicates how much of the total variance in the Y dimension is accounted for by the association of Y with the X variable. Pearson's technique is suitable for describing the relationship between two variables and for making inferences from sample data about the correlation in the population.

  Spearman's rank-order correlation test is used to determine the relationship between two sets of rank-order data

Pearson's ρ	Formulas
For raw data	$$\rho = \frac{\sum XY - (\sum X)(\sum Y)/N}{\sqrt{(SS_X)(SS_Y)}}$$
For deviation data	$$\rho = \frac{\sum\left[(X - \mu_X)(Y - \mu_Y)\right]}{\sqrt{(SS_X)(SS_Y)}}$$
For z-score data	$$\rho = \frac{\sum(z_X z_Y)}{N}$$
t formula for the r statistic	$$t = \frac{r - \rho}{s_r}$$
r for a sample	$$r = \frac{\sum XY - (\sum X)(\sum Y)/n}{\sqrt{(SS_X)(SS_Y)}}$$
Standard error	$$s_r = \sqrt{\frac{1 - r^2}{n - 2}}$$
Spearman rank-order correlation	$$rho = 1 - \frac{6\sum d^2}{n(n^2 - 1)}$$

CONCEPT REVIEW ANSWERS

16.1. Factors that might be involved here include nutrition, smoking, general health, prenatal care, and so on. For example, pregnant women who choose to use crack throughout their pregnancies may tend to take less care over their general health. Their eating habits may be different from women who rarely or never use crack. Numerous variables could be involved here other than crack.

Note: I do not mean to suggest that the evidence relating crack use to newborn health is not strong. In fact, it is very strong. Correlational evidence with humans and experimental evidence with animals is very convincing. (*Women should not use drugs (unless prescribed by their physician) or alcohol during pregnancy.*)

16.2. The figure below indicates the rating of violence and preference for five sports by women.

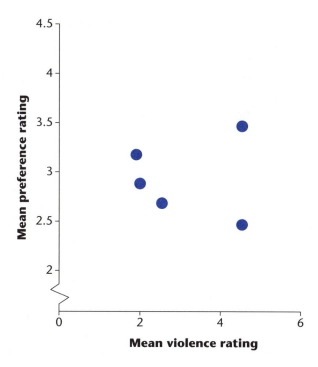

With the exception of one data point (hockey), there does seem to be a trend that less violent sports are preferred by women. Let's look at the scattergram that indicates the rating of violence and preference for five sports by men.

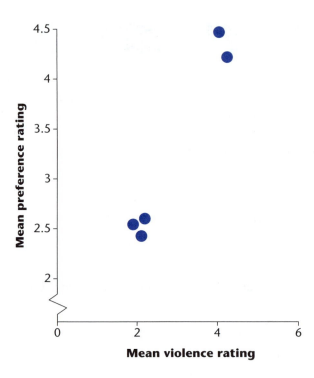

There may be a suggestion of a trend here. The three sports that the men rated as less violent were also rated as less preferred. The two sports that they rated as more violent were preferred. I think it's an interesting little study that could be pursued on a wider scale.

16.3. A. "People who brush with 'Brand X' toothpaste have fewer cavities."

It's hard to know what this statement means. The advertiser wants you to believe that using Brand X toothpaste *causes* a reduction in cavities. Perhaps people who choose Brand X happen to be people with exceptionally good teeth. Perhaps people with good teeth like the look of Brand X. Or perhaps people who can afford good dental care can afford the more expensive Brand X. Who knows? Now read the statement again and ask yourself this question. People who use Brand X have fewer cavities than whom? *People who don't brush their teeth?* We just don't know.

B. My best guess is that women who choose this discipline of study are not the "marrying kind." In other words, the kinds of women who choose this discipline may be different, at the outset, from the kinds of women who choose other disciplines. It is not the discipline that "caused" the effect. The groups may have been different to begin with.

EXERCISES

1. For the data provided below, plot a scattergram. What is the direction of the correlation?

Participant	X	Y
1	12	34
2	12	37
3	14	40
4	17	41
5	18	56
6	20	55
7	21	56
8	25	60

2. For the data provided below, plot a scattergram. What is the direction of the correlation?

Participant	X	Y
1	11	102
2	11	100
3	12	98
4	14	90
5	14	92
6	15	84
7	17	79
8	21	65

3. Determine ρ for the data given in Exercise 1. Use the raw score formula

4. Determine ρ for the data given in Exercise 2. Use the deviation–score formula. How much of the variance is accounted for by the association?

5. For the data below, determine ρ using the z-score formula.

Participant	X	Y
1	1	3
2	2	3
3	4	5
4	6	4
5	7	5
6	10	8

6. An administrator at a small junior college is curious about the relationship between student performance in chemistry (a "hard science") and psychology (a "soft science"). She has the final exam scores for 15 students who took both courses. She finds the correlation (r) between the two exams to be .64. At $\alpha = .05$, use a nondirectional alternative to test the hypothesis that there is no correlation in the population from which her sample was drawn.

7. Determine the Pearson correlation between the "intelligence" test scores and the "creativity" test scores given below. What do you conclude about the relationship?

	Intelligence Test	Creativity Test
Peter	122	15
Dan	102	35
Susan	135	20
David	110	22
Larry	140	12
Marilyn	130	10
Lori	128	15

8. A sociologist was interested in the relationship between the IQs of fathers and sons. He obtained the IQ scores of 20 fathers and the IQ scores of the oldest son of each. Compute the Pearson correlation on his data. Does there seem to be a relationship?

IQ Father	*IQ* Son	*IQ* Father	*IQ* Son
112	125	110	105
123	120	114	112
100	89	103	99
98	117	115	110

IQ Father	*IQ* Son	*IQ* Father	*IQ* Son
109	90	118	117
125	123	138	124
132	128	128	130
120	117	120	100
117	100	100	115
109	113	101	105

9. The data below reflect mean reaction times of 15 pilots and their scores on an overall physical fitness test. Compute the Pearson correlation. Does there seem to be a relationship?

Fitness Score	Reaction Time	Fitness Score	Reaction Time
10	0.4	55	3.8
12	2.5	61	5.9
14	1.2	71	5.3
24	2.4	72	6.0
30	4.5	80	4.9
36	3.0	89	6.2
44	4.2	98	5.6
49	4.6		

10. A marriage counsellor tests each of her 15 couples on a test of marital satisfaction and a test of communication skills. Compute Pearson's correlation. Is the relationship positive or negative?

Satisfaction	Communication	Satisfaction	Communication
2.30	6.0	4.01	7.8
2.48	7.2	4.11	8.0
2.64	3.5	4.26	6.0
3.18	2.4	4.28	8.2
3.40	5.0	4.38	8.9
3.58	4.0	4.49	7.5
3.78	5.8	4.58	7.0
3.89	6.3		

11. Construct a scattergram for the following data:

Participant	X	Y
1	78	65
2	66	43
3	54	38
4	89	79
5	46	67
6	70	67
7	55	69
8	95	80
9	64	72
10	86	62

12. A researcher asked his 20 students how many hours they studied per week on average. At the end of their first year, the researcher recorded the grade point average received by each of the 20 students. Construct a scattergram of the data. Does there seem to be a relationship?

Student Number	Grade Point Average	Study Hours Per Week
1	9	16
2	9	9
3	8	13
4	8	10
5	8	8
6	8	8
7	8	10
8	7	9
9	7	9
10	6	4
11	6	15
12	6	10
13	6	6
14	5	6
15	5	7
16	4	4

Student Number	Grade Point Average	Study Hours Per Week
17	3	8
18	3	3
19	2	6
20	1	5

13. The 10 Canadian provinces have been rank-ordered according to crime rate in 2011 and in 2012. Run the rank-order correlation test to see if the rankings are related ($\alpha = .05$). Are they?

Province	2011	2012
British Columbia	1	3
Alberta	2	1
Manitoba	3	5
Saskatchewan	4	4
Ontario	5	2
Quebec	6	8
Prince Edward Island	7	6
Nova Scotia	8	7
New Brunswick	9	9
Newfoundland	10	10

14. Plot the data from Exercise 13 on a scattergram.

15. An ecologist has assessed pollution and crime rate for nine U.S. cities using a standard index. Calculate Spearman's *rho* for the following raw-score data. Remember you must rank the data first. Is there a relationship between crime rate and pollution?

U.S. Cities	Pollution	Crime Rate
Los Angeles	20	3
Denver	17	9
Salt Lake	15	2
Boston	14	4
Chicago	12	10
Dallas	12	1
New York	11	5
Detroit	9	11
Hartford	6	8

16. Compute Spearman's *rho* for the following data.

Variable 1	Variable 2	Variable 1	Variable 2
51	62	72	67
53	69	73	54
55	63	75	53
56	52	75	58
57	53	76	59
59	81	76	49
61	90	76	72
64	84	78	63
66	45	83	69
68	60	87	61
68	65	89	53

Predictive Techniques

LEARNING OBJECTIVES

After reading this chapter, you should be able to do the following:

1. Describe the least squares criterion used to fit the regression line.
2. Calculate the slope and Y intercept for a given set of data.
3. Use the regression equation to predict Y for a given set of data.
4. Describe and calculate the standard error of estimate and the coefficient of determination.
5. Describe and provide an example of regression on the mean.
6. Lay down the regression line for a given set of data.
7. Describe the difference between simple linear regression and multiple regression analyses.
8. Compute the multiple correlation coefficient and partial correlations for a given set of data.
9. Use the multiple regression equation to predict criterion performance for a given set of data.

Half of Young Goths Have Tried Suicide

Teenagers immersed in the goth subculture are far more likely than their peers to have harmed themselves or attempted suicide, research has revealed.

Scientists at Glasgow University who studied 1258 Scots at the ages of 11, 13, 15 and 19, discovered that 47 percent of those identifying themselves as Goths had attempted suicide. An even higher percentage—53—said they had harmed themselves, compared with national rates of between 7 and 14 per cent. Mental health workers last night described the results as "extremely worrying" and said more needs to be done to help troubled teenagers.

Goth stars, such as the rocker Marilyn Manson, have been criticized for appearing to glorify self-harm, but scientists think the subculture actually attracts self-harmers who can find support among peers to help them deal with problems.

The research found that self-harm was more common before becoming a goth or at around the same time, as opposed to afterwards. Even after the researchers took into account factors such as social class, depression, and alcohol use, being a goth was the single strongest predictor of either self-harm or suicide attempt.

Lyndsay Moss, *The Scotsman*, April 2006

When we know that variables are related, we can use this information to make predictions from one variable(s) to another. In the excerpt above, the variable, "being a goth," was said to be a strong predictor of self-harm or suicide attempts.

As discussed in Chapter 16, most colleges and universities correlate high school grades with college performance; most students who do well in high school also do well in college. We can predict how well a person will perform in college if we know his or her high school average. Our prediction is based on how the average student with that particular high school average has done in college in the past. Sometimes we will be wrong, of course, but if the correlation is very strong we usually predict correctly.

The previous chapter discussed the straight line of best fit in a bivariate frequency distribution. Let's look at how that line is determined.

The Regression Line

The straight line of best fit is called the regression line. The mathematical equation that defines it is called the **regression equation**. Figure 17.1 shows

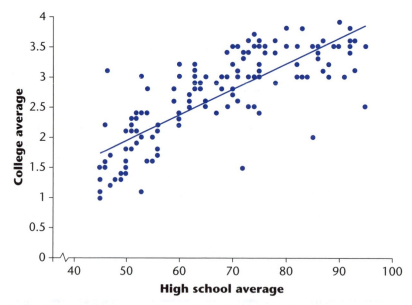

Figure 17.1. The regression line for a bivariate distribution of high school versus college grades.

the **regression line** fitted to a scattergram of high school (%) and college average grades (1–4).

When we use the correlation between two variables to predict one from the other, we use the regression line as our prediction. We take any X value and predict for Y as the point on the regression line corresponding to that X value. Suppose you have just finished high school with a grade point average of 75%. Using the scattergram in Figure 17.2, you can see that we would predict your college average to be 3.

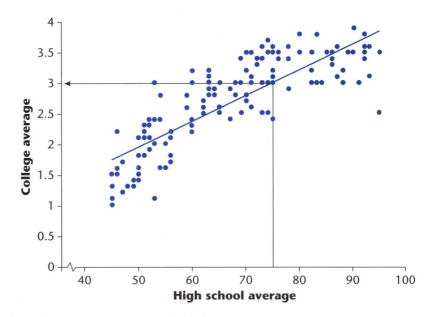

Figure 17.2.   Scattergram of correlation between high school and college grades.

Does that mean that you would get an average of 3 in college? Not necessarily. Our predicted value of 3 is a mean of college grades for students who entered with a high school average of 75%. The accuracy of our prediction for any individual depends on the strength of the correlation: How closely do the Y values hug the regression line?

Regression line: The straight line of best fit

Regression equation: The mathematical equation that defines the regression line

CONCEPT REVIEW 17.1

Below is the line of regression for Y on X. What value of Y would we predict for an X value of 25?

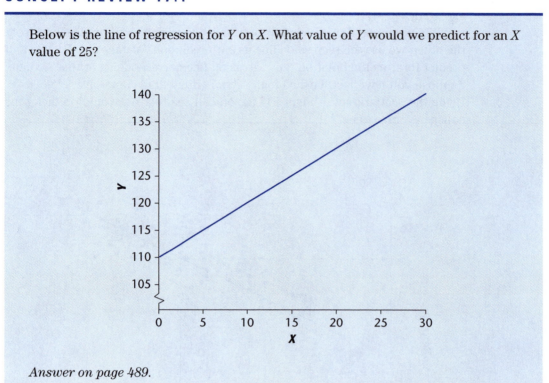

Answer on page 489.

Criterion of Best Fit

To fit the straight line to a bivariate frequency distribution, Pearson used the **least squares criterion**. This criterion dictates that the line be laid down in such a way that the sum of the squared distances between the Y values and the line be as small as possible. In other words, *the sum of the squared distances is a minimum*. Consider the scattergram in Figure 17.3.

The points are the actual values of Y found for each value of X. The straight line is called the line of regression of Y on X. Note that the distances are measured in the Y dimension. The line, Y on X, is laid down so that the sum of the squared distances of the Y values from the regression line is as small as possible in the Y dimension. This may sound familiar. In Chapter 3, we learned one way to define a mean: The value in a distribution about which the sum of the squared deviations is a minimum. The regression line is much like a mean.

> **Least squares criterion:** For the regression line, a mathematical criterion that specifies that the sum of the squared distances of points from the line is a minimum

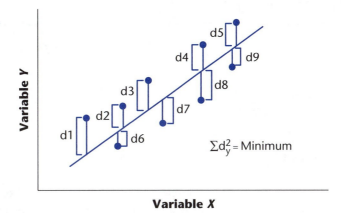

Figure 17.3. The least squares criterion for the regression of *Y* on *X*.

FYI

A different line is fitted to the data when we minimize the sum of the squared discrepancies in the *X* dimension. Consider the scattergram in Figure 17.4.

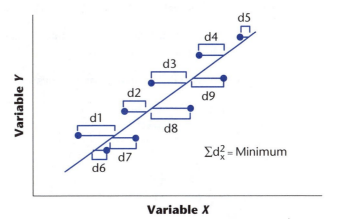

Figure 17.4. The least squares criterion for the regression of *X* on *Y*.

Here the distances are measured in the *X* dimension. This regression line of *X* on *Y* is different from *Y* on *X*. Which line is appropriate is based on how you name your variables and plot your data. We always assume that *X* is known and *Y* is to be predicted; therefore, our regression line is always *Y* on *X*. Keep in mind, however, that you can fit two lines to the same data.

CONCEPT REVIEW 17.2

When we predict a Y value from a known X value, what exactly are we predicting Y to be?

Answer on page 489.

The Regression Equation

The regression line is defined by an equation that takes the same general form as the equation for any straight line. You may recall from your high school math course that the equation for a straight line is

$$Y = \overset{\text{slope}}{b} X + \overset{\text{Y intercept}}{a}$$

In any equation for a straight line, the **slope** indicates the amount of increase in Y that accompanies one unit of increase in X. As you can see below, the regression equation can be expressed in raw score, deviation score, and z-score form. Prime notation ($'$) is used to indicate that Y is a predicted value. σ_Y and σ_X refer to the standard deviation of Y and the standard deviation of X, respectively.

Slope In regression, indicates the amount of change in Y that accompanies one unit of increase in X

The regression equations are as follows:

Raw score	slope	Y intercept
	$Y' = \rho\left(\dfrac{\sigma_Y}{\sigma_X}\right)X$	$+ \left[-\rho\left(\dfrac{\sigma_Y}{\sigma_X}\right)\mu_X + \mu_Y\right]$
Deviation score	$(Y - \mu_Y)' = \rho\left(\dfrac{\sigma_Y}{\sigma_X}\right)(X - \mu_X) +$	0
z score	$z_{Y'} = \rho z_X$	$+ \quad 0$

In the deviation-score and z-score formulas, the **Y intercept** is zero. The regression line passes through the ordinate at zero. In general, the regression line always passes through the mean of Y and the mean of X. When data are in deviation or z-score form, the means are zero and so the regression line must pass through the origin.

In the z-score regression equation, the value of ρ is the slope. When the data are in z-score form, ρ indicates what portion of a *standard deviation* Y increases for one *standard deviation* increase in X.

The regression line can be determined by calculating the slope and the Y intercept of a set of data.

Y intercept In a scattergram, the point on the ordinate crossed by the regression line

CONCEPT REVIEW 17.3

With z-score data, we predict that $z_Y = +1$. The correlation between X and Y is .5. What was the z equivalent for our X score? What is the value of the Y intercept? What does the slope mean in words?

Answer on page 489.

Calculating the Slope

When data are in raw-score form, we can see from the formula above that the formula for the slope of the regression line is

$$b = \rho\left(\frac{\sigma_Y}{\sigma_X}\right)$$

By substituting the raw-score formula for ρ and simplifying the equation, we find that the formula for calculating the slope with raw data is

$$b = \frac{\sum XY - (\sum X)(\sum Y)/N}{\sum X^2 - (\sum X)^2/N}$$

Let's use this formula to calculate the slope of the regression line for the following data:

X	Y	XY	X²
3	5	15	9
5	7	35	25
4	4	16	16

(Continued)

(Continued)

X	Y	XY	X²
7	8	56	49
6	9	54	36
3	5	15	9
2	3	6	4
3	4	12	9
4	3	12	16
5	7	35	25
Total	42	55	256	198
Mean	4.2	5.5		

Using the formula,

$$b = \frac{\sum XY - (\sum X)(\sum Y)/N}{\sum X^2 - (\sum X)^2/N}$$

$$= \frac{256 - (42)(55)/10}{198 - (42)^2/10}$$

$$= \frac{25}{21.6} = 1.16$$

Calculating the *Y* Intercept

The raw-score formula for calculating the *Y* intercept of the regression line is

$$a = \left(-\rho\left(\frac{\sigma_Y}{\sigma_X}\right)\mu_X + \mu_Y\right)$$

Because $-\rho\left(\dfrac{\sigma_Y}{\sigma_X}\right)$ is the slope, *b*, we can simplify the formula to

$$a = \mu_Y - b\mu_X$$

Let's use the previous example to determine the *Y* intercept of the regression line:

$$a = 5.5 - (1.16)(4.2) = 0.63$$

The regression line passes through the y-axis at 0.63. You will recall that all regression lines pass through the point of intersection of the mean of Y and the mean of X. We have enough information to lay down the regression line for our example.

Laying Down the Regression Line

Let's lay down the regression line for the example we've been using. We know that the line crosses the y-axis at 0.63 and that it passes through the intersection of the mean of X (i.e., 4.2) and the mean of Y (i.e., 5.5). We only need to plot these two points and connect them to obtain the regression line. See Figure 17.5.

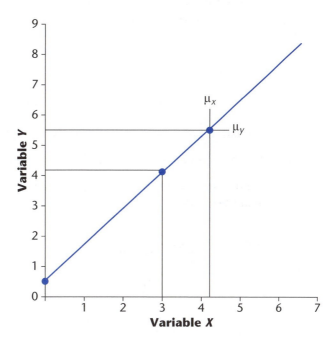

Figure 17.5.   Laying down the regression line.

Let's verify our work by predicting the value of Y for an X value of 3. The raw-score equation is

$$Y' = \rho\left(\frac{\sigma_Y}{\sigma_X}\right)X - \rho\left(\frac{\sigma_Y}{\sigma_X}\right)\mu_X + \mu_Y$$

Because we already know the slope and Y intercept, we can simplify this equation to

$$Y' = bX + a$$

As Figure 17.5 shows, the predicted Y value of 4.11 for an X score of 3 is, indeed, correct.

Using the Regression Equation for Prediction

Let's see how the regression equation can be used to predict Y from X. Suppose a statistics professor kept student test performance scores for many years. She found that performance on the first midterm test correlated reasonably well with the final-grade students received in the course. Here are the data:

First test: $\mu_X = 56.45$ $\sigma_X = 10.25$

Final grade: $\mu_Y = 63.12$ $\sigma_Y = 12.14$

The correlation between the two variables: $\rho = 0.60$

A student in her current class scored 76.0 on the first midterm exam.

Let's use the regression equation to predict the final grade this student will receive in the course.

$$Y' = \rho\left(\frac{\sigma_Y}{\sigma_X}\right)X - \rho\left(\frac{\sigma_Y}{\sigma_X}\right)\mu_X + \mu_Y$$
$$= (0.60)(12.14/10.25)(76.0) - (0.60)(12.14/10.25)(56.45) + 63.12$$
$$= (0.71)(76.0) - (0.71)(56.45) + 63.12$$
$$= 54.01 - 40.11 + 63.12 = 77.02$$

We would predict a final grade of 77.02 for this student.

Take a look at Figure 17.6. The regression equation predicts the average final grade received by students who scored 76.0 on the first midterm test. Because the correlation is not perfect, there will be some error in prediction. The predicted value is the point on the line, but the actual points scatter around the regression line to some degree. How far the points vary from the line determines how much error we will make when we use the regression line as our predictor.

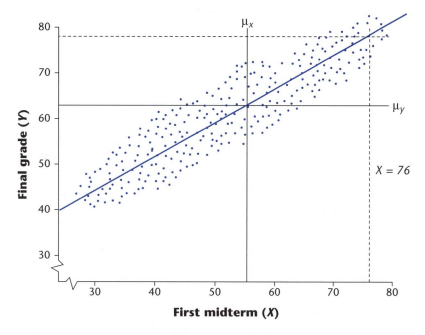

Figure 17.6. Predicting *Y* from *X*.

Error of Prediction: The Standard Error of Estimate

The regression equation states what value of *Y* is expected when *X* has a particular value. *Y'* is not likely to be the actual value corresponding to *X*. For example, a regression equation may predict that a man who is 183 cm tall will weigh 79.5 kg. However, we would not expect a particular 183-cm-tall man to weigh exactly 79.5 kg. The predicted value is an estimate of weights of all men who are 183 cm tall. If the correlation between height and weight is not strong, then we can expect considerable variation in the actual values. Only when there is a perfect correlation, $\rho = \pm 1$, will the actual values precisely equal the predicted values.

The **standard error of estimate**, denoted as σ_{YX}, measures the variability of the actual *Y* values from the predicted *Y* values. Recall that the standard deviation of *Y* is found by the following formula:

$$\sigma_y = \sqrt{\frac{\sum(Y - \mu_Y)^2}{N}}$$

To determine the error encountered when we make predictions between two moderately correlated variables, we measure the variability of the actual *Y* values about the predicted values (Y'). The standard error of estimate indicates the variability of the actual Y values around the regression line. The formula for the standard error of estimate is

$$\sigma_{YX} = \sqrt{\frac{\Sigma(Y - Y')^2}{N}}$$

This measures the magnitude of the error of prediction. When the correlation is perfect, each $Y - Y'$ difference is zero because all the actual Y values fall on the regression line. Therefore, the standard error of estimate is zero, and there is no error in prediction. When the correlation is zero, then Y' equals the mean of Y for all values of X and

$$\sigma_{YX} = \sqrt{\frac{\Sigma(Y - \mu_Y)^2}{N}} = \sigma_Y$$

In other words, the standard error of estimate ranges from zero when $\rho = \pm 1$ to the standard deviation of Y when $\rho = 0$.

The standard error of estimate is a standard deviation and has all the properties of one. The sum of the deviations of the Y values about the regression line is zero, and the sum of the squared deviations of the Y values about the regression line is minimized.

The standard error of estimate can be calculated more easily with the following formula:

$$\sigma_{YX} = \sigma_Y \sqrt{1 - \rho^2}$$

As we saw above, when $\rho = 0$, then $\sigma_{YX} = \sigma_Y$ and when $\rho = \pm 1$, then $\sigma_{YX} = 0$.

Standard error of estimate In regression, the variability of the Y values around the regression line; estimates predictive error

Interpreting the Correlation in Terms of Explained Variance

When X and Y are correlated, Y takes on different values depending on whether X is high or low. If we select a single X value, Y still varies to some extent unless the correlation is perfect. In other words, unless the correlation is ± 1, the actual Y values will vary around the straight line of best fit. With lower correlations, this variability increases.

The total variation in the Y distribution can be partitioned into two components:

1. The variation in Y that is associated with changes in X.

2. The variation inherent in Y that is independent of changes in X.

Let's take a single Y value and look at how its variation can be partitioned into two parts. See Figure 17.7.

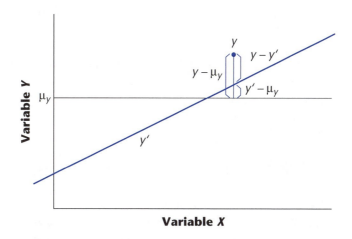

Figure 17.7. Partitioning the Y variance in regression.

Remember that the total variation in Y is based on the deviations of the Y values from the mean of the distribution. If all the deviations were squared, summed, and divided by N, we would have the Y variance.

Look at Figure 17.7. The Y value differs from the mean of the Y distribution. That discrepancy can be partitioned into two components:

1. The difference between the Y value and the point on the straight line of best fit (i.e., Y').

2. The difference between the line (Y') and the mean of the distribution.

If we square all the differences, sum the squares, and then divide each by N, we would have the following:

$$\frac{\sum (Y - \mu_Y)^2}{N} = \frac{\sum (Y - Y')^2}{N} + \frac{\sum (Y' - \mu_Y)^2}{N}$$

$$\sigma_Y^2 = \sigma_{YX}^2 + \sigma_{Y'}^2$$

$$\text{Total } Y \text{ variance} = \begin{pmatrix} \text{Variance in } Y \\ \text{independent of} \\ \text{changes in } X \end{pmatrix} + \begin{pmatrix} \text{Variance in } Y \\ \text{associated with} \\ \text{changes in } X \end{pmatrix}$$

σ_Y^2 = total variance in the Y distribution

σ_{YX}^2 = variance of the actual Y values around the straight line (Y')

$\sigma_{Y'}^2$ = variance of the points on the line of best fit around the mean of the Y distribution

When $\rho = \pm 1$, all the Y values fall exactly on the straight line of best fit, and there is no variation of the Y values from Y'. The value of σ_{YX}^2 is zero; all the variation in Y is due to changes in X. When the correlation is zero, none of the variation in Y is due to changes in X. The value of σ_Y^2 is zero.

Calculating Effect Size: Coefficient of Determination

The correlation coefficient can be interpreted in terms of the *proportion of the total Y variance that is associated with changes in X*. This proportion is called the **coefficient of determination** and is calculated using the formula

$$\frac{\text{Variance in } Y \text{ associated with changes in } X}{\text{Total } Y \text{ variance}} = \frac{\sigma_{Y'}^2}{\sigma_Y^2} = \rho^2$$

Recall that the coefficient of determination, ρ^2, indicates the strength of the relationship between the two variables. It estimates how much of the total Y variation is due to the correlation Y has with X. In correlational research, this then is an estimate of **effect size**. This coefficient, found by squaring the correlation coefficient, tells us how much of the variance in one variable is explained by its relationship or correlation with another variable. A small effect would be a ρ^2 of about .01, a medium effect would be a ρ^2 of about .09, and a large effect would be a ρ^2 of about .25.

Coefficient of determination (ρ^2) In regression, the proportion of the total variance in Y that is explained by the correlation between X and Y; indicates the strength of the relationship between two variables

Effect size An estimate of the size of the treatment effect or relationship

ALERT

Think of the coefficient of determination in terms of how much of the variance in Y can be *explained* and how much is left unaccounted for. Many people find this a more helpful way to think about correlations. For example, if you have a correlation of 0.50, you know that 25% of the total variability of Y is due to the correlation, and the rest is unexplained.

Regression on the Mean

When a value of Y is predicted from a given value of X, Y' can never be farther from its mean than X is from its mean. Unless the correlation is perfect, Y' will be closer to its mean than X is to its mean. This is called **regression on the mean**. It can lead us into some peculiar situations.

Consider the correlation between IQ of parents and their offspring. It's about 0.5. Let's predict the IQ of children whose parents' IQs are two standard deviations below the mean. We will use our z-score formula.

$$z_{Y'} = 0.5(2) + 0 = +1$$

For parents whose IQ scores are two standard deviations below the mean, we will predict their offspring to be only one standard deviation below the mean. Similarly, for parents whose scores are two standard deviations above the mean, we will predict their offspring to be one standard deviation above the mean. As you can see, the predicted values regress toward the mean.

Figure 17.8 shows the z scores of Y that we would predict for various z scores of X, when ρ is 0, 0.5, and 1. When ρ is 0, we predict that the z score of Y will be the mean (which in any z distribution is 0). When ρ is 1, the z score of Y will be the same as the z score of X. But when ρ is 0.5, the predicted value of Y tends toward the mean.

Regression on the mean occurs because the predicted Y score cannot be farther away from the mean of its distribution than its X counterpart. We must always predict that Y will be no farther away from its mean than X is from its mean.

Regression on the mean In regression, refers to the fact that the predicted Y value tends to be closer to its mean than the X value (used to predict Y) is from its mean

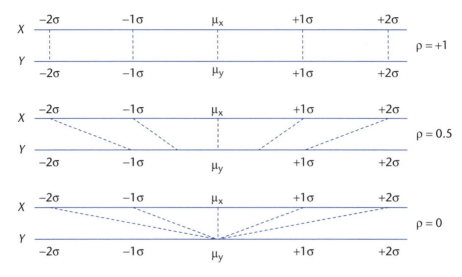

Figure 17.8. Regression on the mean.

CONCEPT REVIEW 17.4

A physical education instructor evaluated the fitness of her 25 students at the beginning of the year and again at the end of the semester. She was disappointed to find that, although her less-fit students improved over the course of the semester, her fitter students did not. Considering what you know about regression on the mean, what would you say to her?

Answer on page 490.

Multiple Regression Analysis

In simple linear regression, Y is predicted from knowledge of X. The strength of the correlation between X (often called the **predictor variable**) and Y (often called the **criterion variable**) determines the accuracy of the prediction.

Multiple regression analysis, on the other hand, is a technique used to predict Y (the criterion variable) from a set of predictor variables (X_1, X_2, etc.). This analysis provides an index of the relationship between the criterion variable and each of the predictor variables, in the form of a regression coefficient. Imagine that the U.S. Air Force is interested in screening applicants for military flying school. They might use various measures to predict an applicant's future performance as a pilot trainee. Perhaps they have a standard aptitude test that has been shown to be correlated with success. Perhaps, in addition, they assess the applicant's general physical fitness. They could use each of these predictor variables to predict the applicant's likelihood of benefiting from training. A multiple **regression analysis** will provide a measure of the kinds of predictor information most useful in predicting success in training school.

> **Predictor variable** In regression, the variable used to predict the value of another, the criterion variable
>
> **Criterion variable** In regression, the variable being predicted from information about another, the predictor, variable
>
> **Regression analysis** An inferential technique used to predict the value of a variable from known values of a correlated variable

The Multiple Correlation Coefficient

We will use multiple regression *(MR)* to stand for the **multiple correlation** coefficient between all predictors and the criterion.

The equation for multiple correlation from two predictor variables is as follows:

$$MR = \sqrt{\frac{\rho_{y_1}^2 + \rho_{y_2}^2 - 2\rho_{y_1}\rho_{y_2}\rho_{X_1 X_2}}{1 - \rho_{X_1 X_2}^2}}$$

Y = criterion variable

X_1 = first predictor variable

X_2 = second predictor variable

Therefore,

$\rho_{y_1}^2$ = square of the correlation coefficient between the criterion variable and the first predictor variable

$\rho_{y_2}^2$ = square of the correlation coefficient between the criterion variable and the second predictor variable

$\rho_{X_1 X_2}$ = correlation coefficient between the first and second predictor variables

Let's use our air force example to see how this equation would be used.

Suppose the air force had determined that the correlation between the standard aptitude test and success in flying school is 0.58, the correlation between their physical fitness measure and success is 0.52, and the correlation between physical fitness and aptitude is 0.32. You can see that the aptitude measure is a better predictor of flying school success than is the fitness measure. What we will find out with multiple regression is whether combining both predictor measures is a better predictor of success than either alone. We can write then that

$\rho_{y_1} = 0.58$, the correlation between aptitude and success

$\rho_{y_2} = 0.52$, the correlation between physical fitness and success

$\rho_{X_1 X_2} = 0.32$, the correlation between physical fitness and aptitude

Using these values in the multiple correlation equation,

$$MR = \sqrt{\frac{\rho_{y_1}^2 + \rho_{y_2}^2 - 2\rho_{y_1}\rho_{y_2}\rho_{X_1 X_2}}{1 - \rho_{X_1 X_2}^2}}$$

$$MR = \sqrt{\frac{0.58^2 + 0.52^2 - 2(0.58)(0.52)(0.32)}{1 - 0.32^2}}$$

$$= 0.68$$

You can see that using both predictor measures produces a correlation coefficient that is higher than each separate coefficient, allowing us to better predict success.

Multiple correlation In regression, the correlation between all predictor variables and the criterion variable

Using Multiple Correlation for Prediction

In simple linear regression, we used the correlation coefficient to predict from X to Y. We can do the same here. We use a multiple regression equation to predict the criterion variable from predictor variables. As with linear regression, we need to determine the Y intercept. Unlike simple linear regression, we also need to calculate slopes for each predictor variable. Each slope tells us how much change occurs in Y for a unit change in one X variable when all other predictor variables are held constant. With two predictor variables, the multiple regression equation is as follows:

$$Y' = b_1 X_1 + b_2 X_2 + a$$

$a = Y$ intercept

$b_1 =$ slope for predictor variable X_1

$b_2 =$ slope for predictor variable X_2

You can see that the predicted value of Y is equal to a linear combination of Xs, each weighted by a value of b.

The equations for the slopes are as follows:

$$b_{X_1} = \left(\frac{\sigma_Y}{\sigma_{X_1}}\right)\left(\frac{\rho_{y_1} - \rho_{y_2}\rho_{X_1 X_2}}{1 - \rho_{X_1 X_2}^2}\right)$$

$$b_{X_2} = \left(\frac{\sigma_Y}{\sigma_{X_2}}\right)\left(\frac{\rho_{y_2} - \rho_{y_1}\rho_{X_1 X_2}}{1 - \rho_{X_1 X_2}^2}\right)$$

$\sigma_Y =$ standard deviation of the criterion variable

$\sigma_{X_1} =$ standard deviation of the first predictor variable

$\sigma_{X_2} =$ standard deviation of the second predictor variable

The bs, or slopes, indicate the relationship between the criterion variable (Y) and each predictor variable.

The equation for the Y intercept is

$$a = \mu_Y - b_1\mu_{X_1} - b_2\mu_{X_2}$$

$\mu_Y =$ mean of the criterion variable

$\mu_{X_1} =$ mean of the first predictor variable

$\mu_{X_2} =$ mean of the second predictor variable

Let's use our air force example to predict performance for two applicants. Suppose the following data have been collected for the aptitude test, the physical fitness test, and flying school performance.

Flying school performance (Y)

$$\mu_Y = 64.8$$

$$\sigma_Y = 12.6$$

Aptitude test norms (1)

$$\mu_{X_1} = 432$$

$$\sigma_{X_1} = 65$$

Physical fitness norms (2)

$$\mu_{X_2} = 73.2$$

$$\sigma_{X_2} = 1.4$$

The correlations were as follows:

$\rho_{y_1} = 0.58$, the correlation between aptitude and success

$\rho_{y_2} = 0.52$, the correlation between physical fitness and success

$\rho_{X_1 X_2} = 0.32$, the correlation between physical fitness and aptitude

Suppose our first candidate for flying school obtained an aptitude score of 390 and a physical fitness score of 8.2, and our second candidate obtained an aptitude score of 512 and a physical fitness score of 7.0. Let's use our equations to predict the flying school performance of each applicant.

Step 1. Determine the slopes.

$$b_{X_1} = \left(\frac{\sigma_Y}{\sigma_{X_1}}\right)\left(\frac{\rho_{y_1} - \rho_{y_2}\rho_{X_1 X_2}}{1 - \rho_{X_1 X_2}^2}\right)$$

$$= \left(\frac{12.6}{65}\right)\left(\frac{0.58 - (0.52)(0.32)}{1 - 32^2}\right) = 0.09$$

$$b_{X_2} = \left(\frac{\sigma_Y}{\sigma_{X_2}}\right)\left(\frac{\rho_{y_2} - \rho_{y_1}\rho_{X_1 X_2}}{1 - \rho_{X_1 X_2}^2}\right)$$

$$= \left(\frac{12.6}{1.4}\right)\left(\frac{0.52 - (0.58)(0.32)}{1 - 32^2}\right) = 3.35$$

Step 2. Determine the Y intercept.

$$a = \mu_Y - b_1\mu_1 - b_2\mu_2$$
$$= 64.8 - 0.09(432) - 3.35(7.2) = 1.8$$

Step 3. Determine the predicted values of Y for each applicant. For the first applicant:

$$Y' = b_1 X_1 + b_2 X_2 + a$$
$$= 0.09(390) + 3.35(8.2) + 1.8 = 64.37$$

For the second applicant:

$$Y' = b_1 X_1 + b_2 X_2 + a$$
$$= 0.09(512) + 3.35(7.0) + 1.8 = 71.33$$

If we had to choose between the two, we might be wise to select the second applicant.

With simple linear regression, the strength of the correlation coefficient determines the amount of predictive error. With multiple regression, the strength of the multiple correlation determines predictive error. With simple linear regression, predictive error was measured by the standard error of estimate. One formula for the standard error of estimate is

$$\sigma_{YX} = \sigma_Y \sqrt{1 - \rho^2}$$

The formula for the standard error of multiple estimate is similar.

$$\sigma_{ME} = \sigma_Y \sqrt{1 - MR^2}$$

For our above example, the standard error of multiple estimate is

$$\sigma_{ME} = 12.6\sqrt{1 - 0.68^2} = 9.24$$

You can see that with a very strong multiple correlation, the standard error of multiple estimate tends toward zero; with a very weak multiple correlation, the standard error tends toward the standard deviation of the criterion variable, Y.

Partial Correlation

The multiple correlation equation estimates the combined influence of predictor variables on a criterion measure. This may allow the researcher to make a more accurate prediction of the criterion variable.

Partial correlation techniques, on the other hand, are used to measure the relationship between two variables when a third variable has an influence on them both. In other words, it assesses the correlation between the two variables of interest by ruling out the influence of the third variable known to be involved. The formula for partial correlation is as follows:

$$R_p = \frac{\rho_{y_1} - \rho_{y_2}\rho_{x_1 x_2}}{\sqrt{\left(1 - \rho_{y_2}^2\right)\left(1 - \rho_{x_1 x_2}^2\right)}}$$

Suppose there is a positive correlation between age and income level. Older people make more money than younger people. This would seem to make sense because the longer a person is in the workforce, the more promotions and therefore the higher income he or she can obtain. Can you think of another variable that might be correlated with both age and income?

How about years of education? We might imagine that older people have more education than younger people and that better-educated people earn higher salaries. The question then is "What is the true relationship between age and income level if the years of education factor is held constant?" This is a problem that could be solved with partial correlation. Let's determine the partial correlation between age and income. Suppose the following:

$\rho_{y_1} = 0.60$, correlation between age and income

$\rho_{y_2} = 0.63$, correlation between age and years of education

$\rho_{x_1 x_2} = 0.77$, correlation between years of education and income

$$R_p = \frac{0.60 - (0.63)(0.77)}{\sqrt{\left(1 - 0.63^2\right)\left(1 - 0.77^2\right)}}$$

$$= 0.23$$

Although the correlation between age and income was quite high (i.e., 0.60), once the influence of years of education is removed, the correlation is not nearly as impressive.

Partial correlation In regression, the correlation between two variables when a third has been held constant

FYI

Correlational and regression analyses are very common in the social sciences, particularly for researchers working in areas where experimental designs are not possible or are ethically unacceptable. Multiple correlation and multiple regression analyses are powerful and complicated techniques that cannot be presented with any degree of detail here. Interested students should consult upper-level statistics books for more comprehensive coverage of these useful techniques.

FOCUS ON RESEARCH

Eating disorders are seen in many young women and can result in serious health problems, even death. This was the area of interest of Piran and Cormier (2005)[1] of the University of Toronto.

THE RESEARCH PROBLEM

Piran and Cormier (2005) examined three variables that they thought might predict disordered eating in women. They wanted to determine how much of the variability in eating disorder measures, the *criterion* variable, could be explained by the *predictor* variables.

THE VARIABLES

Self-silencing is the tendency to put the needs of others first at the expense of one's own needs. *Anger suppression* is the tendency to not express anger outwardly. The third variable was *body objectification* or the tendency to treat one's body as an object to be looked at. Eating disorder behaviors and attitudes were obtained using several common measures.

THE RESULTS

Some of the results are as follows. Self-silencing was found to be a significant predictor of disordered eating behavior on several measures, explaining 8% to 22% of the variance. When anger suppression was added, an additional 1% to 3% of the variance was explained. When body objectification was added to the other two predictors, 4% to 30% of the variance was also explained.

THE CONCLUSIONS

The authors concluded that the tendency in our society for women to internalize certain values or ways of thinking about themselves can have a negative effect on their health. They called for more awareness and better education of families, schools, and the media about these issues.

This example illustrates the application of multiple regression analysis. In fields where numerous variables may be involved, such as in the understanding of complex interpersonal relationships, this sort of analysis can be very useful.

---

[1]Piran, N., & Cormier, H. C. (2005). The social construction of women and disordered eating patterns. *Journal of Counseling Psychology, 52*(4), 549–558.

SUMMARY OF TERMS AND FORMULAS

When the *correlation* between two variables is known, we may use knowledge of performance on the first variable to predict performance on the second variable. A *regression line* is fitted to the correlational data, and the point that lies on the line is the predicted value of Y for a given X value.

When the correlation between variables is not perfect, some predictive error will occur. The measure of predictive error is called the *standard error of estimate*.

The *coefficient of determination*, ρ^2, can be interpreted in terms of the proportion of the total variance in Y that can be explained or accounted for by the relationship of Y to X.

Regression on the mean occurs in prediction whenever the correlation between X and Y is not perfect. The predicted value will tend to be closer to its mean than was the value used in the prediction.

Multiple correlation is used to predict from several predictor variables to a criterion variable. It often allows a more accurate prediction than simple linear correlation. *Partial correlation* is used to estimate the individual influence of a variable on another by holding constant other variables known to have an effect.

Regression equation for predicting Y from X	
Raw score	$Y' = \rho\left(\dfrac{\sigma_Y}{\sigma_X}\right)X - \rho\left(\dfrac{\sigma_Y}{\sigma_X}\right)\mu_X + \mu_Y$
Deviation score	$(Y - \mu_Y)' = \rho\left(\dfrac{\sigma_Y}{\sigma_X}\right)(X - \mu_X)$
z score	$z_{Y'} = \rho z_X$
Slope of the regression line	$b = \rho\left(\dfrac{\sigma_Y}{\sigma_X}\right)$
Raw data	$b = \dfrac{\sum XY - (\sum X)(\sum Y)/N}{\sum X^2 - (\sum X)^2/N}$
Y intercept of the regression line	$a = -\rho\left(\dfrac{\sigma_Y}{\sigma_X}\right)\mu_X + \mu_Y$

Standard error of estimate	$$\sigma_{YX} = \sqrt{\dfrac{\sum(Y-Y')^2}{N}}$$ $$\sigma_{YX} = \sigma_Y\sqrt{1-\rho^2}$$
Multiple correlation coefficient	$$MR = \sqrt{\dfrac{\rho_{Y_1}^2 + \rho_{Y_2}^2 - 2\rho_{Y_1}\rho_{Y_2}\rho_{X_1X_2}}{1-\rho_{X_1X_2}^2}}$$
Multiple regression equation	$$Y' = b_1X_1 + b_2X_2 + a$$
Slopes for multiple regression	
For first and second predictor variable	$$b_1 = \left(\dfrac{\sigma_Y}{\sigma_{X_1}}\right)\left(\dfrac{\rho_{Y_1} - \rho_{Y_2}\rho_{X_1X_2}}{1-\rho_{X_1X_2}^2}\right)$$ $$b_2 = \left(\dfrac{\sigma_Y}{\sigma_{X_2}}\right)\left(\dfrac{\rho_{Y_2} - \rho_{Y_1}\rho_{X_1X_2}}{1-\rho_{X_1X_2}^2}\right)$$
Standard error of multiple estimate	$$\sigma_{ME} = \sigma_Y\sqrt{1-MR^2}$$
Partial correlation	$$R_P = \dfrac{\rho_{Y_1} - \rho_{Y_2}\rho_{X_1X_2}}{\sqrt{\left(1-\rho_{Y_2}^2\right)\left(1-\rho_{X_1X_2}^2\right)}}$$

CONCEPT REVIEW ANSWERS

17.1. The point on the regression line corresponding to an X value of 25 is 135, so that is the Y value we would predict.

17.2. We predict Y to be the mean of all actual values of Y associated with the particular X value we are using.

17.3. Our X score must have been +2.

$$z_{Y'} = 0.5(2) + 0 = +1$$

The Y intercept is zero. The slope or correlation coefficient tells us that for every one standard deviation that X increases, Y increases by one-half standard deviation.

17.4. You should explain to her that the students who scored high on the fitness variable would be expected to score lower on subsequent testing. Their scores should regress toward the mean. Likewise, the low scores obtained by the less-fit students will tend to increase on subsequent testing. This is a statistical phenomenon, and the instructor should not fret about her physical education training.

EXERCISES

1. A professor collected the following data on the number of hours per week students spend studying and their scores on tests.

Hours/Week	Test Scores	Hours/Week	Test Scores
8	75	2	35
8	50	5	50
2	50	7	65
4	45	4	60
4	65	2	50
9	60	1	50
10	80	7	70
10	95		

   a. Calculate the slope for the above data (use the raw-score equation).
   b. Calculate the Y intercept for the above data.
   c. Plot the regression line. Be precise.

2. If Russell tells you he studies 7.5 hours/week, circle the test score on the graph from Exercise 1(c) that you would predict for him. Verify the predicted value with your equation.

3. Suppose $\rho = 0.60$, $\sigma_Y = 4.2$, $\sigma_X = 3.0$, $\mu_X = 8.6$, and $\mu_Y = 12.0$.
   Determine Y' for an X value of

   a. 2
   b. 8
   c. 5

4. If $\rho = -0.60$, find the z score in Y that should be predicted for

   a. a score ½ standard deviation below the mean in X
   b. $z_X = 1.5$
   c. a score equal to the mean of X

5. Consider the following data:

X	Y
22	12
16	16
16	11
15	13
13	10
11	9
11	12
9	7
7	3
4	2

   a. Calculate Pearson's ρ using the raw-score formula and the deviation score formula.
   b. How much of the variance is accounted for by the correlation between the two variables?

6. Using the data in Exercise 5, calculate the slope (b) and the Y intercept (a) to determine the predicted Y values for each of the following given X values.
   a. $X = 9$
   b. $X = 13$
   c. $X = 17$

7. Consider the following data:

X	Y	X	Y
43	19	72	46
49	18	73	40
52	23	77	53
61	27	77	52
64	34	78	40
65	21	80	69
70	45	83	67

    a. Calculate Pearson's ρ using the deviation score formula.

    b. Determine the slope (b) and the Y intercept (a) for the above data.

    c. Plot the regression line.

8. A researcher finds that the correlation between psychological disorder in mothers and psychological disorder in their children is 0.45. The correlation between psychological disorder in fathers and their children is 0.25. The correlation between parents in terms of disorder is 0.15. Determine the multiple correlation where the child's psychological health is the criterion and the psychological health of the parents are the predictor variables.

9. If the correlation between the IQs of mothers and their children is 0.50, the correlation between the IQs of fathers and their children is 0.45, and the correlation between the IQs of parents is 0.35, determine the multiple correlation using the child's IQ as the criterion variable.

10. Using the data from Exercise 9, predict the IQ of a child whose mother's IQ is 132 and whose father's IQ is 125. Assume that the mean and standard deviation of each distribution of IQs is 100 and 15, respectively.

Choosing the Appropriate Test of Significance

LEARNING OBJECTIVES

After reading this chapter, you should be able to do the following:

1. Choose the appropriate parametric test of significance for a given research problem.
2. Choose the appropriate nonparametric test of significance for a given research problem.

Congratulations! Here we are at the end of our journey. Elsewhere in this book, I talk about the important distinction between *doing a statistical analysis* and *determining which analysis should be done*, given the nature of the data and the research question. In this book, I have tried to teach you how to do a lot of statistical analyses even though it is very unlikely that you will ever do any of these again! You will use computer software, like I do. Far more important than actually doing the analysis is knowing which one should be done. But I do not believe you can be competent at determining the appropriate analysis without first knowing exactly how each is done.

Beginning in Chapter 9, I started to teach you how to choose the appropriate analysis for a given research problem. In this final chapter, you will use your skills to examine various research problems and determine which analysis, of all the tests of significance you have learned, is the most appropriate. But before we begin, read each of the statements below that I have taken from various newspapers and magazines, and think about what the statements mean given what you now know about statistics and research.

> *High heels pose high risk!*
>
> *Women can tell which guys might be interested in becoming dads just by looking at their faces!*
>
> *Guaranteed improvement in 30 days or less!*
>
> *Lesbians' brains vary from those of straight women.*
>
> *. . . guaranteed to reduce the appearance of fine lines and wrinkles!*
>
> *No other product does a better job at disinfecting than . . .*
>
> *Preferred by eight out of 10 doctors, for pain relief*
>
> *I lost 30 lbs in 10 days! (results not typical, your results will vary)*

Nonparametric Versus Parametric Analysis

As we have learned how to decide which test of significance is appropriate, this decision-making process has become more complicated. In this chapter, we will go through the steps involved in deciding which we should use of all the tests of significance we have studied. This is meant to be a guide in decision making only. For example, parametric analyses, although robust, may not be appropriate when their assumptions are badly violated. It isn't possible to cover all the intricacies involved in selecting the appropriate statistical analysis here, but this chapter should help you with many common research problems and data types.

A progression of questions and answers has to be dealt with when choosing the most appropriate test of significance. The first step is to determine what kinds of data have been collected by the investigator. We need to decide among three possibilities.

First, if the data are *measures of performance* where means will be computed to compare groups, then we will usually choose a parametric test. Parametric tests of significance test hypotheses about specific population parameters such as the population mean or the difference between population means. These tests assume that measurement is at least on an interval scale and that the population distributions are normal with equal variability.

When the research design or the type of data do not permit us to make the assumptions necessary for a parametric approach, we should use a **nonparametric technique** to analyze the data. Nonparametric techniques have weaker assumptions. Parametric analyses can tolerate some violations of their assumptions and may be more powerful than their nonparametric counterparts. Much of the time, though, nonparametric tests are more powerful than the parametric approach if violations of parametric analysis are serious, such as *unequal sample sizes* and *heterogeneity of variances*. In such situations, we may choose to convert our measurement data to ranks. Deciding whether parametric assumptions have been violated is a difficult process, and I will not include such examples here.

Second, if the data are not measures but are *rank-order data*, we will choose a nonparametric test.

Third, if the data are neither rank orders nor measures, we need to determine if they are *frequency counts*. When the observations are frequency counts, percentages, or proportions, we will likely be interested in a chi-square analysis.

Once the kind of data has been determined, we continue with the steps in choosing the appropriate test.

Nonparametric techniques: Used to make inferences about entire populations rather than population parameters; fewer assumptions about the nature of the data are made compared with parametric techniques

ALERT

Remember that categorical data are data in which participants have been classified on some variable. In other words, the performance measures of participants are not analyzed per se, but rather are used to classify participants into categories.

Choosing the Appropriate Parametric Test of Significance

To determine the appropriate procedure to test a parametric hypothesis, several questions must be answered about the nature of the data and research design.

The flow diagram in Figure 18.1 shows the progression of steps we follow when deciding on the appropriate parametric test.

Let's go through each step involved in deciding which test is most appropriate.

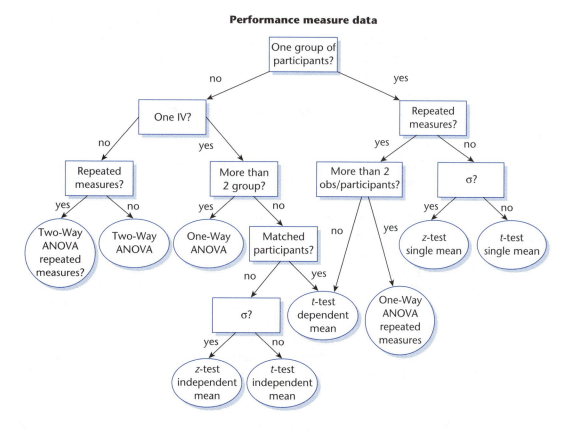

Figure 18.1.   Choosing the appropriate parametric test of significance.

Let's use this step-by-step approach to determine the appropriate test of significance for the following examples.

Example A: A sociologist wishes to compare the annual salaries of American men and women in similar occupations. She randomly selects 35 women from a variety of occupational groups. She randomly selects a man in the same occupation as each woman to a second group. She wishes to determine if women and men get "equal pay for equal work."

Step 1. How many groups?

The sociologist wishes to compare the salaries of men and women in similar occupations. She has two groups in her study.

Step 2. How many independent variables?

The issue is whether salary depends on gender. Although gender, as you may recall from Chapter 1, is not a true independent variable but rather an organismic variable, you may treat it as an independent variable as far as our statistical analysis is concerned.

Step 3. Are participants matched or independently assigned?

Because the sociologist did not independently assign participants to groups but rather matched her participants according to occupation, you will run a *t test for dependent means* on the salary data.

Example B: A research team composed of a nutritionist, a physician, a physical education expert, and a sports psychologist developed an exercise and diet program designed to improve physical fitness. They randomly select 30 people to participate in the program and 30 others to serve as a control group. The physical fitness of all participants is measured first. Physical fitness of the experimental participants is measured again halfway through the program, at the end of the program, and 6 months later. The participants in the control group are evaluated at the same times as the experimental participants. The researchers are interested in whether the experimental participants improve in fitness and, if so, whether any gains in physical fitness are maintained once the program is finished.

Step 1. There is more than one group of participants: an experimental and a control group.

One group in the experiment	If there is only one group of participants, then you must determine whether each participant provides one observation or more than one observation. In other words, you have to determine if repeated measures have been taken.
One group— repeated measures	If each participant contributes more than one data point, then simply determine how many measures each participant contributes. If each participant contributes two observations, you run a t test for dependent samples. If each participant contributes more than two observations, you run a one-way ANOVA with repeated measures.
One group— no repeated measures	If you have determined that each participant in the group provides only one data point or observation, then you should run a z test or a t test for the population mean. A z test is appropriate when the population standard deviation is known, and a t test is appropriate if it must be estimated.
More than one group in the experiment	If you have two or more groups in the study, you must determine how many independent variables are involved. Do you have several groups of participants under different levels of one independent variable, or do you have groups being treated with more than one independent variable?
One independent variable	With more than two groups of participants, each group under a different level of a single independent variable, you have only one test of significance to choose: One-way ANOVA. With only two groups of participants, you need to determine whether participants have been matched, that is, a matched-groups design. If they have, you run a t test for dependent means. If participants have not been matched but, rather, have been independently assigned to the two groups, you have one more question to answer. If you know the population standard deviations, you run a z test for the difference between means. If you do not know the population standard deviations, you run a t test for independent means.
Two independent variables	If you determine that the experimental design involves two independent variables, then you run an analysis of variance. If participants have been randomly and independently assigned to all levels of both independent variables, you choose a two-way ANOVA. If one of the independent variables involves measures on the same participants, that is, a repeated measures design, then you run a two-way ANOVA with repeated measures.

Step 2. This example has two independent variables. One independent variable is participation in the fitness program. The other is time of testing. This study is a pretest–posttest kind of study. Recall that the dependent variable, fitness, is measured at different times throughout and after the program for both groups of participants.

Step 3. You are testing the same participants for fitness at different times, so you have a repeated measures design. Measures are repeated on the time-of-testing variable. You run a *two-way mixed ANOVA*, with participation in the program as the between-participants variable and time of measurement as the within-participants variable.

Example C: The mayor of a small town in Kennebunkport is concerned about the standard of living of his townspeople. From U.S. census data, he discovers that the mean income of people living in similar small towns across the country is $42 000 with a standard deviation of $6 500. He randomly selects 100 people from the census files for his town and records the annual income of each. He finds the mean income of his sample is only $38 000. How would he determine if the residents of Kennebunkport earn significantly less than other Americans living in similar small towns?

Step 1. This study is a good exercise in differentiating between a sample and a population. Many students think that there are two groups: one from Kennebunkport and the other from towns across the United States. However, the mayor randomly selected one group of participants from his town, and that is the sample. The information obtained from the census is population information. The mayor did not randomly select participants from towns across the United States. Rather, he is asking whether the people in his town are a random sample from the population of all townspeople.

Step 2. There are no repeated measures in this study. The mayor recorded income for each member of his sample.

Step 3. You do know the population standard deviation, and so you will run a *z test for a single mean*. The mayor wants to know if his townspeople differ in annual income from all Americans living in similar small towns.

Choosing the Appropriate Nonparametric Test of Significance

Let's now go through the decision-making steps to choose the appropriate nonparametric test of significance. We will first consider situations in which the data do not satisfy the requirements of a parametric approach.

Testing for Identical Rank-Order Populations

The following flow diagram (Figure 18.2) illustrates the steps involved in choosing the appropriate test of significance when data are rank orders.

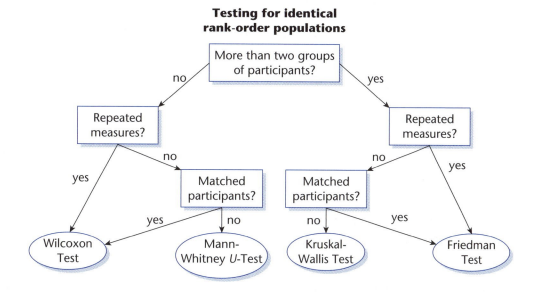

Figure 18.2.   Choosing the appropriate test for rank-order data.

Let's go through each step involved in deciding which test is most appropriate.

More than two groups in the experiment	You must determine if repeated measures have been taken or if participants have been matched.
Repeated measures or matched participants	Use the *Friedman test*, the nonparametric alternative to the one-way repeated measures ANOVA.
No repeated measures/ participants not matched	The appropriate analysis is the *Kruskal-Wallis procedure*. This is analogous to a one-way ANOVA.
Two groups or fewer in the experiment	You must determine if repeated measures have been taken or if participants have been matched in some way.
Repeated measures or matched participants	If participants have contributed more than one observation or participants have been matched, then you use the *Wilcoxon Signed-Ranks test*.
No repeated measures/ participants not matched	When participants have not been matched, run the nonparametric equivalent of a *t* test for independent groups, the *Mann-Whitney U test*.

Let's use our step-by-step approach to determine the appropriate test of significance for the following examples.

Example D: A rating scale was used to evaluate the morale of 15 employees at a meat-packing plant before and after several new policies regarding working conditions were put into effect. The psychologist in charge of this study wanted to know if the new policies improved morale.

Step 1. How many groups?

There is one group of 15 people in the study.

Step 2. Have repeated measures been taken?

Because each participant was tested before and after the new policies were implemented, this is a repeated-measures design. The appropriate analysis is a *Wilcoxon Signed-Ranks test*.

Example E: Five groups of eight rats each were used to investigate the effects of exercise on caloric intake. The exercise level of each group was controlled by access time to a running wheel. The lowest exercise group was allowed 2 minutes access to the wheel, the next group 5 minutes, the next group 8 minutes, and so on. Caloric intake was recorded for each animal in terms of the number of pellets of rat chow consumed per day.

Step 1. How many groups?

Because we have five groups of participants in this study we need go no farther. The appropriate nonparametric analysis is the *Kruskal-Wallis test*.

Example F: A graduate student in special education was interested in the effects of Spanish immersion education on the reading of Grade 1 children. She compared 18 children from a Spanish immersion program with 18 children in a regular Grade 1 program by recording the number of books each child borrowed from the library in a week.

Step 1. How many groups?

There are two groups of children in this study.

Step 2. Were repeated measures taken?

The children were measured once only.

Step 3. Were participants matched?

The children were not matched on a variable, and so the *Mann-Whitney U test* is the appropriate analysis for this study.

Example G: Three new reading programs were developed at an inner-city school in response to complaints from parents that their children were below average in reading skills. In order to evaluate the effectiveness of the new programs, children were randomly selected to participate in the study. Each child was evaluated for reading level and matched with two other children of equal ability. One child from each matched triad was randomly assigned to each of the three programs. After the program was completed, all the children were again evaluated for reading skills, and the results of this final evaluation were used to evaluate program effectiveness.

Step 1. How many groups?

There are three groups of participants in this study.

Step 2. Were repeated measures taken?

Although two measures were taken from each child, the first measure was used only to match children of equal ability. The statistical analysis was done only on the final measure of reading ability.

Step 3. Were participants matched?

Yes; the initial measure of reading ability was used to create triads of children with equal reading ability. This is a dependent-groups design and the appropriate analysis is the *Friedman test*, the nonparametric alternative to a one-way repeated measures ANOVA.

Testing for Differences Between Obtained and Expected Frequencies

When a research design uses percentage, proportion, or frequency as its measure, then a chi-square analysis is likely to be the most appropriate procedure. In these designs, participants are classified into categories based on some measure. Chi-square analyses compare obtained frequencies with those expected, given a particular hypothesis. Deciding which chi-square test is appropriate involves answering a series of questions about the nature of the data.

The following flow diagram (Figure 18.3) illustrates this process.

**Testing for differences between
obtained and expected frequencies**

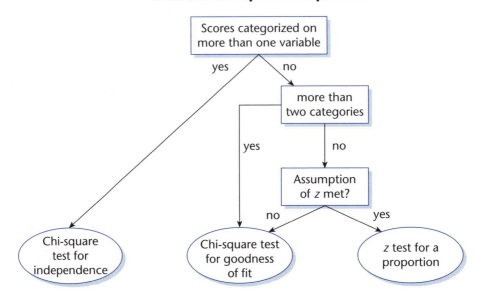

Figure 18.3.   Choosing the appropriate test for comparing obtained and expected
frequencies.

Let's go through the steps to decide on a chi-square analysis.

One variable classification	If the scores have been classified into categories or levels of one variable only, you must determine how many categories were used.
Two categories	With one variable and only two categories, you may run a *chi-square test for goodness of fit* with 1 *df*. If the assumptions required for a *z* test have been met, then a *z test for a proportion* is also an appropriate analysis.
More than two categories	With one variable and more than two categories, a *chi-square test for goodness of fit* is appropriate, with the number of degrees of freedom = number of categories −1.
Two variable classification	If the scores have been classified on two variables simultaneously and all categories are mutually exclusive, the appropriate analysis is a *chi-square test for independence*. The degrees of freedom = (number of rows - 1) (number of columns - 1).

Let's decide which test is appropriate for the following examples.

Example H: A San Francisco city planner, whose job involves making decisions about traffic over city bridges, decides to gather some data on bridge use. He wants to know if there is a difference in bridge use depending on the day of the week. He monitors flow over each of five bridges in the city by using a traffic counter to count the number of cars passing over each bridge 24 hours a day, 7 days a week.

Step 1. How many variables?

In this case, the city planner has two variables of interest, day of the week and bridge. He will run a *chi-square test for independence* to determine if bridge use depends on day of the week. He has 24 *df* (6×4).

Example I: A sociologist interviews 150 randomly selected citizens to determine their opinion about the Free Trade Agreement between Canada and the United States. She places each individual into one of five categories: (1) strongly in favor of, (2) moderately in favor of, (3) no opinion about, (4) moderately against, and (5) strongly against the Free Trade Agreement. She also places each individual into one of three socioeconomic groups: (1) upper class, (2) middle class, and (3) lower class. She is interested in knowing whether socioeconomic status and opinion are related.

Step 1. How many variables?

The researcher classified her participants simultaneously on two variables, (1) opinion and (2) socioeconomic status. She will run a *chi-square test for independence* with 8 *df*.

Example J: A blue-jeans manufacturer randomly selects 100 young women and asks them if they prefer stone-washed or acid-treated blue jeans. He wants to know if there is preference for one type of jean over the other.

Step 1. How many variables?

The women are classified on one variable: preference.

Step 2. How many categories?

There are two categories of the preference variable and so a *chi-square test for goodness of fit* ($df = 1$) is appropriate. *A z test for a proportion* is also appropriate.

Example K: A botanist plants 100 seeds in each of three planters. Each planter is exposed to different amounts of light for a 3-week period. She then counts the number of seeds that germinate under high-light, moderate-light, and low-light conditions.

Step 1. There is one variable: light condition.

Step 2. There are three categories of the light variable, and so a *chi-square test for goodness of fit* with 2 *df* will be used.

EXERCISES .

Part A: For each of the following research studies, determine the most appropriate parametric test of significance.

A.1. A research group of behavior analysts is interested in the effects of diet and exercise on the development of anorexia nervosa in laboratory animals. An initial study is designed to determine the effect of caloric intake and amount of exercise on weight loss. They randomly assign 12 laboratory rats to each of six treatment groups. Animals in three of the six groups receive a low-calorie diet; the rest receive a moderate-calorie diet. In addition, one group from each diet type is put on a low-exercise program, one group is put on a moderate-exercise program, and the last group is put on a high-exercise program. The researchers measure the weight of each animal before and after the program. They will use amount of weight loss as their measure.

A.2. A social psychologist is investigating group-helping behavior. She randomly assigns 20 participants to each of three groups. Each participant is left in a waiting room and told that the experimenter will arrive shortly. In the Alone group, participants are alone in the waiting room. In the One-Other group, the participant waits with another person who, unknown to the participant, is a confederate of the experimenter. In the Five-Others group, the real participant is in the waiting room with five other people, all confederates. Three minutes after the participant has been waiting, a loud crash and a moan are heard outside the waiting room. The confederates of the experiment ignore these sounds. The experimenter records how long it takes for the real participants to respond to the sounds of distress. She suspects that as the number of bystanders increases, so will the time taken to help.

A.3. A physician is interested in the relationship between maternal weight-gain and birth weight. Although the fashion has been for pregnant women to gain less weight than they used to, the physician is worried about the effects of this trend on the weight of newborns. She randomly selects 50 women from her practice. At the time of birth, she compares the weights of the newborns of the 35 women who gained 10 kg or more with the weights of the children born to the 15 women who gained less than 10 kg.

A.4. The principal of a bilingual school has decided to respond to the recent criticism that the children in French immersion are behind in certain areas of English, such as reading and writing. She hires a researcher, who randomly selects 20 French immersion children starting kindergarten and gives them a standard English language knowledge test. She gives the same English test to several children starting English kindergarten. Using these scores, she matches an English child with each French immersion child. At the end of Grade 1, she retests all the children with a standard English language knowledge test. She will compare the performance of the French immersion and English children on this last test.

Part B: For each of the following research studies, determine the most appropriate nonparametric test of significance.

B.1. Officials at a state college were concerned about class attendance. The dean of student services decided to do a study to see if attendance differed between faculties. She monitored classes on the sciences, the arts, and commerce and recorded student absences over a period of several weeks. Her data indicated that attendance was poorest in science classes. What nonparametric technique could she use to see if there was a significant difference in attendance?

B.2. A sports psychologist randomly selected 25 hockey season ticket holders in Edmonton, Alberta. She interviewed each hockey fan about the controversial Gretzky trade to Los Angeles immediately after the trade was announced in 1988, to determine if Edmontonians believed that it was Gretzky or the team owner, Peter Pocklington, who had initiated the trade. Twenty years later, the psychologist reinterviewed the 25 people to determine if their feelings beliefs had changed over the years.

B.3. Eight sets of identical twins suffering from a mild form of dyslexia participated in a study to investigate the effects of a new bio-feedback program on attention span. All of the children learned a series of tasks involving motor, perceptual, and cognitive skills. One twin from each set was given bio-feedback during the learning sessions; the other twin was not given bio-feedback. Several measures of the rate and quality of learning were taken. What nonparametric procedure should be used to evaluate the effectiveness of the bio-feedback training?

Part C: For each of the following research studies, determine the frequency test you would use and specify the number of degrees of freedom.

C.1. A day-care worker offers two kinds of toys to her group of 35 children. Action toys (such as building blocks, puzzles, etc.) require active participation on the part of the children. Cuddly toys (such as dolls, stuffed animals, etc.) fill a nurturing need. The day-care worker wonders if gender (girls vs. boys) makes a difference in choice (action vs. cuddly).

C.2. A professor of women's studies polls a random sample of 300 women and asks them how they feel about the abortion issue. She categorizes them into one of six groups based on whether they have any children (yes or no) and how they feel about abortion on demand (pro, con, or undecided). She wishes to know if having children makes a difference on how women feel about abortion on demand.

C.3. A researcher has found that twice as many middle-aged students prefer studying at home with correspondence courses as opposed to attending night school. She randomly selects 150 young students and asks them which they would prefer. She wants to know if the younger group resembles the older group in preference.

Toolbox

This appendix consists of two parts. The first section presents most of the computational formulas used in the text. I hope this section will be a handy reference. The second section contains the test summaries found in the text. Both sections are arranged in alphabetical order. You are encouraged to refer to the appropriate chapter before beginning any analysis.

Toolbox of Computational Formulas

One-Way Anova

Sums of Squares

Total

$$SS_{TOT} = \sum X_{tot}^2 - \frac{(\sum X_{tot})^2}{n_{tot}}$$

Between groups

$$SS_{BG} = \frac{(\sum X_1)^2}{n_1} + \frac{(\sum X_2)^2}{n_2} + \cdots + \frac{(\sum X_k)^2}{n_k} - \frac{(\sum X_{tot})^2}{n_{tot}}$$

Within groups

$$SS_{WG} = SS_{TOT} - SS_{BG}$$

Mean Squares

Between groups

$$MS_{BG} = \frac{SS_{BG}}{k-1}$$

Within groups

$$MS_{WG} = \frac{SS_{WG}}{n_{tot} - k}$$

F Ratio

$$F = \frac{MS_{BG}}{MS_{WG}}$$

Two-Way Anova

Sums of Squares

Total

$$SS_{TOT} = \Sigma X_{tot}^2 - \frac{(\Sigma X_{tot})^2}{n_{tot}}$$

Between groups

$$SS_{BG} = \frac{(\Sigma X_{A_1 B_1})^2 + (\Sigma X_{A_1 B_2})^2 + \cdots + (\Sigma X_{A_a B_b})^2}{n} - \frac{(\Sigma X_{tot})^2}{n_{tot}}$$

A

$$SS_A = \frac{(\Sigma X_{A_1})^2 + (\Sigma X_{A_2})^2 + \cdots + (\Sigma X_{A_a})^2}{bn} - \frac{(\Sigma X_{tot})^2}{n_{tot}}$$

B

$$SS_B = \frac{(\Sigma X_{B_1})^2 + (\Sigma X_{B_2})^2 + \cdots + (\Sigma X_{B_b})^2}{an} - \frac{(\Sigma X_{tot})^2}{n_{tot}}$$

$A \times B$

$$SS_{A \times B} = SS_{BG} - SS_A - SS_B$$

Within groups

$$SS_{WG} = SS_{TOT} - SS_{BG}$$

Mean Squares

$$MS_A = \frac{SS_A}{df_a}$$

$df_a = (a - 1)$, where a is the number of levels of A

$$MS_B = \frac{SS_B}{df_b}$$

$df_b = (b - 1)$, where b is the number of levels of B

$$MS_{A \times B} = \frac{SS_{A \times B}}{df_{a \times b}}$$

$df_{axb} = (df_{bg} - df_a - df_b)$ or $(df_a)(df_b)$

Within groups

$$MS_{WG} = \frac{SS_{WG}}{n_{tot} - k}$$

F Ratios

F for the *A* main effect
$$\frac{MS_A}{MS_{WG}}$$

F for the *B* main effect
$$\frac{MS_B}{MS_{WG}}$$

F for the interaction
$$\frac{MS_{A \times B}}{MS_{WG}}$$

One-Way Anova With Repeated Measures

Sums of Squares

Total
$$SS_{TOT} = \sum X_{tot}^2 - \frac{(\sum X_{tot})^2}{kn}$$

Between participant
$$SS_P = \frac{(\sum X_{P_1})^2 + (\sum X_{P_2})^2 + \cdots + (\sum X_{P_n})^2}{k} - \frac{(\sum X_{tot})^2}{kn}$$

Within participant
$$SS_{WP} = SS_{TOT} - SS_P$$

Treatment
$$SS_T = \frac{(\sum X_{T})^2 + (\sum X_{T_2})^2 + \cdots + (\sum X_{T_k})^2}{n} - \frac{(\sum X_{tot})^2}{kn}$$

Participant by treatment
$$SS_{P \times T} = SS_{WP} - SS_T$$

Mean Squares

Treatment
$$MS_T = \frac{SS_T}{k-1}$$

Participant by treatment
$$MS_{P \times T} = \frac{SS_{P \times T}}{(n-1)(k-1)}$$

F Ratio

$$F = \frac{MS_T}{MS_{S \times T}}$$

Two-Way Anova With Repeated Measures

Sums of Squares

Total

$$SS_{TOT} = \sum X^2_{tot} - \frac{(\sum X_{tot})^2}{abn}$$

Between participants

$$SS_P = \frac{(\sum X_{p_1})^2 + (\sum X_{p_2})^2 + \cdots + (\sum X_{p_{an}})^2}{b} - \frac{(\sum X_{tot})^2}{abn}$$

A

$$SS_A = \frac{(\sum X_{a_1})^2 + (\sum X_{a_2})^2 + \cdots + (\sum X_{a_a})^2}{bn} - \frac{(\sum X_{tot})^2}{abn}$$

Participants within groups

$$SS_{P(gps)} = SS_P - SS_A$$

Within participants

$$SS_{WP} = SS_{TOT} - SS_P$$

B

$$SS_B = \frac{(\sum X_{b_1})^2 + (\sum X_{b_2})^2 + \cdots + (\sum X_{b_b})^2}{an} - \frac{(\sum X_{tot})^2}{abn}$$

$A \times B$

$$SS_{A \times B} = \frac{(\sum X_{a_1 b_1})^2 + (\sum X_{a_1 b_2})^2 + \cdots + (\sum X_{a_a b_b})^2}{n}$$

$$- \frac{(\sum X_{tot})^2}{abn} - SS_A - SS_B$$

Participants within groups

$$SS_{P(gps) \times B} = SS_{WP} - SS_B - SS_{A \times B}$$

Mean Squares

A

$$MS_A = \frac{SS_A}{a-1}$$

Participants within groups $\times B$

$$MS_{P(gps)} = \frac{SS_{P(gps)}}{a(n-1)}$$

B

$$MS_B = \frac{SS_B}{b-1}$$

$A \times B$

$$MS_{A \times B} = \frac{SS_{A \times B}}{(a-1)(b-1)}$$

Participants within groups $\times B$

$$MS_{P(gps) \times B} = \frac{SS_{P(gps) \times B}}{a(n-1)(b-1)}$$

F Ratios

$$F_A = \frac{MS_A}{MS_{P(gps)}}$$

$$F_B = \frac{MS_B}{MS_{P(gps) \times B}}$$

$$F_{A \times B} = \frac{MS_{A \times B}}{MS_{P(gps) \times B}}$$

Chi-Square Formula

$$\chi^2 = \Sigma \frac{(0-E)^2}{E}$$

Combinations

$$_nC_r = \frac{n!}{r!(n-r)!r!}$$

Confidence Intervals

Difference

$$(\mu_1 - \mu_2) = (\bar{X}_1 - \bar{X}_2) \pm z_{crit}(\sigma_{\bar{x}_1 - \bar{x}_2})$$

Mean

$$\mu = \bar{X} \pm z_{crit}\sigma_{\bar{x}}$$

Proportion

$$P = p \pm z_{crit}(\sigma_p)$$

When σ is estimated with *s*

Difference-Independent

$$(\mu_1 - \mu_2) = (\bar{X}_1 - \bar{X}_2) \pm t_{crit}(s_{\bar{x}_1 - \bar{x}_2})$$

Difference-Dependent

$$\mu_{\bar{D}} = \bar{D} \pm t_{crit}(s_{\bar{D}})$$

Mean

$$\mu = \bar{X} \pm t_{crit}s_{\bar{x}}$$

Deviation Score

$$X - \mu$$

Friedman Test Statistic

$$\chi_r^2 = \frac{12}{nk(k+1)} \left[(\Sigma R_1)^2 + (\Sigma R_2)^2 + (\Sigma R_3)^2 + \cdots + (\Sigma R_k)^2 \right] - 3n(k-1)$$

Kruskal-Wallis *H*

$$H = \frac{12}{n_{tot}(n_{tot}+1)} \left[\frac{(\Sigma R_1)^2}{n_1} + \frac{(\Sigma R_2)^2}{n_2} + \cdots + \frac{(\Sigma R_k)^2}{n_k} \right] - 3(n_{tot}+1)$$

Mann-Whitney *U*

$$U_1 = n_1 n_2 + \frac{n_1(n_1+1)}{2} - \Sigma R_1$$

$$U_2 = n_1 n_2 + \frac{n_2(n_2+1)}{2} - \Sigma R_2$$

Mean

Population

Raw score

$$\mu = \frac{\Sigma X}{N}$$

Data in a frequency distribution

$$\mu = \frac{\Sigma fX}{N}$$

Mean for combined subgroups

when sums are known

$$\mu_c = \frac{\Sigma X + \Sigma Y}{N_x + N_y}$$

when means are known

$$\mu_c = \frac{N_x \mu_x + N_y \mu_y}{N_x + N_y}$$

when $N_x = N_y$

$$\mu_c = \frac{\mu_x + \mu_y}{2}$$

Sample

Raw score

$$\bar{X} = \frac{\sum X}{n}$$

Data in a frequency distribution

$$\bar{X} = \frac{\sum fX}{n}$$

Median

$$Mdn = L + \frac{\left[N\left(\dfrac{50}{100}\right) - cf_b \right]i}{f_w}$$

Pearson's Coefficient of Correlation

Raw score

$$\rho = \frac{\sum XY - (\sum X)(\sum Y)/N}{\sqrt{(SS_X)(SS_Y)}}$$

Deviation score

$$\rho = \frac{\sum \left[(X - \mu_X)(Y - \mu_Y) \right]}{\sqrt{(SS_X)(SS_Y)}}$$

z score

$$\rho = \frac{\sum (z_X z_Y)}{N}$$

When estimating ρ with r:

$$r = \frac{\sum XY - (\sum X)(\sum Y)/n}{\sqrt{(SS_X)(SS_Y)}}$$

Percentile

$$P_{PR} = L + \frac{\left[N\left(\dfrac{PR}{100}\right) - cf_b \right]i}{f_w}$$

Percentile Rank

$$PR_X = \frac{\left[f_w\left(\dfrac{X - L}{i}\right) - cf_b \right]100}{N}$$

Permutations

$$_nP_r = \frac{n!}{(n-r)!}$$

Probability

Binomial Probability

$$_nC_r p^r q^{n-r} = \frac{n!}{(n-r)!r!}p^r q^{n-r}$$

Compound

Dependent events

$$p(A \text{ and } B) = p(A) \bullet p(B \mid A)$$

Independent events

$$p(A \text{ and } B) = p(A) \bullet p(B)$$

$p(A \text{ or } B)$

Not mutually exclusive

$$p(A) + p(B) - p(A \text{ and } B)$$

Mutually exclusive

$$p(A) + p(B)$$

Conditional

$$p(B \mid A) = \frac{\# B \mid A \text{ has occurred}}{\# O \mid A \text{ has occurred}}$$

Simple

$$p(A) = \frac{\# A}{\# O}$$

Range

$$H - L + 1$$

Regression Formulas

Simple Linear Regression

Raw score

$$Y' = \rho\left(\frac{\sigma_Y}{\sigma_X}\right)X - \rho\left(\frac{\sigma_Y}{\sigma_X}\right)\mu_X + \mu_Y$$

Deviation score

$$(Y - \mu_Y)' = \rho\left(\frac{\sigma_Y}{\sigma_X}\right)(X - \mu_X)$$

z score

$$z_{Y'} = \rho z_X$$

Slope of the regression line

$$b = \rho\left(\frac{\sigma_Y}{\sigma_X}\right)$$

Slope for raw data

$$b = \frac{\sum XY - (\sum X)(\sum Y)/N}{\sum X^2 - (\sum X)^2/N}$$

Intercept of the regression line

$$a = -\rho\left(\frac{\sigma_Y}{\sigma_X}\right)\mu_X + \mu_Y$$

Multiple Regression

Multiple correlation coefficient

$$MR = \sqrt{\frac{\rho_{Y_1}^2 + \rho_{Y_2}^2 - 2\rho_{Y_1}\rho_{Y_2}\rho_{X_1 X_2}}{1 - \rho_{X_1 X_2}^2}}$$

Multiple regression equation

$$Y' = b_1 X_1 + b_2 X_2 + a$$

Partial correlation

$$R_P = \frac{\rho_{Y_1} - \rho_{Y_2}\rho_{X_1 X_2}}{\sqrt{(1 - \rho_{Y_2}^2)(1 - \rho_{X_1 X_2}^2)}}$$

Scheffé

F' statistic

$$F' = \frac{C}{s_c}$$

Scheffé's critical F

$$F_s = \sqrt{(k-1)F_{crit}}$$

Comparison

$$C = c_1\bar{X}_1 + c_2\bar{X}_2 + \cdots + c_k\bar{X}_k$$

Standard error

$$s_c = \sqrt{MS_{error}\left(\frac{c_1^2}{n_1} + \frac{c_2^2}{n_2} + \cdots + \frac{c_k^2}{n_k}\right)}$$

Spearman Rank-Order Correlation Coefficient

$$rho = 1 - \frac{6\sum d^2}{n(n^2 - 1)}$$

Standard Deviation

Population

Raw data

$$\sigma = \sqrt{\frac{\sum X^2 - (\sum X)^2/N}{N}}$$

Data in frequency distribution

$$\sigma = \sqrt{\frac{\sum fX^2 - (\sum fX)^2/N}{N}}$$

Estimate of σ

$$s = \sqrt{\frac{SS}{n-1}} = \sqrt{\frac{\sum X^2 - (\sum X)^2/n}{n-1}}$$

Standard Errors for z Tests

Difference

$$\sigma_{\bar{X}_1 - \bar{X}_2} = \sqrt{\frac{SS_1 + SS_2}{n_1 + n_2}\left(\frac{1}{n_1} + \frac{1}{n_2}\right)}$$

$$\sigma_{\bar{X}_1 - \bar{X}_2} = \sqrt{\frac{SS_1 + SS_2}{n(n)}} \quad \text{if } n_1 = n_2$$

where $SS = \sum X^2 - \left(\sum X\right)^2 / n$

Mean

$$\sigma_{\bar{X}} = \frac{\sigma}{\sqrt{n}}$$

Proportion

$$\sigma_P = \sqrt{\frac{PQ}{n}}$$

Standard Errors: Estimates for t Tests

Difference

Independent samples

$$s_{\bar{X}_1 - \bar{X}_2} = \sqrt{s_{\bar{X}_1}^2 + s_{\bar{X}_2}^2}$$

$$s_{\bar{X}_1 - \bar{X}_2} = \sqrt{\frac{SS_1 + SS_2}{n_1 + n_2}\left(\frac{1}{n_1} + \frac{1}{n_2}\right)} \quad n_1 \neq n_2$$

$$s_{\bar{X}_1 - \bar{X}_2} = \sqrt{\frac{SS_1 + SS_2}{n(n-1)}} \quad n_1 = n_2$$

where $SS = \sum X^2 - \dfrac{\left(\sum X\right)^2}{n}$

Dependent samples

$$s_{\bar{D}} = \sqrt{\frac{\sum D^2 - \left(\sum D\right)^2 / n}{n(n-1)}}$$

Mean

$$s_{\bar{X}} = \frac{s}{\sqrt{n}} = \sqrt{\frac{SS}{n(n-1)}}$$

Standard Error of Estimate

$$\sigma_{YX} = \sqrt{\frac{\sum(Y - Y')^2}{N}} = \sigma_Y\sqrt{1 - \rho^2}$$

Standard Error of Multiple Estimate

$$\sigma_{ME} = \sigma_Y \sqrt{1 - MR^2}$$

Standard Error for Pearson's r

$$s_r = \sqrt{\frac{1 - r^2}{n - 2}}$$

t Ratios

Population mean $\qquad t = \dfrac{\overline{X} - \mu_{\overline{X}}}{s_{\overline{X}}}$

Difference between means

Independent means $\qquad t = \dfrac{\overline{X}_1 - \overline{X}_2}{s_{\overline{X}_1 - \overline{X}_2}}$

Dependent means $\qquad t = \dfrac{\overline{D} - \mu_{\overline{D}}}{s_{\overline{D}}}$

r $\qquad t = \dfrac{r - \rho}{s_r}$

Planned comparison $\qquad t = \dfrac{\overline{X}_1 - \overline{X}_2}{\sqrt{2MS_{error} / n}}$

Treatment Effect Estimates

Cohen's $d = \dfrac{M_1 - M_2}{SD}$

Eta squared $\eta^2 = \dfrac{SS_{treatment}}{SS_{total}}$

Coefficient of determination

$$\frac{\text{Variance in } Y \text{ associated with change in } X}{\text{Total } Y \text{ Variance}} = \frac{\sigma_{Y'}^2}{\sigma_Y^2} = \rho^2$$

Tukey

$$HSD = q(\alpha, df_{error}, k)\sqrt{MS_{error} / n}$$

Variance

Population

Raw score

$$\sigma^2 = \frac{\sum X^2 - (\sum X)^2 / N}{N}$$

Data in frequency distribution

$$\sigma^2 = \frac{\sum fX^2 - (\sum fX)^2 / N}{N}$$

Pooled variance for three combined subgroups

$$\sigma_c^2 = \frac{N_W \sigma_W^2 + N_X \sigma_X^2 + N_Y \sigma_Y^2 + N_W (\mu_W - \mu_c)^2 + N_X (\mu_X - \mu_c)^2 + N_Y (\mu_Y - \mu_c)^2}{N_W + N_X + N_Y}$$

Estimate of σ^2

$$s^2 = \frac{\sum X^2 - (\sum X)^2 / n}{n - 1}$$

Wilcoxon

$$z = \frac{T - \mu_T}{\sigma_T}$$

z Ratios

Difference

$$z = \frac{\bar{X}_1 - \bar{X}_2}{\sigma_{\bar{X}_1 - \bar{X}_2}}$$

Mean

$$z = \frac{\bar{X} - \mu_{\bar{X}}}{\sigma_{\bar{X}}}$$

Proportion

$$z = \frac{p - P}{\sqrt{PQ / n}}$$

Score

$$z = \frac{X - \mu}{\sigma}$$

Mann-Whitney *U*

$$z = \frac{U - n_1 n_2 / 2}{\sqrt{\dfrac{n_1 n_2 (n_1 + n_2 + 1)}{12}}}$$

Wilcoxon *T*

$$z = \frac{T - n(n+1) / 4}{\sqrt{\dfrac{n(n+1)(2n+1)}{24}}}$$

Toolbox of Test Summaries

SUMMARY OF ONE-WAY ANOVA

Hypotheses

H_0: No main effects and no interaction.
H_1: H_0 is false.

Assumptions

1. Participants are randomly selected and independently assigned to groups.
2. Population distributions are normal.
3. Population variances are homogeneous.

Decision Rules

$df_a = a - 1$
$df_b = b - 1$
$df_{a \times b} = (a - 1)(b - 1)$
If $F_{obt} \geq F_{crit}$ reject the H_0
If $F_{obt} < F_{crit}$ do not reject H_0

Formula

$$F \text{ for the } A \text{ main effect} = \frac{MS_A}{MS_{WG}}$$

$$F \text{ for the } B \text{ main effect} = \frac{MS_B}{MS_{WG}}$$

$$F \text{ for the interaction} = \frac{MS_{A \times B}}{MS_{WG}}$$

SUMMARY OF ONE-WAY ANOVA WITH REPEATED MEASURES

Hypotheses

$H_0 : \mu_1 = \mu_2 = \cdots = \mu_k$
$H_1 : H_0$ is false

Assumptions

1. Participants are randomly selected.
2. Population distributions are normal.
3. Population variances are homogeneous.
4. Population covariances are equal.

Decision Rules

$df_t = k - 1$

$df_{p \times t} = (n-1)(k-1)$

If $F_{obt} \geq F_{crit}$ reject H_0

If $F_{obt} < F_{crit}$ do not reject H_0

Formula

$$F = \frac{MS_T}{MS_{P \times T}}$$

SUMMARY OF TWO-WAY ANOVA MIXED DESIGN

Hypotheses

H_0: No main effects and no interaction.
H_1: H_0 is false.

Assumptions

1. Participants are randomly selected with repeated measures on Factor B.
2. Population distributions are normal.
3. Population variances are homogeneous.
4. Population covariances are equal.

Decision Rules

$df_a = a - 1$

$df_b = b - 1$

$df_{a \times b} = (a-1)(b-1)$

$df_{p(gps)} = a(n-1)$

$df_{p(gps) \times b} = a(n-1)(b-1)$

If $F_{obt} \geq F_{crit}$ reject the H_0

If $F_{obt} < F_{crit}$ do not reject H_0

Formula

$$F_A = \frac{MS_A}{MS_{P(gps)}}$$

$$F_B = \frac{MS_B}{MS_{P(gps) \times B}}$$

$$F_{A \times B} = \frac{MS_{A \times B}}{MS_{P(gps) \times B}}$$

SUMMARY OF THE CHI-SQUARE TEST FOR GOODNESS OF FIT

Hypotheses

$H_0 : Os = Es$

$H_1 : Os \neq Es$

Assumptions

1. Participants are randomly selected.
2. Categories are mutually exclusive.

Decision Rules

$df = $ number of categories $- 1$

If $\chi^2_{obt} \geq \chi^2_{crit}$ reject H_0

If $\chi^2_{obt} < \chi^2_{crit}$ do not reject H_0

Formula

$$\chi^2 = \sum \frac{(O - E)^2}{E}$$

SUMMARY OF THE CHI-SQUARE TEST FOR INDEPENDENCE

Hypotheses

H_0: The variables are independent.
H_1: The variables are dependent.

Assumptions

1. Participants are randomly selected.
2. Observations have been classified simultaneously on two independent categories.

Decision Rules

$df = $ (number of rows $- 1$)(number of columns $- 1$)

If $\chi^2_{obt} \geq \chi^2_{crit}$ reject H_0

If $\chi^2_{obt} < \chi^2_{crit}$ do not reject H_0

Formula

$$\chi^2 = \sum \frac{(O - E)^2}{E}$$

SUMMARY OF THE FRIEDMAN TEST

Hypotheses

H_0: Populations are identical.
H_1: Populations are not identical.

Assumptions

1. Participants are randomly selected.
2. Same or matched participants.
3. Measurement scale is ordinal.

Decision Rules

If $\chi_r^2 \geq \chi_{crit}^2$ reject the H_0

If $\chi_r^2 < \chi_{crit}^2$ do not reject the H_0

Formula

$$X_r^2 = \frac{12}{nk(k+1)}\left[(\sum R_1)^2 + (\sum R_2)^2 + (\sum R_3)^2 + \cdots + (\sum R_k)^2\right] - 3n(k+1)$$

SUMMARY OF THE KRUSKAL-WALLIS TEST

Hypotheses

H_0: Populations are identical.
H_1: Populations are not identical.

Assumptions

1. Participants are randomly selected and independently assigned to groups.
2. Measurement scale is ordinal.

Decision Rules

$df = k - 1$

If $H_{obt} \geq \chi^2_{crit}$ reject the H_0

If $H_{obt} < \chi^2_{crit}$ do not reject the H_0

Formula

$$H = \frac{12}{n_{tot}(n_{tot}+1)}\left[\frac{(\sum R_1)^2}{n_1} + \frac{(\sum R_2)^2}{n_2} + \cdots + \frac{(\sum R_k)^2}{n_k}\right] - 3(n_{tot}+1)$$

where k is the number of columns of ranked scores

n is the number of rows, that is, the number of participants or matched participants

$\sum R$ is the sum of the ranks in a column

SUMMARY OF THE MANN-WHITNEY U TEST

Hypotheses

H_0: Populations are identical.
H_1: Populations are not identical.

Assumptions

1. Participants are randomly selected and independently assigned to groups.
2. Measurement scale is ordinal.

Decision Rules

If $U_{obt} < U_{crit}$ reject the H_0

If $U_{obt} \geq U_{crit}$ do not reject the H_0

Formula

$$U_1 = n_1 n_2 + \frac{n_1(n_1 + 1)}{2} - \sum R_1$$

$$U_2 = n_1 n_2 + \frac{n_2(n_2 + 1)}{2} - \sum R_2$$

U_{obt} is the smaller of U_1 and U_2

SUMMARY OF THE PEARSON CORRELATION TEST

Hypotheses

H_0: $\rho = 0$

H_1: $\rho \neq 0, \rho < 0, \rho > 0$

Assumptions

1. Participants are randomly selected.
2. Both populations are normally distributed.

Decision Rules

If $t_{obt} \geq t_{crit}$ reject H_0

If $t_{obt} < t_{crit}$ do not reject H_0

Formula

$$t = \frac{r - \rho}{s_r}$$

SUMMARY OF PLANNED COMPARISONS

Hypotheses

H_0: No difference between population means.
H_1: H_0 is false.

Assumptions

The outcome of the ANOVA need not be significant.

Decision Rules

If $t_{obt} \geq t_{crit}$ reject H_0

If $t_{obt} < t_{crit}$ do not reject H_0

Formula

$$t = \frac{\bar{X}_1 - \bar{X}_2}{\sqrt{2MS_{error} / n}}$$

SUMMARY OF THE SCHEFFÉ TEST

Hypotheses

H_0: No difference between population means.
H_1: H_0 is false.

Assumptions

The outcome of the ANOVA was significant.

Decision Rules

If $F' \geq F_s$ reject the H_0

If $F' < F_s$ do not reject H_0

Formula

$F' = C / s_c$

$F_s = \sqrt{(k-1)F_{crit}}$

SUMMARY OF THE SPEARMAN RANK-ORDER CORRELATION TEST

Hypotheses

H_0: $Rho = 0$
H_1: $Rho \neq 0$, $Rho < 0$, $Rho > 0$

Assumptions

1. Participants are randomly selected.
2. Observations are rank-ordered.

Decision Rules

n = number of pairs of ranks

If $rho_{obt} \geq rho_{crit}$ reject H_0

If $rho_{obt} < rho_{crit}$ do not reject H_0

Formula

$$rho = 1 - \frac{6 \sum d^2}{n(n^2 - 1)}$$

SUMMARY OF t TEST FOR A SINGLE MEAN

Hypotheses

H_0: μ = specified value
H_1: $\mu \neq$, or $<$, or $>$ specified value

Assumptions

1. Participants are randomly selected.
2. Population distribution is normal.

Decision Rules

$df = n - 1$

If $t_{obt} \geq t_{crit}$ reject the H_0

If $t_{obt} < t_{crit}$ do not reject H_0

Formula

$$t = \frac{\bar{X} - \mu}{s_{\bar{X}}}$$

SUMMARY OF t TEST FOR DEPENDENT MEANS

Hypotheses

H_0: $\mu_1 = \mu_2$
H_1: $\mu_1 \neq \mu_2$, $\mu_1 < \mu_2$, $\mu_1 > \mu_2$

Assumptions

1. Participants are randomly selected.
2. Population distributions are normal.
3. Population variances are homogeneous.
4. Repeated measures or matched participants are used.

Decision Rules

$df = n_{pairs} - 1$

If $t_{obt} \geq t_{crit}$ reject H_0

If $t_{obt} < t_{crit}$ do not reject H_0

Formula

$$t = \frac{\bar{D}}{s_{\bar{D}}}$$

SUMMARY OF t TEST FOR INDEPENDENT MEANS

Hypotheses

H_0: $\mu_1 = \mu_2$
H_1: $\mu_1 \neq \mu_2$, $\mu_1 < \mu_2$, $\mu_1 > \mu_2$

Assumptions

1. Participants are randomly selected and independently assigned to groups.
2. Population variances are homogenous.
3. Population distributions are normal.

Decision Rules

$df = n_1 + n_2 - 2$

If $t_{obt} \geq t_{crit}$ reject H_0

If $t_{obt} < t_{crit}$ do not reject H_0

Formula

$$t = \frac{\bar{X}_1 - \bar{X}_2}{s_{\bar{X}_1 - \bar{X}_2}}$$

SUMMARY OF THE TUKEY TEST

Hypotheses

H_0: No difference between population means.
H_1: H_0 is false.

Assumptions

The outcome of the ANOVA was significant.

Decision Rules

Any mean difference $\geq$HSD, reject the H_0

Formula

$$\text{HSD} = q(\alpha, df_{error}, k)\sqrt{MS_{error} / n}$$

SUMMARY OF THE WILCOXON SIGNED-RANKS TEST

Hypotheses

H_0: Populations are identical.
H_1: Populations are not identical.

Assumptions

1. Participants are randomly selected.
2. Same or matched participants.
3. Measurement scale is ordinal.

Decision Rules

If $T_{obt} \leq T_{crit}$ reject the H_0

If $T_{obt} > T_{crit}$ do not reject the H_0

Formula

n is the number of pairs with nonzero differences.
T is the sum of the absolute ranks with the less frequently appearing sign.

SUMMARY OF z TEST FOR A SINGLE MEAN

Hypotheses

H_0: μ = specified value
H_1: $\mu \neq \mu <$, or $\mu >$ specified value

Assumptions

1. Participants are randomly selected.
2. Population distribution is normal.
3. Population standard deviation is known.

Decision Rules

If $z_{obt} \geq z_{crit}$ reject the H_0.

If $z_{obt} < z_{crit}$ do not reject H_0.

Formula

$$z = \frac{\bar{X} - \mu_{\bar{X}}}{\sigma_{\bar{X}}}$$

SUMMARY OF z TEST FOR A PROPORTION

Hypotheses

H_0: P = specified value
H_1: P $\neq$, <, or > specified value

Assumptions

1. Participants are randomly selected.

2. Sampling distribution of the statistic is normal.

3. Observations are dichotomous.

Decision Rules

If $z_{obt} \geq z_{crit}$ reject the H_0

If $z_{obt} < z_{crit}$ do not reject H_0.

Formula

$$z = \frac{\mathrm{p} - \mathrm{P}}{\sqrt{\mathrm{PQ}/n}}$$

SUMMARY OF z TEST FOR INDEPENDENT MEANS

Hypotheses

$H_0: \mu_1 = \mu_2$

$H_1: \mu_1 \neq \mu_2, \mu_1 < \mu_2, \mu_1 > \mu_2$

Assumptions

1. Participants are randomly selected and independently assigned to groups.

2. Population distributions are normal.

3. Population standard deviations are known.

Decision Rules

If $z_{obt} \geq z_{crit}$ reject the H_0

If $z_{obt} < z_{crit}$ do not reject H_0.

Formula

$$z = \frac{\bar{X}_1 - \bar{X}_2}{\sigma_{\bar{X}_1 - \bar{X}_2}}$$

Statistical Tables

Table B.1 *Areas under the normal curve*

z			z			z		
0.00	.0000	.5000	0.50	.1915	.3085	1.00	.3413	.1587
0.01	.0040	.4960	0.51	.1950	.3050	1.01	.3438	.1562
0.02	.0080	.4920	0.52	.1985	.3015	1.02	.3461	.1539
0.03	.0120	.4880	0.53	.2019	.2981	1.03	.3485	.1515
0.04	.0160	.4840	0.54	.2054	.2946	1.04	.3508	.1492
0.05	.0199	.4801	0.55	.2088	.2912	1.05	.3531	.1469
0.06	.0239	.4761	0.56	.2123	.2877	1.06	.3554	.1446
0.07	.0279	.4721	0.57	.2157	.2843	1.07	.3577	.1423
0.08	.0319	.4681	0.58	.2190	.2810	1.08	.3599	.1401
0.09	.0359	.4641	0.59	.2224	.2776	1.09	.3621	.1379
0.10	.0398	.4602	0.60	.2257	.2743	1.10	.3643	.1357
0.11	.0438	.4562	0.61	.2291	.2709	1.11	.3665	.1335
0.12	.0478	.4522	0.62	.2324	.2676	1.12	.3686	.1314
0.13	.0517	.4483	0.63	.2357	.2643	1.13	.3708	.1292
0.14	.0557	.4443	0.64	.2389	.2611	1.14	.3729	.1271
0.15	.0596	.4404	0.65	.2422	.2578	1.15	.3749	.1251
0.16	.0636	.4364	0.66	.2454	.2546	1.16	.3770	.1230
0.17	.0675	.4325	0.67	.2486	.2514	1.17	.3790	.1210
0.18	.0714	.4286	0.68	.2517	.2483	1.18	.3810	.1190
0.19	.0753	.4247	0.69	.2549	.2451	1.19	.3830	.1170
0.20	.0793	.4207	0.70	.2580	.2420	1.20	.3849	.1151
0.21	.0832	.4168	0.71	.2611	.2389	1.21	.3869	.1131
0.22	.0871	.4129	0.72	.2642	.2358	1.22	.3888	.1112
0.23	.0910	.4090	0.73	.2673	.2327	1.23	.3907	.1093
0.24	.0948	.4052	0.74	.2704	.2296	1.24	.3925	.1075
0.25	.0987	.4013	0.75	.2734	.2266	1.25	.3944	.1056
0.26	.1026	.3974	0.76	.2764	.2236	1.26	.3962	.1038
0.27	.1064	.3936	0.77	.2794	.2206	1.27	.3980	.1020
0.28	.1103	.3897	0.78	.2823	.2177	1.28	.3997	.1003
0.29	.1141	.3859	0.79	.2852	.2148	1.29	.4015	.0985
0.30	.1179	.3821	0.80	.2881	.2119	1.30	.4032	.0968
0.31	.1217	.3783	0.81	.2910	.2090	1.31	.4049	.0951
0.32	.1255	.3745	0.82	.2939	.2061	1.32	.4066	.0934
0.33	.1293	.3707	0.83	.2967	.2033	1.33	.4082	.0918
0.34	.1331	.3669	0.84	.2995	.2005	1.34	.4099	.0901
0.35	.1368	.3632	0.85	.3023	.1977	1.35	.4115	.0885
0.36	.1406	.3594	0.86	.3051	.1949	1.36	.4131	.0869
0.37	.1443	.3557	0.87	.3078	.1922	1.37	.4147	.0853
0.38	.1480	.3520	0.88	.3106	.1894	1.38	.4162	.0838
0.39	.1517	.3483	0.89	.3133	.1867	1.39	.4177	.0823
0.40	.1554	.3446	0.90	.3159	.1841	1.40	.4192	.0808
0.41	.1591	.3409	0.91	.3186	.1814	1.41	.4207	.0793
0.42	.1628	.3372	0.92	.3212	.1788	1.42	.4222	.0778
0.43	.1664	.3336	0.93	.3238	.1762	1.43	.4236	.0764
0.44	.1700	.3300	0.94	.3264	.1736	1.44	.4251	.0749
0.45	.1736	.3264	0.95	.3289	.1711	1.45	.4265	.0735
0.46	.1772	.3228	0.96	.3315	.1685	1.46	.4279	.0721
0.47	.1808	.3192	0.97	.3340	.1660	1.47	.4292	.0708
0.48	.1844	.3156	0.98	.3365	.1635	1.48	.4306	.0694
0.49	.1879	.3121	0.99	.3389	.1611	1.49	.4319	.0681

z			z			z		
1.50	.4332	.0668	2.12	.4830	.0170	2.74	.4969	.0031
1.51	.4345	.0655	2.13	.4834	.0166	2.75	.4970	.0030
1.52	.4357	.0643	2.14	.4838	.0162	2.76	.4971	.0029
1.53	.4370	.0630	2.15	.4842	.0158	2.77	.4972	.0028
1.54	.4382	.0618	2.16	.4846	.0154	2.78	.4973	.0027
1.55	.4394	.0606	2.17	.4850	.0150	2.79	.4974	.0026
1.56	.4406	.0594	2.18	.4854	.0146	2.80	.4974	.0026
1.57	.4418	.0582	2.19	.4857	.0143	2.81	.4975	.0025
1.58	.4429	.0571	2.20	.4861	.0139	2.82	.4976	.0024
1.59	.4441	.0559	2.21	.4864	.0136	2.83	.4977	.0023
1.60	.4452	.0548	2.22	.4868	.0132	2.84	.4977	.0023
1.61	.4463	.0537	2.23	.4871	.0129	2.85	.4978	.0022
1.62	.4474	.0526	2.24	.4875	.0125	2.86	.4979	.0021
1.63	.4484	.0516	2.25	.4878	.0122	2.87	.4979	.0021
1.64	.4495	.0505	2.26	.4881	.0119	2.88	.4980	.0020
1.65	.4505	.0495	2.27	.4884	.0116	2.89	.4981	.0019
1.66	.4515	.0485	2.28	.4887	.0113	2.90	.4981	.0019
1.67	.4525	.0475	2.29	.4890	.0110	2.91	.4982	.0018
1.68	.4535	.0465	2.30	.4893	.0107	2.92	.4982	.0018
1.69	.4545	.0455	2.31	.4896	.0104	2.93	.4983	.0017
1.70	.4554	.0446	2.32	.4898	.0102	2.94	.4984	.0016
1.71	.4564	.0436	2.33	.4901	.0099	2.95	.4984	.0016
1.72	.4573	.0427	2.34	.4904	.0096	2.96	.4985	.0015
1.73	.4582	.0418	2.35	.4906	.0094	2.97	.4985	.0015
1.74	.4591	.0409	2.36	.4909	.0091	2.98	.4986	.0014
1.75	.4599	.0401	2.37	.4911	.0089	2.99	.4986	.0014
1.76	.4608	.0392	2.38	.4913	.0087	3.00	.4987	.0013
1.77	.4616	.0384	2.39	.4916	.0084	3.01	.4987	.0013
1.78	.4625	.0375	2.40	.4918	.0082	3.02	.4987	.0013
1.79	.4633	.0367	2.41	.4920	.0080	3.03	.4988	.0012
1.80	.4641	.0359	2.42	.4922	.0078	3.04	.4988	.0012
1.81	.4649	.0351	2.43	.4925	.0075	3.05	.4989	.0011
1.82	.4656	.0344	2.44	.4927	.0073	3.06	.4989	.0011
1.83	.4664	.0336	2.45	.4929	.0071	3.07	.4989	.0011
1.84	.4671	.0329	2.46	.4931	.0069	3.08	.4990	.0010
1.85	.4678	.0322	2.47	.4932	.0068	3.09	.4990	.0010
1.86	.4686	.0314	2.48	.4934	.0066	3.10	.4990	.0010
1.87	.4693	.0307	2.49	.4936	.0064	3.11	.4991	.0009
1.88	.4699	.0301	2.50	.4938	.0062	3.12	.4991	.0009
1.89	.4706	.0294	2.51	.4940	.0060	3.13	.4991	.0009
1.90	.4713	.0287	2.52	.4941	.0059	3.14	.4992	.0008
1.91	.4719	.0281	2.53	.4943	.0057	3.15	.4992	.0008
1.92	.4726	.0274	2.54	.4945	.0055	3.16	.4992	.0008
1.93	.4732	.0268	2.55	.4946	.0054	3.17	.4992	.0008
1.94	.4738	.0262	2.56	.4948	.0052	3.18	.4993	.0007
1.95	.4744	.0256	2.57	.4949	.0051	3.19	.4993	.0007
1.96	.4750	.0250	2.58	.4951	.0049	3.20	.4993	.0007
1.97	.4756	.0244	2.59	.4952	.0048	3.21	.4993	.0007
1.98	.4761	.0239	2.60	.4953	.0047	3.22	.4994	.0006
1.99	.4767	.0233	2.61	.4955	.0045	3.23	.4994	.0006
2.00	.4772	.0228	2.62	.4956	.0044	3.24	.4994	.0006
2.01	.4778	.0222	2.63	.4957	.0043	3.25	.4994	.0006
2.02	.4783	.0217	2.64	.4959	.0041	3.30	.4995	.0005
2.03	.4788	.0212	2.65	.4960	.0040	3.35	.4996	.0004
2.04	.4793	.0207	2.66	.4961	.0039	3.40	.4997	.0003
2.05	.4798	.0202	2.67	.4962	.0038	3.45	.4997	.0003
2.06	.4803	.0197	2.68	.4963	.0037	3.50	.4998	.0002
2.07	.4808	.0192	2.69	.4964	.0036	3.60	.4998	.0002
2.08	.4812	.0188	2.70	.4965	.0035	3.70	.4999	.0001
2.09	.4817	.0183	2.71	.4966	.0034	3.80	.4999	.0001
2.10	.4821	.0179	2.72	.4967	.0033	3.90	.49995	.00005
2.11	.4826	.0174	2.73	.4968	.0032	4.00	.49997	.00003

Source: Runyon, Richard, & Haber, Audrey (1971). *Fundamentals of behavioral statistics* (2nd ed.). Reading, MA: Addison-Wesley. (Copyright by Random House)

Table B.2 *Critical values of t*

	Level of significance for a directional (one-tailed) test					
	.10	.05	.025	.01	.005	.0005
	Level of significance for a nondirectional (two-tailed) test					
df	.20	.10	.05	.02	.01	.001
1	3.078	6.314	12.706	31.821	63.657	636.619
2	1.886	2.920	4.303	6.965	9.925	31.598
3	1.638	2.353	3.182	4.541	5.841	12.941
4	1.533	2.132	2.776	3.747	4.604	8.610
5	1.476	2.015	2.571	3.365	4.032	6.859
6	1.440	1.943	2.447	3.143	3.707	5.959
7	1.415	1.895	2.365	2.998	3.499	5.405
8	1.397	1.860	2.306	2.896	3.355	5.041
9	1.383	1.833	2.262	2.821	3.250	4.781
10	1.372	1.812	2.228	2.764	3.169	4.587
11	1.363	1.796	2.201	2.718	3.106	4.437
12	1.356	1.782	2.179	2.681	3.055	4.318
13	1.350	1.771	2.160	2.650	3.012	4.221
14	1.345	1.761	2.145	2.624	2.977	4.140
15	1.341	1.753	2.131	2.602	2.947	4.073
16	1.337	1.746	2.120	2.583	2.921	4.015
17	1.333	1.740	2.110	2.567	2.898	3.965
18	1.330	1.734	2.101	2.552	2.878	3.922
19	1.328	1.729	2.093	2.539	2.861	3.883
20	1.325	1.725	2.086	2.528	2.845	3.850
21	1.323	1.721	2.080	2.518	2.831	3.819
22	1.321	1.717	2.074	2.508	2.819	3.792
23	1.319	1.714	2.069	2.500	2.807	3.767
24	1.318	1.711	2.064	2.492	2.797	3.745
25	1.316	1.708	2.060	2.485	2.787	3.725
26	1.315	1.706	2.056	2.479	2.779	3.707
27	1.314	1.703	2.052	2.473	2.771	3.690
28	1.313	1.701	2.048	2.467	2.763	3.674
29	1.311	1.699	2.045	2.462	2.756	3.659
30	1.310	1.697	2.042	2.457	2.750	3.646
40	1.303	1.684	2.021	2.423	2.704	3.551
60	1.296	1.671	2.000	2.390	2.660	3.460
120	1.289	1.658	1.980	2.358	2.617	3.373
	1.282	1.645	1.960	2.326	2.576	3.291

Source: From Table III of Fisher, R. A., & Yates, F. (1978). *Statistical tables for biological, agricultural and medical research*. London, England: Longman Group.

Table B.3   Critical values of F

(.05 level in light type, .01 level in boldface)

Degrees of freedom for the numerator

	1	2	3	4	5	6	7	8	9	10	11	12	14	16	20	24	30	40	50	75	100	200	500	—
1	161	200	216	225	230	234	237	239	241	242	243	244	245	246	248	249	250	251	252	253	254	254	254	254
	4,052	**4,999**	**5,403**	**5,625**	**5,764**	**?**	**5,928**	**5,981**	**6,022**	**6,056**	**6,082**	**6,106**	**6,142**	**6,169**	**6,208**	**6,234**	**6,261**	**6,286**	**6,302**	**6,323**	**6,334**	**6,352**	**6,361**	**6,366**
2	18.51	19.00	19.16	19.25	19.30	19.33	19.36	19.37	19.38	19.39	19.40	19.41	19.42	19.43	19.44	19.45	19.46	19.47	19.47	19.48	19.49	19.49	19.50	19.50
	98.49	**99.00**	**99.17**	**99.25**	**99.30**	**99.33**	**99.36**	**99.37**	**99.39**	**99.40**	**99.41**	**99.42**	**99.43**	**99.44**	**99.45**	**99.46**	**99.47**	**99.48**	**99.48**	**99.49**	**99.49**	**99.49**	**99.50**	**99.50**
3	10.13	9.55	9.28	9.12	9.01	8.94	8.88	8.84	8.81	8.78	8.76	8.74	8.71	8.69	8.66	8.64	8.62	8.60	8.58	8.57	8.56	8.54	8.54	8.53
	34.12	**30.82**	**29.46**	**28.71**	**28.24**	**27.91**	**27.67**	**27.49**	**27.34**	**27.23**	**27.13**	**27.05**	**26.92**	**26.83**	**26.69**	**26.60**	**26.50**	**26.41**	**26.35**	**26.27**	**26.23**	**26.18**	**26.14**	**26.12**
4	7.71	6.94	6.59	6.39	6.26	6.16	6.09	6.04	6.00	5.96	5.93	5.91	5.87	5.84	5.80	5.77	5.74	5.71	5.70	5.68	5.66	5.65	5.64	5.63
	21.20	**18.00**	**16.69**	**15.98**	**15.52**	**15.21**	**14.98**	**14.80**	**14.66**	**14.54**	**14.45**	**14.37**	**14.24**	**14.15**	**14.02**	**13.93**	**13.83**	**13.74**	**13.69**	**13.61**	**13.57**	**13.52**	**13.48**	**13.46**
5	6.61	5.79	5.41	5.19	5.05	4.95	4.88	4.82	4.78	4.74	4.70	4.68	4.64	4.60	4.56	4.53	4.50	4.46	4.44	4.42	4.40	4.38	4.37	4.36
	16.26	**13.27**	**12.06**	**11.39**	**10.97**	**10.67**	**10.45**	**10.29**	**10.15**	**10.05**	**9.96**	**9.89**	**9.77**	**9.68**	**9.55**	**9.47**	**9.38**	**9.29**	**9.24**	**9.17**	**9.13**	**9.07**	**9.04**	**9.02**
6	5.99	5.14	4.76	4.53	4.39	4.28	4.21	4.15	4.10	4.06	4.03	4.00	3.96	3.92	3.87	3.84	3.81	3.77	3.75	3.72	3.71	3.69	3.68	3.67
	13.74	**10.92**	**9.78**	**9.15**	**8.75**	**8.47**	**8.26**	**8.10**	**7.98**	**7.87**	**7.79**	**7.72**	**7.60**	**7.52**	**7.39**	**7.31**	**7.23**	**7.14**	**7.09**	**7.02**	**6.99**	**6.94**	**6.90**	**6.88**
7	5.59	4.74	4.35	4.12	3.97	3.87	3.79	3.73	3.68	3.63	3.60	3.57	3.52	3.49	3.44	3.41	3.38	3.34	3.32	3.29	3.28	3.25	3.24	3.23
	12.25	**9.55**	**8.45**	**7.85**	**7.46**	**7.19**	**7.00**	**6.84**	**6.71**	**6.62**	**6.54**	**6.47**	**6.35**	**6.27**	**6.15**	**6.07**	**5.98**	**5.90**	**5.85**	**5.78**	**5.75**	**5.70**	**5.67**	**5.65**
8	5.32	4.46	4.07	3.84	3.69	3.58	3.50	3.44	3.39	3.34	3.31	3.28	3.23	3.20	3.15	3.12	3.08	3.05	3.03	3.00	2.98	2.96	2.94	2.93
	11.26	**8.65**	**7.59**	**7.01**	**6.63**	**6.37**	**6.19**	**6.03**	**5.91**	**5.82**	**5.74**	**5.67**	**5.56**	**5.48**	**5.36**	**5.28**	**5.20**	**5.11**	**5.06**	**5.00**	**4.96**	**4.91**	**4.88**	**4.86**
9	5.12	4.26	3.86	3.63	3.48	3.37	3.29	3.23	3.18	3.13	3.10	3.07	3.02	2.98	2.93	2.90	2.86	2.82	2.80	2.77	2.76	2.73	2.72	2.71
	10.56	**8.02**	**6.99**	**6.42**	**6.06**	**5.80**	**5.62**	**5.47**	**5.35**	**5.26**	**5.18**	**5.11**	**5.00**	**4.92**	**4.80**	**4.73**	**4.64**	**4.56**	**4.51**	**4.45**	**4.41**	**4.36**	**4.33**	**4.31**
10	4.96	4.10	3.71	3.48	3.33	3.22	3.14	3.07	3.02	2.97	2.94	2.91	2.86	2.82	2.77	2.74	2.70	2.67	2.64	2.61	2.59	2.56	2.55	2.54
	10.04	**7.56**	**6.55**	**5.99**	**5.64**	**5.39**	**5.21**	**5.06**	**4.95**	**4.85**	**4.78**	**4.71**	**4.60**	**4.52**	**4.41**	**4.33**	**4.25**	**4.17**	**4.12**	**4.05**	**4.01**	**3.96**	**3.93**	**3.91**
11	4.84	3.98	3.59	3.36	3.20	3.09	3.01	2.95	2.90	2.86	2.82	2.79	2.74	2.70	2.65	2.61	2.57	2.53	2.50	2.47	2.45	2.42	2.41	2.40
	9.65	**7.20**	**6.22**	**5.67**	**5.32**	**5.07**	**4.88**	**4.74**	**4.63**	**4.54**	**4.46**	**4.40**	**4.29**	**4.21**	**4.10**	**4.02**	**3.94**	**3.86**	**3.80**	**3.74**	**3.70**	**3.66**	**3.62**	**3.60**
12	4.75	3.88	3.49	3.26	3.11	3.00	2.92	2.85	2.80	2.76	2.72	2.69	2.64	2.60	2.54	2.50	2.46	2.42	2.40	2.36	2.35	2.32	2.31	2.30
	9.33	**6.93**	**5.95**	**5.41**	**5.06**	**4.82**	**4.65**	**4.50**	**4.39**	**4.30**	**4.22**	**4.16**	**4.05**	**3.98**	**3.86**	**3.78**	**3.70**	**3.61**	**3.56**	**3.49**	**3.46**	**3.41**	**3.38**	**3.36**
13	4.67	3.80	3.41	3.18	3.02	2.92	2.84	2.77	2.72	2.67	2.63	2.60	2.55	2.51	2.46	2.42	2.38	2.34	2.32	2.28	2.26	2.24	2.22	2.21
	9.07	**6.70**	**5.74**	**5.20**	**4.86**	**4.62**	**4.44**	**4.30**	**4.19**	**4.10**	**4.02**	**3.96**	**3.85**	**3.78**	**3.67**	**3.59**	**3.51**	**3.42**	**3.37**	**3.30**	**3.27**	**3.21**	**3.18**	**3.16**

(Continued)

Table B.3   (Continued)

(.05 level in light type, .01 level in boldface)

Degrees of freedom for the numerator

	1	2	3	4	5	6	7	8	9	10	11	12	14	16	20	24	30	40	50	75	100	200	500	—
14	4.60	3.74	3.34	3.11	2.96	2.85	2.77	2.70	2.65	2.60	2.56	2.53	2.48	2.44	2.39	2.35	2.31	2.27	2.24	2.21	2.19	2.16	2.14	2.13
	8.86	**6.51**	**5.56**	**5.03**	**4.69**	**4.46**	**4.28**	**4.14**	**4.03**	**3.94**	**3.86**	**3.80**	**3.70**	**3.62**	**3.51**	**3.43**	**3.34**	**3.26**	**3.21**	**3.14**	**3.11**	**3.06**	**3.02**	**3.00**
15	4.54	3.68	3.29	3.06	2.90	2.79	2.70	2.64	2.59	2.55	2.51	2.48	2.43	2.39	2.33	2.29	2.25	2.21	2.18	2.15	2.12	2.10	2.08	2.07
	8.68	**6.36**	**5.42**	**4.89**	**4.56**	**4.32**	**4.14**	**4.00**	**3.89**	**3.80**	**3.73**	**3.67**	**3.56**	**3.48**	**3.36**	**3.29**	**3.20**	**3.12**	**3.07**	**3.00**	**2.97**	**2.92**	**2.89**	**2.87**
16	4.49	3.63	3.24	3.01	2.85	2.74	2.66	2.59	2.54	2.49	2.45	2.42	2.37	2.33	2.28	2.24	2.20	2.16	2.13	2.09	2.07	2.04	2.02	2.01
	8.53	**6.23**	**5.29**	**4.77**	**4.44**	**4.20**	**4.03**	**3.89**	**3.78**	**3.69**	**3.61**	**3.55**	**3.45**	**3.37**	**3.25**	**3.18**	**3.10**	**3.01**	**2.96**	**2.98**	**2.86**	**2.80**	**2.77**	**2.75**
17	4.45	3.59	3.20	2.96	2.81	2.70	2.62	2.55	2.50	2.45	2.41	2.38	2.33	2.29	2.23	2.19	2.15	2.11	2.08	2.04	2.02	1.99	1.97	1.96
	8.40	**6.11**	**5.18**	**4.67**	**4.34**	**4.10**	**3.93**	**3.79**	**3.68**	**3.59**	**3.52**	**3.45**	**3.35**	**3.27**	**3.16**	**3.08**	**3.00**	**2.92**	**2.86**	**2.79**	**2.76**	**2.70**	**2.67**	**2.65**
18	4.41	3.55	3.16	2.93	2.77	2.66	2.58	2.51	2.46	2.41	2.37	2.34	2.29	2.25	2.19	2.15	2.11	2.07	2.04	2.00	1.98	1.95	1.93	1.92
	8.28	**6.01**	**5.09**	**4.58**	**4.25**	**4.01**	**3.85**	**3.71**	**3.60**	**3.51**	**3.44**	**3.37**	**3.27**	**3.19**	**3.07**	**3.00**	**2.91**	**2.83**	**2.78**	**2.71**	**2.68**	**2.62**	**2.59**	**2.57**
19	4.38	3.52	3.13	2.90	2.74	2.63	2.55	2.48	2.43	2.38	2.34	2.31	2.26	2.21	2.15	2.11	2.07	2.02	2.00	1.96	1.94	1.91	1.90	1.88
	8.18	**5.93**	**5.01**	**4.50**	**4.17**	**3.94**	**3.77**	**3.63**	**3.52**	**3.43**	**3.36**	**3.30**	**3.19**	**3.12**	**3.00**	**2.92**	**2.84**	**2.76**	**2.70**	**2.63**	**2.60**	**2.54**	**2.51**	**2.49**
20	4.35	3.49	3.10	2.87	2.71	2.60	2.52	2.45	2.40	2.35	2.31	2.28	2.23	2.18	2.12	2.08	2.04	1.99	1.96	1.92	1.90	1.87	1.85	1.84
	8.10	**5.85**	**4.94**	**4.43**	**4.10**	**3.87**	**3.71**	**3.56**	**3.45**	**3.37**	**3.30**	**3.23**	**3.13**	**3.05**	**2.94**	**2.86**	**2.77**	**2.69**	**2.63**	**2.56**	**2.53**	**2.47**	**2.44**	**2.42**
21	4.32	3.47	3.07	2.84	2.68	2.57	2.49	2.42	2.37	2.32	2.28	2.25	2.20	2.15	2.09	2.05	2.00	1.96	1.93	1.89	1.87	1.84	1.82	1.81
	8.02	**5.78**	**4.87**	**4.37**	**4.04**	**3.81**	**3.65**	**3.51**	**3.40**	**3.31**	**3.24**	**3.17**	**3.07**	**2.99**	**2.88**	**2.80**	**2.72**	**2.63**	**2.58**	**2.51**	**2.47**	**2.42**	**2.38**	**2.36**
22	4.30	3.44	3.05	2.82	2.66	2.55	2.47	2.40	2.35	2.30	2.26	2.23	2.18	2.13	2.07	2.03	1.98	1.93	1.91	1.87	1.84	1.81	1.80	1.78
	7.94	**5.72**	**4.82**	**4.31**	**3.99**	**3.76**	**3.59**	**3.45**	**3.35**	**3.26**	**3.18**	**3.12**	**3.02**	**2.94**	**2.83**	**2.75**	**2.67**	**2.58**	**2.53**	**2.46**	**2.42**	**2.37**	**2.33**	**2.31**
23	4.28	3.42	3.03	2.80	2.64	2.53	2.45	2.38	2.32	2.28	2.24	2.20	2.14	2.10	2.04	2.00	1.96	1.91	1.88	1.84	1.82	1.79	1.77	1.76
	7.88	**5.66**	**4.76**	**4.26**	**3.94**	**3.71**	**3.54**	**3.41**	**3.30**	**3.21**	**3.14**	**3.07**	**2.97**	**2.89**	**2.78**	**2.70**	**2.62**	**2.53**	**2.48**	**2.41**	**2.37**	**2.32**	**2.28**	**2.26**
24	4.26	3.40	3.01	2.78	2.62	2.51	2.43	2.36	2.30	2.26	2.22	2.18	2.13	2.09	2.02	1.98	1.94	1.89	1.86	1.82	1.80	1.76	1.74	1.73
	7.82	**5.61**	**4.72**	**4.22**	**3.90**	**3.67**	**3.50**	**3.36**	**3.25**	**3.17**	**3.09**	**3.03**	**2.93**	**2.85**	**2.74**	**2.66**	**2.58**	**2.49**	**2.44**	**2.36**	**2.33**	**2.27**	**2.23**	**2.21**
25	4.24	3.38	2.99	2.76	2.60	2.49	2.41	2.34	2.28	2.24	2.20	2.16	2.11	2.06	2.00	1.96	1.92	1.87	1.84	1.80	1.77	1.74	1.72	1.71
	7.77	**5.57**	**4.68**	**4.18**	**3.86**	**3.63**	**3.46**	**3.32**	**3.21**	**3.13**	**3.05**	**2.99**	**2.89**	**2.81**	**2.70**	**2.62**	**2.54**	**2.45**	**2.40**	**2.32**	**2.29**	**2.23**	**2.19**	**2.17**
26	4.22	3.37	2.98	2.74	2.59	2.47	2.39	2.32	2.27	2.22	2.18	2.15	2.10	2.05	1.99	1.95	1.90	1.85	1.82	1.78	1.76	1.72	1.70	1.69
	7.72	**5.53**	**4.64**	**4.14**	**3.82**	**3.59**	**3.42**	**3.29**	**3.17**	**3.09**	**3.02**	**2.96**	**2.86**	**2.77**	**2.66**	**2.58**	**2.50**	**2.41**	**2.36**	**2.28**	**2.25**	**2.19**	**2.15**	**2.13**

Table B.3 (Continued)

(.05 level in light type, .01 level in boldface)

Degrees of freedom for the numerator

	1	2	3	4	5	6	7	8	9	10	11	12	14	16	20	24	30	40	50	75	100	200	500	—	
27	4.21	3.35	2.96	2.73	2.57	2.46	2.37	2.30	2.25	2.20	2.16	2.13	2.08	2.03	1.97	1.93	1.88	1.84	1.80	1.76	1.74	1.71	1.68	1.67	27
	7.68	**5.49**	**4.60**	**4.11**	**3.79**	**3.56**	**3.39**	**3.26**	**3.14**	**3.06**	**2.98**	**2.93**	**2.83**	**2.74**	**2.63**	**2.55**	**2.47**	**2.38**	**2.33**	**2.25**	**2.21**	**2.16**	**2.12**	**2.10**	
28	4.20	3.34	2.95	2.71	2.56	2.44	2.36	2.29	2.24	2.19	2.15	2.12	2.06	2.02	1.96	1.91	1.87	1.81	1.78	1.75	1.72	1.69	1.67	1.65	28
	7.64	**5.45**	**4.57**	**4.07**	**3.76**	**3.53**	**3.36**	**3.23**	**3.11**	**3.03**	**2.95**	**2.90**	**2.80**	**2.71**	**2.60**	**2.52**	**2.44**	**2.35**	**2.30**	**2.22**	**2.18**	**2.13**	**2.09**	**2.06**	
29	4.18	3.33	2.93	2.70	2.54	2.43	2.35	2.28	2.22	2.18	2.14	2.10	2.05	2.00	1.94	1.90	1.85	1.80	1.77	1.73	1.71	1.68	1.65	1.64	29
	7.60	**5.42**	**4.54**	**4.04**	**3.73**	**3.50**	**3.33**	**3.20**	**3.08**	**3.00**	**2.92**	**2.87**	**2.77**	**2.68**	**2.57**	**2.49**	**2.41**	**2.32**	**2.27**	**2.19**	**2.15**	**2.10**	**2.06**	**2.03**	
30	4.17	3.32	2.92	2.69	2.53	2.42	2.34	2.27	2.21	2.16	2.12	2.09	2.04	1.99	1.93	1.89	1.84	1.79	1.76	1.72	1.69	1.66	1.64	1.62	30
	7.56	**5.39**	**4.51**	**4.02**	**3.70**	**3.47**	**3.30**	**3.17**	**3.06**	**2.98**	**2.90**	**2.84**	**2.74**	**2.66**	**2.55**	**2.47**	**2.38**	**2.29**	**2.24**	**2.16**	**2.13**	**2.07**	**2.03**	**2.01**	
32	4.15	3.30	2.90	2.67	2.51	2.40	2.32	2.25	2.19	2.14	2.10	2.07	2.02	1.97	1.91	1.86	1.82	1.76	1.74	1.69	1.67	1.64	1.61	1.59	32
	7.50	**5.34**	**4.46**	**3.97**	**3.66**	**3.42**	**3.25**	**3.12**	**3.01**	**2.94**	**2.86**	**2.80**	**2.70**	**2.62**	**2.51**	**2.42**	**2.34**	**2.25**	**2.20**	**2.12**	**2.08**	**2.02**	**1.98**	**1.96**	
34	4.13	3.28	2.88	2.65	2.49	2.38	2.30	2.23	2.17	2.12	2.08	2.05	2.00	1.95	1.89	1.84	1.80	1.74	1.71	1.67	1.64	1.61	1.59	1.57	34
	7.44	**5.29**	**4.42**	**3.93**	**3.61**	**3.38**	**3.21**	**3.08**	**2.97**	**2.89**	**2.82**	**2.76**	**2.66**	**2.58**	**2.47**	**2.38**	**2.30**	**2.21**	**2.15**	**2.08**	**2.04**	**1.98**	**1.94**	**1.91**	
36	4.11	3.26	2.86	2.63	2.48	2.36	2.28	2.21	2.15	2.10	2.06	2.03	1.98	1.93	1.87	1.82	1.78	1.72	1.69	1.65	1.62	1.59	1.56	1.55	36
	7.39	**5.25**	**4.38**	**3.89**	**3.58**	**3.35**	**3.18**	**3.04**	**2.94**	**2.86**	**2.78**	**2.72**	**2.62**	**2.54**	**2.43**	**2.35**	**2.26**	**2.17**	**2.12**	**2.04**	**2.00**	**1.94**	**1.90**	**1.87**	
38	4.10	3.25	2.85	2.62	2.46	2.35	2.26	2.19	2.14	2.09	2.05	2.02	1.96	1.92	1.85	1.80	1.76	1.71	1.67	1.63	1.60	1.57	1.54	1.53	38
	7.35	**5.21**	**4.34**	**3.86**	**3.54**	**3.32**	**3.15**	**3.02**	**2.91**	**2.82**	**2.75**	**2.69**	**2.59**	**2.51**	**2.40**	**2.32**	**2.22**	**2.14**	**2.08**	**2.00**	**1.97**	**1.90**	**1.86**	**1.84**	
40	4.08	3.23	2.84	2.61	2.45	2.34	2.25	2.18	2.12	2.07	2.04	2.00	1.95	1.90	1.84	1.79	1.74	1.69	1.66	1.61	1.59	1.55	1.53	1.51	40
	7.31	**5.18**	**4.31**	**3.83**	**3.51**	**3.29**	**3.12**	**2.99**	**2.88**	**2.80**	**2.73**	**2.66**	**2.56**	**2.49**	**2.37**	**2.29**	**2.20**	**2.11**	**2.05**	**1.97**	**1.94**	**1.88**	**1.84**	**1.81**	
42	4.07	3.22	2.83	2.59	2.44	2.32	2.24	2.17	2.11	2.06	2.02	1.99	1.94	1.89	1.82	1.78	1.73	1.68	1.64	1.60	1.57	1.54	1.51	1.49	42
	7.27	**5.15**	**4.29**	**3.80**	**3.49**	**3.26**	**3.10**	**2.96**	**2.86**	**2.77**	**2.70**	**2.64**	**2.54**	**2.46**	**2.35**	**2.26**	**2.17**	**2.08**	**2.02**	**1.94**	**1.91**	**1.85**	**1.80**	**1.78**	
44	4.06	3.21	2.82	2.58	2.43	2.31	2.23	2.16	2.10	2.05	2.01	1.98	1.92	1.88	1.81	1.76	1.72	1.66	1.63	1.58	1.56	1.52	1.50	1.48	44
	7.24	**5.12**	**4.26**	**3.78**	**3.46**	**3.24**	**3.07**	**2.94**	**2.84**	**2.75**	**2.68**	**2.62**	**2.52**	**2.44**	**2.32**	**2.24**	**2.15**	**2.06**	**2.00**	**1.92**	**1.88**	**1.82**	**1.78**	**1.75**	
46	4.05	3.20	2.81	2.57	2.42	2.30	2.22	2.14	2.09	2.04	2.00	1.97	1.91	1.87	1.80	1.75	1.71	1.65	1.62	1.57	1.54	1.51	1.48	1.46	46
	7.21	**5.10**	**4.24**	**3.76**	**3.44**	**3.22**	**3.05**	**2.92**	**2.82**	**2.73**	**2.66**	**2.60**	**2.50**	**2.42**	**2.30**	**2.22**	**2.13**	**2.04**	**1.98**	**1.90**	**1.86**	**1.80**	**1.76**	**1.72**	
48	4.04	3.19	2.80	2.56	2.41	2.30	2.21	2.14	2.08	2.03	1.99	1.96	1.90	1.86	1.79	1.74	1.70	1.64	1.61	1.56	1.53	1.50	1.47	1.45	48
	7.19	**5.08**	**4.22**	**3.74**	**3.42**	**3.20**	**3.04**	**2.90**	**2.80**	**2.71**	**2.64**	**2.58**	**2.48**	**2.40**	**2.28**	**2.20**	**2.11**	**2.02**	**1.96**	**1.88**	**1.84**	**1.78**	**1.73**	**1.70**	

Table B.3   (Continued)

(.05 level in light type, .01 level in boldface)

Degrees of freedom for the numerator

	1	2	3	4	5	6	7	8	9	10	11	12	14	16	20	24	30	40	50	75	100	200	500	—	
50	4.03	3.18	2.79	2.56	2.40	2.29	2.20	2.13	2.07	2.02	1.98	1.95	1.90	1.85	1.78	1.74	1.69	1.63	1.60	1.55	1.52	1.48	1.46	1.44	**50**
	7.17	**5.06**	**4.20**	**3.72**	**3.41**	**3.18**	**3.02**	**2.88**	**2.78**	**2.70**	**2.62**	**2.56**	**2.46**	**2.39**	**2.26**	**2.18**	**2.10**	**2.00**	**1.94**	**1.86**	**1.82**	**1.76**	**1.71**	**1.68**	
55	4.02	3.17	2.78	2.54	2.38	2.27	2.18	2.11	2.05	2.00	1.97	1.93	1.88	1.83	1.76	1.72	1.67	1.61	1.58	1.52	1.50	1.46	1.43	1.41	**55**
	7.12	**5.01**	**4.16**	**3.68**	**3.37**	**3.15**	**2.98**	**2.85**	**2.75**	**2.66**	**2.59**	**2.53**	**2.43**	**2.35**	**2.23**	**2.15**	**2.06**	**1.96**	**1.90**	**1.82**	**1.78**	**1.71**	**1.66**	**1.64**	
60	4.00	3.15	2.76	2.52	2.37	2.25	2.17	2.10	2.04	1.99	1.95	1.92	1.86	1.81	1.75	1.70	1.65	1.59	1.56	1.50	1.48	1.44	1.41	1.39	**60**
	7.08	**4.98**	**4.13**	**3.65**	**3.34**	**3.12**	**2.95**	**2.82**	**2.72**	**2.63**	**2.56**	**2.50**	**2.40**	**2.32**	**2.20**	**2.12**	**2.03**	**1.93**	**1.87**	**1.79**	**1.74**	**1.68**	**1.63**	**1.60**	
65	3.99	3.14	2.75	2.51	2.36	2.24	2.15	2.08	2.02	1.98	1.94	1.90	1.85	1.80	1.73	1.68	1.63	1.57	1.54	1.49	1.46	1.42	1.39	1.37	**65**
	7.04	**4.95**	**4.10**	**3.62**	**3.31**	**3.09**	**2.93**	**2.79**	**2.70**	**2.61**	**2.54**	**2.47**	**2.37**	**2.30**	**2.18**	**2.09**	**2.00**	**1.90**	**1.84**	**1.76**	**1.71**	**1.64**	**1.60**	**1.56**	
70	3.98	3.13	2.74	2.50	2.35	2.23	2.14	2.07	2.01	1.97	1.93	1.89	1.84	1.79	1.72	1.67	1.62	1.56	1.53	1.47	1.45	1.40	1.37	1.35	**70**
	7.01	**4.92**	**4.08**	**3.60**	**3.29**	**3.07**	**2.91**	**2.77**	**2.67**	**2.59**	**2.51**	**2.45**	**2.35**	**2.28**	**2.15**	**2.07**	**1.98**	**1.88**	**1.82**	**1.74**	**1.69**	**1.62**	**1.56**	**1.53**	
80	3.96	3.11	2.72	2.48	2.33	2.21	2.12	2.05	1.99	1.95	1.91	1.88	1.82	1.77	1.70	1.65	1.60	1.54	1.51	1.45	1.42	1.38	1.35	1.32	**80**
	6.96	**4.88**	**4.04**	**3.56**	**3.25**	**3.04**	**2.87**	**2.74**	**2.64**	**2.55**	**2.48**	**2.41**	**2.32**	**2.24**	**2.11**	**2.03**	**1.94**	**1.84**	**1.78**	**1.70**	**1.65**	**1.57**	**1.52**	**1.49**	
100	3.94	3.09	2.70	2.46	2.30	2.19	2.10	2.03	1.97	1.92	1.88	1.85	1.79	1.75	1.68	1.63	1.57	1.51	1.48	1.42	1.39	1.34	1.30	1.28	**100**
	6.90	**4.82**	**3.98**	**3.51**	**3.20**	**2.99**	**2.82**	**2.69**	**2.59**	**2.51**	**2.43**	**2.36**	**2.26**	**2.19**	**2.06**	**1.98**	**1.89**	**1.79**	**1.73**	**1.64**	**1.59**	**1.51**	**1.46**	**1.43**	
125	3.92	3.07	2.68	2.44	2.29	2.17	2.08	2.01	1.95	1.90	1.86	1.83	1.77	1.72	1.65	1.60	1.55	1.49	1.45	1.39	1.36	1.31	1.27	1.25	**125**
	6.84	**4.78**	**3.94**	**3.47**	**3.17**	**2.95**	**2.79**	**2.65**	**2.56**	**2.47**	**2.40**	**2.33**	**2.23**	**2.15**	**2.03**	**1.94**	**1.85**	**1.75**	**1.68**	**1.59**	**1.54**	**1.46**	**1.40**	**1.37**	
150	3.91	3.06	2.67	2.43	2.27	2.16	2.07	2.00	1.94	1.89	1.85	1.82	1.76	1.71	1.64	1.59	1.54	1.47	1.44	1.37	1.34	1.29	1.25	1.22	**150**
	6.81	**4.75**	**3.91**	**3.44**	**3.14**	**2.92**	**2.76**	**2.62**	**2.53**	**2.44**	**2.37**	**2.30**	**2.20**	**2.12**	**2.00**	**1.91**	**1.83**	**1.72**	**1.66**	**1.56**	**1.51**	**1.43**	**1.37**	**1.33**	
200	3.89	3.04	2.65	2.41	2.26	2.14	2.05	1.98	1.92	1.87	1.83	1.80	1.74	1.69	1.62	1.57	1.52	1.45	1.42	1.35	1.32	1.26	1.22	1.19	**200**
	6.76	**4.71**	**3.88**	**3.41**	**3.11**	**2.90**	**2.73**	**2.60**	**2.50**	**2.41**	**2.34**	**2.28**	**2.17**	**2.09**	**1.97**	**1.88**	**1.79**	**1.69**	**1.62**	**1.53**	**1.48**	**1.39**	**1.33**	**1.28**	
400	3.86	3.02	2.62	2.39	2.23	2.12	2.03	1.96	1.90	1.85	1.81	1.78	1.72	1.67	1.60	1.54	1.49	1.42	1.38	1.32	1.28	1.22	1.16	1.13	**400**
	6.70	**4.66**	**3.83**	**3.36**	**3.06**	**2.85**	**2.69**	**2.55**	**2.46**	**2.37**	**2.29**	**2.23**	**2.12**	**2.04**	**1.92**	**1.84**	**1.74**	**1.64**	**1.57**	**1.47**	**1.42**	**1.32**	**1.24**	**1.19**	
1000	3.85	3.00	2.61	2.38	2.22	2.10	2.02	1.95	1.89	1.84	1.80	1.76	1.70	1.65	1.58	1.53	1.47	1.41	1.36	1.30	1.26	1.19	1.13	1.08	**1000**
	6.66	**4.62**	**3.80**	**3.34**	**3.04**	**2.82**	**2.66**	**2.53**	**2.43**	**2.34**	**2.26**	**2.20**	**2.09**	**2.01**	**1.89**	**1.81**	**1.71**	**1.51**	**1.54**	**1.44**	**1.38**	**1.28**	**1.19**	**1.11**	
α	3.84	2.99	2.60	2.37	2.21	2.09	2.01	1.94	1.88	1.83	1.79	1.75	1.69	1.64	1.57	1.52	1.46	1.40	1.35	1.28	1.24	1.17	1.11	1.00	**α**
	6.64	**4.60**	**3.78**	**3.32**	**3.02**	**2.80**	**2.64**	**2.51**	**2.41**	**2.32**	**2.24**	**2.18**	**2.07**	**1.99**	**1.87**	**1.79**	**1.69**	**1.59**	**1.52**	**1.41**	**1.36**	**1.25**	**1.15**	**1.00**	

Source: Snedecor, G. W., & Cochran, W. G. (1967). *Statistical methods* (6th ed.). Ames, IA: Iowa State University Press.

Table B.4   *Critical values of chi-square*

df	\.20	\.10	\.05	\.02	\.01	\.001
			Level of significance for a nondirectional test			
1	1.64	2.71	3.84	5.41	6.64	10.83
2	3.22	4.60	5.99	7.82	9.21	13.82
3	4.64	6.25	7.82	9.84	11.34	16.27
4	5.99	7.78	9.49	11.67	13.28	18.46
5	7.29	9.24	11.07	13.39	15.09	20.52
6	8.56	10.64	12.59	15.03	16.81	22.46
7	9.8	12.02	14.07	16.62	18.48	24.32
8	11.03	13.36	15.51	18.17	20.09	26.12
9	12.24	14.68	16.92	19.68	21.67	27.88
10	13.44	15.99	18.31	21.16	23.21	29.59
11	14.63	17.28	19.68	22.62	24.72	31.26
12	15.81	18.55	21.03	24.05	26.22	32.91
13	16.98	19.81	22.36	25.47	27.69	34.53
14	18.15	21.06	23.68	26.87	29.14	36.12
15	19.31	22.31	25.00	28.26	30.58	37.70
16	20.46	23.54	26.30	29.63	32.00	39.29
17	21.62	24.77	27.59	31.00	33.41	40.75
18	22.76	25.99	28.87	32.35	34.80	42.31
19	23.90	27.20	30.14	33.69	36.19	43.82
20	25.04	28.41	31.41	35.02	37.57	45.32
21	26.17	29.62	32.67	36.34	38.93	46.80
22	27.30	30.81	33.92	37.66	40.29	48.27
23	28.43	32.01	35.17	38.97	41.64	49.73
24	29.55	33.20	36.42	40.27	42.98	51.18
25	30.68	34.38	37.65	41.57	44.31	52.62
26	31.80	35.56	38.88	42.86	45.64	54.05
27	32.91	36.74	40.11	44.14	46.96	55.48
28	34.03	37.92	41.34	45.42	48.28	56.89
29	35.14	39.09	42.69	46.69	49.59	58.30
30	36.25	40.26	43.77	47.96	50.89	59.70
32	38.47	42.59	46.19	50.49	53.49	62.49
34	40.68	44.90	48.60	53.00	56.06	65.25
36	42.88	47.21	51.00	55.49	58.62	67.99
38	45.08	49.51	53.38	57.97	61.16	70.70
40	47.27	51.81	55.76	60.44	63.69	73.40
44	51.64	56.37	60.48	65.34	68.71	78.75
48	55.99	60.91	65.17	70.20	73.68	84.04
52	60.33	65.42	69.83	75.02	78.62	89.27
56	64.66	69.92	74.47	79.82	83.51	94.46
60	68.97	74.40	79.08	84.58	88.38	99.61

Source: From Fisher, R. A., & Yates, F. (1978). *Statistical tables for biological, agricultural and medical research.* London, England: Longman Group.

Table B.5 *Studentized range points for Tukey test*

Error df	α	r = 2	3	4	5	6	7	8	9	10	11	12	13	14	15	16	17	18	19	20	α	Error df
5	.05	3.64	4.60	5.22	5.67	6.03	6.33	6.58	6.80	6.99	7.17	7.32	7.47	7.60	7.72	7.83	7.93	8.03	8.12	8.21	.05	5
	.01	5.70	6.98	7.80	8.42	8.91	9.32	9.67	9.97	10.24	10.48	10.70	10.89	11.08	11.24	11.40	11.55	11.68	11.81	11.93	.01	
6	.05	3.46	4.34	4.90	5.30	5.63	5.90	6.12	6.32	6.49	6.65	6.79	6.92	7.03	7.14	7.24	7.34	7.43	7.51	7.59	.05	6
	.01	5.24	6.33	7.03	7.56	7.97	8.32	8.61	8.87	9.10	9.30	9.48	9.65	9.81	9.95	10.08	10.21	10.32	10.43	10.54	.01	
7	.05	3.34	4.16	4.68	5.06	5.36	5.61	5.82	6.00	6.16	6.30	6.43	6.55	6.66	6.76	6.85	6.94	7.02	7.10	7.17	.05	7
	.01	4.95	5.92	6.54	7.01	7.37	7.68	7.94	8.17	8.37	8.55	8.71	8.86	9.00	9.12	9.24	9.35	9.46	9.55	9.65	.01	
8	.05	3.26	4.04	4.53	4.89	5.17	5.40	5.60	5.77	5.92	6.05	6.18	6.29	6.39	6.48	6.57	6.65	6.73	6.80	6.87	.05	8
	.01	4.75	5.64	6.20	6.62	6.96	7.24	7.47	7.68	7.86	8.03	8.18	8.31	8.44	8.55	8.66	8.76	8.85	8.94	9.03	.01	
9	.05	3.20	3.95	4.41	4.76	5.02	5.24	5.43	5.59	5.74	5.87	5.98	6.09	6.19	6.28	6.36	6.44	6.51	6.58	6.64	.05	9
	.01	4.60	5.43	5.96	6.35	6.66	6.91	7.13	7.33	7.49	7.65	7.78	7.91	8.03	8.13	8.23	8.33	8.41	8.49	8.57	.01	
10	.05	3.15	3.88	4.33	4.65	4.91	5.12	5.30	5.46	5.60	5.72	5.83	5.93	6.03	6.11	6.19	6.27	6.34	6.40	6.47	.05	10
	.01	4.48	5.27	5.77	6.14	6.43	6.67	6.87	7.05	7.21	7.36	7.49	7.60	7.71	7.81	7.91	7.99	8.08	8.15	8.23	.01	
11	.05	3.11	3.82	4.26	4.57	4.82	5.03	5.20	5.35	5.49	5.61	5.71	5.81	5.90	5.98	6.06	6.13	6.20	6.27	6.33	.05	11
	.01	4.39	5.15	5.62	5.97	6.25	6.48	6.67	6.84	6.99	7.13	7.25	7.36	7.46	7.56	7.65	7.73	7.81	7.88	7.95	.01	
12	.05	3.08	3.77	4.20	4.51	4.75	4.95	5.12	5.27	5.39	5.51	5.61	5.71	5.80	5.88	5.95	6.02	6.09	6.15	6.21	.05	12
	.01	4.32	5.05	5.50	5.84	6.10	6.32	6.51	6.67	6.81	6.94	7.06	7.17	7.26	7.36	7.44	7.52	7.59	7.66	7.73	.01	
13	.05	3.06	3.73	4.15	4.45	4.69	4.88	5.05	5.19	5.32	5.43	5.53	5.63	5.71	5.79	5.86	5.93	5.99	6.05	6.11	.05	13
	.01	4.26	4.96	5.40	5.73	5.98	6.19	6.37	6.53	6.67	6.79	6.90	7.01	7.10	7.19	7.27	7.35	7.42	7.48	7.55	.01	
14	.05	3.03	3.70	4.11	4.41	4.64	4.83	4.99	5.13	5.25	5.36	5.46	5.55	5.64	5.71	5.79	5.85	5.91	5.97	6.03	.05	14
	.01	4.21	4.89	5.32	5.63	5.88	6.08	6.26	6.41	6.54	6.66	6.77	6.87	6.96	7.05	7.13	7.20	7.27	7.33	7.39	.01	
15	.05	3.01	3.67	4.08	4.37	4.59	4.78	4.94	5.08	5.20	5.31	5.40	5.49	5.57	5.65	5.72	5.78	5.85	5.90	5.96	.05	15
	.01	4.17	4.84	5.25	5.56	5.80	5.99	6.16	6.31	6.44	6.55	6.66	6.76	6.84	6.93	7.00	7.07	7.14	7.20	7.26	.01	
16	.05	3.00	3.65	4.05	4.33	4.56	4.74	4.90	5.03	5.15	5.26	5.35	5.44	5.52	5.59	5.66	5.73	5.79	5.84	5.90	.05	16
	.01	4.13	4.79	5.19	5.49	5.72	5.92	6.08	6.22	6.35	6.46	6.56	6.66	6.74	6.82	6.90	6.97	7.03	7.09	7.15	.01	
17	.05	2.98	3.63	4.02	4.30	4.52	4.70	4.86	4.99	5.11	5.21	5.31	5.39	5.47	5.54	5.61	5.67	5.73	5.79	5.84	.05	17
	.01	4.10	4.74	5.14	5.43	5.66	5.85	6.01	6.15	6.27	6.38	6.48	6.57	6.66	6.73	6.81	6.87	6.94	7.00	7.05	.01	
18	.05	2.97	3.61	4.00	4.28	4.49	4.67	4.82	4.96	5.07	5.17	5.27	5.35	5.43	5.50	5.57	5.63	5.69	5.74	5.79	.05	18
	.01	4.07	4.70	5.09	5.38	5.60	5.79	5.94	6.08	6.20	6.31	6.41	6.50	6.58	6.65	6.73	6.79	6.85	6.91	6.97	.01	
19	.05	2.96	3.59	3.98	4.25	4.47	4.65	4.79	4.92	5.04	5.14	5.23	5.31	5.39	5.46	5.53	5.59	5.65	5.70	5.75	.05	19
	.01	4.05	4.67	5.05	5.33	5.55	5.73	5.89	6.02	6.14	6.25	6.34	6.43	6.51	6.58	6.65	6.72	6.78	6.84	6.89	.01	
20	.05	2.95	3.58	3.96	4.23	4.45	4.62	4.77	4.90	5.01	5.11	5.20	5.28	5.36	5.43	5.49	5.55	5.61	5.66	5.71	.05	20
	.01	4.02	4.64	5.02	5.29	5.51	5.69	5.84	5.97	6.09	6.19	6.28	6.37	6.45	6.52	6.59	6.65	6.71	6.77	6.82	.01	
24	.05	2.92	3.53	3.90	4.17	4.37	4.54	4.68	4.81	4.92	5.01	5.10	5.18	5.25	5.32	5.38	5.44	5.49	5.55	5.59	.05	24
	.01	3.96	4.55	4.91	5.17	5.37	5.54	5.69	5.81	5.92	6.02	6.11	6.19	6.26	6.33	6.39	6.45	6.51	6.56	6.61	.01	
30	.05	2.89	3.49	3.85	4.10	4.30	4.46	4.60	4.72	4.82	4.92	5.00	5.08	5.15	5.21	5.27	5.33	5.38	5.43	5.47	.05	30
	.01	3.89	4.45	4.80	5.05	5.24	5.40	5.54	5.65	5.76	5.85	5.93	6.01	6.08	6.14	6.20	6.26	6.31	6.36	6.41	.01	
40	.05	2.86	3.44	3.79	4.04	4.23	4.39	4.52	4.63	4.73	4.82	4.90	4.98	5.04	5.11	5.16	5.22	5.27	5.31	5.36	.05	40
	.01	3.82	4.37	4.70	4.93	5.11	5.26	5.39	5.50	5.60	5.69	5.76	5.83	5.90	5.96	6.02	6.07	6.12	6.16	6.21	.01	
60	.05	2.83	3.40	3.74	3.98	4.16	4.31	4.44	4.55	4.65	4.73	4.81	4.88	4.94	5.00	5.06	5.11	5.15	5.20	5.24	.05	60
	.01	3.76	4.28	4.59	4.82	4.99	5.13	5.25	5.36	5.45	5.53	5.60	5.67	5.73	5.78	5.84	5.89	5.93	5.97	6.01	.01	
120	.05	2.80	3.36	3.68	3.92	4.10	4.24	4.36	4.47	4.56	4.64	4.71	4.78	4.84	4.90	4.95	5.00	5.04	5.09	5.13	.05	120
	.01	3.70	4.20	4.50	4.71	4.87	5.01	5.12	5.21	5.30	5.37	5.44	5.50	5.56	5.61	5.66	5.71	5.75	5.79	5.83	.01	
∞	.05	2.77	3.31	3.63	3.86	4.03	4.17	4.29	4.39	4.47	4.55	4.62	4.68	4.74	4.80	4.85	4.89	4.93	4.97	5.01	.05	∞
	.01	3.64	4.12	4.40	4.60	4.76	4.88	4.99	5.08	5.16	5.23	5.29	5.35	5.40	5.45	5.49	5.54	5.57	5.61	5.65	.01	

r = number of means or number of steps between ordered means

Source: Pearson, E. S., & Hartley, H. O. (1966–1972). *Biometrika tables for statisticians* (3rd ed., Vol. 1). New York, NY: Cambridge University Press, 1966. (Copyright by the Biometrika Trustees)

Table B.6 Critical values of Mann-Whitney U

Critical values of the Mann-Whitney U. For a one-tailed test at a = 0.05 (*light type*) and a = 0.025 (**boldface type**) and for a two-tailed test at a = 0.10 (*light type*) and a = 0.05 (**boldface type**).

Each cell is shown as *light* / **bold** (— = no critical value).

n2 \ n1	1	2	3	4	5	6	7	8	9	10	11	12	13	14	15	16	17	18	19	20
1	—	—	—	—	—	—	—	—	—	—	—	—	—	—	—	—	—	—	—	0/—
2	—	—	—	—	0/—	0/—	0/—	1/0	1/0	1/0	1/0	2/1	2/1	2/1	3/1	3/1	3/2	4/2	4/2	4/2
3	—	—	0/—	0/—	1/0	2/1	2/1	3/2	3/2	4/3	5/3	5/4	6/4	7/5	7/5	8/6	9/6	9/7	10/7	11/8
4	—	—	0/—	1/0	2/1	3/2	4/3	5/4	6/4	7/5	8/6	9/7	10/8	11/9	12/10	14/11	15/11	16/12	17/13	18/13
5	—	0/—	1/0	2/1	4/2	5/3	6/5	8/6	9/7	11/8	12/9	13/11	15/12	16/13	18/14	19/15	20/17	22/18	23/19	25/20
6	—	0/—	2/1	3/2	5/3	7/5	8/6	10/8	12/10	14/11	16/13	17/14	19/16	21/17	23/19	25/21	26/22	28/24	30/25	32/27
7	—	0/—	2/1	4/3	6/5	8/6	11/8	13/10	15/12	17/14	19/16	21/18	24/20	26/22	28/24	30/26	33/28	35/30	37/32	39/34
8	—	1/0	3/2	5/4	8/6	10/8	13/10	15/13	18/15	20/17	23/19	26/22	28/24	31/26	33/29	36/31	39/34	41/36	44/38	47/41
9	—	1/0	3/2	6/4	9/7	12/10	15/12	18/15	21/17	24/20	27/23	30/26	33/28	36/31	39/34	42/37	45/39	48/42	51/45	54/48
10	—	1/0	4/3	7/5	11/8	14/11	17/14	20/17	24/20	27/23	31/26	34/29	37/33	41/36	44/39	48/42	51/45	55/48	58/52	62/55
11	—	1/0	5/3	8/6	12/9	16/13	19/16	23/19	27/23	31/26	34/30	38/33	42/37	46/40	50/44	54/47	57/51	61/55	65/58	69/62
12	—	2/1	5/4	9/7	13/11	17/14	21/18	26/22	30/26	34/29	38/33	42/37	47/41	51/45	55/49	60/53	64/57	68/61	72/65	77/69
13	—	2/1	6/4	10/8	15/12	19/16	24/20	28/24	33/28	37/33	42/37	47/41	51/45	56/50	61/54	65/59	70/63	75/67	80/72	84/76
14	—	2/1	7/5	11/9	16/13	21/17	26/22	31/26	36/31	41/36	46/40	51/45	56/50	61/55	66/59	71/64	77/67	82/74	87/78	92/83
15	—	3/1	7/5	12/10	18/14	23/19	28/24	33/29	39/34	44/39	50/44	55/49	61/54	66/59	72/64	77/70	83/75	88/80	94/85	100/90
16	—	3/1	8/6	14/11	19/15	25/21	30/26	36/31	42/37	48/42	54/47	60/53	65/59	71/64	77/70	83/75	89/81	95/86	101/92	107/98
17	—	3/2	9/6	15/11	20/17	26/22	33/28	39/34	45/39	51/45	57/51	64/57	70/63	77/67	83/75	89/81	96/87	102/93	109/99	115/105
18	—	4/2	9/7	16/12	22/18	28/24	35/30	41/36	48/42	55/48	61/55	68/61	75/67	82/74	88/80	95/86	102/93	109/99	116/106	123/112
19	—	4/2	10/7	17/13	23/19	30/25	37/32	44/38	51/45	58/52	65/58	72/65	80/72	87/78	94/85	101/92	109/99	116/106	123/113	130/119
20	0/—	4/2	11/8	18/13	25/20	32/27	39/34	47/41	54/48	62/55	69/62	77/69	84/76	92/83	100/90	107/98	115/105	123/112	130/119	138/127

Critical values of the Mann-Whitney U. For a one-tailed test at a = 0.01 (*light type*) and a = 0.005 (**boldface type**) and for a two-tailed test at a = 0.02 (*light type*) and a = 0.01 (**boldface type**).

Each cell is shown as *light* / **bold** (— = no critical value).

n2 \ n1	1	2	3	4	5	6	7	8	9	10	11	12	13	14	15	16	17	18	19	20
1	—	—	—	—	—	—	—	—	—	—	—	—	—	—	—	—	—	—	—	—
2	—	—	—	—	—	—	—	—	—	—	—	—	0/—	0/—	0/—	0/—	0/—	0/—	1/0	1/0
3	—	—	—	—	—	0/—	0/—	0/—	1/0	1/0	1/0	2/1	2/1	2/1	3/2	3/2	4/2	4/2	4/3	5/3
4	—	—	—	0/—	0/0	1/0	1/1	2/1	3/1	3/2	4/2	5/3	5/3	6/4	7/5	7/5	8/6	9/6	9/7	10/8
5	—	—	0/—	0/0	1/1	2/1	3/2	4/3	5/4	6/5	7/6	8/7	9/7	10/8	11/9	12/10	13/11	14/12	15/13	16/13
6	—	—	0/—	1/1	2/2	3/3	4/4	6/5	7/6	8/7	9/9	11/10	12/11	13/12	15/13	16/15	18/16	19/18	20/19	22/20
7	—	—	0/0	1/1	3/3	4/4	6/6	7/7	9/9	11/10	12/12	14/13	16/15	17/16	19/18	21/19	23/21	24/22	26/24	28/25
8	—	—	1/0	2/2	4/4	6/6	7/7	9/9	11/11	13/13	15/15	17/17	20/18	22/20	24/22	26/24	28/26	30/28	32/30	34/32
9	—	—	1/1	3/3	5/5	7/7	9/9	11/11	14/13	16/16	18/18	21/20	23/22	26/24	28/27	31/29	33/31	36/33	38/36	40/38
10	—	—	1/1	3/3	6/6	8/8	11/11	13/13	16/16	19/18	22/21	24/24	27/26	30/29	33/31	36/34	38/37	41/39	44/42	47/44
11	—	—	1/1	4/4	7/7	9/9	12/12	15/15	18/18	22/21	25/24	28/27	31/30	34/33	37/36	41/39	44/42	47/45	50/48	53/51
12	—	—	2/2	5/5	7/8	11/11	14/14	17/17	21/20	24/24	28/27	31/31	35/34	38/37	42/41	46/44	49/47	53/51	56/54	60/58
13	—	0/0	2/2	5/5	8/9	12/12	16/16	20/18	23/23	27/27	31/31	35/34	39/38	43/42	47/45	51/49	55/53	59/57	63/60	67/64
14	—	0/0	2/2	6/6	10/10	13/13	17/17	22/22	26/26	30/30	34/34	38/38	43/42	47/46	51/50	56/54	60/58	65/63	69/67	73/71
15	—	0/0	3/3	7/7	11/11	15/15	19/19	24/24	28/28	33/33	37/37	42/42	47/46	51/51	56/55	61/60	66/64	70/69	75/73	80/78
16	—	0/0	3/3	7/7	12/12	16/16	21/21	26/26	31/31	36/36	41/41	46/46	51/51	56/56	61/61	66/66	71/71	76/76	82/82	87/87
17	—	0/0	4/4	8/8	13/13	18/18	23/23	28/28	33/33	38/38	44/44	49/49	55/55	60/60	66/66	71/71	77/77	82/82	88/88	93/93
18	—	0/0	4/4	9/9	14/14	19/19	24/24	30/30	36/36	41/41	47/47	53/53	59/59	65/65	70/70	76/76	82/82	88/88	94/94	100/100
19	—	1/0	4/4	9/9	15/15	20/20	26/26	32/32	38/38	44/44	50/50	56/56	63/63	69/69	75/75	82/82	88/88	94/94	101/101	107/107
20	—	1/0	5/5	10/10	16/16	22/22	28/28	34/34	40/40	47/47	53/53	60/60	67/67	73/73	80/80	87/87	93/93	100/100	107/107	114/114

Source: From Kirk, R. E. (1978). *Introductory statistics*. Pacific Grove, CA: Wadsworth–Brooks/Cole.

Table B.7   Critical values of Wilcoxon T

	Level of significance for a one-tailed test			
	0.05	0.025	0.01	0.005
	Level of significance for a two-tailed test			
N	0.10	0.05	0.02	0.01
5	0	—	—	—
6	2	0	—	—
7	3	2	0	—
8	5	3	1	0
9	8	5	3	1
10	10	8	5	3
11	13	10	7	5
12	17	13	9	7
13	21	17	12	9
14	25	21	15	12
15	30	25	19	15
16	35	29	23	19
17	41	34	27	23
18	47	40	32	27
19	53	46	37	32
20	60	52	43	37

Source: From Kirk, R. E. (1978). *Introductory statistics.* Pacific Grove, CA: Wadsworth–Brooks/Cole.

Table B.8   Critical values of Spearman rho

	Significance level for a directional test at			
	.05	.025	.005	.001
	Significance level for a nondirectional test at			
n	.10	.05	.01	.002
5	.900	1.000		
6	.829	.886	1.000	1.000
7	.715	.786	.929	.953
8	.620	.715	.881	.917
9	.600	.700	.834	.879
10	.564	.649	.794	.855
11	.537	.619	.764	.826
12	.504	.588	.735	.797
13	.484	.561	.704	.772
14	.464	.539	.680	.750
15	.447	.522	.658	.730
16	.430	.503	.636	.711
17	.415	.488	.618	.693
18	.402	.474	.600	.676
19	.392	.460	.585	.661
20	.381	.447	.570	.647
21	.371	.437	.556	.633
22	.361	.426	.544	.620
23	.353	.417	.532	.608
24	.345	.407	.521	.597
25	.337	.399	.511	.587
26	.331	.391	.501	.577
27	.325	.383	.493	.567
28	.319	.376	.484	.558
29	.312	.369	.475	.549
30	.307	.363	.467	

Source: CRC (1968). *CRC Handbook of tables for probability and statistics* (2nd ed.). Boca Raton, FL: CRC Press.

Table B.9   *Values of r at the 5% and 1% levels of significance (two-tailed test)*

Degrees of Freedom (*df*)	5%	1%	Degrees of Freedom (*df*)	5%	1%
1	.997	1.000	24	.388	.496
2	.950	.990	25	.381	.487
3	.878	.959	26	.374	.478
4	.811	.917	27	.367	.470
5	.754	.874	28	.361	.463
6	.707	.834	29	.355	.456
7	.666	.798	30	.349	.449
8	.632	.765	35	.325	.418
9	.602	.735	40	.304	.393
10	.576	.708	45	.288	.372
11	.553	.684	50	.273	.354
12	.532	.661	60	.250	.325
13	.514	.641	70	.232	.302
14	.497	.623	80	.217	.283
15	.482	.606	90	.205	.267
16	.468	.590	100	.195	.254
17	.456	.575	125	.174	.228
18	.444	.561	150	.159	.208
19	.433	.549	200	.138	.181
20	.423	.537	300	.113	.148
21	.413	.526	400	.098	.128
22	.404	.515	500	.088	.115
23	.396	.505	1000	.062	.081

Source: Fisher, R. A., & Yates, F. (1978). Statistical tables for biological, agricultural and medical research. London, England: Longman Group. Part of this table is reprinted from Snedecor, G. W., & Cochran, W. G. (1967). *Statistical methods* (6th ed.). Ames, IA: Iowa State University Press.

Table B.10   *Critical Values of c_r^2 for the Friedman Test*

N	$k = 3$ $\alpha = .05$	$k = 3$ $\alpha = .01$	$k = 4$ $\alpha = .05$	$k = 4$ $\alpha = .01$
2	–	–	6.0	−9.0
3	6.000	–	7.4	9.6
4	6.500	8.000	7.8	
5	6.400	8.400		
6	7.000	9.000		
7	7.143	8.857		
8	6.250	9.000		
9	6.222	8.667		

Basic Summation Rules

X and Y refer to distributions of scores.

c refers to a constant in a distribution of scores such as the mean of the distribution.

$$\sum(X-Y) = \sum X - \sum Y$$

$$\sum(X+Y) = \sum X + \sum Y$$

$$\sum cX = c\sum X$$

$$\sum c = Nc$$

$$(X-Y)^2 = X^2 - 2XY + Y^2$$

$$(X+Y)^2 = X^2 + 2XY + Y^2$$

$$\sum(X-Y)^2 = \sum X^2 - 2\sum XY + \sum Y^2$$

$$\sum(X+Y)^2 = \sum X^2 + 2\sum XY + \sum Y^2$$

Answers to Exercises

Chapter 1

1. a. Each value differs from the others in some qualitative way.
   b. The values differ in quantity. X_2 is larger than X_1.
   c. The difference between X_2 and X_1 is the same amount as the difference between X_3 and X_2.
   d. X_4 is twice as large as X_2.

2. a. ordinal: all we know is the order of the finish not the distance between each horse
   b. ratio: time to finish has a true zero point and ratio statements can be made
   c. nominal: male and female jockeys differ in kind not quantity
   d. nominal: post positions differ in name only; Post 1 is not quantitatively different than Post 2.

3. a. This is most likely a question to be answered with correlational statistics. The researcher is interested in the relationship between income and attitude about free trade. This study may also use inferential statistics. Chapter 16 discusses how correlation can be a descriptive or an inferential technique.
   b. Because the researcher wants to know how all New Yorkers feel about free trade, he will probably use inferential statistics to generalize from the sample of New Yorkers he interviews to the population as a whole.
   c. This researcher will most likely use correlational techniques to examine the relationship between abused children and abusing parents.
   d. This is an example of the use of inference to generalize from the sample (every 10th person) to all the shoppers in the mall.
   e. The professor needs to describe how the students did on the midterm and to present some summary of the results to the class. He will choose descriptive measures to do this.
   f. The consultant is using a test to screen applicants. This would involve predictive techniques because she will predict the applicants' suitability as police persons use their results on the test to do so.

4. a. constant: only one temperature is the highest of the day
   b. constant: number of children delivered in one year does not vary
   c. variable: different students vary in terms of religious affiliation
   d. constant: only boys are enrolled so gender does not vary
   e. variable: different species of birds are seen so species vary

5.

	Independent Variable	Dependent Variable
a	Blood-alcohol	Reaction time
b	Training	Crisis control effectiveness
c	Training	Grades
d	Labels	Perception
e	Feeding schedule	Rate of weight gain
f	Exercise	Fitness

6. a. continuous: aptitude could in theory be measured with infinite precision
    b. discrete: number of students is discrete in that certain values cannot occur (e.g., half a student)
    c. continuous: reaction time could in theory be measured with infinite precision
    d. continuous: temperature could in theory be measured with infinite precision
    e. discrete: socioeconomic class has only certain values (e.g., upper, middle, lower)
    f. discrete: curriculum subject has only certain values (e.g., English, chemistry)
    g. continuous: age could in theory be measured with infinite precision
    h. discrete: gender has only two values
    i. discrete: dress size has only certain values (large, medium, small for example)

7. Brand of pain reliever—independent variable; rating—dependent variable.

8. a. ordinal   d. interval   g. ratio
    b. ratio   e. nominal   h. nominal
    c. nominal   f. nominal   i. ordinal

9. a. 11   c. 6
    b.   4   d. 2

10. a. observation   d. verbal report
     b. observation   e. standardized test
     c. verbal report   f. observation

11. There are several possible threats to internal validity in this example. Proactive history might differ between the two groups. The participants were not randomly assigned, and the 8:00 a.m. class may well be different from the later class. Early-morning classes may have more students sleeping than classes later in the day. If the students talked to each other during the course of the study, then retroactive history could also threaten internal validity. Investigator bias might be involved because the professor is both conducting the research and evaluating the results. He may also unintentionally treat his experimental group more differently than he thinks.

12. This is an example of a study with no hope for internal validity. The teacher has no control group. She didn't test her participants before she introduced her new technique. If she finds they do well, she has no way of knowing what the responsible variables are.

13. This example is a slight improvement over Example 12 because the teacher has administered a pretest. Internal validity is in doubt, however, because she has no control over the effects of the pretest on the posttest results. Testing itself can affect performance. Factors such as retroactive history, maturation, and investigator bias are also causes for concern.

14. This investigator has taken some trouble to control for factors affecting internal validity by using random selection, by using a placebo control group, and by using a double-blind technique. He could not randomly assign participants to groups, but his placebo control will help mitigate changes in memory due to maturation, and so on. The major problem here will be with attrition. The experiment spans a 2-year period. Thus, we would expect that the group of 80- to 90-year-olds may lose more participants than the younger groups.

Chapter 2

1. a.

Class Interval	After	Before
64–66	1	0
61–63	0	0
58–60	0	0
55–57	2	0
52–54	0	0
49–51	0	1
46–48	3	1
43–45	0	0
40–42	4	4
37–39	1	2
34–36	2	0
31–33	4	2
28–30	3	3
25–27	1	3
22–24	2	5
19–21	2	2
16–18	0	2

b.

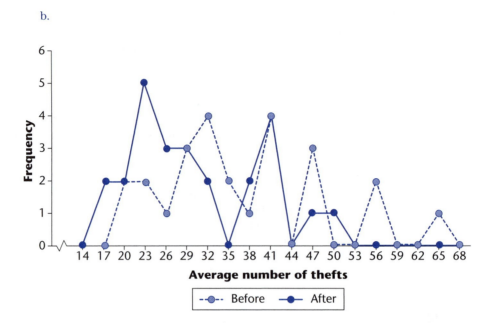

2.	X	f
	25	1
	24	0
	23	0
	22	0
	21	0
	20	0
	19	0
	18	1
	17	0
	16	0
	15	3
	14	1
	13	1
	12	1
	11	1
	10	1
	9	1
	8	2
	7	1
	6	1

3.	X	rf
	90	0.05
	89	0.05
	88	0.05
	87	0.00
	86	0.00
	85	0.00
	84	0.10
	83	0.05
	82	0.00
	81	0.00
	80	0.05
	79	0.05
	78	0.05
	77	0.10
	76	0.00
	75	0.05
	74	0.00
	73	0.00
	72	0.10
	71	0.20
	70	0.10

4.	X	cf
	21	25
	20	24
	19	23
	18	21
	17	20
	16	18
	15	14
	14	11
	13	8
	12	4
	11	4
	10	3

5. Bar graph of student major

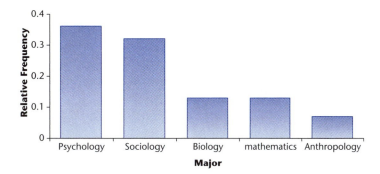

6. Bar graph of opinion

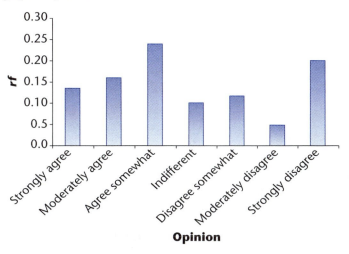

7. Bar graph of residents by region

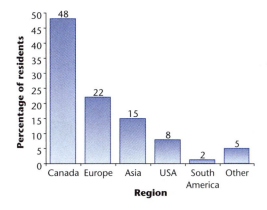

8.

Interval	f
46–50	1
41–45	2
36–40	2
31–35	0
26–30	0
21–25	1
16–20	0
11–15	2
6–10	5
1–5	1

9. Frequency polygon of Exercise 8 data

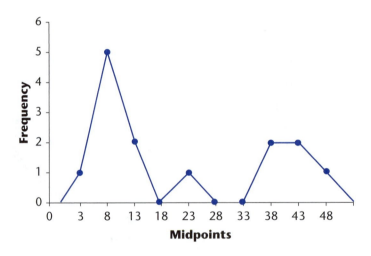

10. Histogram of Exercise 8 data

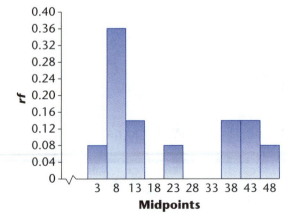

11. Ogive of Exercise 8 data

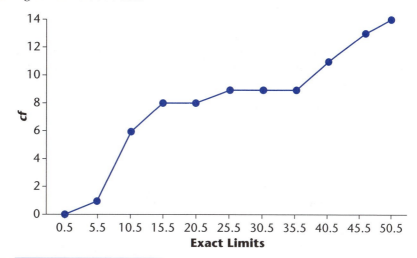

12.

Interval	rf
84–90	0.04
77–83	0.02
70–76	0.00
63–69	0.09
56–62	0.15
49–55	0.19
42–48	0.12
35–41	0.10
28–34	0.06
21–27	0.10
14–20	0.04
7–13	0.04
0–6	0.05

13. Histogram of Exercise 12 data

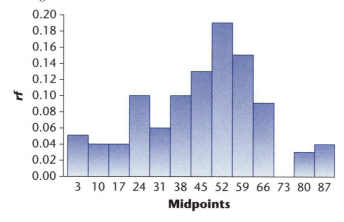

14. a. 1.95 to 2.05   d. 24.5 to 29.5
    b. 2.55 to 2.65   e. 24.45 to 29.55
    c. 1.5 to 4.5   f. 24.495 to 29.505

15. Bar graph. Type of entrée is a discrete variable so a bar graph should be used. Relative frequency. Relative frequency would make it easier to compare summer and winter customer choices.

16. Frequency Polygon

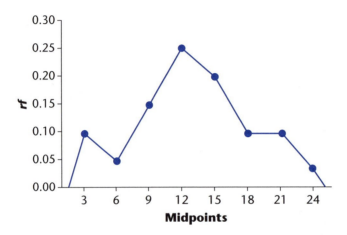

17. Bar graph of disorder by gender

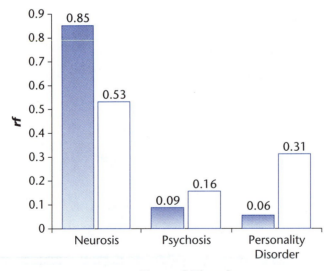

18.

```
1 | 0   0   1   5   6
2 | 1   3   3   5   6   7   8
3 | 1   2   3   7   7   8   9   9
4 | 2   2   3   6   6   8   9   9
5 | 0   1   2   8   9   9   9   9
6 | 1   4   4   5   6   7   7   8
7 | 2   3   3   4   5   7
8 | 4   5   5   6   7   8
9 | 0   0   3   4   5   6
```

19.

a. Table 2.1

Simple frequency distribution of weights

X	F	X	f	X	f	X	f
164	1	144	0	124	1	104	2
163	0	143	0	123	2	103	3
162	0	142	1	122	1	102	2
161	0	141	1	121	2	101	2
160	0	140	0	120	0	100	3
159	2	139	0	119	3	99	0
158	0	138	1	118	1	98	3
157	1	137	1	117	3	97	2
156	0	136	3	116	4	96	1
155	2	135	1	115	2	95	0
154	1	134	2	114	2	94	1
153	1	133	3	113	1	93	1
152	0	132	1	112	0	92	0
151	1	131	2	111	2	91	2
150	1	130	2	110	2	90	2
149	0	129	3	109	3	89	0
148	0	128	2	108	3	88	1
147	0	127	1	107	0	87	0
146	0	126	0	106	3	86	1
145	0	125	1	105	3	85	1

b. Table 2.2

Grouped frequency distribution of weights

Apparent Limits	Exact Limits	MP	f	rf	cf	crf
160–164	159.5–164.5	162	1	0.01	100	1.00
155–159	154.5–159.5	157	5	0.05	99	0.99
150–154	149.5–154.5	152	4	0.04	94	0.94
145–149	144.5–149.5	147	0	0.00	90	0.90

(Continued)

(Continued)

Apparent Limits	Exact Limits	MP	f	rf	cf	crf
140–144	139.5–144.5	142	2	0.02	90	0.90
135–139	134.5–139.5	137	6	0.06	88	0.88
130–134	129.5–134.5	132	10	0.10	82	0.82
125–129	124.5–129.5	127	7	0.07	72	0.72
120–124	119.5–124.5	122	6	0.06	65	0.65
115–119	114.5–119.5	117	13	0.13	59	0.59
110–114	109.5–114.5	112	7	0.07	46	0.46
105–109	104.5–109.5	107	12	0.12	39	0.39
100–104	99.5–104.5	102	12	0.12	27	0.27
95–99	94.5–99.5	97	6	0.06	15	0.15
90–94	89.5–94.5	92	6	0.06	9	0.09
85–89	84.5–89.5	87	3	0.03	3	0.03

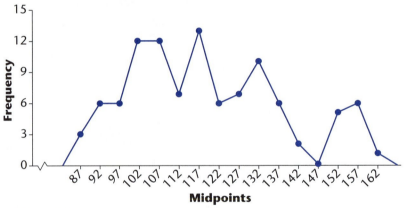

c. *Figure 2.1.*   Frequency polygon of weights.

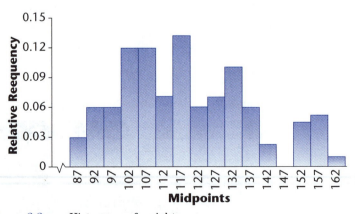

d. *Figure 2.2.*   Histogram of weights.

Chapter 3

1. *DATA SET A*
   $N = 15$
   $\Sigma X = 114$
   $\mu = 7.60$
   $Mo = 11, 9, 8, 7, 5, 3$
   $Mdn = 7.75$
   Negative skew

   DATA SET B
   $N = 10$
   $\Sigma X = 22$
   $\mu = 2.20$
   $Mo = 2$
   $Mdn = 1.83$
   Positive skew

2. *DATA SET A*
   $N = 19$
   $\Sigma fX = 139$
   $\mu = 7.32$
   $Mo = 7$
   $Mdn = 7.25$
   Positive skew

   DATA SET B
   $N = 65$
   $\Sigma fX = 1\ 490$
   $\mu = 22.92$
   $Mo = 17$
   $Mdn = 19.71$
   Positive skew

3. Frequency polygon for Exercise 2, Data Set *B*

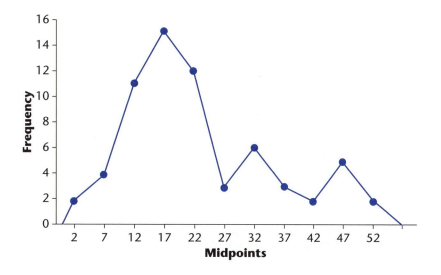

4. $\mu = 7$ $Mo = 8$ $Mdn = 7.67$ negative skew

5. $\mu = 3$ $Mo = 2$ $Mdn = 2.25$ positive skew

6. $\mu_c = 5.44$

7. $\mu = 19.73$ $Mo = 12$ $Mdn = 18.5$ positive skew

8. $\mu = 6.79$ $Mo = 5$ $Mdn = 6.2$ positive skew

9. $\mu = 113.85$ $Mo = 107$ $Mdn = 113.14$ positive skew

10. $\mu = 10.1$ $Mo = 8$ $Mdn = 9.5$ positive skew

11. a. It is limited at zero.

b. Mean: Because it is positively skewed the mean will have the highest value

12. $\mu = 12.7$ $Mdn = 12.68$ $Mo = 11.8$ positive skew

13. a. The dress manufacturer should choose mode. This is the only reasonable measure of average for an ordinal measure such as dress size. Median or mean dress size would be of little help because it is possible that no woman could wear this average size.

b. The median will divide the entire group into two groups of equal sizes.

c. Most rating scale studies report the median response as their measure of average. With so few alternatives, the mode is likely to be of little use. The data are not really amenable to the computation of a mean.

d. The median is the most appropriate measure of average for an open-ended distribution.

Chapter 4

1. *DATA SET A*
$\Sigma X = 200$
$N = 10$
$\mu = 20$
$\Sigma(X - \mu) = 0$
$SS = 1\ 198$
$\sigma^2 = 119.80$
$\sigma = 10.94$

   DATA SET B
$\Sigma X = 49$
$N = 7$
$\mu = 7$
$\Sigma(X - \mu) = 0$
$SS = 104$
$\sigma^2 = 14.86$
$\sigma = 3.85$

2. *DATA SET A*
$\Sigma X = 42$
$\Sigma X^2 = 314$
$(\Sigma X)^2 = 1\ 764$
$(\Sigma X)^2/N = 252$
$\sigma^2 = 8.86$
$\sigma = 2.98$

   DATA SET B
$\Sigma fX = 152$
$\Sigma fX^2 = 1\ 020$
$(\Sigma fX)^2 = 23\ 104$
$(\Sigma fX)^2/N = 888.62$
$\sigma^2 = 5.05$
$\sigma = 2.25$

3.

X	$X - \mu_X$	Y	$Y - \mu_Y$
2	−2	12	−16
4	0	23	−5
6	2	50	22
7	3	35	7
4	0	20	−8
3	−1		
2	−2		

$\mu_X = 4$

$\mu_Y = 28$

4. $\mu = 5.86$ $\Sigma(X - \mu)^2 = 48.86$ $N = 7$
   $\sigma^2 = 6.98$ $\sigma = 2.64$ Range $= 10 - 2 + 1 = 9$

5. $\mu = 3$ $\sigma^2 = 7.25$ $\sigma = 2.69$ Range $= 8 - 0 + = 9$

6. $\Sigma X^2 = 130$ $\Sigma X = 24$ $(\Sigma X)^2/N = 72$ $\sigma^2 = 7.25$ $\sigma = 2.69$

7. $(\Sigma f X)^2/N = 875.84$ $\Sigma f X^2 = 937$ $\sigma^2 = 3.22$ $\sigma = 1.79$ Range $= 6$

8. $\sigma^2 = 30.85$ $\sigma = 5.55$

9. $\sigma_c^2 = 9.16$

10. In Distribution A, most of the scores were close to the mean of 98, and very few were as high as 112. This score indicates better performance in Distribution A than in Distribution B.

11.
	GROUP 1	GROUP 2
μ	23.42	21.53
σ	1.95	3.31
Median	23.92	21.92
Skew	Slight negative	Slight negative

12. $\mu = 6.40$ $\sigma = 1.43$ Skew: slight positive

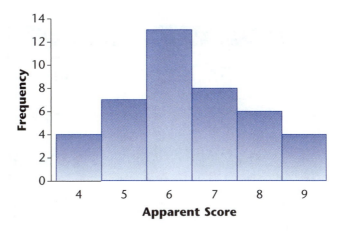

13. a. SIQ (semi-interquartile range) $= (23.5 - 11)/2 = 6.25$

    b. SIQ $= (22.5 - 10)/2 = 6.25$

Chapter 5

1. $P_{50} = 121.5$ $P_{75} = 129.5$ $P_{90} = 133.25$ $PR_{117} = 30.83$

2. $z = -2$

3.

X	z
4	−1.02
6	−0.30
8	0.42
9	0.78
11	1.49
3	−1.37

4. Maria did better on her math test: $z_{grammar} = 1$; $z_{math} = 1.5$

5. A positively skewed distribution.

6. 62% of the scores were at or below a score value of 89%.

7. d

8. $X = 3(3) + 54 = 63$

9. $X = 1.30(3) + 64 = 67.9$

10. a. $P_{30} = 59.25$ $\quad$ $P_{45} = 71.93$ $\quad$ $P_{85} = 84.50$
    b. $PR_{83} = 81.25$ $\quad$ $PR_{54} = 18.75$ $\quad$ $PR_{78} = 66.25$
    c. and d.

X	f	fX	X²	fX²	X − μ	z
98	1	98	9 604	9 604	27.5	1.93
93	3	279	8 649	25 947	22.5	1.58
88	1	88	7 744	7 744	17.5	1.23
83	5	415	6 889	34 445	12.5	0.88
78	7	546	6 084	42 588	7.5	0.53
73	7	511	5 329	37 303	2.5	0.18
68	1	68	4 624	4 624	−2.5	−0.18
63	2	126	3 969	7 938	−7.5	−0.53
58	4	232	3 364	13 456	−12.5	−0.88
53	5	265	2 809	14 045	−17.5	−1.23
48	4	192	2 304	9 216	−22.5	−1.58
Sum		2 820		206 910		

$\mu = 70.50$

$\sigma = 14.23$

11. a. $P_{30} = 105.75$
    b. $P_{95} = 155.5$

    c. $P_{127} = 68.5$
    d. $P_{139} = 87.4$

12. $PR_{130} = 52.6$

    $Mdn = 129.5$

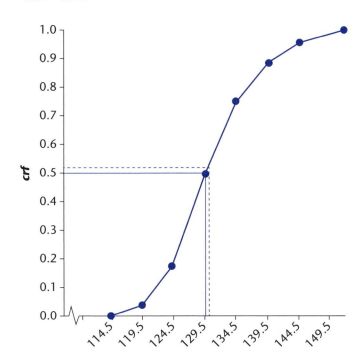

13. a. $\Sigma X = 528$
    b. $\Sigma X^2 = 19\ 106$
    c. $N = 15$
    d. $(\Sigma X)^2 = 278\ 784$
    e. $\mu = 35.2$
    f. $(\Sigma X)^2/N = 18\ 585.6$
    g. $\sigma^2 = 34.69$
    h. $\sigma = 5.89$
    i. z scores (ordered from high to low): 0.81, 0.81, 0.81, 0.81, 0.64, 0.64, 0.47, 0.47, 0.47, 0.30, 0, –1.2, 1.2, –1.4, –2.4
    j. $\Sigma z = 0$

14. a. z-score Test 1 = 0.33 z-score Test 2 = 0.4

       He did better on Test 2 because he was farther above the mean.

    b. Ben's $z = 2.83$ Tom's $z = 3.13$

       Tom is farther above the mean than Ben, so relatively speaking, Tom is richer.

Chapter 6

1. .9876
2. .9386
3. .0250

4. ±1.64
5. +1.28

6. a. 0.50
   b. 2.5
   c. 50
   d. 95
   e. 99

7. a. $z = (80 - 72)/12 = 0.66$ Area $= 25.14\%$
   b. $z = (66 - 72)/12 = -0.5$ Area $= 31\%$
   c. $X = 72 \pm (0.84)(12) = 61.92$ and 82.08
   d. $X = 72 - 1.64(12) = 52.35$
   e. 5% of 5 000 $= 250$
   f. 110
   g. $X = 63.96$

8. $z = (63 - 50)/10 = 1.30$

   Area between 0 and 1.30 is .4032; area below 0 is .5

   Total area below the score of 63 is .5 + .4032 = .9032; $PR_{63} = 90.32$

9. $z = 20.84$ $P_{20} = 41.6$

10. $z = (70 - 112)/12 = -3.50$
    $z = (150 - 112)/12 = 3.17$

    Area $= .4998 + .4992 = .9990$

11. $z = \pm 1.64$

12. 451.6 and 648.4

13. 50/10 000 $= 0.005$
    $z = -2.58$
    $X = 550 - (2.58)60 = 395.20$

14. $z = (500 - 550)/60 = -0.83$
    $z = (600 - 550)/60 = 0.83$

    Area $= 2(.2967) = .5934$

    Number of scores $= 0.5934(10\ 000) = 5934$

Chapter 7

1. a, c, d
2. a, c, d

3. a. $p = (A \text{ and } B) = .80 \bullet .70 = .56$
    b. $p = (A \text{ or } B) = .80 + .70 - .56 = .94$

4. a. $p = .15 \bullet .25 = .04$ c. $p = .15 + .75 - (.15)(.75) = .79$
    b. $p = 0.85 \bullet .25 = .21$ d. $p = .75 \bullet .15 = .11$

5. a. $p = .25 \bullet .15 = .025$
    b. $p = .10 + .25 - (.25)(.15) = .325$

6. a. $p = .31$ c. $p = .33$
    b. $p = .003$ d. $p = .04$

7. $p = {}_6C_2(3/8)^2(5/8)^4 = .32$

8. ${}_6P_6 = 720$

9. 56

10. ${}_{10}P_4 = 5040$

11. a. 1/48   d. 46/48
    b. 1/48   e. 4/48
    c. 2/48

12. a. $1/48 \bullet 1/47$
    b. $2/48 \bullet 1/47$
    c. $4/48 \bullet 3/47$

13. a. 36   b. 4

14. 2/36

15. 1/4 and 2/4

16. a. 4 outcomes
    b. $p = 2/36$

17. Row totals: 4, 13, 33, 25, 45, 6, 0, 2, 1
    Column totals: 58, 37, 34

    Total: 129

    a. $p = .45$ b. $p = .09$ c. $p = .01$ d. $p = .98$

18. a. $p = (.0005)4$ b. $p = .0192$ c. $p = .0196$

Chapter 8

1. a. $\Sigma X = 130$ d. $\Sigma X^2 = 2\,708$
    b. $(\Sigma X)^2/N = 2414.29$ e. $\mu = 18.57$
    c. $N = 7$ f. $\sigma = 6.48$

2. $\mu = 5$ $\sigma = 3.64$

3.

Samples	Sample Mean	Samples	Sample Mean	Samples	Sample Mean
1, 1	1.00	11, 2	6.50	4, 7	5.50
2, 1	1.50	1, 4	2.50	7, 7	7.00
4, 1	2.50	2, 4	3.00	11, 7	9.00
7, 1	4.00	4, 4	4.00	1, 11	6.00
11, 1	6.00	7, 4	5.50	2, 11	6.50
1, 2	1.50	11, 4	7.50	4, 11	7.50
2, 2	2.00	1, 7	4.00	7, 11	9.00
4, 2	3.00	2, 7	4.50	11, 11	11.00
7, 2	4.50				

4.

$\bar{X}$	f	$f\bar{X}$	$\bar{X}^2$	$f\bar{X}^2$
11	1	11	121	121
9	2	18	81	162
7.5	2	15	56.3	112.5
7	1	1	49	49
6.5	2	13	42.3	84.5
6	2	12	36	72
5.5	2	11	30.3	60.5
4.5	2	9	2.3	40.5
4	3	12	16	48
3	2	6	9	18
2.5	2	5	6.25	12.5
2	1	2	4	4
1.5	2	3	2.25	4.5
1	1	1	1	1
Sum	25	125		790

$\mu_{\bar{X}} = 5$

$\sigma_{\bar{X}} = 2.57$

5. a. $p = 0$
    b. $p = 12/25$
    c. $p = 4/25$

6. a. $\mu_{\bar{X}} = 75$ and $\sigma_{\bar{X}} = 1$
    b. $\mu_{\bar{X}} = 75$ and $\sigma_{\bar{X}} = 1.5$
    c. $\mu_{\bar{X}} = 75$ and $\sigma_{\bar{X}} = 3$

7. $p = .9050$

8. Standard error of the mean $= 3.20$
   a. $z = 3.75, p \sim .0001$
   b. $z = 1.56, p = .8812$
   c. $z = -3.125, p = .0009$

9. a. $100 \pm 1.96(3.20) = 106.27$ and $93.73(95\% \text{ CI})$
   b. $100 \pm 2.58(3.20) = 108.26$ and $91.74(99\% \text{ CI})$

10. Standard error of the difference $= 16.04$
    a. $z = 1.37, p = .0853$
    b. $z = 1.87, p = .0307$
    c. $z = 2.94, p = .0016$

11. Standard error $= 0.97$
    a. $z = -0.30, p = .3821$
    b. $z = -2.06, p = .0197$
    c. $z = -0.51, p = .3050$

12. Standard error of the proportion $= 0.06$
    a. $z = 1.41, p = .0793$
    b. $z = -0.28, p = .3897$
    c. $z = -1.97, p = .0244$

13. Standard error of the proportion $= 0.02$
    $z = -3.72$
    $p = .0001$

Chapter 9

1. $H_0: \mu = 79$
   $H_1: \mu \neq 79$
   $z = 2.14$

   Fail to reject. No evidence that the students are different from all students.

2. 95% CI: $(85 \pm 5.49) = 79.51$ to 90.49
   99% CI: $(85 \pm 7.22) = 77.78$ to 92.22

3. $H_0: P = .50$ $H_1: P > .50$ $p = 29/52 = .56$

$$z = \frac{.56 - .50}{\sqrt{\dfrac{(.5)(.5)}{52}}} = 0.86$$

Fail to reject. No evidence that Claire is a better than chance guesser.

4. H_0: $\mu = 250$ $\qquad$ H_1: $\mu \neq 250$

$$z = \frac{245 - 250}{3.5\sqrt{49}} = -10$$

Reject. The mean breaking strength of this manufacturer's seat belts is not 250 kg.

5. H_0: $P = .75$ $\qquad$ H_1: $P > .75$ $\qquad$ $p = .81$

$$z = \frac{.81 - .75}{\sqrt{\dfrac{(.75)(.25)}{100}}} = 1.39$$

Fail to reject. No evidence that more than 75% of retired couples prefer apartment living.

6. 99% CI: $[48 \pm 2.58(20/10)] = 42.84$ to 53.16

7. H_0: $P = .70$ $\qquad$ H_1: $P \neq .70$ $\qquad$ $p = .60$ $\qquad$ $z = 1.54$

Fail to reject. No evidence that the true proportion is not .70.

8. H_0: $P = .50$ $\qquad$ H_1: $P \neq .50$ $\qquad$ $z = 1.76$

Fail to reject. No evidence that Candidate A is ahead of Candidate B.

9. a. H_0: $\mu = 85$ $\qquad$ H_1: $\mu < 85$
   b. Critical z value $= -1.64$
   c. $z_{obt} = \dfrac{82 - 85}{9.5/\sqrt{49}} = \dfrac{-3}{1.36} = 2.21$
   d. Decision: Reject the null

   There is a statistically significant loss of weight after participating in the program.

10. a. H_0: $P = .25$ $\qquad$ H_1: $P > .25$
    b. Critical z value $= 2.33$
    c. Obtained z value $= 4.50$
    d. Reject.
    e. Brad guessed significantly better than chance.

11. a. H_0: $\mu = 1.1$ $\qquad$ H_1: $\mu \neq 1.1$
    b. Critical z value $= \pm 2.58$
    c. Obtained z value $= -2.53$
    d. Fail to reject.
    e. No evidence that the company's claim is untrue.

12. $\mu_1 - \mu_2 = (115 - 118) \pm 2.58(2)$
    $C(-8.16 \leq \mu_1 - \mu_2 \leq 2.16) = .99$

Chapter 10

1. t test for dependent means (this is a within-participants design).

2. t test for dependent means (participants are not independently assigned to groups).

3. t test for independent means (participants have not been matched; the population of interest is male children with IQs more than 120).

4. a. 28, $t_{.05} = \pm 2.048$ b. 15, $t_{.05} = \pm 2.131$

5. $H_0: \mu_A = \mu_B$ $H_1: \mu_A \neq \mu_B$ $t_{.01} = \pm 2.98$

	Program A	Program B
ΣX	106	118
ΣX^2	1 448	1 816
$(\Sigma X)^2$	11 236	13 924
$(\Sigma X)^2/n$	1404.5	1740.5

$$t = \frac{13.25 - 14.75}{\sqrt{\dfrac{43.5 + 75.5}{8(7)}}} = -1.03$$

Fail to reject the null.

6. $H_0: \mu_1 = \mu_2$ $H_1: \mu_1 \neq \mu_2$
   $df = 14$ $t_{.01} = \pm 2.98$
   $\Sigma D = -48$ $\Sigma D^2 = 552$
   $t = -3.2/1.38 = -2.323$

   Fail to reject. No evidence that the speaker made a difference.

7. $H_0: \mu_1 = \mu_2$ $H_1: \mu_1 < \mu_2$ $df = 38$
   Reject. Female survivors of acquaintance rape had significantly lower self-esteem ratings than woman who were not assaulted ($t(38) = -4.40$, $p < .01$).

8. $s_{\bar{X}_1 - \bar{X}_2} = \sqrt{\dfrac{425}{23}\left(\dfrac{1}{15} + \dfrac{1}{10}\right)} = 1.755$

   $C(1.36 \leq \mu_1 - \mu_2 \leq 8.64) = .95$

9. a. Rejecting a true null hypothesis (α).
   b. Failing to reject a false null hypothesis (β).
   c. The probability of rejecting a false null hypothesis($1 - \beta$).

10. a. Use a dependent samples design to decrease error variance.
    b. Use a larger alpha level.
    c. Increase sample size.

11. a. $H_0: \mu = 28$ $H_1: \mu \neq 28$ e. Obtained t value $= -1.33$
    b. $df = 15$ f. Fail to reject. No evidence that the training
    c. Critical t value $= \pm 2.131$ had an effect on assertiveness.
    d. $s = 6.74$

12. a. $H_0: \mu_1 = \mu_2$ $H_1: \mu_1 \neq \mu_2$ e. $p > \alpha$
    b. $df = 14$
    c. $t_{crit} = \pm 2.98$
    d. $t = -3/1.36 = -2.21$

    f. Fail to reject. There is no statistical evidence that the workshop and lecture groups differed in logical decision-making scores.

13. a. $H_0: \mu_1 = \mu_2$ $H_1: \mu_1 > \mu_2$ d. $t = 2.5$
    b. $df = 9$ e. $p < .05$
    c. $t_{.05} = +1.83$

    f. Reject. The DNA significantly improved running speed.

14. a. $H_0: \mu_1 = \mu_2$ $H_1: \mu_1 \neq \mu_2$ e. $p > \alpha$
    b. $df = 16$
    c. $t_{.05} = \pm 2.12$
    d. $t = 0.82$

    f. Fail to reject. There is no evidence that the noise and silence groups differed in number of problems solved.

15. a. $df = 27$
    b. $t_{.05} = \pm 2.052$ and $t_{.01} = \pm 2.771$
    c. Standard error $= 1.51$

    d. $C(-0.76 \leq (\mu_1 - \mu_2) \leq 5.42) = .95$
    e. $C(-1.85 \leq (\mu_1 - \mu_2) \leq 6.51) = .99$

Chapter 11

1.

	SS	df	MS	F
BG	141.3	3	47.10	3.54
WG	1 278	96	13.31	

$F_{.05} = 2.70$, Reject

2.

	SS	df	MS	F
BG	433.2	2	216.6	24.27
WG	107.1	12	8.93	

Reject

3.

	SS	df	MS	F
BG	54.45	1	54.45	14.39
WG	68.10	18	3.78	

Reject. Training had a significant effect on speed.

4.

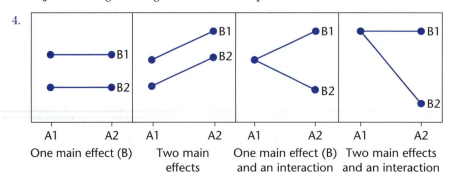

| One main effect (B) | Two main effects | One main effect (B) and an interaction | Two main effects and an interaction |

5.

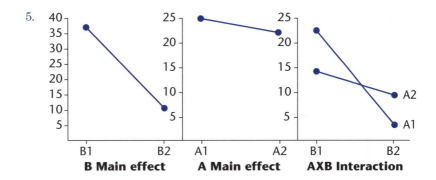

	B Main effect	A Main effect	AXB Interaction

6.

Source	SS	df	MS	F	p
A	28.13	1	28.13	21.14	<.01
B	28.13	1	28.13	21.14	<.01
A × B	12.5	1	12.5	9.40	<.01
WP	37.25	28	1.33		
Total	106	31			

There was a significant main effect of cartoon content and presence of authority figure. There was significant interaction between cartoon content and presence/absence of authority figure.

7. a. $SS_{TOT} = 141.14$ d. $H_0: \mu_1 = \mu_2 = \mu_3$ e. F_{cnt} (2, 18) = 3.55
   b. $SS_{BG} = 56.00$ $H_1: H_0$ is false
   c. $SS_{WG} = 85.14$

f.

Source	SS	df	MS	F	p
Between	56.00	2	28.00	5.92	<.05
Within	85.14	18	4.73		
Total	141.14	20			

g. Reject. The means of the three groups are not equal.

8.

Source	SS	df	MS	F	p
Between	16.39	3	5.46	0.98	>.05
Within	133.86	24	5.58		

Reject.

9.

Source	SS	df	MS	F	p
A	16.67	1	16.67	0.11	<.05
B	8.17	1	8.17	0.05	<.05
A × B	383.99	1	383.99	2.58	<.05
WG	2981.00	20	149.05		
Total	3389.83	23			

Fail to reject. No main effects and no interaction.

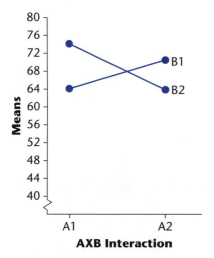

AXB Interaction

10.

Source	SS	df	MS	F	p
A	23.11	1	23.11	9.41	<.01
B	19.01	1	19.01	7.74	<.01
A × B	35.11	1	35.11	14.29	<.01
WS	186.75	76	2.46		

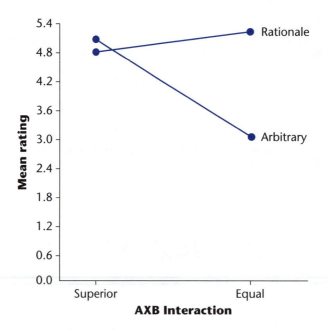

AXB Interaction

Reject. Both main effects and the interaction were significant. Ratings were higher in the rationale condition. Ratings were higher when the command was given by a superior. However, the interaction indicates that the rationale-arbitrary difference only occurred when the command giver was an equal.

Chapter 12

1.

Source	df
a. Total	99
b. Between participants	19
c. Within participants	80
d. Between treatment	4
e. Participant by treatment	76

2.

Source	SS	df	MS	F	p
Between participants	197.33	9			
Within participants	1569.33	20			
Treatment	695.27	2	347.63	7.16	<.01
$P \times T$	874.07	18	48.56		
Total	1766.67	29			

Reject.

3.

Source	SS	df	MS	F	p
A	50	3	16.67	2.67	<.01
$P_{(gps)}$	200	32	6.25		
B	700	2	350		<.01
$A \times B$	550	6	91.67	2.93	<.05
$P_{(gps) \times B}$	2 000	64	31.25		

Both main effects were significant. There was an interaction.

4.

Source	SS	df	MS	F	p
P	3559.81	15			
A	17.52	1	17.52	0.07	>.05
$P_{(gps)}$	3542.29	14	221.39		
WP	1194.67	32			
B	401.79	2	200.90	18.18	<.01
$A \times B$	439.35	2	219.68	19.88	<.01
$P_{(gps) \times B}$	353.52	28	11.05		
Total	4754.48	47			

The B main effect (type of relationship) and the interaction were significant.

5.

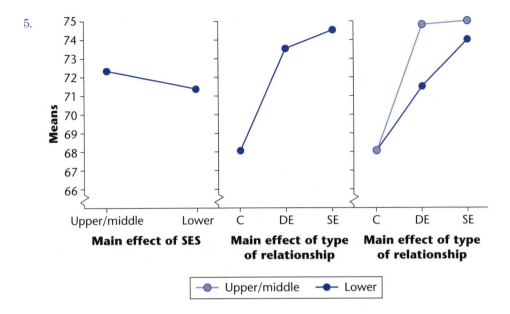

Main effect of SES   **Main effect of type of relationship**   **Main effect of type of relationship**

○— Upper/middle   ●— Lower

6. *F*s are as follows: $A = 2.24,$ $B = 2.75,$ $A \times B = 2.05$

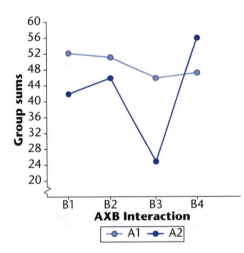

AXB Interaction

○— A1   ●— A2

Source	SS	df	MS	F	p
A	10.56	1	10.56	2.24	>.05
$P_{(gps)}$	65.88	14	4.71		
B	36.56	3	12.19	2.75	>.05
A × B	27.31	3	9.10	2.05	>.05
$P_{(gps)}$ × B	186.13	42	4.432		
Total	326.44	63			

7.

Source	SS	df	MS	F	p
A	17.83	2	8.92	6.64	<.01
$P_{(gps)}$	36.14	27	1.34		
B	1.54	2	0.77	15.17	>.01
A × B	35.04	4	3.9	0.60	<.05
$P_{(gps) \times B}$	35.04	54	0.65		
Total	125.59	89	89		

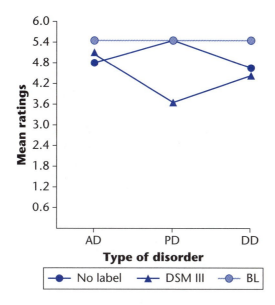

One main effect and the interaction were significant.

8.

Source	SS	df	MS	F	p
A	1 602.47	2	801.23	7.66	<.01
$P_{(gps)}$	2 822.60	27	104.54		
B	2 588.07	2	1 294.03	15.17	>.01
$A \times B$	205.47	4	51.37	0.60	<.05
$P_{(gps) \times B}$	4 607.80	54	85.33		
Total	11 826.4	89			

Chapter 13

1. $t_{crit} = \pm 2.083$ standard error $= 7.05$

Comparison	t
$A_1 B_1$ vs. $A_1 B_2$	−1.30
$A_1 B_1$ vs. $A_2 B_2$	−0.90
$A_1 B_1$ vs. $A_2 B_1$	0.07
$A_1 B_2$ vs. $A_2 B_1$	0.40
$A_1 B_2$ vs. $A_2 B_2$	1.37
$A_2 B_1$ vs. $A_2 B_2$	0.97

There are no significant differences.

2. $t_{crit} = \sim \pm 2.66$ standard error $= 0.50$

Group 2 vs	t
Group 1	4.6
Group 3	4.1
Group 4	4.8

All three groups were significantly different from Group 2.

3. $F_s = 2.79$

a. $C = 1.6$	b. $C = 4.20$	c. $C = 5.00$
$s_c = 1.33$	$s_c = 1.15$	$s_c = 1.33$
$F' = 1.20$	$F' = 3.65$	$F' = 3.76$
Fail to reject	Reject	Reject

4. $q(.05, 9, 3) = 3.95$

ANOVA

$SS_{TOT} = 78.25$	$\bar{X}_c - \bar{X}_a = 5.00*$
$SS_{BG} = 50$	$\bar{X}_c - \bar{X}_b = 2.50$
$SS_{WG} = 28.25$	$\bar{X}_b - \bar{X}_a = 2.5$
$MS_{WG} = 3.14$	*significantly different
$HSD = 3.50$	

5.

	SS	df	MS	F
Between	28.40	2	14.20	9.28
Within	9.20	6	1.53	

	1 vs. 2	1 vs. 3	3 vs. 2	2 and 3 vs. 1	1 and 3 vs. 2	1 and 2 vs 3
C	4.6	3.9	0.7	4.25	2.65	1.60
s_c	1.01	1.01	1.01	0.87	0.87	0.87
F'	4.55*	3.86*	0.69	4.89*	3.05	1.84
$F_s = 3.21$ * significant at .05 level						

6. a.

	SS	df	MS	F	p
Between	9.66	3	3.22	29.27	<.01
Within	2.24	20	0.11		
Total	11.9	23			
$F_s = 3.05$					

b. Mirage versus Eclipse

$\quad C = 0.79 \qquad s_c = 0.19 \qquad F' = 4.16*$

c. Average of Mirage, Dancer, and Mark IV versus Eclipse

$\quad C = 1.19 \qquad s_c = 0.16 \qquad F' = 7.44$

d. Tukey's HSD = 0.54

Mirage versus Eclipse = 0.78*	Dancer versus Eclipse = 0.98*
Mark IV versus Eclipse = 1.78*	Dancer versus Mirage = 0.20*
Mark IV versus Mirage = 1.00*	Mark IV versus Dancer = 0.80*

* significantly different

7. a. HSD $= 2.31$

    b. $NH - NL = 1.87$ $CH - NH = 1.50$ $CL - NH = 0.63$

    $CH - NL = 3.37^*$ $CL - NL = 2.50^*$ $CH - CL = 0.87$

    * significantly different

8. $MS_{error} = 5.58$ a. $C = 1.36$ b. $s_c = 0.89$

    c. $F_s = 3.00$ d. $F' = 1.53$

    e. No significant difference

Chapter 14

1. a. $df = 5$ and $\chi^2_{.05} = 11.07$

    b. $df = 1$ and $\chi^2_{.01} = 6.64$

    c. $df = 12$ and $\chi^2_{.05} = 21.03$

    d. $df = 1$ and $\chi^2_{.01} = 6.64$

2. a. H_0: No difference in preference H_1: Preference differs

    b. $df = 2$ c. $\chi^2_{.05} = 5.99$

	Light Ale	Pilsner	Malt
O	35	20	45
E	33.33	33.33	33.33
$O - E$	1.67	−13.33	11.67
$(O - E)^2/E$	0.08	5.33	4.08

    d. $\chi^2 = 9.50$ e.   Reject: Preference differs

3. a. H_0: Strain and performance are independent

    H_1: Performance depends on strain

    b. $df = 1$ c. $\chi^2_{.05} = 3.84$

    d. $\chi^2 = 7.72$ e. Reject. Problem-solving success depends on Strain.

4.

Censorship Attitude	Expected Frequencies of Piety		
Attitude	High	Medium	Low
Pro	11.90	11.43	11.67
Neutral	20.40	19.60	21.00

    a. H_0: Attitude and piety are independent H_1: Attitude and piety are dependent

    b. $df = 4$ c. $\chi^2_{.01} = 13.28$

    d. $\chi^2 = 25.35$ e. Reject. Attitude about censorship depends on piety.

5. $\chi^2 = 4.3$. Fail to reject. No evidence that children prefer one cereal over the other.

6. $\chi^2 = 42.67$. Reject. The college students are different from the general population.

7. $\chi^2 = 8$. Reject. Children prefer Popsicles.

8. $\chi^2 = 0.04$. Fail to reject. No evidence that type of purchase depends on gender.

9. $\chi^2 = 18.3$. Reject. Attitude about legalization of marijuana depends on strength of religious values.

10. $\chi^2 = 28.51$. Reject. Hair color and popularity are dependent.

11. $\chi^2 = 4.19$. Fail to reject. No evidence that the claim is incorrect.

12. $\chi^2 = 12.8$. Reject. The book had a significant effect on Peter's wins (it reduced them).

13. $\chi^2 = 35.88$. Reject. What the party goers wore depended on their position.

14. $\chi^2 = 44.6$. Reject. Type of crime and type of family were dependent.

15. $\chi^2 = 46.59$. Reject. Political affiliation depends on occupation.

Chapter 15

1.

Liberal Arts		Church Work	
Scores	Ranks	Scores	Ranks
7	7.5	2	1
8	9	3	2
9	10	4	3
10	11.5	5	4
11	13	6	5.5
12	14	6	5.5
14	15	7	7.5
18	16	10	11.5

$U_1 = 4$ $U_2 = 60$ $U_{crit} = 7$, for a two-tailed test at $\alpha = .01$
Reject because $4 < 7$. The populations from which the two groups come are not identical.

2.

Before	After	Difference	Rank
2	2.5	−0.5	−2.5
3.5	2.5	1	5
1.5	2	−0.5	−2.5
2.5	2.5	0	drop
3	1.5	1.5	7
4	4.5	−0.5	−2.5
1	2.5	−1.5	−7
3	2.5	0.5	2.5
1.5	3	−1.5	−7

$T = 14.5$ Number of pairs used $= 8$ $T_{crit} = 3$

Do not reject. There is no evidence that viewing a violent cartoon affects aggressiveness of children.

3.

	Eclipse		Mirage		Dancer	
	Score	Rank	Score	Rank	Score	Rank
	4.8	9	3.1	2	2.9	1
	5.2	10	3.9	6	3.3	3
	6.0	13	4.7	8	3.5	4
	6.1	14	5.3	11	3.6	5
	6.5	15	5.4	12	4	7
Sum		61		39		20
Sum^2		3 721		1 521		400

$H = 8.42$ Critical value of chi-square $= 5.99$

Reject. The ratings of the three boats differ.

4. a. ΣR Group 1 $= 574$ ΣR Group 2 $= 416$
    b. $U_1 = 163$ $U_2 = 321$
    c. $z = -1.85$ d. Fail to reject

5. a.

	R_1	R_2	R_3
Σ	120.50	344.5	570
$\Sigma^2 / 15$	968.02	7 912.02	21 660

    b. $H = 39.04$ c. $\chi^2_{crit} = 5.99$ d. Reject

6.

Time 1	Rank	Time 2	Rank	Time 3	Rank	Time 4	Rank
43	1	46	2	47	3	50	4
40	1.5	42	3	40	1.5	45	4
39	1	40	2	42	3	43	4
44	3	39	1	45	4	40	2
36	2	40	3	35	1	41	4
42	1	43	2	45	3	46	4
39	2	42	4	40	3	38	1
37	2	40	3	35	1	41	4

Friedman $\chi^2 = 6.86$ $df = 3$ $p = .08$

Do not reject. There is no statistical evidence that quality of life changes over time.

Chapter 16

1. Positive correlation.

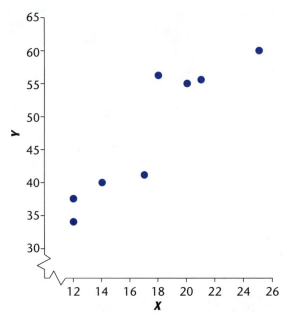

2. Negative correlation

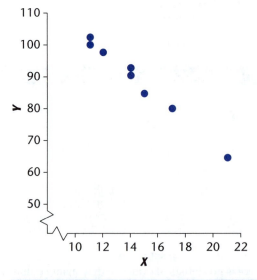

3.

	X	Y	X²	Y²	XY
Sums	139	379	2 563	18 703	6 893

$\rho = 0.93$

4.

	$(X - \mu_X)(Y - \mu_Y)$	$(X - \mu_X)^2$	$(Y - \mu_Y)^2$
Sums	−292.25	79.88	1 081.50

$\mu_X = 14.38$ $\mu_Y = 88.75$

$\rho = -0.99$ $\rho^2 = 0.98$

5.

	z_X	z_Y	z_{XY}
	−1.29	−0.98	1.27
	−0.97	−0.98	0.95
	−0.32	0.19	−0.06
	0.32	−0.39	−0.13
	0.65	0.19	0.13
	1.61	1.96	3.16
Sum			5.31

$\rho = 0.88$

6. $H_0 : \rho = 0$ $H_1 : \rho \neq 0$ $t_{.05} = \pm 2.16$ $s_r = 0.21$ $t = 3$

There is a significant relationship between performances on the two exams.

7.

	$(X - \mu_X)(Y - \mu_Y)$	$(X - \mu_X)^2$	$(Y - \mu_Y)^2$
Sums	−557.57	1112.86	425.71

$\mu_X = 123.86$ $\mu_Y = 18.43$ $\rho = -0.81$

It seems intelligence and creativity scores are correlated.

8. $\rho = 0.59$. It seems that scores are positively correlated.

9. $\rho = 0.88$. It seems that reaction time and fitness scores are positively correlated.

10. $\rho = .0.53$. There seems to be a positive relationship.

11.

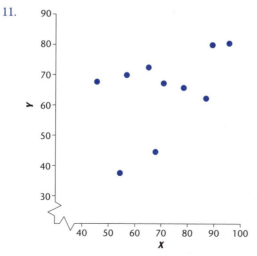

12.

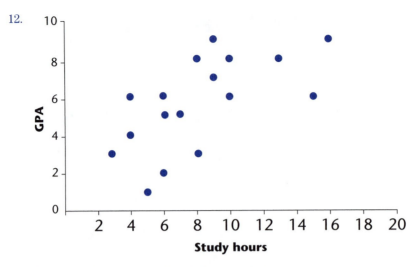

It appears that students who study more do better.

13.

	Ranks		d	d²
British Columbia	1	3	−2	4
Alberta	2	1	1	1
Manitoba	3	5	−2	4
Saskatchewan	4	4	0	0
Ontario	5	2	3	9
Quebec	6	8	−2	4
Prince Edward Island	7	6	1	1
Nova Scotia	8	7	1	1
New Brunswick	9	9	0	0
Newfoundland	10	10	0	0

$\Sigma d^2 = 24$ $rho = 0.86$ $rho_{crit} = 0.65$

Reject. There is a significant relationship between the rankings.

14.

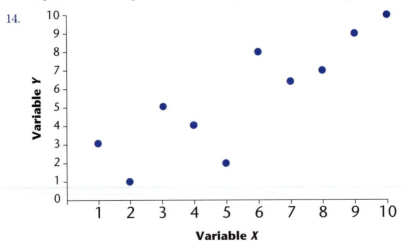

15.

X rank	Y rank	D	d²
1	7	−6	36
2	3	−1	1
3	8	−5	25
4	6	−2	4
5.5	2	3.5	12.25
5.5	9	−3.5	12.25
7	5	2	4
8	1	7	49
9	4	5	25

Rho = -0.40. No evidence of a relationship between crime rate and pollution.

16. $\Sigma d^2 = 2\,050$ *rho* = −0.16, *ns*

Chapter 17

1.

	X	Y	XY	X²	Y²
Sums	83	900	5 485	593	57 350

a. $b = 3.78$ $\mu_X = 5.53$ $\mu_Y = 60$

b. $a = 39.11$

c.
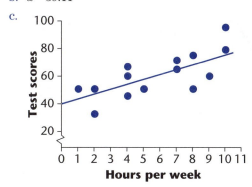

2. $Y' = bX + a = 3.78(7.5) + 39.11 = 67.43$

3. a. $Y' = 6.46$ b. $Y' = 11.50$ c. $Y' = 8.98$

4. a. 0.3   b. −0.9   c. 0

5.

	X	Y	X²	Y²	XY	$(X - \mu_X)^2$	$(Y - \mu_Y)^2$	$(X - \mu_X)(Y - \mu_Y)$
Sums	124	95	1 778	1 077	1 344	240	175	166

a. $\rho = 0.81$ b. $\rho^2 = 0.66$

6. Slope = 0.69 Y intercept = 0.94

X	Y'
9	7.15
13	9.91
17	12.68

7.

	$(X - \mu_X)^2$	$(Y - \mu_Y)^2$	$(X - \mu_X)(Y - \mu_Y)$
Sums	1987.43	3721.43	2395.57

$\mu_X = 67.43$ $\mu_Y = 39.57$
$\sigma_X = 11.91$ $\sigma_Y = 16.30$

a. $\rho = 0.88$
b. $b = 1.20$ $a = -41.35$
c.

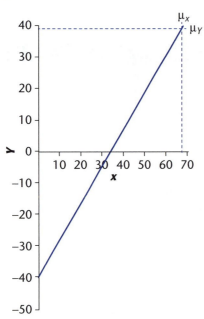

8. $MR = 0.49$

9. $MR = 0.58$

10. $b_1 = 0.39$ $b_2 = 0.31$
    $a = 29.63$ $Y' = 120.32$

Chapter 18

A.1. Two-way ANOVA

A.2. One-way ANOVA

A.3. t test for independent means

A.4. t test for dependent means

B.1. Kruskal-Wallis test

B.2. Wilcoxon test

B.3. Friedman test

C.1. Chi-square test for independence with 1 df

C.2. Chi-square test for independence with 2 df

C.3. Chi-square test for goodness of fit with 1 df or a z test for a proportion

Glossary of Terms

Σ Sign for summation

a priori Before the fact; in inference, refers to expected outcomes or intended comparisons prior to data collection

Abscissa The horizontal axis on a graph; x-axis

Absolute frequency (f) The number of times a score occurs in a distribution

Alternative hypothesis (H_1) States a value of a parameter or relationship between parameters that is different from that specified in the null hypothesis and corresponds to the research hypothesis

ANOVA (analysis of variance) A family of statistical tests used to evaluate the significance of differences between means of two or more groups

Apparent limits The upper and lower scores of a class interval used in the construction of a grouped frequency distribution

Bar graph A graph used to depict the frequency distribution of discrete variables

Between-group variance In ANOVA, variability among the means of different treatment conditions

Between-participants design Different participants are randomly assigned to the control and treatment group

Bimodal Describes a distribution with two values of high frequency

Binomial variable A variable having only two outcomes of interest (also called dichotomous)

Central limit theorem Defines the relationship between various random sampling distributions and the normal distribution

Chi-square test A nonparametric analysis used to test hypotheses about frequencies of categorical or discrete variables

Class interval The span of scores used to group data in a grouped frequency distribution

Coefficient of determination (ρ^2) In regression, the proportion of the total variance in Y that is explained by the correlation between X and Y; indicates the strength of the relationship between two variables

Combination (C) In probability, a set of events where order or sequence is irrelevant

Combined mean (μ_c) The grand mean of all the scores in all groups when two or more groups are combined

Completely randomized factorial design In ANOVA, a fully crossed experimental design in which different participants serve in each treatment combination

Conceptual hypothesis States relationship between theoretical concepts

Confidence interval (CI) A range of values computed from sample data within which a parameter of interest has a known probability of falling

Constant A characteristic of things, people, or events that does not vary

Continuous variable A variable that, in theory, can take on an infinite number of values within a given interval

Control group The group that is not exposed to the independent variable

Correlation Describes a linear relationship between two variables

Correlational hypothesis States the expected relationship between two or more variables

Criterion variable In regression, the variable being predicted from information about another, the predictor, variable

Critical region In hypothesis testing, the region within which a sample statistic must fall if the null hypothesis is to be rejected

Critical value The value of a statistic corresponding to a given significance level; used to make decisions about rejection or nonrejection of a null hypothesis

Cumulative frequency (cf) Summing frequencies from the bottom of a frequency distribution up for each value or interval

Degrees of freedom (df) The number of values free to vary once certain constraints have been placed on data; important in several statistical procedures

Dependent events In probability, when the occurrence of one event affects the probability of occurrence of another event

Dependent samples t test Parametric test for the significance of the difference between means of samples of same or matched participants

Dependent variable In experiments, a measure of the behavior of participants expected to be influenced by the independent variable, that is the variable manipulated by the researcher

Derived score A score obtained by transforming raw scores

Descriptive statistics Procedures for summarizing the characteristics of populations

Deviation score The difference between a score and the mean of its distribution

Directional alternative Hypothesis that states a value of a parameter or relationship between parameters that is different from that stated in the null and in a specific direction

Discrete variable A variable that has a finite set of possible values

Effect size An estimate of the size of the treatment effect or relationship

Empirical Based on real observations

Error term The denominator of a significance test ratio; estimates the inherent variability among participants free of treatment effects

Error variance Variability between participants that is free of treatment effects

Exact limits Mathematically precise start and end points of a score or interval; also called real limits

Experiment-wise error rate Overall probability in an experiment that the null will be rejected in error (Type I error)

Experimental research hypothesis States the expected relationship between an independent variable and a dependent variable

External validity The extent to which research outcomes generalize to other situations and participants

f The number of times a particular score occurs in a distribution; stands for frequency

F **distribution** In ANOVA, the relative frequency distribution of the F statistic

F **ratio** In ANOVA, the ratio of two unbiased variance estimates

Factor In ANOVA, an independent variable

Frequency polygon Graph used to depict the frequency distribution of continuous variables

Friedman test Nonparametric alternative to one-way repeated measures ANOVA

Grouped frequency distribution Table indicating class intervals and their associated frequencies

Histogram Graph used to depict the frequency distribution of continuous variables

Homogeneity of variance Equal variances in populations

Homoscedasticity In regression, equal variability of Y values around the regression line throughout the bivariate distribution

Honestly significant difference (HSD) Value used in the Tukey test to assess the significance of mean differences

Independent events In probability, events where the occurrence of one has no effect on the probability of occurrence of the other

Independent samples *t* test Test for the significance of the difference between means of samples of independent (uncorrelated) participants

Independent variable In experiments, the variable controlled by the experimenter and expected to have an effect on the behavior of the participants

Inferential statistics Procedures used to generalize from a sample(s) to the population(s) from which it was (they were) drawn

Interaction effect In ANOVA, the effect of combinations of levels of independent variables on the dependent variable

Internal validity The extent to which an observed relationship or outcome reflects the manipulations of the research variables

Interquartile range The distance between the 75th and 25th percentiles; a measure of variability

Interval estimation Inferential procedure that estimates the probable location of population parameters or relationships between parameters from sample data

Interval variable A variable with values ordered by quantity and where intervals between values are equal in size

Interval width Span of the class interval in a grouped frequency distribution

Kruskal-Wallis test Nonparametric alternative to the one-way ANOVA, used for rank-order data

Kurtosis Shape characteristic of a frequency distribution that describes variability or peakedness

Least squares criterion In regression, rule used to fit the regression line to a bivariate frequency distribution such that the sum of the squared distances of points from the line is minimized

Leptokurtic Describes a distribution that is more peaked (less variable) than the normal distribution

Linearity of regression In regression, refers to a relationship between two variables that is best described by a straight line

Main effect In ANOVA, the effect of an independent variable (factor) on performance of groups, the dependent variable

Mann-Whitney *U* test Nonparametric alternative to the t test for independent groups, used for rank-order data

Matched groups design A research design in which each participant in one treatment group is similar to a cohort in another treatment group on some variable thought to be related to the dependent variable

Mean The arithmetic average of all the scores in a distribution

Mean square In ANOVA, an unbiased estimate of the population variance calculated by dividing sum of squares by degrees of freedom

Median The score at or below which exactly 50% of the scores lie; the middle score in a distribution

Mesokurtic A distribution with moderate peakedness; an example is the normal distribution

Midpoint The middle value of an interval in a grouped frequency distribution

Mode The most frequently occurring score in a distribution

Multimodal A distribution having three or more frequency peaks or points of central tendency

Multiple correlation In regression, the correlation between all predictor variables and the criterion variable

Mutually exclusive events In probability, events that cannot occur together

Mutually exclusive interval Nonoverlapping interval in a grouped frequency distribution such that each score falls in only one interval

N The total number of observations in a population distribution

n The total number of observations in a sample

Negatively skewed distribution An asymmetrical distribution where the bulk of the scores are high with a few low scores; graphically the tail of the distribution points to the left

Nominal variable A variable having values that differ in quality but not in quantity

Nondirectional alternative Hypothesis that negates the null but does not specify a direction

Nonlinearity In regression, a relationship between two variables that is best described as a curve rather than a straight line

Nonparametric techniques Used to make inferences about entire populations rather than population parameters; fewer assumptions about the nature of the data are made compared with parametric techniques

Null hypothesis (H_0) In hypothesis testing, states the expected value of a parameter or expected relationship between parameters given certain assumptions; is the hypothesis to be rejected in favor of the alternative or research hypothesis

One-tailed test A statistical test where the region of rejection lies in one tail only; the outcome is expected to be in a specific direction

Open-ended distribution A frequency distribution where the exact upper or lower limit of the distribution is unknown

Operationalize To make measurable or observable

Ordinal variable A variable that has values that differ in quantity; intervals are not assumed to be equal in size

Ordinate The vertical axis of a graph; y-axis

Organismic variable Inherent characteristic of the participant that cannot be controlled by the researcher

Parameter A summary characteristic of a population

Partial correlation In regression, the correlation between two variables when a third has been held constant

Participant variable Characteristic of the participant that cannot be controlled by the researcher

Percentile or **percentile point (*P*)** Score point at or below which a particular percentage of cases fall

Percentile rank (*PR*) The percentage of cases falling at or below a particular score

Permutation In probability, an ordered sequence of events

Planned comparisons Statistical comparisons among means planned in advance of data collection; a multiple comparison procedure

Platykurtic Describes a distribution that is flatter (more variable) than the normal distribution

Population The entire set of individuals, items, events, or data points of interest

Positive correlation Describes two variables that increase and decrease together in a linear fashion

Positively skewed distribution An asymmetrical distribution where the bulk of the scores are low with a few high scores; graphically the tail of the distribution points to the right

Post hoc After the fact

Post hoc comparisons Statistical comparisons among means decided after the data have been examined

Power (1 – β) The probability that a significance test will lead to rejection of a false null hypothesis

Predictive statistics Provide tools for making predictions about an event, based on available information

Predictor variable In regression, the variable used to predict the value of another, the criterion variable

Quartile The 25th, 50th, 75th, and 100th percentile of a distribution

Random sample A sample collected such that all members of the population are equally likely to be included

Random sampling distribution A theoretical relative frequency distribution of the values of some statistic computed for all possible samples of some fixed size(s) drawn with replacement from a population; important in statistical inference

Range The difference between the highest and lowest score plus one unit in a distribution; the span of a distribution

Ratio variable A quantitative variable with equal intervals and a true zero point

Real limits Mathematically precise start and end points of numbers or intervals; also called exact limits

Region of nonrejection (or region of acceptance) Outcomes in this area lead to non-rejection of the null

Region of rejection In hypothesis testing, area beyond the critical value; sample outcomes lying in this area lead to rejection of the null

Regression analysis An inferential technique used to predict the value of a variable from known values of a correlated variable

Regression equation In regression, the mathematical equation that defines the regression line

Regression line In regression, the straight line fit to a bivariate frequency distribution

Regression on the mean In regression, refers to the fact that the predicted Y value tends to be closer to its mean than the X value (used to predict Y) is from its mean

Relative frequency (rf) The number of times a score occurs in a distribution, divided by the total number of scores

Repeated measures design An experimental design where participants serve in more than one treatment group

Research hypothesis States expected relationship between measurable events

Sample A subset of a population

Sampling fluctuation Refers to the fact that samples drawn from the same population will yield summary measures that vary; variability of these measures depends on sample size

Scattergram A graphic representation of a bivariate frequency distribution; sometimes called scatterplot or scattergraph

Score A quantitative (numeric) value

Semi-interquartile range Half the span of the middle 50% of the distribution; half the distance between the third and first quartiles

Significance Used in statistics to refer to an outcome that led to the rejection of the null hypothesis and is therefore unlikely to have occurred by chance alone

Significance level (α) The level of probability at which we will reject the null; alpha level

Slope In regression, indicates the amount of change in Y that accompanies one unit of increase in X

Standard deviation (σ) The average deviation of scores from the mean

Standard error Standard deviation of a random sampling distribution

Standard error of estimate In regression, the variability of the Y values around the regression line; estimates predictive error

Standard error of the difference The standard deviation of the sampling distribution of the difference

Standard normal curve Theoretical bell-shaped distribution; the normal curve

Statistic A summary characteristic of a sample

Statistical hypothesis States expected relationship between statistical properties of data

Statistically significant outcome An outcome leading to rejection of the null hypothesis

Sum of squares (SS) The sum of the squared deviations of scores from the mean

Symmetrical distribution One that is a mirror image about its center

t score (or t ratio) The deviation of a particular value from the mean of its distribution expressed in relationship to an unbiased estimate of the standard deviation of that distribution

t **test** Parametric test of significance of means or mean differences

Theoretical Based on theoretical or hypothetical observations

Total variability Variability of all the scores from the combined mean

Treatment Refers to some manipulation by the researcher; an independent variable

Treatment group (or experimental group) In an experiment, the group that is exposed to a different level of the independent variable than the control group

Two-tailed test A statistical test where the region of rejection lies in both tails

Type I error Rejecting the null hypothesis in error; the probability of a Type I error is determined by the significance level

Type II error Failure to reject the null when, in fact, it is false

Unbiased estimate An estimate of a parameter that, on average, exactly equals the value of the parameter

Unimodal Term used to describe distributions with one value of highest frequency; graphically having one peak

Value A property of a variable; can be quantitative or qualitative

Variable A characteristic of things, people, or events that varies

Variance The average of the squared deviations of scores from the mean of the distribution

Wilcoxon test A nonparametric equivalent to the *t* test for independent samples

Within-participants design (or repeated measures design) An experimental design in which participants serve under all levels of the independent variable

X_N The last score in the X distribution

Y **intercept** In a scattergram, the point on the ordinate crossed by the regression line

Yates correction An adjustment used in special cases of chi-square tests when expected frequencies are small

z **score** A derived score indicating the distance of a score from its mean in units of standard deviation

z **test** Parametric test of significance of means, mean differences, or proportions

References

Ambrose, S. E., Fey, M. E., & Eisenberg, L. S. (2012). Phonological awareness and print knowledge of preschool children with cochlear implants. *Journal of Speech, Language, and Hearing Research, 55*(3), 811–823.

Austin, V., Shah, S., & Muncer, S. (2005). Teacher stress and coping strategies used to reduce stress. *Occupational Therapy International, 12*(2), 63–80.

Cohen, J. (1992). A power primer. *Psychological Bulletin, 112*(1), 155–159.

Dickson-Spillmann, M., & Siegrist, M. (2011). Consumers' knowledge of healthy diets and its correlation with dietary behaviour. *Journal of Human Nutrition and Dietetics, 24*, 54–60. doi:10.1111/j.1365-277X.2010.01124.x

Dysart, J. E., Lawson, V. Z., & Rainey, A. (2012). Blind lineup administration as a prophylactic against the postidentification feedback effect. *Law and Human Behavior, 36*(4), 312–319. doi:10.1037/h0093921

Geisser, S., & Greenhouse, S. W. (1958). An extension of Box's results on the use of the *F*-distribution in multivariate analysis. *Annals of Mathematical Statistics, 29*, 885–891.

Gonzalez, A. Q., & Koestner, R. (2005). Parental preference for sex of newborn as reflected in positive affect in birth announcements. *Sex Roles, 52*(5/6), 407–411.

Hechler, T., Beumont, P., Marks, P., & Touyz, S. (2005). How do clinical specialists understand the role of physical activity in eating disorders? *European Eating Disorders Review, 13*, 125–132.

Hill, K. (2012, January 28). Marketers for acai berry products fined for unfounded claims. *Science-Based Life*. Retrieved from http://sciencebasedlife.wordpress.com/2012/01/28/marketers-for-acai-berry-products-fined-for-unfounded-claims/

Merikangas, K. R., He, J. P., Burstein, M., Swanson, S. A., Avenevoli, S., Cui, L., . . . Swendsen, J. (2010). Lifetime prevalence of mental disorders in U.S. adolescents: Results from the National Comorbidity Survey Replication—Adolescent Supplement (NCS-A). *Journal of American Academy of Child and Adolescent Psychiatry, 49*(10), 980–989.

Moss, L. (2006, April 14). Half of young goths have tried suicide. *The Scotsman*. Retrieved from http://www.scotsman.com/news/health/half-of-young-goths-have-tried-suicide-1-1113963

Nduru, M. (2006). Medical brain drain puts Southern Africa in a quandary: The figures tell it all. Inter Press Service, Johannesburg. Retrieved from http://www.ipsnews.net/2006/04//world-health-day-medical-brain-dran-puts-southern-africa-in-a-quandary/

Piran, N., & Cormier, H. C. (2005). The social construction of women and disordered eating patterns. *Journal of Counseling Psychology, 52*(4), 549–558.

Resendes, J., & Lecci, L. (2012). Comparing the MMPI-2 scale scores of parents involved in parental competency and child custody assessments. *Psychological Assessment*. doi:10.1037/a0028585

Szymanowicz, A., & Furnham, A. (2011). Do intelligent women stay single? Cultural stereotypes concerning the intellectual abilities of men and women. *Journal of Gender Studies, 20*(1), 43–54.

Thabane, L., Childs, A., & Lafontaine, A. (2005). Determining the level of statistician participation on Canadian-based research ethics boards. IRB: *Ethics & Human Research, 27*(2), 11–14.

Tukey, J. W. (1977). *Exploratory data analysis*. Reading, MA: Addison-Wesley.

Index

⑤SAGE researchmethods

The essential online tool for researchers from the world's leading methods publisher

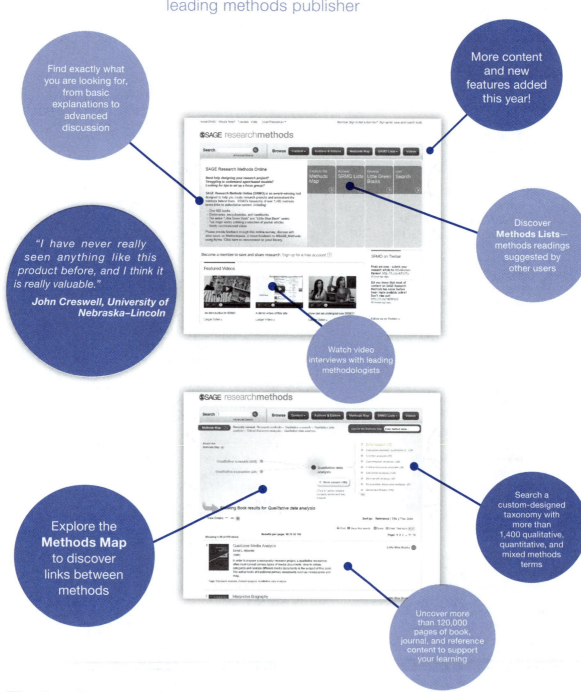

Find exactly what you are looking for, from basic explanations to advanced discussion

More content and new features added this year!

"I have never really seen anything like this product before, and I think it is really valuable."

John Creswell, University of Nebraska–Lincoln

Discover **Methods Lists**— methods readings suggested by other users

Watch video interviews with leading methodologists

Explore the **Methods Map** to discover links between methods

Search a custom-designed taxonomy with more than 1,400 qualitative, quantitative, and mixed methods terms

Uncover more than 120,000 pages of book, journal, and reference content to support your learning

Find out more at
www.sageresearchmethods.com